Fort Kent

Ashland

MAINE

Calais

Lubec

Bangor

Bar Harbor

ugusta

Boothbay
Harbor

Maine
Pages 278–303

*Atlantic
Ocean*

vincetown

Connecticut
Pages 198–229

Rhode Island
Pages 172–197

Boston
Pages 54–131

Massachusetts
Pages 136–171

0 kilometers   10
0 miles   10

EYEWITNESS TRAVEL

NEW ENGLAND

EYEWITNESS TRAVEL

NEW ENGLAND

DK | Penguin Random House

Produced by St. Remy Media Inc., Montréal, Canada

President Pierre Léveillé
Vice President, Finance Natalie Watanabe
Managing Editor Carolyn Jackson
Managing Art Director Diane Denoncourt
Production Manager Michelle Turbide
Director, Business Development Christopher Jackson
Editor Neale McDevitt
Art Directors Michel Giguère, Anne-Marie Lemay
Senior Research Editor Heather Mills
Researchers Tal Ashkenazi, Jessica Braun, Genevieve Ring
Picture Researcher Linda Castle
Map Coordinator Peter Alec Fedun
Senior Editor, Production Brian Parsons
Indexer Linda Cardella Cournoyer
Prepress Production Martin Francoeur, Jean Sirois

Main Contributors Eleanor Berman, Patricia Brooks, Tom Bross, Patricia Harris, Pierre Home-Douglas, Helga Loverseed, David Lyon

Photographers Alan Briere, Ed Homonylo, David Lyon

Illustrators Gilles Beauchemin, Martin Gagnon, Vincent Gagnon, Stéphane Jorisch, Patrick Jougla, Luc Normandin, Jean-François Vachon

Maps Dimension DPR

Printed and bound in China

First published in the UK in 2001
by Dorling Kindersley Limited
80 Strand, London WC2R 0RL

16 17 18 19 10 9 8 7 6 5 4 3 2 1

Reprinted with revisions 2003, 2004, 2005, 2006, 2007, 2009, 2010, 2012, 2014, 2016

**The information in this
DK Eyewitness Travel Guide is checked regularly.**
Every effort has been made to ensure that this book is as up-to-date as possible at the time of going to press. Some details, however, such as telephone numbers, opening hours, prices, gallery hanging arrangements, and travel information are liable to change. The publishers cannot accept responsibility for any consequences arising from the use of this book, nor for any material on third party websites, and cannot guarantee that any website address in the book will be a suitable source of information. We value the views of our readers very highly. Please write to DK Eyewitness Travel Guides, Dorling Kindersley, 80 Strand, London WC2R 0RL, UK, or email: travelguides@dk.com.

...age: Nubble Lighthouse, near Old York, on the south coast of Maine

...d Lighthouse, Cape Elizabeth, Maine

Contents

Vermont's dazzling fall foliage

West Quoddy Head Light, Maine

Boston

New England
Region by Region

Travellers'
Needs

Mansion in Waterbury, Vermont

Survival Guide

Costumed interpreter at Plimoth
Plantation, Plymouth,
Massachusetts

Mark Twain House in
Hartford, Connecticut

HOW TO USE THIS GUIDE

This guide helps you to get the most from your visit to New England. *Introducing New England* maps the region and sets it in its historical and cultural context. Each of the six states, along with the city of Boston, has its own chapter describing the important sights using maps, pictures, and detailed illustrations. Suggestions on restaurants, accommodations, shopping, entertainment, and outdoor activities are covered in *Travelers' Needs*. The *Survival Guide* has tips on everything from changing currency in New England to getting around in Boston.

Boston

Boston has been divided into five sightseeing areas, each one opening with a list of the sights described. All the sights are numbered and plotted on an *Area Map*. The detailed information for each sight is presented in numerical order, making it easy to locate within the chapter.

Sights at a Glance lists the chapter's sights by category: Historic Streets and Squares; Historic Buildings, Churches, Museums, and Theaters; Waterfront Sights; Gardens and Zoos; and Parks and Cemeteries.

1 Area map
For easy reference, the sights are numbered and located on a map. The sights are also shown on the *Boston Street Finder* on pages 126–31.

A locator map shows where you are in relation to other areas of the city center.

2 Street-by-Street map
This gives a bird's-eye view of the heart of each sightseeing area.

A suggested route for a walk covers the more interesting streets in the area.

All pages relating to Boston have yellow thumb tabs.

Stars indicate the sights that no visitor should miss.

3 Detailed information on each sight
All the sights in Boston are described individually. Addresses, telephone numbers, opening hours, and information on admission charges and wheelchair access are also provided. The key to all the symbols used in the information block is shown on the back flap.

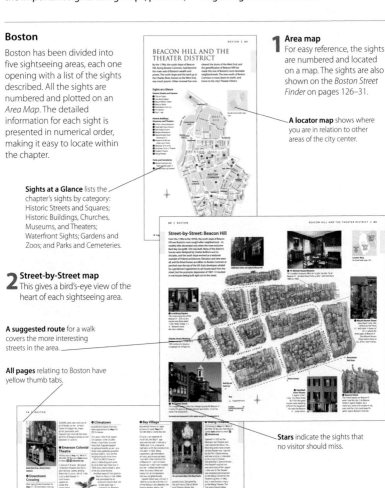

New England Region by Region

In this book, New England has been divided into the six states, each of which has a separate chapter. The most interesting sights to visit have been numbered on the *Regional Map*.

1 Introduction

The landscape, history, and character of each state is described here, showing how the area has developed over the centuries and what it has to offer visitors today.

Each state of New England can be quickly identified by its color coding, which is shown on the inside front cover.

2 Regional map

This shows the road network and gives an illustrated overview of the whole state. All the sights are numbered, and there are also useful tips on getting around the state.

Story boxes explore specific subjects further.

3 Detailed information

All the important towns and other places to visit are described individually. They are listed in order, following the numbering on the *Regional Map*. Within each town or city, there is detailed information on important buildings and other sights.

For all the top sights, a Visitors' Checklist provides the practical information you will need to plan your visit.

4 The top sights

These are given two or more pages. Historic buildings are dissected to reveal their interiors; museums and galleries have color-coded floor plans; national parks have maps showing facilities and trails.

Stars indicate the best features and works of art.

INTRODUCING NEW ENGLAND

DISCOVERING NEW ENGLAND

The following tours have been designed to take in as many of the region's highlights as possible, while keeping long-distance travel to a minimum. First comes a two-day tour of Boston and suggested day trips, followed by the highlights of Eastern Massachusetts. These itineraries can be followed individually or combined to form a week-long tour. Next come two seven-day tours covering the northern and southern parts of New England. A car is essential for these tours, but the region is quite simple to navigate. This is a lively destination and the area's cultural calendars are always buzzing, so be sure to consult with the states' visitor resources to learn about current happenings and special events. Pick, combine, and follow your favorite tours, or simply dip in and out and be inspired.

Waterplace Park, Rhode Island
A 175,000-sq-ft (16,250-sq-m) walkway in downtown Providence, with cobblestone paths, Venetian-style footbridges, and free concerts in summers.

A Week in Southern New England

- Feel the energy of lively **Providence** while pausing for a glimpse of the city's past with a stroll down **Benefit Street's Mile of History**.

- Relax on a cruise around picturesque **Newport**.

- Appreciate Connecticut's nautical past and present with visits to **Mystic Seaport** and the **Mystic Aquarium**.

- Enjoy a white clam pie at one of **New Haven's** famous pizzerias, and walk off the calories while touring **Yale University's** historic campus.

- Explore **Hartford's** many historical attractions.

- Visit the charming small towns that populate the **Berkshires**.

CANADA

UNITED STATES

VERMONT

Lake Champlain

Burlington

Bretton Woods

White Mountain National Forest

Green Mountains

Lake Winni-pesaukee

Squam Lake

Meredith · Wolfeboro

Killington

Woodstock

Weirs Beach

NEW HAMPSHIRE

NEW YORK

Massachusetts Museum of Contemporary Art

Lexington

Concord

Pittsfield

Lenox

MASSACHUSETTS

Great Barrington

The Berkshires

Norfolk

Providence

Litchfield Hills

Hartford

RHODE ISLAND

Kent

CONNECTICUT

Newpor

Bethlehem

Mohegan Sun · Foxwoods

Mystic

Essex · Stonington

New Haven · Groton

Guilford Madison New London

0 kilometers 75

0 miles 75

◀ Painting of Boston Harbor circa 1750

A Week in Northern New England

- Explore **Mount Desert Island's** many charms, from the **Acadia National Park** to the town of **Bar Harbor**.
- Shop till you drop in Portland's **Old Port District**.
- Be one with nature in New Hampshire's **Lakes Region**.

- Take a hike, hit the slopes, or admire fall foliage in New Hampshire's scenic **White Mountains**.
- Fish, bike, or enjoy a canoe ride surrounded by Vermont's majestic **Green Mountains**.
- Enjoy a **Lake Champlain** pleasure cruise or stroll in bustling **Church Street**.

Portland Head Light, Maine
Erected in 1791 as part of Fort William, Portland Head Light is Maine's oldest lighthouse and is also one of the most-photographed lighthouses in the world.

MAINE

Bar Harbor
Acadia National Park
Mount Desert Island
Penobscot Bay

...ago
...e
Portland

Atlantic Ocean

...mouth

Peabody Essex Museum
Collections of China trade treasures, historic furniture, and Asian art in a soaring building by top architect Moshe Safdie.

Provincetown
Cape Cod
Cape Cod Bay
Hyannis   Chatham
...eyard
...aven
Edgartown   Nantucket
...artha's
...eyard

Key

— A Week in Northern New England
— A Week in Southern New England
— A Week in Eastern Massachusetts

A Week in Eastern Massachusetts

- Explore **Salem's** many historic sights and the world-class **Peabody Essex Museum**.
- Soak in all the culture that **Boston** has to offer.
- Visit one of **Cape Cod's** inviting iconic towns such as **Hyannis** or **Provincetown**.

- Indulge in a relaxing visit to celeb-favorites **Martha's Vineyard** and **Nantucket**.
- Step back in time with a visit to **Plimoth Plantation**.
- Appreciate the area's role in the American Revolution at **Minute Man National Historical Park** in **Concord** and **Lexington**.

Boston Common and the Public Garden

Two Days in Boston

Boston's importance in American history has left it with a unique architectural heritage. The city's wealth of sights, along with its many parks and gardens, make it a fascinating city to explore.

- **Arriving** Logan Airport, nestled on the water's edge in East Boston, is New England's primary air hub. From the airport, the MBTA provides a variety of transport options via bus, train, and boat. Boston's South Station and Back Bay Stations both provide direct rail and bus service throughout the area.

Day 1
Morning Compact and walkable, **Boston** can be easily explored on foot. Begin your day at **Boston Common and the Public Garden** *(pp68–9)*. The city's primary green spaces are great for people-watching. If the Swan Boats are operating, indulge your inner child with a calming ride. Grab a coffee and stroll the **Back Bay's** *(pp98–9)* world-class shops before the crowds arrive.

Afternoon Score a bite at one of **Kenmore Square's** casual cafés, then take a tour of **Fenway Park**, the country's oldest baseball park and a true icon of the city. Continue your culture crawl with a relaxing afternoon

at one of the nearby museums – the **Museum of Fine Arts** *(pp110–13)* or the **Isabella Stewart Gardner Museum** *(p109)*. Stroll the handsome streets of trendy **South End** and round off the day at one of the city's hottest tables, which you will have to reserve in advance.

Day 2
Morning Explore some of New England's priciest real estate in the historic **Beacon Hill** *(pp64–5)* neighborhood. Grab a warming beverage and peruse the numerous high-end boutiques and antique shops that line the neighborhood's primary artery, beautiful **Charles Street** *(p66)*.

Evening Head towards the waterfront to enjoy the city's major water-based attraction, the **New England Aquarium** *(pp94–5)*. Join the steady stream of visitors who fill **Quincy Market** *(p84)* to shop, dine, and watch colorful street performers. Be

Charlestown Navy Yard and the USS *Constitution*

sure to check out neighboring **Faneuil Hall** *(p84)*, one of the city's most historic sights. Later, stroll through the atmospheric **North End** *(pp88–9)*. Stop by **Paul Revere House** *(p92)* and **Old North Church** *(p91)*; both are particularly photogenic at night.

Day Trips from Boston

The cities and towns that surround Boston hold a treasure of historical and cultural offerings to satisfy any traveler's interests.

- **Arriving** Since the MBTA public transport system covers much of the Greater Boston area, including Charlestown and Cambridge, there is no need to hire a rental car.

Charlestown
Situated a short walk from the North End, on the north bank of the Charles River, **Charlestown** *(pp122–3)* exudes history. Simply follow the well-marked **Freedom Trail** *(p58)* and you'll arrive at the **Bunker Hill Monument**, site of the infamous Battle of Bunker Hill. Head back towards the water to visit the historic **Charlestown Navy Yard and USS Constitution**, pride of the post-revolutionary American Navy. Give your feet a rest by hoisting a pint (and some filling pub grub) at one of the nation's oldest watering holes, the **Warren Tavern**. Don't leave town without exploring other historical spaces such as **City Square** and the **John Harvard Mall**.

Cambridge
While often grouped with Boston, **Cambridge** *(pp114–21)* is a unique city in its own right, renowned for its strong liberal bent and youthful population. To best appreciate the city's place in worldwide academia, begin your visit by exploring the campuses of **Harvard University** and the **Massachusetts Institute of Technology (MIT)**. Harvard's **museums** alone rival those of many major cities. In the

DISCOVERING NEW ENGLAND | **13**

afternoon, visit important historic sights such as **Christ Church** and **Cambridge Common**, before exploring dining and shopping options in Harvard, Central, Kendall, and Inman squares.

A Week in Eastern Massachusetts

- **Transport** Though parking can be difficult in Eastern Massachusetts, a car is recommended to follow this itinerary.

Day 1: Salem

Infamous as the city that tried and executed witches in the late 1600s, **Salem** *(pp140–43)* today is a vibrant, entrepreneurial city. Explore its unique history at the **Salem Witch Museum** and **Salem Witch Trial Memorial**. Admire one of the region's best art collections with a visit to the **Peabody Essex Museum**, then take a stroll along the pedestrian-only **Essex Street Mall**, stopping to browse colorful costume shops and occult boutiques. Appreciate the city's rich maritime history by visiting the **Salem Maritime National Historic Site**, then enjoy a meal of fresh seafood by the water.

Day 2: Boston

Pick a day from the Boston itinerary on p12.

Day 3: Cape Cod

Take a ferry, plane, bus, or drive to "**The Cape**" *(pp160–63)*, as locals call it. Stop at key commercial destination **Hyannis**, which has the fascinating **JFK Museum**. Then drive north, visiting idyllic **Chatham**, where you can marvel at the area's natural beauty and shifting shoreline, and onwards to festive, colorful **Provincetown**.

Day 4: Martha's Vineyard or Nantucket

Take in **Martha's Vineyard's** *(pp156–7)* key attractions, from rustic natural seascapes to the bustling town of **Vineyard Haven** and the old whaling port of **Edgartown**. Alternatively, take a ferry ride to **Nantucket** *(p157)*, then hire a bicycle to explore the charming, gray-shingled neighborhoods that dot the island. If time allows, hop aboard a **whale-watch** and try to spot finbacks, minkes, and humpbacks.

Day 5: Plymouth

Step back in time with a visit to one of America's most authentic living-history museums, **Plimoth Plantation** *(pp154–5)*, where costumed staff recreate the settlement c.1627. Be sure to go through the exhibits devoted to Wampanoag (Native American) life in the same era. Head into **Plymouth** *(p152)* to explore historical relics such as the *Mayflower II* and **Plymouth Rock**. A meal of fresh lobster on

Gothic-style façade of the Salem Witch Museum, Massachusetts

the waterfront provides a perfect end to a historic day.

Day 6: Boston

Pick a day from the Boston itinerary on p12.

Day 7: Concord and Lexington

The opening skirmishes of the American Revolution, in what is now **Minute Man National Historical Park** *(p148)*, forever link these neighboring towns. Explore the historical markers, statues, and battlegrounds found in the park, then visit Concord's literary attractions including the **Old Manse**, home to author Nathaniel Hawthorne, **Emerson House**, where writer Ralph Waldo Emerson lived, and **Walden Pond**, where essayist Henry David Thoreau lived in a cabin for a year.

The 17th-Century English Village at Plimoth Plantation, Massachusetts

A Week in Northern New England

- **Airports** Arrive at Portland International Jetport or Bangor International Airport, and depart from Burlington International Airport.

- **Transport** While hiring a car will make for an easier journey, various bus and rail services connect major New England cities and towns.

Bass Harbor Head Light, Mount Desert Island, Maine

Day 1: Mount Desert Island

An easy drive from either of Maine's major airports, **Mount Desert Island** condenses the fabled Maine coast and woods into a single magical spot. Explore the intimate fishing villages that dot the southwest corner, and make time to take the seasonal, 27-mile **Loop Road** for a taste of the fabled **Acadia National Park** (pp292–3). Spend the night in **Bar Harbor**, the area's busiest port, filled with restaurants, shops, and lodging options.

Days 2 and 3: Portland

Though it has burned down four times since its establishment in 1633, **Portland** (pp284–7), Maine's hub remains one of America's most inviting small cities. Take a stroll along **Congress Street** and through the restored **Old Port District**. The working waterfront, where you can grab an inexpensive seafood meal, and nearby beaches all add to the city's charm and atmosphere. Spend the afternoon appreciating

one of the country's largest Winslow Homer collections at the **Portland Museum of Art**.

Start Day 3 getting to know the city's history at sites such as the **Victoria Mansion**, **Wadsworth-Longfellow House**, and **Neal Dow Memorial**. No visit to Portland is complete without stopping by the **Portland Observatory** or driving to **Portland Head Light** to snap some postcard-worthy photos.

Day 4: New Hampshire's Lakes Region

Sporty types love New Hampshire's largest lake, **Lake Winnipesaukee** (p268). Ringed by mountains, the lake is dotted with 274 islands and numerous sheltered bays and harbors. Hit the water in a canoe, motorboat, or waterskis, or simply jump in for a swim. Visit **Wolfeboro**, **Meredith**, and **Weirs Beach**, just a few of the charming small towns worth exploring. Those seeking a calming respite or looking to bird-watch should visit **Squam Lake**, best known as the setting for the 1981 film *On Golden Pond*. Finish the day with a visit to historic **Portsmouth** (pp256–7), one of southern New Hampshire's iconic cities.

Day 5: White Mountains

More than 20 summits define the rugged north country of New Hampshire, of which 1,200 sq miles (3,116 sq km) is set aside as the **White Mountain National Forest** (p269). This is the place in northern New

England to make the most of the outdoors: there is summer hiking and climbing, superb fall foliage, and winter skiing. Expect to see wonderful scenery and tumbling waterfalls as you drive onwards to **Bretton Woods** (p271) for your overnight stop.

Day 6: Green Mountains

Another day of outdoor activity beckons. **The Green Mountains** (p248) form the backbone of Vermont, running north-south from the Massachusetts border to Quebec. Use one of the charming ski towns of **Killington** (pp244–5) or **Woodstock** (p251) as your base for exploring this fascinating region. It's worth taking the ski gondola up the mountain for the view alone. Options include fishing, hiking, mountain biking, camping, canoeing, skiing, and snowshoeing. State Route 100, which runs between the east and west ranges, is among the most striking roads in the country for fall foliage.

Day 7: Burlington

This friendly, colorful **college town** (pp236–9) is situated on New England's largest lake, **Lake Champlain** (p240). Enjoy a narrated cruise on the **Spirit of Ethan Allen III**, the lake's largest cruise ship, to best appreciate the city's setting and history. See what's on at the **University of Vermont** and its **Robert Hull Fleming Museum**. Round off your tour with dinner on scenic **Church Street**, the city's pedestrian artery.

Squam Lake, New Hampshire

For practical information on travelling around New England, see pp374–9

Providence Place Mall, Rhode Island

A Week in Southern New England

- **Airports** Arrive at T. F. Green Airport, located just south of Providence, and depart from Hartford's Bradley International Airport or New York's Albany International Airport.

- **Transport** While hiring a car will make for an easier journey, various bus and rail services connect major New England cities and towns.

Day 1: Providence

Providence (pp178–81) is Rhode Island's largest city, chock full of things to keep a traveler busy. Stroll through the **Waterplace Park** and **Riverwalk** before visiting the city's huge, and very popular, **Providence Place Mall** (pp344–5). Uphill from here are the eclectic neighborhood shops and cheap ethnic eateries situated near the **Brown University** campus. From there take in **Benefit Street's Mile of History**, which includes more than 100 houses ranging in style from Colonial and Federal to Greek Revival and Victorian. For a peek into the city's impressive history, visit the **John Brown House**, **Governor Stephen Hopkins House**, and the **First Baptist Church in America**.

Days 2 and 3: Newport

The small city of **Newport** (pp186–91) packs an amazing amount of history into a few square miles. To best appreciate the distinct shoreline, take a pleasure cruise from the waterfront. Later, walk some (or all) of the 3.5-mile (5.5-km) **Cliff Walk**, stopping to wonder at some of the nation's most ornate, historic mansions such as the **Breakers**.

On Day 3, visit the **Naval War College Museum** (the site of America's first naval college), the **Redwood Library and Athenaeum** (the country's oldest continuously operated library), and **Touro Synagogue**, the nation's first synagogue. Sports fans can't leave town without exploring the **International Tennis Hall of Fame**. End the day with a nightcap at the **White Horse Tavern**, which has been pulling pints since 1673.

Day 4: Southeastern Connecticut

In the southeastern corner of the state resides the historic town of **Mystic**, whose **Mystic Seaport** (pp218–19) museum allows you to walk the decks of a ship or watch carpenters replank a vessel. From there, head to the town's popular aquarium. Gain a sense of New England of yesteryear as you pass through the nearby towns of **Stonington**, **New London**, and **Groton**. Visit one of the region's gargantuan casino resorts, **Foxwoods** and **Mohegan Sun**, for a lively night to remember.

Day 5: Connecticut Coast and New Haven

Tour the **Yale University** (pp226–9) campus, almost a living museum with its imposing Gothic architecture and historical artifacts. Walk the parks of **New Haven** (pp224–9), and be sure to sample a local pizza. The town is known for its old-school, thin-crust pies (Frank Pepe's is perhaps the most famous). Enjoy a lazy drive along the coast, stopping to visit the charming small towns of **Madison**, **Guilford**, and **Essex** (p220).

Day 6: Hartford and Litchfield Hills

Explore **Hartford's** (pp202–205) wealth of grand buildings and institutions, from the ornate Victorian-Gothic **Connecticut State Capitol** in Bushnell Park to America's first public art museum, the **Wadsworth Atheneum**. The city was also a hotbed of 19th-century publishing and writing; visit **Mark Twain House** (pp204–205) and adjacent **Harriet Beecher Stowe Center** to better appreciate the city's literary history. Tucked into the northwest corner of the state, not far from Hartford, are the undulating **Litchfield Hills** (pp212–13). Enjoy a leisurely drive through some of the area's most bucolic scenery, or step into cold mountain streams to practice fly-fishing. Try to pass through the idyllic 18th- and 19th-century communities of **Bethlehem**, **Norfolk**, and **Kent** (p213), which are filled with white churches and tidy town greens.

Day 7: The Berkshires

Seemingly a world apart from Boston, calmer Western Massachusetts contains the famous **Berkshires** (pp170–71). Tour the Colonial-era villages of the hilly region's south, including **Great Barrington** or the former mill towns of **Pittsfield** and **North Adams**. Follow music lovers from across the globe to **Lenox**, home of the esteemed summertime institution **Tanglewood**. Visit the **Massachusetts Museum of Contemporary Art (MASS MoCA)** (p168). Nature lovers can skip the artistic trappings in favor of challenging hikes over mountaintop trails with sweeping views.

Putting New England on the Map

Northern New England shows the region at its most rural.
Vermont is famous for its rolling farmland, and New
Hampshire for its White Mountains and the spectacular passes
between the peaks. Sparsely populated Maine is covered in
dense forest and an intricate network of lakes, streams, and
rivers, with a rugged coastline. Southern New England has
traditionally been the industrial and cultural hub of the
region, with Boston its capital. Massachusetts is the historical
center of the New England colonies. Tiny Rhode Island
contains some of New England's most extravagant mansions,
and Connecticut's proximity to New York City has graced
many of its towns and cities with a cosmopolitan flavor.

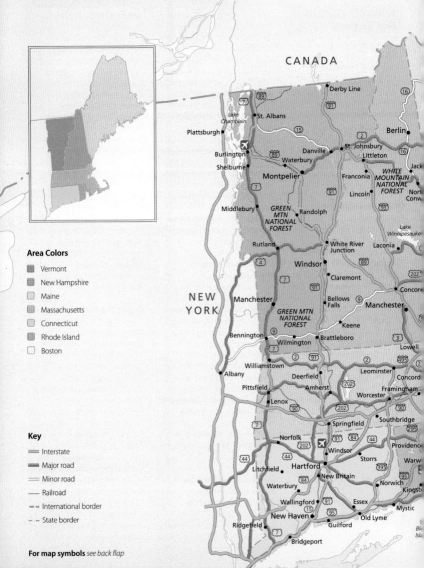

Area Colors

- Vermont
- New Hampshire
- Maine
- Massachusetts
- Connecticut
- Rhode Island
- Boston

Key

‒‒‒ Interstate

━━━ Major road

═══ Minor road

⎯⎯ Railroad

‒ ‒ International border

– – State border

For map symbols *see back flap*

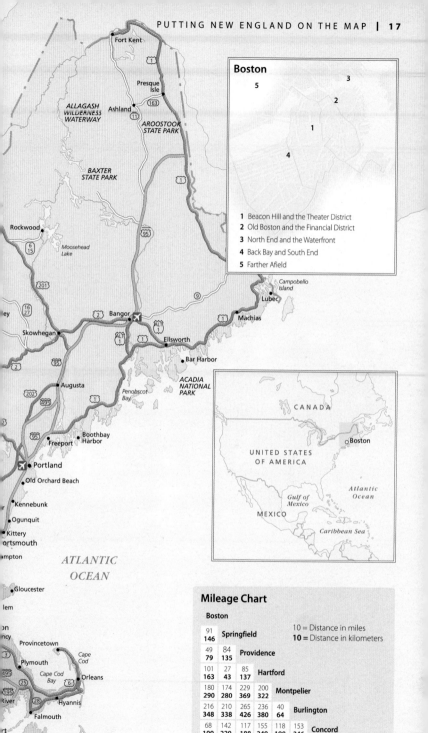

Boston

5

3

2

1

4

1 **Beacon Hill and the Theater District**
2 **Old Boston and the Financial District**
3 **North End and the Waterfront**
4 **Back Bay and South End**
5 **Farther Afield**

Campobello
Island

Lubec

Machias

ALLAGASH
WILDERNESS
WATERWAY

Fort Kent

Presque
Isle

Ashland

AROOSTOOK
STATE PARK

BAXTER
STATE PARK

Rockwood

Moosehead
Lake

Bangor

Skowhegan

Ellsworth

Bar Harbor

Augusta

ACADIA
NATIONAL
PARK

Penobscot
Bay

Boothbay
Harbor

Freeport

Portland

Old Orchard Beach

Kennebunk

Ogunquit

Kittery

ortsmouth

ampton

**ATLANTIC
OCEAN**

Gloucester

lem

Provincetown

Plymouth

Cape
Cod

Orleans

Cape Cod
Bay

Hyannis

Falmouth

Martha's
Vineyard

Nantucket
Island

CANADA

UNITED STATES
OF AMERICA

Boston

Gulf of
Mexico

Atlantic
Ocean

MEXICO

Caribbean Sea

Mileage Chart

Boston

91	**Springfield**							
146								
49	84	**Providence**						
79	**135**							
101	27	85	**Hartford**					
163	**43**	**137**						
180	174	229	200	**Montpelier**				
290	**280**	**369**	**322**					
216	210	265	236	40	**Burlington**			
348	**338**	**426**	**380**	**64**				
68	142	117	155	118	153	**Concord**		
109	**229**	**188**	**249**	**190**	**246**			
164	254	213	264	197	234	153	**Augusta**	
264	**409**	**343**	**425**	**317**	**377**	**246**		
106	189	155	202	171	209	85	59	**Portland**
171	**304**	**249**	**325**	**275**	**336**	**137**	**95**	

10 = Distance in miles
10 = Distance in kilometers

A PORTRAIT OF NEW ENGLAND

For many people, New England is white-steepled churches, craggy coastlines, and immaculate village greens. However, the region is also home to the opulence of Newport, Rhode Island, the beautiful suburban communities of Connecticut, and the self-assured sophistication of Boston – as well as the picture-postcard villages, covered bridges, timeless landscapes, and back-road gems.

From its beginning, the region has been shaped by both geography and climate. Early explorers charted its coastline, and communities soon sprang up by the sea, where goods and people could be ferried more easily from the Old World to the New. Much of the area's early commerce depended heavily on the ocean, from shipping and whaling to fishing and boat-building. Inland the virgin forests and hilly terrain of areas such as New Hampshire, Vermont, and Maine created communities that survived and thrived on independence. The slogan "Live free or die" on today's New Hampshire license plates is a reminder that the same spirit still lives on.

New England winters are long and harsh, and spring can bring unpredictable weather. As the 19th-century author Harriet Martineau (1802–76) declared, "I believe no one attempts to praise the climate of New England." Combined with the relatively poor growing conditions of the region – glaciers during the last Ice Age scoured away much of New England's precious soil – this has meant that farming has always been a struggle against the capricious forces of nature. To survive in these northeastern states required toughness, ingenuity, and resourcefulness, all traits that became ingrained in the New England psyche. Indeed, the area today is as much a state of mind as it is a physical space.

Few places in America – if any – are richer in historical connections. This is where European civilization first gained a toehold in America. And even long after the American Revolution (1775–83), New England continued to play an important role in the life of the developing nation, supplying many of its political and

Victorian cottage in the Trinity Park district in Oak Bluffs, Massachusetts

◀ The scenic village of Stowe, Vermont

Former frontier outpost, Old Fort Western in Augusta, Maine – a view into New England's past

intellectual leaders. That spirit endures. An intellectual confidence, some may call it smugness, persists; some people would say it is with good reason, since it was New England that produced the first flowering of American culture. Writers such as Henry David Thoreau (1817–62), Ralph Waldo Emerson (1803–82), Louisa May Alcott (1832–88), and Herman Melville (1819–91) became the first American writers of an international caliber. Even today, New England still figures prominently in the arts and letters, and its famous preparatory schools and the Ivy League universities and other institutions of higher learning continue to draw some of America's best and brightest to the region.

Statue of Samuel de Champlain

Mountains and Seashore

From the heights of the White Mountains – the highest terrain in the northeastern US – to the windswept seashore of Cape

New-England-born Louisa May Alcott

Cod, New England offers a stunning range of landscapes. And, while industrialization and urbanization have left their stamp, there is plenty of the wild past still in the present. The woods of Maine, for example, look much as they did when American writer and naturalist Henry David Thoreau visited them more than 150 years ago. Vermont's Green Mountains would be instantly recognizable by the explorer Samuel de Champlain (1567–1635), who first saw them more than 400 years ago. But it is not only the countryside that has endured; there are homes scattered throughout New England that preserve an array of early American architectural styles, from Colonial to Greek Revival. Just as the terrain is varied, so, too, is New England's population. The earliest settlers to the region were mostly of English and Scottish stock. Even by the early 19th century New England was still a relatively homogenous society, but this changed dramatically during the mid-1800s as waves of Irish immigrants arrived, driven from their homeland by the potato famines.

This altered the political balance of the area. Whereas the earliest leaders tended to be of British ancestry – men such as

Machine shed inside the Boott Cotton Mills Museum in Lowell, Massachusetts

President John Adams (1735–1826) and John Hancock (1737–93), signatories of the Declaration of Independence – now Irish-born politicians came to the fore. In 1884 one such man, Hugh O'Brien (1827–95), won the mayoral race in Boston. Meanwhile immigrants from Italy, Portugal, and eastern Europe also arrived, as well as an influx of French-Canadians, who flocked to the mill towns looking for employment. Still, the Irish represented a sizable part of the New England community and their impact on New England society and politics continued to grow, culminating in the election of John F. Kennedy (1917–63) in 1960 as America's first Roman Catholic president. Today some of the fourth-, fifth-, and sixth-generation Irish Americans have ascended to the top of New England's social hierarchy, although there remains a special cachet for people who can trace their ancestry directly to the Pilgrims who first came here aboard the *Mayflower*.

Outdoor Activities

Despite the area's proximity to some of America's most populated areas – a mere 40-mile (64-km) commute separates Stamford, Connecticut, and New York City – it offers a wealth of outdoor activities. There is something here to keep just about any sports enthusiast satisfied. For canoeists and white-water rafters, there are the beautiful Allagash and Connecticut rivers and a captivating collection of lakes. For skiers, resorts such as Killington, Stowe, and Sugarloaf offer some of the best skiing in the eastern US. The region's heavy snowfalls provide a wonderful base for cross-country skiers and snowshoers as well. There's biking on the back roads of New Hampshire and excellent hiking on the Appalachian Trail

White-water rafting on the Kennebec River, Maine

and Vermont's Long Trail, considered by many as one of the best hiking trails in the world.

Of course, many popular outdoor activities center around the ocean. There's kayaking among the islands and inlets of the Maine shoreline, windsurfing off Cape Cod, and ample opportunities for sailing, fishing, swimming, and scuba diving up and down the entire New England coast.

Fisherman holding up a large striped bass

The Landscape and Wildlife of New England

Considering its proximity to major cities, rural New England boasts a surprisingly diverse collection of wildlife, including many species of birds, moose, bears, beavers, and, rarely, bobcats. The topography of the region includes rolling hills, dense woodlands, rugged mountains, and a coastline that is jagged and rocky in some areas and sandy and serene in others. Northern Maine has the closest thing to wilderness found in the eastern United States, with hundreds of square miles of trackless land and a vast network of clear streams, rivers, and lakes. New England is also home to the White and Green Mountains of the Appalachian chain.

Bald eagles are found around water, making Maine their favorite New England state.

Coastline

From the crenelated coastline of Maine, which measures almost 3,500 miles (5,630 km) in length, to the sandy beaches of Connecticut, the New England shoreline is richly varied. Here visitors find various sea and shore birds, many attracted by the food provided by the expansive salt marshes that have been created by barrier beaches. A few miles offshore, there is excellent whale-watching.

Mountain Landscape

The western and northern parts of New England are dominated by the Appalachian Mountains, a chain that extends from Georgia to Canada. The highest point is 6,288-ft (1,917-m) Mount Washington, also known for drastic weather changes at its summit. Birch and beech trees are plentiful at elevations up to 2,000 ft (610 m). At the higher elevations, pine, spruce, and fir trees are most common.

The great blue heron is the largest of the North American herons. This elegant bird is easily spotted in wetlands and on lakeshores.

White-tailed deer can be found in a range of habitats, from forest edges to open woodland. They are frequently spotted on mountainsides up to 2,000 ft (610 m).

Whales are plentiful off the coast, particularly in the Gulf of Maine, from early spring to mid-October. Finbacks, minke, and right whales are most common, but humpbacks put on the best show, often leaping out of the water.

Coyotes were once all but extinct in the region, but their numbers are on the rise again. They tend to live in forested and mountainous areas, but might be seen in urban areas.

National Wildlife Refuge System

With 234,400 sq miles (607,100 sq km) under its control, the National Wildlife Refuge System (NWRS) offers protection for some of the country's most ecologically rich areas. The NWRS began in 1903, when President Theodore Roosevelt (1858–1919) established Pelican Island in Florida as a refuge for birds. Thirty-five refuges are located in New England, including eleven in Massachusetts, five in Rhode Island, four in New Hampshire, ten in Maine, one in Connecticut, and one in Vermont. They offer some of the best bird-watching in the region. See www.fws.gov/refuges for more information.

Rachel Carson National Wildlife Refuge, a vast wetland stop for migratory birds

Lakes and Rivers

The rivers and lakes of New England provide fishermen, canoeists, and vacationers in general with a world of outdoor pleasures. The network of waterways is particularly extensive in Maine, which has more lakes than any state in the northeastern United States. Among the rivers, the Connecticut is New England's longest, at more than 400 miles (644 km) in length. It runs from the Canadian border along the Vermont-New Hampshire border and through Massachusetts and Connecticut.

Forests

The logging industry and the switch to agricultural and grazing land – especially for sheep – decimated many of the forests of New England in the 19th and early 20th centuries, but the tide has turned. Vermont, for example, has far more forests today than it did 100 years ago. In the lower elevations, the trees are mostly deciduous, such as ash, maple, and birch, but higher up in the mountains coniferous trees such as balsam fir predominate.

Mallard ducks are a frequent sight throughout New England wetlands. The birds can be seen from April to October, when they migrate to warmer climes.

The pigeon hawk, also known as the merlin, can be found throughout New England, even in urban areas.

Moose are common in Maine, northern Vermont, and New Hampshire. Although they can be spotted in the woods, they are most often seen along the shores of lakes. Drivers should be wary of moose, especially at dawn and dusk.

Chipmunks are seen virtually throughout rural New England, especially in the forests.

Raccoons are commonly seen in wooded areas. They often pay visits to campsites, brazenly foraging for food with dexterous paws.

Fall Foliage

The cool weather in the fall signals more than back-to-school time in New England. It also sounds a clarion call to hundreds of thousands of visitors to head outdoors to gaze in wonder at one of nature's most splendid offerings: the annual changing of leaf colors. Planning foliage tours is an inexact science, however. Generally, leaves start to change earliest in more northern areas and higher up mountainsides. On some mountains in northern New England, for example, the leaves will begin changing color as early as August. In general, the peak period varies from early October in the northern part of the region to late October in the southern section. But this can differ, depending on the weather. Cooler temperatures than normal tend to speed up the leaf-changing timetable, and vice versa.

The fall harvest can produce some impressive pumpkins

Blue sky
The rich palette created by the foliage is made even more dramatic by a backdrop of a deep-blue fall sky.

Vermont's Fall Colors

While each of the New England states offers something for "leaf peepers," none can top Vermont. With its rich mix of deciduous trees, the Green Mountain State is anything but just green in late September and October. Inns and hotels tend to be booked up months in advance on the key weekends as the Vermont countryside swells with one of its biggest influxes of out-of-state visitors.

Forest floor
Fallen leaves are more than just beautiful to the eye. They will eventually decay and replenish the humus layer.

Nature's paint box
One of the most remarkable features of the fall foliage season is how it transforms the scenery. Here Quechee Gorge, Vermont's Grand Canyon, has changed its verdant green cloak for one of many colors.

Maple leaf
The maple tree is one of the most common trees in New England. Its leaves change to yellow, red, or orange.

Why Leaves Turn

The changing of leaf colors is not just a capricious act of nature. It is a direct response to the changing realities of the seasons. As daylight hours diminish, the leaves of deciduous trees stop producing the green pigment chlorophyll. With the disappearance of chlorophyll, other pigments that had been hidden behind the chlorophyll's color now burst into view. More pigments are produced by sugars that remain trapped in the leaves. The result is a riotous display that makes this the high point of the year for many visitors. Two of the most spectacular areas for color are Litchfield Hills, Connecticut *(see pp212–13)*, and Penobscot Bay, Maine *(pp290–91)*. Foliage hotlines give updates and are listed on page 379.

Fall hiking
Hikers should wear bright clothing and stick to well-marked trails and paths in the fall, as this is also hunting season in the area.

A single crimson leaf aglow on the forest floor

The Appalachian Trail

The Appalachian Trail is one of the longest footpaths in the world at 2,180 miles (3,508 km). From its southern terminus at Springer Mountain in the state of Georgia to its northernmost point on the summit of Mount Katahdin, Maine, the trail crosses 14 states and two national parks as it winds its way through forests, meadows, and mountains. The trail travels through five of the six New England states, missing only Rhode Island, and reaches its highest point in the northeast on windswept Mount Washington *(see p271)* in New Hampshire. Each year about 400 intrepid souls, called "thru hikers," complete the journey in a single trip. The vast majority of people, however, choose to walk the trail in smaller, more manageable sections. The trail is usually marked by rectangular white blazes painted on trees and rocks, and overnight hikers can take advantage of more than 250 primitive shelters along the route.

Locator Map

- New England
- - - Appalachian Trail

0 kilometers 50

0 miles 50

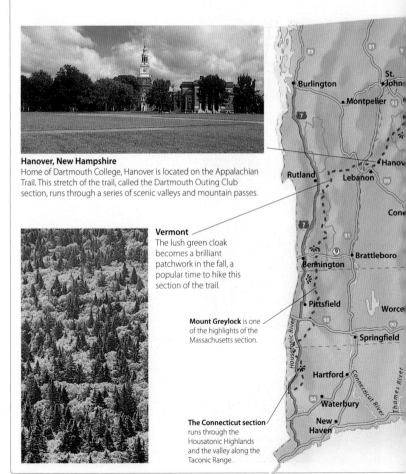

Hanover, New Hampshire
Home of Dartmouth College, Hanover is located on the Appalachian Trail. This stretch of the trail, called the Dartmouth Outing Club section, runs through a series of scenic valleys and mountain passes.

Vermont
The lush green cloak becomes a brilliant patchwork in the fall, a popular time to hike this section of the trail.

Mount Greylock is one of the highlights of the Massachusetts section.

The Connecticut section runs through the Housatonic Highlands and the valley along the Taconic Range.

Burlington

St. John

Montpelier

Rutland

Hanov

Lebanon

Con

Brattleboro

Bennington

Pittsfield

Worce

Springfield

Hartford

Waterbury

New Haven

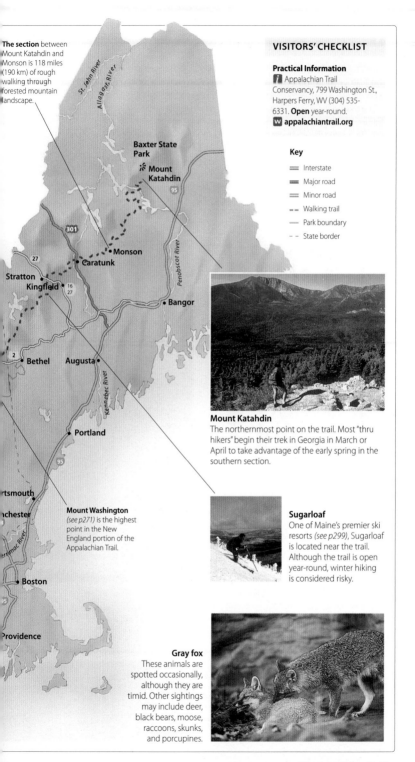

The section between Mount Katahdin and Monson is 118 miles (190 km) of rough walking through forested mountain landscape.

Baxter State Park

Mount Katahdin

Monson

Caratunk

Stratton

Kingfield

Bangor

Bethel

Augusta

Portland

rtsmouth

nchester

Boston

Providence

Mount Katahdin
The northernmost point on the trail. Most "thru hikers" begin their trek in Georgia in March or April to take advantage of the early spring in the southern section.

Mount Washington *(see p271)* is the highest point in the New England portion of the Appalachian Trail.

Sugarloaf
One of Maine's premier ski resorts *(see p299)*, Sugarloaf is located near the trail. Although the trail is open year-round, winter hiking is considered risky.

Gray fox
These animals are spotted occasionally, although they are timid. Other sightings may include deer, black bears, moose, raccoons, skunks, and porcupines.

Maritime New England

It was the sea that helped open up the region to settlement in the 17th century. The sea also provided New Englanders with a way of life. In the early years, ships worked the fertile waters off Cape Cod for whales, fish, and lobster. Whaling reached its zenith in the 19th century, when hundreds of whaleboats fanned out to the uttermost ends of the Earth. Today the best places to explore the area's rich maritime history are the New Bedford Whaling National Historical Park and the New Bedford Whaling Museum in New Bedford, Massachusetts *(see p125)*, Mystic Seaport *(see pp218–19)*, Connecticut, and the Penobscot Marine Museum in Searsport, Maine *(see p290)*.

Ropes and pulleys were important for hoisting sails and lowering the whaleboats.

Antique whaling harpoons
Harpoons and lances were hand-forged in New Bedford. Harpoons were thrown to attach a line to the whale. When the leviathan tired of pulling boat and men, the lance was used for the kill.

New England's Whalers

Competition in 19th-century whaling was fierce. In 1857 some 330 whalers sailed out of New Bedford, Massachusetts, alone. The *Catalpa*, portrayed by C. S. Raleigh in his late 1800s painting, is an example of a well-outfitted whaler.

Whaleboats were lowered into the water to hunt and harpoon whales. Whale oil was used for illumination and was a valuable commodity.

Maritime art
Maritime influences still appear throughout New England. This contemporary chest by Harriet Scudder depicts an early whaling scene.

The Ice Trade

The cold winters of northern New England provided the source of a valuable export in the 19th century. In the days before mechanical refrigeration, ice from the region's frozen rivers, lakes, and ponds was cut up into large blocks, packed in sawdust, and shipped as far away as India. To keep the ice from melting, engineers designed ships with special airtight hulls. The ice trade finally collapsed in the late 1800s, when mechanical methods for keeping perishables cool began to make ice obsolete for refrigeration in an increasing number of places in the world.

Harvesting ice

Barks were popular whaling vessels in the 19th century because they were maneuverable and could undertake long voyages.

Scrimshaw
New England sailors killed long periods of inactivity on the sea making etchings on whale teeth or jawbones. Ink and tobacco juice added color.

Whale carcasses were secured to the sides of the ship so that the blubber could be stripped and boiled onboard for its oil.

Lighthouses
Nearly 200 lighthouses dot New England's coast, testimony to the area's maritime ties.

Lobster industry
In colonial times, lobster was so common it was used as fertilizer. Today it is considered a delicacy.

New England Architecture

New England architecture encompasses a variety of styles. In the early years of colonization, the influences of England predominated. But after the Revolutionary War (1775–83), the new republic wanted to distance itself from its colonial past. Drawing on French Neo-Classicism, the newest European style of the late 18th century, American architects brought into being a distinctive American version known as Federal. In its efforts to define itself, New England did not reject foreign ideas, however, as evidenced by the Greek Revival style of the early 19th century and the adaptation of English and French Revival styles for the next 100 years.

Center Church in West Hartford, Connecticut

Colonial Style

Colonial style, the style of the period when America was still a British colony, has two aspects: the homes of ordinary people and the more elaborate architecture of public buildings, mansions, and churches. The large wooden houses built in towns and rural areas in New England between 1607 and 1780 constitute one of the area's architectural treasures. Numerous examples survive, and the style has many regional variations. The famous Connecticut "saltbox" houses are an example. They featured distinctive close-cropped eaves and a long back roof that projected over a kitchen lean-to.

Eleazer Arnold House chimney, Lincoln, Rhode Island

Roof
Shingles became the main roofing material and were frequently used for walls as well.

Chimney
The large chimney provided a vital outlet for smoke.

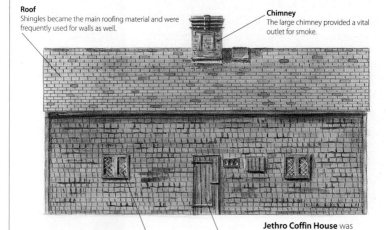

Jethro Coffin House was built in 1686 and is the oldest surviving structure in Nantucket, Massachusetts. A slot beside the front door allowed inhabitants to see who was standing outside.

Windows
Small casement windows were fitted with diamond-shaped panes of glass imported from England.

Door
In keeping with the practical Colonial aesthetics, doors featured a simple, vertical-board design.

Casement window

Georgian Style

The term "Georgian," or "Palladian," refers to the mainstream Classical architecture of 18th-century England, which drew on the designs of 16th-century Italian architect Andrea Palladio (1508–80). In the colonies and England, these elegant buildings marked the presence of the British ruling class.

Pedimented dormers, Ladd Gilman House, in Exeter, New Hampshire

Roof
Roofs were less steeply pitched than earlier Colonial-era designs. A delicate balustrade crowns the roof.

Windows
Georgian windows were usually double-hung sash with six panes.

Doors
Doors featured a raised-panel design with six or more panels and Classical moldings.

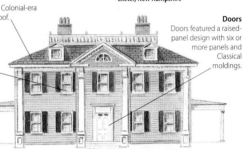

Longfellow House – Washington's Headquarters in Cambridge, Massachusetts, built in 1759. Its façade has Classical columns and a triangular pediment.

Federal Style

American architects viewed the Federal style as a distinctive national statement. Some Federal buildings drew on both Greek and Roman architecture, representing the tenets of democracy and republicanism. Federal style is more restrained than Georgian, with less intricate woodwork.

The Colony House in Newport *(see pp186–91)*, Rhode Island

Fanlights
Fanlights, frequent in Georgian architecture, were also found in Neo-Classical design.

Roof
Neo-Classical roofs were often flat.

Façade
Neo-Classical façades were less decorated than Georgian. Often stories were separated by bands of stone called string courses.

Gardner-Pingree House in Salem, Massachusetts, is known for its graceful proportions.

Greek Revival Style

Popular between 1820 and 1845, this style is a more literal version of Classical architecture than the Federal style. Greek Revival buildings typically borrowed the façades of ancient Greek temples, often sensitively re-creating them in wood.

Samuel Russell House in Middletown, Connecticut, features a white exterior common in Greek Revival structures.

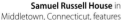

Providence, Rhode Island, church door

Façade
The "temple fronts" of Greek Revival buildings were inspired by the archaeological discoveries in Greece and Turkey in the 18th century.

Columns
These Corinthian columns faithfully follow conventions of ancient Greek architecture.

Colleges and Universities

New England is not only the cradle of American civilization, it is also the birthplace of higher education in the New World. Harvard University *(see pp116–21)* was founded in 1636, only 16 years after the Pilgrims arrived at Plymouth Rock *(see pp152–3)*. Four of the country's eight renowned Ivy League colleges are located in New England: Harvard, Brown *(see p179)*, Dartmouth *(see p267)*, and Yale *(see pp226–9)*. Here higher learning goes hand in hand with tradition and culture. Many of America's most famous art collections and natural history museums are found on campus grounds. As well, many of the top-ranked liberal arts colleges are found here, including Bowdoin and all-women Smith and Wellesley Colleges.

1764 Rhode Island College, later Brown University, is founded in Providence, Rhode Island

1852 The Harvard crew wins inaugural Harvard-Yale Regatta – beginning one of the longest rivalries in US college sports

1778 Phillips Academy is founded by educator Samuel Phillips in Andover, Massachusetts

1781 John Phillips, uncle of Samuel, founds Phillips Exeter Academy in Exeter, New Hampshire

1636 Harvard University is founded in Cambridge, Massachusetts; 12 students enroll in the inaugural year

1701 Puritan clergymen found Collegiate School in Saybrook, Connecticut

1801 Daniel Webster graduates from Dartmouth and goes on to an illustrious career as US statesman and orator

1640	1680	1720	1760	1800	184

1640	1680	1720	1760	1800	184

1642 Physics becomes a mandatory subject at Harvard, using text by Aristotle

1777 Brown's University Hall building is used as barracks for Colonial troops during War of Independence

1817 Harvard Law School is established

1832 Yale Art Gallery is founded after US artist John Trumbull donates around 100 pieces of art from his personal collection

1717 Collegiate School is moved to New Haven, Connecticut, and is renamed Yale in 1718 in honor of benefactor Elihu Yale

1844 Yale graduate Samuel Morse sends world's first telegraphic message in Morse code

1853 Franklin Pierce, graduate of Bowdoin College in Brunswick, Maine, is elected 14th president of the United States

1861 Massachusetts Institute of Technology (MIT) is founded

1868 William Dubois is born. Dubois would go on to become the first black person to earn a Ph.D. from Harvard

1919 Philanthropist and Brown University graduate John D. Rockefeller, Jr. donates 8 sq miles (20 sq km) of Maine's Mount Desert Island for use as a preserve. His further gifts would form almost one-third of Acadia National Park *(see pp292–3)*

1925 S. J. Perelman graduates from Brown; goes on to win Academy Award for screenplay of *Around the World in 80 Days* (1956)

1957 *The Cat in the Hat*, written by Dartmouth alumnus Theodor Geisel (Dr. Seuss), is published

1992 Yale graduate Bill Clinton is elected 42nd president of the United States

2004 MIT completes Stata Center, designed by Frank Gehry, to house computer science and artificial intelligence laboratories

2008 Harvard Law School graduate Barack Obama is elected as the first African-American president of the United States

2010 University of Connecticut women's basketball team sets college record for most consecutive wins by either men's or women's teams

2012 Expanded Yale Art Gallery opens

2014 Expanded Harvard Art Museums open

| 1880 | 1920 | 1960 | 2000 | 2040 |

| 1880 | 1920 | 1960 | 2000 | 2040 |

1946 Percy Bridgman becomes first Harvard physicist to receive Nobel Prize in Physics

1969 Women are admitted to Yale's undergraduate program

2000 Yale graduate George W. Bush is elected 43rd president, following in the footsteps of his father George H. W. Bush – Yale graduate and 41st president

1877 Former slave Inman Page becomes first African-American to graduate from Brown

1861 Yale awards country's first Ph.D. degrees

New England Boarding Schools

New England boasts the most prestigious collection of college preparatory, or "prep," schools in the US. The two preeminent institutions are Phillips Academy in Andover, Massachusetts, and Phillips Exeter Academy *(see p260)* in Exeter, New Hampshire. Both are private, coeducational schools and attract the sons and daughters of some of the country's wealthiest and most influential families. Other prominent prep schools include Choate Rosemary Hall in Wallingford, Connecticut, and Groton in Groton, Massachusetts.

Campus of Phillips Exeter Academy

Literary New England

Writing in his seminal work *Democracy in America* (1835), French historian Alexis de Tocqueville (1805–59) declared, "The inhabitants of the United States have, then, at present, no literature." Less than two decades later, that scenario had changed radically. By then, writers such as Ralph Waldo Emerson (1803–82), Henry David Thoreau (1817–62), and Nathaniel Hawthorne (1804–64) were creating works that would take their place among the classics of 19th-century literature – and that was just in one town, Concord *(see pp148–9)*, Massachusetts. Since that first flowering, New England writers have been taking their place among the best in the world.

Author Nathaniel Hawthorne (1804–64)

Ralph Waldo Emerson, speaking to Transcendentalists in Concord

Father of Transcendentalism

Born in Boston, Ralph Waldo Emerson graduated from Harvard University in 1821 and became the pastor of the Second Church (Unitarian) in Boston in 1829. In many ways Emerson turned his back on his formal religious education in the 1830s when he founded the Transcendentalism movement. Among other things, Emerson's writings espoused a system of spiritual independence in which each individual was responsible for his or her own moral judgments. Moving to

Concord in 1834, the popular essayist and lecturer soon became known as the "Sage of Concord" for his insightful teachings.

Concord was also the birthplace of Emerson's most famous disciple, Henry David Thoreau. A one-time school teacher, Thoreau worked as a pencil maker before quitting to undertake his lifelong study of nature. Deeply influenced by the Transcendentalist belief that total unity with nature was achievable, Thoreau built a small cabin at Walden Pond *(see p149)* in 1845, living as a recluse for the next two years. In 1854 his work *Walden; or, Life in the Woods,* was published, in which he outlined how people could escape a life of "quiet desperation" by paring

away the extraneous, anxiety-inducing trappings of the industrial age and living in harmony with the natural world.

19th-Century Literary Flowering

It was also in Concord that Nathaniel Hawthorne penned *Mosses from an Old Manse* in 1846. Hawthorne later returned to his hometown, Salem *(see pp140–41)*, Massachusetts, where he wrote his best-known work, *The Scarlet Letter* (1850). Moving to Lenox in western Massachusetts, Hawthorne became friends with Herman Melville (1819–91), who wrote his allegorical masterpiece *Moby-Dick* (1851) in neighboring Pittsfield. The book drew its inspiration from the voyage that

Illustration from Herman Melville's *Moby-Dick*

Henry David Thoreau's simple grave in Concord, Massachusetts

The porch of the Robert Frost house in New Hampshire

Melville made from New Bedford, Massachusetts, to the South Seas aboard the New England whaler *Acushnet*.

Like Melville, Mark Twain (1835–1910) was not a New Englander by birth. However, it was during his long stay in Hartford *(see pp202–205)*, Connecticut, that he penned the novels that would vault him into worldwide prominence, including *The Adventures of Tom Sawyer* (1876), *The Adventures of Huckleberry Finn* (1885), and *A Connecticut Yankee in King Arthur's Court* (1889).

19th-Century Women Authors

Although opportunities for women were limited in 19th-century America, several New England female writers still managed to leave their mark on literature. One of the region's most famous – and mysterious – literary figures was Emily Dickinson (1830–86). Born in Amherst *(see pp166–7)*, Massachusetts, she was educated at the Mount Holyoke Female Seminary *(see p166)* before withdrawing from society in her early 20s. Living the rest of her life in her family's home, Dickinson wrote more than 1,000 poems – the vast majority of which remained unpublished until after her death. Today her finely crafted poems are admired for their complex rhythms and intensely personal lyrics.

Cover of sheet music for Harriet Beecher Stowe's *Uncle Tom's Cabin*

The greatest single indictment of the slavery that would catapult America into civil war came from the pen of Harriet Beecher Stowe (1811–96), who would later become Mark Twain's next-door neighbor in Hartford. *Uncle Tom's Cabin; or, Life Among the Lowly* (1852) told the story of a slave family's desperate flight for freedom to a rapt, largely sympathetic audience worldwide. Louisa May Alcott (1832–88) – yet another Concord resident – left a lasting and loving portrait of domestic life in the United States during the Civil War (1861–5) in *Little Women* (1868), a perennial favorite of children.

20th Century

In the 20th century, New England continued to play a defining role in American literature, spawning native writers as diverse as "Beat" chronicler Jack Kerouac *(see p146)* and the "Chekhov of the suburbs," John Cheever (1912–82). The region has also provided a fertile base for transplanted New Englanders. The poet Robert Frost (1874–1963), a native of San Francisco, lived most of his life in Vermont and New Hampshire, and the mountains, meadows, and people of the region figure prominently in his poetry, which won the Pulitzer Prize an unprecedented four times. Poet and novelist John Updike (1932–2009) lived much of his life in Ipswich, Massachusetts, and set both *Couples* (1968) and *The Witches of Eastwick* (1984) in the northeast. Novelist John Irving was born in Exeter, New Hampshire, in 1942. Much of his later fiction is set in New England, including *The World According to Garp* (1978) and *Cider House Rules* (1985). Perhaps the area's best-known living writer is horror master Stephen King (b.1947), a longtime resident of Bangor, Maine. Boston-born mystery writer Dennis Lehane (b.1966) sets his novels in gritty working-class neighborhoods.

Fright master and longtime Bangor resident Stephen King

NEW ENGLAND THROUGH THE YEAR

New England is really a year-round tourist destination – depending on what it is people are looking to do. Generally, spring is the shortest season. Occurring sometime between April and June, spring in New England can be short-lived but glorious; wildflowers bursting forth in colorful bloom provide a feast for the eyes. Summer is the busiest period for tourism. With the good weather stretching from mid-June into early September, this part of the year is characterized by warm temperatures that have people flocking to lakes and the ocean. Fall is when New England is at its most beautiful, with its lush forests changing from green to a riot of gold, red, and orange. The peak period for fall foliage generally occurs from mid-September to late October. Winter, which usually lasts from December through to mid-April, is often marked by heavy snowfalls – a boon for winter-sport enthusiasts.

Cars decorated with flowers in Nantucket's Daffodil Festival

Spring

New England's shortest season is sometimes little more than a three-week interval between winter and summer. As well as being the prime time for maple-syrup tapping, spring brings with it a host of festivals.

April
Boston Marathon *(third Monday, April)*, Boston, MA. America's oldest and most prestigious marathon.
Patriot's Day *(third Monday, April)*, Lexington and Concord, MA. Costumed reenactments of the pivotal battles that were waged at the outset of the Revolutionary War.
Daffodil Festival *(late April)*, Nantucket, MA. The town is decked out in millions of yellow daffodils.

May
Lilac Sunday *(early May)*, Boston, MA. The celebration of the Arnold Arboretum historic lilac collection includes tours, performances, and picnics amid the blooms.
Moose Mania *(mid-May– mid-June)*, Greenville, ME. Moose sightings, craft fairs, and other events.
Cape Cod Maritime Days *(May)*, Cape Cod, MA. Celebration of seaside life with lectures, boat rides, kayaking, and kite-flying.
Brimfield Antique Show *(May, July, and September)*, Brimfield, MA. Dealers from across the US gather at this show to sell their wares.
Vermont Artisans' Open Studios *(late May)*, statewide. Artists welcome visitors.

Patriot's Day celebration in Lexington, Massachusetts

A juggler performing as part of the award-winning Circus Smirkus

Waterfire *(May–October)*, Providence, RI. This dazzling art event features 100 bonfires, which are lit on the city's three rivers.

Early June
Cambridge River Festival *(early June)*, Cambridge, MA. This community festival features food and arts.
Discover Jazz Festival *(early June)*, Burlington, VT. Jazz, blues, and gospel are the highlights of this popular festival.
Circus Smirkus *(early June– mid-August)*. This international youth circus performs around New England.

Summer

New England summers can be hot and humid. This is vacation time for students and families, making the region a very busy place, especially the coastline and beaches.

Average daily hours of sunshine

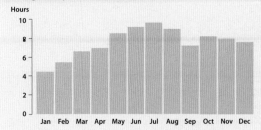

Hours

Jan Feb Mar Apr May Jun Jul Aug Sep Oct Nov Dec

Sunshine Chart
New England's weather can vary greatly from year to year. Generally, the short spring is cloudy and wet, giving way to better weather in June. July and August are usually the sunniest months. Bright fall days out among the colorful foliage are spectacular.

Late June
Gaspee Days *(mid-June)*, Cranston and Warwick, RI. Reenactment of the burning of a British schooner.
Secret Garden Tour *(mid-June)*, Newport, RI. Private gardens open to the public for self-guided walking tour.
International Festival of Arts and Ideas *(mid-June–July)*, New Haven, CT. A showcase of performance, visual arts, literature, film, and family events.
Jacob's Pillow Dance Festival *(mid-June–late August)*, Becket, MA. Ballet, jazz, and modern dance feature in the country's oldest dance festival.
Windjammer Days *(late June)*, Boothbay Harbor, ME. Shoreside events complement parade of graceful sailboats.
Antique Tractor Festival *(late June)*, Norridgewock, ME. Antique machinery demonstrations, crafts, tractor pulls, and a flea market.
Block Island Race Week *(late June)*, Block Island, RI. The largest sailing event on the coast.
Vermont Quilt Festival *(late June–early July)*, Essex Junction, VT. A quilting celebration.
Williamstown Theater Festival *(late June–August)*, Williamstown, MA. Featuring classical and new theater productions.

July
Independence Day Celebrations *(July 4th)*, throughout New England. Parades, fireworks, and concerts.
Tanglewood Music Festival *(early July–late August)*, Lenox, MA.

Boston Symphony and Boston Pops orchestras give concerts on this grand estate *(see p171)*.
Riverfest *(July)*, Hartford, CT. Fireworks and free concerts along the Connecticut River.
Vermont Cheesemakers Festival *(mid-July)*, Shelburne, VT. More than 40 makers of cheese and other products offer samples.
American Independence Festival *(mid-July)*, Exeter, NH. Beer festival, fireworks, and reenactments.
Newport Regatta *(mid-July)*, Newport, RI. This huge regatta attracts some 200 boats.
Guilford Craft Expo *(mid-July)*, Guilford, CT. This event features pottery, glass, jewelry, folk art, and quilts.
Lowell Folk Festival *(late July)*, Lowell, MA. Dance troupes, musicians, and ethnic food in historic Downtown Lowell.
Newport Folk Festival *(late July–early August)*, Newport, RI. One of the country's top folk festivals, held at Fort Adams State Park.

August
Maine Lobster Festival *(early August)*, Rockland, ME. Lobster and live entertainment are on the menu at this event.
League of New Hampshire Craftsmen Annual Fair *(early August)* Newbury, NH. The oldest crafts fair in the US features craft demonstrations, workshops, performing arts, and 200 booths selling high-quality crafts.
Addison County Fair *(early August)*, New Haven, VT. This is one of the state's largest agricultural fairs.

One of many festivals celebrating New England's nautical past

Newport Jazz Festival *(early August)*, Newport, RI. International jazz stars gather to perform at this festival.
Mystic Outdoor Arts Festival *(mid-August)*, Mystic, CT. This art show attracts 300 artists.
Wild Blueberry Festival *(mid–late August)*, Machias, ME. Foot races, pie-eating contests, and musical comedy celebrate the berry harvest.
Brooklyn Fair *(late August)*, Brooklyn, CT. The country's oldest continuously running agricultural fair has ox-pulls and livestock shows.
Champlain Valley Fair *(late August–early September)*, Essex Junction, VT. Horse shows and midway rides are part of this huge fair.
Classic Yacht Regatta *(late August–early September)*, Newport, RI. More than 100 vintage wooden yachts are on parade in this regatta.
Thomas Point Beach Bluegrass Festival *(late August–early September)*, Brunswick, ME. World-class lineup of musicians.

July 4th road markings

Average monthly precipitation

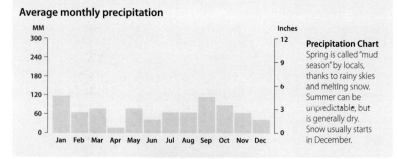

Precipitation Chart
Spring is called "mud season" by locals, thanks to rainy skies and melting snow. Summer can be unpredictable, but is generally dry. Snow usually starts in December.

Autumn

Many people consider the fall to be New England's most beautiful season. Bright, crisp autumn days are made more glorious by the brilliant fall foliage (see pp24–5).

September

Pawtucket Arts Festival (early September), Pawtucket, RI. Music and food for all tastes and colorful dragon-boat races are some of the highlights of this festival.

International Seaplane Fly-In (early September), Greenville, ME. Spectators gather on the shores of Moosehead Lake to observe floatplane competitions and sample local food.

Windjammer Festival (early September), Camden, ME. A celebration of Maine's fleet of classic sailing ships.

Vermont State Fair (early September), Rutland, VT. One of the most popular agricultural fairs in the state.

Woodstock Fair (early September), South Woodstock, CT. The state's second-oldest agricultural fair includes crafts, go-kart races, livestock shows, and petting zoos for children.

Norwalk Oyster Festival (early September), East Norwalk, CT. This nationally acclaimed celebration includes music, nautical displays, and lots of oyster sampling.

The Big "E" (last two weeks of September), Eastern States Exhibition Ground, West Springfield, MA. One of New England's biggest fairs, with rodeos, rides, and a circus.

A costumed reveler at Haunted Happenings, Salem, Massachusetts

Harvest Festivals (late September), throughout New England. Parades, apple picking, and hay-rides are some of the events held around the region to celebrate the fall harvest.

Sugar Hill Antique Show (late September), Sugar Hill, NH. A popular, long-running antique show attracts numerous dealers and their wares.

Fryeburg Fair (late September–early October), Fryeburg, ME. Maine's oldest county fair emphasizes its agricultural roots, but also offers midway rides and live entertainment.

Northeast Kingdom Fall Foliage Festival (late September–early October), throughout northern Vermont. Different towns hold foliage-related bus tours, hiking parties, and family events.

October

Mount Greylock Ramble (Columbus Day), Adams, MA. The whole community climbs the state's highest mountain.

Jack-O-Lantern Spectacular (October), Providence, RI. Roger Williams Park Zoo displays 5,000 carved pumpkins.

Haunted Happenings (October), Salem, MA. A month-long festival celebrating the city's witch-related past (see pp140–43) and Halloween.

Wellfleet Oysterfest (mid-October), Wellfleet, MA. Local cuisine, road race, oyster shuck-off, and music.

Chowder Days (mid-October), Mystic, CT. Enjoy chowder and a range of family activities at Mystic Seaport.

Brilliant colors, heralding Northeast Kingdom Fall Foliage Festival

Average monthly temperature

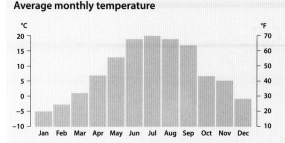

Temperature Chart
New England temperatures vary greatly through the year. In the summer, temperatures of 90° F (32° C) are quite frequent, while the thermometer can dip to 0° F (−18° C) or lower in winter. In general, it is warmer along the coast and in the southern section of New England.

November

Dinner in a Country Village (*November–March*), Old Sturbridge Village, Sturbridge, MA. Dinners cooked on open hearths relieve the winter chill.

Holiday Craft Exhibition and Sale (*mid-November–December 31*), Brookfield, CT. Craft artists put unique wares up for sale.

Thanksgiving Celebration (*mid- to late-November*), Plymouth, MA. Thanksgiving traditions of the past are celebrated in historic homes. Visitors can also enjoy a Thanksgiving dinner at Plimoth Plantation (*see pp154–5*).

Holiday Light Fantasia (*late November–early January*), Hartford, CT. Holiday lights line a 2-mile (3-km) route through Goodwin Park.

Winter

New England winters are often marked by heavy snowfalls, particularly in the mountainous areas farther inland. Temperatures can also plunge drastically overnight and from one day to the next. This, of course, is a boon for people who enjoy winter sports, as New England has some of the most popular ski centers in the eastern US.

December

Christmas at Newport Mansions (*late November–December*), Newport, RI. Three mansions are decked out for the holidays.

Festival of Trees and Traditions (*early December*), Hartford, CT. Hundreds of beautiful trees and

A traditional Thanksgiving dinner celebration

wreaths are on display at Wadsworth Athenaeum.

Festival of Lights (*early December*), Wickford Village, RI. This family-oriented festival includes tree- and window-decorating competitions, hayrides, and live music.

Christmas Tree Lighting (*early December*), Boston, MA. The huge tree in front of the Prudential Tower and Shopping Center is lit up with bright lights.

Candlelight Stroll (*mid-December*), Portsmouth, NH. The town's historic Strawbery Banke district (*see pp258–9*) is resplendent with antique Christmas decorations.

Boston Tea Party Reenactment (*mid-December*), Boston, MA. Costumed interpreters bring to life the famous protest that precipitated the Revolutionary War.

New Year's Eve Celebrations (*December 31*), throughout New England. Family-oriented festivities including fireworks, ice carvings, and performances can be found around the region.

January

Vermont Farm Show (*late January*), Barre, VT. Vermont's premier winter show includes a variety of agricultural displays and livestock exhibits.

Chinese New Year (*late January–early March*), Boston, MA. The location for this colorful festival is Boston's Chinatown.

February

National Toboggan Championships (*February*), Camden, ME. Daredevils of all sizes and ages come to compete in this high-speed, often hilarious, event.

Stowe Derby (*late February*), Stowe, VT. This is one of the oldest downhill and cross-country skiing races in the country.

March

Boston Flower and Garden Show (*March*), Boston, MA. Meticulous landscaped gardens and thousands of new blooms announce the end of winter.

St. Patrick's Day Parades (*mid-March*), Boston and Holyoke, MA. Two of New England's oldest and largest celebrations.

Maple Season (*late March*), throughout New England. Visitors can see how maple sap is collected and made into syrup.

Musicians in Boston's St. Patrick's Day Parade

THE HISTORY OF NEW ENGLAND

The early history of New England is the history of the United States itself, for it is here that Europeans first gained a toehold in America and where much of the drama of forming a new country was played out. But even after the rest of the country had been populated, New England continued to exert influence on the political, economic, and intellectual life of the country.

No one can say for sure which Europeans first made landfall in New England. Some historians claim that the Vikings, after first reaching Newfoundland around AD 1000, eventually ventured as far south as Massachusetts. Others suggest that Spanish, Portuguese, or Irish explorers were the first Old World visitors. But one thing is sure: none of these peoples actually discovered the area. Native Americans already had called the region home for several thousand years. They were descendants of nomads from central Asia who had journeyed to what is now Alaska via the then-dry Bering Strait between 25,000 and 12,000 BC. Slowly they migrated east.

The earliest fossil evidence of human activity in the area dates back to 9000 BC. By the time the first European came ashore, the region was populated by about 20,000 Native Americans. Most of them were members of the Algonquin "nation," a loose conglomeration of a dozen or so tribes that occasionally engaged in violent internecine struggles. Their inability to unite would later prove a fatal flaw when confronted by a common foe – white settlers. Unlike their Asian ancestors, the Algonquins, also known as Abenakis ("people of the dawn"), had given up nomadic life. They ate moose, deer, birds, and fish, but grew crops, too – maize, called Indian corn, beans, and pumpkins.

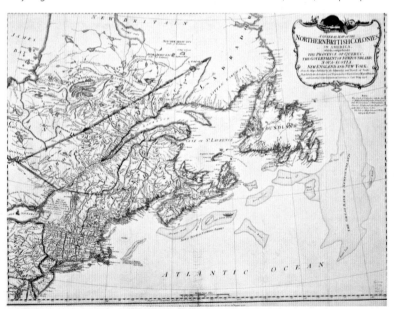

Map of the Northeast, printed in England a month after the Declaration of Independence was signed

◀ *Native American Indians Cooking and Preparing Food* c.1850 by J. Fumagalli

Embarkation and Departure of Columbus from the Port of Palos, undated painting by Ricardo Balaca

The Age of Discovery

The voyage of Christopher Columbus (1451–1506) to the New World in 1492 fired the imagination of maritime nations in Europe. Soon seafarers from England, France, and Spain were setting forth to explore the New World on behalf of their respective kings and queens. In 1497 the Italian explorer John Cabot (c.1425–99) reached New England from Bristol, England, and claimed the land, along with all the territory north of Florida and east of the Rocky Mountains, for his English patron, Henry VII (1457–1509). By the end of the 16th century, helped largely by the 1588 defeat of the Spanish Armada, England was beginning to achieve mastery of the seas.

In 1606 England's King James I (1566–1625) granted a charter to two ventures to establish settlements in America. The Virginia Company was assigned an area near present-day Virginia; the Plymouth Company was granted rights to a more northern colony. This second group ran into trouble early on. One of its

King James I (1566–1625)

ships strayed off course and was captured by the Spanish near Florida. Another ship made it to New England, but had to turn back to England before winter arrived. In May 1607 two ships left Plymouth, England, with approximately 100 colonists. Three months later they made landfall at the mouth of the Kennebec River, where the settlers constructed Fort St. George. Their first winter proved to be an especially cold and snowy one, and the furs and mineral wealth fell far short of what the colonists expected. After just a year, the so-called Popham Colony was abandoned.

Despite this inauspicious beginning, the Plymouth Company hired surveyor John Smith (1580–1631) to conduct a more extensive evaluation of the territory. In 1614 Smith sailed along the Massachusetts coast, observing the region. His findings, published in *A Description of New England*, not only coined the name of the region, but also painted a glowing picture of this new land and its "greatnesse" of fish and

25,000–12,000 BC Central Asian nomads cross Bering Strait to become first North Americans

7,000–1,000 BC Warming temperatures lead to development of New England's forests

25,000 BC

10,000 BC

AD 1000

1500

10,000 BC Humans move into New England area after deglaciation

AD 1000 Vikings sail to Newfoundland, Canada, and move south along the coast

Leif Eriksson in Viking boat

timber. Of all the places in the world, concluded Smith, this would be the best to support a new colony.

Colonial New England

While the explorers of the early 17th century probed the shoreline of New England, events were taking place in Europe that would have a far-reaching impact on the settlement of the New World. The Reformation of the 16th century and the birth of the Protestant faith had created an upheaval in religious beliefs – particularly in England, where Henry VIII (1491–1547) had severed ties with Rome and had made sure that parliament declared him head of the Church of England.

Protestant Puritans believed that the Church of England, despite its claim to represent a reformed Christianity, was still rife with Catholic practices and that their faith was being debased in England, especially after James I, who was suspected of having Catholic sympathies, succeeded Elizabeth I in 1603. Puritans were persecuted for their beliefs and found themselves facing a stark choice: stay at home to fight against overwhelming odds or start anew somewhere else.

A small, radical faction of Puritans, known as Separatists, emigrated to the Netherlands. The lifestyle of the Dutch did not live up to the

Puritan governor addresses Colonists in 1621

demanding standards of the Separatists' stern orthodoxy. As a result, they negotiated a deal with the Plymouth Company to finance a "pilgrimage" to America. In September 1620 they set sail. After a grueling 66-day voyage, their ship, the *Mayflower*, landed at what is now Provincetown *(see p160)*, Massachusetts.

It was a short-lived stay. The barren, sandy coast seemed a forbidding place, so the ship sailed on to Plymouth Rock *(see pp152–3)*, where the fatigued Pilgrims disembarked on December 26, 1620. During the winter of 1620–21, half of the Pilgrims succumbed to scurvy and the rigors of a harsh New England winter. But with the arrival of spring, the worst seemed to be behind them. The settlers found an ally among the indigenous people in Squanto (d.1622), a member of the Pawtuxet tribe who had been taken to England in 1605. Squanto had returned to the New World in 1615, and when word reached him that the English had arrived he soon helped negotiate a 50-year peace treaty between the Pilgrims and the chief of the local Wampanoag tribe. Squanto also taught the newcomers how to live in their adopted home. He showed them how to shoot and trap, and told them which crops to grow. The first harvest was celebrated in the fall of 1621 with a three-day feast of Thanksgiving.

Pilgrims board the *Mayflower* in 1620

1497 John Cabot explores North American coast

1607 First North American colony founded at Jamestown

1614 John Smith names territory New England

1620 Pilgrims land at Plymouth, Massachusetts, aboard the *Mayflower*

1500

1600

1615

1620

1492 Christopher Columbus discovers the New World

1602 Captain Bartholomew Gosnold lands on Massachusetts coast

John Smith

1616 Smallpox epidemic kills large number of New England Indians

First feast of Thanksgiving

1621 Pilgrims celebrate feast of Thanksgiving

The Battle of Bunker Hill

The first major battle of the Revolutionary War took place in Boston on June 17, 1775, and actually was fought on Breed's Hill. The Americans had captured heavy British cannon on Breed's and Bunker hills overlooking Boston Harbor, which gave them a commanding position. Britain's first two attacks on Breed's Hill were repelled by the outnumbered defenders. The Colonial soldiers were running low on ammunition, however, which gave rise to commander Colonel William Prescott's orders, "Don't fire until you can see the whites of their eyes!" Reinforced with 400 fresh troops, British forces made a bayonet charge and seized the hill, forcing the Americans to retreat to nearby Bunker Hill. The British suffered more than 1,000 casualties to approximately 150 for the Americans. The battle reinforced the confidence of the American troops that had first been kindled by their successes at Lexington and Concord.

Bunker Hill Monument, a granite obelisk, honors Colonial casualties.

In the Heat of the Battle
John Trumbull's 1786 painting The Death of General Warren at the Battle of Bunker's Hill, June 17, 1775 *depicts the hand-to-hand combat of the skirmish, fought mainly with bayonets and muskets. Victory came at a price. As one British soldier commented, "It was such a dear victory, another such would have ruined us."*

Colonial General Joseph Warren dies in final moments of battle after being shot in the head.

Declaration of Independence
Less than a year after the battle, the Second Continental Congress adopted the Declaration of Independence, which outlined the framework for democracy in the United States.

Attack on Breed's Hill
Prior to the infantry assault on the Colonial position, British men-of-war bombarded Breed's Hill with cannonade. Portions of nearby Charlestown caught fire and burned during the bombing.

A British officer
prevents grenadier's coup de grâce.

British Firelocks
Loading a musket involved shaking gunpowder into a pan just above the trigger, as well as into the barrel itself. The powder in the barrel was then tamped down with a small rod. This time-consuming process meant that soldiers stood unprotected on the battlefield as they reloaded.

British troops storm Colonial positions with renewed vigor after having suffered massive casualties on their first two attempts.

British Major John Pitcairn collapses into his son's arms after being shot in the chest, only to die while receiving medical treatment for his wounds.

Colonel William Prescott

Born in Groton, Massachusetts, William Prescott (1726–95) led the Colonial forces during the battle of Bunker Hill. In the initial stages of the fight, British warships bombarded the Americans' fortified position with heavy cannon. The untested Colonial troops were taken aback, especially when a private was decapitated by a cannonball. Sensing his men were disheartened, Prescott, covered in the slain soldier's blood, leaped atop the redoubt wall and paced back and forth in defiance of the bombs bursting around him. His brave gesture galvanized the troops, who went on to make one of the most courageous stands of the Revolutionary War.

Death of Metacomet (King Philip) in 1676

Colonial New England

From this modest beginning, the settlement began slowly to prosper and expand. Within five years the group was self-sufficient. Nine years later the Massachusetts Bay Company was founded, which sent 350 people to Salem (*see pp140–43*).

A second, much larger group joined the newly appointed governor, John Winthrop (c.1587–1649), and established a settlement at the mouth of the Charles River. They first called their new home Trimountain, but renamed it Boston in honor of the town some of the settlers had left in England.

During the 1630s, immigrants started spreading farther afield, creating settlements along the coast of Massachusetts and New Hampshire, and even venturing inland.

However, the colonists' gain proved to be the Natives' loss. Initial cooperation between both groups gave way to competition and outright hostility as land-hungry settlers moved into Indian territory. War first erupted with the Pequot tribe in 1637, which resulted in their near annihilation as a people. The hostility reached its peak at the outset of King Philip's War (1675–6), when several hundred members of the Narragansett tribe were killed by white settlers near South Kingston, Rhode Island.

Weakening Ties

The sheer distance dividing England and New England and the fact that communication could move no faster than windborne ships meant that there was very little contact between Old World and New. The colonists were largely self-governing, and there was no representation from them in the British parliament. Efforts by London to tighten control over the colonies were sporadic and in most cases successfully resisted until the Seven Years' War between Britain and France (1756–63) assured British domination of North America. Ironically, British success created the conditions that lessened the colonists' dependence on the mother country and also led to their growing estrangement. The colonies, especially New England, would come to feel that they no longer had to rely on British protection against the French in Canada and their Indian allies. Moreover, Britain's efforts after 1763 to derive a revenue from the colonies to help

England's George III (1738–1820)

1636 Harvard is founded, becoming America's first college

Harvard booster

1656 Puritans of Massachusetts Bay Colony begin systematic persecution of newly arrived Quakers with imprisonment, banishment, and hanging

1675–6 King Philip's War ends when Wampanoag chief Metacomet is betrayed and killed

| 1630 | 1660 | 1675 | 1690 |

1630 Puritans led by John Winthrop found Boston

1636 Murder of two colonists, supposedly by Pequot Indians, sparks the beginning of Pequot War

Salem gravestone

1692 Salem witch trials begin, leading to the execution of 20 people

cover the debt incurred by the war and to contribute to imperial defense met growing resistance. The cry of "No taxation without representation" would become a rallying call to arms for the independence movement, with the most vocal protests coming from New England.

The taxation issue came to a head under the reign of King George III (1738–1820), who ascended the throne of Great Britain in 1760. The Hanoverian king believed that the American colonists should remain under the control of Britain, and enacted a series of heavy taxes on various commodities, such as silk and sugar. In 1765 the British parliament passed the Stamp Act, which placed a tax on commercial and legal documents, newspapers, agendas, and even playing cards and dice. The act had a galvanizing effect throughout New England as its incensed inhabitants banded together and refused to use the stamps. They even went so far as to hold stamp-burning ceremonies.

Parliament eventually repealed the act in 1766, but this did not end the issue. In fact, at the same time that the Stamp Act was rescinded, it was replaced by the Declaratory Act, which stated that every part of the British Empire would continue to be taxed however the parliament saw fit. To make sure that the colonists would not flout the law, the British sent two regiments to

Paul Revere's 1770 engraving of the Boston Massacre

British stamp for American colony goods

Boston to enforce its control. The troops, called Redcoats for their distinctive uniforms, proved decidedly unpopular. A series of small skirmishes between them and local sailors and workers culminated in the Boston Massacre (March 5, 1770), in which the British soldiers opened fire on an unruly crowd, killing five, including a free black man, Crispus Attucks.

Revolutionary Spirit

After the massacre, an uneasy truce ensued. A simmering distrust remained between the two sides, and it only needed a suitable provocation to boil over again. That provocation came in the form of yet another proclamation – this one giving the East India Company the right to market tea directly in America, thus bypassing American merchants. When three ships arrived in Boston Harbor in 1773 with a shipment to unload, a group of about 60 men, including local politicians Samuel Adams (1722–1803) and John Hancock (1737–93), disguised themselves with Indian headdresses and then boarded the ships. They dumped 342 tea chests, valued at £18,000, into the harbor. The Boston Tea Party (see p93) was celebrated by the

Protesters during the 1773 Boston Tea Party

704 The *Boston ews Letter*, America's st newspaper, is ublished

1737 John Hancock, an original signatory of the Declaration of Independence, is born

John Hancock's signature

1773 New taxes spur Boston Tea Party

1710	1725	1740	1750	1770

1713 Boatyard in Gloucester, Massachusetts, produces America's first schooner

1770 British soldiers kill five in Boston Massacre

Crowd in Philadelphia celebrating the signing of the Declaration of Independence on July 4, 1776

colonists as a justifiable act of defiance against an oppressive regime. Parliament responded by passing the Intolerable Acts of 1774. These included the closing of the port of Boston by naval blockade until payment was made for the tea that had been destroyed.

On September 5, 1774, 56 representatives from the various American colonies, including New England, met in Philadelphia to establish the First Continental Congress to consider how to deal with grievances against Britain. The first concrete step toward nationhood had been taken.

Minute Men repelling the British, who were trying to march through to Concord

Although the British troops garrisoned in Boston in the mid-1770s represented a formidable force, a large part of New England lay beyond their control. In the countryside, locals stockpiled arms. In 1775 the royal governor of Massachusetts, General Thomas Gage (1721–87), learned about such a cache at Concord *(see pp148–9)*, 20 miles (32 km) west of Boston. He ordered 700 British soldiers to travel there under cover of darkness and destroy the arms.

The Americans were tipped off by dramatic horseback rides from Boston by Paul Revere and William Dawes. By the time the troops arrived at Lexington a few miles to the east of Concord, 77 colonial soldiers had set up a defensive formation, slowing the British advance. The Redcoats pressed onward to Concord, where close to 400 American patriots, called Minute Men for their ability to muster at a moment's notice, repelled the British attack. By the end of that day, April 19, 1775, 70 British had been killed and the casualty toll was 273. American losses were 95.

| 1774 British Navy imposes blockade of Boston Harbor | 1775 Battles at Concord and Lexington mark beginning of Revolutionary War | 1781 Colonial forces win decisive battle over British at Yorktown, Virginia | 1789 George Washington becomes first president of the United States |
| | | 1783 Treaty of Paris signals end to Revolutionary War | |

George Washing...

| | 1775 | 1780 | 1785 | 1790 | 1795 |

| 1774 First Continental Congress held in Philadelphia | 1776 Second Continental Congress ratifies the Declaration of Independence | 1791 First mechanical cotton mill of Samuel Slater at Pawtucket, Rhode Island | |

Slater Mill

Boston shipbuilding c.1850

The days of discussion were now clearly over. Colonial leaders signed the Declaration of Independence on July 4, 1776, and the American Revolution had begun. For the next six years the war would be waged first on New England soil, but then mostly beyond its borders at such key places as the Valley Forge encampment, Pennsylvania, and Yorktown, Virginia. Although the fighting ceased in 1781, the war officially came to an end with the signing of the 1783 Treaty of Paris.

A New Industrial Power

The fledgling United States of America was rich in natural resources, especially in New England. The region had excellent harbors that gave it access to the West Indies, Europe, and farther afield, where a developing maritime trade *(see pp28–9)* with the spices, teas, and other riches of the Far East proved increasingly lucrative. Indeed, New England ships became a familiar sight at docks from Nantucket *(see p157)* to New Guinea and from Portsmouth *(see pp256–9)* to Port-au-Prince, Haiti.

Antique harpoon

New England also became a world center for the whaling industry, as local ships plied the Seven Seas in search of the leviathans of the deep, which were killed for their oil, baleen, and blubber. The burgeoning shipbuilding industry that had sprung up along the coast also supplied a fleet of fishing boats that trolled the Grand Banks and the waters off Cape Cod, returning with their holds full of cod and halibut.

Ultimately it was an invention of the Industrial Revolution that transformed New England into an economic powerhouse. In the late 18th century, the first of Richard Arkwright's (1732–92) cotton spinning machines was imported to North America from England and installed on the Blackstone River at Pawtucket *(see pp176–7)*, Rhode Island. Previously cotton had been processed on individual looms in homes. Arkwright's device permitted cotton spinning to be carried out on factory-sized machines, which increased productivity a thousandfold. Soon mills sprang up, mainly in Massachusetts, in

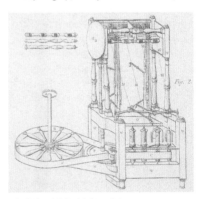

Richard Arkwright's sketch for his revolutionary cotton spinning machine

1800 National census results: 5.3 million people

Noah Webster

1805	1810	1815	1820	1825

1806 *Compendious Dictionary of the English Language*, written by New Haven's Noah Webster, is published

1820 Maine gains independence from Massachusetts and becomes 20th state in the Union towns such as Lowell *(see p146)*, Waltham, and Lawrence. By the mid-19th century, New England held two-thirds of America's cotton mills. The region offered two main advantages: a ready supply of rivers to power the mills' machinery and an increasing flow of cheap labor. Escaping the potato famine in the 1840s, numerous Irish immigrants fled to Massachusetts, where the mill towns beckoned with dormitory housing for their employees. Despite their numbers, however, this group faced discrimination. In Boston many such newcomers settled in squalid tenements along the city's waterfront. Eventually the Irish would come to dominate Boston politics, but for much of the 19th century they faced a daily struggle just to survive.

Irish farmer contemplating failed crop

The extent of industrialization was felt in a relatively small area of New England, mostly Massachusetts, Rhode Island, and Connecticut. In the hinterland of Vermont, New Hampshire, and Maine, farming and logging remained the key industries well into the 20th century. These far-flung regions provided some of the manpower for the heartland's factories, as people left the hardscrabble life of subsistence farming for new lives farther south. Northern New England also helped supply the factories with some of their raw materials. The forests of Vermont, for example, were hacked down to make grazing land for sheep, which supplied wool for the textile mills.

Abolitionist New England

New England's role in 19th-century America was not merely one of economic powerhouse. The region also dominated the fields of education, science, politics, and architecture, as well as serving as the cultural heart of the nation, with Boston and its environs producing some of the nation's most influential writers and thinkers. The Massachusetts capital was also the center of a prominent protest against slavery, which was firmly entrenched in the southern states and reviled in much of the North.

William Lloyd Garrison (1805–79) began publishing a newspaper called *The Liberator* in 1831. In Garrison's view, "There is only one theme which should be dwelt upon till our whole country is free from the curse – SLAVERY." His polemics in *The Liberator* drew the wrath of pro-slavery forces. The House of Representatives of the southern state of Georgia offered $5,000 for his arrest. But Garrison continued publishing his newspaper, never missing an issue until it ceased publication at the end of the Civil War in 1865, when slavery had been expunged from American society.

Some residents of New England towns went beyond merely reading and writing about the injustices of slavery. Stirred by Garrison and the so-called

Abolitionist William Lloyd Garrison

Colt six-shooters	**1835** Connecticut's Samuel Colt invents the six-shooter handgun	**1851–2** *Uncle Tom's Cabin* appears in serial form in *The National Era* newspaper	**1861** Civil War begins
1830		**1845**	**1860**
1831 Abolitionist William Lloyd Garrison publishes first edition of anti-slavery newspaper *The Liberator*	**1840** Ireland's first potato famine devastates country	**1851** *Moby-Dick*, written by Herman Melville in the southern Berkshires, is published	**1865** Civil War ends, leaving some 620,000 Americans dead

abolitionist movement, some anti-slavery exponents offered safe houses for what came to be known as the Underground Railroad. This loosely connected network of escape routes helped slaves fleeing the South make their way to freedom in the North and in Canada, beyond the reach of slave hunters. Towns such as New Bedford (see p125), Massachusetts, Portland (see pp284–7), Maine, and Burlington (see pp236–9), Vermont, served as key "stations" on the slaves' road to freedom. The Underground Railroad was immortalized in Harriet Beecher Stowe's novel Uncle Tom's Cabin; or, Life Among the Lowly (1852).

Cover of sheet music based on Harriet Beecher Stowe's Uncle Tom's Cabin by artist Louisa Corbauy

Declining Power

In the latter part of the 19th century there were signs that the days of New England's industrial preeminence were over. The transcontinental railroad had opened up the West to an army of new immigrants, which flooded in after the Civil War. The New World was a far, far bigger place than it had been when the Pilgrims landed, and the opportunities were boundless. The Great Plains encompassed thousands of square miles of arable land that New England farmers could only dream about. And, for those looking for a more temperate climate, many other areas of the US now beckoned.

Meanwhile, the exploitation of natural resources and the development of new technologies were changing the face of industry. The discovery of

Child laborer in cotton-spinning plant

petroleum meant that whale oil lost its economic importance, while steam engines offered a way of powering mills that no longer required river waterpower – one of the natural advantages upon which the region had relied.

These problems were compounded by the fact that local labor was organizing to fight for better pay and working conditions, driving some factories to move to the South, where labor costs were cheaper. Between 1880 and 1923, the South's share of the cotton-weaving industry rose from 6 percent to almost 50 percent.

The call for unionization even reached into the ranks of the police force, sparking one of America's most bitter labor

1884 The Adventures of Huckleberry Finn, a novel written by Mark Twain at his home in Hartford, Connecticut, is published

Modern Red Sox fan

1875   1890   1910

1882 Massachusetts-born poet/philosopher Ralph Waldo Emerson dies

1897 Country's first subway is opened in Boston

1903 Boston Red Sox win first World Series baseball championship

alph Waldo Emerson

confrontations. In 1919, Boston's men in blue sought to affiliate themselves with the American Federation of Labor. The city's police commissioner refused the request, and the entire force went on strike. Boston was beset by a wave of crime and riots, prompting the governor to send in the militia. By the time order was restored, at least five people had been killed and dozens had been wounded.

The loss of New England's economic importance was accompanied by a wave of change in the social makeup of the region. What had long been a homogenous society – largely Protestant and of English or Scottish descent – was transformed by a rapid influx of immigrants. By the turn of the 20th century more than two-thirds of the residents of Massachusetts had at least one parent born outside the country.

The Depression of the 1930s hit the inhabitants of New England particularly hard. Unemployment in some towns topped 40 percent and wages plunged dramatically. World War II provided a temporary boost to the economy as shipyards and munition factories worked

Women making shell casings in a munitions plant during World War II

overtime to provide the military with the tools of their trade. However, with the return of peace, New England struggled to find its way in the new post-war era, and its economy continued to have its difficulties. The glory days, at least economically speaking, seemed to be irretrievable.

New England Rebirth

Even in its worse decline, as factories crumbled and residents headed for greener pastures, New England still possessed advantages that set the stage for recovery. One important factor was its concentration of higher educational institutions (*see*

Unknown artist's depiction of Harvard University campus c.1857

Calvin Coolidge

1914–18 World War I

1915

1923 Vermont's Calvin Coolidge is sworn in as country's 30th president by his father

1925

1929 Stock market crash marks beginning of Great Depression

Depression soup kitchen

1935

1939–45 World War II: US enters conflict in 1941

1945

1954 World's first nuclear submarine is built in Groton, Connecticut

1955

Falmouth Heights Beach in Cape Cod

pp32–3). As the Manufacturing Age gave way to the Information Age beginning in the 1960s, knowledge and adaptability became increasingly valuable commodities. With their well-endowed research facilities, venerable institutions such as Harvard University *(see pp116–21)* and the Massachusetts Institute of Technology *(see p115)* attracted a new generation of young entrepreneurs looking to cash in on this newest opportunity. Meanwhile a son of one of Boston's most prominent families was proving that New England's impact on the national political scene was not over yet. John F. Kennedy *(see p108)*, the great-grandson of an Irish potato-famine immigrant, became America's first Catholic president in 1960.

Starting in the mid-1980s, companies producing computer software and biomedical technology set up shop in the Boston suburbs and southern New Hampshire. The meteoric growth of high-tech industries represented a second revolution of sorts – proving far more valuable than the Industrial Revolution of the previous century. Meanwhile certain businesses, such as the insurance trade, weathered the shifts in the economy better than traditional manufacturing ventures, with Hartford *(see pp202–205)*, Connecticut,

continuing to serve as the insurance capital of the nation.

One thing that all the economic upheavals did not change was New England's stunning physical beauty: the craggy coastline of Maine, the beaches of Cape Cod *(see pp160–63)*, the picturesque Vermont villages, and the coiled-up mountains of New Hampshire. As America became more prosperous and its workers had more free time in which to spend their mounting disposable income, tourism became an even bigger business than manufacturing had once been. The skiers, fishermen, beachcombers, antique hunters, campers, and others who flocked to the Northeast year-round pumped billions of dollars into the states' economies. By the 1990s tourism ranked alongside man-ufacturing as one of New England's most profitable industries.

Somehow, it seems fitting. After all, it was the beauty of the area that had helped convince people such as John Smith, more than four centuries ago, that New England had a viable future. And now, that same natural beauty is proving to be both timeless and lucrative, helping to bring about a renaissance in the prosperity of the place where American society had begun so tenuously so many years before.

Vermont's trademark rural landscape

1961 Massachusetts-born John F. Kennedy becomes first Catholic president

1963 President Kennedy is assassinated in Dallas

1990 Thieves make off with artwork valued at $100 million from Boston's Isabella Stewart Gardner Museum

2008 Boston Celtics win their 17th NBA championship

2004 Red Sox "reverse the curse" and win Baseball World Series

2009 Senator Edward M. Kennedy (D-Mass) dies

2013 Terrorists bomb Boston Marathon

1960   **1970**   **1980**   **1990**   **2000**   **2010**   **2020**

1968 Senator Robert Kennedy is assassinated in Los Angeles

Robert F. Kennedy

1999 John F. Kennedy, Jr. dies in plane crash off Martha's Vineyard

2004 Massachusetts legally recognizes gay marriage

2011 Boston Bruins win hockey's Stanley Cup

2015 New England Patriots win fourth Super Bowl since 2002

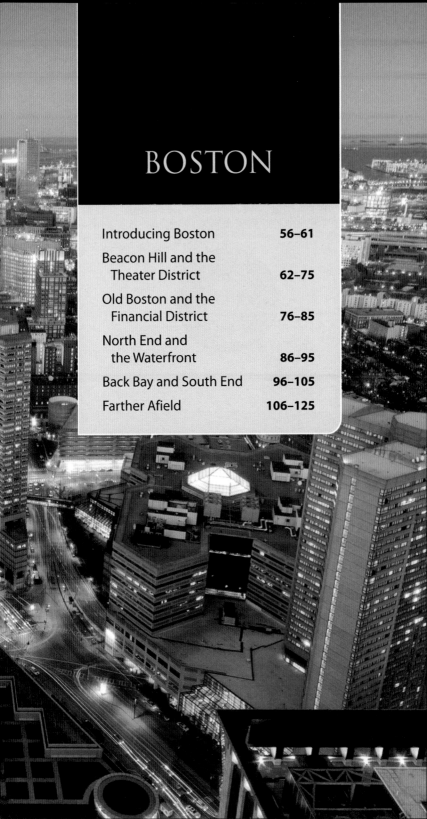

BOSTON

Boston's Best

The city of Boston's Athenian self-image is manifested in dozens of museums, galleries, and archives, paramount of which is the Museum of Fine Arts. The city's importance in America's history has left it with a unique legacy of old buildings, with much fine religious and civic architecture, including Trinity Church and Massachusetts State House. This strong architectural heritage continues to the present day, and includes modern structures such as the John Hancock Tower. Boston's wealth of sights, along with its many parks and gardens, make it a fascinating city to explore.

Boston Common and Public Garden
At the heart of the city, the spacious common, and smaller, more formal Public Garden, provide open space for both sport and relaxation.

Trinity Church
Perhaps Boston's finest building, this Romanesque Revival masterpiece by Henry Hobson Richardson was completed in 1877.

John Hancock Tower
Dominating the Back Bay skyline, with its mirrored façade reflecting the surroundings, the John Hancock Tower is New England's tallest building.

CHARLES ST

BEACON STREET

ARLINGTON ST

BOYLSTON STREET

HUNTINGTON AVE

COLUMBUS AVENUE

WASHINGTON ST

| 0 kilometers | 0.5 |
| 0 miles | 0.5 |

Museum of Fine Arts
One of the largest museums in North America, the MFA is famous for its Egyptian, Greek, and Roman art, and French Impressionist paintings.

◀ Brightly lit city of Boston at night

Old State House
The seat of British colonial government until independence, the building later undertook many different uses. It now houses a museum.

Old North Church
Dating from 1723, this is Boston's oldest surviving church. Due to its role in the Revolution, it is also one of the city's most important historical sites.

New England Aquarium
This aquarium displays a huge array of creatures from the world's oceans. Researchers here are also involved in key international fish and whale conservation programs.

Boston Common and Public Garden

Massachusetts State House
Built in the 1790s as the new center of state government, the Charles-Bulfinch-designed State House sits imposingly at the top of Beacon Hill.

John F. Kennedy Library and Museum
The nation's 35th president is celebrated here in words and images – video clips of the first president to fully use the media make this a compelling museum.

CAUSEWAY

HANOVER ST

COMMERCIAL ST

CONGRESS ST

ATLANTIC AVE

SUMMER ST

The Freedom Trail
From Boston Common to Paul Revere House

Boston has more sites directly related to the American Revolution than any other city. The most important of these sites, as well as some relating to other freedoms gained by Bostonians, have been linked together as "The Freedom Trail." This 2.5-mile (4-km) walking route, marked in red on the sidewalks, starts at Boston Common and eventually ends at Bunker Hill in Charlestown. This first section weaves its way through the central city and Old Boston.

Elegant Georgian steeple of Park Street Church

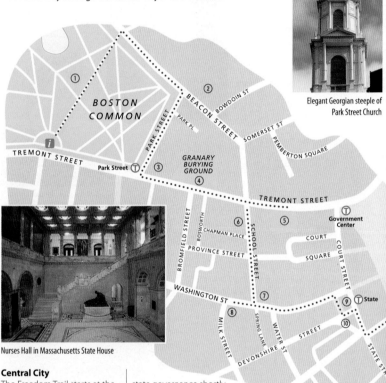

Nurses Hall in Massachusetts State House

Central City

The Freedom Trail starts at the Visitor Information Center on Boston Common ① (see pp68–9). This is where angry colonials rallied against their British masters and where the British forces were encamped during the 1775–6 military occupation. Political speakers still expound from their soapboxes here, and the Common remains a center of activity.

Walking toward the northwest corner of the Common gives a great view of the Massachusetts State House ② (see pp72–3) on Beacon Street, designed by Charles Bulfinch as the new center of

state governance shortly after the Revolution. Along Park Street, at the end of the Common, you will come to Park Street Church ③ (see p70), built in 1810 and a bulwark of the antislavery movement. The church took the place of an old grain storage facility, which gave its name to the adjacent Granary Burying Ground ④, one of Boston's earliest cemeteries and the final resting place of patriots John Hancock and Paul Revere (see p124). Continuing along Tremont Street you will come to King's Chapel and Burying Ground ⑤ (see p80). The tiny cemetery

is Boston's oldest, containing, among others, the grave of city founder John Winthrop. As the name suggests, King's Chapel was the principal Anglican church in Puritan Boston, and more than half of its congregation fled to Nova Scotia at the outbreak of the Revolution. The box pew on the right just inside the front entrance was reserved for condemned prisoners to hear their last sermons before going to the gallows on Boston Common.

Heart of Old Boston

Head back along Tremont Street and turn down School Street, where a hopscotch-like mosaic embedded in the sidewalk commemorates the site of the First Public School ⑥, established in 1635. At the bottom of the street is the Old Corner Bookstore ⑦ *(see p81)*, a landmark more associated with Boston's literary emergence of 1845–65 than with the Revolution.

The Old South Meeting House ⑧, a short way to the south on Washington Street, is a graceful, white-spired brick church, modeled on Sir Christopher Wren's English country churches. As one of the largest meeting halls in Revolutionary Boston, "Old South's" rafters rang with many a fiery speech urging revolt against the British. A few blocks along, the Old State House ⑨ presides over the head of State Street. The colonial government

building, it also served as the first state legislature, and the merchants' exchange in the basement was where Boston's colonial shipping fortunes were made. The square in front of the Old State House is the Boston Massacre Site ⑩, where British soldiers opened fire on a taunting mob in 1770, killing five and providing ideal propaganda for revolutionary agitators.

Follow State Street down to Congress Street and turn left to reach Faneuil Hall ⑪, called the "Cradle of Liberty" for the history of patriotic speeches made in its public meeting hall. Donated to the city by Huguenot merchant Peter Faneuil, the building was Boston's first marketplace.

The red stripe of the Freedom Trail comes in handy when negotiating the way to the North End and the Paul Revere House ⑫ on North Square. Boston's oldest house, it was home to the man known for his famous "midnight ride" *(see p124)*.

Tips for Walkers

Starting point: Boston Common. Maps at Boston Common Visitor Center.
Length: 2.5 miles (4 km).
Getting there: Park Street Station ("T" Green and Red lines) to start. Free guided tours leave from National Park Visitor Center at Faneuil Hall. Follow red stripe on sidewalk for the full route.
🔲 thefreedomtrail.org

Faneuil Hall, popularly known as "the Cradle of Liberty"

Old State House, the seat of colonial government

Walk

① Boston Common
② Massachusetts State House
③ Park Street Church
④ Granary Burying Ground
⑤ King's Chapel and Burying Ground
⑥ First Public School Site
⑦ Old Corner Bookstore
⑧ Old South Meeting House
⑨ Old State House
⑩ Boston Massacre Site
⑪ Faneuil Hall
⑫ Paul Revere House

0 meters 200
0 yards 200

Key
••• Walk route

For map symbols *see back flap*

The Freedom Trail

From Old North Church to Bunker Hill Monument

Distances begin to stretch out on the second half of the Freedom Trail as it meanders through the narrow streets of the North End, then continues over the Charles River to Charlestown, where Boston's settlers first landed. The sites here embrace two wars – the War of Independence and the War of 1812.

Copp's Hill terrace, at the edge of Copp's Hill Burying Ground

The North End

Following the Freedom Trail through the North End, allow time to try some of the Italian cafés and bakeries along the neighborhood's main thoroughfare, Hanover Street. Cross

Gravestone at Copp's Hill Burying Ground

through the Paul Revere Mall to reach Old North Church ⑬ (see p91), whose spire is instantly visible over the shoulder of the statue of Paul Revere on horseback. Sexton Robert Newman hung two lanterns in the belfry here, signaling the advance of British troops on Lexington and Concord in 1775. The church retains its 18th-century interior, including the traditional box pews.

The crest of Copp's Hill lies close by on Hull Street. Some of Boston's earliest gallows stood here, and Bostonians would gather in boats below to watch the hangings of heretics and pirates. Much of the hilltop is covered by Copp's Hill Burying Ground ⑭. This was established

in 1660, and the cemetery holds the remains of several generations of the Mather family – Boston's influential 17th- and 18th-century theocrats – as well as the graves of many soldiers of the Revolution.

Boston's first free African-American community, "New Guinea," covered the west side of Copp's Hill. A broken column marks the grave of Prince Hall, head of the Black Masons, distinguished veteran of the Revolution, and prominent political leader in the early years of the Republic. The musketball-chipped tombstone of patriot Daniel Malcolm records that he asked to be buried "in a stone grave 10 feet deep" to rest beyond the reach of British gunfire.

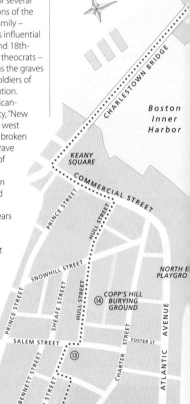

Traditional box pews inside Old North Church

Walk

⑬ Old North Church
⑭ Copp's Hill Burying Ground
⑮ Charlestown Navy Yard and the USS *Constitution*
⑯ Bunker Hill Monument

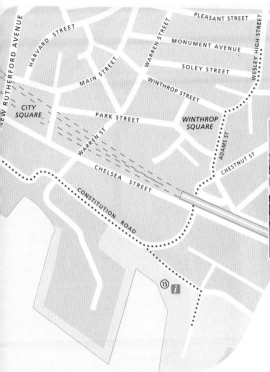

Bunker Hill Monument from
Charlestown harborfront

Key

• • • Walk route

| 0 meters | | 200 |
| 0 yards | | 200 |

Charlestown

The iron bridge over the Charles River that links the North End in Boston with City Square in Charlestown dates from 1899. Across the bridge, turn right along Constitution Road, following signs to Charlestown Navy Yard ⑮. The National Park Service now operates the Visitor Center at Building 5, with a film and exhibits about the historic role of the Navy Yard and the history of the 18th- through to 20th-century warships that are berthed at its piers. The colonial navy had been no match for the might of Britain's naval forces during the Revolution, and building a more formidable naval force became a priority. This was one of several shipyards that were set up around 1800. Decommissioned in 1974, the yard is now maintained by the National Park Service. In Dry Dock 1 until 2018, the USS Constitution is probably the

Lion carving,
USS *Constitution*

most famous ship in US history and still remains the flagship of the US Navy. Built at Hartt's shipyard in the North End, she was completed in 1797. In the War of 1812, she earned the nickname "Old Ironsides" for the resilience of her live oak hull against cannon fire. Restored for her bicentennial, the *Constitution* is currently undergoing another restoration. The granite obelisk that towers above the

Charlestown waterfront is Bunker Hill Monument ⑯, commemorating the battle of June 17, 1775 that ended with a costly victory for British forces against an irregular colonial army, which finally ran out of ammunition. British losses were so heavy, however, that the battle would presage future success for the colonial forces. As a monument to the first large-scale battle of the Revolution, the obelisk, based on those of ancient Egypt, was a prototype for others across the US.

Defensive guns at Charlestown Navy Yard opposite the North End

For map symbols *see back flap*

BEACON HILL AND THE THEATER DISTRICT

By the 1790s, the south slope of Beacon Hill, facing Boston Common, had become the main seat of Boston's wealth and power. The north slope and the land up to the Charles River, known as the West End, was much poorer. Urban renewal has now cleared the slums of the West End, and the gentrification of Beacon Hill has made this one of Boston's most desirable neighborhoods. The area south of Boston Common is more down-to-earth, and home to the city's Theater District.

Sights at a Glance

Historic Streets and Squares

1. Charles Street
2. Louisburg Square
3. Mount Vernon Street
6. Beacon Street
14. Downtown Crossing
16. Chinatown
17. Bay Village

Historic Buildings, Museums, and Theaters

4. Nichols House Museum
5. Hepzibah Swan Houses
8. Park Street Church
10. Boston Athenaeum
11. *Massachusetts State House pp72–3*
12. Museum of African American History
13. Museum of Science
15. Emerson Colonial Theatre
18. Shubert Theatre
19. Wang Theatre

Parks and Cemeteries

7. *Boston Common and Public Garden pp62–3*
9. Granary Burying Ground

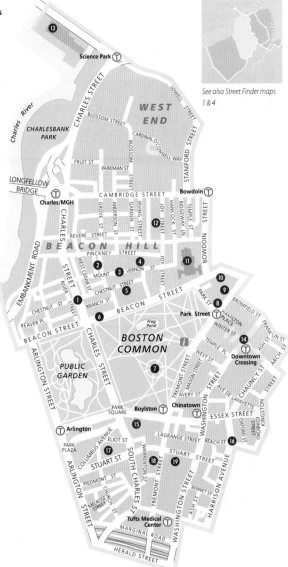

See also Street Finder maps 1 & 4

0 meters 250
0 yards 250

◄ A typical fall day in Boston

For map symbols *see back flap*

Street-by-Street: Beacon Hill

From the 1790s to the 1870s, the south slope of Beacon
Hill was Boston's most sought-after neighborhood – its
wealthy elite decamped only when the more exclusive
Back Bay *(see pp96–105)* was built. Many of the district's
houses were designed by Charles Bulfinch and his
disciples, and the south slope evolved as a textbook
example of Federal architecture. Elevation and view were
all, and the finest homes are either on Boston Common or
perched near the top of the hill. Early developers abided
by a gentleman's agreement to set houses back from the
street, but the economic depression of 1807–12 resulted
in row houses being built right out to the street.

Cobblestone street, once typical of Beacon Hill

❷ Louisburg Square
The crowning glory of the
Beacon Hill district, this
square was developed
in the 1830s. Today, it is
still Boston's most
desirable address.

**Charles Street Meeting
House** was built in the early
19th century to house a
congregation of Baptists.

❶ ★ Charles Street
This elegant street is the main shopping area for Beacon Hill.
Lined with upscale grocers and antique stores, it also has
some fine restaurants.

For hotels and restaurants in this region see pp310–13 and pp324–9

PINCKNEY STREET

LOUISBURG SQUARE

MOUNT VERNON STREET

CEDAR STREET

CHARLES STREET

CHESTNUT STREET

Back Bay and
South End

Key

— Suggested route

0 meters   50

0 yards   50

Locator Map
See Street Finder maps 1 & 4

❹ ★ Nichols House Museum
This modest museum offers an insight into the life of Beacon Hill resident Rose Nichols, who lived here from 1885 to 1960.

WALNUT STREET

❸ Mount Vernon Street
Described in the 19th century as the "most civilized street in America," this is where the developers of Beacon Hill (the Mount Vernon Proprietors) chose to build their own homes.

→ Massachusetts State House

BEACON STREET

↓ Boston Common

❺ Hepzibah Swan Houses
Elegant in their simplicity, these three Bulfinch-designed houses were wedding gifts for the daughters of a wealthy Beacon Hill proprietress.

❻ Beacon Street
The finest houses on Beacon Hill were invariably built on Beacon Street. Elegant, Federal-style mansions, some with ornate reliefs, overlook the city's most beautiful green space, Boston Common.

Charles Street, lined with shops catering to the residents of Beacon Hill

❶ Charles Street

Map 1 B4. Ⓣ Charles/MGH.

This street originally ran along the bank of the Charles River, although subsequent landfill has removed it from the riverbank by several hundred feet. The main shopping and dining area of the Beacon Hill neighborhood, the curving line of Charles Street hugs the base of Beacon Hill, giving it a quaint, village-like air. Many of the houses remain residential on the upper stories, while street level and cellar levels were converted to commercial uses long ago. Though most of Charles Street dates from the 19th century, widening in the 1920s meant that some of the houses on the west side acquired new façades. The Charles Street Meeting House, designed by Asher Benjamin in 1807, was built for a Baptist congregation that practiced immersion in the then-adjacent river. It is now a commercial building. Two groups of striking Greek Revival row houses are situated at the top of Charles Street, between Revere and Cambridge Streets. Charles Street was one of the birthplaces of the antique trade in the US and now has a high concentration of antique dealers.

❷ Louisburg Square

Map 1 B4. Ⓣ Charles/MGH, Park Street.

Home to millionaire politicians, best-selling authors, and corporate moguls, Louisburg Square is perhaps Boston's most prestigious address. Developed in the 1830s as a shared private preserve on Beacon Hill, the square's tiny patch of greenery surrounded by a high iron fence sends a clear signal of the square's continued exclusivity. On the last private square in the city, the narrow, Greek Revival bow-fronted town houses sell for a premium over comparable homes elsewhere on Beacon Hill. Even the on-street parking spaces are deeded. The traditions of Christmas Eve carol singing and candlelit windows are said to have begun on Louisburg Square. A statue of Christopher Columbus, presented by a wealthy Greek merchant in 1850, stands at its center.

❸ Mount Vernon Street

Map 1 B4. Ⓣ Charles/MGH, Park Street.

In the 1890s the novelist Henry James called Mount Vernon Street "the most civilized street in America," and it still retains that air of urbane culture. Most of the developers of Beacon Hill, who called themselves the Mount Vernon Proprietors, chose to build their private homes along this street. Architect Charles Bulfinch envisioned Beacon Hill as a district of large freestanding mansions on spacious landscaped grounds, but building costs ultimately dictated much denser development. The sole remaining example of Bulfinch's vision is the second Harrison Gray Otis House, built in 1800 at No. 85 Mount Vernon Street. The current Greek Revival row houses next door (Nos. 59 – 83), graciously set back from the street by 30 ft (9 m), were built to replace the single mansion belonging to Otis's chief development partner, Jonathan Mason. The original mansion was torn down after Mason's death in 1836. The three Bulfinch-designed houses at Nos. 55, 57, and 59 Mount Vernon Street were built by Mason for his daughters. No. 55 was ultimately passed on to the Nichols family in 1885.

Columbus Statue, Louisburg Square

Oliver Wendell Holmes and the Boston Brahmins

In 1860, Oliver Wendell Holmes wrote that Boston's wealthy merchant class of the time constituted a Brahmin caste, a "harmless, inoffensive, untitled aristocracy" with "their houses by Bulfinch, their monopoly on Beacon Street, their ancestral portraits and Chinese porcelains, humanitarianism, Unitarian faith in the march of the mind, Yankee shrewdness, and New England exclusiveness." So keenly did he skewer the social class that the term has persisted. In casual usage today, a Brahmin is someone with an old family name, whose finances derive largely from trust funds, and whose politics blend conservatism with *noblesse oblige* toward those less fortunate. Boston's Brahmins founded most of the hospitals, performing arts bodies, and museums of the greater metropolitan area.

Oliver Wendell Holmes
(1809–94)

Drawing room of the Bulfinch-designed
Nichols House Museum

4 Nichols House Museum

55 Mount Vernon St. **Map** 1 B4.
Tel (617) 227-6993. Ⓣ Park Street.
Open Apr–Oct: 11am–4pm Tue–Sat;
Nov–Mar: 11am–4pm Thu–Sat.
🅿 ♿ ⬤

The Nichols House Museum was designed by Charles Bulfinch in 1804 and offers a rare glimpse into the tradition-bound lifestyle of Beacon Hill. Modernized in 1830 by the addition of a Greek Revival portico, the house is nevertheless a superb example of Bulfinch's domestic architecture. It also offers an insight into the life of a true Beacon Hill character. Rose Standish Nichols moved into the house at 13 when her father purchased it in 1885. She left it as a museum in her 1960 will. A woman ahead of her time, strong-willed and

famously hospitable, Nichols was, among other things, a self-styled landscape designer who traveled extensively around the world to write about gardens.

5 Hepzibah Swan Houses

13, 15 & 17 Chestnut St. **Map** 1 B4.
Ⓣ Park Street. **Closed** to the public.

The only woman who was ever a member of the Mount Vernon Proprietors, Mrs. Swan had these houses built by Bulfinch as wedding presents for her daughters in 1806, 1807, and 1814. Some of the most elegant and distinguished houses on Chestnut Street, they are backed by Bulfinch-designed stables that face onto Mount Vernon Street. The deeds restrict the height of the stables to 13 ft (4 m) so that her daughters would still have a view over Mount Vernon Street. In 1863–5, No. 13 was home to Dr. Samuel Gridley Howe, abolitionist and educational pioneer who, in 1833, founded the first school for the blind in the US.

6 Beacon Street

Map 1 B4. Ⓣ Park Street.

Beacon Street is lined with urban mansions facing Boston Common. The 1808 William Hickling Prescott House at No. 55, designed by Asher Benjamin, offers tours of rooms in Federal, Victorian, and Colonial Revival styles on Wednesdays and Saturdays between May and October. The American Meteorological Society in No. 45 was built as Harrison Gray Otis's last and finest house. It had 11 bedrooms and an elliptical room behind the front parlor, where the walls and even the doors are curved.

The elite Somerset Club stands at Nos. 42–43 Beacon Street. Between the 1920s and the 1940s, Irish Catholic mayor James Michael Curley would lead election night victory marches to the State House, pausing at the Somerset Club to taunt the Boston Brahmins inside.

The Parkman House at No. 33 Beacon Street is now a city-owned meeting center. It was the home of Dr. George Parkman, who was murdered by Harvard professor and fellow socialite Dr. John Webster in 1849. Boston society was torn apart when the presiding judge, a relative of Parkman, sentenced Webster to be hanged.

Elegant Federal-style houses on Beacon Street, overlooking
Boston Common

❼ Boston Common and Public Garden

Acquired by Boston in 1634 from first settler William Blackstone, the 232,300-sq-yard Boston Common served for two centuries as common pasture, military drill ground, and gallows site. British troops camped here during the 1775–6 military occupation. As Boston grew in the 19th century, the Boston Common became a center for open-air civic activity and remains so to this day. By contrast, the 116,150-sq-yard Public Garden is more formal. When the Charles River mud flats were first filled in the 1830s, a succession of landscape plans were plotted for the Public Garden before the city chose the English-style garden scheme of George F. Meacham in 1869. The lagoon was added to the garden two years later.

The Public Garden, a popular green space in the heart of the city

Make Way for Ducklings
Based on the classic children's story by Robert McCloskey, this sculpture is of a duck and her brood of ducklings.

★ George Washington Statue
Cast by Thomas Ball from bronze, with a solid granite base, this is one the finest memorial statues in Boston. It was dedicated in 1869.

VISITORS' CHECKLIST

Practical Information
Map 1 B4.
Open 24 hrs
Visitors' Center: 139 Tremont St.;
(617) 426-3115. **Open** 8:30am–
5pm Mon–Fri, 9am–5pm Sat & Sun
(winter: shorter weekend hours).
Swan Boats: Boston Public
Garden. **Tel** (617) 522-1966.
Open Mid-Apr–mid-Sep: 10am–
5pm daily (subject to change).
🆆 swanboats.com
🆆 bostonusa.com

Transport
Ⓣ Park Street, Boylston,
Arlington

Lagoon Bridge
This miniature, ornamental bridge over the Public Garden lagoon was designed by William G. Preston in 1869 in a moment of whimsy. The lagoon it "spans" was constructed in 1861.

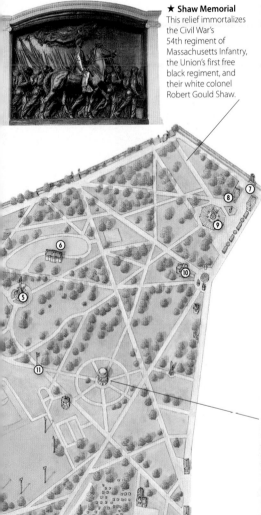

★ **Shaw Memorial**
This relief immortalizes the Civil War's 54th regiment of Massachusetts Infantry, the Union's first free black regiment, and their white colonel Robert Gould Shaw.

KEY

① **The Swan Boats**, originally inspired by Wagner's *Löhengrin*, have been a feature of the Public Garden lake since 1877.

② **Statue of Reverend William Ellery Channing**

③ **The Ether Monument** memorializes the first use of anesthesia in 1846.

④ **Statue of Edward Everett Hale**

⑤ **The Soldiers and Sailors Monument**, erected in 1877, features prominent Bostonians from the time of the Civil War.

⑥ **The Frog Pond** turns into a public outdoor skating rink during winter months.

⑦ **Blackstone Memorial Tablet** recalls the purchase of the common in 1634 and is cited as proof that it belongs to the people.

⑧ **Park Street subway**

⑨ **Brewer Fountain** was purchased at the Paris Expo of 1867.

⑩ **Visitors' Center**

⑪ **The Flagstaff**

Parkman Bandstand
This bandstand was built in 1912 to memorialize George F. Parkman, who bequeathed $5 million for the care of Boston Common and other parks in the city.

Central Burying Ground
This graveyard, which dates from 1756, holds the remains of many British and American casualties from the Battle of Bunker Hill (1775). The portraitist Gilbert Stuart is also buried here.

0 meters 100
0 yards 100

Park Street Church at the corner of Tremont and Park Streets

❽ Park Street Church

1 Park St. **Map** 1 C4. **Tel** (617) 523-3383. Ⓣ Park Street. **Open** Jul & Aug: 9am–4pm Tue–Fri, 9am–3pm Sat; Sep–Jun: by appointment. ✝ 8:30am, 11am, 4pm Sun. ✉ ♿
Ⓦ parkstreet.org

Park Street Church's 217-ft (65-m) steeple has punctuated the intersection of Park and Tremont Streets since its dedication in 1810. Designed by English architect Peter Banner, who adapted a design by the earlier English architect Christopher Wren, the church was commissioned by parishioners wanting to establish a Congregational church in the heart of Boston. The church was, and still is, one of the city's most influential pulpits.

Contrary to popular belief, the sermons of Park Street ministers did not earn the intersection the nickname of "Brimstone Corner." Rather, the name came about because during the War of 1812 the US militia, based in Boston, stored its gunpowder in the church basement as safekeeping against bombardment from the British Navy.

In 1829, William Lloyd Garrison (1805–79), fervently outspoken firebrand of the movement to abolish slavery, gave his first abolition speech from the Park Street pulpit.

In 1849 a speech entitled "The War System of Nations" was addressed to the American Peace Society by Senator Charles Sumner. Much later, in 1893, the anthem *America the Beautiful* by Katharine Lee Bates debuted at a Sunday service. Today the church continues, as always, to be involved in religious, political, cultural, and humanitarian activities.

❾ Granary Burying Ground

Tremont St. **Map** 1 C4. Ⓣ Park Street. **Open** 9am–5pm daily.

Named after the early grain storage facility that once stood on the adjacent site of Park Street Church, the Granary Burying Ground dates from 1660. Buried here were three important signatories to the Declaration of Independence – Samuel Adams, John Hancock, and Robert Treat Paine, along with Paul Revere, Benjamin Franklin's parents, merchant-philanthropist Peter Faneuil, and victims of the Boston Massacre.

The orderly array of gravestones, often featured in films and television shows set in Boston, is the result of modern grounds-keeping. Few stones, if any, mark the actual burial site of the person memorialized. In fact, John Hancock may not be here at all. On the night he was buried in 1793, graverobbers cut off the hand with which he had signed his name to the Declaration of Independence, and some believe that the rest of his body was removed during 19th-century construction work.

❿ Boston Athenaeum

101/2 Beacon St. **Map** 1 C4. **Tel** (617) 227-0270. Ⓣ Park Street. **Open** 9am–8pm Mon–Thu, 9am–5:30pm Fri, 9am–4pm Sat, noon–4pm Sun. 🅿
Ⓦ bostonathenaeum.org

Organized in 1807, the collection of the Boston Athenaeum quickly became one of the country's leading private libraries. Sheep farmer Edward Clarke Cabot won the 1846 design competition to house the library, with plans for a gray sandstone building based on Palladio's Palazzo da Porta Festa in Vicenza, a building Cabot knew from a book in the Athenaeum's collection. Included in over half a million volumes are rare manuscripts, maps, and newspapers. Among the

Granary Burying Ground, final resting place for Revolutionary heroes

Stone frieze decoration on the Renaissance-Revival-style Athenaeum

Athenaeum's major holdings are the personal library that once belonged to George Washington and the theological library supplied by King William III of England to the King's Chapel *(see p80)*. In its early years the Athenaeum was Boston's chief art museum, but when the Museum of Fine Arts was proposed, it graciously donated much of its art, including unfinished portraits of George Washington purchased in 1831 from the widow of the painter Gilbert Stuart.

⓫ Massachusetts State House

See pp72–3.

⓬ Museum of African American History

46 Joy St. **Map** 1 C3. **Tel** (617) 725-0022. Ⓣ Park Street. **Open** 10am–4pm Mon–Sat (Jun–Aug: 9:30am–5pm daily). **Closed** public hols. 🖼️ 🎥 🅦 afroammuseum.org

Built from town-house plans designed by Asher Benjamin, the African Meeting House (the centerpiece of the museum) was dedicated in 1806. The oldest black church building in the United States, it was the political and religious center of Boston's African-American society. The interior is plain but rang with the oratory of some of the 19th century's most fiery abolitionists: from Sojourner Truth and Frederick Douglass to William

Lloyd Garrison, who founded the New England Anti-Slavery Society in 1832. The meeting house basement was Boston's first school for African-American children until the adjacent Abiel Smith School was built in 1831. When segregated education was barred in 1855, however, the Smith School closed. The meeting house became a Hasidic synagogue in the 1890s, as most of Boston's African-American community moved to Roxbury and Dorchester. The synagogue closed in the 1960s, and in 1987 the African Meeting House reopened as the linchpin site on the Black Heritage Trail.

⓭ Museum of Science

Science Park. **Map** 1 B2. **Tel** (617) 723-2500. Ⓣ Science Park. **Open** 9am–5pm Mon–Thu & Sat–Sun (Jul–early Sep: 9am–7pm), 9am–9pm Fri. **Closed** Thanksgiving, Dec 25. 🖼️ 🅑 🎥 🅦 mos.org

The Museum of Science straddles the Charles River atop the flood control dam that sits at the mouth of the Charles River. The campus that has developed around it includes a large-format IMAX cinema and planetarium.

With more than 700 interactive exhibits covering natural history, medicine, astronomy, the physical sciences, and computing, the Science Museum is largely oriented to families. The Mugar Omni Theater contains a five-story domed screen with a multidimensional wrap-around sound system, and shows mostly films with a natural science theme. The Charles Hayden Planetarium offers laser shows as well as shows about stars, planets, and other celestial phenomena.

Black Heritage Trail

In the first US census in 1790, Massachusetts was the only state to record no slaves. During the 19th century, Boston's substantial free African-American community lived principally on the north slope of Beacon Hill and in the adjacent West End. The Black Heritage Trail links several key sites, ranging from the African Meeting House to several private homes, which are not open to visitors. Among them are the 1797 George Middleton House (Nos. 5–7 Pinckney Street), the oldest standing house built by African Americans on Beacon Hill, and the Lewis and Harriet Hayden House (No. 66 Phillips Street). Escaped slaves, the Haydens made their home a haven for runaways in the "Underground Railroad" of safe houses between the South and Canada. The walking tour also leads through mews and alleys, like

Holmes Alley, once an escape route for slaves on the run

Holmes Alley at the end of Smith Court, once used by fugitives to flee professional slave catchers.

Free tours of the Black Heritage Trail are led by National Park Service rangers – (617) 742-5415 – from Memorial Day weekend through August, 10am, noon, and 2pm Monday through Saturday, departing from the Shaw Memorial. Self-guided tour maps are available at the Museum of African American History.

⓫ Massachusetts State House

The cornerstone of the Massachusetts State House was laid on July 4, 1795, by Samuel Adams and Paul Revere. Completed on January 11, 1798, the Charles Bulfinch-designed center of state government served as a model for the US Capitol Building in Washington and as an inspiration for many of the state capitols around the country. Later additions were made, but the original building remains the archetype of American government buildings. Its dome, sheathed in copper and gold, serves as the zero mile marker for Massachusetts, making it, as Oliver Wendell Holmes *(see p67)* remarked, "the hub of the universe."

The State House, from Boston Common

★ **House of Representatives**
This elegant oval chamber was built for the House of Representatives in 1895. The Sacred Cod, which now hangs over the gallery, came to the State House when it first opened in 1798, and it has since hung over any place where the representatives have met.

KEY

① **The Wings** of the State House, thought by many to sit incongruously with the rest of the structure, were added in 1917.

② **The Great Hall** is the latest addition to the State House. Built in 1990, it is lined with marble and topped by a glass dome, and is used for state functions.

③ **Administrative offices** can be found on the upper floors of the building.

④ **The dome** was sheathed in copper in 1802 to prevent water leakage, and, in 1872, gilded in 23-carat gold.

Main Staircase
Beautiful stained-glass windows decorate the main staircase. They illustrate the varied state seals of Massachusetts from its inception as a colony through to modern statehood.

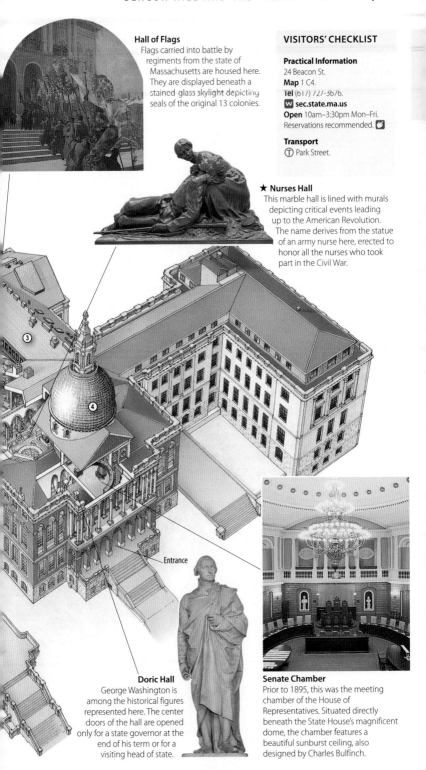

Hall of Flags
Flags carried into battle by regiments from the state of Massachusetts are housed here. They are displayed beneath a stained glass skylight depicting seals of the original 13 colonies.

VISITORS' CHECKLIST

Practical Information
24 Beacon St.
Map 1 C4.
Tel (617) 727-3676.
w sec.state.ma.us
Open 10am–3:30pm Mon–Fri.
Reservations recommended.

Transport
Ⓣ Park Street.

★ **Nurses Hall**
This marble hall is lined with murals depicting critical events leading up to the American Revolution. The name derives from the statue of an army nurse here, erected to honor all the nurses who took part in the Civil War.

Entrance

Doric Hall
George Washington is among the historical figures represented here. The center doors of the hall are opened only for a state governor at the end of his term or for a visiting head of state.

Senate Chamber
Prior to 1895, this was the meeting chamber of the House of Representatives. Situated directly beneath the State House's magnificent dome, the chamber features a beautiful sunburst ceiling, also designed by Charles Bulfinch.

Brattle Book Shop, a Boston literary landmark

⑭ Downtown Crossing

Washington, Winter & Summer Sts. **Map** 4 F1. Ⓣ Downtown Crossing.

As an antidote to heavy traffic congestion, this shopping-district crossroads, located at the intersection of Washington, Winter, and Summer Streets, was laid out as a pedestrian zone between 1975 and 1978. Downtown's single remaining department store is Macy's, although the area also offers a range of other outlets, including bookstores, camera stores, and a jewelry district. Street vendors and summer lunchtime concerts create a lively scene.

The busy Macy's department store is one of a chain found throughout the US, with the most well-known store in New York. Across Summer Street, the building that housed Filene's Department Store remains a local landmark. A decade-long redevelopment maintained the original 1912 Beaux-Arts façade and added a sleek condominium tower. The complex also features restaurants and shops, including a Roche Brothers food store and casual café and a branch of the clothing chain Primark. Nearby is the French bakery Paul's first full-service restaurant in the United States.

Another well-known store in the area is Brattle Book Shop, just off Washington Street on West Street. Founded in 1825, this bibliophiles' treasure-house is packed with more than

250,000 used, rare, and out-of-print books, as well as back issues of magazines, maps, prints, postcards, and manuscripts. Outside the store are bins of bargain books priced between $1 and $5.

⑮ Emerson Colonial Theatre

106 Boylston St. **Map** 4 E2. **Tel** (617) 482-9393. Ⓣ Boylston. **Open** phone to check. ♿ ⓦ **citicenter.org**

Clarence H. Blackall designed 14 Boston theaters during his architectural career, among them the Colonial, which is the city's oldest theater in continuous operation under the same name. Although plain outside, the interior is impressively opulent. Designed by H. B. Pennell, the Rococo lobby has chandeliers, gilded trim, and lofty arched ceilings. The auditorium is decorated with figures, frescoes, and friezes.

Cherub, Emerson Colonial Theatre

The theater opened on December 20, 1900 with an extravagant performance of the melodrama *Ben Hur*. Today the theater is best remembered for premiering lavish musical productions, such as *Ziegfeld Follies*.

⑯ Chinatown

Bounded by Kingston, Kneeland, Washington & Essex Sts. **Map** 4 E2. Ⓣ Chinatown.

This area is the third-largest Chinatown in the US after those in San Francisco and New York. Pagoda-topped telephone booths, as well as a three-story gateway guarded by four marble lions, set the neighborhood's Asian tone.

The first 200 Chinese to settle in New England came by ship from San Francisco in 1870, recruited to break a labor strike at a shoe factory.

Another wave of immigration from California in the 1880s was prompted by an economic boom that led to job openings in construction. Boston's Chinese colony was fully established by the turn of the 19th century.

Political turmoil in China immediately following World War II, and more recent arrivals from Vietnam, Laos, Korea, Thailand, and Cambodia, have swelled Chinatown's population. Along with the area's garment and textile industries, restaurants, bakeries, food markets, and dispensers of Chinese medicine are especially numerous along the main thoroughfare of Beach Street, as well as on Tyler, Oxford, and Harrison Streets.

Chinatown Gate (*paifang*) with a foo lion on each side

⑰ Bay Village

Bounded by Tremont, Arlington & Charles St. South. **Map** 4 D2.
Ⓣ Tufts Medical Center, Boylston.

Originally an expanse of mud flats, the Bay Village area was drained in the early 1800s and initially became habitable with the construction of a dam in 1825. Many carpenters, cabinetmakers, artisans, and house painters involved in the construction of Beacon Hill's pricier town houses built their own modest but well-crafted residences here. As a result there are many similarities between the two neighborhoods.

Fayette Street was laid out in 1824 to coincide with the visit of the Marquis de Lafayette, the French general who allied himself with George Washington. Bay Street, located just off Fayette Street, features a single dwelling and is generally regarded as the city's shortest street. In 1809, author Edgar Allan Poe was born in a boarding house on Carver Street, where his parents were staying while touring with a traveling theatrical company. Poe was never fond of Boston (he called residents "Frogpondians"), but the city honored him with a statue. Erected in October 2014 on the corner of Boylston Street and Charles Street South, it depicts Poe in mid-stride, with a flowing cape and a suitcase overflowing with manuscripts. A raven is at his side.

During Prohibition in the 1920s, clandestine speakeasies gave Bay Village its bohemian ambience. More recently, the neighborhood has become a center for Boston's gay community.

⑱ Shubert Theatre

265 Tremont St. **Map** 4 E2. **Tel** (617) 482-9393. Ⓣ Boylston, Tufts Medical Center. **Open** phone to check. ♿
Ⓦ citicenter.org

The 1,500-seat Shubert Theatre rivals the Colonial Theatre for its long history of staging major pre-Broadway musical

The vast Grand Lobby of the Wang Theatre

productions. Designed by the architects Charles Bond and Thomas James, the theater features a white Neo-Classical façade with a pair of Ionic columns flanking a monumental, Palladian-style window over the entrance. The theater first opened its doors in 1910, and during its heyday many stars walked the boards, including Sarah Bernhardt, W. C. Fields, Cary Grant, Mae West, Humphrey Bogart, Ingrid Bergman, Henry Ford, and Rex Harrison. Today, dance, theater, musicals, and opera are showcased here.

⑲ Wang Theatre

270 Tremont St. **Map** 4 E2. **Tel** (617) 482-9393. Ⓣ Boylston, Tufts Medical Center. **Open** phone to check. ♿
Ⓦ citicenter.org

Opened in 1925 as the Metropolitan Theatre and later named the Music Hall, New England's most ornate variety theater was inspired by the Paris Opera House, and was originally intended to be a movie theater. Designed by Clarence Blackall, the theater's auditorium was once one of the largest in the world. The theater was restored and renamed as the Wang Center for the Performing Arts in 1983, but is now known simply as the Wang Theatre. The five-story Grand Lobby and seven-story auditorium are designed in Renaissance Revival style, with gold chandeliers, stained glass, ceiling murals, and jasper pillars.

Today the theater hosts Broadway road shows, visiting dance and opera companies, concerts, motion-picture revivals, and local productions. The Wang, Shubert, and Emerson Colonial theaters are managed by the Citi Performing Arts Center.

The History of Boston's Theater District

Boston's first theater opened in 1793 on Federal Street. Fifty years later, with patronage from the city's social elite, Boston had become a major tryout town and boasted a number of lavish theaters. The US premiere of Handel's *Messiah* opened in 1839, the US premiere of Gilbert and Sullivan's *HMS Pinafore* in 1877, and the premiere of Tchaikovsky's *First Piano Concerto* in 1875. In the late 19th century theaters came under fire from the censorious Watch and Ward Society. Later, in the 20th century, dramas such as Tennessee Williams' *A Streetcar Named Desire* and Eugene O'Neill's *Long Day's Journey into Night* debuted here. Musicals included *Ziegfeld Follies*, Gershwin's *Porgy and Bess*, and works by Rodgers and Hammerstein.

A Streetcar Named Desire, starring a young Marlon Brando and Jessica Tandy

OLD BOSTON AND THE FINANCIAL DISTRICT

This is an area of Boston where old and new sit one on top of the other. Some of its sights, situated in the older part of the district closest to Boston Common, predate the American Revolution. Much of what can be seen today, though, was built much more recently. The north of the district is home to Boston's late 20th-century, modernist-style City Hall and Government Center, while to the east is the city's bustling Financial District. This once formed part of Boston's harbor waterfront, a district built on mercantile wealth. Today, the wharves and warehouses have been replaced by skyscrapers belonging to banks, insurance companies, and high-tech industries.

Sights at a Glance

Historic Buildings and Churches

1. Omni Parker House
2. King's Chapel and Burying Ground
3. Old City Hall
4. Old Corner Bookstore
5. Old South Meeting House
6. *Old State House pp82–3*
7. Government Center
8. Faneuil Hall
9. Quincy Market
10. Custom House
11. Post Office Square Park

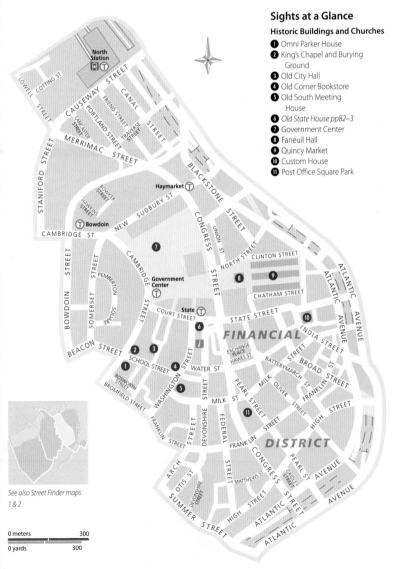

See also Street Finder maps 1 & 2

0 meters	300
0 yards	300

◀ Quincy Market and the distinctive Custom House tower by night

For map symbols *see back flap*

Street-by-Street: Colonial Boston

An important part of Boston's Freedom Trail *(see pp58–61)* runs through this historic core of the city, the site of which predates American Independence. Naturally, the area is now dominated by 19th- and 20th-century development, but glimpses of a colonial past are prevalent here and there in the Old State House, King's Chapel and its adjacent burying ground, and the Old South Meeting House. Newer buildings of interest include the Omni Parker House, as well as the towering skyscrapers of Boston's financial district, located on the northwest edges of this area.

Irish Famine memorial, Washington Street

Government Center

SCHOOL STREET

❷ ★ King's Chapel and Burying Ground
A church has stood here since 1688, although the current building dates from 1749. The adjacent cemetery is the resting place of some of the most important figures in US history.

❶ Omni Parker House
This hotel *(see p312)* first opened its doors in 1855, then underwent many renovations. Famed for its opulence, the hotel also gained a reputation in the 19th century as a meeting place for Boston intellectuals. The current building was erected in 1927.

❸ Old City Hall
This building served as Boston's City Hall from 1865 to 1969. Today it houses a steak house.

0 meters	50
0 yards	50

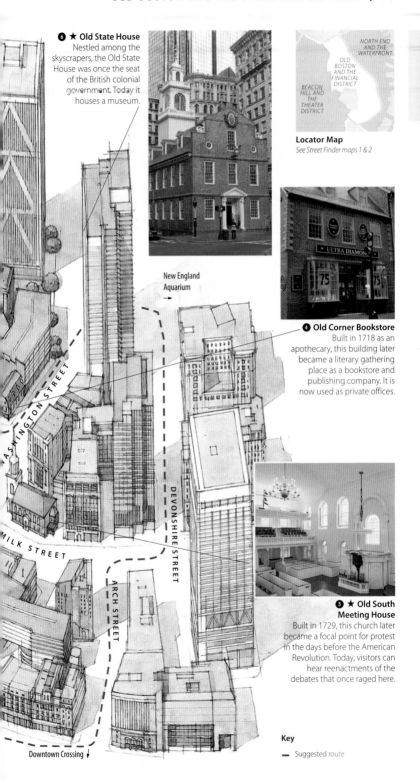

❻ ★ Old State House
Nestled among the skyscrapers, the Old State House was once the seat of the British colonial government. Today it houses a museum.

Locator Map
See Street Finder maps 1 & 2

New England Aquarium →

❹ Old Corner Bookstore
Built in 1718 as an apothecary, this building later became a literary gathering place as a bookstore and publishing company. It is now used as private offices.

WASHINGTON STREET

DEVONSHIRE STREET

MILK STREET

ARCH STREET

❺ ★ Old South Meeting House
Built in 1729, this church later became a focal point for protest in the days before the American Revolution. Today, visitors can hear reenactments of the debates that once raged here.

Downtown Crossing ↓

Key
— Suggested route

❶ Omni Parker House

60 School St. **Map** 1 C4. **Tel** (617) 227-8600. ⓣ Park Street, State, Government Center.
Ⓦ omnihotels.com

Harvey D. Parker, raised on a farm in Maine, became so successful as the proprietor of his Boston restaurant that he achieved his ambition of expanding the property into a first-class, grand hotel. His Parker House opened in 1855, with a façade clad in white marble, standing five stories high, and featuring the first passenger elevator ever seen in Boston. It underwent several, rapid transformations during its early years, with additions made to the main structure in the 1860s and a 10-story, French château-style annex completed later that century. The building saw many successive transform-ations, and its latest 14-story incarnation has stood across from King's Chapel on School Street since 1927.

This hotel attained an instant reputation for luxurious accommodations and fine, even lavish, dining, typified by 11-course menus prepared

Simply decorated, pure white interior of King's Chapel on Tremont Street

by a French chef. Among Parker House's many claims to fame are its Boston Cream Pie, which was first created here, and the word "scrod," a uniquely Bostonian term for the day's freshest seafood, still in common usage. Two former Parker House employees later became recognized for quite different careers. Vietnamese revolutionary leader Ho Chi Minh worked in the hotel's kitchens around 1915, while black activist Malcolm X was a busboy in Parker's Restaurant in the 1940s.

❷ King's Chapel and Burying Ground

58 Tremont St. **Map** 1 C4. **Tel** (617) 523-1749. ⓣ Park Street, State, Government Center. **Open** late May–mid-Sep: 10am–5pm Mon–Sat, 1:30–5pm Sun; mid-Sep–May: call for hours. ✞ 11am Sun, 6pm Wed. Music Recitals: 12:15pm Tue.
Ⓦ kings-chapel.org

British Crown officials were among those who attended Anglican services at the first chapel on this site, which was built in 1688. When New England's governor decided a larger church was needed, the present granite edifice – begun in 1749 – was constructed around the original wooden chapel, which was dismantled and heaved out the windows of its replacement. After the Revolution, the congregation's religious allegiance switched from Anglican to Unitarian. The sanctuary's raised pulpit – dating from 1717 and shaped like a wine glass – is one of the oldest in the US. High ceilings and clear glass windows enhance the sense of spacious-ness. The bell inside the King's Chapel is the largest ever cast by Paul Revere (see p124).

Among those interred in the adjacent cemetery, Boston's oldest, are John Winthrop and Elizabeth Pain, the inspiration for adulteress Hester Prynne in Nathaniel Hawthorne's moralistic novel *The Scarlet Letter*.

Parker House Guests

Boston's reputation as the "Athens of America" was widely acknowledged when members of a distinguished social club began meeting for lengthy dinners and lively intellectual exchanges in 1857. Their get-togethers took place on the last Saturday of every month at Harvey Parker's fancy new hotel. Regular participants included New England's literary elite *(see pp34–5)*: Henry Wadsworth Longfellow, Ralph Waldo Emerson, Nathaniel Hawthorne, and Henry David Thoreau, to name a few. Charles Dickens participated while

John Wilkes Booth, infamous Parker House guest

staying at the Parker House during his American speaking tours, and used his sitting-room mirror to rehearse the public readings he gave at Tremont Temple next door. The mirror now hangs on a mezzanine wall. In 1865, actor John Wilkes Booth, in town to see his brother, a fellow thespian, stayed at the hotel and took target practice at a nearby shooting gallery. Ten days later, at Ford's Theatre in Washington, he pulled a pistol and shot Abraham Lincoln.

❸ Old City Hall

45 School St. **Map** 2 D4. Ⓣ Park Street, State, Government Center.

This building is a wonderful example of French Second Empire architectural gaudiness and served as Boston's City Hall for over a century from 1865 to 1969. It was eventually superseded by the rakishly imposing new City Hall structure at nearby Government Center *(see p84)*. Now the renovated 19th-century building features a steak house.

Previous occupants of the Old City Hall have included such flamboyant mayors as John "Honey Fitz" Fitzgerald and James Michael Curley. There are also statues here which memorialize Josiah Quincy, the second mayor of Boston, after whom Quincy Market is named, as well as Benjamin Franklin, who was born on nearby Milk Street in 1706.

19th-century French-style façade of Boston's Old City Hall

❹ Old Corner Bookstore

1 School St. **Map** 2 D4. Ⓣ Park Street, State, Government Center. **Closed** to the public.

A dormered gambrel roof crowns this brick landmark, which opened as Thomas Crease's apothecary shop in 1718 and was reestablished as the Old Corner Bookstore in 1829. Moving in 16 years later, the Ticknor & Fields publishing company became a gathering place for a notable roster of authors: Emerson, Hawthorne, Longfellow, Thoreau, early feminist writer Margaret Fuller, and *Uncle Tom's Cabin* novelist Harriet Beecher Stowe. The firm is often credited with carving out the first distinctively American literature. The earliest editions of the erudite *Atlantic Monthly* periodical were also printed here under editor James Russell Lowell before he handed the reins over to William Dean Howells. Julia Ward Howe's rousing tribute to American Civil War bravado, "The Battle Hymn of the Republic," first appeared in in the *Atlantic's* February 1862 issue. No publishing activities take place at the Old Corner Bookstore anymore.

❺ Old South Meeting House

310 Washington St. **Map** 2 D4. **Tel** (617) 482-6439. Ⓣ Park Street, State, Government Center. **Open** Apr–Oct: 9:30am–5pm daily; Nov–Mar: 10am–4pm daily. 🅰 📷 ♿ 📱 Ⓦ oldsouthmeetinghouse.org

Built in 1729 for Puritan religious services, this edifice, with a tall octagonal steeple, had colonial Boston's biggest capacity for town meetings – a fact capitalized upon by a group of rebellious rabble-rousers calling themselves the Sons of Liberty. Their outbursts against British taxation and other royal annoyances drew increasingly large and vociferous crowds to the pews and upstairs galleries.

During a candlelit protest rally on December 16, 1773, fiery speechmaker Samuel Adams flashed the signal that led to the Boston Tea Party *(see p93)* down at Griffin's Wharf several hours later. The British retaliated by turning Old South Meeting House into an officers' tavern and stable for General John Burgoyne's 17th Lighthorse Regiment of Dragoons. It was saved from destruction and became a museum in 1877. Displays and a smartphone

Many consider the Old Corner Bookstore the cradle of American literature

audio tour entitled "If These Walls Could Speak" relive those raucous days as well as more recent occurrences well into the 20th century. The Meeting House offers a series of lectures covering a wide range of New England topics and also holds chamber music concerts and other musical performances. The downstairs shop has a broad selection of merchandise, including books and the ubiquitous tins of "Boston Tea Party" tea.

Directly across Washington Street, sculptor Robert Shure's memorial to the victims of the 1845–9 Irish Potato Famine was added to the small plaza here in 1998.

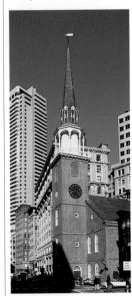

Old South Meeting House, in stark contrast to the modern city

❻ Old State House

Dwarfed by the towers of the Financial District, this was the seat of British colonial government between 1713 and 1776. The royal lion and unicorn still decorate each corner of the eastern facade. After independence, the Massachusetts legislature took possession of the building, and it has had many uses since, including produce market, merchants' exchange, Masonic lodge, and Boston City Hall. Its wine cellars now function as a downtown subway station. The Old State House houses two floors of Bostonian Society memorabilia and a multimedia show about the Boston Massacre.

Old State House amid the skyscrapers of the Financial District

West Façade

A Latin inscription, relating to the first Massachusetts Bay colony, runs around the outside of this crest. The relief in the center depicts a local Native American.

Keayne Hall

This is named after Robert Keayne, who, in 1658, gave £300 to the city so that the Town House, predating the Old State House, could be built. Exhibits in the room depict events from the Revolution.

Entrance

KEY

① **A gold sculpture** of an eagle, symbol of America, can be seen on the west façade.

② **The tower** is a classic example of Colonial style. In 18th-century paintings and engravings it can be seen clearly above the Boston skyline.

③ **The Declaration of Independence** was read from this balcony in 1776. In the 1830s, when the building was City Hall, the balcony was enlarged to two tiers.

★ Central Staircase

A fine example of 19th-century workmanship, the central spiral staircase has two beautifully crafted wooden handrails. It is one of the few such staircases still in existence in the US.

For hotels and restaurants in this region see pp310–13 and pp324–9

Site of the Boston Massacre

Stone marker noting the site
of the Boston Massacre

A brass-and-stone marker below the balcony on the eastern façade of the Old State House indicates the site of the Boston Massacre. After the Boston Tea Party, this was one of the most inflammatory events leading up to the American Revolution. On March 5, 1770, an angry mob of colonists taunted British guardsmen with insults, rocks, and snowballs. The soldiers opened fire, killing five colonists. A number of articles relating to the Boston Massacre are exhibited inside the Old State House, including a musket found near the site and a coroner's report detailing the incident.

VISITORS' CHECKLIST

Practical Information
Washington & State Sts.
Map 2 D4.
Tel (617) 720-1713.
W bostonhistory.org
Open 9am–5pm daily (reduced hours Jan, extended hours Jul & Aug).

Transport
Ⓣ State.

British Unicorn and Lion
A royal symbol of Britain, the original lion and unicorn were torn down when news of the Declaration of Independence reached Boston in 1776.

★ East Façade
This façade has seen many changes. An earlier clock from the 1820s was removed in 1957 and replaced with an 18th-century replica of the sundial that once hung here. The clock has now been reinstated.

Council Chamber
Once the chambers for the royal governors, and from 1780 chambers for the first governor of Massachusetts (John Hancock), this room has seen many key events. Among them were numerous impassioned speeches made by Boston patriots.

City Hall and Government Center, a main city focal point

❼ Government Center

Cambridge, Court, New Sudbury & Congress Sts. **Map** 2 D3. Ⓣ Government Center.

This city center development was built on the site of what was once Scollay Square, demolished as part of the trend for local urban renewal that began in the early 1960s. This trend had already seen the building of the strikingly Modernist concrete and brick new City Hall, which stands on the eastern side of the square and houses government offices.

Some viewed the development as controversial; others did not lament what was essentially a disreputable cluster of saloons, burlesque theaters, tattoo parlors, and scruffy hotels. The overall master plan for Government Center was inspired by the outdoors vitality and spaciousness of Italian piazzas. Architects I. M. Pei & Partners re-created some of this feeling by surrounding Boston's new City Hall with a vast terraced plaza covering 271,050 sq yards, paved with 1,800,000 bricks. Its spaciousness makes it an ideal place for events such as skateboard contests, political and sports rallies, food fairs, patriotic military marches, and concerts.

❽ Faneuil Hall

Dock Sq. **Map** 2 D3. Ⓣ Government Center, Haymarket, State. Great Hall: **Open** 9am–5pm daily (closed for events). ♿ 📷 🏛 🅦 nps.gov/bost

A gift to Boston from the wealthy merchant Peter Faneuil in 1742, this Georgian, brick landmark has always functioned simultaneously as a public market and town meeting place. Master tinsmith Shem Drowne modeled the building's grasshopper weathervane after the one on top of the Royal Exchange in the City of London, England. Revolutionary gatherings packed the hall, and as early as 1763 Samuel Adams used the hall as a platform to urge the American colonies to unite and fight for independence against British oppression; hence the building's nickname "Cradle of Liberty" and the bold posture of the statue of Sam Adams at the front of the building. Toward the end of the 18th century, architect Charles Bulfinch was commissioned to expand the building in order to accommodate larger crowds. The work was completed in 1806, and Faneuil Hall then remained unchanged until 1898, when it was further expanded according to Bulfinch stipulations. This Freedom Trail landmark also houses the visitor center of the Boston

Sam Adams statue, in front of Faneuil Hall

National Historical Park. Opposite the building is the information center for the Boston Harbor Islands.

❾ Quincy Market

Between Chatham & Clinton Sts. **Map** 2 D3. **Tel** (617) 523-1300. Ⓣ State, Government Center. **Open** 10am–9pm Mon–Sat, noon–6pm Sun. ♿ 🅦 faneuilhallmarketplace.com

This immensely popular shopping and dining complex attracts nearly 18 million people every year. It was developed from the buildings of the old Quincy Market, which was the city's meat, fish, and produce market. These buildings had fallen into disrepair before they underwent a widely acclaimed restoration in the 1970s. The 535-ft- (163-m-) long Greek-Revival-style colonnaded market hall with a spectacular central rotunda is flanked by the North and South Market buildings. These individual warehouses have also been refurbished to accommodate numerous boutiques, stores, restaurants, and pubs, as well as upstairs business offices. In 2015 the city opened a new fresh market opposite the Haymarket subway station on the Rose Kennedy Greenway. The year-round Boston Public Market features only locally sourced produce and specialty foods.

Gallery of the Greek Revival main dome in Quincy Market's central hall

⑩ Custom House

3 McKinley Square. **Map** 2 E3. **Tel** (617) 310-6300. Ⓣ Aquarium. Museum: **Open** 8am–9pm daily. Tower: **Open** 2pm Sat–Thu. 🖼 🅦 **marriott. com/vacationclub**

Before landfill altered downtown topography, early Boston's Custom House perched at the water's edge. A temple-like Greek Revival structure with fluted Doric columns, the granite building had a skylit dome upon completion in 1847. Since 1915, however, it has supported a 495-ft (150-m) tower with a four-sided clock. For the best part of the 20th century, the Custom House was Boston's only bona fide skyscraper.

The building contains a small maritime museum and an observatory, both of which are open to the public. The latter offers stunning views of the harbor and the Financial District skyscrapers that tower over it.

The Langham Boston Hotel in Post Office Square Park

Greek Revival Custom House tower, one of Boston's most striking sights

⑪ Post Office Square Park

Franklin, Pearl, High & Congress sts. **Map** 2 D4. Ⓣ State, Aquarium.

Officially named Norman B. Leventhal Park, and occupying land reclaimed when a parking garage was demolished, this beautifully landscaped park is a small island of green amid the soaring skyscrapers of the Financial District. Vines climb a 143-ft- (44-m-) long trellis along one side of the park, and a fountain made of green glass cascades on the square's Pearl Street side. A focal point for the entire Financial District throughout the year, the Post Office Square Park comes into its own in the summer months, when a small kiosk sells luncheon fare, jazz concerts are often held at midday, and office workers fill the benches and lounge on the well-kept lawns. The green space is blanketed with free Wi-Fi access.

The square is surrounded by several notable buildings, not least the former main post office on Congress Street after which the park is named. The 1929–31 Art Deco masterpiece of geometric and botanical ornamentation that used to be occupied by the post office now houses the John W. McCormack courthouse. The Langham Boston hotel *(see p312)* is housed in a classic Renaissance Revival showpiece completed in 1922 that once housed the Federal Reserve Bank. Among the original features that have been carefully preserved are the painted dome and murals by N. C. Wyeth. Perhaps the most notable edifice on the square is the "wedding-cake"-style 1947 late Art Deco building on the south side of Franklin Street. Originally constructed as the headquarters for the New England Telephone Company, this landmark building also recalls the neighborhood's connection to telephone history. The laboratory of telephone pioneer Alexander Graham Bell was located on nearby Court Street.

Alexander Graham Bell (1847–1922)

A native of Edinburgh, Scotland, and son of a deaf mother, Bell moved to Boston in 1871 to start a career teaching speech to the deaf. Two years later he was appointed as professor of vocal physiology at Boston University. Bell worked in his spare time on an apparatus for transmitting sound by electrical current. History was made on March 17, 1876, when Bell called to his assistant in another room: "Mr. Watson, come here. I want you." The first demonstration of the "telephone" took place in Boston on May 10, 1876, at the Academy of Arts and Sciences. By 1878, he had set up the first public telephone exchange in New Haven, Connecticut.

NORTH END AND THE WATERFRONT

This was Boston's first neighborhood, and one that has been key to the city's fortunes. Fringed by numerous wharves, the area prospered initially through shipping and shipbuilding, with much of America's early trade passing through its warehouses. The more recent importance of finance and high-tech industries, however, has seen the waterfront evolve, its old warehouses transformed into luxury apartment blocks and offices. Away from the waterfront, the narrow streets of the North End have historically been home to European immigrants, drawn by the availability of work. The area's Italian heritage is evident in the cafés, delis, restaurants, and religious festivals that make it one of the city's most distinct communities.

Sights at a Glance

Historic Sites and Churches

❶ Copp's Hill Burying Ground
❸ Old North Church *p91*
❹ Paul Revere Mall
❺ Paul Revere House

Waterfront Sights

❷ Institute of Contemporary Art
❻ Waterfront Wharves
❼ *New England Aquarium pp94–5*
❽ Boston Tea Party Ships and Museum
❾ Children's Museum

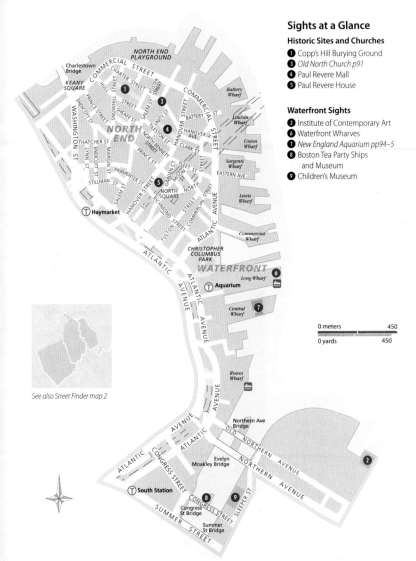

See also Street Finder map 2

◀ Sailboats on the Charles River with the Boston skyline in the background

For map symbols *see back flap*

Street-by-Street: North End

The main arteries of this area are Hanover and Salem Streets. Topped by the Old North Church, Salem Street is indicative of this area's historical connections – indeed the Old North Church is one of Boston's premier Revolutionary sights. In general the area consists of narrow streets and alleys, with four- and five-story tenements, many of which are now expensive condominiums. Hanover Street, like much of the area, has a distinctly Italian feel, while just south of here is North Square, site of the famous Paul Revere House *(see p92)*.

Clough House was built by Ebenezer Clough, who helped build the Old North Church. It houses an 18th-century-style chocolate shop.

❶ Copp's Hill Burying Ground
During the American Revolution, the British used this low hilltop to fire cannon at American positions across Boston Harbor. Created in 1659, it is the city's second oldest graveyard.

❸ ★ Old North Church
Built in 1723 and famous for the part it played in Paul Revere's midnight ride *(see p124)*, this is Boston's oldest religious building. On festive occasions, the North End still rings with the sound of its bells.

HULL STREET

SHEAFE STREET

SALEM STREET

NORTH BEN

PRINCE STREET

Charlestown

Government Center

Key

— Suggested route

| 0 meters | 50 |
| 0 yards | 50 |

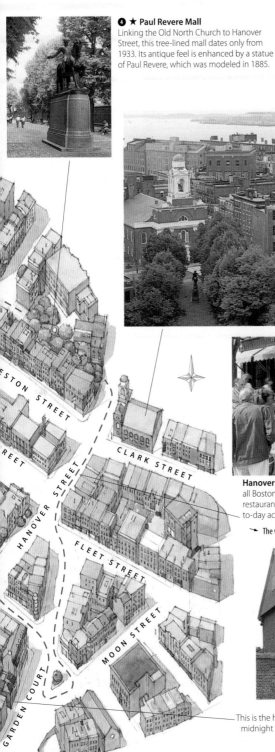

❹ ★ Paul Revere Mall
Linking the Old North Church to Hanover Street, this tree-lined mall dates only from 1933. Its antique feel is enhanced by a statue of Paul Revere, which was modeled in 1885.

Locator Map
See Street Finder map 2

St. Stephen's Church echoes the North End's Italian theme, though only by chance. Long before the first Italians arrived, Charles Bulfinch incorporated Italian Renaissance features and a bell tower into his renovation of an earlier church building.

Hanover Street is the most Italian of all Boston's streets, brought to life by restaurants and cafés, as well as the day-to-day activities of its ethnic community.

➤ The waterfront

❺ ★ Paul Revere House
This is the house where Paul Revere began his midnight ride *(see p124)*. Revere's home from 1770 to 1800, it is now a museum.

Slate tombstones of Boston's early settlers, Copp's Hill Burying Ground

❶ Copp's Hill Burying Ground

Entrances at Charter & Hull Sts.
Map 2 D2. Ⓣ Government Center, North Station. **Open** 9am–5pm daily.

Existing since 1659, this is Boston's second-oldest cemetery after the one by King's Chapel (*see p80*). Nicknamed "Corpse Hill," the real name of the hill occupied by the cemetery derives from a local man by the name of William Copp. He owned a farm on its southeastern slope from 1643, and much of the cemetery's land was purchased from him. His children are buried here. Other more famous people interred here include Robert

Quiet, leafy street, typical of the area around Copp's Hill

Newman, the sexton who hung Paul Revere's signal lanterns in the belfry of Old North Church (*see p91*), and Edmund Hartt, builder of the USS *Constitution* (*see p123*). Increase, Cotton, and Samuel Mather, three generations of a family of highly influential colonial period Puritan ministers, are also buried here. Hundreds of Boston's Colonial-era black slaves and freedmen are also buried here, including Prince Hall, a free black man who founded the African Freemasonry Order in Massachusetts.

During the British occupation of Boston, the site was used by British commanders who had an artillery position here. They would later exploit the prominent hilltop location during the Revolution, when they directed cannon fire from here across Boston harbor toward American positions in Charlestown. King George III's troops were said to have used the slate headstones for target practice, and pockmarks from their musket balls are still visible on some of them.

Copp's Hill Terrace, directly across Charter Street, is a prime observation point for

Decorative column, Copp's Hill

views over to Charlestown and Bunker Hill. It is also the site where, in 1919, a 2.3-million-gallon molasses tank exploded, creating a huge, syrupy tidal wave that killed 21 people.

❷ Institute of Contemporary Art

100 Northern Ave. **Map** 2 F5. **Tel** (617) 478-3100. Ⓣ Courthouse. **Open** 10am–5pm Tue, Wed, Sat, Sun (to 9pm Thu, Fri). ♿ 📷 🎫 🅦 **icaboston.org**

Since 1936, when it introduced Americans to the then-radical work of German Expressionism, the Institute of Contemporary Art has made a point of championing cutting-edge innovation and avant-garde expression. Over the years, the ICA has pushed the envelope of the definition of art, showing creations often outside the usual art-world boundaries, such as an entire exhibition devoted to blowtorches. The ICA was also in the vanguard of showing and interpreting video art when the technology was still in its infancy. For its first 70 years, the ICA was an exhibiting but not a collecting institution, in part on the theory that the definition of "contemporary" changes from minute to minute. That focus changed in 2006 when the ICA moved from its quaint Back Bay building to a dramatic new wood, steel, and glass structure cantilevered above the Harbor Walk on Fan Pier on the South Boston waterfront. The 65,000-sq-ft (6,040-sq-m) museum is the creation of the design firm Diller Scofidio + Renfro, and includes a 325-seat performing arts theater with clear walls that allow the harbor to serve as a stage backdrop, as well as a media center and art lab for educational programs. The vastly expanded facilities also allow the ICA to focus on collecting 21st-century art.

❾ Old North Church

Christ Episcopal Church is the official name of Boston's oldest surviving religious edifice, which dates from 1723. It was built of brick in the Georgian style similar to that of St. Andrew's-by-the-Wardrobe in Blackfriars, London, designed by Sir Christopher Wren. The church was made famous on April 18, 1775, when sexton Robert Newman, aiding Paul Revere *(see p124)*, hung a pair of signal lanterns in the belfry. These were to warn the patriots in Charlestown of the westward departure of British troops, on their way to engage the revolutionaries.

VISITORS' CHECKLIST

Practical Information
193 Salem St. **Map** 2 E2.
Tel (617) 858-8231.
🌐 oldnorth.com
Open Mar–May, Nov & Dec:
9am–5pm daily; Jan & Feb:
10am–4pm daily; Jun–Oct
9am–6pm daily. 🕇 9am, 11am.
📷 🚫 ♿ ♿ (call for tours)

Transport
Ⓣ Haymarket, Aquarium,
North Station.

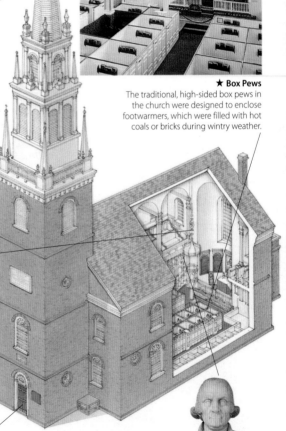

Tower
The tower of the Old North Church contains the first set of church bells in North America cast in 1745.

★ **Box Pews**
The traditional, high-sided box pews in the church were designed to enclose footwarmers, which were filled with hot coals or bricks during wintry weather.

Chandeliers
The church's distinctive chandeliers were brought from England in January 1724 for the first Christmas season.

Entrance

★ **Bust of George Washington**
This marble bust of the first US president, modeled on an earlier one by Christian Gullager, was presented to the church in 1815.

❹ Paul Revere Mall

Hanover St. **Map** 2 E2. Ⓣ Haymarket, Aquarium. ♿

This brick-paved plaza gives the crowded neighborhood of the North End a precious stretch of open space between Hanover and Unity Streets. A well-utilized municipal resource, the Mall is always full of local people: children, teenagers, young mothers, and older residents chatting in Italian and playing cards or checkers. Laid out in 1933, and originally called the Prado, its focal point is Cyrus Dallin's equestrian statue of local hero Paul Revere, which was originally modeled in 1885. However, it was not sculpted and placed here until 1940. Bronze bas-relief plaques on the mall's side walls commemorate a number of North End residents who have played an important role in the history of Boston. Benches, a fountain, and twin rows of linden trees complete the space, which has a distinctly European feel.

At the north end of the Mall, across Unity Street, is Old North Church (see p91), one of the city's most important historical sites. To the south is busy Hanover Street, which is lined with numerous Italian cafés and restaurants.

Paul Revere House kitchen, as it was in the 18th century

❺ Paul Revere House

19 North Sq. **Map** 2 E2. **Tel** (617) 523-2338. Ⓣ Haymarket, Aquarium. **Open** mid-Apr–Oct: 9:30am–5:15pm daily; Nov–mid-Apr: 9:30am–4:15pm daily. **Closed** Jan–Mar: Mon. 🎧 ♿ 📷 🏛 call for hours. 🅦 paulreverehouse.org

The city's oldest surviving clapboard frame house is historically significant, for it was here in 1775 that Paul Revere began his legendary horseback ride to warn his compatriots in Lexington of the impending arrival of British troops. This historic event was later immortalized in a boldly patriotic, epic poem by Henry Wadsworth Longfellow (see p114). It begins "Listen, my children, and you shall hear of the midnight ride of Paul Revere."

Revere, a Huguenot descendant, was by trade a versatile gold- and silversmith, copper engraver, and maker of church bells and cannons. He and his second wife, Rachel, mother of eight of his 16 children, owned the house from 1770 to 1800. Small leaded casement windows, an overhanging upper story, and nail-studded front door all contribute to make it a fine example of 18th-century Early American architecture. By the mid-19th century the house had become a decrepit tenement. It was saved from demolition by preservationists' efforts led by one of Revere's great-grandsons. Period artifacts provide a good picture of domestic life in Colonial times.

In the courtyard is a large bronze bell, cast by Paul Revere for a church in 1804 – Revere made nearly 200 church bells.

Other buildings on the campus include the early 18th-century Pierce-Hichborn House, the earliest brick town house remaining in New England, and a visitor center with historic exhibitions and a gift shop.

The Rose Fitzgerald Kennedy Greenway connects Boston's downtown with the waterfront

Rowes Wharf development, typical of Boston's waterfront regeneration

❻ Waterfront Wharves

Atlantic Ave. **Map** 2 E4. ⓣ Aquarium.

Boston's waterfront is fringed by many wharves, reminders of the city's past as a key trading port. One of the largest of these is Long Wharf, established in 1710 to accommodate the boom in early maritime commerce. Once extending 2,000 ft (610 m) into Boston Harbor and lined with shops and warehouses, Long Wharf provided mooring for the largest ships of the time. Many sightseeing excursion boats depart from here.

Harbor Walk connects Long Wharf with other adjacent 19th-century wharves, including Rowes Wharf, a good example of waterfront revitalization, with the Boston Harbor Hotel, restaurants, and a marina. Long Wharf is also a good access point to the Rose Fitzgerald Kennedy Greenway, a 1.5-mile (2.5-km) linear park

created in 2008 on land reclaimed from the removal of an elevated highway. It features fountains, public art, a Boston-themed carousel, and numerous food trucks.

❼ New England Aquarium

See pp94–5.

❽ Boston Tea Party Ships & Museum

306 Congress St. **Map** 2 E5. **Tel** (617) 338-1773. ⓣ South Station. **Open** 10am–5pm daily (winter: 4pm). 🖼 🅦 bostonteapartyship.com

Griffin's Wharf, where the Boston Tea Party took place on December 16, 1773, was buried beneath landfill many years ago. Replicas of two British East India Company ships involved in the Tea Party now anchor on the Fort Point Channel, a short

distance south of the old Griffin's Wharf site. After boarding the ships and even tossing tea overboard, visitors can enter an interactive museum where exhibits put that historic act of protest into a broader context, explaining how the political tensions between Boston and the British Crown led up to the American Revolution.

❾ Children's Museum

308 Congress St. **Map** 2 E5. **Tel** (617) 426-6500. ⓣ South Station. **Open** 10am–5pm daily (to 9pm Fri). 🖼 🅵 🅦 bostonchildrensmuseum.org

Overlooking Fort Point Channel, a pair of rejuvenated 19th-century redbrick wool warehouses contain one of the country's best children's museums. The expansive museum offers a host of interesting exhibits. Youngsters play games, join learning activities, and hoist themselves up the 30-ft (9-m) New Balance climbing structure in the lobby. The Art Studio provides a hands-on recycling area with materials for projects. Visits to a silk merchant's house transplanted from Kyoto (Boston's sister city) inject a multicultural dimension, while careers can be sampled as children work on a mini-construction site.

A towering milk bottle in front of the museum serves as a summer ice-cream stand, and mazes, giant boulders, and performance spaces grace an outdoor park.

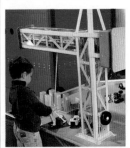

Playing on the mini-construction site at Boston's Children's Museum

❼ New England Aquarium

The waterfront's prime attraction dominates Central Wharf. Designed by a consortium of architects in 1969, the aquarium's core encloses a vast four-story ocean tank, which contains an innumerable array of marine animals. A curving walkway runs around the outside of the tank from top to bottom and provides viewpoints of the interior of the tank from different levels. Also resident at the aquarium are colonies of penguins, playful harbor seals, anacondas, rays, sea turtles, and mesmerizing seadragons. The facility also includes a superb IMAX theater.

Shark and Ray Touch Tank
The largest shark and ray touch tank on the East Coast is surrounded by shallow edges and viewing windows.

★ **Penguin Exhibit**
One of the most popular attractions of the aquarium, the penguin pool runs around the base of the giant tank. It contains more than 80 penguins.

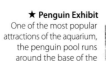

★ **Whale Watch**
A naturalist aboard an aquarium boat explains marine ecology on 3- to 4-hour educational trips to Stellwagen Bank to see whales and seabirds.

Main entrance

Harbor Seals
An outdoor tank covered by a steel canopy is home to a lively colony of harbor seals.

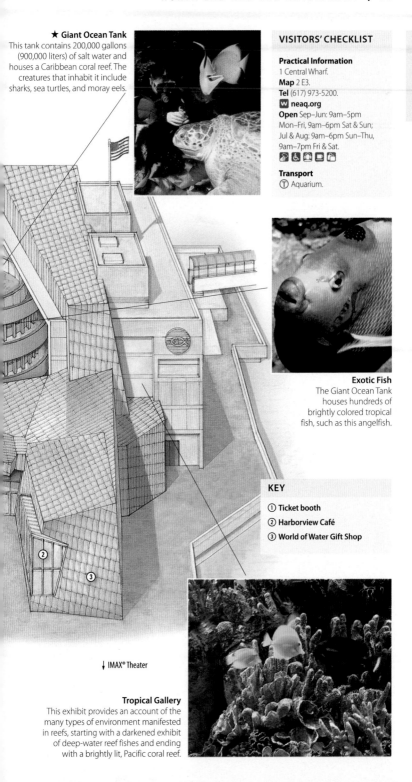

★ Giant Ocean Tank
This tank contains 200,000 gallons (900,000 liters) of salt water and houses a Caribbean coral reef. The creatures that inhabit it include sharks, sea turtles, and moray eels.

VISITORS' CHECKLIST

Practical Information
1 Central Wharf.
Map 2 E3.
Tel (617) 973-5200.
Ⓦ **neaq.org**
Open Sep–Jun: 9am–5pm Mon–Fri, 9am–6pm Sat & Sun; Jul & Aug: 9am–6pm Sun–Thu, 9am–7pm Fri & Sat.

Transport
Ⓣ Aquarium.

Exotic Fish
The Giant Ocean Tank houses hundreds of brightly colored tropical fish, such as this angelfish.

KEY

① Ticket booth
② Harborview Café
③ World of Water Gift Shop

↓ IMAX® Theater

Tropical Gallery
This exhibit provides an account of the many types of environment manifested in reefs, starting with a darkened exhibit of deep-water reef fishes and ending with a brightly lit, Pacific coral reef.

BACK BAY AND SOUTH END

Until the 19th century Boston was situated on a narrow peninsula surrounded by tidal marshes. Projects to fill Back Bay began in the 1850s and were made possible by new inventions such as the steam shovel. The Back Bay was filled by 1880, and developers soon moved in.

Planned along French lines, with elegant boulevards, Back Bay is now one of Boston's most exclusive neighborhoods. The more bohemian South End, laid out on an English model of town houses clustered around squares, is home to many artists and much of Boston's gay community.

Sights at a Glance

Historic Streets and Squares
1. The Esplanade
4. Commonwealth Avenue
5. Newbury Street
7. Copley Square
8. Boylston Street

Historic Buildings, Churches, and Museums
2. Gibson House Museum
3. First Baptist Church
6. *Trinity Church pp102–103*
9. Boston Public Library

10. John Hancock Tower
11. Berklee Performance Center
12. Boston Center for the Arts

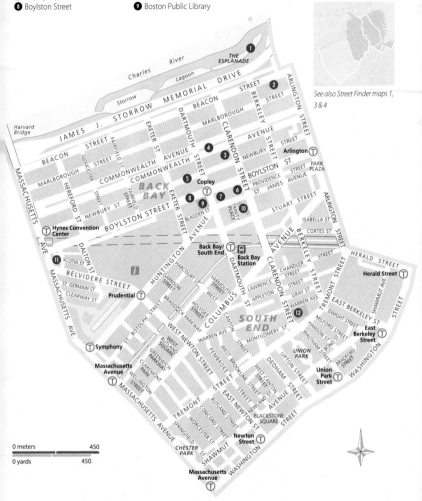

See also Street Finder maps 1, 3 & 4

0 meters 450
0 yards 450

◀ Interior of the historic Boston Public Library

For map symbols *see back flap*

Street-by-Street: Back Bay

This fashionable district unfolds westward from the Public Garden (see pp68–9) in a grid that departs radically from the twisting streets found elsewhere in Boston. Commonwealth Avenue, with its grand 19th-century mansions and parkland, and Newbury and Boylston Streets are its main arteries. Newbury Street is a magnet for all of Boston wanting to indulge in some upscale shopping, whereas the more somber Boylston Street bustles with office workers. Copley Square anchors the entire area and is the site of Henry Hobson Richardson's magnificent Trinity Church (see pp102–103) and the 60-story John Hancock Tower (see p105), which is the tallest building in New England.

Weekly summer and fall farmers' market, Copley Square

❼ Copley Square
This square was a marsh until 1870. It took on its present form only in the late 20th century as buildings around its edges were completed. A farmers' market, concerts, and folk-dancing feature regularly.

COMMONWEALTH AVEN

N E W B

Fenway Park

DARTMOUTH STREET

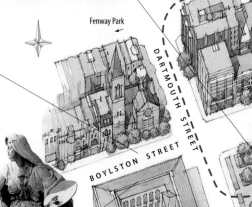

❽ Boylston Street
The site of the Prudential Tower and Shopping Center and the Hynes Convention Center, Boylston Street is also the location of the fabulous New Old South Church (see p104).

BOYLSTON STREET

BOYLSTON STREET

❾ ★ Boston Public Library
One of the first free public libraries in the world, this building was designed by Charles McKim. Inside are murals by John Singer Sargent.

↓
South
End

For hotels and restaurants in this region see pp310–13 and pp324–9

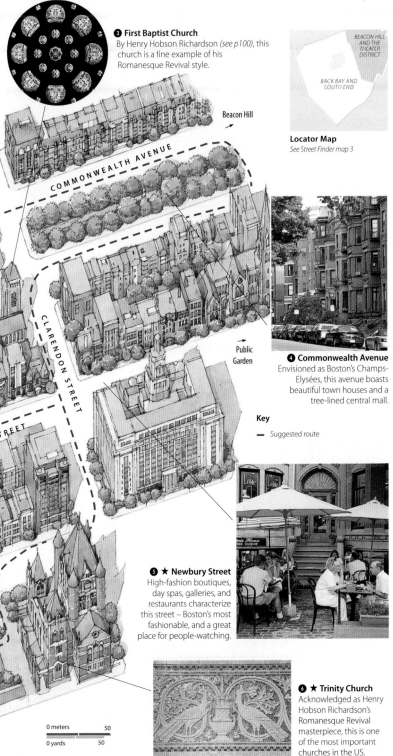

❸ **First Baptist Church**
By Henry Hobson Richardson *(see p100)*, this church is a fine example of his Romanesque Revival style.

Locator Map
See Street Finder map 3

Beacon Hill

COMMONWEALTH AVENUE

CLARENDON STREET

TREET

Public Garden

❹ **Commonwealth Avenue**
Envisioned as Boston's Champs-Elysées, this avenue boasts beautiful town houses and a tree-lined central mall.

Key

— Suggested route

❺ ★ **Newbury Street**
High-fashion boutiques, day spas, galleries, and restaurants characterize this street – Boston's most fashionable, and a great place for people-watching.

❻ ★ **Trinity Church**
Acknowledged as Henry Hobson Richardson's Romanesque Revival masterpiece, this is one of the most important churches in the US.

0 meters 50
0 yards 50

❶ The Esplanade

Map 3 C1. ⓣ Charles/MGH.
Open 24 hrs daily. ♿

Running along the Boston side of the Charles River, between Longfellow Bridge and Dartmouth Street, are the parkland, lagoons, and islands known collectively as the Esplanade. The park is used extensively for in-line skating, cycling, and strolling. It is also the access point for boating on the river (including gondola rides) and the site of the city's leading outdoor concert space.

In 1929, Arthur Fiedler, then the young conductor of the Boston Pops Orchestra, chose the Esplanade for a summer concert series that became a tradition. The Hatch Memorial Shell was constructed in 1939, and its stage is widely used by musical ensembles and other groups throughout the summer. Fourth of July concerts by the Boston Pops, which are followed by fireworks, can attract upward of 500,000 spectators.

Fountains at the Esplanade, next to the Charles River

❷ Gibson House Museum

137 Beacon St. **Map** 3 C1. **Tel** (617) 267-6338. ⓣ Arlington. **Open** Tours at 1pm, 2pm & 3pm Wed–Sun. ⧉ ⧉
⧉ ⓦ thegibsonhouse.org

Among the first houses built in the Back Bay, the Gibson House preserves its original Victorian decor and furnishings throughout all six stories. The 1860 brownstone and redbrick structure was designed in the popular Italian Renaissance

The original Victorian-style library of the Gibson House Museum

Revival style for the widow Catherine Hammond Gibson, who was one of the few women to own property in this part of the city. Her grandson Charles Hammond Gibson, Jr., a noted eccentric, poet, travel writer, horticulturalist, and bon vivant, arranged for the house to become a museum after his death in 1954. As a prelude to this, Gibson began to rope off the furniture in the 1930s, thus inviting his guests to sit on the stairs to drink martinis made with his own bathtub gin.

One of the most modern houses of its day, the Gibson House boasted such technical advancements as gas lighting, indoor plumbing in the basement, and coal-fired central heating. Visitors can see a full dinner setting in the dining room or admire the whimsical Turkish pet pavilion. It is Gibson's preservation of the 1860s decor (with some modifications in 1888) that makes the museum a true time capsule of Victorian life in Boston.

Detail of Bartholdi's frieze atop the distinctive square tower of the First Baptist Church

❸ First Baptist Church

110 Commonwealth Ave. **Map** 3 C2. **Tel** (617) 267-3148. ⓣ Arlington, Copley. **Open** for Sunday worship. ✝ 11am Sun. ⧉ ♿

The Romanesque-style First Baptist Church on the corner of Commonwealth Avenue and Clarendon Street was Henry Hobson Richardson's first major architectural commission and became an instant landmark when it was finished in 1872. Viewed from Commonwealth Avenue, it is one of the most distinctive buildings of the city skyline.

Richardson considered the nearly freestanding bell tower, which he modeled roughly on Italian campaniles, to be the church's most innovative structure. The square tower is topped with a decorative frieze and arches protected by an overhanging roof. The frieze was modeled in Paris by Bartholdi, the sculptor who created the Statue of Liberty, and was carved in place by Italian artisans after the stones were set. The faces in the frieze, which depict the sacraments, are likenesses of prominent Bostonians of that time, among them Henry Wadsworth Longfellow and Ralph Waldo Emerson. The trumpeting angels at the corners of the tower gave the building its nickname, "Church of the Holy Bean Blowers."

Four years after the church was completed, the Unitarian congregation dissolved because it was unable to bear the expense of the building. The church stood vacant until 1881, when the First Baptist congregation from the South End took it over.

❹ Commonwealth Avenue

Map 3 B2. ⓣ Arlington, Copley, Hynes Convention Center.

Back Bay was Boston's first fully planned neighborhood, and architect Arthur Gilman made Commonwealth Avenue, modeled on the elegant boulevards of Paris, the centerpiece of the design. At 200 ft (61 m) wide, with a 10-ft (3-m) setback from the sidewalks to encourage small gardens in front of the buildings, Commonwealth became an arena for America's leading domestic architects in the second half of the 19th century. A walk from the Public Garden to Massachusetts Avenue is like flicking through a catalog of architectural styles. Few of the grand buildings on either side of the avenue are

open to the public, but strollers on the central mall of the avenue encounter a number of historic figures in the form of bronze statues. Some have only tangential relationships to the city, like Alexander Hamilton, the first secretary of the US Treasury. The end of the mall features a heroic bronze of Leif Eriksson, erected as a historically unsupported flight of fancy that the Norse explorer landed at Boston. The patrician statue of abolitionist William Lloyd Garrison is said to capture the man's air of moral superiority. The best-loved memorial depicts sailor and historian Samuel Eliot Morison dangling his feet from a rock.

William Lloyd Garrison statue on Commonwealth Avenue

❺ Newbury Street

Map 3 C2. ⓣ Arlington, Copley, Hynes Convention Center.

Newbury Street is a Boston synonym for "stylish." The Taj Boston, formerly the Ritz-Carlton Hotel, at Arlington Street sets an elegant tone for the street that continues with a mix of prestigious and often

well-hidden art galleries, stylish boutiques, and some of the city's most *au courant* restaurants. Churches provide vestiges of a more decorous era. The **Church of the Covenant** at No. 67 Newbury contains the world's largest collection of Louis Comfort Tiffany stained-glass windows and an elaborate Tiffany lantern. A chorus and orchestra perform sacred music each Sunday (Sep–May) at Emmanuel Church on the corner of Berkeley Street.

Most of Newbury Street was constructed as town-house residences, but the desirability of these spaces for retail operations has pushed residents to the upper floors, while ground and subsurface levels are devoted to chic boutiques and eateries. Modern-day aspiring celebrities may be spotted at the sidewalk tables of Newbury's "hottest" restaurants, such as Sonsie (see p325).

⌂ Church of the Covenant
67 Newbury St. **Tel** (617) 266-7480.
🕙 10:30am Sun. ♿ 🅿 ♿ 📷 🏛
🅦 **cotcbos.org**

Stylish Newbury Street, with its elegant shops, galleries, and restaurants, the epitome of Boston style

❻ Trinity Church

Routinely voted one of America's finest buildings, this masterpiece by Henry Hobson Richardson dates from 1877. Trinity Church was founded in 1733 near Downtown Crossing, but the congregation moved the church to this site in 1871. The church is a granite and sandstone Romanesque structure standing on wooden piles driven through mud into bedrock, surmounted with granite pyramids. John LaFarge designed the interior, while some of the windows are designed by Edward Burne-Jones and executed by William Morris.

Bas-relief in Chancel
On the wall of the chancel, behind the altar, are a series of gold bas-reliefs. This one shows St. Paul before King Agrippa.

★ North Transept Windows
Designed by Edward Burne-Jones and executed by William Morris, the three stained-glass windows above the choir relate the story of Christmas.

Parish House

KEY

① **The Pulpit** is covered with carved scenes from the life of Christ, as well as portraits of great preachers through the ages.

② **The Bell Tower** was inspired by the Renaissance cathedral at Salamanca, central Spain.

③ **John LaFarge's** lancet windows show Christ in the act of blessing. They were designed at the request of Phillips Brooks – he wanted LaFarge to create an inspirational design for the west nave, which he could look at while preaching.

Chancel
Designed by Charles Maginnis, the present-day chancel was not dedicated until 1938. The seven windows by Clayton & Bell of London show the life of Christ.

David's Charge to Solomon
Located in the baptistry, to the right of the chancel, this beautiful window is also the result of a partnership between Edward Burne-Jones and William Morris. The story shown is one of the few in the church from the Old Testament.

VISITORS' CHECKLIST

Practical Information
Copley Sq.
Map 3 C2. **Tel** (617) 536-0944.
🌐 trinitychurchboston.org
Open 9am–5pm Mon–Sat (to 6pm Tue–Thu), 1–5:30pm Sun.
7:45am, 9am, 11:15am, 6pm Sun. Concerts: Sep–mid-June: 12:15pm Fri.

Transport
Ⓣ Copley.

★ **West Portico**
Richardson disliked the original flat façade of Trinity Church, and so modeled the deeply sculpted west portico after St. Trophime in Arles, France. It was added after his death.

③

Carving of Phillips Brooks and Christ

Phillips Brooks

Born in Boston in 1835 and educated at Harvard, Brooks was a towering charismatic figure. Rector of Trinity Church from 1869, he gained a reputation for powerful sermons. From 1872 Brooks worked closely with Henry Hobson Richardson on the design of the new Trinity Church – at least five sculpted likenesses of him can be seen in and around the building.

Main entrance

The New Old South Church on the corner of Copley Square

❼ Copley Square

Map 3 C2. Ⓣ Copley.

Named after John Singleton Copley, the great Boston painter born nearby in 1737, Copley Square is a hive of civic activity surrounded by some of Boston's most striking architecture. Summer activities include weekly farmers' markets, concerts, and even folk-dancing.

The inviting green plaza took years to develop; when Copley was born it was just a marshy riverbank, which remained unfilled until 1870. Construction of the John Hancock Tower in 1975 anchored the southeastern side of Copley Square, and the Copley Place development completed the square on the southwestern corner in 1984. Today's Copley Square, a wide open space of trees, grass, and fountains, took shape in the heart of the city in the 1990s, after various plans to utilize this hitherto wasted space were tendered.

A large plaque honoring the Boston Marathon, which ends at the Boston Public Library, was set in the sidewalk in 1996 to coincide with the 100th race. As well as pushcart vendors, the plaza has a booth for discounted theater, music, and dance tickets.

❽ Boylston Street

Map 3 C2. Ⓣ Boylston, Arlington, Copley, Hynes Convention Center.

The corners of Boylston and Berkeley streets represent Boston architecture at its most diverse. The stately French Academic-style structure on the west side was erected for the Museum of Natural History, a forerunner of the Museum of Science *(see p71)*. It has gone on to house upscale shops and restaurants. The east side spouts a Robert A. M. Stern tower and a Philip Johnson office building that resembles a table radio. Boston jeweler Shreve, Crump & Low occupied the Art Deco building at the corner of Arlington Street until relocating nearby to Newbury Street.

Some notable office buildings stand on Boylston Street. The lobby of the New England building at No. 501 features large historical murals and dioramas depicting the process of filling Back Bay. The central tower of the Prudential Tower and Shopping Center dominates the skyline on upper Boylston Street. Adjoining the Prudential is the Hynes Convention Center. It was significantly enlarged in 1988 to accommodate the city's burgeoning business in hosting conventions.

The Italian-Gothic-style **New Old South Church**, which is located at the corner of Dartmouth, was built in 1874–5 by the congregation that had met previously at the Old South Meeting House *(see p81)*.

🛈 **New Old South Church**

645 Boylston St. **Tel** (617) 536-1970. **Open** 8am–8pm Mon–Fri, 8:30am–5pm Sat, 8:30am–7:30pm Sun. 🕇 6pm Thu, 9am, 11am, 6pm Sun. ✉ ♿ 🖳 oldsouth.org

❾ Boston Public Library

Copley Square. **Map** 3 C2. **Tel** (617) 536-5400. Ⓣ Copley. General Library: **Open** 9am–9pm Mon–Thu, 9am–5pm Fri–Sat, 1–5pm Sun. **Closed** public hols; Jun–Sep: Sun. 🎞 2:30pm Mon, 6pm Tue & Thu, 11am Wed, Fri & Sat, 2pm Sun. ♿ 🖳 🖳 bpl.org

Founded in 1848, the Boston Public Library was America's first metropolitan library for the public. It quickly outgrew its original building, hence the construction of the Italian *palazzo*-style Copley Square building in 1887–95. Designed by Charles McKim, the building is a marvel of fine wood and marble detail. Bates Hall, on the second floor, is particularly noted for its soaring barrel-vaulted ceiling. Sculptor Daniel Chester French fashioned the library's huge bronze doors, Edward Abbey's murals of the Quest for the Holy Grail line the book request room, and John Singer Sargent's murals of Judaism and Christianity cover a third-floor gallery. The library's collection is housed in the 1971 Boylston Street addition, a Modernist structure by architect Philip Johnson.

The vast Bates Hall in the Boston Public Library, noted for its high barrel-vaulted ceiling

❿ John Hancock Tower

200 Clarendon St. **Map** 3 C2.
Ⓣ Copley. **Closed** to the public.

The tallest building in New England, the 790-ft (240-m) rhomboid that is the John Hancock Tower cuts into Copley Square, with its mirrored façade reflecting the surroundings, including from one angle the original Hancock building, built in 1947, with its red and blue lights that forecast the local weather. The innovative design has created a 60-story office building with 10,344 windows that shares the square with its 19th-century neighbors, the Romanesque Trinity Church and the Italian Renaissance Revival Copley Plaza Hotel, without dwarfing them. It was designed by Henry Cobb of the architect firm of I. M. Pei & Partners and its construction was completed in 1975.

⓫ Berklee Performance Center

136 Massachusetts Ave. **Map** 3 A3.
Tel (617) 266-7455. Ⓣ Hynes Convention Center. **Open** call or consult website for concert details.
Ⓦ berkleebpc.com

The largest independent music college in the world, Berklee College of Music has produced a number of jazz, rock, and pop stars, including producer and arranger Quincy Jones, Dixie Chicks singer Natalie Maines, and jazz-pop pianist/vocalist Diana Krall.

Berklee students as well as faculty frequently use the Berklee Performance Center as a showcase, and often as a venue for making live recordings. The warm acoustics and intimate relationship between the performers and the audience produce what is known among audiophiles as "the Berklee sound."

Back Bay and the Charles River seen from the John Hancock Tower

⓬ Boston Center for the Arts

539 Tremont St. **Map** 4 D3. **Tel** (617) 426-5000. Ⓣ Back Bay/South End. Cyclorama: **Open** 9am–5pm Mon–Fri. Mills Gallery: **Open** noon–5pm Wed & Sun; noon–9pm Thu–Sat. **Closed** public hols. 🎭 for performances. ✉ ♿ Ⓦ bcaonline.org

The centerpiece of a resurgent South End, the BCA complex includes four stages, an art gallery, and artists' studios as well as the Boston Ballet Building, home to the company's educational programs, rehearsal space, and administrative offices. The Tremont Estates Building at the corner of Tremont Street, an organ factory in the years after the Civil War, now houses artists' studios, rehearsal space, and an art gallery. The largest of the BCA buildings is the circular, domed Cyclorama, which opened in 1884 to exhibit the 50-ft (15-m) by 400-ft (121-m) painting *The Battle of Gettysburg* by the French artist Paul Philippoteaux. The painting was removed in 1889 and is now displayed at Gettysburg National Historic Park. It now serves as performance and exhibition space.

The Stanford Calderwood Pavilion, with a 360-seat and a 200-seat theater, opened in 2004 as the first new theater in Boston in 75 years. **The Mills Gallery** houses exhibitions focusing on emerging contemporary artists, with a strong emphasis on multimedia installations and shows with confrontational, and often provocative, themes.

Richardsonian Romanesque is a popular architectural style in Back Bay

❶ John F. Kennedy Library and Museum

Columbia Point, Dorchester.
Tel (617) 514-1600. Ⓣ JFK/U Mass.
Open 9am–5pm daily. **Closed** Jan 1,
Thanksgiving, Dec 25. 🗐 🚹 🗐 🔍
Ⓦ jfklibrary.org

The soaring white concrete and glass building of the John F. Kennedy Library stands sentinel on Columbia Point near the mouth of Boston Harbor. Exhibitions chronicle the 1,000 days of the Kennedy presidency and include a re-creation of the Oval Office. Kennedy was among the first politicians to grasp the power of media. The museum takes full advantage of film and video footage to use the president's own words and image to tell his story, including his campaign for the Democratic Party nomination and landmark television debates with Republican opponent Richard M. Nixon.

Gripping film clips capture the anxiety of nuclear brinkmanship during the Cuban missile crisis, as well as the inspirational spirit of the space program and the founding of the Peace Corps. The combination of artifacts, displays, and television footage

Spectators enjoying a baseball game at Fenway Park

evoke both the euphoria of "Camelot" and the numb horror of the assassination.

Two of the president's brothers are also recognized for their contributions to American history. Within the Kennedy Library, the re-created office of Attorney General Robert F. Kennedy touches on both his deft handling of race relations and his key advisory role to his brother. Adjacent to the library, the Edward M. Kennedy Institute for the United States Senate opened in 2015. Tours, exhibits, and a full-scale re-creation of the US Senate Chamber in Washington, DC, promote understanding of the legislative process and celebrate Ted Kennedy's 46 years as senator.

❷ Fenway Park

4 Yawkey Way. **Tel** (617) 226-6661.
Ⓣ Kenmore. **Open** through the year,
check website for details on events.
🗐 🗐 daily. **Ⓦ redsox.com**

Whatever their loyalties, sports fans from all over the world flock to this civic icon, the home of the wildly popular Boston Red Sox. Opened in 1912, this is the oldest Major League baseball park and a shrine to the national pastime.

Tickets to games during the baseball season (April to October) can be hard to come by, but one-hour tours are offered daily throughout the year. Knowledgeable tour guides provide visitors with a behind-the-scenes look at the park's many intricacies, including a stop atop the fabled Green Monster, which stands 37 ft (11 m) above left-field. The venue has also become a popular summertime concert space, hosting big-name acts such as Bruce Springsteen and the Rolling Stones.

❸ Arnold Arboretum

125 Arborway, Jamaica Plain.
Tel (617) 524-1718. Ⓣ Forest Hills.
🚍 39. **Open** sunrise–sunset daily.
Visitor Center: **Open** 10am–5pm Thu–
Tue (Nov–Mar: noon–4pm Thu–Tue).
Closed public hols. 🚹 🗐
Ⓦ arboretum.harvard.edu

Founded by Harvard University in 1872 as a living catalog of all the indigenous and exotic trees and shrubs adaptable to

Dramatic, modern structure of the John F. Kennedy Library and Museum

New England's climate, the Arboretum is planted with more than 15,000 labeled specimens. It is the oldest arboretum in the US and a key resource for botanical and horticultural research. The Arboretum also serves as a park where people jog, stroll, read, and paint.

The park's busiest time is on Lilac Sunday in early May, when tens of thousands come to revel in the sight and fragrance of the lilac collection, one of the largest in the world. The range of the Arboretum's collections guarantees flowers from late March into November, beginning with cornelian cherry and forsythia. Blooms shift in late May to azalea, magnolia, and wisteria, then to mountain laurel and roses in June. Sweet autumn clematis bursts forth in September, and native witch hazel blooms in October and November. The Arboretum also has fine fall foliage in September and October.

A large scale model of the Arboretum can be seen in the Visitors' Information Center just inside the main gate.

❹ John F. Kennedy National Historic Site

83 Beals St., Brookline. **Tel** (617) 566-7937. ⓣ Coolidge Corner. **Open** late May–Oct: 9:30am–5pm Wed–Sun. ⬚ ✉ ♿ 🎧 📷 ⓦ nps.gov/jofi

The first home of the late president's parents, this Brookline house saw the birth of four of nine Kennedy children, including JFK on May 29, 1917. Although the Kennedys moved to a larger house in 1921, the Beals Street residence held special memories for the family, who repurchased the house in 1966 and furnished it with their belongings circa 1917 as a memorial to John F. Kennedy. The guided tour includes a taped interview with JFK's mother, Rose. A walking tour takes in other neighborhood sites relevant to the family's early years.

Central courtyard of the *palazzo*-style Isabella Stewart Gardner Museum

❺ Isabella Stewart Gardner Museum

25 Evans Way. **Tel** (617) 566-1401. ⓣ MFA. **Open** 11am–5pm Wed–Mon (to 9pm Thu). **Closed** Jan 1, Thanksgiving, Dec 25. ⬚ ✉ 📷 Concerts: (call for schedule). ⓦ **gardnermuseum.org**

The only thing more surprising than a Venetian *palazzo* on The Fenway is the collection of more than 2,500 works of art inside. Advised by scholar Bernard Berenson, the strong-willed Isabella Stewart Gardner turned her wealth to collecting art in the late 19th century, acquiring a notable collection of Old Masters and Italian Renaissance pieces. Titian's *Rape of Europa*, for example, is considered his best painting in a US museum. The eccentric "Mrs. Jack" had an eye for her contemporaries as well. She purchased the first Matisse to enter an American collection and was an ardent patron of James McNeill Whistler and John Singer Sargent. The paintings, sculptures, and tapestries are displayed on three levels around a stunning skylit courtyard. Mrs. Gardner's will stipulates the collection should remain assembled in the manner that she originally intended. Her intentions were thwarted in 1990, when thieves stole 13 priceless works, including a rare Rembrandt seascape. On a more positive note, a wing designed by the Italian architect Renzo Piano opened in 2012 with gallery space and a performance hall for the Gardner's concert series.

The Emerald Necklace

Best known as designer of New York's Central Park, Frederick Law Olmsted based himself in Boston, where he created parks to solve environmental problems and provide a green refuge for inhabitants of the 19th-century industrial city. The Emerald Necklace includes the green spaces of Boston Common and the Public Garden (*see pp68–9*) and Commonwealth Avenue (*see p101*). To create a ring of parks, Olmsted added the Back Bay Fens (site of beautiful rose gardens and gateway to the Museum of Fine Arts and the Isabella Stewart Gardner Museum), the rustic Riverway, Jamaica Pond (sailing and picnicking), Arnold Arboretum, and Franklin Park (a golf course, zoo, and cross-country ski trails). The 5-mile (8-km) swath of parkland makes an excellent bicycle tour or ambitious walk.

Jamaica Pond, part of Boston's fine parklands

❻ The Museum of Fine Arts

This is the largest art museum in New England and one of the great encyclopedic art museums in the United States. Its collection includes around 450,000 objects, ranging from Egyptian artifacts to paintings by John Singer Sargent. The MFA's original 1909 Beaux-Arts-style building was augmented in 2010 by the 53 galleries of the Art of the Americas Wing, designed by Foster and Partners. In 2011, the museum transformed its west-facing wing, designed in 1981 by I. M. Pei, into the Linde Family Wing for Contemporary Art.

Linde Family Wing

★ Egyptian Mummies
Among the museum's Egyptian and Nubian art is this tomb group of Nes-mut-aat-neru (767–656 BC) of Thebes.

American Silver
The revolutionary Paul Revere *(see p124)* was also a noted silversmith and produced many beautiful objects, such as this ornate teapot.

Fenway Entrance

Calderwood Courtyard

Sha
Cou

★ Japanese Temple Room
This room was created in 1909 to provide a space in which to contemplate Buddhist art. The MFA has one of the finest Japanese collections outside Japan.

Huntingdon Entrance

★ Copley Portraits
John Singleton Copley (1738–1815) painted the celebrities of his day, hence this portrait of a dandyish John Hancock *(see p25)*.

Lower Ground

Head of Aphrodite
This rare example of ancient Greek sculpture dates from about 330–300 BC.

Level 3

Level 2

Level 1

VISITORS' CHECKLIST

Practical Information
Avenue of the Arts, 465 Huntington Ave.
Tel (617) 267-9300.
🌐 mfa.org
Open 10am–4:45pm Sat–Tue, 10am–9:45pm Wed–Fri.
Closed most public hols.
🅿 ♿ 📷 📱 Lectures, concerts, and films: 📽 📱 📸

Transport
Ⓣ MFA.

Sargent Murals
John Singer Sargent spent the last years of his life creating artwork for the MFA. Originally commissioned to produce three paintings, Sargent instead constructed these elaborate murals, which were unveiled in 1921 and can still be seen today. He went on to create the works of art in the adjacent colonnade until his death in 1925.

Gallery Guide
The Linde Family Wing (west side) displays contemporary art and houses a restaurant and the museum store. European, Classical, Far Eastern, and Egyptian art and artifacts occupy the original MFA building. Arts from North, Central, and South America are displayed over four levels in the Art of the Americas Wing. Works on display are subject to change.

Key
▢ Art of Europe
▢ Contemporary Art
▨ Art of Asia, Oceania, and Africa
▢ Art of the Ancient World
▨ Art of the Americas
▢ Special/Temporary exhibitions
▢ Non-exhibition space

★ Impressionist Paintings
Boston collectors were among the first to appreciate French Impressionism. *Dance at Bougival* (1883) by Renoir is typical of the MFA collection.

Exploring the Museum of Fine Arts

In addition to the major collections noted below, the Museum of Fine Arts has important holdings in the arts of Africa, Oceania, and the ancient Americas. The museum also houses collections of works on paper, contemporary art, and musical instruments. Several galleries are devoted to temporary thematic exhibitions. Other features of the museum include a seminar room, lecture hall, and well-stocked bookstore. The museum also offers several eateries, ranging from an open courtyard café to a fine-dining restaurant.

and tall clocks. The museum's period rooms display decorative arts in their historical context. They include furnishings and the reproduced decor of three c.1800 rooms from a Peabody mansion designed by Federal period master architect and woodcarver Samuel McIntyre.

Boston Harbor by the Luminist painter Fitz Henry Lane (1804–65)

American Paintings, Decorative Arts, and Sculpture

In addition to extensive holdings from throughout the continent, the Art of the Americas Wing features one of the finest collections of art of the United States, including more than 2,000 paintings. A dedicated gallery offers selections from the museum's 60 portraits by John Singleton Copley, the leading American painter of the 18th century. Other prominent early artists include Charles Willson Peale. Other works on display are 19th-century landscapes, including harbor scenes by Fitz Henry Lane, an early Luminist painter, lush society portraits by John Singer Sargent, and those of other late 19th-century artists who constituted the "Boston School." On show there are also notable seascapes by Winslow Homer, who often painted on

the Massachusetts coast, as well as the muscular figure portraiture of Thomas Eakins. The MFA also houses a sampling of works by 20th-century masters, including Stuart Davis, Jackson Pollock, Georgia O'Keeffe, and Arthur Dove.

The museum's holdings of American silver are superb. As well as works by John Coney, there are two cases containing tea services and other pieces by Paul Revere *(see p92)*. The MFA also traces the development of the Boston style of 18th-century furniture through a definitive collection of desks, high chests,

European Paintings, Decorative Arts, and Sculpture

This collection of European paintings and sculpture ranges from the 7th to the late 20th century. It showcases numerous masterpieces by English, Dutch, French, Italian, and Spanish artists, including various portraits by the 17th-century Dutch painter Rembrandt. The collection of works from 1550 to 1700 is impressive both for the quality of art and for its size; it includes paintings by Francisco de Zurbarán, El Greco, Titian, and Peter Paul Rubens.

Boston's 19th-century collectors enriched the MFA with wonderful French art: the museum features several paintings by Jean-François Millet (the MFA has, in fact, the largest collection of his work in the world), as well as by other well-known 19th-century French artists, such as Edouard Manet, Pierre-Auguste Renoir, and Edgar Degas. Among popular favorites are *Waterlilies* (1905) by Claude Monet and *Dance at Bougival* (1883) by Renoir. The MFA's Monet holdings are among the world's largest, and there is also a good collection of paintings by Vincent van Gogh and Paul Gauguin.

Where Do We Come From? What Are We? Where Are We Going? by Paul Gauguin (1848–1903)

For hotels and restaurants in this region see pp310–13 and pp324–9

Part of the Processional Way of Ancient Babylonia (6th century BC)

Early 20th-century European art is also exhibited.

The gallery of European Modernism chronicles the major movements of 20th-century art, from Fauvism in the early 1900s through to 1960, with particular emphasis on Expressionist works by Oskar Kokoschka, Ernst Kirchner, Max Beckmann, and Kathe Kollwitz.

The MFA is also renowned for its collections of European decorative arts and sculpture, which are among the most significant in the US. The collections of English silver and porcelain, considered to be some of the world's most comprehensive, are complemented by extensive holdings of 18th-century French decorative arts.

Ancient Egyptian, Nubian, and Near Eastern Art

The MFA's collection of Egyptian and Nubian materials is unparalleled outside of Africa, and it derives primarily from MFA-Harvard University excavations along the Nile, which began in 1905. Artifacts from three millennia include many objects from the Pyramid Age and such signature pieces as a painted coffin, the burial goods of a 2000 BC governor, and the famous sculpture simply known as "Boston Green Head." Also on display are some exceptional Babylonian, Assyrian, and Sumerian reliefs. Works from ancient Nubia, the cultural region around the Nile stretching roughly between the modern African cities of Aswan and Khartoum, encompass gold and silver artifacts, ceramics, and jewels.

Other highlights from the Egyptian and Nubian collections include two monumental sculptures of Nubian kings from the Great Temple of Amen at Napata (620–586 BC and 600–580 BC). A few of the galleries are set up to re-create Nubian burial chambers, which allows cuneiform wall carvings to be displayed in something akin to an original setting; a superb example is the offering chapel of Sekhem-ankh-Ptah from Sakkara (2450–2350 BC).

Tang Dynasty Chinese Horse (8th century)

Classical Art

The MFA boasts one of America's top collections of Greek ceramics. In particular, the red- and black-figured vases dating from the 6th and 5th centuries BC are exceptional. The Classical galleries of the museum are

Roman fresco, excavated from a Pompeian villa (1st century AD)

intended to thematically highlight the influence of Greek arts. Three new galleries spotlight wine, poets, and performers in ancient Greece. The gallery for ancient coins displays 500 pieces from Greece and Rome. The Roman collection features grave markers, portrait busts, and a series of wall panel paintings unearthed in Pompeii on an MFA expedition in 1900–1.

Asian Art

The Asian collection is one of the most extensive that can be found under one roof. A range of works from India, the Near East, and central Asia is exhibited. Among the highlights are Indian sculpture and changing displays of Islamic miniature paintings and Indian narrative paintings. Elsewhere, works from Korea feature some Buddhist paintings and sculptures, jewelry, and ornaments.

The museum also boasts calligraphy, ceramics, and stone sculptures from China and the largest collection of Japanese art outside Japan. Extensive holdings and limited display space mean that exhibitions change often, but the MFA's collections of Japanese and Chinese scroll and screen paintings are, nevertheless, unmatched in the West. The strength of the MFA's Japanese art collection is largely due to the efforts of enthusiasts such as Ernest Fenollosa and William Sturgis Bigelow. In the 19th century, they encouraged the Japanese to maintain their traditions, and preserved Buddhist temple art when the Japanese imperial government had withdrawn subsidies from these institutions. This collection is considered to contain some of the finest examples of Asian temple art in the world.

⑦ Cambridge

Part of the greater Boston metropolitan area, Cambridge is, nonetheless, a city in its own right and has the mood and feel of such. Principally a college town, it is dominated by Harvard University and other college campuses. It also boasts a number of important historic sights, such as Christ Church and Cambridge Common, which have associations to the American Revolution. Harvard Square is the area's main entertainment and shopping district.

Site of the Washington Elm, on Cambridge Common

🏛 Longfellow House – Washington's Headquarters National Historic Site

105 Brattle St. **Tel** (617) 876-4491. **Open** Jun–Oct: 10am–4:30pm Wed– Sun. ✉ ♿ 📷 🌐 **nps.gov/long**

This house on Brattle Street, like many around it, was built by Colonial-era merchants loyal to the British Crown during the Revolution. It was seized by American revolutionaries and served as George Washington's headquarters during the Siege of Boston.

The poet Henry Wadsworth Longfellow boarded here in 1837, was given the house as a wedding present in 1843, and lived here until his death in 1888. He wrote his most famous poems here, including *Tales of a Wayside Inn* and *The Song of Hiawatha*. Longfellow's status as literary dean of Boston meant that Nathaniel Hawthorne and Charles Sumner, among others, were regular visitors.

🏛 Harvard Square

ℹ (617) 491-3434. ♿ 🌐 **harvardsquare.com**

Even Bostonians think of Harvard Square as a stand-in for Cambridge – the square was the original site of Cambridge from around 1630. Dominating the square is the Harvard Cooperative Society ("the Coop"), a local institution that sells inexpensive clothes, posters, and books.

Street musician, Harvard Square

Harvard's large student population is very much in evidence here, adding color to the character of the square. Many trendy boutiques, inexpensive restaurants, and friendly cafés cater to their needs. Street performers abound, especially on the weekends, and the square has long been a place where pop trends begin. Club Passim, for example, has incubated many successful singer-songwriters since Joan Baez first debuted here in 1959.

🏛 Cambridge Common

Set aside as common pasture and military drill ground in 1631, Cambridge Common has served as a center for religious, social, and political activity ever since. George Washington took command of the Continental Army here on July 3, 1775, beneath the Washington Elm, now marked by a stone. The common served as the army's encampment from 1775 to 1776. In 1997 the first monument in the US to commemorate the victims of the Irish Famine was unveiled on the common.

⛪ Christ Church

Garden St. **Tel** (617) 876-0200. **Open** 8am–5pm Mon–Fri & Sun, 8am–3pm Sat. ⛪ 7:45am, 10:15am Sun (Sep–Jun also 5:30pm), 12:10pm Wed. ✉ ♿ 🌐 **cccambridge.org**

With its square bell tower and plain, gray shingled edifice, Christ Church is a restrained example of an Anglican church. Designed in 1761 by Peter Harrison, the architect of Boston's King's Chapel *(see p80)*, Christ Church came in for rough treatment as a barracks for Continental Army troops in 1775 – British loyalists had almost all fled Cambridge by this time. The army even melted down the organ pipes to cast musket balls. The church was restored for services on New Year's Eve 1775, when George Washington and his wife, Martha, were among the worshipers. Anti-Anglican sentiment remained strong in Cambridge, and Christ Church did not have its own rector again until the 19th century.

Simple interior of Christ Church, designed prior to the Revolution in 1761

For hotels and restaurants in this region see pp310–13 and pp324–9

🖼 Radcliffe Institute for Advanced Study

Brattle St. **Tel** (617) 495-8601.
🛗 🌐 **radcliffe.edu**

Radcliffe College was founded in 1879 as the Collegiate Institution for Women, when 27 women began to study by private arrangement with Harvard professors. By 1943, members of Harvard's faculty no longer taught separate undergraduate courses to the women of Radcliffe, and in 1999 Radcliffe ceased its official existence as an independent college. It is now an institute for advanced study promoting scholarship of women's culture. The first Radcliffe building was the 1806 Federal-style mansion, Fay House, on the northern corner of what became Radcliffe Yard. Schlesinger Library, on the west side of the yard, is considered a significant example of Colonial Revival architecture. The

Stained glass, Radcliffe Institute

library's most famous holdings are an extensive collection of cookbooks and reference works on gastronomy.

🖼 MIT

77 Massachusetts Ave. **Tel** (617) 253-4795. MIT Museum **Open** 10am–5pm daily. 🖼 Hart Nautical Gallery **Open** 10am–5pm daily. List Visual Arts Center **Open** noon–6pm Tue–Sun (to 8pm Thu). 🖼 🛗 📷 🌐 **mit.edu**

Chartered in 1861 to teach "exactly and thoroughly the fundamental principles of positive science with application to the industrial arts," the Massachusetts Institute of Technology has evolved into one of the world's leading universities in engineering and the sciences. Several architectural masterpieces dot MIT's 0.2-sq-mile (0.6-sq-km) campus along the Charles River, including Eero Saarinen's Kresge Auditorium and Kresge Chapel, built in 1955. The Wiesner

VISITORS' CHECKLIST

Practical Information
ℹ Harvard Square Information Booth: (617) 497-1630.
Cambridge Office of Tourism.
(617) 441-2884 or (800) 862-5678.
📧 Sun.
🌐 **harvard.edu**
🌐 **cambridge-usa.org**

Transport
Ⓣ Harvard. 🚌 1, 69.

Building is a major collaboration between architect I. M. Pei and several artists, including Kenneth Noland, whose relief mural dominates the atrium. The building houses the **List Visual Arts Center**, noted for its avant-garde art.

The **Hart Nautical Gallery** in the Rogers Building focuses on marine engineering, with exhibits ranging from models of ships to exhibits of the latest advances in underwater research. The **MIT Museum** blends art and science with exhibits such as Harold Edgerton's groundbreaking stroboscopic flash photographs, and the latest holographic art.

Harvard Square Area

① Cambridge Common
② Christ Church
③ Harvard Square
④ Harvard University Museums
   (see pp118–21)
⑤ Harvard Yard
   (see pp116–17)
⑥ Longfellow House – Washington's Headquarters National Historic Site
⑦ Radcliffe Institute for Advanced Study

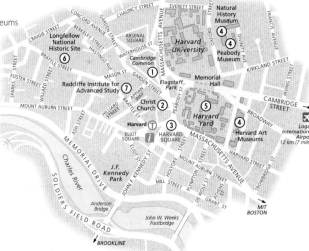

Harvard Yard

In 1636 Boston's well-educated Puritan leaders founded a college in Newtowne. Two years later cleric John Harvard died and bequeathed half his estate and all his books to the fledgling college. The colony's leaders bestowed his name on the school and rechristened the surrounding community Cambridge after the English city where they had been educated. The oldest university in the US, Harvard is now one of the world's most prestigious centers of learning. The university has expanded to encompass more than 400 buildings, but Harvard Yard is still at its heart.

Holden Chapel
Built in 1742, the chapel was the scene of revolutionary speeches and was later used as a demonstration hall for human dissections.

★ Old Harvard Yard
This leafy yard dates from the founding of the college in 1636. Freshman dormitories dot the yard, and throughout the year it is a focal point for students.

Harvard University
Information Center

★ John Harvard Statue
This statue celebrates Harvard's most famous benefactor. Almost a place of pilgrimage, graduates and visitors invariably pose for photographs here.

★ Widener Library
This library memorializes Harry Elkins Widener, who died on the *Titanic* in 1912. With more than 3 million volumes, it is the world's largest university library.

For hotels and restaurants in this region see pp310–13 and pp324–9

★ **Memorial Church**
This church was built in 1931 and copies earlier styles. For example, the steeple is modeled on that of the Old North Church *(see p91)* in Boston's North End.

VISITORS' CHECKLIST

Practical Information
Massachusetts Ave.
Open 24 hrs.
Closed Commencement (date varies, late May–early Jun). ♿
🎦 🎬 Lectures, concerts and films: Harvard Film Archive:
Tel (617) 495-4700.
Films shown Fri–Mon.
W **harvard.edu**
Harvard Information Center:
Tel (617) 495-1573.
Harvard Box Office:
Tel (617) 496-2222.

Transport
Ⓣ Harvard.

Peabody Museum and Harvard Museum of Natural History *(see pp120–21)*

Sever Hall
One of the most distinctive of Harvard's Halls, this Romanesque style-building was designed by Henry Hobson Richardson.

KEY

① **University Hall**, designed by Charles Bulfinch, was built in 1816.

② **Massachusetts Hall**, built in 1720, is Harvard's oldest building.

③ **Hollis Hall** was used as barracks by George Washington's troops during the American Revolution.

④ **Memorial Hall**, a Ruskin Gothic building, memorializes Harvard's Union casualties from the Civil War.

⑤ **Harvard Art Museums** *(see pp118–20)*

⑥ **Tercentenary Theater**

Carpenter Center for Visual Arts
Opened in 1963, the Carpenter Center is the only building in the US designed by the avant-garde Swiss architect Le Corbusier.

0 meters   50
0 yards   50

Harvard University Museums

Harvard's museums were conceived to revolutionize the process of education; students were to be taught by allowing them access to artifacts from around the world. Today, this tradition continues, with the museums housing some of the world's finest university collections: art from the Americas, Europe, North Africa, the Mediterranean, and Asia at the Harvard Art Museums; archaeological finds in the Peabody Museum; and a vast collection of artifacts in the Harvard Museum of Natural History.

The exterior of the Harvard Art Museums, with a distinctive glass roof

Harvard Art Museums

32 Quincy St. **Tel** (617) 495-9400.
Open 10am–5pm daily. **Closed**
Dec 24 and major hols. ♿ ♿ 📷
w harvardartmuseums.org

Formerly housed in separate buildings, the Fogg Art, Busch-Reisinger, and Arthur M. Sackler museums now occupy a single expanded facility designed by the Italian architect Renzo Piano.

The eco-friendly complex provides greater access to the museums' collections, which feature works of art ranging from the ancient world to the present day. The heart of the facility is the Calderwood Courtyard. This interior space is modeled on the façade of the canon's house at the 15th-century church of San Biagio in Montepulciano, Italy. It is open to the public free of charge, as are the adjoining museum shop and café. Keep an eye out for contemporary sculptures and a stunning series of eight 12th-century French and Spanish capitals that flank the courtyard.

Piano's design incorporates entrances on two sides, but nods to the original geography of the three institutions. The lion's share of the Fogg collections is located on the Quincy Street–Harvard Yard side of the building on three levels; the majority of the Busch-Reisinger collections is on the Prescott Street side on level one; the Sackler collections largely occupy the Prescott Street–Broadway corner of the building on three levels. Because collections from the three museums sometimes overlap, galleries devoted to a particular region or era may have works from more than one museum.

The **Fogg Art Museum** was created in 1895, when Harvard began to build its own art collection. The museum is renowned for its extensive collection of European and American paintings, sculpture, decorative arts, and works on paper from the post-Classical period to the present day. Located on the first floor, the Maurice Wertheim Collection of Impressionist and Post-Impressionist paintings and

Guide to Harvard Art Museums

The Fogg Art, Busch-Reisinger and Arthur M. Sackler Museums exhibit approximately 250,000 pieces across the building's first three floors. The fourth-floor Art Study Center and fifth-floor Lightbox Gallery offer further opportunity to examine and explore their collections.

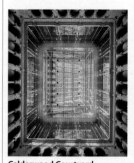

Calderwood Courtyard
Renovated by the Italian architect Renzo Piano, the courtyard features an impressive glass roof.

First floor

Buddhist sculptures, part of the Sackler's Asian and Indian collections

For hotels and restaurants in this region see pp310–13 and pp324–9

sculptures includes works by Renoir, Manet, and Degas.

The Fogg's second-floor galleries feature early Italian Renaissance painting, 17th-century art from France and the British Isles, and 18th-century American portraiture. Highlights here include a glass-walled gallery that contains several terracotta models of angels and saints by the Roman Baroque sculptor Gian Lorenzo Bernini, who used these as sketches for his large-scale marble and bronze sculpture.

Another gallery explores the Fogg's collection of works by the Pre-Raphaelites, including portraits by Dante Gabriel Rossetti and Edward Burne-Jones, alongside paintings and sculpture from other cultures and eras that resonated with the Pre-Raphaelites.

The **Busch-Reisinger Museum**, which was founded in 1903 as the school's Germanic Museum, focuses on that country's art and design from after 1880, with an emphasis on German

Expressionism. It is the only facility in North America devoted exclusively to the art of the German-speaking regions of central and northern Europe. The museum owns an important collection of paintings and sculptures by 20th-century masters such as Max Beckmann, Wassily Kandinsky, László Moholy-Nagy, Paul Klee, Oskar Kokoschka, Emil Nolde, and Franz Marc, along with Austrian Secession art, 1920s abstraction, and medieval sculpture.

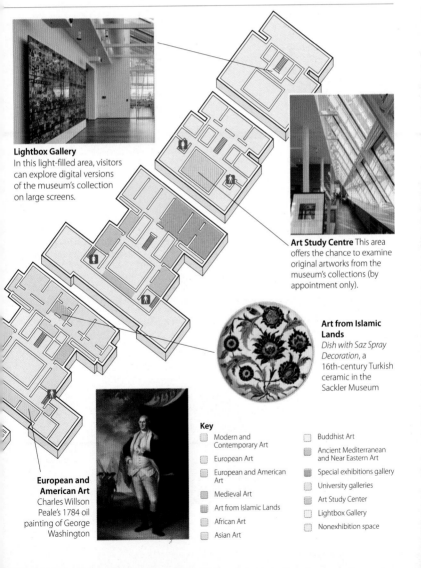

Lightbox Gallery
In this light-filled area, visitors can explore digital versions of the museum's collection on large screens.

Art Study Centre This area offers the chance to examine original artworks from the museum's collections (by appointment only).

Art from Islamic Lands
Dish with Saz Spray Decoration, a 16th-century Turkish ceramic in the Sackler Museum

European and American Art
Charles Willson Peale's 1784 oil painting of George Washington

Key
- Modern and Contemporary Art
- European Art
- European and American Art
- Medieval Art
- Art from Islamic Lands
- African Art
- Asian Art
- Buddhist Art
- Ancient Mediterranean and Near Eastern Art
- Special exhibitions gallery
- University galleries
- Art Study Center
- Lightbox Gallery
- Nonexhibition space

Mummy Portrait of a Woman with Earrings, from 2nd-century Egypt; Sackler Museum

One of the highlights is *Light Prop for an Electric Stage (Light-Space Modulator)* (1930), a fascinating moving installation by the Hungarian artist Moholy-Nagy.

Also noteworthy is the variety of renowned postwar and contemporary art from the likes of Georg Baselitz, Anselm Kiefer, Gerhard Richter, and Joseph Beuys. Harvard was a safe haven for many Bauhaus artists, architects, and designers fleeing Nazi Germany, and both Walter Gropius and Lyonel Feininger chose the Busch-Reisinger as the depository of their personal papers and drawings.

Named for a famous philanthropist, physician, and art collector, the **Arthur M. Sackler Museum** is home to Harvard's collection of ancient, Asian, Islamic, and late Indian art. The Sackler galleries are located on the first, second, and third floors.

The Sackler holds a world-renowned collection of archaic Chinese jades, many of which are on display on the first floor, alongside bronze ritual vessels and weapons from China. Nearby is a large glass-walled gallery filled with Chinese and Korean Buddhist sculpture, which can be contemplated in a serene, light-filled environment.

Examples from the Sackler's collection of Chinese and Korean ceramics are on the second floor, alongside Buddhist paintings and sculpture from China and Japan.

Also on display is the museum's famed *Tale of Genji* album, from Japan, around 1509. It is the world's oldest complete illustrated edition of the work, which is widely considered to be the world's first novel. Notable works in various forms, such as vases, bronzes, and coins from Greece, Rome, Egypt, and the Near East, as well as objects from ancient Mediterranean and Byzantine civilizations, are displayed on the third floor.

Galleries on the second floor hold the Sackler's collections from Islamic lands and India. They include works on paper (paintings, drawings, calligraphy, and manuscript illustrations), as well as Islamic ceramics from the 8th to the 19th centuries.

On the third floor, three gallery spaces present rotating installations programmed in consultation with Harvard faculty to support specific coursework or in partnership with other Harvard museums. Adjacent, is a special exhibition gallery that provides a space for curatorial staff to present important new research on artists and artistic practice. The "special exhibitions" gallery space tends to be the most challenging for visitors, as the exhibitions often call into question the very idea of "art" and often weigh art and artifacts

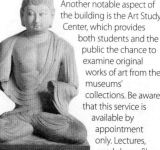

An 8th-century Chinese sculpture of seated Buddha, Sackler Museum

in the context of a broader social order. It is also usually the busiest gallery in the museum.

At the top level of the Harvard Art Museums complex is the Lightbox Gallery, where visitors can use large screens to digitally explore the museums' collections. This glass-walled space overlooks the courtyard below and also allows visitors to glimpse into the labs of the Straus Center for Conservation and Technical Studies, a training ground for fine arts conservation and research. Another notable aspect of the building is the Art Study Center, which provides both students and the public the chance to examine original works of art from the museums' collections. Be aware that this service is available by appointment only. Lectures, workshops, films, performances, special events, and other programs are held throughout the year. Check the calendar on the website for details.

Peabody Museum of Archaeology and Ethnology

11 Divinity Ave. **Tel** (617) 496-1027. **Open** 9am–5pm daily. **Closed** Jan 1, Thanksgiving, Dec 24, 25. 🖼 🖾 📷 Ⓦ **peabody.harvard.edu**

The Peabody Museum of Archaeology and Ethnology was founded in 1866 as the first museum in the Americas devoted solely to anthropology. The many collections, which

Frog mask fom Easter Island in the South Pacific, Peabody Museum

For hotels and restaurants in this region see pp313–14 and pp329–31

include several million artifacts and more than 500,000 photographic images, come from all around the world. Initially, in the 19th century, the museum's pioneering archaeological and ethnological research began relatively close to home with excavations of Mayan sites in Central America. The Peabody also conducted some of the first and most important research on the precontact Anasazi people of the American Southwest and on the cultural history of the later Pueblo tribes of the same region. Joint expeditions sponsored by the Peabody Museum and the Museum of Fine Arts *(see pp110–11)* also uncovered some of the richest finds of dynastic and predynastic Egypt. Research continued in all these areas well into the 20th century and later broadened to embrace the cultures of the islands of the South Pacific.

The Hall of the North American Indian on the ground level was completely overhauled so that the artifacts could be displayed in a way that puts them in the context of the time when they were gathered, when European and Native cultures first came into contact. For example, the Native American tribes of the Northern Plains are interpreted largely through an exhibition detailing the Lewis and Clark expedition of 1804–6; these two explorers undertook to find a route, by water, from East to West Coast, and on their way collected innumerable artifacts. Other outstanding exhibits include totem carvings by Pacific Northwest tribes and a wide range of historic and contemporary Navajo weavings. The third floor is devoted to Central American anthropology,

Native American totem pole, Peabody Museum

with casts of some of the ruins uncovered at Copán in Honduras and Chichen Itza in Mexico. The fourth floor concentrates on Polynesia, Micronesia, and other islands of the Pacific, with striking collections of ceremonial objects, such as masks. Small vessels used for fishing and near-island trading hang overhead.

Harvard Museum of Natural History

26 Oxford St. **Tel** (617) 495-3045. **Open** 9am–5pm daily. **Closed** Jan 1, Thanksgiving, Dec 24, 25. 🅿 ♿ 📷 📹 🅦 hmnh.harvard.edu

The Harvard Museum of Natural History is actually three museums rolled into one, all displayed on a single floor of a turn-of-the-century classroom building. It includes the collections of the **Mineralogical and Geological Museum**, the **Museum of Comparative Zoology**, and the **Botanical Museum**. The straightforward presentation of labeled objects exudes an infectious, old-fashioned charm, yet their initial appearance belies the fact that these are some of the most complete collections of their kind.

The mineralogical galleries include some of Harvard University's oldest specimen collections, the oldest of which dates from 1783. Virtually every

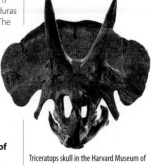

Triceratops skull in the Harvard Museum of Natural History

New England mineral, rock, and gem type is represented here, including rough and cut gemstones and one of the world's premier meteorite collections.

The zoological galleries owe their inception to the great 19th-century biologist Louis Agassiz and include his personal arachnid collection. The collection of taxidermied bird, mammal, and reptile specimens is comprehensive, and there is also a collection of dinosaur skeletons. Children are most fascinated by the giant kronosaurus (a type of prehistoric sea serpent) and the skeleton of the first triceratops ever described in scientific literature. There are also fossil exhibits of the earliest invertebrates and reptiles, as well as skeletons of still-living species, including a collection of whale skeletons.

The collections in the botanical galleries include the Ware Collection of Blaschka Glass Models of Plants, popularly known as the "glass flowers." Between 1887 and 1936, father and son artisans Leopold and Rudolph Blaschka created these 3,000 exacting models of 850 plant species. Each species is illustrated with a scientifically accurate life-size model and magnified parts. While the handblown models were created as teaching aids, they are a unique accomplishment in the glassblowers' art and are as prized for their aesthetic qualities as their scientific utility.

Amethyst specimen in the Harvard Museum of Natural History

❽ Charlestown

Situated on the north bank of the Charles River, directly opposite the North End, Charlestown exudes history. The site of the Battle of Bunker Hill, when American troops suffered huge losses in their fight for independence, today the district forms a major part of Boston's Freedom Trail (see pp58–61). As well as sights from the American Revolution, visitors can see USS Constitution, pride of the post revolutionary American Navy, which took part in the 1812 war with Britain. Also of interest is the Charlestown Navy Yard.

Granite obelisk of the Bunker Hill Monument, erected in 1843

🏛 Bunker Hill Monument

Monument Square. **Tel** (617) 242-5641. **Open** 9am–5pm daily. **Closed** Jan 1, Thanksgiving, Dec 25. Ⓦ nps.gov/bost

In the Revolution's first pitched battle between British and colonial troops, which took place on June 17, 1775, the British won a Pyrrhic victory on the battlefield but failed to create an escape route from the Boston peninsula to the mainland. Following the battle, American irregulars were joined by other militia to keep British forces penned up until the Continental Army, under the command of General George Washington, forced their evacuation by sea the following March 17, still celebrated in the Boston area as Evacuation Day.

The citizens of Charlestown began raising funds for the Bunker Hill Monument in 1823, laid the cornerstone in 1825, and dedicated the 221-ft (67-m) granite obelisk in 1843. There is

no elevator, but the 294-step climb to the top is rewarded with spectacular views.

The ground-level museum, completely accessible for the disabled, focuses on the strategies and significance of the Battle of Bunker Hill. High-efficiency lighting fully illuminates the monument at night and reveals the pyramid that caps the obelisk – a design echoed at the tops of the pylons of the nearby Leonard P. Zakim Bunker Hill Bridge. Be aware that, during the winter months, the monument may be closed due to ice and snow accumulation on the stairs.

🏛 City Square

When John Winthrop arrived with three shiploads of Puritan refugees in 1630, they settled first in the marshes at the base of Town Hill, now City Square. A small public park now marks the site of Winthrop's Town House, the very first seat of Boston government.

Municipal art in City Square

🏛 John Harvard Mall

Ten families founded Charlestown in 1629, a year before the rest of Boston was settled. They built their homes and a palisaded fort on Town Hill, a spot now marked by John Harvard Mall. Several bronze plaques within the small enclosed park commemorate events in the early history of the Massachusetts Bay Colony (see p46), one plaque proclaiming "this low mound of earth the memorial of a mighty nation." A small monument pays homage to John Harvard, the young cleric who ministered to the Charlestown settlers and who left his name, half his estate, and all his books to the fledgling college at Newtowne when he died in 1638 (see pp116–17).

🏛 Warren Tavern

2 Pleasant St. **Tel** (617) 241-8142. **Open** lunch, dinner daily, brunch Sat–Sun. Ⓦ warrentavern.com

Dating from 1780, Warren Tavern was one of the first buildings erected after the British burned Charlestown. It was named after Joseph Warren, president of the Provincial Congress in 1774 and a general in the Massachusetts Army. He enlisted as a private with the Continental Army for the Battle of Bunker Hill, where he was killed. The tavern, once derelict, has been restored to its 18th-century style. By contrast, the food is modern fare.

Old-fashioned clapboard houses on Warren Street

USS *Constitution*, built in 1797, moored in Charlestown Navy Yard

On decommissioning, the facility was transferred to the National Park Service to interpret the art and history of naval shipbuilding. The yard was designed by Alexander Parris, architect of Quincy Market (*see p84*), and was one of the first examples of industrial architecture in Boston.

Dry dock No. 1, built in 1802, was the one of the first docks that could be drained of water – its first occupant was USS *Constitution*. Visitors can also board the World War II destroyer USS *Cassin Young*.

🚇 Charlestown Navy Yard

Visitor Center, Building 5. **Tel** (617) 242-5601. **Open** 9am–5pm daily. **Closed** Jan 1, Thanksgiving, Dec 25. ♿ 🅿 🌐 nps.gov/bost

Boston's deep harbor and long tides made Charlestown a logical site for one of the US Navy's first shipyards, established in 1800. For 174 years, as the Navy moved from wooden sailing ships to steel giants, Charlestown Navy Yard played a key role in supporting the US Atlantic fleet.

🚢 USS Constitution

Charlestown Navy Yard. **Tel** (617) 242-5601. **Open** 2–6pm Tue–Fri, 10am–6pm Sat & Sun (subject to change). Photo ID required for those aged 18 and older. ♿ 🅿 Museum **Open** Apr–Oct: 9am–6pm daily; Nov–Mar: 10am–5pm daily. **Closed** Jan 1, Thanksgiving, Dec 25. 📷 ♿ 🌐 ussconstitutionmuseum.org

The oldest commissioned warship afloat, the USS *Constitution* was built in the North End and christened in 1797. She saw immediate action in the Mediterranean protecting American shipping from the Barbary pirates.

In the War of 1812, she won fame and her nickname of "Old Ironsides" when cannonballs bounced off her in a battle with the British ship *Guerriere*. She won 42 battles, lost none, captured 20 vessels, and was never boarded by an enemy. She was nearly scuttled several times. In 1830, Oliver Wendell Holmes penned the poem *Old Ironsides*, which rallied public support to save the ship, while on another occasion, in the 1920s, schoolchildren sent in their pennies and nickels to salvage her. She underwent an overhaul for her 1997 bicentennial, able to carry her own canvas into the wind for the first time in a century. A small museum documents her history. She is currently in Dry Dock 1 for restoration through mid-2018. The top deck is open to visitors.

VISITORS' CHECKLIST

Practical Information
📷 Wed.

Transport
🚌 93. ⛴ from Long Wharf.
Ⓣ Community College.

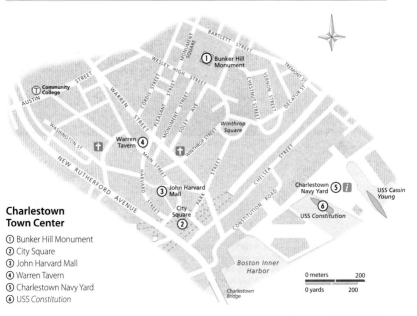

Charlestown Town Center

① Bunker Hill Monument
② City Square
③ John Harvard Mall
④ Warren Tavern
⑤ Charlestown Navy Yard
⑥ USS *Constitution*

For map symbols see back flap

BOSTON STREET FINDER

The key map below shows the area of Boston covered by the *Street Finder* maps, which can be found on the following pages. Map references, given throughout this guide, for sights, restaurants, hotels, shops, and

entertainment venues refer to the grid on the maps. The first figure in the map reference indicates which *Street Finder* map to turn to (1 to 4), and the letter and number that follow refer to the grid reference on that map.

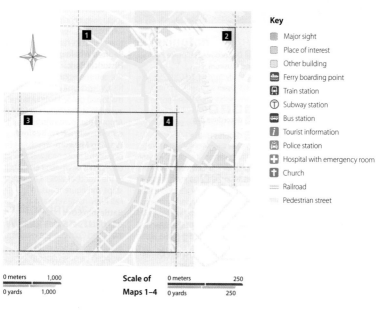

Key

- ▦ Major sight
- ▦ Place of interest
- ▢ Other building
- 🚢 Ferry boarding point
- 🚉 Train station
- Ⓣ Subway station
- 🚌 Bus station
- ℹ️ Tourist information
- 🚓 Police station
- ✚ Hospital with emergency room
- ✝ Church
- ▦ Railroad
- ▦ Pedestrian street

Scale of Maps 1–4

0 meters 1,000
0 yards 1,000

0 meters 250
0 yards 250

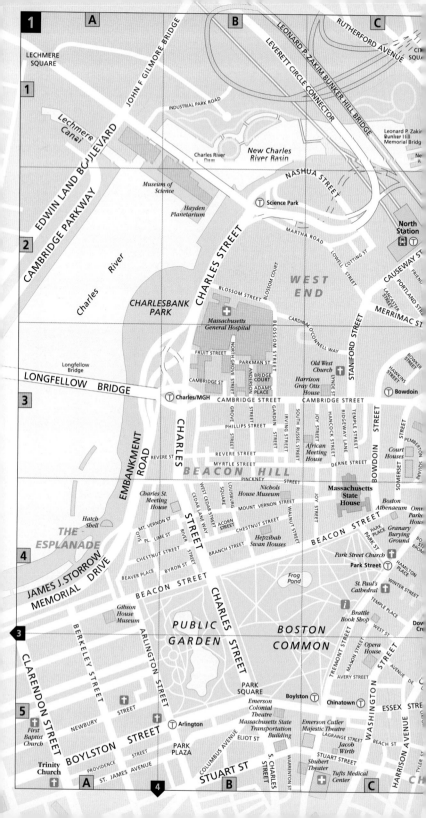

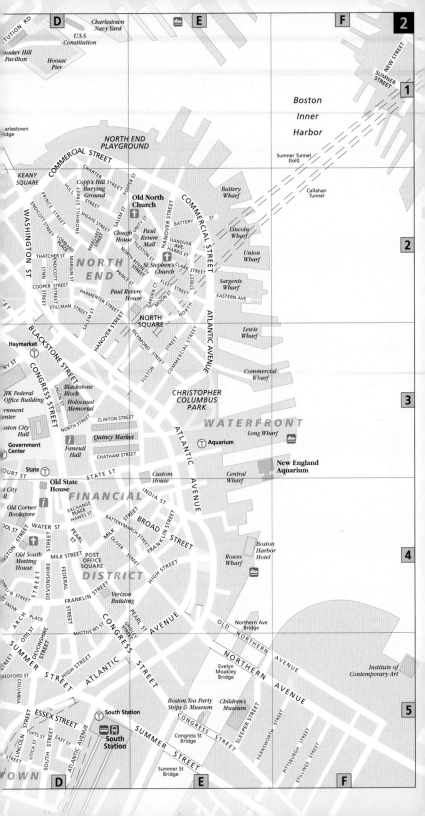

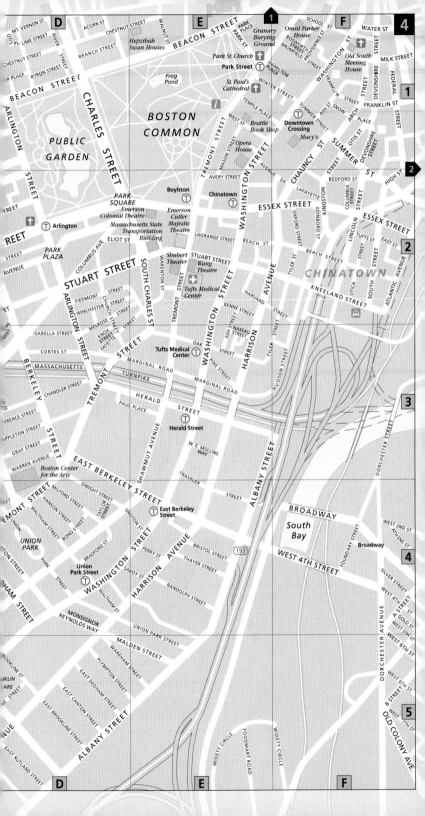

NEW ENGLAND REGION BY REGION

New England at a Glance

Tucked away in the northeasternmost corner of the United States, New England is rich in history and natural beauty. Many of the country's earliest settlements were established within these six states, with the seeds of the Revolutionary War taking root most firmly in Massachusetts. Interspersed along large tracts of rural countryside, heavy forests, and sweeping coastlines, Ivy League universities and college towns bring an influx of modernity to this historically significant region.

Vermont's fall foliage usually peaks in mid-October.

The Salem Towne House in Old Sturbridge Village was built in 1796. Located in Sturbridge, Massachusetts, the village is one of New England's most popular living-history museums *(see p164)*.

Mark Twain House in Hartford, Connecticut, is where the famous US author penned many of his most beloved works. The house was commissioned in 1873 for the then-hefty sum of $45,000 *(see pp204–205)*.

Newport

Lake Champlain

Ber

Danville

Montpelier

Nc Cor

Middlebury

Lincoln

VERMONT
(See pp230–251)

Rutland

White River Junction

Laconia

NEW HAMPSHIRE
(See pp252–277)

Bellows Falls

Concord

Bennington

Lo

MASSACHUSE
(See pp136–171

Lenox

Springfield

Southb

Norfolk

Provide

RHO ISLA
(See pp17

Hartford

CONNECTICUT
(See pp198–229)

New Haven

Old Lyme

| 0 kilometers | 100 |
| 0 miles | 50 |

◀ Lush autumn forest surrounding Jordan Pond, Acadia National Park, Maine

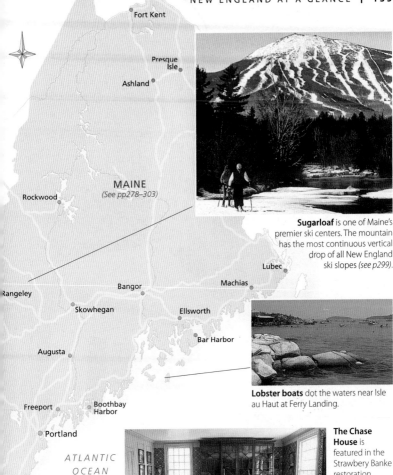

Fort Kent

Presque Isle

Ashland

MAINE
(See pp278–303)

Rockwood

Sugarloaf is one of Maine's premier ski centers. The mountain has the most continuous vertical drop of all New England ski slopes (see p299).

Lubec

Rangeley

Bangor

Machias

Skowhegan

Ellsworth

Bar Harbor

Augusta

Lobster boats dot the waters near Isle au Haut at Ferry Landing.

Freeport

Boothbay Harbor

Portland

ATLANTIC OCEAN

The Chase House is featured in the Strawbery Banke restoration project in Portsmouth, New Hampshire (see pp258–9).

Portsmouth

Gloucester

...ston

Provincetown

Plymouth

Orleans

The Breakers is one of Newport, Rhode Island's most opulent mansions. Designed after 16th-century palaces in Italy, the 70-room masterpiece was used as the summer "cottage" for the wealthy Vanderbilt family (see pp190–91).

River

Hyannis

Falmouth

MASSACHUSETTS

Of all the New England states, Massachusetts may have the most diverse mix of natural and man-made attractions. Miles of wide sandy beaches beckon along the eastern seaboard; green mountains and rich culture characterize the Berkshire Hills in the west. America's early architecture has been well protected, from the lanes of Boston to villages dotting coast and countryside.

Many of America's pivotal events have been played out against the backdrop of Massachusetts. In 1620 a group of 102 English Pilgrims sailing to the Virginia Colony were blown off course and forced to land farther north. Their colony at Plymouth *(see pp152–3)* was the first permanent English settlement in North America. More than 100 years later, the seeds of the American Revolution took strongest root in Boston, blossoming into the nation of the United States and forever altering the course of world history.

Massachusetts has always been New England's industrial and intellectual hub. The machinery of the American Industrial Revolution chugged to life in the early 19th century in Lowell *(see p146)* and other mill towns. Later the high-tech labs in Cambridge *(see pp114–21)* would help lead the nation into the computer age. In 1944, scientists at Harvard University *(see pp116–17)*, the oldest and most prestigious college in the nation, developed the world's first digital computer. Today the venerable university attracts visitors from around the world wanting to tour its beautiful campus and explore the multitude of treasures in its magnificent museums.

Travelers can also tread the same ground as some of the country's most influential leaders. Quincy *(see p125)* honors the father and son team of John Adams (1735–1826) and John Quincy Adams (1767–1848), the nation's second and sixth presidents. Fashionable Hyannis Port on Cape Cod *(see pp158–63)* is home to the Kennedy clan *(see p163)* compound. Of course, the Cape is best known for its expanse of sand dunes and beaches along the Cape Cod National Seashore *(see pp158–9)*.

Part of the stunning sculpture collection at Chesterwood in Stockbridge

◀ Pumpkins laid out in front of an old-style building in Chatham, Massachusetts

Exploring Massachusetts

Massachusetts is a wonderful destination for travelers in that such a diverse array of attractions is squeezed into a relatively small area. Art, music, theater, and dance can be found in abundance in many of the state's larger urban areas and busy college towns. Scenic seascapes, historic villages, and whale-watching junkets await along the coast and Cape Cod *(see pp158–63)*. Understandably, the coastal beaches are popular spots in summer. Venturing inland, visitors will come upon centuries-old towns, verdant forests and meadows, and countless opportunities for antiquing. As is the case with all the New England states, fall is one of the most beautiful times of year to visit.

Blooming wildflowers beside the Deerfield River

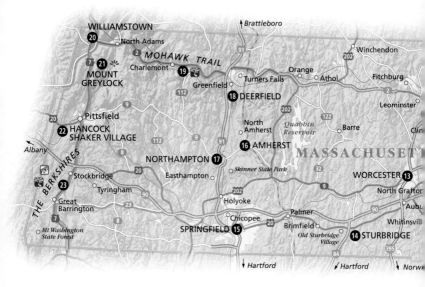

Getting Around

Interstate 93 and Interstate 95 are the two largest and most popular north-south routes leading into Boston. Interstate 495 loops outside Boston, thereby bypassing much of the heavy traffic. Highway 2 and Interstate 90 are the two biggest east-west routes. Boston's Logan International Airport is New England's largest airport. Amtrak has rail links between Boston and New York City and Boston and Portland, Maine, with stops in between. Bus lines such as American Eagle, Concord Trailways, Greyhound, and Peter Pan service most of Massachusetts. Passenger and car ferries sail year-round from Cape Cod (leaving from Woods Hole) to Martha's Vineyard and from Hyannis to Nantucket. Advance reservations are essential for cars.

Brant Point, at the entrance to Nantucket Harbor

For hotels and restaurants in this region see pp313–14 and pp329–31

Sights at a Glance

1. Salem
3. Lowell
4. Sudbury
5. Nashoba Valley
6. Concord
7. Plymouth
8. Duxbury
9. Martha's Vineyard
10. Nantucket Island
11. *Cape Cod National Seashore pp158–9*
12. Cape Cod
13. Worcester
14. Sturbridge
15. Springfield
16. Amherst
17. Northampton
18. Deerfield
20. Williamstown
21. Mount Greylock State Reservation
22. Hancock Shaker Village
23. The Berkshires

Tours

2. North Shore *pp144–5*
19. Mohawk Trail *pp168–9*

The impressive Minute Man Visitor Center in Lincoln

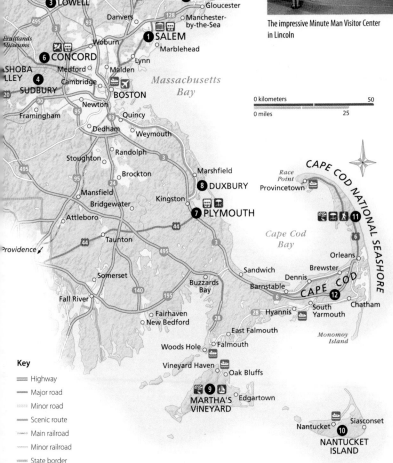

Key

— Highway
— Major road
····· Minor road
— Scenic route
–··– Main railroad
— Minor railroad
═══ State border
△ Summit

For additional map symbols *see back flap*

● Salem

Although it is best known for the infamous witch trials of 1692, which resulted in the execution of 20 innocent people, this coastal town has other, less sensational claims to fame. Founded in 1626 by Roger Conant (1592–1679), Salem grew to become one of New England's busiest 18th- and 19th-century ports, its harbor filled with clipper ships carrying treasures from around the globe. Present-day Salem is a bustling, good-natured town that has the ability to celebrate its rich artistic and architectural heritage, all the while playing up its popular image as the witchcraft capital of America.

An 1842 whaling scene from the Peabody Essex Museum

Exploring Salem

Salem's main attractions are situated in clusters in the harbor and downtown areas. The historic water-front can be explored on foot, as can the busy area along Essex and Liberty streets (see pp142–3).

Photo opportunities for Salem visitors

🏛 Peabody Essex Museum

East India Sq. **Tel** (978) 745-9500, or (866) 745-1876. **Open** 10am–5pm Tue–Sun.
W pem.org

The dramatic Moshe Safdie building allows the Peabody Essex soaring galleries to display its collection of more than one million objects, including some of the world's largest holdings of Asian art and artifacts. Among the exhibits are treasures brought back from the Orient, the Pacific, and Africa by Salem's sea captains. Highlights include jewelry, porcelain figures, ritual costumes, scrimshaw, and figureheads.

The museum also displays the only complete Qing Dynasty house outside China.

🏛 Salem Witch Museum

19 1/2 Washington Sq. N. **Tel** (978) 744-1692 or (800) 544-1692. **Open** Jul & Aug: 10am–7pm daily; Sep–Jun: 10am–5pm daily. **Closed** Jan 1, Thanksgiving, Dec 24 & 25.
W salemwitchmuseum.com

Salem's most-visited sight commemorates the town's darkest hour. In 1692, 150 people were jailed and 20 executed after being charged with practicing witchcraft. According to some, Nathaniel Hawthorne – who was profoundly disturbed by reports of the events – added a "w" to his last name to distance himself from other descendants of Judge Hathorne, the man

Salem City Center

① Peabody Essex Museum
② Salem Witch Museum
③ Salem Witch Trial Memorial
④ Salem Maritime National Historic Site
⑤ Custom House
⑥ House of Seven Gables Historic Site

| 0 meters | 300 |
| 0 yards | 300 |

Key

▪ Street-by-Street map see pp142–3

Salem Witch Museum, commemorating the infamous 1692 witch trials

VISITORS' CHECKLIST

Practical Information

🏛 38,000. ℹ 2 New Liberty St., (978) 740-1650. 🎭 Maritime Festival (Jul), Haunted Halloween (Oct).

Ⓦ salem.org

Transport

🚢 From Boston's Long Wharf.

✈ 14 miles (22 km) S in Boston.

who presided over the witch trials. Exhibits in the Gothic-style building trace the history of witches and witchcraft and evolving perceptions of witches up to the present day. The town capitalizes on its association with witches each year in October with one of the nation's largest and most colorful celebrations of Halloween.

🏛 Salem Witch Trial Memorial

Charter St. **Open** dawn to dusk.
Located next to the old cemetery, this memorial provides a place for quiet contemplation and public acknowledgment of this tragic event in local history. The memorial was dedicated by Nobel laureate Elie Wiesel in 1992 on the 300th anniversary of the witch trials.

🏚 Salem Maritime National Historic Site

Visitor Center, 2 New Liberty St.
Tel (978) 740-1650. **Open** 10am–5pm Wed–Sun. **Closed** Jan 1, Thanksgiving, & Dec 25. 🅿 🎥 ♿ Ⓦ nps.gov/ sama

Salem's heyday as a maritime center has been preserved here. At its peak, the town's harbor was serviced by some 50 wharves. Today this waterfront complex maintains three wharves, including the 2,100-ft (640-m) Derby Wharf. The *Friendship*, a reconstruction of an East Indiaman sailing ship built in 1797, is moored here when it is not on tour during the summer.

🏚 Custom House

See Salem Maritime National Historic Site for details.
The Federal-style Custom House (1819) was established to collect taxes on imports and now forms part of the Salem Maritime National Historic Site. In the 1840s author Nathaniel Hawthorne (1804–64) worked as a surveyor here. The redbrick structure, described in his novel *The Scarlet Letter* (1850), contains his office and desk.

Clock Tower at Abbot Hall in Marblehead

🏚 House of Seven Gables Historic Site

115 Derby St. **Tel** (978) 744-0991.
Open mid-Jan–Jun, Nov & Dec 10am–5pm daily; Jul–Oct: 10am–7pm daily. **Closed** first 2 weeks Jan, Thanksgiving, Dec 25. 🅿 🎥 obligatory. ♿ partial. 📷 Ⓦ 7gables.org

Fans of author Nathaniel Hawthorne should make a pilgrimage to this 1668 house. The Salem-born writer was so taken with the Colonial-style home that he used it as the setting in his novel *House of Seven Gables* (1851). As well as its famous seven steeply pitched gables, the house also has a secret staircase. The site also contains other early homes, including Hawthorne's birthplace, a gambrel-roofed 18th-century residence moved from Union Street in 1958.

Environs

Just 4 miles (6 km) from town lies the area's most picturesque spot: Marblehead. When President George Washington (1732–99) visited, he said it had "the look of antiquity." This still holds true. Settled in 1629 and perched on a rocky peninsula, this village displays its heritage as a fisherman's enclave and a thriving port. Crisscrossed by hilly, twisting lanes, the historic district is graced with a wonderful mix of merchants' homes, shipbuilders' mansions, and fishermen's cottages. With more than 200 houses built before the Revolutionary War and nearly 800 built during the 1800s, the district is a catalog of American architecture. Included among the historic buildings is the spired **Abbot Hall**, the seat of local government built in 1876, where *The Spirit of '76* painting (1875) by Archibald Willard (1836–1918) hangs. Built in 1768 for a wealthy business-man, the **1768 Jeremiah Lee Mansion** has a sweeping entrance hall, mahogany woodwork, and superb wallpaper. A drive along the shoreline reveals the lighthouse at Point O'Neck (1835).

🏚 Abbot Hall

Washington Sq. **Tel** (781) 631-0000.
Open call for hours. ♿

🏚 1768 Jeremiah Lee Mansion

161 Washington St. **Tel** (781) 631-1768.
Open Jun–Oct: 10am–4pm Thu–Sat.
🅿 🎥 Ⓦ marbleheadmuseum.org

Street-by-Street: Historic Salem

Like many New England towns, Salem is enjoying something of a rebirth. Downtown renewal programs have revitalized the city core, particularly around Essex Street. Specialty shops, cobblestone walkways, restaurants, and a pedestrian mall offer visitors an array of diversions, including stores specializing in the occult. Travelers are best served by stopping by the Regional Visitor Center operated by the National Park Service, where they can watch a 27-minute film on the region's history and pick up maps to guide their tour.

Peabody Essex Museum
houses the 1765 portrait of Sarah Erving by John S. Copley.

Old Town Hall
The redbrick building is now a popular venue for concerts.

Old Burying Point Cemetery

Salem Witch Village traces the history of witches by looking at their traditions, legends, and – ultimately – their persecution.

DERBY SQUARE

ESSEX STREET

FRONT STREET

LAFAYETTE ST.

CENTRAL STREET

CHARTER STREET

NEW LIBERTY STREET

DERBY STREET

Salem Witch Trials

In 1692 Salem was swept by a wave of hysteria in which 200 citizens were accused of practicing witchcraft. In all, 150 people were jailed and 19 were hung as witches, while another man was crushed to death with stones. No one was safe: two dogs were executed on the gallows for being witches. Not surprisingly, when the governor's wife became a suspect, the trials came to an abrupt and officially sanctioned end.

Early accused:
Rebecca Nurse

Key

░ Pedestrian mall

▬ Suggested route

0 yards	50
0 meters	50

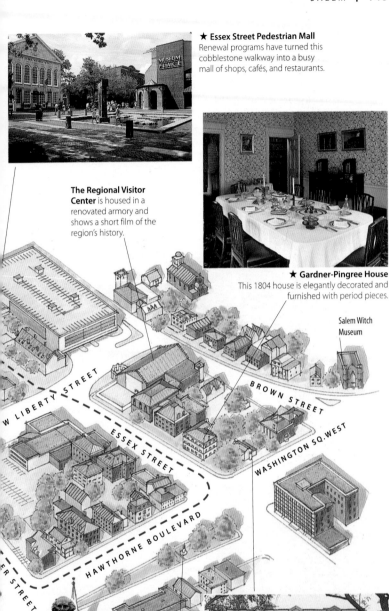

★ **Essex Street Pedestrian Mall**
Renewal programs have turned this cobblestone walkway into a busy mall of shops, cafés, and restaurants.

The Regional Visitor Center is housed in a renovated armory and shows a short film of the region's history.

★ **Gardner-Pingree House**
This 1804 house is elegantly decorated and furnished with period pieces.

Salem Witch Museum

W LIBERTY STREET

BROWN STREET

ESSEX STREET

WASHINGTON SQ. WEST

HAWTHORNE BOULEVARD

ER STREET

To waterfront

Statue of Nathaniel Hawthorne honors the Salem-born author of *The Scarlet Letter* (1850).

Crowninshield Bentley House
Built in 1727, this house typifies the architectural style of mid-18th-century dwellings.

❷ Tour of the North Shore

The scenic tip of the North Shore is a favorite escape for harried Bostonians and vacationers who come for the quaint towns, sandy beaches, and whale-watching excursions that are found here in abundance. Ipswich, founded in 1633, still has more than 40 houses built before 1725. It is also known for its sandy beaches, marshes, dunes and seafood, especially clams. The rocky shores of Cape Ann hold diverse pleasures, including artists' colonies, mansions, and opportunities for swimming and boating.

Fishermen casting into the surf on a North Shore beach

⑧ Ipswich
A wealth of 17th-century architecture makes this a fine town to explore.

Antiquing
Antique stores can be found throughout the North Shore region, particularly in Essex along Main Street.

① Manchester-by-the-Sea
A scenic harbor, luxurious mansions, and a wide beach are town highlights.

② **Magnolia**
This Gloucester village is known for magnificent summer homes and the Medieval-style Hammond Castle Museum.

③ Gloucester
Famous for its *Fisherman's Memorial* statue, this is a lively town with a busy harbor.

Key
- Tour route
- Other road

0 kilometers   3

0 miles   3

For hotels and restaurants in this region see pp313–14 and pp329–31

The World's First Fried Clam

The town of Essex has a proud culinary distinction: it was here that the clams were first fried. In 1916 Lawrence "Chubby" Woodman and his wife were selling raw clams by the road. Following a friend's suggestion, they tried deep-frying a clam. The popularity of the new-dish snack helped Woodman open his own restaurant – still one of the region's most popular today.

Fried clams to go from Woodman's restaurant in Essex

Tips for Drivers

Tour length: 31 miles (50 km) with detour to Wingaersheek Beach.
Starting point: Rte. 127 in Manchester-by-the-Sea.
Stopping-off points: Seafood abounds in places such as Gloucester, Rockport, Essex, and Newburyport. Lodgings are plentiful, but reservations are advised during the peak period of June to October.

⑦ **Wingaersheek Beach**
One of the North Shore's most popular beaches, Wingaersheek affords a view of the Annisquam lighthouse.

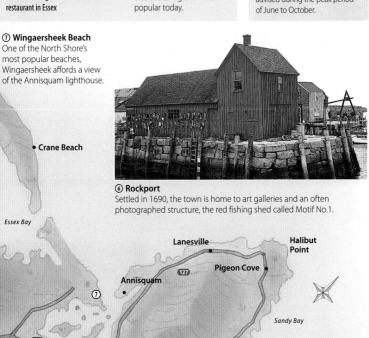

• Crane Beach

⑥ **Rockport**
Settled in 1690, the town is home to art galleries and an often photographed structure, the red fishing shed called Motif No.1.

Essex Bay

Lanesville

Halibut Point

Annisquam

127

Pigeon Cove

⑦

Sandy Bay

128

• Riverdale

⑥

⑤ **Eastern Point Light**
The view from the lighthouse takes in the rocky shoreline and, on clear days, Boston's skyscrapers.

128

③

127

127

④

Long Beach

Gloucester Harbor

127

Eastern Point Light ⑤

④ **Rocky Neck**
Home to one of America's oldest art colonies, Rocky Neck lays claim to fine seafood restaurants.

For map symbols *see back flap*

Power looms on display in the Boott Cotton Mills Museum

❸ Lowell

106,000. ✈ 30 miles (48 km) S in Boston. 🚌 ℹ 40 French St., 2nd Floor, (978) 459-6150. **ⓦ merrimackvalley.org**

Lowell has the distinction of being the country's first industrial city, paving the way for the American Industrial Revolution. In the early 19th century, Boston merchant Francis Cabot Lowell (1775–1817) opened a cloth mill in nearby Waltham and equipped it with his new power loom. The increase in production was so great that the mill quickly outgrew its quarters and was moved to the town of East Chelmsford (later renamed for Lowell). Set on 0.6 sq miles (1.6 sq km) and using power provided by a steep drop in the Merrimack River, the business expanded to include 10 giant mill complexes, which employed more than 10,000 workers.

While the town prospered, it was at the expense of its workers, many of whom were unskilled immigrants exploited by the greedy mill owners. Eventually laborers organized and there were many strikes. The most successful was the 1912 Bread and Roses Strike, which began in neighboring Lawrence and spread to Lowell. While that confrontation helped improve conditions for workers, the relief was temporary. In the 1920s companies began to move south in search of

cheaper labor. The death knell came in 1929. The country was rocked by the Great Depression and the mills closed, leaving Lowell a ghost town.

In 1978 the **Lowell National Historical Park** was established to rehabilitate more than 100 downtown buildings and preserve the town's unique history. The Market Mills Visitor Center on Market Street offers a free introductory video show, walking tour maps, guided walks with rangers, and tickets for summer canal boat tours of the waterways. From March to November, antique trolleys take visitors to the **Boott Cotton Mills Museum**, the centerpiece of the park, where 88 vintage power looms produce a deafening clatter. Interactive exhibits trace the Industrial Revolution and the growth of the labor movement. Also in Lowell, the **American Textile History Museum** traces the evolution of textiles, from Colonial-era weavers to today's high-tech fabrics made from recycled materials.

Lowell has non-industrial attractions as well. The **New England Quilt Museum** displays both antique and contemporary examples of the quilt-maker's art, and sponsors talks and symposia on quilt scholarship and trends in current fiber arts. Painter James McNeill Whistler (1834–1903), most famous for his portrait of his mother, was born in Lowell while his father was in charge of the railroad works for

the city's mills. Whistler's birthplace is now a **museum** that displays prints of some of his work, but focuses more on 19th- and 20th-century American art.

🏛 **Lowell National Historical Park**
246 Market St. **Tel** (978) 970-5000. **Open** Mar–Oct: 9am–5pm daily, Nov–Feb: 9am–4:30pm Mon–Sat, 10am–5pm Sun. 🅿 for canal tours only. 🅒 🅑 ⓦ **nps.gov/lowe**

🏛 **Boott Cotton Mills Museum**
115 John St. **Tel** (978) 970-5000. **Open** late May–Nov: 9:30am–4:30pm daily (call for opening hours off-season). 🅿 🅑

🏛 **American Textile History Museum**
491 Dutton St. **Tel** (978) 441-0400. **Open** 10am–5pm Wed–Sun. **Closed** public hols. 🅿 🅒 🅑 ⓦ **athm.org**

🏛 **New England Quilt Museum**
18 Shattuck St. **Tel** (978) 452-4207. **Open** 10am–4pm Tue–Sat, also open noon–4pm Sun May–Dec. **Closed** public hols. 🅿 🅑 ⓦ **nequiltmuseum.org**

🏛 **Whistler House Museum of Art**
243 Worthen St. **Tel** (978) 452-7641. **Open** 11am–4pm Wed–Sat. 🅿 ⓦ **whistlerhouse.org**

Bedroom display at the New England Quilt Museum in Lowell

Lowell's Jack Kerouac

Lowell native Jack Kerouac was the leading chronicler of the "beat generation," a term that he coined to describe members of the disaffected Bohemian movement of the 1950s. Although he lived elsewhere for most of his adult life, his remains are buried in the town's Edson Cemetery. Excerpts from Kerouac's most famous novel, *On the Road* (1957), and other of his writings are inscribed on granite pillars in the Kerouac Commemorative Park on Bridge Street.

Jack Kerouac (1922–69)

Part of the Fruitlands Museums' Shaker collection

❹ Sudbury

🏙 18,000. ✈ 24 miles (39 km) E in Boston.

The picturesque town of Sudbury is home to a number of historic sites, including the 1797 First Parish Church and the 1723 Loring Parsonage. Longfellow's Wayside Inn, one of the nation's oldest inns, was built in 1716 and was immortalized in Henry Wadsworth Longfellow's poetry collection entitled *Tales of a Wayside Inn* (1863). In the 1920s the building was purchased by industrialist Henry Ford (1863–1947), who restored it, filled it with antiques, and surrounded it with other relocated structures, such as a rustic gristmill, a schoolhouse, and a general store.

Today, the inn serves both as a mini-museum of Colonial America as well as offering cozy overnight rooms and hearty American fare in its pub-like restaurant.

❺ Nashoba Valley

ℹ 100 Sherman Ave., Devens (978) 772-6976.

Fed by the Nashoba River, Nashoba Valley is an appealing world of meadows and orchards and colonial towns built around village greens. The region is particularly popular in May when the apple trees are in bloom, and again in fall when the apples are ripe for picking and the surrounding hills are ablaze in autumn colors.

The **Fruitlands Museums**, the valley's major attraction, comprises four museums, two outdoor sites, and a restaurant on beautiful hilltop grounds that include nature trails and picnic areas with valley views. Founder Clara Endicott Sears (1863–1960), a philosopher, writer, collector, and early preservationist, built her home here in 1910 and began gathering properties of historical significance. Her first acquisition was Fruitlands, the "New Eden" commune based partly on vegetarianism and self-sufficiency initiated by Bronson Alcott (1799–1888) and fellow Transcendentalists. Alcott was the father of author Louisa May Alcott (1832–88) and was the model for the character of Mr. March in her book *Little Women*

Fruitlands Museums' rocking horse

(1868). The restored farmhouse now serves as a museum and includes memorabilia of Alcott, Ralph Waldo Emerson (1803–82), and other Transcendentalist leaders.

Five years later, Sears acquired a building in nearby Shaker Village. The 1790 structure, the first office building in the village, now houses a collection of traditional Shaker furniture, clothing, and artifacts. The Native American Gallery includes objects from New England and throughout the United States.

Another of the region's attractions is the **Nashoba Valley Winery**, a beautiful 0.1-sq-mile (0.2-sq-km) orchard that produces wines from grapes, as well as apples, pears, peaches, plums, blueberries, strawberries, and elderberries. More than 100 varieties of apples are grown here. On weekends the winery offers tours.

🏛 **Fruitlands Museums**
102 Prospect Hill Rd., Harvard. **Tel** (978) 456-3924. **Open** mid-Apr–mid-Nov: 10am–4pm Mon & Wed–Fri, 10am–5pm Sat & Sun. 🅿 ♿ partial. 🌐 fruitlands.org

🍷 **Nashoba Valley Winery**
100 Wattaquadock Hill Rd., Bolton. **Tel** (978) 779-5521. **Open** year-round: 11am–5pm daily. Winery tours: year-round: 11am–4pm Sat & Sun. 🅿 🌐 nashobavalleywinery.com

Henry Wadsworth Longfellow's Wayside Inn, one of the nation's oldest

❻ Concord

The peaceful suburban face of modern Concord masks an eventful past. This small town was central to two important chapters in US history. The first was the Battle of Lexington and Concord on April 19, 1775, which signaled the beginning of the Revolutionary War. The second spanned several generations, as 19th-century Concord blossomed into the literary heart and soul of the US, when many of the nation's leading authors and thinkers of the time lived here. The influence of both important periods is in full evidence today.

North Bridge in Minute Man National Historical Park

Exploring Concord
At Concord's center lies **Monument Square**. After besting American militia on Lexington Green, British troops marched through Concord and out Monument Street. At North Bridge, they clashed with the Minute Men. The first pitched battle of the Revolutionary War ended in a British retreat.

🏛 Minute Man National Historical Park
North Bridge Visitor Center: 174 Liberty St. **Tel** (978) 369-6993. **Open** Apr–Nov: 9am–5pm Tue–Sat; Dec–Mar: 11am–3pm daily. **Closed** Jan 1, Thanksgiving, Dec 25. Minute Man Visitor Center: Rte. 2A, Lincoln. **Tel** (781) 674-1920. **Open** Apr–Oct: 9am–5pm daily. **Closed** winter. 🚻 🅆 nps.gov/mima

Following their April 19, 1775, victory on Lexington Green (*see p124*), British troops proceeded to Concord. Forces deployed to secure **North Bridge** were ambushed by a Colonial militia of ordinary citizens known as Minute Men, who believed the British were burning Concord. The brief ensuing battle turned into a running rout down Battle Road as three British companies fled back to their Boston barracks.

This 1.5-sq-mile (4-sq-km) park preserves the site and tells the story of the American victory. The Minute Man Visitor Center also features a massive battle mural

Minute Man statue in Concord

and a 22-minute multimedia show called "Road to Revolution." The Battle Road Trail traces the 5-mile (8-km) path followed by the British as they advanced from Lexington to Concord – the same route they took in their retreat back to Boston.

The park's North Bridge Unit is the place where the first major engagement was fought. This so-called "shot heard 'round the world" set off the war. Across the bridge is the famous **Minute Man statue** by Concord native Daniel Chester French (1850–31). A short trail leads from the bridge to the **North Bridge Visitor Center**. A reenactment of the battle takes place every year in April in Concord and Lexington.

🏛 Concord Museum
Jct of Lexington Rd. & Cambridge Tpk. **Tel** (978) 369-9609. **Open** Jan–Mar: 11am–4pm Mon–Sat, 1–4pm Sun; Apr–Dec: 9am–5pm Mon–Sat, noon–5pm Sun (Jun–Aug: 9am–5pm Sun). 📷 ♿ 🅆 concord museum.org

The museum's eclectic holdings include decorative arts from the 17th, 18th, and 19th centuries, and the lantern that Paul Revere ordered hung in the steeple of Old North Church to warn of the British advance (*see p124*).

🏛 The Old Manse
269 Monument St. **Tel** (978) 369-3909. **Open** mid-Mar–mid-Apr, Nov & Dec: noon–5pm Sat & Sun; mid-Apr–Oct: noon–5pm Tue–Sun. 📷 🅐
🅆 thetrustees.org
The parsonage by the North Bridge was built in 1770 by the grandfather of writer Ralph

Along the Battle Road, by John Rush, located in the Minute Man Visitor Center

Concord's Old Manse: home to 19th-century literary giants

Waldo Emerson (1803–82), who lived here briefly. Author Nathaniel Hawthorne (1804–64) and his wife rented the house during the first three years of their marriage (loving inscriptions are scratched into the windows). The house got its name from Hawthorne's *Mosses from an Old Manse* (1846), the collection of short stories he wrote here.

🌐 Emerson House

28 Cambridge Tpk. **Tel** (978) 369-2236. **Open** mid-Apr–late Oct: 10am–4:30pm Thu–Sat, 1–4:30pm Sun & public hols. 🕮
Ralph Waldo Emerson lived in this house from 1835 until his

death in 1882, writing essays, organizing lecture tours, and entertaining friends and admirers. Much of Emerson's furniture, writings, books, and family memorabilia is on display.

🌐 Walden Pond State Reservation

915 Walden St. **Tel** (978) 369-3254. **Open** call for hours. 🕮 🕮 🕮
🌐 **mass.gov/dcr/**
Essayist Henry David Thoreau (1817–62) lived in relative isolation at Walden Pond from July 1845 to September 1847. During his stay, he compiled the material for his seminal work *Walden; or, Life in the Woods* (1854). In the book, he called for a return to simplicity in everyday life and respect for nature. Because of Thoreau's deep influence on future generations of environmentalists, Walden

Pond is widely considered to be the birthplace of the conservationist movement.
The pond itself is surrounded by 0.6 sq miles (1.5 sq km) of mostly undeveloped woodlands. The area is popular for walking, fishing, and swimming, and today is far from the solitary spot that Thoreau described, even though the reservation limits the number of visitors to no more than 1,000 people at one time.

VISITORS' CHECKLIST

Practical Information
🗺 17,750. ℹ 58 Main St. (978) 369-3120. 🎫 Battle of Concord Reenactment (Apr). 🌐 **concord chamberofcommerce.org**

Transport
✈ 21 miles (34 km) W in Boston.

Fisherman on the tranquil waters of Walden Pond

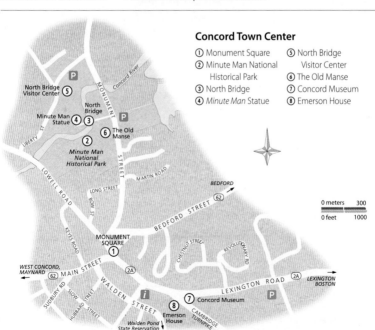

Concord Town Center

① Monument Square
② Minute Man National Historical Park
③ North Bridge
④ *Minute Man* Statue
⑤ North Bridge Visitor Center
⑥ The Old Manse
⑦ Concord Museum
⑧ Emerson House

0 meters 300
0 feet 1000

For map symbols *see back flap*

Mayflower II, replica of the original Pilgrim sailing ship

❼ Plymouth

🏙 52,000. ✈ 40 miles (64 km) NW in Boston. 🚢 to Provincetown (seasonal). ℹ 130 Water St. (508) 747-7533 or (800) USA-1620.
🌐 visit-plymouth.com

In 1620, 102 pilgrims aboard the ship *Mayflower* sailed into Plymouth harbor and established what is considered to be the first permanent English settlement in the New World. Today the town bustles with tourists exploring the sites of America's earliest days, including **Plimoth Plantation** *(see pp154–5)*, which is 2.5 miles (4 km) from town. The plantation is a living-history museum of the English colonists and Native Americans of the area. Plymouth itself is a popular seaside resort, complete with a 3.5-mile-(6-km-) long beach, harbor cruises, and fishing excursions. In the fall, the surrounding bogs turn ruby red as the annual cranberry harvest gets underway. Plymouth is popular for its "Progress," which takes place most Fridays in August at 6pm and on Thanksgiving Day at 10am. Visitors come to witness the

solemn reenactment of the Pilgrims' slow procession to Burial Hill, where a short service is held.

Most of the historic sights can be accessed on foot by the Pilgrim Path that stretches along the waterfront and downtown areas. A seasonal sightseeing trolley connects sights and features a 40-minute history of the town. Ensconced in a monument at the harbor is the country's most famous boulder, Plymouth Rock, marking the spot where the Pilgrims are said to have first stepped ashore. The ***Mayflower II***, a replica of the 17th-century sailing ship that carried the Pilgrims over from England, is moored by Plymouth Rock. At just 106 ft (32 m) in length, the vessel seems far too small to have made a transatlantic voyage, especially considering the horrific weather it encountered. Walking along the cramped deck, visitors will marvel at the Pilgrims' courage. Even after surviving the brutal crossing, many Pilgrims succumbed to illness and

Fully functioning water wheel at Plimoth Grist Mill

malnutrition during their first winter in Plymouth. Their remains are buried across the street on Coles Hill, which is fronted by a statue of Massasoit, the Wampanoag Indian chief who allied himself with the newcomers and aided the survivors by teaching them the growing and use of native corn. It was with Massasoit and his people that the Pilgrims celebrated their famous first Thanksgiving. Coles Hill offers a panoramic view of the harbor.

Burial Hill at the head of the Town Square was the site of an early fort and the final resting place of many members of the original colony, including Governor William Bradford (1590–1656). Most Fridays in August, citizens dressed in Pilgrim garb walk from Plymouth Rock to the hill to reenact the church service attended by the 51 survivors of the first winter. Perched on a hilltop overlooking town, the 81-ft (25-m) National Monument to the Forefathers is dedicated to the Pilgrims who made the dangerous voyage to the New World. The Pilgrim Mother Fountain was erected in honor of the women who made the original voyage. Eighteen adult women set sail from England, but only four of them survived.

Statue of Massasoit

Opened in 1824, the **Pilgrim Hall Museum** is one of America's oldest public museums, housing the largest existing collection of Pilgrim-era artifacts, such as the only known portrait of a *Mayflower* passenger, as well as such personal items as bibles, cradles, and the sword of one of the most colorful Pilgrims, Myles Standish (c.1584–1656), a former soldier of fortune who went on to found nearby Duxbury. Exhibitions explore Pilgrim history as well as Native American culture and history, and the interactions between the two groups. To

◀ Scenic boardwalk at Duxbury Beach

Pilgrim Hall exhibits furniture, armor, and art

appreciate how quickly the Pilgrims progressed from near castaways to hardy settlers, take in the **Plimoth Grist Mill**, a 1970 reconstruction of the 1636 original destroyed by fire in 1847. The restored mill grinds cornmeal with power from a 14-ft (4-m) water wheel.

Plymouth has several historic homes of special interest. Among them is **Spooner House**, constructed in 1749 and continuously occupied by one family until 1954, when James Spooner left his home to the Plymouth Antiquarian Society. Its accumulation of artifacts provides a history of Plymouth life. An American crafts shop can be found in the town's oldest home, c.1640 **Richard Sparrow House**.

The original section of the **Mayflower Society House** was built in 1754 and extensively renovated in 1898. What was the old kitchen is now the office for the General Society of Mayflower Descendants. Its research library has one of the finest genealogical collections in the United States.

Travelers will encounter many of the state's 19 sq miles (49 sq km) of cranberry bogs along the roads of south-eastern Massachusetts inland from Plymouth. Introduced to the English colonists by Native

Americans, the cranberry was first cultivated commercially on Cape Cod in the mid-19th century; about a century later, the center of both growing and processing moved to the Plymouth area. During the autumn harvest season, visitors may see the rectangular bogs flooded as paddle-wheel harvesters thrash the submerged bushes, causing the red berries to separate from the plants and float to the surface, where they are harvested by skimming.

🏛 **Mayflower II**
State Pier. **Tel** (508) 746-1622. **Open** late Mar–Nov: 9am–5pm daily. 🅿

🏛 **Pilgrim Hall Museum**
75 Court St. **Tel** (508) 746-1620. **Open** year-round: 9:30am–4:30pm daily. **Closed** Jan. 🅿

🏚 **Plimoth Grist Mill**
6 Spring Lane. **Tel** (508) 747-4544. **Open** Apr–Nov: 9am–5pm daily.

🏚 **Spooner House**
27 North St. **Tel** (508) 746-0012. **Open** Jun–Aug: 2–6pm Thu & Sun, Sep–mid-Oct: 2–6pm Sat. 🅿

🏚 **Richard Sparrow House**
42 Summer St. **Tel** (508) 747-1240. **Open** Apr–late Dec: 10am–5pm daily; late Dec–Apr: 10am–5pm Thu–Sat. 🅿 ♿ call first. 📷

🏚 **Mayflower Society House**
4 Winslow St. **Tel** (508) 746-3188. **Open** call for hours. 🅿

❽ Duxbury

🏔 15,350. ✈ 34 miles (54 km) N in Boston. 🛈 130 Water St., Plymouth (508) 747-7533.

Duxbury was settled in 1628 by a group of Pilgrims who found that the Plymouth colony was getting too crowded. Two who made the move, John Alden (c.1598–1687) and Myles Standish (c.1584–1656), were on the *Mayflower* crossing. Today the town is best known for its 9-mile- (14-km-) long beach.

The last home of Alden and his wife was the 1653 **Alden House**. The structure has several features of note, including gunstock beams and a ceiling plastered with crushed clam and oyster shells.

King Caesar House, the home of another prominent resident, is one of the town's grandest structures. Ezra Weston II, an 18th-century shipping magnate, had a fortune large enough to earn him the nickname "King Caesar." It also allowed him the luxury of building this stately Federal mansion in 1808. Today the house is furnished with period pieces, French wallpaper, and a small museum celebrating the region's maritime history.

The **Art Complex Museum** has everything from Asian and European art to Shaker furniture and contemporary New England art. A traditional Japanese tea ceremony is held on the last Sunday of the month, June through August.

Shaker piece at Art Complex Museum

🏚 **Alden House**
105 Alden St. **Tel** (781) 934-9092. **Open** Jun–early Sep: noon–4pm Wed–Sat. 🅿 ♿ (first floor only).

🏚 **King Caesar House**
120 King Caesar Rd. **Tel** (781) 934-6106. **Open** Jul & Aug: 1–4pm Wed–Sun.

🏛 **Art Complex Museum**
189 Alden St. **Tel** (781) 934-6634. **Open** Mar–mid-Jan: 1–4pm Wed–Sun.

For hotels and restaurants in this region see pp313–14 and pp329–31

Plimoth Plantation

Plimoth Plantation is a painstakingly accurate re-creation of the Pilgrims' 1627 village, right down to the 17th-century breeds of livestock. Costumed interpreters portray actual original colonists going about their daily tasks of salting fish, gardening, and musket drills. In the parallel Wampanoag Village, descendants of the people who have lived here for 12,000 years speak in modern language about the experiences of the Wampanoag and explore the story of one 17th-century man, Hobbamock, and his family.

Plimoth Plantation
Costumed interpreters mingle with visitors on the village's busy central street.

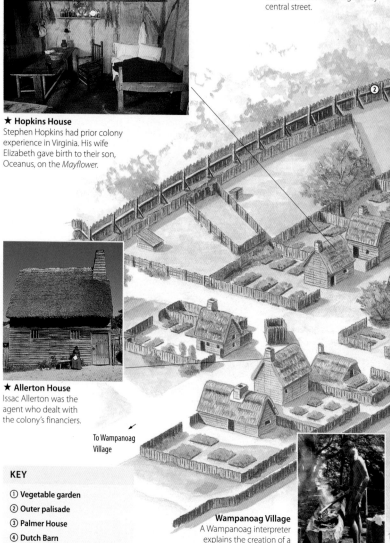

★ **Hopkins House**
Stephen Hopkins had prior colony experience in Virginia. His wife Elizabeth gave birth to their son, Oceanus, on the *Mayflower*.

★ **Allerton House**
Issac Allerton was the agent who dealt with the colony's financiers.

To Wampanoag Village

KEY

① Vegetable garden
② Outer palisade
③ Palmer House
④ Dutch Barn

Wampanoag Village
A Wampanoag interpreter explains the creation of a dugout canoe.

Key

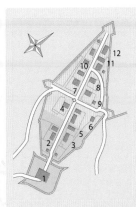

- ☐ Illustrated
- ☐ Not illustrated
1. Fort/Meetinghouse
2. Standish and Alden Houses
3. Winslow and Cooke Houses
4. Bradford House
5. Allerton House
6. Cow Shed
7. Hopkins House
8. Brewster and Browne Houses
9. Dutch Barn
10. Fuller House
11. Forge
12. Storehouse

VISITORS' CHECKLIST

Practical Information

Rte. 3A. 🛈 137 Warren Ave. (508) 746-1622. **Open** late Mar–Nov: 9:30am–5pm daily. 🅿 ♿ limited access to certain parts of site; wheelchairs available upon request. 📷 **W** **plimoth.org**

★ Storehouse
Everyday provisions were stored here, along with furs and other goods to be shipped to England.

Local Reeds
Used for thatching, reeds were long-lasting, easily repaired, and virtually waterproof.

The Cow Shed
Cows and other livestock were housed in what was often called the "beasthouse." It opens into an enclosed paddock.

0 meters   10
0 yards   10

Martha's Vineyard scene: fishing boat outside fishing shack

❶ Martha's Vineyard

🏛 13,900. ✈ West Tisbury.
🚢 Woods Hole; Hyannis; Falmouth;
New Bedford. 🛈 Beach Rd., Vineyard
Haven (508) 693-0085 or (800) 505-
4815. 🆆 mvy.com

"The Vineyard", as the locals call
it, is the largest of all New
England's vacation islands at
108 sq miles (280 sq km). Just
a 45-minute boat ride from
shore, it is blessed with a
mesmerizing mix of scenic
beauty and the understated
charm of a beach resort.
Bicycle trails abound here and
opportunities for hiking, surf
fishing, and some of the best
sailing in the region add to the
Vineyard's lure. Each town has
its own distinctive mood and
architectural style, making for
interesting exploring.

Vineyard Haven
Most visitors arrive on Martha's
Vineyard aboard ferries that sail
into this waterfront town, which

was largely destroyed by fire
in the 1800s. Vineyard Haven is
sheltered between two points
of land known as East and West
Chop, each with its own
landmark lighthouse.

Edgartown
As the center of the island's
whaling industry in the early
1800s, Edgartown was once
home to wealthy sea captains
and merchants. The streets are
lined with their homes.

Victorian home with gingerbread
ornamentation in Oak Bluffs

The main building of the
Martha's Vineyard Museum
complex is the c.1730 Thomas
Cooke House. The beautiful
12-room structure is filled
with antique furniture, ship
models, scrimshaw, and gear
used by whalers.

At the eastern end of the
waterfront, visitors can catch the
ferry to Chappaquiddick Island,
a rural outpost that is popular for
its beaches and opportunities
for bird-watching, surf fishing,
canoeing, and hiking. This quiet
enclave was made famous by a
fatal accident in 1969, when a
car driven by Senator Edward
Kennedy (1932–2009) went off
the bridge, killing a young
woman passenger.

🏛 **Martha's Vineyard Museum**
59 School St. **Tel** (508) 627-4441.
Open 10am–5pm Mon–Sat (mid-Oct–
mid-Jun: to 4pm; Jan–mid-Mar: open
Sat only). **Closed** public hols. Cooke
House: **Closed** mid-Oct–mid-Jun. ♿
♿ 📷 🆆 mvmuseum.org

Oak Bluffs
Tourism began on Martha's
Vineyard in 1835, when local
Methodists began using the
undeveloped area to pitch their
tents during their summer
revival meetings. The setting
proved popular as people came
in search of sunshine and
salvation. Gradually the tent
village gave way to a town of
colorful gingerbread cottages,
boarding houses, and stores,
and was named Cottage City. In
1907 it was renamed Oak Bluffs.
The town is home to the **Flying
Horses Carousel**, the oldest
continuously operating carousel
in the country. Today's children
delight in riding on it as much
as those of the 1870s.

🎠 **Flying Horses Carousel**
Oak Bluffs Ave. **Tel** (508) 693-9481.
Open Apr–mid-Oct: call for hours.
📷 ▣

Western Shoreline
Unlike the Vineyard's busier
eastern section, the western
shoreline is tranquil and rural.
The area, which includes the
towns of North and West
Tisbury, Menemsha, and

Whale-watching

Whale off the coast of Martha's
Vineyard

From April to mid-October the
waters off Nantucket Island and Cape
Cod come to life with the antics of
finback, right, minke, and humpback
whales. These gentle behemoths
bang their massive tails, blow clouds
of bubbles, and sometimes fling their
entire bodies into the air only to
come crashing down in mammoth
back or belly flops. Whales are most
numerous during July and
August, and cruises are offered
from many ports, including
Provincetown and Barnstable on
the Cape, Vineyard Haven on
Martha's Vineyard, and the Straight
Wharf in the town of Nantucket.

Colored cliffs of Aquinnah on western shore of Martha's Vineyard

Aquinnah (formerly Gay Head but renamed in 1998), is graced by a number of private homes and pristine beaches, many of which are strictly private.

Tiny West Tisbury remains a rural village of picket fences, a white-spired church, and a general store. In Menemsha, a working fishing fleet fills the harbor, and the weathered fishermen's shacks, fish nets, and lobster traps look much as they did a century ago. Windswept Aquinnah at the western edge of the island is famous for its steep multi-hued clay cliffs – a favorite subject of photographers.

❿ Nantucket Island

🏠 9,000 (year-round). ✈ West Tisbury. ⛴ Hyannis, Harwichport & Oak Bluffs. ℹ Zero Main St. (508) 228-1700. 🅆 **nantucketchamber.org**

Lying off the southern tip of Cape Cod *(see pp160–63)*, Nantucket Island is a 14-mile-(22-km-) long enclave of tranquility. With only one town to speak of, the island remains an untamed world of kettle ponds, cranberry bogs, and lush stands of wild grapes and blueberries, punctuated by the occasional lighthouse.

In the early 19th century the town of Nantucket was the envy of the whaling industry, with a fleet of about 100 vessels. The town's

Brant Point Light on Nantucket Island

architecture reflects those glory days, with the magnificent mansions of sea captains and merchants – made rich from their whaling profits – lining Main Street. Today the town has the nation's largest concentration of pre-1850s houses.

The **Nantucket Historical Association** (NHA) operates 11 historical buildings in town. One of the most important sites is the Whaling Museum on Broad Street. The expanded museum features a restored 1847 spermaceti candle factory and a rare complete 46-ft (14-m) skeleton of a sperm whale recovered from Nantucket beach. Historic exhibits include ship models, ships' logs, maps and charts, tools, letters, manuscripts, business documents, and genealogical materials, as well as more than 45,000 photographs and examples of scrimshaw that highlight the era when Nantucket was the world's leading whaling port. Additional buildings of interest include the Hawden House, built in 1845, which focuses on the lifestyle of the well-off whaling merchants, and the Quaker Meeting House. From an initial meeting in 1701, Quakerism grew to be the religion of Nantucket's elite. The meeting house is still a tiny but active congregation. Also open for tours are the 1686 Jethro Coffin House, which is the oldest house on the

island, and the 18th-century Old Mill, a wind-powered grain mill restored to operating condition.

🏛 Nantucket Historical Association (NHA)

15 Broad St. **Tel** (508) 228-1894. Historic buildings: **Open** call for hours. 📷 📁 ♿ Whaling Museum only. 🏠 🅆 **nha.org**

Environs
Just 8 miles (13 km) from the town of Nantucket lies the tiny village of **Siasconset**. The village, which is called "Sconset" by locals, is located on the eastern shore of the island and easily lives up to the description offered by one 18th-century visitor: "Perfectly unconnected with the real world and far removed from its perturbations." Set between cranberry bogs and rose-covered bluffs overlooking the Atlantic Ocean, the village's narrow lanes are lined with miniature cottages that are among the oldest of the island. Many of these fishermen's shanties are constructed out of wood rescued from shipwrecks, accounting for Sconset's old nickname, "Patchwork Village."

Once Sconset was a summer colony for actors, attracting such luminaries of the American stage as Lillian Russell (1861–1922) and Joseph Jefferson (1829–1905), who made the 35-minute ride from the town of Nantucket via an island railroad. Today there are only a few inns remaining. The majority of Sconset's summer visitors own or rent homes, a fact that serves to keep the beaches uncrowded and the village peaceful.

⓫ Cape Cod National Seashore

Stretching more than 40 miles (64 km) from Chatham in the south to Provincetown in the north, Cape Cod National Seashore is one of the Eastern Seaboard's true gems. With the backing of President John Kennedy (1917–63), the seashore was established in 1961 to protect the fragile sand dunes and beaches, salt marshes, glacial cliffs, and woodlands. While the delicate landscape has been under federal protection since then, certain features have been added, including bike trails, hiking paths, and specially designated dune trails for off-road vehicles. Historical structures are interspersed among the seashore's softly beautiful natural features.

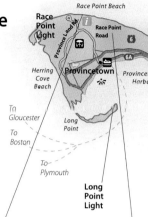

★ Old Harbor Life-Saving Station
This 1897 station houses a museum containing turn-of-the-century rescue equipment and shipwreck paraphernalia. During the summer months, traditional rescue methods are sometimes demonstrated.

★ Province Lands Area
The barren, windswept landscape of the Province Lands Area has long been an inspiration for writers and artists. Here, beech forests give way to dramatic parabolic dunes and white sand beaches.

Overview
Visitors get an overview of the area in the park's visitor centers.

Key

━━ Major road

═══ Minor road

-- Walking trail

— Park boundary

For hotels and restaurants in this region see pp313–14 and pp329–31

★ **Atwood Higgins House**
This 1730s Colonial-style home typifies the
houses of early settlers to the region.

★ **Atlantic White
Cedar Swamp Trail**
A nature trail, part of
which is a boardwalk
over swamp, leads
through forested
swampland and
stands of scrub oak
and pitch pine to
Marconi Station.

Marconi Beach
This broad and sandy expanse near South Wellfleet is named
after Guglielmo Marconi (1874–1937), who transmitted the
world's first wireless message from this area in 1903.

Wildflowers
These flowers
bloom throughout
the seasons at the
National Seashore.

For map symbols *see back flap*

⑫ Cape Cod

Millions of visitors arrive each summer to enjoy the boundless beaches, natural beauty, and quaint colonial villages of Cape Cod. Extending some 70 miles (113 km) into the sea, the Cape is shaped like an upraised arm, bent at the elbow with the Atlantic Ocean and the Cape Cod National Seashore *(see pp158–9)* and ending with the fist at Provincetown. Crowds are heaviest along Route 28, where beaches edge the warmer waters of Nantucket Sound and Buzzard's Bay. Towns along Route 6A, the old Kings Highway, retain their colonial charm, with many of the old homes now serving as antique shops and inns.

Fishermen on their boat in Provincetown harbor

Exploring the Lower Cape

First-time visitors to Cape Cod are almost always confused when they are given directions by locals. This is because residents have divided the Cape into three districts with names that do not make much sense. The Mid- and Upper Cape is actually the southernmost portion closest to the mainland, while the Lower Cape is the northernmost section.

The Lower, or Outer, Cape takes in the long elbow of the peninsula that curls northward and forms Cape Cod Bay. The towns of Chatham, Brewster, Orleans, Eastham, Wellfleet, Truro, and Provincetown are all located in this section.

Provincetown

This picturesque town at the northern tip of the Cape has a colorful history. The Pilgrims first landed here in 1620 and stayed for five weeks before pushing on to the mainland. During that time they drew up the Mayflower Compact, a forerunner of the American Constitution. "P-Town," as it is called, later grew into a major 18th-century fishing center. By the beginning of the 20th century, P-Town had become a bustling artists' colony. Today this popular and eccentric town is one of New England's most vibrant destinations and a popular gay resort. However, in the summer months the town's population can swell from 3,500 to more than 30,000.

Pilgrim Monument

The place where the Pilgrims first landed is marked by a bronze plaque on Commercial Street and commemorated by the tallest granite structure in the US, the 252-ft (77-m) **Pilgrim Monument**. On a clear day, the view from the top extends all the way to Boston. Eclectic displays in the adjacent **museum** include exhibits of Pilgrim history as well as marine and Arctic artifacts.

The **Whydah Pirate Museum** is named for a ship that sank in a storm off Cape Cod after being captured by pirates. It exhibits artifacts such as gold dubloons, weapons, clothing, and West African gold jewelry. The region's rich cultural history is celebrated in the galleries of the **Provincetown Art Association and Museum**, where works by local artists are displayed. One of the town's busiest locales is MacMillan

Wharf, the center of nautical activity, including the jumping-off point for whale-watching cruises *(see p156)*.

🏛 **Pilgrim Monument and Provincetown Museum**
High Pole Hill Rd. **Tel** (508) 487-1310. **Open** Apr–Nov: 9am–5pm daily (Jun–mid-Sep: to 7pm). 🖼 ♿

🏛 **Whydah Pirate Museum**
16 MacMillan Wharf. **Tel** (508) 487-8899. **Open** mid-May–Oct: 10am–5pm daily (Jun–Aug: extended hours). 🖼 ♿ 🔲

🏛 **Provincetown Art Association and Museum**
460 Commercial St. **Tel** (508) 487-1750. **Open** call for hours. 🖼 ♿

Environs

Just 17 miles (27 km) south of Provincetown lies Wellfleet, an early whaling center that possesses one of the Cape's largest concentrations of art

Busy streets of Cape Cod's Provincetown in the summertime

galleries. Farther down the Cape is Eastham, home to the **Old Schoolhouse Museum**, a one-room school built in 1869. Neighboring Orleans is a commercial center with access to the very beautiful Nauset Beach and its much-photographed lighthouse.

Old Schoolhouse Museum
Nauset Rd., Eastham. **Tel** (508) 255-0788. **Open** call for opening hours.

Chatham

Chatham rests on the very point of the Cape's "elbow," the place where Nantucket Sound meets the Atlantic Ocean. An attractive, upscale community, it offers fine inns, a Main Street filled with attractive shops, and a popular summer playhouse. Housed in an 1887 Victorian train station, the **Railroad Museum** contains models, photos, memorabilia, and vintage trains that can be boarded. Fishing boats unload their catch at the pier every afternoon, and the surrounding waters offer good opportunities for amateur anglers to fish for bluefish and bass.

Chatham is also the best place to plan a trip to the **Monomoy National Wildlife Refuge**. Encompassing two islands, this huge reserve attracts migrating birds and is a nesting habitat for such endangered birds as the piping plover and the roseate tern. Deer are spotted here, as are the numerous gray and harbor seals that bask on the rocks.

Railroad Museum
Depot Rd. **Tel** (508) 945-5199. **Open** mid-Jun–mid-Sep: 10am–4pm Tue–Sat.

Monomoy National Wildlife Refuge
Wikis Way, Morris Island. **Tel** (508) 945-0594. Visitor Center: **Open** late May–mid-Sep: 10am–6pm daily. Call for off-season hours and info on boat services. **w** monomoy.fws.gov

Brewster

Named for Elder William Brewster (1567–1644), who was a passenger on the *Mayflower*, Brewster is another town graced with handsome 19th-century houses of wealthy sea captains. It is also home to a particularly lovely church, the 1834 First Parish Brewster Unitarian Universalist Church. Some pews are marked with names of prominent captains.

Children will love the interactive exhibits on display at the **Cape Cod Museum of Natural History**. An observation area looking out on the salt-marsh habitat of birds gives visitors close-up views of the natural world. The 3,571,900-sq-ft (331,850-sq-m) grounds are laced with three walking trails with boardwalks that cross salt marshes. The museum also offers interesting guided "eco-treks" and cruises to nearby Nauset Marsh and Monomoy Islands.

Naturalists can continue with a more hands-on kind of exploration at any of Brewster's

VISITORS' CHECKLIST

Practical Information
200,000. Jct Rtes 132 & 6, Hyannis; Rte. 25, Plymouth (508) 362-3225 or (888) 33-CAPECOD. Cape Cod Maritime Week (May), Annual Bourne Scallop Festival (Sep). **w** capecodchamber.org

Transport
Barnstable Municipal Airport. Elm Ave, Hyannis. Ocean St., Hyannis; Railroad Ave, Woods Hole

eight beaches along Cape Cod Bay. These strands taper gradually toward the ocean, and about 1 mile (1.6 km) of tidal flats is revealed at low tide. The dramatic flats attract a wide variety of visitors, from photographers, to children who like to search for sea life, to clam diggers.

Cape Cod Museum of Natural History
869 Rte. 6A. **Tel** (508) 896-3867. **Open** Jun–Sep: 9:30am–4pm daily. Call for winter opening hours. **Closed** public hols. **w** ccmnh.org

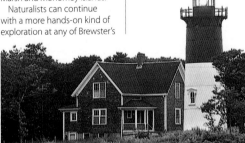
Red and white Nauset Light on the Lower Cape

Provincetown Artist Colony

Artists, writers, and poets have long been inspired by the sublime natural beauty of Provincetown. The town's first art school opened in 1901 and Hans Hofmann (1880–1966), Jackson Pollock (1912–56), Mark Rothko (1903–70), and Edward Hopper (1882–1967) are among the many prominent artists who have spent time here. Today the town is famous for its art galleries, both large and small. The roster of resident writers includes John Dos Passos (1896–1970), Tennessee Williams (1911–83), Sinclair Lewis (1885–1951), and Eugene O'Neill (1888–1953), whose earliest plays were staged at the Provincetown Playhouse.

Visitor to one of Provincetown's many art galleries

Exploring the Mid- and Upper Cape

Stretching from Bourne and Sandwich in the west to Yarmouth and Harwich in the east, Cape Cod's Mid- and Upper sections offer travelers a broad range of vacation experiences. Be it sunbathing on the tranquil beaches of Nantucket Sound by day or partaking in the fashionable nightlife of Hyannis once the sun has set over Cape Cod Bay, this section of the Cape has a little something for every taste.

Hyannis boatbuilder and his remodeled Russian torpedo boat

Dennis

This gracious village has developed into a vibrant artistic center and is home to the 1927 **Cape Playhouse**, America's oldest professional summer theater, as well as some of the Cape's finest public golf courses. The list of stage luminaries who started their career here is impressive. Playhouse grads include eventual Academy Award-winners Humphrey Bogart, Bette Davis, and Henry Fonda. The Playhouse complex also includes the **Cape Cod Museum of Art**, displaying the works of Cape Cod artists. A short drive to the east, the Scargo Hill Tower is open to the public and offers brilliant views of the surrounding landscape.

Cape Playhouse
820 Rte. 6A. **Tel** (508) 385-3911. **Open** call for show times.

Cape Cod Museum of Art
Cape Playhouse grounds. **Tel** (508) 385-4477. **Open** late May–mid-Oct: 10am–5pm Tue–Sat, noon–5pm Sun; call for winter hours. **Closed** public hols; mid-Oct–late May: Mon. ccmoa.org

Hyannis
The Cape's largest village is also a busy shopping center and the transportation hub for regional train, bus, and air service. The harbor is full of yachts and sightseeing boats. Surprisingly, one of Hyannis' most popular forms of transportation does not float. The **Cape Cod Central Railroad** takes travelers for a

scenic two-hour round-trip to the Cape Cod canal. Hyannis was one of the Cape's earliest summer resorts, attracting vacationers as far back as the mid-1800s. In 1874 President Ulysses S. Grant (1822–85) vacationed here, followed by President Grover Cleveland (1837–1908) years later. The most famous estate is the Kennedy compound, summer playground of one of America's most famous political dynasties. The heavily screened compound is best seen from the water aboard a sightseeing cruise.

After John Kennedy's assassination in 1963, a simple monument was erected in his honor: a pool and fountain and a circular wall bearing Kennedy's profile. The **John F. Kennedy Hyannis Museum** on the ground floor of the Old Town Hall covers the years he spent vacationing here, beginning in the 1930s, and includes photos, oral histories, and family videos.

Cape Cod Central Railroad
Tel (508) 771-3800 or (888) 797-7245. **Open** late May–late Oct: Tue–Sun; call for trip times and departure points. capetrain.com

John F. Kennedy Hyannis Museum
397 Main St. **Tel** (508) 790-3077. **Open** call for hours.

Barnstable
This attractive harbor town is the hub of Barnstable County, a widespread region extending to both sides of the Cape. The **Coast Guard Heritage Museum**, located in an 1856 customs house, displays artifacts from the Lighthouse, Livesaving, and Revenue Cutter services. A film

Popular sightseeing mode of transportation: Cape Cod Central Railroad

For hotels and restaurants in this region see pp313–14 and pp329–31

The Kennedy Clan

The center of the Kennedy compound in Hyannis Port is the "cottage" that multi-millionaire Joseph Kennedy (1888–1969) and his wife Rose (1890–1995) bought in 1926. The much-expanded structure was a vacation retreat for the Kennedys and their nine children. John Fitzgerald Kennedy (1917–63), the country's 35th president, and his brothers and sisters continued to summer here long after they had started families of their own. In 1999, JFK's son, John Jr, was flying to the compound for a family wedding when his plane crashed off Martha's Vineyard.

John and Jacqueline Kennedy at their cottage in Hyannis Port

shows lifesaving techniques. The harbor is home to whale-watching cruises, and conservation properties offer fine hiking.

Coast Guard Heritage Museum
Rte. 6A, 3353 Main St. **Tel** (508) 362-8521. **Open** mid-Jun–Oct: 10am–3pm Tue–Sat. **W** coastguardheritage museum.org

Falmouth

Falmouth, settled by Quakers in 1661, grew into a resort town in the late 19th century. The picturesque village green and historic Main Street reflect a Victorian heritage.

Falmouth's coastline is ideal for boating, windsurfing, and sea kayaking. As well, the town is graced with 12 miles (19 km) of beaches. Old Silver is the most popular beach, but Grand Avenue has the most dramatic views of Vineyard Sound. Nature lovers will find walking and hiking trails, salt marshes, tidal pools, and opportunities for beach-combing and bird-watching. The 3.3-mile (5-km) Shining Sea Bike Path offers vistas of beach, harbor, and woodland on the way to Woods Hole.

Woods Hole

This is home to the world's largest independent marine science research center, the Woods Hole Oceanographic Institution (WHOI).

Visitors to the **WHOI Exhibit Center** can explore two floors of displays and videos explaining coastal ecology and highlighting some of the organization's findings. Exhibits include a replica of the interior of the *Alvin*, one of the pioneer vessels developed for deep-sea exploration.

WHOI Exhibit Center
15 School St. **Tel** (508) 289-2663. **Open** Apr–Dec: call for hours. donation. Jul & Aug by appt.

Sandwich

The oldest town on the Cape is straight off a postcard: the First Church of Christ overlooks a picturesque pond fed by the brook that powers the water wheel of a colonial-era gristmill. The church has what is said to be the oldest church bell in the US, dating to 1675. The **Dexter Grist Mill**, built in 1654, has been restored and is grinding again, producing cornmeal that is available at the gift shop.

Antique bottle in Glass Museum

Another industry is celebrated at the **Sandwich Glass Museum**. Between 1825 and 1888, local entrepreneurs invented a way to press glass that was prized for its colors. Nearly 5,000 pieces of Sandwich glass are handsomely displayed here.

The most unique attraction in Sandwich is **Heritage Museums and Gardens**, a 3,267,000-sq-ft (303,500-sq-m) garden and museum built around the collection of pharmaceutical magnate and inveterate collector

Josiah Kirby Lilly, Jr (1893–1966). The artifacts fill three buildings. The American History Museum, a replica of a Revolutionary War fort, includes military miniatures and antique firearms. A collection of 37 antique cars is displayed in a reproduction of a Shaker barn. The Art Museum contains everything from folk art and a collection of Currier and Ives prints to changing exhibits and a working 1912 carousel – a favorite with visitors. Outside, the grounds are planted with more than 1,000 varieties of trees, shrubs, and flowers, including superb rhododendrons.

Dexter Grist Mill
Maine & Water Sts. **Tel** (508) 888-4910. **Open** call for hours.

Sandwich Glass Museum
129 Main St. **Tel** (508) 888-0251. **Open** Feb & Mar: 9:30am–4pm Wed–Sun; Apr–Dec: 9:30am–5pm daily. **W** sandwichglass museum.org

Heritage Museums and Gardens
67 Grove St. **Tel** (508) 888-3300. **Open** Apr–mid-Oct: 10am–5pm daily. **W** heritagemuseums andgardens.org

Film star Gary Cooper's 1930 Duesenberg, Heritage Museums and Gardens

Old Sturbridge Village

At the heart of this living-history museum are about 40 vintage buildings that have been restored and relocated from all over New England. Laid out like an early 19th-century village, Old Sturbridge is peopled by costumed interpreters who go about their daily activities. A blacksmith works the forge, farmers tend crops, and millers work the gristmill. Inside buildings, visitors will find re-created period settings, early American antiques, and demonstrations of such crafts as spinning and weaving. A gallery, education center, and workshops illuminate 19th-century life.

VISITORS' CHECKLIST

Practical Information
Rte. 20, Sturbridge. **Tel** (508) 347-3362 or (800) 733-1830.
Open mid-Apr–mid-Oct: 9:30am–5pm daily; mid-Oct–mid-Apr: 9:30am–4pm Tue–Sun.
Closed Dec 25. 🎫 📷 call for times. ♿ some buildings. 🖊 🖥 🎦 🅦 osv.org

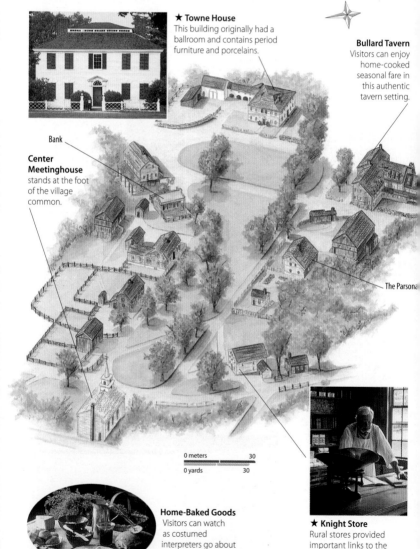

★ Towne House
This building originally had a ballroom and contains period furniture and porcelains.

Bullard Tavern
Visitors can enjoy home-cooked seasonal fare in this authentic tavern setting.

Bank

Center Meetinghouse stands at the foot of the village common.

The Parsona

0 meters 30
0 yards 30

Home-Baked Goods
Visitors can watch as costumed interpreters go about such daily activities as preparing food.

★ Knight Store
Rural stores provided important links to the outside world by stocking imported goods.

⓭ Worcester

🏙 181,000. ✈ Worcester Airport.
🚌 🚉 ℹ 91 Prescott St. (508) 753-2920.

Worcester has always been on the cutting edge. During the American Industrial Revolution, local designers developed the nation's first mechanized carpet weavers and envelope folders. This spirit of invention reached its pinnacle in 1926, when Worcester native Dr. Robert Goddard (1882–1945) launched the world's first liquid-fuel rocket.

Not all of Worcester's forward thinking has been reserved for the development of new machines, however. Over time this city, which is built on seven hills, became home to 10 colleges and universities plus a center for biological research that in the 1950s developed the first birth-control pill.

Central Massachusetts' premier event space, the **DCU Center**, contains an indoor arena and convention center. Located in the heart of downtown Worcester, the complex is within walking distance of numerous shops, restaurants, and bars. The facility hosts an assortment of events, from big-name concerts and sporting events to family shows and conventions. The arena holds nearly 15,000 spectators and has hosted the likes of Frank Sinatra, Katy Perry, and local icons Aerosmith.

Housed in a handsome late 19th-century stone building, the **Worcester Art Museum** has distinguished itself as an important repository. Its impressive collection contains some 35,000 objects spanning 5,000 years, including a 12th-century chapter house that was rebuilt stone by stone on the premises. The museum's holdings of East and West Asian art and Japanese woodblock prints are balanced wonderfully by a good number of works by such Western masters as Claude Monet (1840–1926), Thomas

Gainsborough (1728–88), and Pablo Picasso (1881–1973).

Just 2 miles (3 km) from downtown, the **Ecotarium** promotes a better understanding of the region's environment and its wildlife. Interactive exhibits invite hands-on learning experiences. The surrounding grounds contain a wildlife center for injured and endangered animals, and New England's only tree canopy walkway (summer only). The 2,613,600-sq-ft (242,800-sq-m) grounds also hold a planetarium.

DCU Center
50 Foster St. **Tel** (508) 755-6800.
Open year-round, check website for details on events. 🌐 **dcucenter.com**

🏛 Worcester Art Museum
55 Salisbury St. **Tel** (508) 799-4406.
Open year-round: 11am–5pm Wed–Fri & Sun, 10am–5pm Sat. 🎨 ♿
🌐 **worcesterart.org**

🦎 Ecotarium
222 Harrington Way. **Tel** (508) 929-2700. **Open** year-round: 10am–5pm Tue–Sat, noon–5pm Sun. 🎨 ♿
🌐 **ecotarium.org**

Environs
North Grafton, 10 miles (16 km) southeast, has a long history of clock-making. In the early 19th century brothers Benjamin, Simon, Ephraim, and Aaron Willard were regarded as some of New England's best craftsmen, designing new styles for timepieces. The timepieces were given such names as Eddystone Lighthouse, Skeleton, and Act of Parliament. Today more than 70 Willard timepieces and elegant

tall clocks are on display in the family's original 18th-century homestead.

🏛 Willard House and Clock Museum
11 Willard St., North Grafton. **Tel** (508) 839-3500. **Open** Apr–Dec: 10am–4pm Wed–Sat, 1–4pm Sun; Jan–Mar: Fri–Sun only. 🎨 📷 obligatory.
♿ partial. 🌐 **willardhouse.org**

⓮ Sturbridge

Sturbridge's roots are literally in the land. Soon after its founding in 1729, residents planted apple orchards, some of which are still in operation. The town's main attraction is its living-history museum: Old Sturbridge Village (see p164).

The 1748 Parsonage in Old Sturbridge Village

Environs
Located 9 miles (14 km) west, the village of Brimfield blossoms three times each year as America's flea market capital. The Brimfield Antique Show attracts hundreds of dealers, filling every field, sidewalk, and front porch in town. Treasure hunters descend to the village by the thousands to shop for wares ranging from valuable antiques to the truly kitsch.

Scraping recent layers of paint off an antique carousel horse at the Brimfield flea market

⑮ Springfield

🏙 153,000. ✈ 15 miles (24 km) SW in Windsor Locks, CT. 🚌 🚆 ℹ 1441 Main St. (413) 787-1548 or (800) 723-1548. 🌐 valleyvisitor.com

Now a center for banking and insurance, Springfield owes much of its early success to guns. The **Springfield Armory** – the first armory in the US – was commissioned by George Washington (1732–99) to manufacture arms for the Colonial forces fighting in the Revolutionary War. Today the historic armory is part of the National Park Service and maintains one of the most extensive and unique firearms collections in the world.

In 1891 Dr. James Naismith (1861–1939), an instructor at the International YMCA Training Center, now Springfield College, invented the game of basketball. **Basketball Hall of Fame** traces the development of the game from its humble beginnings, in which peach baskets were used as nets, to its evolution as one of the world's most popular team sports. Along with its collection of basketball memorabilia, the state-of-the-art museum features interactive displays. Children and adults can play against former stars in virtual reality games or test their own shooting skills.

Court Square on Main Street is the revitalized center of the city, lined with 19th-century churches, civic and commercial buildings, and a 300-ft- (91-m-) high tower housing carillon bells. Nearby is **The Quadrangle**, a group of

Emblem of the Basketball Hall of Fame in Springfield

five museums of art, science, and history. The G.W.V. Smith Art Museum displays a noted collection of Oriental decorative arts and Japanese armor. Galleries at the Museum of Fine Arts contain European and American paintings, sculpture, and decorative arts. Children love the Springfield Science Museum, with its live animal center, planetarium, and Dinosaur Hall, with a life-size model of *Tyrannosaurus rex*. The Connecticut Valley Historical Museum concentrates on Colonial-era history, while the Wood Museum of Springfield History displays locally made cars and motorcycles.

The Dr. Seuss National Memorial sculpture features the beloved characters of popular children's author and Springfield native Theodor Geisel (1904–91), better known as Dr. Seuss.

🏛 Springfield Armory National Historic Site
One Armory Sq. **Tel** (413) 734-8551. **Open** 9am–5pm daily. **Closed** Jan 1, Thanksgiving, Dec 25. 🎟 🔊

🏛 Basketball Hall of Fame
1000 W Columbus Ave. **Tel** (413) 781-6500. **Open** 10am–4pm Tue–Fri & Sun, 10am–5pm Sat. **Closed** Thanksgiving, Dec 25, Mon & Tue (Jan–Apr). 🎟 🎟 🔊 🌐 hoophall.com

🏛 The Quadrangle
State & Chestnut Sts. **Tel** (413) 263-6800. Five museums: **Open** year-round: call for hours. 🎟 🔊 partial. 🌐 springfieldmuseums.org

Environs
Some 11 miles (18 km) north, the hamlet of South Hadley is home to **Mount Holyoke College** (1837), the nation's oldest women's college. Poet Emily Dickinson (1830–86) was one of Mount Holyoke's most famous students. The 1.2-sq-mile (3.2-sq-km) campus encompasses two lakes and a series of nature trails. College sites worth a visit include the **Art Museum** and the **Talcott Greenhouse**, which is located in a Victorian-style greenhouse.

Farther north in Hadley, the summit of 954-ft (291-m) Mount Holyoke in **Skinner State Park** offers a panorama

Dinosaur model dwarfing visitor in Springfield's Science Museum

of the oxbow bend in the Connecticut River. The park is well-known for massive laurel displays in June and flaming foliage in autumn.

🏛 Mount Holyoke College Art Museum
Mount Holyoke College. **Tel** (413) 538-2245. **Open** 11am–5pm Tue–Fri, 1–5pm Sat & Sun. 🔊

🌼 Talcott Greenhouse
Mount Holyoke College. **Tel** (413) 538-2116. **Open** year-round: 9am–4pm Mon–Fri, 1–4pm Sat & Sun. 🔊

🚩 Skinner State Park
Rte. 47. **Tel** (413) 586-0350. **Open** May–Oct: dawn–dusk. 🐾 on weekends.

⑯ Amherst

🏙 23,000. ✈ 41 miles (66 km) S in Windsor Locks, CT. 🚌 🚆 ℹ 28 Amity St. (413) 253-0700.

This idyllic college town is home to three different institutes of higher learning. The most popular with visitors is Amherst College, with its central green and traditional ivy-covered buildings. Founded in 1821 for underprivileged youths hoping to enter the ministry, the school has grown into one of the most selective small colleges in the US. The college's excellent **Mead Art Museum** includes the Rotherwas Room, an ornately paneled English hall c.1600. Minerals, fossils, and bones star in the **Beneski Museum of Natural History**, also on the college campus. Poet Emily

Dickinson was one of Amherst's most famous citizens. In her early 20s, Dickinson withdrew from society and spent the rest of her life in the family home, where she died in 1886. The second-floor bedroom of the **Emily Dickinson Museum** has been restored to the way it was during the years 1855–86, when the reclusive poet wrote her most important verse. Her work remained unpublished until after her death. Over time critics proclaimed it to be the work of a poetic genius. The **Jones Library** has displays on Dickinson's life and works, as well as collections on poet Robert Frost, who taught at Amherst College in the 1940s.

Mead Art Museum
Amherst College. **Tel** (413) 542-2335. **Open** 9am–5pm Tue–Thu, Sat & Sun, 9am–8pm Fri. **Closed** mid-Dec–late Jan.

Beneski Museum of Natural History
Amherst College. **Tel** (413) 542-2165. **Open** year-round: 11am–4pm Tue–Sun.

Emily Dickinson Museum
280 Main St. **Tel** (413) 542-8161. **Open** Mar–Dec: call for hours. obligatory.

Jones Library
43 Amity St. **Tel** (413) 256-4090. **Open** 9am–5:30pm Mon–Wed, Fri & Sat, 9am–8:30pm Tue & Thu, 1–5pm Sun. **Closed** Jun–Aug: Sun. Special collections: **Open** year-round: 2–5pm Mon & Sat, 10am–5pm Tue–Fri.

⓱ Northampton
🏙 30,000. ✈ 36 miles (58 km) S in Windsor Locks, CT. 🚌
ℹ 99 Pleasant St. (413) 584-1900.

A lively center for the arts and known for its bar scene, Northampton has a well-preserved Victorian-style Main Street lined with craft galleries and shops. The town is also home to the 1871 **Smith College**, the largest privately endowed women's college in the nation. The handsome campus has a notable **Museum of Art** and the **Lyman Plant House and Conservatory**, known for its flower shows and the arboretum

Beautiful bloom at Smith College's Lyman Plant House

and gardens. South of Northampton in Holyoke, visitors can explore the trails in the 3-sq-mile (7-sq-km) **Mount Tom State Reservation**. Nearby is the Norwottuck Rail Trail, a popular walking and biking path that runs along an old railroad bed connecting Northampton to neighboring Amherst.

Smith College Museum of Art
Elm St., Northampton. **Tel** (413) 585-2760. **Open** 10am–4pm Tue–Sat, noon–4pm Sun.

Lyman Plant House and Conservatory
College Lane, Northampton. **Tel** (413) 585-2740. **Open** year-round: 8:30am–4pm daily. **Closed** Thanksgiving, Dec 25–Jan 1.

Mount Tom State Reservation
125 Reservation Rd., Holyoke. **Tel** (413) 534-1186. **Open** year-round: 8am–dusk daily. Visitor center: **Open** Memorial Day–mid-Oct: Wed–Sun. Call for hours. partial.

⓲ Deerfield
🏙 5,300. ✈ 52 miles (84 km) S in Windsor Locks, CT. ℹ 18 Miner St., Greenfield (413) 773-9393.

A one-time frontier outpost that was almost annihilated by Indian raids in the late 17th century, Deerfield survived and its farmers prospered, building gracious clapboard homes along the mile-(1.6-km-) long center avenue known simply as "The Street."

Sixty of these remain within **Historic Deerfield** and are carefully preserved. Some of the buildings now serve as museums, exhibiting a broad range of period furniture and decorative arts, including silverware, ceramics, and textiles. The Flynt Center of Early New England Life schedules changing exhibitions on early life in western Massachusetts. Visitors seeking a photo opportunity can drive to the summit of **Mount Sugarloaf State Reservation** in South Deerfield for views of the Connecticut River Valley.

Historic Deerfield
The Street, Old Deerfield. **Tel** (413) 775-7214. **Open** Dec–Mar: call for hours; Apr–Nov: 9:30am–4:30pm daily. **Closed** Thanksgiving, Dec 24, Dec 25. W historic-deerfield.org

Mount Sugarloaf State Reservation
US 116, South Deerfield. **Tel** (413) 665-2928. **Open** May–Dec: 8am–dusk daily.

White clapboard house and picket fence in historic Deerfield

⑲ Tour of the Mohawk Trail

Originally an Indian trade route, this trail was a popular artery for early pioneers. In 1914 the trail, which stretches for 63 miles (100 km) from Orange to North Adams along Route 2, became a paved road. The choicest section of the route, from Greenfield to North Adams, was the first officially designated scenic drive in New England. This twisting road offers magnificent mountain views, particularly in the sharp hairpin curves leading into North Adams, and is one of the most popular fall foliage routes.

② Charlemont
A modest statue here, *Hail to the Sunrise*, honors the Mohawk tradition.

③ Hairpin Turn
This sharp bend in the road offers soaring views of Mount Greylock.

Mount Greylock

Hoosic River

Key

▬ Tour route

═ Other road

④ North Adams
North Adams is near America's only naturally formed marble bridge.

⑳ Williamstown

🏔 8,000. ✈ 47 miles (75 km) W in Albany, NY. 🚌 ℹ Jct Rtes 2 & 7 (413) 458-9077 or (800) 214-3799.

Art lovers make pilgrimages to The **Sterling and Francine Clark Art Institute** to see its private art collection, strong on French Impressionists, including more than 30 Renoirs, and housed in a post-modern building. The grounds of this hilltop museum also include trails through forest and meadow that are open to hikers and, in winter, snowshoers. The **Williams College Museum of Art** is also notable for a collection that ranges from ancient Assyrian stone reliefs to Andy Warhol's (1927–87) final self-portrait.

The summertime Williamstown Theater Festival, founded in 1954, is known for its high-quality productions, which often feature big-name Broadway and Hollywood stars.

Degas statue at Clark Institute

A 19th-century Steinway at the Sterling and Francine Clark Art Institute

🏛 **Sterling and Francine Clark Art Institute**
225 South St. **Tel** (413) 458-2303. **Open** 10am–5pm Tue–Sun (Jul & Aug: daily). 🎟 (Jun–Oct only). ▱ ♿
ⓦ clarkart.edu

🏛 **Williams College Museum of Art**
Main St. **Tel** (413) 597-2429. **Open** 10am–5pm Thu–Tue (Jun–Aug: 10am–5pm daily). ♿ ⓦ wcma.org

Environs
More art can be found 7 miles (11 km) east in North Adams at the **Massachusetts Museum of Contemporary Art** (MASS MoCA). Seven interconnected buildings, part of a 19th-century factory, with enormous indoor spaces, elevated walkways, and outdoor courtyards display cutting-edge art. The complex is able to house sculptures and paintings that are too large for most conventional museums.

🏛 **Massachusetts Museum of Contemporary Art**
1040 MASS MoCA Way. **Tel** (413) 662-2111. **Open** 11am–5pm Wed–Mon (Jul–Sep: 10am–6pm daily). 🎟 ♿
🏠 ⓦ massmoca.org

① Shelburne Falls
This small, 19th-century village, with its many original houses, is divided by the Deerfield River. The river is spanned by an old trolley bridge decked in flowers.

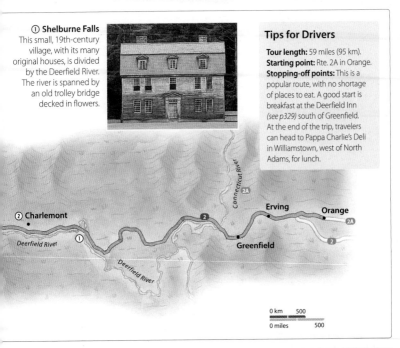

② Charlemont · ① · Erving · Orange · Greenfield
Deerfield River · Connecticut River

0 km 500
0 miles 500

㉑ Mount Greylock State Reservation

Off Rte. 7, Lanesborough. **Open** (Auto road open late-May–Oct.) (413) 499-4262. **mass.gov/dcr/parks**

The Appalachian Trail *(see pp26–7)*, the popular 2,000-mile (3,200-km) hiking path running from Georgia to Maine, crosses Mount Greylock's summit. At 3,491 ft (1,064 m), Greylock is the highest peak in Massachusetts and offers panoramic views of five states. The auto road to the summit is open from late May through October. Hiking trails in the 2-sq-mile (5-sq-km) park remain open and are particularly popular during fall foliage season. At the summit visitors can climb Veterans' Memorial Tower for an even more panoramic view.

㉒ Hancock Shaker Village

Rte. 20, outside Pittsfield. **Tel** (413) 443-0188. **Open** mid-Apr–late May: 10am–4pm daily; late May–Oct: 10am–5pm daily. **hancockshakervillage.org**

Founded in 1783, this was the third in a series of 19 Shaker settlements established in the Northeast and Midwest as utopian communities. The Shakers, so-called because they often trembled and shook during moments of worship and prayer, believed in celibacy and equality of the sexes, with men and women living separately but sharing authority and responsibilities. At its peak in the 1830s, there were 300 residents living in the village. Now the community has no resident Shakers.

Authentic Shaker door latch at Hancock Shaker Village

Twenty of the 100 original buildings have been restored, including the tri-level round stone barn, cleverly designed so that as many as 52 head of cattle could be fed by a single farmhand from a central core. The Brick Dwelling can house up to 100 people, and has a meeting room used for weekday worship and a communal dining room, where traditional Shaker fare is served on select evenings.

Presentations on the Shaker way of life include demonstrations of chair-, broom-, and oval box-making. In the Discovery Room visitors may try on reproduction Shaker clothing and also try their hand at crafts such as weaving. An orientation exhibit and videos in several buildings provide historical background.

Summit Veteran's Memorial Tower atop Mount Greylock

For map symbols *see back flap*

Picturesque Bash Bish Falls in Mount Washington State Forest

㉓ The Berkshires

✈ 37 miles (60 km) NE in Albany, NY.
🚉 Pittsfield. 🛈 3 Hoosac St., Adams
(413) 743-4500; (800) 237-5747.
Ⓦ berkshires.org

Visitors have long been attracted to the peaceful wooded hills, green valleys, rippling rivers, and waterfalls of this western corner of Massachusetts. Among the first tourists were writers such as Henry Wadsworth Longfellow (1807–82), Herman Melville (1819–91), and Nathaniel Hawthorne (1804–64). When the three wrote about the natural beauty of the area, the location caught the attention of many of the region's wealthy people, who began to spend their summers here. Now the region is a year-round playground, popular for its culture as well as for the

ample opportunities it provides for outdoor recreation.

The area is speckled with small towns and country villages. Great Barrington to the south and Pittsfield to the north are the commercial centers of the region, while Lenox and Stockbridge are cultural meccas. The old cotton and woolen mills in Housatonic are finding new life as art galleries, and Main Street of Sheffield is lined with interesting little antique shops.

Among the most popular walking and hiking trails in the Berkshires are Bartholemew's Cobble in Sheffield and Bash Bish Falls in the **Mount Washington State Forest**. A trail leads to the summit of Monument Mountain and affords beautiful views. Reputedly, it was on a hike up the mountain that Herman Melville first met Nathaniel Hawthorne, forming a friendship that resulted in Melville's dedicating his novel *Moby-Dick* to his fellow author.

🏞 Mount Washington State Forest
Rte. 41 S. **Tel** (413) 528-0330.
Open sunrise–sunset. 🖼

Pittsfield

Although primarily a commercial hub, Pittsfield has a growing cultural scene, including the award-winning **Barrington Stage Company**. The town's literary shrine is

Life-size model of *Stegosaurus* at Berkshire Museum in Pittsfield

Arrowhead, an 18th-century home in the shadow of Mount Greylock, where Herman Melville lived from 1850 to 1863 and where he wrote his masterpiece *Moby-Dick*. The **Berkshire Museum** has a large collection of items covering the disciplines of history, natural science, and fine art. The museum's aquarium has 20 tanks for local and exotic sea creatures. The galleries are notable for their works by such 19th-century American masters as George Inness (1825–94) and Frederic Church (1826–1900).

🎭 Barrington Stage Company
30 Union St. **Tel** (413) 236-8888.
Ⓦ barringtonstageco.org

🏠 Arrowhead
780 Holmes Rd. **Tel** (413) 442-1793.
Open late May–mid-Oct: 9:30am–5pm daily; rest of year by appt.
🎫 🖼 ♿ first floor only. 🏠 🖼
Ⓦ mobydick.org

🏛 Berkshire Museum
39 South St. **Tel** (413) 443-7171. **Open** 10am–5pm Mon–Sat, noon–5pm Sun.
Closed public hols. 🖼 ♿ 🏠 🖼
Ⓦ berkshiremuseum.org

Lenox
In the late 19th century the gracious village of Lenox became known as the "inland Newport" for the lavish summer "cottages" built by prominent families such as the Carnegies and the Vanderbilts. Before the 1929 Great Depression, there were more than 70 grand estates gracing the area. While some of the millionaires have since moved away, many of their lavish homes remain in service as schools, cultural institutions, resorts, and posh inns. One of the more prominent mansions is **The Mount**, built in 1902 by

Gathering hay by oxcart at Hancock Shaker Village

Typical town house in the village of Lenox

Pulitzer Prize-winning author Edith Wharton (1862–1937).

Lenox gained new status as a center of culture in 1937 when the 0.8-sq-mile (2-sq-km) Tanglewood estate became the summer home of the Boston Symphony Orchestra. Music lovers flock for concerts to the 1,200-seat Seiji Ozawa Hall or the open Music Shed, where many enjoy picnicking and listening to the music on the surrounding lawn. Jazz and popular concerts are interspersed with the classical program. Tanglewood's name is credited to Nathaniel Hawthorne, who lived in a house on the estate at one time and wrote some of his short stories here.

The Mount
2 Plunkett St. **Tel** (413) 551-5111.
Open mid-May–Oct: 10am–5pm daily. 🎟 🚫 ♿ 📷 ✉
W edithwharton.org

Stockbridge
Stockbridge was founded in 1734 by missionaries seeking to educate and convert the local

Figures of *Andromeda* and *Memory* at Chesterwood

Mohegan Indians. The simple **Mission House** (c.1739) was built by Reverend John Sergeant for his bride. Today the house contains period pieces and Indian artifacts.

The town's quaint main street, dominated by the 1897 Red Lion Inn, has been immortalized in the popular paintings of Norman Rockwell (1894–1978), one of America's most beloved illustrators. The painter lived in Stockbridge for 25 years, and the country's largest collection of Rockwell originals can be seen at the **Norman Rockwell Museum**.

Stockbridge has been home to its share of prominent residents, including sculptor Daniel Chester French (1850–1931), who summered at his **Chesterwood** estate. It was here that French created the working models for his famous *Seated Lincoln* (1922) for the Lincoln Memorial in Washington, DC. The models remain in the studio along with other plaster casts. During the summer months the grounds are used to exhibit sculpture. **Naumkeag Museum and Gardens** is a graceful 1885 mansion built for Joseph H. Choate, US Ambassador to the UK and one of the era's leading attorneys. The 26-room house is appointed with its original furnishings and an art collection that spans three centuries. Of note is the exhibit of Chinese porcelains. With their formal gardens, the grounds are also a work of art.

🏠 **Mission House**
19 Main St. **Tel** (413) 298-3239.
Open Memorial Day–Columbus Day; call for tour hours. 🎟 ✉

🏛 **Norman Rockwell Museum**
Rte. 183. **Tel** (413) 298-4100. **Open** May–Oct: 10am–5pm daily; Nov–Apr: 10am–4pm Mon–Fri, 10am–5pm Sat & Sun. **Closed** Jan 1, Thanksgiving, Dec 25. 🎟 🚫 ♿ 📷 W nrm.org

🏠 **Chesterwood**
4 Williamsville Rd. **Tel** (413) 298-3579.
Open late May–Oct: 10am–5pm daily. 🎟 🚫 ♿ partial. ✉
W chesterwood.org

🏛 **Naumkeag Museum and Gardens**
Prospect Hill. **Tel** (413) 298-3239.
Open Memorial Day–Columbus Day: 10am–5pm daily. 🎟 ✉

Relaxed setting for the Tanglewood summer concert series

The Arts in the Berkshires

The Berkshires region has one of America's richest summer menus of performing arts. As well as Boston Symphony Orchestra concerts at Tanglewood, Aston Magna presents baroque concerts at several locations. The Berkshire Choral Festival is held in Sheffield, and the Barrington Stage Company performs in Pittsfield. The Jacob's Pillow Dance Festival in Becket, the oldest such event in the nation, presents leading international companies. The Berkshire Theater Festival and the Williamstown Theater Festival are among the oldest and most respected summer theaters in the nation. Shakespeare & Company presents acclaimed productions of the Bard's works, as well as thought-provoking new plays.

RHODE ISLAND

With an area of just over 1,200 sq miles (3,100 sq km), Rhode Island is the smallest of the 50 states. However, its historic towns, unspoiled wilderness areas, and a pristine shoreline dotted with inlets and tranquil harbors make the place a lively and easily explored holiday destination.

For such a small state, "Little Rhody" was founded on big ideals. Driven from the Massachusetts Bay colony in 1636 for his outspoken beliefs on religious freedom, clergyman Roger Williams (1604–83) established a settlement on the banks of Narragansett Bay. He called the town Providence and founded it upon the tenets of freedom of speech and religious tolerance – principles that would be formally introduced in the First Amendment to the US Constitution in 1781. This forward-thinking spirit made Rhode Island the site of America's first synagogue and Baptist church and some of the nation's earliest libraries, public schools, and colleges. In May 1776 Rhode Island followed the lead of New Hampshire and formally declared its independence from British rule.

Although its 400-mile (645-km) shoreline is considered small in comparison to those of neighboring states, Rhode Island has earned its nickname, the Ocean State. In the 17th century, its port towns were primary players in the burgeoning maritime trade with the West Indies. Today some 120 public beaches provide opportunities for swimming, scuba diving, boating, windsurfing, and fishing. Pleasure craft can be seen skimming the waters of Narragansett Bay. Home to the America's Cup yacht races between 1930 and 1985, Newport is well-known as one of the world's great yachting centers. But not all of Rhode Island's allure is found on the waterfront. More than 50 percent of the state is covered in woodland. The 28 state parks are ideal for outdoor activities; three allow camping.

Fishing at dusk on beautiful Narragansett Bay

◄ Castle Hill Lighthouse on Narragansett Bay, Newport

Exploring Rhode Island

Not an island at all, the state of Rhode Island does, however, contain dozens of islets and peninsulas along the Atlantic coastline. They dot Narragansett Bay, which takes a huge bite out of the eastern portion of the state. Craggy cliffs, grass-covered bluffs, and golden sand beaches mark the shoreline of the Ocean State, which offers an abundance of opportunities for fishing, swimming, boating, surfing, and other aquatic activities. Inland numerous lakes, reservoirs, and swamps (in South County) maintain the maritime atmosphere. Most activity in Rhode Island centers around its two major cities, Providence *(see pp178–81)* and Newport *(see pp186–91)*, but the smaller roads across the western part of the state are perfect for tranquil country drives.

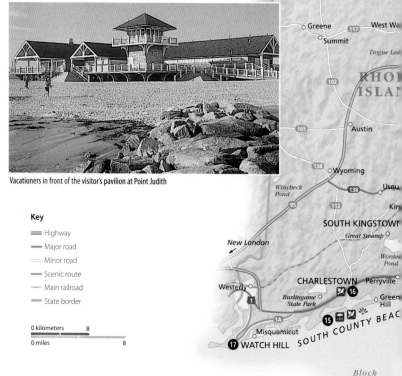

Vacationers in front of the visitor's pavilion at Point Judith

Key

═══ Highway
─── Major road
∷∷∷ Minor road
─── Scenic route
─── Main railroad
─── State border

0 kilometers   8
0 miles   8

Sights at a Glance

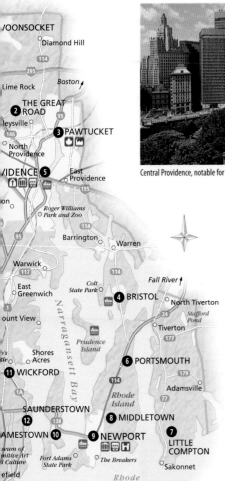

Central Providence, notable for its blend of the historic and modern

Getting Around

Highway 146 follows the Blackstone River Valley south to Providence where it connects with Interstate 95, forming the major north-south artery in the state. For scenery, travelers should stay on Route 1A as it hugs Narragansett Bay and Block Island Sound. An alternative route is 114, which island-hops down the eastern region of the state through Bristol (see p177) to Newport.

Amtrak operates rail lines running from Boston through Providence and down as far as Westerly.

Rhode Island Public Transit Authority (RIPTA) provides bus services throughout most of the state, with an hourly service between Providence and Newport and a summer service to several South County beaches (see pp194–5).

Ferry services to Block Island run year-round from Point Judith (see pp194–5) and seasonally from Newport, Rhode Island, and Fall River, Massachusetts.

Yachts by the score in the harbor at Newport

For map symbols see back flap

Classroom display at the Museum of Work and Culture, Woonsocket

❶ Woonsocket

🚇 44,000. 🛈 175 Main St.,
Pawtucket (401) 724-2200.
🌐 **tourblackstone.com**

A major manufacturing center
located on the busy Blackstone
River, Woonsocket was
transformed from a relatively
small village to a booming mill
town by the development of
the local textile industry in the
19th and early 20th centuries.
Although the textile industry
declined after World War II, the
city remains one of the major
manufacturing hubs.

The **Museum of Work and
Culture** focuses on the impact
of the Industrial Revolution
on the region. The day-to-day
lives of the factory owners,
managers, and immigrant
workers are examined and
explained with the help of a
re-created 1934 union hall,
hands-on displays, models,
and multimedia exhibits.

🏛 **Museum of Work and Culture**
42 S Main St. **Tel** (401) 769-9675.
Open 9:30am–4pm Tue–Fri,
10am–4pm Sat, 1–4pm Sun. 🅿 ♿

❷ The Great Road

🛈 (401) 724-2200.
🌐 **tourblackstone.com**

An often-overlooked gem, the
stretch of Great Road (Route
123) between Saylesville and
Lime Rock follows the course of
the Moshassuck River for 0.6
mile (1 km) and yields eight
historically significant buildings.
Four of these buildings are open
for limited hours and include
the 1693 **Eleazer Arnold
House** and the 1704 **Friends
Meetinghouse**, Rhode Island's
oldest Quaker meeting house in
continuous use. Constructed in

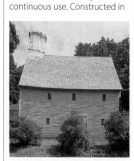

Eleazer Arnold House near Lincoln on the
Great Road

1807 as a toll station and later
serving as a hotel, **North Gate**,
just off the Great Road, now
contains a small museum
room decked out with early
18th-century furniture. Farther
along the road, **Hannaway
Blacksmith Shop** is a one-story,
19th-century structure restored
for blacksmith demonstrations
and special events.

🏛 **Eleazer Arnold House**
487 Great Rd. **Tel** (401) 728-9696.
Open 11am–4pm Sat & Sun. 🅿
🎦 obligatory.

🏛 **Friends Meetinghouse**
374 Great Rd. **Tel** (401) 762-5726.
🎦 obligatory; call for appt.

🏛 **North Gate**
Rte. 246. **Tel** (401) 725-2847.
🎦 obligatory; call for appt.

🏛 **Hannaway Blacksmith Shop**
677 Great Rd. **Tel** (401) 726-0597.
Open 8am–noon Sat & Sun.

❸ Pawtucket

🚇 73,000. 🛈 175 Main St. (401) 724-
2200. 🌐 **tourblackstone.com**

This bustling industrial city, built
on hills sliced by the Blackstone,
Moshassuck, and Ten Mile rivers
is generally acknowledged to
be the birthplace of America's
Industrial Revolution. It was here
in 1793 that mechanical engineer
Samuel Slater (1768–1835) built
the country's first water-powered
cotton-spinning mill.

A major historic landmark, the
**Slater Mill Living History
Museum** includes the restored
Slater Mill and the 1810
Wilkinson Mill, complete with
an authentic 19th-century
machine shop and the only
8-ton (7-tonne) water wheel in

Pawtucket's Slater Mill Living History Museum, home of the first water-powered cotton-spinning mill in the US

For hotels and restaurants in this region see pp314–15 and pp331–3

McCoy Stadium, playing field of the Pawtucket Red Sox baseball team

the US. Also on the site, the 1758 Sylvanus Brown House is furnished with the machinery and personal effects of Sylvanus Brown, a millwright and pattern-maker.

At the 0.3-sq-mile (0.8-sq-km) **Slater Memorial Park** on the Ten Mile River, there are hiking trails, paddleboats, tennis courts, picnic areas, sunken gardens, and a seasonal 1895 Looff carousel. The park is also home to the city's oldest dwelling, the 1685 **Daggett House**, which contains exhibits of 17th-century furnishings and antiques.

The **Pawtucket Red Sox** baseball team plays games at McCoy Stadium. This Boston Red Sox minor league team may relocate to Providence after the 2017 season.

Pawtucket Red Sox logo

🏛 **Slater Mill Living History Museum**
Roosevelt & Slater Aves. **Tel** (401) 725-8638. **Open** Mar, Apr & Nov: 11am–3pm Sat & Sun; May–Oct: 10am–4pm Tue–Sun. ♿ 🅿 ♿

🏞 **Slater Memorial Park**
Newport Ave. **Tel** (401) 728-0500 ext 252. **Open** year-round: 8:30am–dusk daily. ♿ 🅿 for carousel only.

🏛 **Daggett House**
Slater Park off Rte. 1A. **Tel** (401) 722-6931. 🅿 obligatory; call for appt. ♿

Pawtucket Red Sox
McCoy Stadium, Columbus Ave. **Tel** (401) 724-7300. **Open** Apr–early Sep; call for schedule. ♿ ♿
🌐 **pawsox.com**

❹ Bristol

🏛 21,650. 🛈 16 Cutler St., Warren (401) 245-0750.
🌐 **eastbaychamberri.org**

Bristol blossomed in the late 18th century when its status as a major commercial, fishing, whaling, and shipbuilding center made it the nation's fourth-busiest port. The many elegant Federal and Victorian mansions lining Hope, High, and Thames streets attest to those prosperous days. One such fine home is the 1810 **Linden Place**, where scenes from *The Great Gatsby* (1974) were filmed. The Federal-style mansion was built by General George DeWolf (1772–1844) with money he had made from his sugar plantations in Cuba and the slave trade. Historic walking tours are often available.

The trappings of wealth are also in evidence at **Blithewold Mansion and Gardens**. Built in 1894 for Pennsylvania coal baron Augustus Van Wickle (1856–98), the mansion was rebuilt in 1907. It has many gardens and trees from the Far East. The grounds offer spectacular views of Narragansett Bay.

Boating has always been popular with the rich and famous, and Bristol's history as the producer of America's greatest yachts is traced at the **Herreshoff Marine Museum/ America's Cup Hall of Fame**. The museum is located on

Narragansett Bay, at the site of the legendary Herreshoff Manufacturing Company, which built yachts for eight America's Cup races. Photos, models, and restored ships celebrate the golden age of yachting. The museum also operates a sailing school for adults and children, and hosts classic yacht regattas.

Colt State Park, a 0.7-sq-mile (1.9-sq-km) shoreline park features a 3-mile (5-km) shoreline drive along Narragansett Bay, a bicycle trail, many picnic areas, and playing fields. Also on the park grounds is the **Coggeshall Farm Museum**, a restored 1790s coastal farm with a barn, blacksmith shop, and heirloom breeds of domesticated animals. Cyclists and in-line skaters can tour the picturesque East Bay Bike Path, leading some 14.5 miles (23 km) from Bristol to Providence along the coast-hugging route of an old railroad line.

The peaceful rural idyll of Coggeshall Farm Museum

🏛 **Linden Place**
500 Hope St. **Tel** (401) 253-0390. **Open** May–Columbus Day: 10am–4pm Tue–Sat, noon–4pm Sun. 🅿 🅿 ♿

🏛 **Blithewold Mansion**
101 Ferry Rd. **Tel** (401) 253-2707. Mansion: **Open** mid-Apr–mid-Oct: 10am–4pm Tue–Sat, 10am–3pm Sun; call for winter hours. **Closed** public hols. Grounds: **Open** 10am–5pm daily. 🅿 ♿

🏛 **Herreshoff Marine Museum/ America's Cup Hall of Fame**
1 Burnside St. **Tel** (401) 253-5000. **Open** May–Oct: 10am–5pm Wed–Sun. 🅿 🅿 ♿ 🌐 **herreshoff.org**

🏞 **Colt State Park**
Rte. 114. **Tel** (401) 253-7482. **Open** daily. ♿

🏛 **Coggeshall Farm Museum**
Poppasquash Rd. off Rte. 114. **Tel** (401) 253-9062. **Open** 10am–4pm Tue–Sun. 🅿 ♿ 🌐 **coggeshallfarm.org**

❺ Providence

Sandwiched between Boston and New York on busy I-95, Providence is often overlooked by hurried travelers. This is a pity, since the city is blessed with a rich history well worth exploring. Perched on seven hills, Providence started life as a farming community before taking advantage of its location on the Seekonk River to develop into a flourishing seaport in the 17th century. The city then evolved into a hub of industry in the 19th century, with immigrants from Europe pouring in to work in the burgeoning textile mills.

Interior courtyard at Rhode Island School of Design's Museum of Art

Stately buildings along Benefit Street's Mile of History

Exploring Providence

The city is bisected by the Providence River, with the Downtown district (see pp180–81) on the west bank and College Hill to the east. Walking through College Hill, visitors will pass a large number of 18th-century buildings, including the redbrick colonial Market House, built along the waterway in the 1770s and now part of Rhode Island School of Design (RISD).

🏛 Benefit Street's Mile of History

Benefit St. **Tel** (401) 274-1636. Along Benefit Street's Mile of History there are more than 100 houses ranging in style from Colonial and Federal to Greek Revival and Victorian. This lovely, tree-lined street passes the **RISD Museum of Art**, which houses a small but comprehensive collection of artworks from Ancient Egyptian to contemporary American. Also on Benefit Street is the 1838 Greek Revival **Providence Athenaeum**. This is where author Edgar Allan

Poe (1809–49) courted Sarah Whitman, the woman who was the inspiration for his poem *Annabel Lee* (1849). The library, one of the oldest in America, has a collection dating back to 1753. Other architectural gems include the **First Unitarian Church**, which possesses a 2,500-lb (1,350-kg) bell, the largest ever cast by silversmith and Revolutionary War hero Paul Revere (see p192).

🏛 RISD Museum of Art

224 Benefit St. **Tel** (401) 454-6500. **Open** year-round: 10am–5pm Tue–Sun, 10am–9pm 3rd Thu of month. **Closed** public hols. 🅿 🔊 🚻 **w** risd.edu

🏛 Providence Athenaeum

251 Benefit St. **Tel** (401) 421-6970. **Open** year-round: 9am–7pm Mon–Thu, 9am–5pm Fri & Sat, 1–5pm Sun. **Closed** summer: Sat pm, Sun. **w** providenceathenaeum.org

🏛 First Unitarian Church

310 Benefit St. **Tel** (401) 421-7970. **Open** daily. 🔊 🚻 10:30am Sun.

🏛 First Baptist Church in America

75 N Main St. **Tel** (401) 454-3418. **Open** call for hours. 🅿 🔊 🚻 11am Sun (10am in summer).

Founded in 1638 by Roger Williams and built in 1774–5, the First Baptist Church in

| 0 meters | 250 |
| 0 yards | 250 |

Culinary Archives and Museum

Roger Williams Park and Zoo, Johnson and Wales University
Airport
12 miles (19 km) ✈

America is noted for its Ionic columns, intricately carved wood interior, and large Waterford crystal chandelier.

🏛 Governor Stephen Hopkins House

15 Hopkins St. **Tel** (401) 421-0694. **Open** May–Nov: 1–4pm Sat. 🎫 🚻 obligatory.

The 1707 **Governor Stephen Hopkins House** belonged to one of Rhode Island's two signatories to the Declaration of Independence, and contains fine 18th-century furnishings.

🏛 Brown University

45 Prospect St. **Tel** (401) 863-1000. **Open** call for hours. 🎫 ♿ 🚻 📷

Founded in 1764, Brown is the seventh-oldest college in the US and one of the prestigious Ivy League schools *(see pp32–3).* The campus, a rich blend of Gothic and Beaux-Arts styles, is a National Historic Landmark. The John Hay Library has an eclectic collection

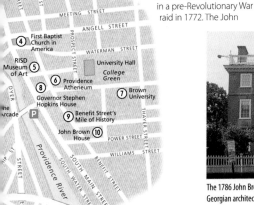
Statue on Brown University campus

that includes artifacts and memorabilia relating to President Abraham Lincoln (1809–65), 5,000 toy soldiers and miniatures, and vintage sheet music. Other buildings of note include University Hall, where French and colonial troops were quartered during the American Revolution; Manning Hall, which houses the University Chapel; the John Carter Brown Library, with its fascinating collection of Americana; and the List Art Center, a striking building designed by Philip Johnson (1906–2005) and featuring classical and contemporary art.

🏛 John Brown House

52 Power St. **Tel** (401) 273-7507. **Open** Dec–Mar: 10:30am–3pm Fri & Sat; Apr–Nov: 1:30–3pm Tue–Fri, 10:30am–3pm Sat. **Closed** public hols. 🎫 🚻 📷 **W** rihs.org

This Georgian mansion was built in 1786 for John Brown (1736–1803) and designed by his brother Joseph (1733–85). A successful merchant and shipowner, John played a lead role in the burning of the British customs ship *Gaspee* in a pre-Revolutionary War raid in 1772. The John

Brown House was the most lavish of its era, introducing Providence to many new architectural elements, including the projecting entrance, Doric portico, and the Palladian window above it. There are Neo-Classical pediments over paired doorways, a grand staircase with twisted balusters, ornate plaster ornamented ceilings, and intricate detailing inside arches over windows and mantels.

Sparing no expense, Brown ordered wallpapers from France and furniture from famed cabinetmakers Townsend and Goddard. The 12-room house has been impeccably restored and is a repository for some of the finest furniture and antiques of that period.

The 1786 John Brown House, an excellent example of Georgian architecture

Providence City Center

For map symbols *see back flap*

Downtown Providence

Downtown Providence, to the west of the Providence River, has undergone several renewal phases. In all, several billion dollars have been pumped into rejuvenation since 1983. Keeping a balance with the old and the new, Providence municipal officials have managed to clean out previously blighted areas by restoring historic buildings, installing more green spaces, and building pedestrian malls and markets. The reclaimed waterfront and developing arts and entertainment district have helped inject new vitality into the city's core. Visitors are best served by exploring on foot so they are free to poke into the numerous shops, cafés, and restaurants.

The Waterfire show, held every summer at Waterplace Park

Exploring Downtown Providence

Providence's rebirth is more than just physical; it is also cultural. The Trinity Repertory Company on Washington Street is home to one of the best theater groups in the country and has performances year-round. Just a block away, the Providence Performing Arts Center, a 1928 movie palace, features Broadway shows, concerts, entertainment for children, and big-screen films, with free lunchtime organ recitals in the spring and fall.

The Trinity Repertory Company, housed in a 1917 historic theater

🌀 Waterplace Park and Riverwalk

Memorial Blvd. **Tel** (401) 751-1177.
Open dawn–dusk daily.

One of the newest and brightest additions to the downtown area is this 174,250-sq-ft (16,200-sq-m) walkway at the junction of the Moshassuck, Providence, and Woonasquatucket rivers. Visitors can stroll the park's cobblestone paths, float under footbridges in

rented kayaks, canoes, or gondolas, or enjoy the free concerts and the Waterfire extravaganza during the summer months.

🏛 The Arcade

65 Weybosset St. **Tel** (401) 454-4568.
♿ 🔲 ✏ 🖥

Known as the "Temple of Trade," this 1828 Greek Revival building has the distinction of being the first indoor shopping mall in the US. The massive, three-story stone complex covers an entire block in Providence's old financial district and has been acclaimed as "one of the three finest commercial buildings in 19th-century America" by New York's Metropolitan Museum of Art. Similar columns on the Westminster entrance match the six 22-ft- (6.7-m-) high Ionic granite columns on Weybosset. Inside a skylight extends the entire length of the building, providing light even on rainy days. After a renovation, the Arcade features boutiques and restaurants at ground level and apartments above.

🔳 Federal Hill

Visitors will know they are in Little Italy once they pass through Federal Hill's impressive arched gateway, decorated with a traditional bronze pine cone. A stripe down the center of the street – in the colors of the Italian flag – confirms that this lively neighborhood in the Federal Hill district is truly Italian in spirit. Bordered by Federal and Broadway streets and Atwells Avenue, the area is marked by Italian groceries, restaurants,

bakeries, import shops, and a pleasant old-world plaza.

🔳 Rhode Island State House

82 Smith St. **Tel** (401) 222-3983.
Open 8:30am–4:30pm Mon–Fri.
Closed public hols. 📷 9am, 10am, 11am, 1pm, 2pm. ♿ 🏠 🖥

Dominating the city landscape, this imposing building was constructed in 1904 by the prominent New York firm McKim, Mead, & White. The white Georgian marble dome is one of the largest self-supported domes in the world. A bronze statue called *Independent Man*, a longtime symbol of Rhode Island's free spirit, tops the magnificent dome. Among the displays in the statehouse are a full-length portrait of President George Washington (1732–99) by Gilbert Stuart (1755–1828), a portrait of Providence resident and Civil War General Ambrose Burnside (1824–81) by Emanuel Leutze

Rhode Island State House, with its white marble dome

For hotels and restaurants in this region see pp314–15 and pp331–3

Roger Williams (1603–1683)

More than an exponent of religious freedom, Roger Williams was also a friend and champion of the area's indigenous inhabitants. He defied the strict restraints of the Massachusetts Bay Colony, believing that all people should be free to worship as they liked without state interference. Banished from Massachusetts for his outspoken views, he established his own colony of Rhode Island and Providence Plantations, obtaining the land from the Narragansett Indians so that "no man should be molested for his conscience sake." It became the country's first experiment in religious liberty.

(1816–68), and the original state charter of 1663.

🏞 Roger Williams Park and Zoo

1000 Elmwood Ave. **Tel** (401) 785-3510. 🚌 Kennedy Plaza. Park **Open** dawn to dusk daily. Zoo **Open** 9am–4pm daily. **Closed** Dec 25.
🏞 zoo. 🎫 ♿ 📷 🚫
W rwpzoo.org

In 1871 Betsey Williams, a direct descendant of Roger Williams, donated 0.2 sq miles (0.4 sq km) of prime real estate to the city for use as parkland. Since that time, another 0.5 sq miles (1.3 sq km) of property have been added to the site. Once farmland, the park now holds gardens and greenhouses, ponds, a lake with paddleboats and rowboats for rent, jogging and cycling paths,

Historic cookbooks from the Culinary Archives and Museum

and a tennis center. Children especially love the carousel and train, the planetarium, and the Museum of Natural History.

Without a doubt, the highlight of the park is the

zoo, which has more than 900 animals and 130 species. Dating back to 1872, the zoo is one of the oldest in the nation, but is constantly updated to meet top animal welfare standards. Its Marco Polo Trek, with camels, snow leopards, and Asian black bears, was enhanced with the addition of endangered red pandas, while a raised viewing deck makes it easier to observe the elephants and giraffes in the Fabric of Africa exhibit.

🏛 Culinary Arts Museum at Johnson & Wales University

315 Harborside Blvd. **Tel** (401) 598-2805. **Open** 10am–5pm Tue–Sat.
🏞 🎫 ♿ W culinary.org

This one-of-a-kind museum contains half a million items relating to the culinary arts – hardly surprising since Johnson & Wales University is devoted to training chefs. The museum was created in 1979, and features Chicago chef Louis Szathmary's vast collection of culinary oddities, including a cannibal eating bowl from Fiji and rings worn by bakers that had been excavated at Pompeii. Other exhibits include an 1833 stagecoach tavern and a mid-20th-century roadside diner.

Roger Williams Park and Zoo, a highlight of downtown Providence

Boats moored at the Sakonnet Wharf near Little Compton

❻ Portsmouth

🏙 16,850. ℹ️ 23 America's Cup Ave., Newport (401) 845-9123 or (800) 976-5122. 🅦 **discovernewport.org**

Portsmouth figures greatly in Rhode Island history. It was the second settlement in the old colony, founded in 1638 just two years after Providence. The town was also the site of the 1778 Battle of Rhode Island, the only major land battle fought in the state during the American Revolution. Bad weather and fierce British resistance forced the US troops to retreat. With the British in hot pursuit, only the courage of the American rear guard enabled most of the soldiers to escape to the sanctuary of Butts Hill Fort. Today some of the fort's redoubts are still visible from Sprague Street, where plaques recount the battle.

Delightful denizens of the Green Animals Topiary Garden

The **Green Animals Topiary Garden** is a more whimsical attraction. Located on a Victorian estate, this lighthearted garden is inhabited by a wild array of topiary creations. In all, some 80 animal shapes – including elephants, camels, giraffes, bears, birds, even a dinosaur – have been trimmed and sculpted from a selection of yew, English boxwood, and California privet. Elsewhere on the grounds, formal flower gardens, a rose arbor, and a museum with an extensive collection of Victorian-era toys delight even the very youngest visitors.

🌱 **Green Animals Topiary Garden**
Cory's Lane. **Tel** (401) 847-1000. **Open** May–early Oct: 10am–5pm daily. 🖼

❼ Little Compton

🏙 3,350. ℹ️ 23 America's Cup Ave., Newport (401) 845-9123 or (800) 976-5122.

Residents of Little Compton relish their isolated nook at the end of a peninsula that borders Massachusetts with good reason: Little Compton is one of the most charming villages in the entire state, protected from the outside world by the surrounding farmlands and woods.

The white-steepled United Congregational Church stands over Little Compton Commons. Beside the church lies the old Commons Burial Ground, with the gravesite of Elizabeth

Padobie (c.1623–1717). The daughter of *Mayflower* Pilgrims Priscilla and John Alden, Padobie was the first white woman born in New England. The 1680 **Wilbor House** was home to eight generations of the Wilbor family. The house is furnished with period pieces and antique household items. Elsewhere on the grounds visitors can explore a one-room schoolhouse and artist's studio. An 1860 barn displays old farm tools, sleighs, a one-horse shay, oxcart, and buggies.

Nearby **Carolyn's Sakonnet Vineyard** is the largest winery in New England. There are free daily wine tastings and guided tours. Beyond the vineyard on Route 77 is Sakonnet Wharf, where the curious can watch fishermen arrive with their catches.

🏠 **Wilbor House**
548 W Main Rd. **Tel** (401) 635-4035. **Open** call for hours. 🖼

Carolyn's Sakonnet Vineyard

◀ The Providence skyline at sunset

Carolyn's Sakonnet Vineyard
162 W Main Rd. **Tel** (401) 635-8486.
Open 10am–6pm Sun–Wed,
10am–8pm Thu–Sat. noon–3pm
daily. **sakonnetwine.com**

Environs
Four miles (6 km) northeast of
Little Compton is Adamsville,
which straddles the
Massachusetts border. On the
Bay State side, **Gray's Grist Mill**
has been grinding Indian flint
corn into meal for johnny cakes
using the same millstones since
1717. The mill is open for tours.

Gray's Grist Mill
638 Adamsville Rd., Westport, MA.
Tel (508) 636-6075. **Open** noon–4pm
Tue–Sat.

Gray's Grist Mill, operating in Adamsville
since the early 18th century

❽ Middletown
19,950. 23 America's Cup Ave.,
Newport (401) 845-9123 or (800)
976-5122.

Nestled between Newport *(see
pp186–91)* and Portsmouth on
Aquidneck Island, Middletown is

Middletown's popular Third Beach

known primarily for its two
popular beaches. **Third Beach**
is located on the Sakonnet
River and is outfitted with a
boat ramp. A steady wind and
relatively calm water make
the beach a favorite among
windsurfers and families with
young children.

Third Beach runs into
the largest and
most beautiful
beach on the
island. Sachuest,
or **Second
Beach**, is widely
considered one of
the best places to surf
in southern New
England. This spacious
strand is rippled with sand
dunes and equipped with
campgrounds. Purgatory Chasm,
a narrow cleft in the rock ledges
on the east side of Easton Point,
provides a scenic outlook over
both the beach and 50-ft-
(15-m-) high Hanging Rock.

Second Beach has yet
another advantage; it is
adjacent to the **Norman Bird**

Inhabitant of the
wildlife area

Sanctuary, a 0.5-sq-mile
(1.3-sq-km) wildlife area with
7 miles (11 km) of walking trails
that are ideal for birding. Some
250 species have been sighted
at this sanctuary, including
herons, egrets, woodcocks,
thrashers, ducks, and swans.
The refuge is home to
numerous four-legged
animals, such as
rabbits and red
foxes. A small
natural history
museum is also
located on the
site, and during the
winter months the
sanctuary trails are
used by cross-country
skiers. Nearby Tiverton Four
Corners is a charming
crossroads village that
combines the bucolic
countryside of riverine Rhode
Island with some of the
commercial sophistication of
Newport. Several galleries sell
clothing, jewelry, weavings,
and pottery made by local
artisans, while cows graze in
the pasture next to the
seasonal ice-cream stand.

Third Beach
Third Beach Rd. **Tel** (401) 849-2822.
Open Memorial Day–Labor Day:
lifeguards on duty 9am–5pm daily.

Second Beach
Third Beach Rd. **Tel** (401) 849-2822.
Open Memorial Day–Labor Day:
lifeguards on duty 8am–6pm daily.

Norman Bird Sanctuary
583 Third Beach Rd. **Tel** (401) 846-
2577. **Open** year-round: 9am–5pm
daily. **Closed** Thanksgiving &
Dec 25.

Waterfowl in Middletown's Norman Bird Sanctuary

❾ Newport

A center of trade, culture, wealth, and military activity for more than 300 years, Newport is a true sightseeing mecca. Historical firsts abound in this small city. America's first naval college and synagogue are here, as are the oldest library in the country and one of the oldest continuously operating taverns. Any visit to the city should include a tour of the mansions from the Gilded Age of the late 19th century, when the rich and famous flocked here each summer to beat New York's heat. These summer "cottage" retreats of the country's wealthiest families, the Vanderbilts and Astors among them, are some of America's grandest private homes.

Public grass courts at the International Tennis Hall of Fame

Advertisement for carved whalebone, or whale ivory

Exploring Newport

Like Italy, Newport has a boot-shaped outline. The city's famous mansions are located on the southeastern heel of the boot, primarily along Bellevue Avenue. Newport's harborfront is to the west, where the laces would be. The main streets, America's Cup Avenue and Thames Street, are notable for restaurants, shops, and colonial buildings. The 1726 **Trinity Church** is on nearby Spring Street.

🏛 Brick Market Museum and Shop

127 Thames St. **Tel** (401) 841-8770. **Open** 10am–5pm daily. 🎥 🚹 📶 ✉

The Brick Market, a commercial hub during the 18th century, is now a museum that provides an excellent introduction to the city's history and architecture. Exhibits include a video of historic Bellevue Avenue. Guided walking tours are also offered.

✡ Touro Synagogue

85 Touro St. **Tel** (401) 847-4794. **Open** call for times. ✡ Shabbat and all Jewish hols. 🎥 🎥 🏛 ✉

America's oldest synagogue, Touro was erected in 1763 by Sephardic Jews who had fled Spain and Portugal in search of religious tolerance. Designed by architect Peter Harrison

(1716–75), it is considered one of the country's finest examples of 18th-century architecture. Services still follow the Sephardic rituals of its founders.

Redwood Library and Athenaeum's stately interior

🏛 Redwood Library and Athenaeum

50 Bellevue Ave. **Tel** (401) 847-0292. **Open** 9:30am–5:30pm Mon–Sat (to 8pm Wed), 1–5pm Sun. **Closed** public hols. 🎥 🚹 📶 **redwoodlibrary.org**

Completed in 1750, the Redwood is the oldest continuously operating library in America and is one of the country's earliest examples of temple-form buildings. In addition to rare books and manuscripts, the library's museum collections contain colonial portraits, sculpture, and furniture.

🏛 International Tennis Hall of Fame

194 Bellevue Ave. **Tel** (401) 849-3990. **Open** 10am–5pm daily. **Closed** Thanksgiving & Dec 25. 🎾 courts available to public. 📶 🚹 🏛 📶 **tennisfame.com**

The hall is housed in the Newport Casino, once a private club for Newport's elite. Founded in 1880, the club installed grass tennis courts to introduce its members to the latest sports rage. The first US National Lawn Tennis Championship, later known as the US Open, was held here in 1881. Today the museum displays everything from antique rackets to the "comeback" outfit worn by Monica Seles (b.1972). The grass courts are the only ones in the US open to the public.

🏖 Cliff Walk

Begins at Memorial Blvd. **Tel** (401) 845-9123. **Open** year-round: dawn–dusk daily. 🎥

This 3.5-mile (5.5-km) walk along Newport's rugged cliffs offers some of the best views of the Gilded-Age mansions. Local fishermen preserved public access to the trail by going to court when wealthy mansion-owners tried to have it closed. The walk was designated a National Recreation Trail in 1975. The Forty Steps, each step named for someone lost at sea, lead to the ocean.

The breathtaking Cliff Walk, popular with residents as well as visitors

⊞ International Yacht Restoration School

449 Thames St. **Tel** (401) 848-5777.
Open call for hours. 🗗 🕭 🐨 iyrs.org

Founded in 1993, this small school provides a fascinating look at yacht restoration. Visitors can observe students from the mezzanine, and tour the waterfront campus. The top-floor library displays artifacts such as miniature model boats and yachting trophies and provides a stunning harbor view.

Students at work at International Yacht Restoration School

🏰 Fort Adams State Park

Harrison Ave. **Tel** (401) 847-2400.
Open sunrise–sunset daily. 🗗

Fort Adams is one of the largest military forts in the US. Completed in 1857 at a cost of $3 million, it was designed to house 2,400 troops.

From this strategic location at the mouth of Newport Harbor, visitors can watch the boat

Fort Adams, centerpiece of Fort Adams State Park

traffic on the harbor as well as the East Passage Narragansett Bay. The surrounding park is popular for swimming, fishing, boating, picnicking, and for playing soccer and rugby. It is also home to the July 4 fireworks and to Newport's world-famous folk and jazz music festivals (*see p37*).

⊞ Newport Mansions

424 Bellevue Ave. **Tel** (401) 847-1000.
Open some mansions are open year-round; call for hours. **Closed** Dec 24 & 25. 🗗 🗗 obligatory. 🕭 partial. 🖾 🐨 newport mansions.org

Built between 1748 and 1902, nine of these summer "cottages," most of them along Bellevue Avenue, are open for guided tours. Modeled on European palaces and decorated with the finest artworks, the mansions were used for only ten weeks of the year. The Breakers (*see*

pp190–91) is one of the finest examples.

🏛 Naval War College Museum

686 Cushing Rd. **Tel** (401) 841-4052.
Open 10am–4:30pm Mon–Fri (Jun–Sep: also noon–4:30pm Sat & Sun).
🗗 🕭

This site preserves the history, art, and science of naval warfare and the heritage of Narragansett Bay. Founded in 1885, the college is the oldest naval institute of higher learning in the world, where education and research is carried out for the US Navy. The museum houses ship models and maritime art. Due to increased security, visitors must call in advance.

Newport City Center

① Trinity Church
② Brick Market Museum and Shop
③ Touro Synagogue
④ Redwood Library and Athenaeum
⑤ International Tennis Hall of Fame

0 meters   300
0 yards   300

Key

▪ Street-by-Street map *see pp188–9*

Around Washington Square

Newport's first settlers were religious moderates fleeing persecution at the hands of Puritans in the Massachusetts Bay colony. With its accessible harbor, the town quickly developed into a thriving seaport. However, its location also made it vulnerable. When Rhode Island declared independence from colonial rule in 1776, British forces occupied the city. Before they were driven out in 1780, the occupying army destroyed much of the town. Thanks to preservation efforts, a number of colonial buildings survive. Several of them can be seen on this tour around historic Washington Square, the center of Newport's political and economic life during Colonial times.

Architectural detail is typical of the Washington Square district.

White Horse Tavern
Granted its liquor license in 1673, the White Horse claims to be the nation's oldest continuously operating tavern. At one time, state legislators gathered here before sitting at Colony House.

St. Paul's Methodist Church was built in 1807. A simple structure, it reflects the continuation of the Colonial style in the decades after independence.

Bank Newport

Rivera House, currently a bank, was once the home of Abraham Rivera, a prominent member of Newport's Jewish and business communities. Rivera laid the cornerstone of Touro Synagogue.

Statue of Oliver Hazard Perry
Oliver Hazard Perry (1785–1819) defeated British forces in a pivotal naval battle in the War of 1812, securing control of Lake Erie for the US. Perry's former home at No. 29 Touro Street faces the statue.

★ **Brick Market Museum and Shop**
The Brick Market, once the center of commerce, has been renovated to house this museum (see p186) that brings to life Newport's economic, social, and sporting past.

Colony House
This grand structure from 1739 was the state's main seat of government until 1900. Rhode Island's declaration of independence was read from the balcony in May 1776, two months before the July 4th proclamation in Philadelphia.

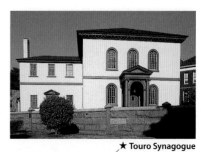

Wanton-Lyman-Hazard House
(c.1697) is the oldest surviving home in Newport.

Newport County
Court House

★ **Touro Synagogue**
Dedicated in 1763, Touro is the oldest synagogue in the country (see p186).

TONE ST

HOZIER

SPRING STREET

TOURO ST

DIVISION ST

SPRING STREET

CLARKE STREET

The Newport Historical Society
is a resource center for studies of Newport history. Open to researchers only, the library holds historic manuscripts and a small art gallery.

AMES STREET

Artillery
Company

Key

— Suggested route

Pineapple Symbolism

While on trade missions to Africa and the West Indies, Newport's sailors ate fresh fruit to ward off scurvy. What they did not eat, they brought home to their families. It became tradition in Newport to place a pineapple on the gatepost when the seagoing man of the house had returned safely. In time, the fruit became a local symbol of hospitality and was often incorporated into the front door's transom or applied directly to the door itself. Pineapples appear on many old Newport homes.

0 meters   25

0 yards   25

The Breakers

The architecture and ostentation of the Gilded Age of the late 1800s reached its pinnacle with the Breakers, the summer home of railroad magnate Cornelius Vanderbilt II (1843–99). Completed in 1895, the four-story, 70-room limestone structure surpassed all other Newport mansions in extravagance. US architect Richard Morris Hunt (1827–95) modeled the building after the 16th-century palaces in Turin and Genoa. Its interior is adorned with marble, alabaster, stained glass, gilt, and crystal.

The Structure
Built in the Italian Renaissance style, the Breakers is alleged to have cost more than $10 million – a huge sum of money in 1895.

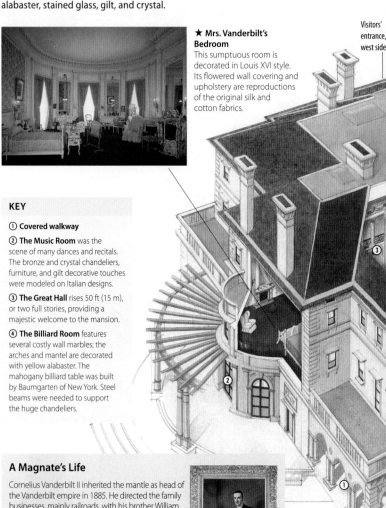

★ **Mrs. Vanderbilt's Bedroom**
This sumptuous room is decorated in Louis XVI style. Its flowered wall covering and upholstery are reproductions of the original silk and cotton fabrics.

Visitors' entrance, west side

KEY

① **Covered walkway**

② **The Music Room** was the scene of many dances and recitals. The bronze and crystal chandeliers, furniture, and gilt decorative touches were modeled on Italian designs.

③ **The Great Hall** rises 50 ft (15 m), or two full stories, providing a majestic welcome to the mansion.

④ **The Billiard Room** features several costly wall marbles; the arches and mantel are decorated with yellow alabaster. The mahogany billiard table was built by Baumgarten of New York. Steel beams were needed to support the huge chandeliers.

A Magnate's Life

Cornelius Vanderbilt II inherited the mantle as head of the Vanderbilt empire in 1885. He directed the family businesses, mainly railroads, with his brother William for 11 years, before suffering a paralyzing stroke. He convalesced at the Breakers, but died in 1899 at the age of 56. At the time of his death, the local gossip held that he had more money than the US Mint.

Cornelius Vanderbilt II

★ The Dining Room
The most richly adorned room in the mansion, the two-story, 2,400-sq-ft (220-sq-m) dining room has two huge crystal chandeliers and a stunning arched ceiling.

VISITORS' CHECKLIST

Practical Information
Ochre Point Ave. **Tel** (401) 847-1000. **Open** 9am–5pm daily (Jul–Oct: to 6pm, Nov & Dec: to 4pm, Jan–mid-Mar: 10am–4pm). **Closed** Thanksgiving, Dec 25.
w newportmansions.org

Transport
67.

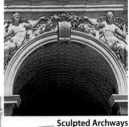

Upper Loggia
The upper loggia offers a view of the sunrise over the Atlantic Ocean. Its ceiling is painted to look like canopies against a clouded sky.

Sculpted Archways
Ornately carved archways are inspired by Italian Renaissance-style palazzi.

★ The Morning Room
The ceiling of this east-facing room is adorned with paintings of the Four Seasons, the mahogany doors with the Four Elements. All cornices, pilasters, and panels were made in France and shipped to Newport.

Sunbathing on the rocks at Beavertail Lighthouse and State Park

⑩ Jamestown

🏙 5,000. ℹ️ 23 America's Cup Ave.,
Newport (401) 845-9123 or (800)
976-5122.

Named for England's King
James II (1633–1701),
Jamestown is located on
Conanicut Island and linked
to Newport *(see pp186–91)*
and the mainland by a pair
of bridges. During the
Revolutionary War, British
troops torched much of the
town, sparing very few of the
houses from that era.

The town is best known for
the **Beavertail Lighthouse and
State Park**, perched at the
southernmost tip of the island.
The first lighthouse here was
built in 1749 and was
subsequently replaced by the
present structure in 1856. As
with many New England
lighthouses, the coastal vistas
from Beavertail are beautiful.
The winds, currents, and surf
can be heavy at times, but on
calm days hiking, climbing, and
sunbathing on the rocks are
favorite pastimes.

Situated on the site of an
early fort and artillery battery,
Fort Wetherill State Park
offers great scenic outlooks,
picnic tables, and a boat ramp.
The park is a popular place
for saltwater fishing, boating,
and scuba diving. Legend
has it that notorious privateer
Captain Kidd (1645–1701)
stashed some of his plundered
loot in the park's Pirate Cave.

**Beavertail Lighthouse and
State Park**
Beavertail Pt. **Tel** (401) 423-9941. Park:
Open dawn to dusk daily. Lighthouse:
Open call for hours. 🛒 ♿

Fort Wetherill State Park
Fort Wetherill Rd. **Tel** (401) 423-1771.
Open dawn to dusk daily. 🛒 ♿

⑪ Wickford

ℹ️ 4808 Tower Hill Rd., Wakefield
(401) 789-4422 or (800) 548-4662.
🌐 southcountyri.com

Considered a part of North
Kingstown (population 26,000),
the quaint village of Wickford
lies in the northern-most point
of Washington County, also
known as South County.
Wickford's many 18th- and
19th-century houses are a
magnet for artists and
craftsmen. John Updike *(see*

p35), author of *Rabbit Run* (1960),
had family roots here. The 1745
Updike House on Pleasant Street
is just one of some 60 buildings
constructed before 1804.

Day-trippers hailing from
Providence and Connecticut
are apt to jam Wickford's
picturesque harbor and
shopping streets. At the corner
of Brown and Phillips Streets,
the Kayak Center of Rhode
Island offers extensive paddling
tours on Narragansett Bay.

Old Narragansett Church
(more commonly called Old
St. Paul's) is one of the oldest
Episcopal churches in the US,
dating back to 1707, with box
pews, an organ from 1660, and
an upstairs gallery to which
plantation slaves were relegated.
Artist Gilbert Stuart (1755–1828)
was baptized here in a silver
baptismal font given to the

Wickford's tranquil harbor

Smith's Castle, just outside of Wickford

church as a gift by England's Queen Anne (1665–1714).

Environs

One mile north of town is **Smith's Castle**, one of America's oldest plantation houses. In 1678 settler Richard Smith built a dwelling on the site. Hardly a castle, the structure served as a garrison for the soldiers who had participated in the 1675 Great Swamp Fight against the Narragansett Indians. The battle resulted in a mass slaughter of Indians, which set off a chain of tragic events culminating in the retaliatory destruction of the garrison and the death of 40 soldiers. Later the structure was rebuilt and acquired by the Updike family in 1692. Subsequent additions and renovations transformed the structure into one of the most handsome plantation houses on the Rhode Island shore. The house contains fine paneling, 17th- and 18th-century furnishings, china, and a chair once owned by Roger Williams (see pp173, 181).

🏠 **Smith's Castle**
55 Richard Smith Dr. **Tel** (401) 294-3521. **Open** call for hours. ♿ 📷

⑫ Saunderstown

ℹ 8045 Post Rd., North Kingstown (401) 295-5566.

Located between Wickford and Narragansett, this town has two main attractions. The gambrel-roofed **Gilbert Stuart Birthplace** was built in 1751 along the Mattatuxet River. Stuart (1755–1828), whose portraits of US presidents were

to bring him lasting fame, was born here. His best-known portrait, that of George Washington, graces the US one-dollar bill.

On the first floor of the house, Stuart's father built a large kitchen and snuff mill, the first in America, powered by a wooden water wheel. The upstairs living quarters are furnished with authentic period pieces.

Also in town is the 18th-century **Silas Casey Farm**. Still in operation, the farm has been occupied by the same family since 1702. The 0.6-sq-mile (1.5-sq-km) property is ringed by almost 30 miles (48 km) of stone walls. Organic vegetables are grown on the farm and sold at a farmers' market on Saturday mornings.

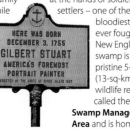

Plaque at Stuart Birthplace

🏠 **Gilbert Stuart Birthplace**
815 Gilbert Stuart Rd. **Tel** (401) 294-3001. **Open** 10am–4pm Thu–Mon (mid-Jun–Aug: 10am–4pm daily). **Closed** mid-Oct–Apr. ♿ 📷

🏠 **Silas Casey Farm**
2325 Boston Neck Rd. **Tel** (401) 295-1030. **Open** Jun–mid-Oct: 1–5pm Tue & Thu, 9am–2pm Sat. **Closed** mid-Oct–May. ♿ 📷 ♿

⑬ South Kingstown

🏕 26,700. ℹ 230 Old Tower Hill Rd., Wakefield. **Tel** (401) 783-2801.

South Kingstown is a 55-sq-mile (142-sq-km) town that encompasses 15 villages,

including Kingstown, Green Hill, Wakefield, and Snug Harbor. The town is home to the **Museum of Primitive Art and Culture**. Located in an 1856 post office, the museum displays weapons, tools, and implements of aboriginal cultures around the world, including a range of artifacts from prehistoric New England.

After visiting the museum, travelers can enjoy some of the region's outdoor charms. Sightseers, particularly those with cameras, will want to make the trek to the top of the observation post at Hannah Robinson Rock and Tower, where they are greeted with expansive views of the Atlantic Ocean and the Rhode Island seashore.

The South County Bike Path is a 5.6-mile (9-km) paved trail, starting at the Kingstown train station, which takes cyclists through Great Swamp, the scene of the 1675 slaughter of 2,000 Narragansett Indians at the hands of soldiers and settlers – one of the bloodiest battles ever fought in New England. The swamp is now a pristine 5-sq-mile (13-sq-km) wildlife refuge called the **Great Swamp Management Area** and is home to creatures such as coyotes, mink, wild turkeys, and ring-necked pheasants. Nature trails lead visitors through dense woodland, past a dike to a boardwalk into a marsh. Birders should use binoculars and visit the refuge during the spring songbird migration. Avoid hunting season.

🏛 **Museum of Primitive Art and Culture**
1058 Kingstown Rd. **Tel** (401) 783-5711. **Open** Sep–Jun: 10am–2pm Wed. 📷

🦌 **Great Swamp Management Area**
Liberty Lane off Great Neck Rd. **Tel** (401) 789-0281. **Open** dawn to dusk daily. 📷

Whale-watching off Point Judith, a popular summer activity

⓮ Narragansett

▲ 18,000. ✈ TF Green Airport.
🛈 36 Ocean Rd. (401) 783-7121.

In the late 19th century this town's waterfront area gained national fame as a fashionable resort, complete with a large casino. In 1900 a devastating fire razed the 1884 casino and many of the lavish hotels. All that remains of the ornate 1884

casino are **The Towers**, two stone towers linked by a Romanesque-Revival-style arch.

Today rolling dice have given way to rolling waves, as the town beach offers some of the best surfing on the East Coast. Nearby the **South County Museum** depicts early Rhode Island life with displays of children's toys, farm tools, weapons, a cobbler's shop, a general store, and a working print shop.

🏛 **The Towers**
35 Ocean Rd. **Tel** (401) 782-2597.
Open call for tours & events schedule or visit the website.
Ⓦ thetowersri.com

🏛 **South County Museum**
Strathmore St. off Rte. 1. **Tel** (401) 783-5400. **Open** May, Jun, Sep: 10am–4pm Fri & Sat; Jul & Aug: 10am–4pm Tue–Sat. 🖼

Environs
Located at the south end of the Narragansett peninsula, **Point Judith** and **Galilee** are departure points for numerous whale-watching cruises, sightseeing boat tours, ferries to Block Island (*see pp196–7*), and charters for deep-sea fishing.

Toward the end of World War II, a German U-boat was sunk just 2 miles (3 km) off the Point Judith Lighthouse. Today the lighthouse affords beautiful views of the ocean. Galilee is famous for its Blessing of the Fleet festival in late July. The Galilee Salt Marsh is popular for birding.

⓰ Charlestown

▲ 6,000. ✈ 🚉 🛈 4945 Old Post Rd. (401) 364-3878.

This small town stretches along 4 miles (6.4 km) of lovely beaches, encompassing the largest saltwater marsh in the state and several points. It is also a convenient base for nature lovers. The 3-sq-mile (8-sq-km) **Burlingame State Park** on Watchaug Pond is equipped with campgrounds, nature trails, swimming and picnic areas, trails for road and mountain bikes, as well as fishing and boating. Birders will enjoy the Audubon Society's **Kimball Wildlife Sanctuary**, located on the south side of the park. The sanctuary is a habitat for many

⓯ South County Beaches

Driving along Highway 1 between Narragansett and Watch Hill, travelers will pass some 100 miles (161 km) of pristine white sand beaches. These thin strands of sand are all that separate Block Island Sound from a series of tidal salt ponds, some of which have been designated national wildlife refuges. The ponds are big lures for bird-watchers hoping to study the egrets, sandpipers, and herons that swim and wade in the salty marshes. Many of the beaches are free to the public, except for parking fees.

Key
▰▰ Major road
▭▭ Other road

⑤ **Misquamicut State Beach**
The state's largest beach has gentle surf and a nearby old-time amusement park with rides for children.

To Westerly

Haversham
Quonochont Pond
Quonochontaug
Weekapaug
Westerly State Airport
Winnapaug Pond
Winnapaug Road
Watch Hill Road
Atlantic Avenue
Watch Hill

kinds of waterfowl and migrating birds, and has a network of easy footpaths.

More outdoor enjoyment can be found at the 0.3-sq-mile (0.7-sq-km) **Ninigret Park**. Tracks lead cyclists and bladers through the grounds, which are graced with a swimming pond, tennis and basketball courts, baseball fields, a bicycle course, a playground, and an 18-hole disc-golf course. Every clear Friday night, the park leaves the gates open to allow visitors to participate in stargazing activities at the **Frosty Drew**

Observatory, which is open year-round. (The facility is unheated, so dress accordingly.)

🏞 Burlingame State Park
Rte. 1A. **Tel** (401) 322-8910.
Open Apr–early Sep: dawn–dusk daily. 🏕 for camping facilities.

🏞 Kimball Wildlife Sanctuary
Prosser Trail. **Tel** (401) 949-5454.
Open dawn–dusk daily.

🏞 Ninigret Park
Rte. 1A. **Tel** (401) 364-1222.
Open dawn–dusk daily. 🚻 ♿

🏞 Frosty Drew Observatory
61 Park Lane, Ninigret Park.

Tel (401) 364-9508. **Open** year-round: Fri (weather allowing).
🅦 frostydrew.org ♿

⑰ Watch Hill

ℹ 1 Chamber Way, Westerly (401) 596-7761.

A village within the town of Westerly, Watch Hill has been an upscale beach haven for the rich and famous since the 19th century. Strolls along Bay Street yield beautiful views of the gingerbread-trimmed Victorian houses on rocky hills above the beach. Visitors to Watch Hill can enjoy the relaxed atmosphere, with a little window-shopping or sunbathing at the beach. The 1867 **Flying Horse Carousel** on the beach is a favorite of children. The vantage point of the Watch Hill Lighthouse offers views of neighboring Connecticut's Fishers Island.

🎠 Flying Horse Carousel
Bay St. **Tel** (401) 348-6007. **Open** mid-Jun–Labor Day: 11am–9pm daily (from 10am Sat & Sun); late May–mid-Jun & Labor Day–mid-Oct: weekends only. 🚻 📷 ⊘

Nature trails through the Kimball Wildlife Sanctuary

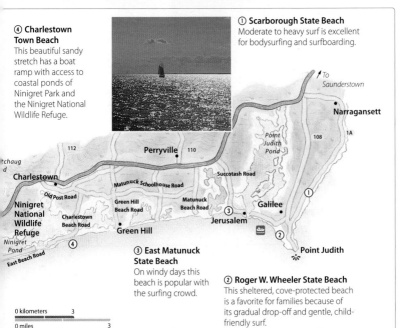

④ **Charlestown Town Beach**
This beautiful sandy stretch has a boat ramp with access to coastal ponds of Ninigret Park and the Ninigret National Wildlife Refuge.

① **Scarborough State Beach**
Moderate to heavy surf is excellent for bodysurfing and surfboarding.

To Saunderstown

Narragansett

112 — Perryville — 110

*chaug
d*

Charlestown

Ninigret National Wildlife Refuge

Ninigret Pond

East Beach Road

Old Post Road

Charlestown Beach Road

Matunuck Schoolhouse Road

Green Hill Beach Road

Green Hill

Succotash Road

Matunuck Beach Road

③

Jerusalem

Galilee

①

②

Point Judith

Point Judith Pond

108

1A

③ **East Matunuck State Beach**
On windy days this beach is popular with the surfing crowd.

② **Roger W. Wheeler State Beach**
This sheltered, cove-protected beach is a favorite for families because of its gradual drop-off and gentle, child-friendly surf.

0 kilometers 3
0 miles 3

⑱ Tour of Block Island

Lying 13 miles (21 km) off the coast, the haven of Block Island has long been a favorite getaway spot for New Englanders. With 25 percent of its wild landscape under protection, Block Island is a wonderful destination for outdoor enthusiasts who enjoy such activities as swimming, fishing, sailing, bird-watching, kayaking, canoeing, and horseback riding. Some 30 miles (48 km) of natural trails entice hikers and cyclists alike to experience the island's natural beauty firsthand.

Colorful lobster buoys ashore on Block Island

④ Great Salt Pond

Completely protected from the ocean, Great Salt Pond has three marinas and is an excellent spot for kayaking and fishing. New Harbor is Block Island's prime marina and boating center.

③ Rodman's Hollow

Nature trails lead hikers through the glacial depression of Rodman's Hollow Natural Area. The wildlife refuge is home to hawks and white-tailed deer. One path takes visitors to the beach at Black Rock Point at the southern extremity of the island.

Key

 Tour route

--- Other road

```
0 meters        500
0 yards         500
```

Dead Man's Cove

Cormorant Point

Gre
P

Grace Cove Road

Champlin Road

Beacon Hill

West Side Road

Beacon Hill Road

Center Road

Cooneymus Road

Cooneymus Swamp

Dickens Road

Black Rock Road

Lakeside Drive

③

Black Rock Point

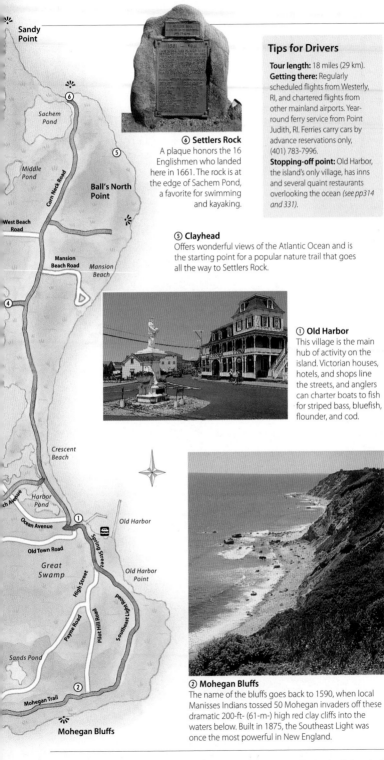

Tips for Drivers

Tour length: 18 miles (29 km).
Getting there: Regularly scheduled flights from Westerly, RI, and chartered flights from other mainland airports. Year-round ferry service from Point Judith, RI. Ferries carry cars by advance reservations only, (401) 783-7996.
Stopping-off point: Old Harbor, the island's only village, has inns and several quaint restaurants overlooking the ocean *(see pp314 and 331).*

⑥ Settlers Rock
A plaque honors the 16 Englishmen who landed here in 1661. The rock is at the edge of Sachem Pond, a favorite for swimming and kayaking.

⑤ Clayhead
Offers wonderful views of the Atlantic Ocean and is the starting point for a popular nature trail that goes all the way to Settlers Rock.

① Old Harbor
This village is the main hub of activity on the island. Victorian houses, hotels, and shops line the streets, and anglers can charter boats to fish for striped bass, bluefish, flounder, and cod.

② Mohegan Bluffs
The name of the bluffs goes back to 1590, when local Manisses Indians tossed 50 Mohegan invaders off these dramatic 200-ft- (61-m-) high red clay cliffs into the waters below. Built in 1875, the Southeast Light was once the most powerful in New England.

For map symbols see back flap

CONNECTICUT

Connecticut is quintessential New England. Its quiet charm is evident everywhere, in scenic villages replete with white steepled churches, immaculate village greens, covered bridges, and old-fashioned clapboard houses ringed by stone walls. Even the state's most bustling cosmopolitan centers contain enclaves of picturesque serenity that invite visitors to poke about at their leisure.

The third-smallest state in the US, Connecticut is brimming with history. One of the country's original 13 colonies, Connecticut has always been a trendsetter, beginning with its adoption in 1639 of the Fundamental Orders of Connecticut – the New World's first constitution. It was on Connecticut soil that the nation's first public library, law school, and amusement park were built. Scholars and soldiers can thank the fertile minds of state residents for giving them the first dictionary and pistol; gourmands, for the hamburger and corkscrew; and children, for the three-ring circus, lollipop, and Frisbee.

Water has played an important role in shaping the state. The Housatonic, Naugatuck, Connecticut, and Thames rivers have been feeding the interior woodlands for thousands of years and acted as the main transportation arteries for early inhabitants. Fueled by waterpower, mill towns sprang up along the rivers, eventually giving way to larger commercial centers. Today these waterways are the arenas of canoeists looking for their next adventure. Houseboats and tour boats offer road-weary passengers unique views of the picturesque towns that hug the banks.

Autumn's annual explosion of color makes it the favorite time of year for visitors to meander along Connecticut's byways, hike the Berkshires, wander the Appalachian Trail (see pp26–7), and indulge in the seasonal bounty of country inns. In addition, the state calendar bulges with eclectic events. Old-fashioned county fairs are held concurrently with cutting-edge performing arts showcases and regattas. When people have had their fill of ballooning and antiquing, they can sample the wares in one of the state's late-summer oyster festivals.

Mystic Seaport's calm harbor

◀ Tower of the Center Church in downtown Hartford

Exploring Connecticut

Compact enough to cross in a few hours, Connecticut has treasures that entice travelers to stay for days. The magnificent shoreline, stretching 105 miles (170 km) from Greenwich near the New York State line northeast to Rhode Island, is scalloped by coves, inlets, and harbors, and dotted with state parks, beaches, and marinas. The coast is punctuated by historically significant houses, culminating in Mystic Seaport *(pp218–19)*, a recreated 18th- and 19th-century seafaring village. The area also attracted America's Impressionist artists. Their works are shown in the state's many museums *(pp206–207)*. Inland hills and valleys are dotted with tiny postcard-perfect villages.

Hartford's Bushnell Park

Beach at Mount Tom State Park

Getting Around

Hugging the coast, Interstate 95 serves as the primary east-west link. Interstate 84 follows a similar route from Danbury through Hartford and beyond. The major north-south artery is Interstate 91. Metro North runs trains from New York City to New Haven. Amtrak's New York-Boston line makes stops along Connecticut's shoreline. Several major bus companies, including Peter Pan and Greyhound, offer interstate services. Seasonal ferries operate New London-Block Island, Rhode Island, and year-round services run New London-Orient Point, New York, as well as Bridgeport–Port Jefferson.

Sights at a Glance

1. Hartford *pp202–205*
2. Farmington
3. New Britain
4. Dinosaur State Park
5. Wethersfield
6. Litchfield Hills *pp212–13*
7. Simsbury
8. Windsor
9. New England Air Museum
10. Old New-Gate Prison and Copper Mine
11. Coventry
12. Lebanon
13. Norwich
14. Foxwoods Resort Casino
15. New London
16. Mystic
17. Old Lyme
18. Essex
19. Gillette Castle *pp222–3*
20. Madison
21. Guilford
22. The Thimbles
23. New Haven *pp224–9*

Tour

24. Coastal Fairfield *pp228–9*

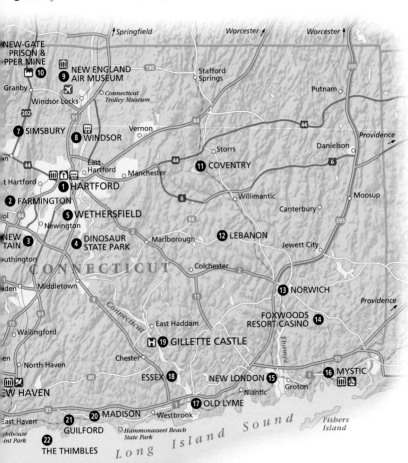

Boat tours cruising the 365 picturesque islands of The Thimbles

Key

▬ Highway
▬ Major road
▭ Minor road
▬ Scenic route
⋯ Main railroad
— Minor railroad
▬ State border
△ Summit

For additional map symbols *see back flap*

❶ Hartford

Serving first as an ancient Saukiog Indian settlement and later as a Dutch trading post, Connecticut's capital was founded in 1636 by the Reverend Thomas Hooker (1586–1647) and a group of 100 Englishmen from the Massachusetts Bay Colony. By the late 19th century, Hartford was basking in its Golden Age, thanks to both an economic boom in the insurance industry and a cultural flowering typified by resident authors Mark Twain (*see pp204–205*) and Harriet Beecher Stowe (*see pp34–5*). An ambitious revitalization program has helped breathe new life into the downtown core.

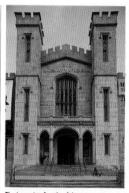

The imposing façade of the Wadsworth Atheneum

Exploring Hartford

Approaching the city by car, travelers are greeted by sunlight gleaming off the gold-leaf dome of the hilltop **State Capitol**. Many of Hartford's most popular attractions are easily accessed on foot from the Old State House, which has an information office for tourists.

🏛 Old State House

800 Main St. **Tel** (860) 522-6766. **Open** year-round: 10am–5pm Mon–Fri. **Closed** public hols, Tue in summer. 🎫 ♿ 🏛 🅿 🅆 ctosh.org

The 1796 State House, designed by Charles Bulfinch (1763–1844), is the country's oldest Capitol building. Its graceful center hall, grand staircase, and ornate cupola make the Old State House one of the nation's finest examples of Federal architecture. An interactive audio tour highlights points of interest such as the Great Senate Room and the courtroom where the slave ship *Amistad* trial of 1839 was held. Outdoors there is a seasonal farmers' market.

🏛 Center Church and Ancient Burying Ground

675 Main St. Church **Tel** (860) 249-5631. **Open** by appt. 🎫 by appt. Burying Ground: **Tel** (860) 280-4145. **Open** 10am–4pm daily.

Five stained-glass windows designed by US artist Louis Comfort Tiffany (1848–1933) grace the 1807 Center Church (First Church of Christ in Hartford). The church's Ancient Burying Ground contains some 415 headstones dating back to 1648, including that of Hartford's founding father, Thomas Hooker. Across Main Street is the 527-ft- (160-m-) high Travelers Tower office building, the tallest man-made observation post in the state.

🏛 Wadsworth Atheneum

600 Main St. **Tel** (860) 278-2670. **Open** 11am–5pm Wed–Sun (from 10am Sat & Sun; to 8pm first Thu of month). **Closed** pub hols. 🎫 (reduced fee 5–8pm first Thu of month). 🎫 ♿ 📷 🏛 🅆 wadsworthatheneum.org

Established in 1842, this museum has the distinction of being the oldest continuously operating public art museum in the country. Its extensive collection has 45,000 pieces and spans five centuries. It is particularly strong in Renaissance, Baroque, and Impressionist works, as well as in European decorative arts. The museum is noted for its extensive collection of American paintings, including works by Thomas Cole (1801–48) and Frederic Church (1826–1900). Outside in the Burr Mall is the monumental red steel sculpture called *Stegosaurus* (1973) by Connecticut resident Alexander Calder (1898–1976).

Alexander Calder's *Stegosaurus*

🌳 Bushnell Park

Trinity and Elm Sts. **Tel** (860) 232-6710. **Open** year-round. 🎫 May–Sep. ♿ Carousel **Open** Tue–Sun; call for hours. 🎫

Shaded by 100 tree varieties, the 1,742,400-sq-ft (161,900-sq-m) park is the lush creation of noted landscape architect and Hartford native Frederick Law Olmsted (1822–1903). Children adore the park's 1914 Bushnell Carousel, with its 48 hand-carved horses, ornate "lovers' chariots," and refurbished Wurlitzer band organ. The 115-ft- (35-m-) tall Soldiers and Sailors Memorial Arch honors those who saw duty in the American Civil War (1861–5).

East Senate Chambers of Hartford's Old State House

For hotels and restaurants in this region see pp315–16 and pp333–5

State Capitol

210 Capitol Ave.
Tel (860) 240-0222.
Open 9am–5pm Mon–Fri,
tours every hour 9:15am–
1:15pm Mon–Fri (also
2:15pm Jul & Aug).

The State Capitol
was designed by
Richard Upjohn
(1828–1903) in
the high-Victorian-
Gothic style. It is
constructed primarily
of marble and granite
and has a golden
dome. Highlights of the
grand interior are the oak
woodwork and the ornate
oak charter chair.

The Bushnell

166 Capitol Ave. Box office **Tel** (860)
987-5900. call (860) 987-6033 for
tour schedule. **bushnell.org**
This leading performing arts
venue features Broadway-
style extravaganzas as well as
more modest productions.
Highlights of the free tours
include the historic theater,
a state-of-the-art modern
stage, and a 14-ft (4.27-m)
chandelier by Seattle glass
artist Dale Chihuly.

Soldiers and Sailors
Memorial

Harriet Beecher Stowe Center

77 Forest St. **Tel** (860) 522-
9258. **Open** year-round:
9:30am–4:30pm Mon–Sat,
noon–4:30pm Sun. **Closed**
public hols, Tue (Jan–Mar).
obligatory. first
floor. **harriet
beecherstowe.org**

Located next to the
Mark Twain House
(see pp204–205), this
home is adorned
with gingerbread
ornamentation typical
of late 19th-century Victorian
design. Harriet Beecher Stowe's
fame as the author of the anti-
slavery novel *Uncle Tom's Cabin*
(1852) overshadowed her skill
as an interior decorator,
demonstrated by the
elegance of her

VISITORS' CHECKLIST

Practical Information
124,000. 100 Pearl St.,
(860) 525-8629.
letsgoarts.org

Transport
Bradley International Airport.
1 Union Place.

1871 home. The Stowes lived
here until Harriet's death in 1896.

Elizabeth Park Rose Gardens

Prospect Ave. **Tel** (860) 231-9443.
Gardens **Open** dawn to dusk daily.
Each year in this 3,920,400-sq-ft
(364,200-sq-m) park more than
900 varieties of roses bloom on
around 15,000 bushes. The park
has delightful herb, perennial,
and rock gardens.

The Connecticut State Capitol, overlooking Bushnell Park

Hartford City Center

① Old State House
② Center Church
③ Wadsworth Atheneum
④ Bushnell Park
⑤ State Capitol
⑥ The Bushnell

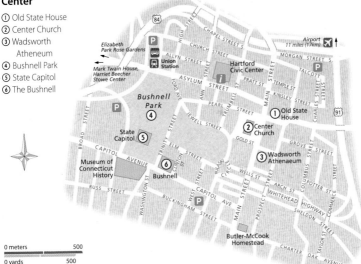

0 meters 500
0 yards 500

Mark Twain House and Museum

Mark Twain (1835–1910) – a former Mississippi riverboat pilot, humorist, and author – lived here from 1874 to 1891 and penned six novels. Based on a floor plan sketched out by Twain's wife, Olivia, the 19-room home is a masterpiece of the Picturesque-Gothic style. The home's expansive upper balconies, peaked gables, towering turrets, and painted brick combine the sense of high style and playfulness personified by its owners. The adjoining museum has extensive exhibits on Twain and his times, including a film by award-winning New England documentary filmmaker Ken Burns.

North face of Mark Twain House, showing peaked gable and turret

★ **Billiard Room**
Twain worked on some of his best-known works, including *The Adventures of Tom Sawyer* (1876), in the tranquility of the Billiard Room.

★ **Library**
The ornate fireplace mantel, carved in Scotland in the 1850s, was purchased by the Clemenses in 1873.

KEY

① **Turret-style bay windows**

② **The Conservatory** has a statue of Venus, similar to works by Karl Gerhardt (1853–1940). Twain helped finance Gerhardt's studies in Europe.

③ **The decorative treatment** of the railings is indicative of the "Stick" style of the 1870s.

★ **Master Bedroom**
Twain rhapsodized about the Master Bedroom, claiming it possessed "the most comfortable bedstead that ever was [and one that brings] peace to the sleepers."

VISITORS' CHECKLIST

Practical Information
351 Farmington Ave.
Tel (860) 247-0998.
Open 9:30am–5:30pm daily.
Closed Tue (Mar only), Jan 1,
Easter Sunday, Thanksgiving, Dec
24 & 25. 🅿 🎥 obligatory, last
tour 4:30pm. ♿ first floor only.
🆆 **marktwainhouse.org**.

Transport
🚌 all buses marked E
Farmington Ave.

Entrance
The massive wooden door leads into the Entrance Hall, famous for its silver stenciling applied by Louis C. Tiffany's firm in 1881.

Mark Twain

Raised in the frontier town of Hannibal, Missouri, on the banks of the Mississippi River, young Samuel Langhorne Clemens (better known as Mark Twain) was exposed to a strange cast of characters. Steamboat captains, gamblers, circus performers, actors, and minstrel showmen were just some of the people who passed through the town. As an adult, Twain worked as a typesetter, printer, miner, journalist, soldier, lecturer, editor, and even steamboat captain before finally trying his hand at writing full-time in 1870.

Graceful exterior of the Hill-Stead Museum in Farmington

❷ Farmington

🏠 21,050. 🚹 33 E Main St., Avon (860) 676-8878 or (800) 493-5266.

Perched on the banks of the surging Farmington River, this quiet enclave has long been the starting point for canoeists, fishermen, and bird-watchers. The skies above the Farmington River Valley are also a busy place, popular with hang-gliders and hot-air balloonists taking in the spectacular vistas from on high. Several companies offer champagne flights over the scenic valley, while others offer candlelit tours of the town's historic homes.

The interior of the **Hill-Stead Museum** has remained unchanged since the 1946 death of its original owner Theodate Pope Riddle (1867–1946). Pope, one of the country's first female architects, designed the Colonial-Revival mansion, which was completed in 1901. Her will stipulated that upon her death nothing in the house could be changed, altered, or moved. The result is a fascinating home frozen in the Edwardian period. On display is the Pope family's fine collection of French and American Impressionist paintings, including works by Edgar Degas (1834–1917), Edouard Manet (1832–83), Mary Cassatt (1845–1926), and James Whistler (1834–1903). The museum also contains splendid examples of American and European furniture and decorative arts. Particularly noteworthy on the grounds of the 0.2-sq-mile (0.6-sq-km) estate is the sunken garden. The **Stanley-Whitman House** is a well-preserved example of

the framed overhang style of early 18th-century architecture of New England. The house, furnished with Colonial pieces, is often used as a venue for craft demonstrations and exhibits. Elsewhere in Farmington, admirers of old cemeteries will find many markers of interest in the Ancient Burying Ground, with gravestones dating back to 1661. In the Riverside Cemetery, one tombstone marks the grave of Foone, an African slave who drowned in the town's canal after being freed in the *Amistad* trial (*see p202*).

🏛 **Hill-Stead Museum**
35 Mountain Rd. **Tel** (860) 677-4787.
Open 10am–4pm Tue–Sun.
Closed public hols. 🚫
📷 obligatory. ♿ partial.
🌐 **hillstead.org**

🏠 **Stanley-Whitman House**
37 High St. **Tel** (860) 677-9222.
Open May–Oct: noon–4pm Wed–Sun; Nov–Apr: call for hours.
📷 📷 ♿ partial.

Environs

Twenty miles (32 km) south of Farmington lies the blue-collar town of Waterbury. The town is proud of its ethnic roots, as

Arts of the West by Thomas Hart Benton at the New Britain Museum of American Art

Impressionist Art Trail

Between 1885 and 1930 Connecticut was a magnet for many American artists. Childe Hassam (1859–1935), J. Alden Weir (1852–1919), Willard Metcalf (1858–1925), and others depicted marshes, seascapes, harbors, and farms in a style called American Impressionism. Their works are in nine museums on a self-guided trail that winds from Greenwich to New London.

Sights at a Glance

① Bruce Museum, Greenwich
② Bush-Holley Historic Site, Cos Cob
③ Weir Farm, Ridgefield and Wilton
④ Yale University Art Gallery, New Haven
⑤ New Britain Museum of American Art, New Britain
⑥ Hill-Stead Museum, Farmington
⑦ Wadsworth Atheneum, Hartford
⑧ Florence Griswold Museum, Old Lyme
⑨ Lyman Allyn Art Museum, New London

evidenced by its 240-ft- (73-m-) tall Clock Tower, modeled on the city hall in Siena, Italy. A hands-on exhibit at the **Mattatuck Museum** relates the state's industrial history, including Waterbury's role as the "Brass City" during the 19th and early 20th century.

Ⅲ Mattatuck Museum
144 W Main St., Waterbury. **Tel** (203) 753-0381. **Open** year-round: 10am–5pm Tue–Sat, noon–5pm Sun. **Closed** public hols. 🅿 🅲 🅴 🖴 w mattatuckmuseum.org

❸ New Britain

🅼 73,000. 🅸 One Constitution Plaza, 2nd Floor, Hartford (860) 787-9640.

New Britain is midway between Boston and New York. Travelers to either city should stop to visit the **New Britain Museum of American Art**, whose distinguished collection spans art from the Colonial era to the present. Almost every major US artist is represented here, including Georgia O'Keeffe (1887–1986), Andrew Wyeth (b.1917), Alexander Calder (1898–1976), and Isamu Noguchi (1904–88). The American Impressionist collection is also important. One gallery is dedicated to the seminal "Arts of Life in America" mural series by Thomas Hart Benton.

Ⅲ New Britain Museum of American Art
56 Lexington St., New Britain. **Tel** (860) 229-0257. **Open** 11am–5pm Tue–Wed & Fri, 11am–8pm Thu, 10am–5pm Sat, noon–5pm Sun. 🅿 w nbmaa.org

❹ Dinosaur State Park

400 West St., Rocky Hill. **Tel** (860) 529-8423. Park: **Open** 9am–4:30pm daily. Exhibit center: **Open** 9am–4:30pm Tue–Sun. **Closed** public hols. 🅿 w dinosaurstatepark.org

During the lower Jurassic period some 200 million years ago, the dinosaurs that roamed this region literally left their mark on the land. Today some 500 prehistoric tracks are preserved beneath this park's huge geodesic dome. Also on

One of 500 ancient tracks at Dinosaur State Park

display is a life-size model of an 8-ft (2-m) *Dilophosaurus*, the creature that most likely left the prints. Two large dioramas tell the story of the Connecticut Valley during the Triassic and Jurassic periods. Highlights of this exhibit are a model *Coelophysis* and a cast of a skeleton unearthed in New Mexico. A thrill for children and amateur paleontologists is the chance to make plaster casts of the tracks from May through October. (Call ahead to find out what to bring.) The park also has 2.5 miles (4 km) of hiking trails through a variety of habitats.

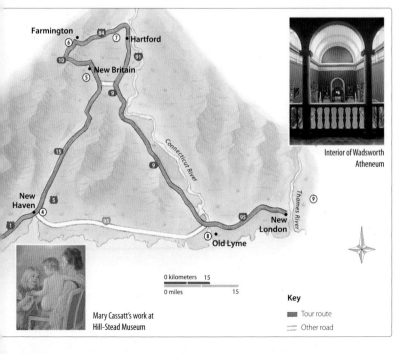

Interior of Wadsworth Atheneum

Mary Cassatt's work at Hill-Stead Museum

| 0 kilometers | 15 |
| 0 miles | 15 |

Key

▬▬ Tour route

═ ═ Other road

❺ Street-by-Street: Wethersfield

Now an affluent Hartford suburb, Wethersfield began as the state's first settlement in 1634. In 1640 its citizens held an illegal public election – America's first act of defiance against British rule. The town also hosted the 1781 Revolutionary War conference between George Washington (1732–99) and his French allies, during which they finalized strategies for the decisive American victory in Yorktown. Preserved within a 12-block area, Old Wethersfield stands as a primer of American architecture, with numerous houses from the 18th to 20th centuries. The centerpiece is the Webb-Deane-Stevens Museum, a trio of dwellings depicting the differing lifestyles of three 18th-century Americans: a wealthy merchant, a diplomat, and a leather tanner.

A Connecticut-River-style entrance built in 1767

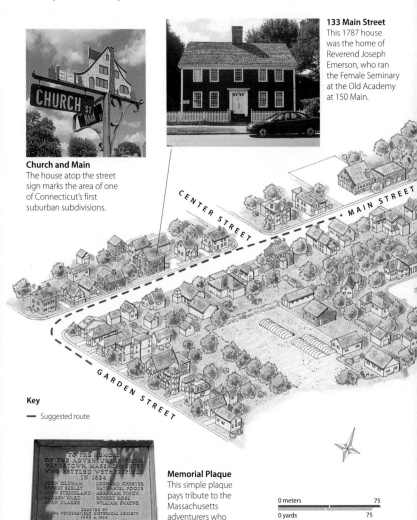

133 Main Street
This 1787 house was the home of Reverend Joseph Emerson, who ran the Female Seminary at the Old Academy at 150 Main.

Church and Main
The house atop the street sign marks the area of one of Connecticut's first suburban subdivisions.

CENTER STREET

MAIN STREET

GARDEN STREET

Key
— Suggested route

Memorial Plaque
This simple plaque pays tribute to the Massachusetts adventurers who settled here in 1634.

0 meters   75
0 yards   75

◀ Gothic façade of the Harkness Tower at Yale University, New Haven

★ **First Church of Christ**
One of only three Colonial meeting houses left in the state, the 1761 church included presidents George Washington (1732–99) and John Adams (1735–1826) among its worshipers.

Ancient Burying Ground
Legend has it that the graves of nine victims of the 1637 Pequot Massacres are buried here.

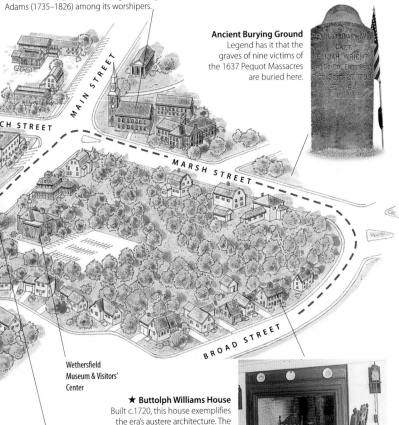

Wethersfield Museum & Visitors' Center

★ **Buttolph Williams House**
Built c.1720, this house exemplifies the era's austere architecture. The parlor is shown on the right.

★ **Webb-Deane-Stevens Museum**
The Joseph Webb House, built in 1752, is part of the Webb-Deane-Stevens Museum. Shown on the right is wallpaper from one of the upstairs bed chambers.

❻ Litchfield Hills

Nestled in the folds and foothills of the Berkshire Hills and Taconic Mountains in the northwesternmost section of Connecticut, the Litchfield Hills region covers some 1,000 sq miles (2,590 sq km), or one-quarter of the state. Many people consider this to be the most scenic part of Connecticut. Anchored by the Housatonic River, the bucolic landscape of woods, valleys, lakes, and wildlife offers unparalleled opportunities for canoeing, kayaking, white-water rafting, tubing, fly-fishing, and hiking. In autumn, traffic along the winding roads can slow as the brilliant fall foliage entrances sightseers. A steady influx of the wealthy into the area has resulted in the gentrification of Litchfield's 26 towns and villages, with boutiques and bistros popping up beside traditional craft shops and historic homes and gardens.

Fishing at Mount Tom State Park outside Litchfield

Bristol

🚹 62,000. 🅸 Litchfield (860) 567-4506.

Bristol's past as a premier clock manufacturing center is celebrated at the American Clock and Watch Museum on Maple Street. Housed in an 1801 mansion, this vast collection includes 5,000 clocks and watches.

Bristol is also home to the Lake Compounce Theme Park, the nation's oldest amusement park. Complete with one of the fastest and longest wooden roller coasters on the East Coast, a white-water raft ride, and a 185-ft- (56-m-) drop tower, the park on Lake Avenue has been entertaining families since 1846. More family fun can be found on Riverside Avenue in the form of the Carousel Museum of New England. Its collection of antique carousel pieces is one of the finest in the world.

Woodbury

🚹 9,400. 🅸 Litchfield (860) 567-4506.

With many shops and dealers, this is a popular haunt for antique lovers. Antique furnishings from the late 18th century can also be found at the Glebe House on Hollow Road. This minister's farmhouse is surrounded by the Gertrude Jekyll Garden, the noted English landscaper's only garden on US soil. The town is

also blessed with five churches from various eras that have been wonderfully preserved.

New Preston

🅸 Litchfield (860) 567-4506.

New Preston offers access to 0.2-sq-mile (0.4-sq-km) Lake Waramaug State Park. The lake is especially beautiful in the autumn, when the glorious colors are reflected on its mirrorlike surface. Visitors can rent canoes for peaceful paddles around the shoreline, and some 80 campsites cater to enthusiasts who want to linger and enjoy the great outdoors. The Hopkins Vineyard, perched above the

lake, offers wine tastings, along with tours of its facilities.

Litchfield

🚹 8,850. 🅸 Northwest Connecticut (860) 567-4506. 🆆 litchfield hills.com

Picturesque Litchfield has many noteworthy historic buildings, such as South Street's 1784 Tapping Reeve House and Law School, the country's first law school.

Just on the outskirts of town on Route 202, Mount Tom State Park has trails leading to the 1,325-ft (404-m) summit. The lake is ideal for scuba diving, swimming, boating, and fishing.

Elegant Bellamy-Ferriday House and Garden in Bethlehem

For hotels and restaurants in this region see pp315–16 and pp333–5

Bethlehem

🏛 3,700. 🛈 Litchfield.

One of the town's highlights is the Bellamy-Ferriday House and Garden, the 18th-century home of Reverend Joseph Bellamy (1719–90), founder of the first theological seminary in America. Located on Main Street, this 13-room house (open May–Oct) displays Ferriday family Delftware, furniture, and Oriental art.

West Cornwall

🛈 Litchfield.

Tiny West Cornwall is best known for its covered bridge. The 1841 bridge, which spans the Housatonic River, is only one of two such spans in the state open to car traffic.

Norfolk

🏛 2,000. 🛈 Litchfield.

Founded in 1758, this small village is located in the northwest corner of the state. Its village green is known for two key reasons: a monument that was designed by architect Stanford White (1853–1906) and US sculptor Augustus Saint-Gaudens *(see pp266–7)*; and the Music Shed. The latter is an auditorium on the Ellen Batell Stoeckel Estate that hosts the highly acclaimed annual Norfolk Chamber Music Festival.

Re-created Algonkian village at the Institute for American Indian Studies

Washington

🏛 3,950. 🛈 Litchfield.

At the Institute for American Indian Studies, situated on Curtis Road, those with a bent for history can examine a pre-contact Algonkian village, artifacts from 10,000 years ago, and exhibits of northwest Connecticut's Woodland Indians. The grounds contain a re-created archaeological dig.

Kent

🏛 2,900. 🛈 Litchfield.

Art lovers should go out of their way to visit this small community. It is well-known for having the highest concentration of galleries in the region, including the interesting Heron American Craft Gallery and the Kent Art Association Gallery.

North of town travelers indulge in outdoor fun at Kent Falls State Park. A short hike into the 0.5-sq-mile (1.2-sq-km) park will reward visitors with stunning views of what many people consider the most impressive waterfall in Connecticut. Picnic facilities overlook the idyllic scene.

Scenic road through Litchfield Hills

Litchfield Hills

The beautiful scenery of Litchfield County attracts many kinds of sightseers. Its scenic roads are perfect for cycling and driving tours. Adventurous travelers can tour the region on hot-air balloon excursions available in Litchfield.

Key

▬ Major road

═ Minor road

Picturesque bridge over the Connecticut River outside the town of Windsor

❼ Simsbury

⛰ 22,000. 🅸 Hartford (860) 787-9640

Originally a quiet colonial farming community, Simsbury grew into something of a boomtown in the early 18th century with the discovery of copper in the region. The wheels of US industry started turning here with the opening of the nation's first steel mill in 1728.

Three centuries of local history are squeezed into the **Phelps Tavern Museum**. The museum is located in the home of sea Captain Elisha Phelps. Period rooms and galleries have been used to create an authentic inn from 1786 to 1849, an era when such wayside inns were central to New England's social life. The tavern museum is part of a 87,100-sq-ft (8,100-sq-m) complex that includes a museum store and award-winning period gardens.

🏛 **Phelps Tavern Museum**
800 Hopmeadow St. **Tel** (860) 658-2500. **Open** Thu–Sat. **Closed** public hols. 🚫 📷 1pm & 2:30pm.

Sea captain's home, Phelps Tavern Museum

❽ Windsor

⛰ 27,800. 🅸 Hartford (860) 787-9640.

Windsor was settled in the early 1630s by Pilgrims from Plymouth *(see pp152–5)*, making it the oldest permanent English settlement in the state – a claim disputed by the residents of nearby Wethersfield *(see pp210–11)*. A drive along Palisado Avenue passes several historic houses.

The 1758 **John & Sarah Strong House** is an old surviving frame structure named after the newlyweds who built it and lived in it for four years before heading west to settle. It has an excellent collection of furnishings reflecting the history of Windsor. Next door is the **Dr. Hezekiah Chaffee House**, a three-story brick Georgian-Colonial built in the mid-18th century. The home is appointed with period furniture and features changing exhibits. Visitors may also tour the adjoining Palisado Green. Here nervous settlers built a walled stockade during the 1637 war with the Pequot Indians. Further down the road

stands the 1780 Georgian home of the state's first senator, Oliver Ellsworth (1745–1807). Today the **Oliver Ellsworth Homestead** contains interior design details from the era, including the original wallpaper.

🏛 **John & Sarah Strong House**
96 Palisado Ave. **Tel** (860) 688-3813. **Open** year-round: 11am–4pm Wed–Sat. **Closed** public hols. 🚫 includes admission to Dr. Hezekiah Chaffee House. 📷

🏛 **Dr. Hezekiah Chaffee House**
108 Palisado Ave. **Tel** (860) 688-3813. **Open** year-round: 11am–4pm Wed–Sat. **Closed** public hols. 🚫 includes admission to John & Sarah Strong House. 📷

🏛 **Oliver Ellsworth Homestead**
778 Palisado Ave. **Tel** (860) 688-8717. **Open** mid-May–mid-Oct: noon–4pm Fri & Sat. 🚫

Environs
Fifteen miles (24 km) north of Windsor, the **Connecticut Trolley Museum** takes visitors on a nostalgic journey. A round-trip through the grounds on an antique trolley highlights permanent displays of classic trolley cars dating from 1894 to 1949. The Connecticut Fire Museum and a Bus Museum are also part of the complex.

🏛 **Connecticut Trolley Museum**
58 North Rd., East Windsor. **Tel** (860) 627-6540. **Open** Apr–mid-Jun: 10am–4:30pm Sat, noon–4pm Sun; mid-Jun–Labor Day: 10am–3:30pm Mon, Wed–Fri, 10am–5pm Sat, noon–4:30pm Sun; off season: call for hours. 🚫 access to both museums. 🅦 ceraonline.org

❾ New England Air Museum

Bradley International Airport, Windsor Locks. **Tel** (860) 623-3305.
Open 10am–5pm daily. **Closed** Jan 1, Thanksgiving, & Dec 25. 🅿 🍴 ♿
📷 🌐 neam.org

Aviation fans can indulge their flights of fancy at the largest aviation museum in the Northeast. The impressive collection of 80 aircraft spans the complete history of aviation beginning with pre-Wright Brothers flying machines right up to present-day jets and rescue helicopters. Located near Bradley International Airport, the museum is housed in and around two cavernous hangars. Highlights include a Bunce-Curtiss Pusher, a vintage 1909 Blériot and a Sikorsky VS-44 Flying Boat, the last of the four-engined flying boats.

To experience the thrill of flying, visitors can strap themselves into a simulator of the Grumman Tracer.

One of the planes on display at the New England Air Museum

Old New-Gate Prison and Copper Mine insignia

❿ Old New-Gate Prison and Copper Mine

ℹ 115 Newgate Rd., East Granby. **Tel** (860) 653-3563. **Closed** until 2017 for renovations. 🅿 🍴 ♿ 📷

When financial woes forced the sale of this less than prosperous 18th-century copper mine, its new proprietors found a novel but grim use for the dark hole in the ground. In 1773 the local government transformed the nation's first chartered copper mine into the state's first colonial prison. Over the course of its infamous career, the jail held everyone from horse thieves to captured British soldiers. New-Gate represented a particularly brutal form of punishment, with prisoners living and sleeping in damp, sunless tunnels. Mercifully, the prison was abandoned in 1827, although tours of its lower chamber still inspire shivers.

⓫ Coventry

🏘 11,350. ℹ Hartford (860) 787-9640.

Coventry is the birthplace of Nathan Hale (1755–76), one of the inspirational heroes of the American Revolution (1775–83). Just minutes before he was to be hanged by the British for being a spy, the 21-year-old Coventry schoolteacher uttered his now famous last words, "I only regret that I have but one life to lose for my country."

The **Nathan Hale Home-stead** is an anomaly in that its namesake never actually lived in the house. The existing structure, located on the site where Hale was born, was built by Hale's brothers and father in 1776, the same year he was executed.

Some of Hale's belongings are on display, including his Bible, army trunk and boyhood "fowling piece." Nearby, Strong-Porter House was built by Hale's great-uncle in 1730.

Between June and October, the Nathan Hale Homestead is the site of the popular **Coventry Regional Farmers' Market**, with organic and heirloom produce for sale. Held on Sundays, this lively market also features live entertainment, food demonstrations, petting animals, and handmade goods from local artisans.

🏠 Nathan Hale Homestead

2299 South St. **Tel** (860) 742-6917.
Open Jun–Aug: noon–4pm Wed–Sat, 11am–4pm Sun; Sep & Oct: noon–4pm Fri & Sat, 11am–4pm Sun. 🅿 🍴 ♿ partial.

🛒 Coventry Regional Farmers' Market

Open Jun–Oct: 11am–2pm Sun.
🌐 coventryfarmersmarket.com

The 1730 Strong-Porter House in Coventry

⑫ Lebanon

6,500. Hartford. New London. Mystic (860) 536-8822 or (800) 863-6569.

This Eastern Connecticut community is steeped in American Revolution history. It was here on the 0.25-sq-mile (0.7-sq-km) common that French hussars trained before joining their American allies in Yorktown for the climactic battle of the conflict. Lebanon native and artist John Trumbull (1756–1843), whose paintings can be seen in Hartford's Wadsworth Atheneum (see p202) and New Haven's Yale University Art Gallery, put down his paintbrush long enough to design the town's 1807 Congregational Church.

Also overlooking the green is the **Governor Jonathan Trumbull's House**. Father to John and governor of the colony and the state of Connecticut from 1769 to 1784, Trumbull was the only governor of the 13 colonies to remain in office before, during and after the Revolutionary War. Behind the house is the **Doctor William Beaumont Homestead**, birthplace of one of the world's pioneers of gastric medicine.

🏠 Governor Jonathan Trumbull's House

169 W Town St. **Tel** (860) 429-7194. **Open** mid-May–mid-Oct: 1–6pm Fri, 10am–5pm Sat, 11am–5pm Sun.

🏠 Doctor William Beaumont Homestead

169 W Town St. **Tel** (860) 642-6579. **Open** mid-May–mid-Oct: noon–4pm Sat.

Environs

Twelve miles (19 km) to the east, Canterbury is home to the

Prudence Crandall Museum. Crandall (1803–90) raised the ire of citizens when, in 1832, she admitted a young black student to her private school for girls. Undaunted by threats of boycotts, Crandall kept the school open and attracted students, many of whom were black, from other states. Public outcry was such that the local government pushed through a law forbidding private schools to admit black children from out of state. Crandall was subsequently jailed and brought to trial. It was only after an angry mob attacked the school in 1834 that the heroic Quaker woman reluctantly closed its doors forever. Today the museum commemorates Crandall's struggle and traces local black history.

🏠 Prudence Crandall Museum

Canterbury Green. **Tel** (860) 546-7800. **Open** call for hours. **Closed** mid-Dec–Mar.

⑬ Norwich

35,000. Mystic (860) 536-8822 or (800) 863-6569.

Norwich has the dubious distinction of being the birthplace of Benedict Arnold (1741–1801), forever synonymous with traitor for betraying colonial forces during the American Revolution. In contrast, the Colonial Cemetery contains graves of soldiers, both American and French, who died fighting for the American cause during the war.

A two-story Colonial structure consisting of a pair of annexed saltboxes, the **Christopher Leffingwell House**, is named

after a financier of the colonial side in the American Revolution. During the war, Leffingwell's house and tavern were used for secret meetings. The interior, full of late 17th- and 18th-century furniture, has never been remodeled, making it of special interest.

🏠 Christopher Leffingwell House

348 Washington St. **Tel** (860) 889-9440. **Open** Apr–Oct: 11am–4pm Sat. **Closed** public hols.

Environs

Located 5 miles (8 km) south of Norwich is the **Shantok Village of Uncas**, final resting place of Native American leader Uncas (d.1683). Inspiration for James Fenimore Cooper's novel *Last of the Mohicans* (1826), Uncas provided early colonists with the plot of land for the original Norwich settlement and sided with them during the Pequot War of the 1630s. An obelisk memorializing Uncas was erected here in 1840.

A Leffingwell sculpture

🏠 Shantok Village of Uncas

Rte. 32 S of Norwich. **Open** dawn to dusk daily.

⑭ Foxwoods Resort Casino

Rte. 2. **Tel** (800) 369-9963. Casino: **Open** 24 hrs daily.

First of the Native American-operated casinos in New England, this gaming facility has hundreds of games tables, more than 4,800 slot machines, and high-stakes bingo and poker. In addition, the 4,000-seat MGM Grand Theater attracts international stars.

Also on casino grounds is the **Mashantucket Pequot Museum**, a state-of-the-art research and exhibition center of Native American history. Multimedia displays and touch-screen computers provide a detailed study of the natural history of the area and its earliest inhabitants. Walking

The War Office in Lebanon, once Jonathan Trumbull's store

For hotels and restaurants in this region see pp315–16 and pp333–5

Life-size Native American figures at the Mashantucket Pequot Museum

through a replica Pequot Village c.1500, visitors come upon life-size figures depicting local Native American life.

🏛 Mashantucket Pequot Museum

110 Pequot Trail. **Tel** (860) 396-6800 or (800) 411-9671. **Open** May–Nov: 9am–5pm Wed–Sat. **Closed** Jan 1, Thanksgiving Eve, Thanksgiving. 🅿 🎫 ♿ 📷 ✏ 🌐 **pequotmuseum.org**

🔟 New London

🏙 26,000. ➡ 🚌 ℹ Mystic (860) 536-8822 or (800) 863-6569.

British forces led by traitor Benedict Arnold razed New London during the American Revolution. Rebounding from the attack, the town enjoyed newfound prosperity with the whaling industry during the 19th century. The four colonnaded Greek-Revival mansions along Whale Oil Row attest to the affluence of that era.

Remarkably, many homes survived Arnold's torching, including the **Joshua Hempsted House**. Built in 1678, the dwelling is insulated with seaweed and represents one of the few 17th-century homes left in the state. Connecticut College houses the **Lyman Allyn Art Museum**, particularly known for

its 19th-century American paintings. Also on campus, the 1-sq-mile (3-sq-km) college Arboretum encompasses a variety of ecosystems, native trees and shrubs, trails, and ponds. At the edge of town is **Monte Cristo Cottage**, boyhood home of Nobel Prize-winning playwright Eugene O'Neill (1888–1953). The two-story cottage, which served as the setting for his Pulitzer Prize-winning play *Long Day's Journey into Night* (1957), is now a research library, with some of O'Neill's belongings on display.

🏠 Joshua Hempsted House

Jct of Hempstead, Jay, & Truman Sts. **Tel** (860) 443-7949. **Open** mid-May–mid-Oct: 1–4pm Sat & Sun (Jul & Aug: also Thu & Fri). 🅿 🎫 obligatory.

🏛 Lyman Allyn Art Museum

625 Williams St. **Tel** (860) 443-2545. **Open** year-round: 10am–5pm Tue–Sat, 1–5pm Sun. **Closed** public hols. 🅿 🎫 by appt. ♿

🏠 Monte Cristo Cottage

325 Pequot Ave. **Tel** (860) 443-5378 ext 227. **Open** late May–early Sep: noon–4pm Thu–Sat, 1–3pm Sun. 🅿

Environs

Directly across the river Thames from New London is the town of Groton. The USS *Nautilus*, the world's first nuclear-powered submarine is berthed at the

Submarine Force Museum on the Naval Submarine Base. **Fort Griswold Battlefield State Park** is where British troops under Benedict Arnold killed surrendered American soldiers in 1781. A 134-ft (41-m) obelisk memorial and a battle diorama mark the event.

🏛 Submarine Force Museum

Crystal Lake Rd. **Tel** (860) 694-3174. **Open** May–Oct: 9am–5pm Wed–Mon; Nov–Apr: 9am–4pm Wed–Mon. **Closed** first week Nov, public hols. ♿

🗺 Fort Griswold Battlefield State Park

Monument & Park Aves. **Tel** (860) 449-6877. Museum: **Open** late May–Labor Day: 9am–5pm Wed–Sun. Park: **Open** year-round: 8am–sunset daily.

Sea-lion sculpture on the rocks at Mystic Aquarium

🔟 Mystic

🏙 2,600. ℹ 27 Coogan Blvd. (860) 546-1641.

When shipbuilding waned, Mystic turned to tourism. Today Mystic Seaport *(see pp218–19)* and **Mystic Aquarium** make the town bustle. Seals and sea lions cavort in the outdoor Seal Island; indoors is a colony of African black-footed penguins and 3,500 sea creatures. They have one of the largest outdoor beluga tanks in the US and there are daily shows in a 14,000-seat theater.

🏛 Mystic Aquarium

55 Coogan Blvd. **Tel** (860) 572-5955. **Open** Apr–Oct: 9am–5pm daily; Nov & Mar: 9am–4pm daily; Dec–Feb: 10am–4pm daily. **Closed** Jan 1, Thanksgiving, Dec 25. 🅿 ♿ ✏ 🌐 **mysticaquarium.org**

World's first nuclear-powered sub, USS *Nautilus*, berthed at Groton

Mystic Seaport

What began as a modest collection of nautical odds and ends housed in an old mill in 1929 has grown into the world's largest maritime museum. The 827,650-sq-ft (76,900-sq-m) working replica of a 19th-century port is a complex of more than 40 buildings open to the public, including a bank, chapel, tavern, cooperage, ship-carver's studio, and one-room schoolhouse from the 19th century. Despite its fascinating exhibits that explore American maritime history, Mystic Seaport's main attraction remains its preservation shipyard and its fleet of antique ships, including the *Charles W. Morgan*, the last remaining vessel of the nation's fleet of 19th-century whalers.

Seagoing Connection
Almost every building sports a nautical motif.

Whaleboat Exhibit
A fully equipped whaleboat contains all the gear carried in such vessels in the late 19th century. It is housed in a shed on Chubb's Wharf.

Shipcarver's Shop
Independent craftsmen carved figureheads and other decorations, such as this American eagle, for shipbuilders.

KEY

① **Middle Wharf**

② **Burrows House** is an early 19th-century home of a shopkeeper and his milliner wife that re-creates coastal domestic life.

③ **Village Green Bandstand** is sometimes used as a concert venue, especially during holiday celebrations.

④ **The *LA Dunton***, a 1921 schooner, is one of the last existing examples of the once-popular New England round-bow fishing vessels.

⑤ **The *Joseph Conrad***, built in Denmark in 1882, is one of the museum's largest ships. It serves as a sail demonstration vessel.

★ **The Charles W. Morgan**
The last wooden whaling ship in the world, the *Charles W. Morgan* was built in 1841. The vessel was completely restored in 2014, and visitors can go aboard and walk the decks.

Thomas Oyster House
Initially used as a culling shop to sort oysters by size, the 1874 building was later used to shuck oysters before shipping them on ice.

The Sabino
Built in 1908 in East Boothbay, Maine, the coal-fueled steamship *Sabino* takes passengers on cruises on the Mystic River.

Lighthouse
This copy of the 1901 Brant Point Lighthouse on Nantucket houses a multimedia exhibit on lighthouse history.

★ Mystic River Scale Model
Inside is a 50-ft- (17-m-) long model giving a bird's-eye view of Mystic c.1870. It has over 250 detailed buildings.

The Harpist by Alphonse Jongers at the Florence Griswold Museum

⓱ Old Lyme

🏙 6,800. 🚹 27 Coogan Blvd., Mystic (860) 536-8822 or (800) 863-6569.

Once a shipbuilding center, Old Lyme is home to numerous 18th- and 19th-century houses. Originally built for merchants and sea captains, many became residences of the artists who established a colony here in the early 1900s.

The **Florence Griswold Museum** is intimately linked to the arts. The mansion became the home of Captain Robert Griswold and his daughter Florence. An art patron, Florence began letting rooms in the 1890s to New York artists looking for a summer by the sea. She hosted Henry Ward Ranger (1858–1916), Childe Hassam (1859–1935), and Clark Voorhees (1871–1933), spawning the Old Lyme Art Colony.

This stop on the American Impressionist Art Trail *(see pp206–207)* features more than 900 works by artists who at one time lived in the house or nearby. Many of Griswold's guests painted on the wall panels of the dining room as thanks for her generosity. There is also a modern gallery which houses changing exhibitions. It is a work of art in itself, with a rippling aluminum canopy entrance, curvilinear walls and skylights to provide soft illumination.

🏛 **Florence Griswold Museum**
96 Lyme St., Old Lyme. **Tel** (860) 434-5542. **Open** year-round: 10am–5pm Tue–Sat, 1–5pm Sun. 🅿 📷 ♿

⓲ Essex

🏙 2,500. 🚹 One Constitution Plaza, 2nd Floor, Hartford (860) 787-9640.

In surveys naming America's top small towns, Essex is often found at the head of the list. Sited on the Connecticut River, the village is surrounded by a series of sheltered coves and has a bustling marina and tree-lined, virtually crime-free streets.

The **Connecticut River Museum**, a restored 1878 warehouse, is perched on a dock overlooking the water. Its collection and exhibits of maritime art and artifacts tell the story of this once-prominent shipbuilding town, where the *Oliver Cromwell* – the first warship built for the American Revolution (1775–83) – was constructed. The museum's conversation piece is a replica of the world's first submersible craft, the *Turtle*, a squat, single-seat vehicle built in 1775. Transportation is also the focus at the **Essex Steam Train & Riverboat Ride**, where guests take an authentic, coal-belching steam engine for a 12-mile (19-km) scenic tour. At the midpoint, passengers can take a 90-minute cruise down the river aboard a riverboat.

🏛 **Connecticut River Museum**
67 Main St. **Tel** (860) 767-8269. **Open** 10am–5pm Tue–Sun (daily late May–early Sep). **Closed** Jan 1, Labor Day, Thanksgiving, Dec 24 & 25. 🅿 📷 ♿

🚂 **Essex Steam Train & Riverboat Ride**
Exit 3 off Rte. 9. **Tel** (860) 767-0103 or (800) 377-3987. **Open** May–Oct: call for ride times. 🅿 📷 ♿
🌐 essexsteamtrain.com

Environs
Five miles (8 km) north of Essex is Chester, home to **The Norma Terris Theatre**, which presents new musicals. Across the Connecticut River the town of East Haddam offers spectacular views of river traffic from the **Goodspeed Opera House**. This late-Victorian "wedding cake" gem is the setting for new musicals and revivals, which are staged from April to December.

🎭 **The Norma Terris Theatre**
N Main St./Rte. 82, Chester. **Tel** (860) 873-8668. **Open** call for show times. 🅿 ♿

🎭 **Goodspeed Opera House**
Rte. 82, East Haddam. **Tel** (860) 873-8668. **Open** call for show times. 🅿 ♿

Replica of the first submersible at Connecticut River Museum

⓳ Gillette Castle

See pp222–3.

⓴ Madison

🏙 16,000. 🚹 One Constitution Plaza, 2nd Floor, Hartford (860) 787-9640.

Madison is a resort town full of antique stores and boutiques, including a specialty store that stocks British kippers, bangers, and pork pies. Several historic homes are open for viewing, including the 1685 **Deacon John Grave House**. The structure has served as tavern, armory, courthouse, and infirmary, but has always belonged to the Graves. One of the oldest artifacts on display is the family's bookkeeping ledger, with entries from 1678 to 1895.

Madison is also home to **Hammonasset Beach State Park**, the largest shoreline park in the state. Poking into Long Island Sound, the peninsula has a 2-mile- (3-km-) long beach that attracts swimmers, sailors, scuba divers, and sunbathers. The park has walking trails, picnic areas, and a 550-site campground.

 Deacon John Grave House
581 Boston Post Rd. **Tel** (203) 245-4798. **Open** mid-Jun–early Sep: call for hours.

Hammonasset Beach State Park
I-95, exit 62. Park: **Tel** (203) 245-2785. Campground reservations: **Tel** (877) 668-2267. Park: **Open** 8am–dusk daily.

The boardwalk at Hammonasset Beach State Park in Madison

㉑ Guilford

20,000. One Constitution Plaza, 2nd Floor, Hartford (860) 787-9640. **ctvisit.com**

In 1639 Reverend Henry Whitfield (1597–1657) led a group of Puritans from Surrey, England, to a wild parcel of land near the West River. There they established the town of Guilford. A year later, fearing an attack by local Mennuncatuk Indians, the colonists built a three-story stronghold out of local granite. The Tudor Gothic-style fort, the oldest stone dwelling of its type in New England, now serves as the **Henry Whitfield State Historical Museum**. The austere interior has a 33-ft-(10-m-) long great hall and 17th-century furnishings.

Guilford is graced by dozens of historic 18th-century homes. Both the **Hyland House**, a classic early saltbox (see p30), and the 1774 **Thomas Griswold House** are open to view. **Dudley Farm**, a 19th-century working farm and living-history museum,

demonstrates the agricultural techniques of the era. In mid-July craftsmen gather on the scenic Guilford Green to celebrate the arts at the annual Guilford Handcraft Exposition (see p37).

Henry Whitfield State Historical Museum
248 Old Whitfield St. **Tel** (203) 453-2457. **Open** May–mid-Dec: 10am–4:30pm Wed–Sun; mid-Dec–Jan: by appt only.

Hyland House
84 Boston St. **Tel** (203) 453-9477. **Open** Jun–Labor Day: 11am–4pm Wed–Sat, noon–4pm Sun. **Closed** Columbus Day. obligatory.

Thomas Griswold House
171 Boston St. **Tel** (203) 453-3176. **Open** call for hours.

Dudley Farm
2351 Durham Rd. **Tel** (203) 457-0770. **Open** May–Oct: 10am–1pm Thu–Sat, 1–4pm Sun.

㉒ The Thimbles

from Stony Creek Dock (203) 488-8905. (203) 777-8550.

From Stony Creek, travelers can cruise to the Thimble islands aboard one of several tour boats that operate in the area. Many of the 365 islands are little more than large boulders visible only at low tide. Some of the privately owned islands sport small communities. One colorful legend about this clutch of islands centers on circus midget General Tom Thumb (1838–83) courting a woman on Cut-In-Two Island. Another has the privateer Captain Kidd (1645–1701) hiding plundered treasure on Money Island while being pursued by the British fleet. Today cruisers watch seals or take in glorious fall colors.

The Thimbles, home to seals, whales, and colorful legends

⑲ Gillette Castle

Ostentatious and bizarre, Gillette Castle is the antithesis of New England architectural grace. However, visitors to the 24-room granite mansion always leave with a smile. Actor William Gillette (1853–1937) based the design of his 1919 dream home on medieval castles, complete with battlements and turrets. The castle is rife with such oddities as Gillette's home-made trick locks, furniture set on wheels and tracks, a cavernous 1,500-sq-ft (139-sq-m) living room, and a series of mirrors starting in his bedroom that permitted him to see who was arriving downstairs in case he wished to be "indisposed" or make a grand entrance.

Park and goldfish pond, a pleasing vista

The View
The castle has a view of the Connecticut River and its traffic. Gillette lived on a houseboat for five years while the castle was constructed.

Castle Grounds
Following Gillette's death, the castle and its 0.2 sq miles (0.5 sq km) of land became a state park. His railroad with its two locomotives used to carry guests on a 3-mile (5-km) tour through the property. Now visitors walk the trails.

KEY

① At the **Main Entrance**, the huge oak door through which visitors must pass is equipped with an elaborate home-made lock.

② **The Study** is where Gillette spent much of his time. The chair at his desk is on a set of small tracks so it can be easily moved back and forth.

③ **Servants' quarters**

④ **The Library** holds the self-educated Gillette's book collection that ranges far and wide.

⑤ **Mezzanine**

⑥ **Outdoor terrace**

William Gillette

An eccentric playwright and actor, Gillette caught the acting bug early, leaving college at age 20 to tread the boards. His most famous role, repeated many times in repertory, was Sherlock Holmes. He was reputed to have made $3 million playing the fictional sleuth. Gillette spent $1 million to build his folly. His will stipulated that it should never fall into the hands of "any blithering saphead."

Castle Exterior
Constructed on a steel framework, the castle is built of fieldstone bought from local farmers and lifted up the hill on an aerial tram designed by Gillette.

④
⑤
⑥
⑥

★ **The Great Hall**
Exposed stone walls are 5 ft (1.5 m) thick in some places, and heavy oak covers steel beams. Gillette had a generator installed to provide power, but the castle is still dark and baronial.

㉓ New Haven

The land on which Connecticut's second most populous city stands was purchased from the Quinnipiac Indians in 1638 for a few knives, coats, and hatchets. The city's location on the coast where the West, Mill, and Quinnipiac Rivers flow into Long Island Sound has helped make it one of the state's major manufacturing centers. Over the centuries, items ranging from clocks and corsets to musical instruments, carriages, and Revolutionary War cannonballs have been made here. In 1716 Yale University *(see pp226–9)* moved from Saybrook to New Haven, establishing the city as a center for education, technology, and research. Today New Haven also offers opportunities for attending theater, opera, dance performances, and concerts.

Amistad Memorial

Tiffany stained-glass window at First Church of Christ

Exploring Downtown New Haven

The 696,950-sq-ft (64,750-sq-m) New Haven Green is the central section of the original nine symmetrical town squares the Puritans laid out in New Haven, the first planned city in America. The Green has been the focal point of local life ever since, serving as the setting for many of New Haven's activities and festivals. Three churches, all built between 1812 and 1815, sit on the Green on Temple Street. United Church on the Green (often called North Church for its northern location) is in the style of London's St. Martin-in-the-Fields. Graced by a beautiful Tiffany stained-glass window, the First Church of Christ (Center Church) is considered an architectural masterpiece of the American Georgian style. The crypt beneath the church holds the remains of some of the city's original colonists. Among the notables buried here are Benedict Arnold's first wife, Margaret, and James Pierpont (1659–1714), one of the founders of Yale University. Trinity Church on the Green was one of the first Gothic-style churches in America.

Looming on the corner of Court and Church Streets is the monumental Greek Revival post office, now the Federal District Court, designed in 1913 by James Gamble Rogers (1867–1947), architect of many of Yale University's Gothic Revival buildings. City Hall faces the Green on Church Street and epitomizes High-Victorian style, with its polychrome limestone-and-sandstone façade. In front of City Hall, the 14-ft- (4-m-) tall bronze Amistad Memorial, which honors Sengbe Pieh (also known as Joseph Cinque), leader of the *Amistad* revolt *(see p202)*, is on the exact site of the jail where the mutinous slaves were held.

In late April the Green becomes the stage for Powder House Day, a reenactment of one of Benedict Arnold's few celebrated moments. At the start of the American Revolution, Arnold, then a captain in the militia, seized control of a municipal arsenal and led his troops to Boston to help bolster the sagging colonial forces.

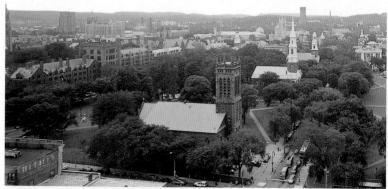

Church spires around New Haven Green

🏛 New Haven Museum and Historical Society
114 Whitney Ave. **Tel** (203) 562-4183. **Open** 10am–5pm Tue–Fri, noon–5pm Sat. **Closed** public hols. 🅿 📷

This handsome Colonial Revival house traces the city's cultural and industrial growth from 1638 to the present. Exhibits include such items as Eli Whitney's cotton gin, the sign that hung over Benedict Arnold's George Street shop, a fine collection of colonial pewter and china, and permanent galleries on the *Amistad* and the city's maritime history.

🏛 Grove Street Cemetery
227 Grove St., gate at N end of High St. **Tel** (203) 787-1443. **Open** year-round: 8am–4pm daily. 🎫 ♿

Established in 1797 and covering 784,100 sq ft (72,850 sq m), this was the first cemetery in the US to be divided into family plots. Walking through its 1848 Egyptian Revival gate, visitors will find a veritable who's who of New Haven. Eli Whitney (1765–1825), Noah Webster (1758–1843), Charles Goodyear (1800–60), and Lyman Beecher (1775–1863) are just some of the distinguished citizens buried in this cemetery.

The colorful 1916 carousel at Lighthouse Point Park

New Haven Parks
Among New Haven's many attractive parks, the 0.1-sq-mile (0.4-sq-km) **Lighthouse Point Park** on Long Island Sound is a standout. The park has nature trails, a picnic grove, swimming facilities, a splash pad, a 1916 Coney-Island-style carousel, and an 1847 lighthouse. **East Rock Park** offers a spectacular view of Long Island Sound, New Haven,

and the harbor and is crisscrossed by 10 miles (16 km) of nature trails. The 0.2-sq-mile (0.5-sq-km) **Edgewood Park** has a duck pond, nature trail, in-line skating rink, and playground. Black Rock Fort, from the Revolutionary War period, and Fort Nathan Hale, vintage Civil War era, offer splendid views of New Haven Harbor.

🏞 Lighthouse Point Park
2 Lighthouse Rd. **Tel** (203) 946-8790. Park: **Open** year-round: dawn–dusk daily. Beach: **Open** Memorial Day–Labor Day: dawn–dusk daily. 🅿 ♿

🏞 East Rock Park
E Rock Park. **Tel** (203) 946-6086. **Open** year-round: 8am–dusk daily.

🏞 Edgewood Park
Edgewood Ave. **Tel** (203) 946-8028. **Open** year-round: dawn–dusk daily. ♿

🏛 Eli Whitney Museum
915 Whitney Ave., Hamden. **Tel** (203) 777-1833. **Open** 10am–3pm Sat, noon–5pm Sun (Jun–Aug: 11am–4pm Sat & Sun). **Closed** public hols. 🅿 ♿ 🌐 eliwhitney.org

On the northern outskirts of New Haven in the suburb of Hamden is the Eli Whitney Museum. One of the nation's earliest inventors, Whitney (1765–1825) was best known for developing the cotton gin, thereby automating the labor-intensive task of separating cotton from its seeds. Another of his inventions, a musket with interchangeable parts, revolutionized manufacturing. The museum contains examples of Whitney's achievements but the primary emphasis is on hands-on children's learning activities which emphasize creativity and inventiveness.

🏞 Connecticut Audubon Coastal Center
1 Milford Point Rd., Milford. **Tel** (203) 878-7440. Center **Open** year-round: 10am–4pm Tue–Sat, noon–4pm Sun. **Closed** gate closed at dusk. 🅿 📷 ♿ 📷 🌐 ctaudubon.org

Just 15 miles (16 km) southwest of New Haven, travelers come upon the Connecticut Audubon Coastal Center, one of the state's best birding sites. This 365,900-sq-ft (34,000-sq-m) bird and wildlife sanctuary and nature center is situated on Long Island Sound at the mouth of the Housatonic River. Visitors can take nature walks along the beach or around the salt marsh and climb a 70-ft (21-m) tower overlooking Long Island Sound.

Eli Whitney Museum in Hamden, just north of New Haven

🏛 Shore Line Trolley Museum
17 River St., East Haven. **Tel** (203) 467-6927. **Open** May–Dec: call for hours. 🅿 ♿ partial. 📷 🌐 shorelinetrolley.org

Five miles (8 km) to the east of New Haven in East Haven is the Shore Line Trolley Museum. The oldest rapid-transit car and first electric freight locomotive are among 100 vintage trolleys from 1878 onward on display. The museum also offers a 3-mile (5-km) trolley ride through salt marshes and woods on the oldest suburban trolley line in the country.

The 1840 lighthouse at Lighthouse Point Park

Yale University

Founded in 1701, this Ivy League school is one of the most prestigious institutions of higher learning in the world. The list of Yale's distinguished alumni includes Noah Webster (1758–1843), who compiled the nation's first dictionary, Samuel Morse (1791–1872), inventor of Morse code, and five US presidents, including George W. Bush (b.1946). While its law and medical schools attract much of the attention, Yale's other graduate programs (ranging from divinity to drama) are no less demanding. In some ways avant-garde, in others staunchly traditional, Yale admitted its first female Ph.D. student before the turn of the 20th century, but didn't become fully coeducational until 1969.

Wrexham Tower, Branford College, on the Yale campus

Exploring Yale Campus

Yale's campus comprises much of New Haven's downtown core, with the main section located on the western flank of the New Haven Green. Campus buildings reflect the architectural eclecticism that runs through the university. **Connecticut Hall** is Yale's oldest building and the only one left of a row of Georgian buildings on the **Old Campus**, Yale's original quadrangle. Nathan Hale *(see p215)* and US President William Howard Taft (1857–1930) had rooms here when they were students. After World War I,

Yale's oldest building, Connecticut Hall, constructed in 1717

James Gamble Rogers (1867–1947) designed the **Memorial Quadrangle**, a beautiful Gothic complex that is now the heart of the campus. Another Rogers design, **Harkness Tower**, completed in 1921, was modeled on St. Botolph's Tower in Boston, England, and has a façade covered with sculptures celebrating Yale's history and traditions. Each day at noon and again at 6pm the beautiful sounds of the bell tower's carillon can be heard throughout New Haven. On the Memorial Gate near the tower, the school's motto is inscribed "For God, for country and for Yale."

Post-World War II architects have left their mark on campus, too. The **Yale School of Art and Architecture** is as controversial today as when it was built in the 1960s. From the outside this 36-level building seems to stand only seven stories tall. The collection of buildings that makes up Ezra Stiles and Morse

Colleges at Broadway and Tower is by architect Eero Saarinen (1910–61), who based the design on an Italian mountain village. Philip Johnson's Kline Biology Tower, Yale's skyscraper, was completed in 1965.

🏛️ **Yale Center for British Art**
1080 Chapel St. **Tel** (203) 432-2800.
Open year-round: 10am–5pm Tue–Sat, noon–5pm Sun. **Closed** public hols. 🅿️ ♿ 📷 🌐 **yale.edu/ycba**

In 1966 Philanthropist Paul Mellon (1907–99) donated his collection of British art to the university. This was no small gift, considering it consisted of more than 50,000 paintings, prints, drawings, watercolors, and rare books and documents. Needing the right space to display its artistic windfall, the university hired American architect Louis Kahn (1901–74) to design an elegant new center. Thus was born this important collection

Library Court in the Yale Center for British Art

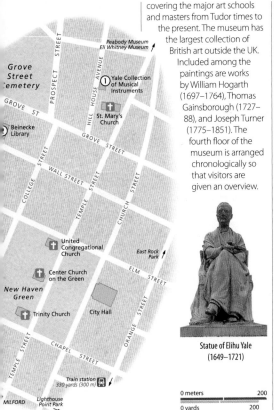

Grove Street Cemetery

New Haven Green

Statue of Elihu Yale
(1649–1721)

0 meters 200
0 yards 200

covering the major art schools and masters from Tudor times to the present. The museum has the largest collection of British art outside the UK. Included among the paintings are works by William Hogarth (1697–1764), Thomas Gainsborough (1727–88), and Joseph Turner (1775–1851). The fourth floor of the museum is arranged chronologically so that visitors are given an overview.

🏛 Sterling Memorial Library
128 Wall St. **Tel** (203) 432-2798.
Closed to the public.

This striking library boasts stained-glass windows and Gothic arches and is the largest on the Yale University campus. It contains some 4 million items, including rare Babylonian tablets.

Gothic entrance to the Sterling Memorial Library

🏛 Beinecke Rare Book and Manuscript Libraries
121 Wall St. **Tel** (203) 432-2977.
Open year-round: 9am–7pm Mon–Thu, 9am–5pm Fri, noon–5pm Sat.
Closed for renovations until Sep 2016.

American architect Gordon Bunshaft (1909–90) built the walls of this library out of translucent marble. This unique design helps filter the sunlight, which could harm the library's illuminated medieval manuscripts and 7,000 books. The library owns a host of rare books and manuscripts, but its prized possession is one of the world's few remaining Gutenberg Bibles.

Yale University Campus

① Yale Collection of Musical
    Instruments
② Beinecke Library
③ Sterling Memorial Library
④ Memorial Quadrangle
⑤ Harkness Tower
⑥ Old Campus
⑦ Connecticut Hall
⑧ Yale Center for British Art
⑨ Yale University Art Gallery
⑩ Yale School of Art
    and Architecture

For map symbols *see back flap*

🏛 Yale University Art Gallery

1111 Chapel St. **Tel** (203) 432-0600.
Open 10am–5pm Tue–Fri (Sep–Jun: until 8pm Thu), 11am–5pm Sat & Sun.
Closed public hols. 🎫 ♿ 📷
W artgallery.yale.edu

This major collection of Asian, African, European, American, and pre-Columbian art comprises more than 100,000 objects and reflects the generosity and taste of Yale alumni and benefactors. While the museum was founded in 1832, its main building was completed in 1953 and is considered architect Louis Kahn's first masterpiece. After a series of alterations, Yale chose to restore the signature window walls, refurbish the geometric ceilings, and reinstate Kahn's open plan to the galleries.

The gallery's vast collection highlights art as far back as ancient Egypt. It is famous for its

Entrance to the Peabody Museum of Natural History

American paintings, furniture, and decorative arts. Among its prized American pieces is John Trumbull's 1786 painting depicting the battle of Bunker Hill. It also includes works by Picasso, van Gogh, Monet, and Pollock.

🏛 Peabody Museum of Natural History

170 Whitney Ave. **Tel** (203) 432-5050.
Open year-round: 10am–5pm Mon–Sat, noon–5pm Sun. **Closed** public hols. 🎫 📷 ♿ 📷 **W** yale.edu/peabody

Visitors entering the museum are dwarfed by the imposing skeleton of a 67-ft- (20-m-) high *Brontosaurus* – an apt introduction to this outstanding museum, famous for its collection of dinosaurs. Children migrate to the Great Hall of Dinosaurs, where they can mingle with the mastodon and socialize with the *Stegosaurus*. Included among the many fossils and realistic dioramas is a 75-million-year-old turtle. *Archelon*, at 10 ft (3 m), ranks as the largest turtle that ever roamed the planet.

㉔ Tour of Coastal Fairfield County

Travelers following Interstate 95 are bound to strike it rich along the "Gold Coast," so nicknamed because of the luxurious estates, marinas, and mansions concentrated between Greenwich and Southport. This, the southernmost corner of the state, has attractions sure to meet everyone's taste. The shoreline is dusted with numerous beaches offering a variety of summer recreation opportunities. Nature preserves, arboretums, planetariums, and the state's only zoo will appeal to naturalists of all ages. People of a more artistic bent can visit the area's numerous small galleries or visit some of its larger, well-established museums.

New Canaan Historical Society building

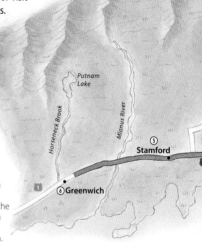

⑥ Greenwich
Blessed with a stunning coastline, this town is home to the Bush-Holley Historic Site, the state's first Impressionist art colony.

⑤ Stamford
This major urban area has a lively downtown and the First Presbyterian Church, which is shaped like a fish.

Stamford's First Presbyterian Church has the largest mechanical-action organ in the state.

The Peabody's third floor has a slightly more contemporary feel, with displays ranging near and far – from daily life in ancient Egypt to modern biodiversity in Connecticut. Elsewhere, visitors can admire exhibits on Native American or Pacific Island cultures, or examine minerals, meteorites, and exhibits on the solar system.

🏛 Yale Collection of Musical Instruments

15 Hillhouse Ave. **Tel** (203) 432-0822. **Open** Sep–Jul: 1–4pm Tue–Fri, 1–5pm Sun. **Closed** Aug. 🅿 🅱 by appt. ♿ partial. **W** yale.edu/musical instruments

A must-stop for the musically inclined, this stunning collection of instruments, considered among the top ten of its kind, has 800 objects, including historic woodwind and stringed instruments. The collection was started by New Haven piano manufacturer Morris Steinert (1831–1912). Steinert's love of music (he also founded the New Haven Symphony) saw him travel to Europe to collect and restore antique instruments, especially claviers and harpsichords, forerunners to his beloved piano. Some of the collection's violins and harpsichords date back centuries. The museum holds a series of concerts from September to April. Many of the concerts are performed using the historic instruments.

Angelic detail on Yale's graceful High Street Bridge

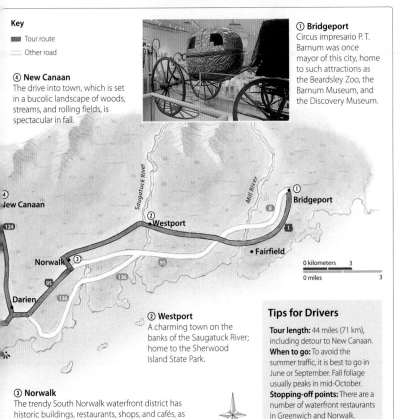

Key

▬▬ Tour route

┄┄┄ Other road

④ New Canaan

The drive into town, which is set in a bucolic landscape of woods, streams, and rolling fields, is spectacular in fall.

① Bridgeport

Circus impresario P. T. Barnum was once mayor of this city, home to such attractions as the Beardsley Zoo, the Barnum Museum, and the Discovery Museum.

② Westport

A charming town on the banks of the Saugatuck River; home to the Sherwood Island State Park.

③ Norwalk

The trendy South Norwalk waterfront district has historic buildings, restaurants, shops, and cafés, as well as the Maritime Aquarium at Norwalk.

Tips for Drivers

Tour length: 44 miles (71 km), including detour to New Canaan.
When to go: To avoid the summer traffic, it is best to go in June or September. Fall foliage usually peaks in mid-October.
Stopping-off points: There are a number of waterfront restaurants in Greenwich and Norwalk.

VERMONT

Vermont was given its name by explorer Samuel de Champlain in 1609. The word means "Green Mountain" in French, and must have seemed most suitable when he gazed upon the fertile landscape. Almost 400 years later, Vermont is still very much an enclave of unspoiled wilderness, with thick forests blanketing the rolling hills and the valley lowlands.

In all there are just about 600,000 people living in Vermont, one of the most rural states in the Union. The countryside is replete with manicured farms where the state's trademark black and white Holstein cattle graze against a backdrop of natural beauty. The pastoral landscape, dotted with pristine villages and covered bridges, evokes the idealized images found in paintings by longtime resident Norman Rockwell *(see p245)*. An anti-billboard law ensures that the countryside is not blighted by obtrusive advertisements.

Vermonters may be small in number, but they are patriotic and often have led the country's conscience on social and political issues. The Stars and Stripes are a familiar sight in Vermont; the American flag, "Old Glory" as is it known, decorates many a front porch.

It is hardly surprising that people from around the world are attracted to this green corner of the US. Each season brings new opportunities to enjoy nature. When the countryside is covered in a blanket of snow, picturesque towns are transformed into bustling ski centers. Outdoor enthusiasts have long known that Vermont possesses some of the best boating, hiking, camping, and fishing in the country. Vermont is also a magnet for painters, writers, musicians, and poets who enrich the cultural life of the state. Regional theaters, museums, and art galleries are prominent attractions. But Vermont is at its scenic best in the fall, when thousands of "leaf peepers" come to see the natural phenomenon of leaves changing color *(see pp24–5)*. What makes the season so special here is the variety of colors that the trees manifest, from the palest mustard to flaming scarlet.

Grazing Holstein cows, a favorite breed in Vermont, in a typical state setting

◄ Lake Champlain boasts beautiful sunsets

Exploring Vermont

Unlike New England's coastal states, with attractions most often found along the water's edge, Vermont's highlights are sprinkled liberally throughout the state. The northeastern region boasts mountains, forests, and the fjordlike Lake Willoughby *(see pp234–5)*. Snaking down the western border, Lake Champlain and its islands *(see p240)* provide the backdrop for the collegial spirit of Burlington *(see pp236–9)* and the one-of-a-kind Shelburne Museum *(see pp242–3)*. Pre-Revolutionary War villages grace the south and provide good base camps for hikers looking to trek the Appalachian Trail *(see pp26–7)* or enjoy the splendor of the Green Mountain National Forest *(see p248)*.

Burlington's waterfront, well used by sailors and boaters

Key

▬▬▬	Highway
▬▬▬	Major road
▪▪▪▪	Minor road
▬▬	Scenic route
▬▬	Main railroad
▬▬	Minor railroad
▬▬▬	International border
▬▬▬	State border
△	Summit

0 kilometers 25
0 miles 25

Sights at a Glance

Montreal ↑
Isle La Motte
North Hero
Grand Isle
Grand Isle **6**
LAKE CHAMPLAIN
89
BURLINGTON **5**
South Burlin
SHELBURNE MUSEUM **7**
11
7
Vergennes
Bristol
MIDDLEBURY **11**
Mt Moosalamoo 799m
30
7
Brandon
Rutla
4
Fair Haven
Poultney
Walling
30
MANCHESTER **13**
Arlington
7
15
9
BENNINGTON
10
Pittsfield

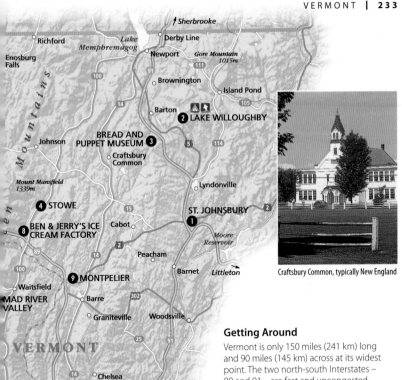

Craftsbury Common, typically New England

Getting Around

Vermont is only 150 miles (241 km) long and 90 miles (145 km) across at its widest point. The two north-south Interstates – 89 and 91 – are fast and uncongested (although traffic is heavier during the fall foliage season). Travelers driving east to west will find the going a little slower. The roads are narrow and village speed limits are usually 25 mph (40 kph). Burlington is the state's transportation hub, with a major airport and Greyhound bus services to many of Vermont's larger towns as well as points in New Hampshire and Massachusetts. Greyhound also runs several buses daily between Burlington and Montreal, Quebec. Amtrak operates two rail lines, both originating in New York, which make a number of stops in the state.

Serene paddling on quiet Amherst Lake, south of Plymouth

For additional map symbols *see back flap*

❶ St. Johnsbury

🏔 7,800. ✈ 77 miles (125 km) W in Burlington. 🚌 ℹ 2000 Memorial Dr. (802) 748-3678 or (800) 639-6379. 🌐 nekchamber.com

This small industrial town, which is the unofficial capital of Vermont's northeast region – also called the "Northeast Kingdom" – sits on a promontory at the convergence of the Moose, Sleeper, and Passumpsic Rivers. The town is named for Saint Jean de Crèvecoeur, who was a friend of Revolutionary War hero Ethan Allen. It was the Frenchman who suggested that "bury" be added to the name because there were too many towns called St. John.

It was here in 1830 that mechanic Thaddeus Fairbanks (1796–1886) invented the platform scale, an easier and more accurate method of weighing than the balances of the time. The Fairbanks scale, as it came to be known, put St. Johnsbury on the map and boosted the growth of other pioneer industries, notably the manufacturing of maple products.

The Fairbanks family collected art and antiques, which now are housed in the **Fairbanks Museum and Planetarium** – one of the area's finest natural history museums. This Romanesque-style brick Victorian building, now on the National Historic Register, contains over 175,000 artifacts, including 4,500 stuffed birds and animals, and tools, dolls, and toys. Also on Main Street is the **St. Johnsbury Athenaeum**

Art on walnut wall panels at St. Johnsbury Athenaeum Art Gallery

Tranquil waters of Lake Willoughby

Art Gallery, a Victorian gem with gleaming woodwork, paneled walls, and circular staircase. The gallery highlights the landscapes of the Hudson River School of painting. Popular in the 19th century, the movement was the first native school of American art, and focuses on the beauty of the natural world. Albert Bierstadt (1830–1902), whose massive canvas *Domes of Yosemite* (1867) hangs here, was one of its leaders.

🏛 Fairbanks Museum and Planetarium
1302 Main St. **Tel** (802) 748-2372. Museum: **Open** 9am–5pm daily. Planetarium: **Open** call for show times. 🚫 ♿ 📷 🌐 fairbanksmuseum.org

🏛 St. Johnsbury Athenaeum Art Gallery
1171 Main St. **Tel** (802) 748-8291. **Open** 10am–5:30pm Mon, Wed & Fri, 2–7pm Tue & Thu, 9:30am–5pm (3pm in summer) Sat. 🚫 ♿ 📷 🌐 stjathenaeum.org

Environs
Nineteen miles (30 km) to the west is Cabot, where one of the state's best-known agricultural products – cheddar cheese – is made. The **Cabot Creamery**, a farmers' cooperative, was started in 1919 and now produces a mind-boggling 100 million lb (45.5 million kg) of cheese a year. The creamery offers tours and free tastings.

🧀 Cabot Creamery
Main St., Cabot, Rte. 215. **Tel** (802) 563-3393 or (800) 837-4261. **Open** May–Oct: 9am–5pm daily; Nov & Dec: 10am–4pm daily; Jan–Apr: 10am–4pm Mon–Sat. **Closed** Jan 1, Thanksgiving. 🚫 ♿ 🌐 cabotcheese.com

❷ Lake Willoughby

Rte. 5A near Barton. **Tel** (802) 239-4147.

Travelers heading east from Barton climb a crest on the road only to be met with the breath-taking view of this beautiful body of water. The narrow glacial lake, which plunges 300 ft (90 m) in certain areas, is flanked by two soaring cliffs: Mount Pisgah at 2,750 ft (840 m) and Mount Hor at 2,650 ft (810 m). Jutting straight out of the water, the mountains give the lake the appearance of a rugged Norwegian fjord or a resort in Switzerland, garnering it the nickname the "Lucerne of America."

With trails leading around both promontories, this is a haven for hikers and swimmers looking for a secluded spot. There are wonderful picnic and camping areas along the beaches at either end of the 5-mile (8-km) lake. Several resorts and bed and breakfast establishments ring the shores. The lake itself offers plenty of recreational opportunities – fishing, boating, scuba diving – and there are three nearby golf courses.

Environs
Because of its isolated location 11 miles (18 km) northwest of Lake Willoughby, Brownington has retained the look of an 18th-century village, with few modern touches. The **Old Stone House** museum documents the history of the region. Twenty-two miles (35 km) to the north of the lake lies Derby Line – really two communities in one. The northern half, which is in Quebec, Canada, is called Rock Island.

The border between Canada and the US runs through the middle of the **Haskell Free Library and Opera House**, a stately granite and brick building constructed in 1904.

Part of the audience sits in the US, but the stage is in Canada. The building's wealthy benefactor, Mrs. Martha Stewart Haskell (1831–1906), wanted both communities to enjoy her gift.

Old Stone House
109 Old Stone House Rd. **Tel** (802) 754-2022. **Open** call for hours. 🚫 obligatory. ♿ 📷

Haskell Free Library and Opera House
93 Caswell Ave. **Tel** (802) 873-3022. Library: **Open** 10am–5pm Tue, Wed & Fri, 10am–6pm Thu, 10am–2pm Sat. Opera House: **Open** May–Oct: call for tours. **Closed** Sun & Mon. 📷

❸ Bread and Puppet Museum

Exit 25 Rte. 122 near Glover. **Tel** (802) 525-3031 or (802) 525-6972. **Open** Jun–Sep: call for hours and show times. 📷 🌐 breadandpuppet.org

An extraordinary place down a quiet rural road, this museum is a century-old, two-story building, which once served as a barn to shelter dairy cattle. The cattle have gone, but every

A selection of fanciful creatures at the Bread and Puppet Museum

The Austrian-style Trapp Family Lodge

inch of space is taken up by paintings, masks, and other theatrical knickknacks, most notably puppets of all shapes and sizes, dressed in outlandish costumes in every style. The props belong to the internationally famous Bread and Puppet Theater company, founded in 1962. Guided tours of the museum are the best way to glimpse the history behind the artistry. The troupe members live communally on the surrounding farm. Their productions are notable for the masterful use of giant puppets.

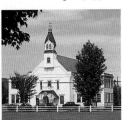
Typical Vermont church in Craftsbury Common

Environs
Small and graceful Craftsbury Common, just 14 miles (22 km) southwest, is pure Americana. Gnarled old trees, planted in 1799 to commemorate the death of George Washington (1732–99), the first president of the US, line the main street. The village green is flanked by handsome clapboard homes with black shutters, and is anchored at one corner by a typical New England church with a white wooden steeple. In winter the area is popular with cross-country skiers.

❹ Stowe

🏠 3,500. ✈ 40 miles (64 km) W in Burlington. ℹ 51 Main St. (802) 253-7321 or (877) 467-8693.
🌐 gostowe.com

It is hardly surprising that the Von Trapp family, whose daring escape from Austria during World War II was the inspiration behind the 1965 movie *The Sound of Music*, chose Stowe as their new home. The pretty village is ringed by mountains, which reminded them of the Alpine region they had left behind. Their Trapp Family Lodge *(see p317)* is part of the 4.2-sq-mile (10.9-sq-km) estate. The giant wooden chalet is one of the area's most popular hotels.

The village has been a major ski and outdoor activity center since the 1930s. In winter it draws hordes of skiers looking to enjoy the region's best slopes *(see pp362–3)*. Mountain Road begins in the village and is lined with chalets, motels, restaurants, and pubs; it leads to the area's highest peak, 4,393-ft (1,339-m) Mount Mansfield. Many local spas and resorts offer gourmet meals, and massages and other health treatments.

In summer there are still opportunities to enjoy the outdoors. Visitors can hike, rock-climb, fish, and canoe, or walk, cycle, or inline skate along the paved, meandering 5.5-mile (8.5-km) Stowe Recreational Path. It winds from Stowe's village church across the West Branch River, then through woodlands.

❺ Burlington

Burlington is one of Vermont's most popular tourist destinations. It is a lively university town with almost half of its population of just over 40,000 made up of students or people associated with the University of Vermont (UVM) and the city's four colleges. One of the oldest universities in the country, UVM was founded in 1791, the same year that Vermont officially joined the United States. Burlington's strategic location on the eastern shore of Lake Champlain *(see p240)* helped it prosper in pioneer times, and today it is Vermont's center of commerce and industry. The town is also rich in grand old mansions, historic landmarks, interesting shops, and restaurants, and has an attractive waterfront. The famed American Revolution patriot Ethan Allen (1738–89), omnipresent throughout the state, has his final resting place here in Greenmount Cemetery.

The restored Flynn Center for the Performing Arts, close to City Hall Place

Exploring Burlington

The center of Burlington is compact and easy to explore on foot. Battery Street, near the waterfront, is the oldest, most historic part of the city and a jumping-off point for ferries to New York State and sightseeing trips around Lake Champlain. More than 200 handsome buildings in the downtown core have been renovated, and visitors will find many architectural landmarks, including the First Unitarian Church *(see pp238–9)*.

Battery Park, at the north end of Battery Street where it meets Pearl Street, was the site of a battle between US soldiers and the British Royal Navy. Burlington saw several skirmishes during the War of 1812, and scuba divers have found military artifacts at the bottom of the lake. Five shipwrecks, three lying close to Burlington, can be explored by divers who register with the Waterfront Diving Center on Battery Street.

These days Battery Park is a much more peaceful place. Lake Champlain is at its widest point here, and visitors who stroll through the park are rewarded with lovely views of Burlington Bay and the backdrop

of the Adirondack Mountains on the other side of the lake. Entertainment is presented in the park on selected evenings in summer.

Burlington's cultural life comes to the fore during its annual jazz festival in June. Venues for this popular concert series include City Hall Stage, Waterfront Park, the Church Street Marketplace *(see pp238–9)*, and the Flynn Center for the Performing Arts. A former vaudeville theater and movie palace, the Flynn has had its Art Deco interior carefully restored, and now stages a variety of cultural events throughout the year. Vermont is well-known for

Statue in Battery Park

Key

Street-by-Street map *see pp238–9*

0 meters 250
0 yards 250

Lake steamer with a full complement of sightseers

its many artists working in craft media. The Frog Hollow Vermont State Craft Center, located on Church Street, serves as a sales gallery for work by artist members and as a source of information on classes in craft media across the state.

🚢 Spirit of Ethan Allen III

Burlington Boat House, College Street. **Tel** (802) 862-8300. **Open** May–Oct: 10am–6:30pm daytime and sunset dinner cruises (reservations necessary). 🚢 🅿 ♿ ✏
W soea.com

Tall-stack steamers used to ply the waters of Lake Champlain. Today visitors can board a three-decker cruise ship, *Spirit of Ethan Allen III*, which holds 363 passengers. During the 90-minute trip, the captain narrates entertaining tales of the Revolutionary War.

🏛 Robert Hull Fleming Museum

61 Colchester Ave. **Tel** (802) 656-2090. **Open** May–mid-Sep: noon–4pm Tue–Fri, 1–5pm Sat & Sun; mid-Sep–Apr: 10am–4pm Tue–Fri (to 7pm Wed), noon–4pm Sat & Sun. **Closed** mid-Dec–mid-Jan, public hols. 🅿 ♿ 📷

The museum is located on the campus of the **University of Vermont**, up on a hillside overlooking the city. Built in 1931, the elegant Colonial Revival building houses a huge collection of artifacts –

Statue of Penelope in the Fleming Museum

more than 25,000 items – ranging from ancient Mesopotamia to modern times. Some of the items on display include European and American paintings and sculptures, as well as Native Indian crafts and glassware.

🐄 Shelburne Farms

1611 Harbor Rd. **Tel** (802) 985-8442. Dairy **Open** mid-May–mid-Oct: 9:30am–3:30pm daily. Farm Store **Open** year-round: 10am–5pm daily. 🚢 🅿 ♿ partial.
W shelburnefarms.org

Seven miles (11 km) south of town are Shelburne Museum (*see pp242–3*) and Shelburne Farms, a historic 2.2-sq-mile (5.7-sq-km) estate. The parklike grounds of the latter include rolling pastures, woodlands, and a working farm. Tours are given of the dairy. There is a children's farmyard.

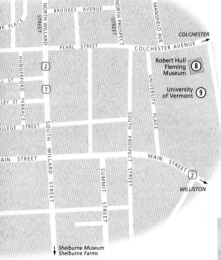

Burlington Town Center

① First Unitarian Church
② Church Street Marketplace
③ City Hall Place
④ Flynn Center for the Performing Arts
⑤ Battery Park
⑥ Waterfront Park
⑦ *Spirit of Ethan Allen III*
⑧ Robert Hull Fleming Museum
⑨ University of Vermont

Part of the stately University of Vermont campus

For map symbols *see back flap*

Street-by-Street: Historic District

The four-block section known as the Church Street Marketplace
is located at the center of the city's historic district. The
neighborhood has been converted into a pedestrian mall
complete with trendy boutiques, patio restaurants, specialty
stores, factory outlets, craft shops, and, naturally, a Ben & Jerry's
(see p240). The marketplace, thronged with shoppers and
sightseers at the best of times, is at its most vibrant in the summer
months, with numerous street performers and musicians adding
color and action. The district also has its share of historical
attractions, including the 1816 First Unitarian Church.

Richardson Building
This 1895 chateau-style
building was a 19th-century
department store.

The Masonic Temple
is Church Street's
tallest structure.

★ **First Unitarian Church**
Standing at the head of
Church Street, the First
Unitarian Church was built
in 1816 and stands as the
oldest house of worship
in Burlington.

**The Burlington Montgomery
Ward Building**, built in 1929, is on the
National Register of Historic Places. Its
graceful lines and colorful façade
typify pre-Depression architecture.

**Central-Union
Blocks**
This was the first
major development
on upper Church
Street. It now
houses restaurants
and pubs.

Pedestrian Mall
This section of the mall – particularly lively on weekends – is popular among students and tourists for its many shops and terraces. Cafés, pubs, and restaurants are housed in Queen Anne-style buildings from the late 1800s.

Merchants Bank was built in 1895 by Burlington architect Sydney Greene.

★ City Hall
This 1928 building marks the southern boundary of the marketplace and is made of local brick, marble, and granite.

Key

▨ Pedestrian mall

— Suggested route

WINOOSKI AVENUE

STREET

COLLEGE STREET

MAIN STREET

0 meters 25
0 yards 25

Abraham Block was once considered the most striking commercial block in the state.

City Hall Park
The park is a popular outdoor concert venue. It features a poured concrete fountain and two granite monuments. One honors those who died in the Civil War; the other, soldiers who died in World War II.

Sailing and boating, popular on beautiful Lake Champlain

❻ Lake Champlain

Vermont-New York border from Whitehall to Alburg. ✈ Burlington. 🚌 ℹ️ 60 Main St., Burlington (802) 863-3489 or (877) 686-5253.
Ⓦ **vermont.org**

Said to be the home of "Champ," a water serpent that could be a distant cousin of Scotland's Loch Ness Monster, Lake Champlain was named for French explorer Samuel de Champlain (1574–1635). He discovered and explored much of the surrounding region. Some 120 miles (190 km) long and 12 miles (19 km) wide, the lake has its western shore in New York State, while the eastern sector is in Vermont. Seasonal hour-long ferry rides run regularly between Burlington and Port Kent, New York.

Sometimes called the sixth Great Lake because of its size, Champlain has 500 miles (800 km) of shoreline and about 70 islands. At the lake's northern end, the Alburg Peninsula and a group of thin islands (North Hero, Isle La Motte, and Grand Isle) give glimpses of the region's colorful past.

At Ste. Anne's Shrine on Isle La Motte is a statue of Champlain. Grand Isle is home to America's oldest log cabin (1783). The villages of North and South Hero were named in honor of brothers Ethan and Ira Allen. Their volunteers, the Green Mountain Boys, helped secure Vermont's status as a separate state.

Some of Lake Champlain's treasures are underwater, preserved in a marine park where scuba divers can explore shipwrecks resting on sandbars and at the bottom of the lake.

Displays at the **Lake Champlain Maritime Museum** at Basin Harbor focus on some of the historic shipwrecks, as well as the numerous steamboats that once plied these waters. Visitors can board a full-scale replica of a 1776 gunboat and visit the Hazelett Watercraft Center, which contains canoes, kayaks, and wooden boats.

🏛 **Lake Champlain Maritime Museum**
4472 Basin Harbor Rd., Vergennes. **Tel** (802) 475-2022. **Open** late May–early Oct: 10am–5pm daily. 🅿️ ♿
Ⓦ **lcmm.org**

❼ Shelburne Museum

See pp242–3.

Gold dome of the Vermont State House in Montpelier

❽ Ben & Jerry's Ice Cream Factory

Rte. 100, Waterbury. **Tel** (802) 882-1240 or (866) 258-6877. **Open** tours: Jul–mid-Aug: 9am–9pm daily; mid-Aug–Oct: 9am–7pm daily; Nov–Jun: 10am–6pm daily. 🅿️ ♿ 🚻 📷
Ⓦ **benjerry.com**

Although Ben Cohen and Jerry Greenfield hail from Long Island, New York, they have done more than any other "flatlanders" to put Vermont's dairy industry on the map. In 1977 these childhood friends paid $5 for a correspondence course on making ice cream and parlayed their knowledge into a hugely successful franchise.

Ben and Jerry use the richest cream and milk from local farms to produce their ice cream and frozen yogurt. The Ben & Jerry trademark is the

Ben & Jerry's bus, gaily decorated with dairy cows

black and white Holstein cow, embellishing everything in the gift shop.

Tours of the factory start every 15 to 30 minutes and run for half an hour. Visitors learn all there is to know about making ice cream. They are given a bird's-eye view of the factory floor, and at the end of the tour a chance to sample the products and sometimes test new flavors.

❾ Montpelier

🏙 8,400. ✈ 40 miles (64 km) NW in Burlington. 🚌 🚉 ℹ️ (877) 887-3678.
Ⓦ **central-vt.com**

Montpelier is the smallest state capital in the US, but its diminutive stature is advantageous. The city is impeccably clean, friendly, and easily seen on foot. Despite its size, Montpelier has a grand, imposing building to house its state politicians and legislators. The **Vermont State House**, which dates back to 1859, replaced an earlier building that was destroyed by fire. It is now a formidable Greek Revival structure, complete with a gilt cupola and giant fluted pillars of granite that were hewn from one of the quarries at neighboring Barre.

The **Vermont History Museum**, run by the local historical society, is housed in a replica of a 19th-century hotel. The museum has an additional center in Barre.

Vermont State House
115 State St. **Tel** (802) 828-2228. **Open** year-round: 8am–4pm Mon–Fri. Jul–Oct: 10am–3:30pm Mon–Fri, 11am–2:30pm Sat. **Closed** public hols.

Vermont History Museum
109 State St. **Tel** (802) 828-2291. **Open** 10am–4pm Tue–Sat. **vermonthistory.org**

Environs
Seven miles (11 km) to the south, Barre (pronounced "berry") is the self-proclaimed granite capital of the world. In the 19th century, Italian and Scottish stonemasons came here to work the pale, white and blue-gray rock.

The region is still a hive of granite-related activity, with several large plants producing stone for tombstones (many have ended up in Barre's Hope Cemetery on Merchant Street), statues, and monuments. In nearby Graniteville, the **Rock of Ages Quarry** is the biggest such operation. Visitors can watch – from the safety of an observation deck – as the stone is being hewn from the

huge 475-ft (134-m) pit. On weekdays visitors can also take a self-guided tour to see artisans at work.

Rock of Ages Quarry
773 Main St., Graniteville. **Tel** (802) 476-3119. **Open** call for hours. **Closed** Jul 4. quarry: late May–mid-Oct; factory: Feb–mid-Dec. **rockofages.com**

⑩ Mad River Valley
Central VT along Rte. 100. Rte. 100, Waitsfield (802) 496-3409 or (800) 828-4748. Waitsfield, mid-May–Columbus Day: 9:30am–1pm Sat. **madrivervalley.com**

Located in central Vermont, Mad River Valley is most famous for outdoor activities that include hiking, cycling, hunting, and especially skiing.

One popular stop is the Mad River Glen ski area (*see p362*), which attracts die-hard traditionalists who enjoy their sport the old-fashioned way – without fancy high-speed gondolas (though there are four chairlifts) and snowmaking equipment. With about four dozen trails, Mad River Glen caters to the country's most skilled skiers – in fact, its motto is "Ski it if you can."

Sugarbush, on the other hand, has more than 100 trails and a vertical drop of 2,650 ft (800 m). It is the polar opposite of Mad River Glen. This trendy resort, which caters to beginners and intermediate skiers as well as those who are more advanced,

Moss Glenn Falls near Warren in Mad River Valley

has the most modern snowmaking facilities and lifts. It was very popular with the 1960s "jet set," but now a more "retro" crowd who own time-share condos frequents the slopes. A state-of-the-art express "people mover" connects what used to be two separate ski areas: Lincoln Peak and Mount Ellen.

Activities in and around Waitsfield, the small, fashionable, and wealthy community that is the center of this tourist region, include hiking, hunting, and – of all things – polo. The local landmark is a round barn, which is one of only a dozen remaining in the state. It is a venue for cultural functions and art exhibits. It sits next to an elegant inn and restaurant that has been converted from an 1806 farmhouse.

Bucolic scenery outside of Waitsfield, a popular summer destination

❼ Shelburne Museum

More than just an eclectic repository, the Shelburne Museum celebrates three centuries of American ingenuity, creativity, and diversity. Here folk art, antique tools, duck decoys, and circus memorabilia are displayed on the same grounds as scrimshaw, and paintings by such US artists as Winslow Homer (1836–1910) and Grandma Moses (1860–1961). Established in 1947 by collector Electra Webb (1888–1960), the museum's 39 exhibition buildings and their contents constitute one of the nation's finest museums.

★ **Circus Building**
The horseshoe-shaped building houses a 500-ft- (152-m-) long miniature circus parade. The west entrance foyer features this 3,500-piece miniature circus.

Museum Store
Handicrafts by New England artisans are sold here.

Round Barn Gallery
All three floors of this 1901 barn feature changing exhibits. The visitor center is located on the top floor.

Key

☐ Illustrated
☐ Not illustrated

1 Museum Store and Entrance
2 Round Barn Gallery
3 Circus Building and Carousel
4 Railroad Station
5 Beach Gallery
6 Beach Lodge
7 *Ticonderoga*
8 Electra Havemeyer Webb Memorial Building
9 Lighthouse
10 Webb Gallery
11 Covered Bridge
12 Meeting House
13 Horseshoe Barny

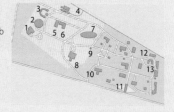

★ **Railroad Station**
The station was built in 1890 in Shelburne, Vermont, and relocated here. It houses a variety of railroad memorabilia, including telegraphy systems, vintage railroad maps, a restored stationmaster's office, and men's and women's waiting rooms.

1871 Lake Champlain Lighthouse
Built to warn ships off reefs in the lake, the building now houses art exhibits and tells of the lives led by lighthouse keepers.

KEY

① **Vintage 1920s carousel**

② **Beach Lodge**, built to resemble an Adirondack hunting lodge, contains a variety of big-game trophies.

③ **Locomotive 220**, a 1915 10-wheel steam locomotive, hauled freight and passenger trains. Engine 220 could pull 12.5 tons (11 tonnes) of dead weight.

★ **Ticonderoga**
A National Historic Landmark, the *Ticonderoga* was still in operation when Webb bought it in 1951. Today the former Lake Champlain steamship is open for visitors to explore.

⓫ Middlebury

🏔 8,500. ✈ 36 miles (58 km) N in Burlington. 🚌 ℹ 93 Court St. (802) 388-7951. 🌐 addisoncounty.com

Middlebury, founded in 1761, is the archetypal New England town. It has not one, but two village greens, or "commons," tall-spired churches, a prestigious college, and a collection of Colonial-era homes. In all Middlebury lays claim to more than 300 buildings that were constructed during the 18th and early 19th centuries. Chief among them are the Congregational Church, the Battell and Beckwith commercial blocks, and the Middlebury Inn, a classic brick Georgian-style hostelry with shuttered windows that dates back to 1827.

The town sits on Otter Creek, which at one time powered the machinery for a thriving wool and grain industry. But the town gets its name from the days of stage coaches when Middlebury served as the transit point on Vermont's main north-south and east-west routes. Morgan horses, one of the first US native breeds, were often seen on this route. Today visitors can tour the **University of Vermont Morgan Horse Farm**, which is dedicated to the preservation and improvement of this versatile and historic breed. Between 60 and 80 stallions, mares, and foals are cared for by agricultural science students. History buffs will enjoy the **Henry Sheldon Museum of Vermont History**, an 1829 house that documents the early 19th century through its collection of furniture, textiles and clothing, and portraits.

Folk art and folk ways meet the 21st century at the **Vermont Folklife Center** where multimedia exhibits using computers and iPods help bring rural culture to life. The center's

Peaceful campus of Middlebury College

Morgan Horse Farm

Heritage Shop features quilts, decoys, baskets, and other objects made by contemporary folk artists. The 0.8-sq-mile (2-sq-km) campus of **Middlebury College** is a delightful place to explore, with graceful architecture, an art gallery, and green spaces. The college's Bread Loaf campus in nearby Ripton is nestled in the Green Mountain National Forest *(see p248)* near the scenic Robert Frost Interpretive Trail. Named for the famous American poet who spent summers here from 1938 to 1962, the path is flanked with quotations from Frost's poems set on plaques.

🅤 **University of Vermont Morgan Horse Farm**
Rte. 23 NW of Middlebury in Weybridge. **Tel** (802) 388-2011. **Open** May–Oct: 9am–4pm daily. 🅿 📷 ♿

🏛 **Henry Sheldon Museum of Vermont History**
1 Park St. **Tel** (802) 388-2117. **Open** Mar–Jan: 10am–5pm Tue–Sat (May–Oct: also 1–5pm Sun). **Closed** Feb. 📷 ♿

🏛 **Vermont Folklife Center**
88 Main St. **Tel** (802) 388-4964. **Open** 10am–5pm Tue–Sat. ♿ 🏫

🎓 **Middlebury College**
College St. **Tel** (802) 443-5000. **Open** year-round: Mon–Fri. ♿ ♿

⓬ Killington

🏔 1,000. 🚏 5 miles (8 km) W in Rutland. ℹ Rte. 4, West Killington (802) 422-3333 or (800) 621-6867. 🌐 killington.com

Outdoor adventurers seeking a lively social life head for this year-round resort. Killington has hundreds of condominiums, vacation homes, ski lodges and B&Bs, golf courses, hiking and bike trails, and an adventure center with water slides and a climbing wall. It operates the largest ski center *(see p362)* in the eastern United States, with 200 runs for alpine skiing and snowboarding spread across seven peaks including nearby Pico Mountain. Killington itself is the second-highest peak in Vermont, at 4,240 ft (1,295 m). Two of the best cross-country ski centers in the eastern US – Mountain Top Inn and Mountain Meadows Cross Country Ski & Snowshoe

One of the numerous trails at Killington, Vermont

Center – are also situated in the Killington area.

The ski season here usually lasts eight months, longer than anywhere else in Vermont, and one of the gondolas that ferry skiers to the peaks runs during the summer and fall as well. It is worth taking a ride to the top for the spectacular views. On a clear day, visitors can glimpse parts of five states and distant Canada. Killington also keeps busy throughout the summer with arts and crafts shows, barbecues, and music festivals.

⓭ Manchester

🏛 3,860. ✈ 33 miles (53 km) N in Rutland. 🚌 ℹ 39 Bonnet St. (802) 362-6313. 🌐 visitmanchestervt.com

Manchester is actually made up of three separate communities: Manchester Depot and Manchester Center, the outlet centers of New England, and Manchester Village. The sum of these parts is a picturesque destination surrounded by mountains, typical of scenic southern Vermont. There are two major ski areas: Stratton, a large complex with more than 90 trails and a hillside ski village with shops and restaurants; and Bromley, a busy, family-oriented ski area.

Manchester has been a popular vacation resort since the 19th century, when wealthy urbanites used to head to the mountains to escape the summer heat. The town's marble sidewalks fringed by old shade trees, the restored Equinox Resort (see p317), and several stately homes evoke that era. Today's tourists take pleasure in following the Equinox Skyline Drive, a toll road, with its panoramic view of the countryside from the crest of Mount Equinox. Many visitors spend their time hunting for brand-name bargains in the designer outlets and factory stores.

One of Manchester's largest and most elegant houses is **Hildene**, a 24-room Georgian Revival manor house built by Robert Lincoln (1843–1926), a lawyer, diplomat, and the son of President Abraham Lincoln (1809–65). Among the mansion's most notable features are its 1,000-pipe Aeolian organ and Lincoln family memorabilia. The grounds are graced with an impeccable formal garden. In winter, 8 miles (14 km) of trails are open to cross-country skiers.

The **Southern Vermont Arts Center** presents music and dance performances and mounts art exhibitions in a stately Georgian mansion as well as a modern museum building. The 522,700-sq-ft (48,550-sq-m) estate features the state's largest sculpture garden. Elsewhere, the

Antique kitchenware on display at elegant Hildene

American Museum of Fly Fishing claims to house the largest collection of fly-fishing paraphernalia in the world. The collection includes hundreds of rods, reels, and flies used by famous people such as singer Bing Crosby, literary giant Ernest Hemingway, and former US president Jimmy Carter.

Manchester is also the site where Charles Orvis established his fly rod shop in 1856; the finest of the company's rods are still built there. The extensive retail operation of the **Orvis Flagship Store** carries the full line of Orvis rods, reels, flies, clothing, and fly-tying equipment and supplies. The store also operates free introductory and intermediate fly-fishing classes on select dates throughout the summer.

🏠 **Hildene**
Rte. 7A. **Tel** (802) 362-1788. **Open** year-round: 9:30am–4:30pm daily. **Closed** Easter, Thanksgiving, Dec 25–27. 🅿 ♿ 📷 🌐 hildene.org

🏛 **Southern Vermont Arts Center**
West Rd. **Tel** (802) 362-1405. **Open** 10am–5pm Tue–Sat, noon–5pm Sun. 🅿 ♿ ✏ 🌐 svac.org

🏛 **American Museum of Fly Fishing**
4104 Main St. **Tel** (802) 362-3300. **Open** Jan–May: 10am–4pm Tue–Sat; Jun–Dec: 10am–4pm Tue–Sun. 🅿 ♿ 🌐 amff.com

🏠 **Orvis Flagship Store**
4180 Main St. **Tel** (802) 362-3750. **Open** 10am–6pm Mon–Fri, 9am–6pm Sat, 10am–5pm Sun. 🌐 orvis.com

Norman Rockwell in Vermont

Painter and illustrator Norman Rockwell, famous for idealized depictions of small-town America, lived in Arlington at the height of his career, from 1939 to 1954. His paintings were so detailed they looked almost like photographs, and the magazine covers that he designed for publications such as *Saturday Evening Post*, the *Ladies' Home Journal*, and *Look*, have become collectors' items. Admirers of his work should be sure to visit the Norman Rockwell Museum in Stockbridge, Massachusetts (see p170).

Norman Rockwell surveys his work surrounded by friends and his son c.1944

⑭ Green Mountain National Forest

ℹ️ Forest Supervisor, Green Mountain National Forest, 231 N Main St., Rutland. **Tel** (802) 747-6700. Hapgood Campground: **Tel** (877) 444-6777 for reservations (all other campgrounds on first-come, first-served basis). **Open** year-round. 🅿️ to campgrounds. 🆆 fs.usda.gov

This huge spine of greenery and mountains runs for 550 sq miles (1,400 sq km) – almost the entire length of the state – along two-thirds of the Green Mountain range. The mountains, many more than 4,000 ft (1,200 m) high, have some of the best ski centers in the eastern United States, including Sugarbush *(see p241)* and Mount Snow *(see p250)*. A large network of snowmobile and cross-country ski trails are also maintained throughout the winter months.

The National Forest is divided into northern and southern sectors, and encompasses six wilderness areas; sections of the forest have remained entirely undeveloped – no roads, no electricity, and even paths may be poorly marked or nonexistent. While hard-core backcountry hikers and campers may enjoy this challenge, the majority of travelers will prefer to roam the less primitive areas of the forest. Picnic sites and campgrounds are found throughout, along with more than 500 miles (805 km) of hiking paths, including the challenging Long and Appalachian trails *(see pp26–7)*.

Many lakes, rivers, and, reservoirs offer excellent boating and fishing opportunities. On land, bike paths (both mountain and road) are numerous and specially designated paths are open to horseback riders. Regardless of their mode of transportation, visitors are encouraged to stay on the paths in order to preserve the delicate ecosystem. Markers indicate designated lookout points and covered bridges. The town of Stratton in the southern portion of the Green Mountain range offers recreational activities such as golf, horseback riding, sailing, and fly-fishing, as well as alpine and cross-country skiing. Stratton Mountain hosts many events. Nearby Bromley Mountain Ski Center has been a popular family resort since the 1930s.

Woodward Reservoir in the Green Mountain National Forest

⑮ Bennington

🏘️ 16,800. 🚆 🚌 ℹ️ Rte. 7 (802) 447-3311 or (800) 229-0252. 🛒 Wed & Fri. 🆆 bennington.com

Although it is tucked away in the southwest corner of the Green Mountain National Forest bordering Massachusetts and New York State, Bennington is no backwoods community.

Dense woodlands of the Green Mountain National Forest

◀ Picturesque countryside during autumn in Vermont

The third-largest city in the state, Bennington is an important manufacturing center and home to Bennington College, the faculty of which once included cutting-edge engineer Buckminster Fuller (1895–1983).

Three covered bridges (just off Route 67) herald the approach to town. These 19th-century wooden structures, built with roofs to protect them

The pulpit of Bennington's First Congregational Church

against the harsh Vermont winter, were nicknamed "kissing bridges," because in the days of horses and buggies they provided a discreet shelter for courting couples to embrace.

Bennington was established in 1749 and a few decades later Ethan Allen arrived on the scene to lead the Green Mountain Boys, a citizen's militia originally created to protect Vermont from the expansionist advances of neighboring New York. Allen would later make his name as a patriot during the Revolutionary War by leading his men into battle and scoring several decisive victories against British forces.

The Revolutionary era comes alive during a walking tour of the **Old Bennington Historic District** just west of the downtown core, where a typical New England village green is ringed by pillared Greek Revival structures and Federal-style brick buildings. The 1806 **First Congregational Church**, with its vaulted plaster and wood ceilings, is a striking and much-photographed local landmark. Next to it is the Old Burying Ground, resting place of five

Vermont governors and the beloved poet Robert Frost *(see p35)*.

Looming over the Historic District is the 306-ft- (93-m-) high **Bennington Battle Monument**, a massive stone obelisk that, when it was built in 1891, was the tallest war monument in the world. It commemorates a 1777 battle in nearby Willoomsac Heights, when the Colonial forces defeated the British Army and their allies, leading to the surrender of their commander, General John Burgoyne (1722–92). An elevator takes visitors to an observation area that affords panoramic views of Vermont and the neighboring states of New York and Massachusetts.

The turbulent times of the Revolutionary War are also recalled at the **Bennington Museum**, where the Military Gallery includes maps, artworks, and artifacts relating to the decisive battle that took place here. The museum is perhaps best known for the Grandma Moses Gallery. Famed folk artist Anna Mary "Grandma" Moses (1860–1961) lived

The 1891 Bennington Battle Monument

in the Bennington area. A farmer's wife with no formal training in art, Moses started painting landscapes as a hobby when she was in her mid-70s. She was "discovered" by the critics in 1940 and was hailed as an important new talent. By the time she died in 1961 at the age of 101, Grandma Moses had produced some 1,600 works of art.

The museum focuses on American art, with an emphasis on the arts of Vermont. The wide-ranging exhibitions feature ceramics produced in Bennington, American glassware, and art and furniture from the city's Gilded Age heyday. The painting collection ranges from folk-art portraits of early Bennington settlers to landscapes and striking modern canvases created in the 1950s through 1970s by a group of avant-garde artists, including Helen Frankenthaler and Jules Olitski, who worked in the Bennington area.

Portrait of Governor Paul Brigham

🏛 **Old Bennington Historic District**
Tel (802) 447-3311 or (800) 229-0252.

⛪ **First Congregational Church**
Monument Ave. **Tel** (802) 447-1223. ⛪ 11am Sun (9:30am Jul & Aug). 📷

🏛 **Bennington Battle Monument**
15 Monument Circle. **Tel** (802) 447-0550. **Open** mid-Apr–late Oct: 9am–5pm daily. 🅿 ♿ 📷

🏛 **Bennington Museum**
75 Main St. **Tel** (802) 447-1571.
Open 10am–5pm Thu–Tue (Jun–Oct: 10am–5pm daily). **Closed** Jan–mid-Feb, Thanksgiving, Dec 25. 🅿 ♿ 📷
🌐 benningtonmuseum.org

For hotels and restaurants in this region see pp316–17 and pp335–6

⑯ Wilmington

🗺 1,950. ✈ 8 miles (13 km) NW in West Dover. ℹ 21 W Main St. (802) 464-8092.

Wilmington is the largest village in the Mount Snow Valley, with several dozen restaurants and stores catering to the tourists who come to enjoy outdoor sports at the nearby mountain. Like so many of Vermont's small towns, its Main Street is lined with restored 18th- and 19th-century buildings, many listed on the National Register of Historic Places.

Standing 3,600 ft (1,100m) tall, **Mount Snow** is named after the original owner of the land, farmer Reuben Snow, although most visitors believe the name refers to the abundance of white stuff that during winter is the resort's raison d'être.

In the late 1990s, more than $35 million was spent on upgrading the ski center, which now has 102 trails, many of them wooded, spread over 1 sq mile (2.5 sq km). Mount Snow was one of the first ski resorts in the US to provide facilities for snowboarders, with dedicated learning areas for beginners and facilities for advanced surfers. The center also opened the first mountain-bike school in the country. Outdoor summer attractions include 45 miles (72 km) of challenging bike trails (some are also ski runs), hiking routes, an inline skate and skateboard park,

Estey organs were manufactured in Brattleboro for more than 100 years

and a climbing wall. The 18-hole **Mount Snow Golf Club** provides a more sedate diversion.

🎿 **Mount Snow**
Rte. 100. **Tel** (802) 464-3333 or (800) 245-7669. **Open** year-round. 🅿 ♿
🌐 mountsnow.com

⛳ **Mount Snow Golf Club**
Rte. 100. **Tel** (802) 464-4254; call for tee times. **Open** 7am–dusk Mon–Fri, 6am–dusk Sat, Sun & public hols. 🅿

⑰ Brattleboro

🗺 12,500. ✈ 20 miles (32 km) NE in Keene, NH. 🚌 🚆 ℹ 180 Main St. (802) 254-4565 or (877) 254-4565. 🗓 May–Oct: Wed & Sat. 🌐 brattleborochamber.org

Perched on the banks of the Connecticut River on the New Hampshire border, Brattleboro is the first major town that northbound travelers encounter as they enter the state. Fort Dummer was established here in 1724, making it the state's first European settlement. For that reason, Brattleboro has adopted the slogan "Where Vermont Begins."

A bustling center of commerce and industry, the town is also a hub of tourism. As is the case with so many other Vermont towns, there is a historic district with many Colonial-era buildings of architectural interest. In the 1840s, after the Vermont Valley Railroad was laid to provide a vital link to the outside world, natural springs were discovered in the area and Brattleboro took on a new personality as a spa town where people came for "cures" and health treatments. The former railroad station is now home to the **Brattleboro Museum and Art Center**, which offers rotating exhibitions by artists of regional and international stature. The Brattleboro Music Center, on Walnut Street, stages a broad range of programs, including a chamber music series. The town's **Estey Organ Museum** is housed in the former factory building

where the famous reed, pipe, and electronic organs were manufactured, prior to being shipped around the world.

🏛 **Brattleboro Museum and Art Center**
10 Vernon St. **Tel** (802) 257-0124. **Open** 11am–5pm Wed–Mon. 🅿 ♿ 🌐 brattleboromuseum.org

🏛 **Estey Organ Museum**
108 Birge St. **Tel** (802) 246-8366. **Open** mid-May–early Oct: 2–4pm Sat & Sun. 🅿 🌐 esteyorgan museum.org

⑱ Grafton

🗺 600. ✈ 47 miles (76 km) N in Rutland. ℹ (802) 228-5830.

A thriving industrial center in the early 19th century, Grafton suffered a steady decline until by the 1960s it was almost a ghost town. But in 1963 Dean Mathey (1890–1972), a wealthy investment banker, established a foundation with the mandate to restore historic structures and revitalize commercial life. Today the village is an architectural treasure trove of 19th-century buildings.

Two tourist attractions are also thriving commercial enterprises. The 1801 Grafton Inn (see p316) is one of the country's oldest hostelries. The **Grafton Village Cheese Company** operates a retail shop next to the inn. On weekdays, visitors can often view the cheddar cheesemaking process at the nearby production facility.

Verdant farmlands around the town of Wilmington

Grafton Village Cheese Company
56 Townshend Rd. **Tel** (802) 843-1062.
Open year-round: 10am–5pm daily.
Closed Tue & Wed in winter.

Environs

Eighteen miles (29 km) to the north lies the hamlet of Plymouth Notch. The tiny community was the birthplace of Calvin Coolidge (1872–1933), the 30th president of the US. The **Calvin Coolidge State Historic Site** encompasses an 1850s general store and post office once run by Coolidge's father, a cheese factory, a schoolhouse, and the Coolidge family home.

In Weston, 21 miles (34 km) west of Plymouth Notch, visitors will find the **Vermont Country Store**. The store is famous for its enormous and eclectic array of merchandise, selected by its owners, the Orton family. Not only are these items highly original – be they badger-hair shaving brushes or handblown glasses that sea captains once used to forecast the weather – they are also always of the highest quality.

Calvin Coolidge State Historic Site
Rte. 100A. **Tel** (802) 672-3773.
Open late May–mid-Oct: 9:30am–5pm daily.

One of the many beautiful homes in the village of Woodstock

Vermont Country Store
Rte. 100, Weston. **Tel** (802) 824-3184.
Open year-round: 9am–5:30pm daily.

⑲ Woodstock

🌆 1,000. ✈ 31 miles (50 km) W in Rutland. 🚌 ℹ 59 Central St. (802) 457-3555 or (888) 496-6378.
🌐 woodstockvt.com

Even in Vermont, a state where historic, picturesque villages are common, Woodstock stands out. Founded in 1761, the town is an enclave of renovated brick and clapboard Georgian houses. The restoration of the town came about as a result of the generosity of philanthropists such as the Rockefeller family and railroad magnate Frederick Billings (1823–90). An early proponent of reforestation, Billings personally financed the planting of 10,000 trees.

Billings Farm & Museum is still a working entity. The 1890 farmhouse has been restored and there are seasonal events such as plowing competitions in the spring and apple-cider pressing in the fall. The museum also traces Vermont's agricultural past with old photographs and exhibits of harvesting implements, butter churns, and ice cutters.

The **VINS Nature Center** is a reserve where injured birds of prey can be cared for until they can be returned to the wild. As well as operating conservation programs and summer day camps for children, the naturalists here give frequent presentations about the owls, falcons, and eagles that have come under their care.

Billings Farm & Museum
River Rd. **Tel** (802) 457-2355.
Open May–Oct: 10am–5pm daily; call for winter hours.
🌐 billingsfarm.org

VINS Nature Center
Rte. 4, Quechee. **Tel** (802) 359-5000.
Open mid-Apr–Oct: 10am–5pm daily; Nov–Apr: call for hours.
🌐 vinsweb.org

Environs

Six miles (10 km) east of town is the stunning Quechee Gorge. The best view of the chasm is on Route 4, which crosses the gorge via a steel bridge. A short hiking trail leads from the parking lot on the east side down to the Ottauquechee River below.

The Rise of Calvin Coolidge

Calvin Coolidge was born in tiny Plymouth to parents who ran a general store. His humble upbringing endowed him with traits that would carry him to the presidency in the 1920s: honesty, frugality, and industry. Known as "Silent Cal," because he wasted little time on small talk, Coolidge guided the US to a period of economic prosperity before the onset of the Great Depression of 1929.

Boyhood home of Calvin Coolidge

Exploring New Hampshire

New Hampshire's compact borders make it ideal for sightseeing. Some attractions can be enjoyed on foot, as with the spectacular boardwalked chasm of Franconia Notch *(see pp276–7)*, or by car, as with a breathtaking fall-foliage tour along the Kancamagus Highway *(see p274)*. The remains of colonial battlements, the Shaker villages at Enfield *(see p266)* and Canterbury *(see pp264–5)*, and the historic homes of poets, politicians, and presidents are sprinkled throughout the state. Called the Granite State for its extensive granite formations and quarries, New Hampshire's rough edges are softened somewhat in its many fine museums. The Currier Museum of Art *(see p262)* is one such establishment, giving visitors the chance to view work by some of the world's great masters.

Bridge over the Flume Gorge in Franconia Notch State Park

Lengthy Cornish-Windsor Bridge outside Cornish

Getting Around

Interstates 93 and 89 are the largest and most popular north-south routes in the state, with numerous smaller roads branching off to more remote areas. Drivers should be aware of two New Hampshire realities: heavier traffic during peak fall-foliage season, especially on the weekends; and moose crossings. While moose sightings are thrilling, collisions with the huge animals can be extremely dangerous. Travelers should drive with caution at all times. The Amtrak "Northeaster" service stops in Exeter, Durham, and Dover. Travelers may also take Amtrak to White River Junction, Vermont, or to Boston and link up with a bus line from there. Commercial bus lines servicing the area include C&J Trailways, Concord Coach Lines, and Greyhound bus lines. The state's largest airport is found in the south in Manchester, although Maine's Portland International Airport is a good jumping-off point for northeastern New Hampshire.

For hotels and restaurants in this region see pp317–18 and pp336–8

Sights at a Glance

Key

▭▭▭ Highway
━━━ Major road
═══ Minor road
━━━ Scenic route
╍╍╍ Main railroad
──── Minor railroad
▪▪▪▪ International border
▭▭▭ State border
△ Summit

Panorama of Saco River Valley from North Conway

| 0 kilometers | 30 |
| 0 miles | 30 |

For additional map symbols see back flap

❶ Portsmouth

When settlers established a colony here in 1623, they called it Strawbery Banke *(see pp258–9)* in honor of the berries blanketing the banks of the Piscataqua River. In 1653 the name was changed to Portsmouth, a reflection of the town's reputation as a hub of maritime commerce. First a fishing port, the town enjoyed prosperity in the 18th century as a link in the trade route between Great Britain and the West Indies. During the years leading up to the American Revolution, the town was a hotbed of revolutionary fervor and the place where colonial naval hero John Paul Jones (1747–92) built his warship, the *Ranger*.

Favorite with tourists: Portsmouth's Market Street

Exploring Portsmouth

Girded by the Piscataqua River and the North and South Mill ponds, compact Portsmouth is easily explored on foot. The town's past permeates the downtown core, especially along busy Market Street. Historic buildings, some constructed in the 19th century by wealthy sea captains, have been restored and turned into museums, boutiques, and restaurants. The city also has a number of brew pubs and microbreweries that produce local ales. More than 70 historic sites, including houses and gardens, can be found along the Portsmouth Harbor Trail, a walking tour of the Historic District.

Beautiful exterior of Moffatt-Ladd House in Portsmouth

🏛 Governor John Langdon House

143 Pleasant St. **Tel** (603)-436-3205. **Open** Jun–mid-Oct: 11am–5pm Fri–Sun. **Closed** Labor Day. 🐾 🎫 ♿

The son of a farmer of modest means, John Langdon (1741–1819) became one of Portsmouth's most prominent citizens. Langdon enjoyed great prosperity as a ship captain, merchant, and shipbuilder before becoming the governor of New Hampshire and a US senator. In 1784 he built this imposing Georgian mansion. The house is known for its ornate Rococo embellishments. The grounds feature a grape arbor and a large rose garden.

🏛 Moffatt-Ladd House

154 Market St. **Tel** (603) 436-8221. **Open** mid-Jun–mid-Oct: 11am–5pm Mon–Sat, 1–5pm Sun. 🐾 🎫 ♿

One of Portsmouth's first three-story homes, this elegant 1763 mansion was built for wealthy maritime trader and sea captain John Moffatt. The house's boxy design was a precursor to the Federal style of architecture that would later become popular throughout the country. The house, located on the Portsmouth Harbor Trail, is graced by a grand entrance hall, a series of family portraits, and period furnishings.

🏛 Wentworth-Gardner House

50 Mechanic St. **Tel** (603) 436-4406. **Open** mid-Jun–mid-Oct: noon–4pm Wed–Sun. **Closed** public hols. 🐾 ♿

Also located on the Portsmouth Harbor Trail, this 1760 house is considered to be one of the best examples of Georgian architecture in the country. The house's beautiful exterior has rows of multi-paned windows, symmetrical chimneys, and a pillared entrance. The interior has 11 fireplaces, hand-painted wallpaper, and graceful carvings that took artisans a year to complete.

John Paul Jones

Born in Scotland, John Paul Jones (1747–92) went to sea as a cabin boy when he was only 12 years old. He worked his way up to being the first mate on a slave ship, then later the commander of a merchant vessel in Tobago. A hard taskmaster, Jones escaped to America before he was to go on trial for the deaths of several sailors he had punished. Regarded as an outlaw by the British, Jones went on to become an illustrious naval commander for the US. During the American Revolution, Jones led a series of daring raids up and down the British coast for which he was awarded a gold medal by Congress.

USS Albacore

Albacore Park, 600 Market St. **Tel** (603) 436-3680. **Open** mid-May–mid-Oct: 9:30am–5pm daily; mid-Oct–mid-Jan & mid-Feb–mid-May: 9:30am–4pm Thu–Mon. 🚻 🖥 ussalbacore.org

This sleek submarine was the fastest underwater vessel of its type when it was launched from the Portsmouth Naval Shipyard in 1953. It gives visitors access to the cramped quarters of submariners and an idea of what life was like for the 55 crew members. Exhibits in the visitor center trace the vessel's history.

🚤 Water Country

Rte. 1 S of Portsmouth. **Tel** (603) 427-1111. **Open** Jun–Labor Day: call for hours. 🚻 🚻 🖥 watercountry.com

Thrilling water rides, a huge wave pool, a pirate ship, and a man-made lagoon await visitors to New England's largest water park. Smaller children can enjoy the slides and fountains in designated areas, while the more adventurous thrill-seekers can careen down looping water slides.

Popular destination on summer days: Water Country

Environs

Around 12 miles (20 km) northwest of Portsmouth, the **Children's Museum of New Hampshire** has interactive exhibits that allow kids to command a submarine, don lab coats to excavate dinosaur fossils, play musical instruments from around the world, and explore visual and textural patterns. There is also a riverside playground and a human-scale kaleidoscope.

🏛 Children's Museum of New Hampshire

6 Washington St., Dover. **Tel** (603) 742-2002. **Open** 10am–5pm Tue–Sat (& Mon in summer), noon–5pm Sun. 🚻 ♿ 🖥 childrens-museum.org

Portsmouth City Center

① Governor John Langdon House
② Moffatt-Ladd House
③ Wentworth-Gardner House

Key

▓ Street-by-Street map *see pp258–9*

Street-by-Street: Strawbery Banke

This outdoor museum near the waterfront depicts more than 300 years of history in the neighborhood where Portsmouth was founded. The 435,600-sq-ft (40,450-sq-m) site contains 40 historic buildings where costumed role-players show life from 1695 to 1955. Houses open to the public are furnished in period style and hold collections of decorative arts, ceramics, and assorted artifacts. Many buildings are set amid gardens cultivated according to their eras, from early pioneer herb gardens to formal Victorian flower beds.

Pitt Tavern
This Revolutionary-War-era inn was frequented by George Washington.

Aldrich House and Garden
The garden of the restored Colonial Revival home of poet Thomas Bailey Aldrich (1836–1907) blooms with flowers celebrated in his verse.

COURT STREET

ATKINSON STREET

COURT STREET

JEFFERSON STREET

WHIDDEN PLACE

WASHINGTON STREET

Key

— Suggested route

0 meters 50
0 yards 50

★ **Chase House**
Built c.1762, this elegant home is furnished with sumptuous pieces from several periods.

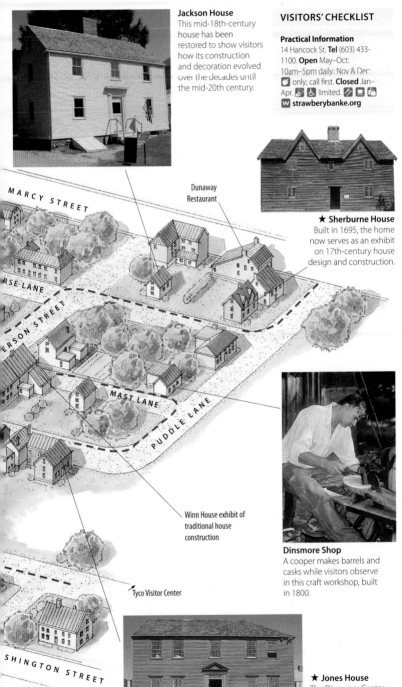

Jackson House
This mid-18th-century house has been restored to show visitors how its construction and decoration evolved over the decades until the mid-20th century.

★ **Sherburne House**
Built in 1695, the home now serves as an exhibit on 17th-century house design and construction.

Dunaway Restaurant

MARCY STREET

RSE LANE

ERSON STREET

MAST LANE

PUDDLE LANE

Winn House exhibit of traditional house construction

Dinsmore Shop
A cooper makes barrels and casks while visitors observe in this craft workshop, built in 1800.

Tyco Visitor Center

SHINGTON STREET

★ **Jones House**
The Discovery Center for Children's Activities entertains and educates youngsters in this c.1790 structure.

❷ Exeter

🏘 14,500. ✈ 15 miles (24 km) E in Portsmouth. 🛈 24 Front St. (603) 772-2411. 🆆 **exeterarea.org**

The quiet little town of Exeter southwest of Portsmouth was much less tranquil during the century and a half leading up to the American Revolution (1775–83). The community sprang up around the falls linking the freshwater Exeter River and the tidal Squamscott River. It was founded in 1638 by the Reverend John Wheelwright (1592–1679), an outspoken cleric who was thrown out of the Massachusetts colony for his radical views.

During the turbulent years leading up to American Independence, outraged townspeople openly defied the British government. They drove off officials who had been dispatched to cut down trees for the British Navy, burned their leaders in effigy, and finally declared independence from Britain, setting a precedent for the rest of the colonies.

Dominating the center of town, Phillips Exeter Academy stands as one of the country's most prestigious preparatory schools. The complex of more than 100 ivy-clad brick buildings fronted by manicured lawns was founded in 1781.

Other points of interest include the **Gilman Garrison House**, a late 17th-century fortified log building, and the **American Independence Museum**, which displays an original copy of the Declaration of Independence in mid-July, and also owns two drafts of the US Constitution.

🏛 Gilman Garrison House
12 Water St. **Tel** (603) 436-3205. **Open** call for opening hours. 📷 🚫 obligatory. ♿

🏛 American Independence Museum
1 Governors Lane. **Tel** (603) 772-2622. **Open** May–Nov: 10am–4pm Tue–Sat. 📷 🚫 obligatory. ♿ 🚻

❸ Hampton

🏘 15,000. ✈ 12 miles (19 km) N in Portsmouth. 🛈 1 Lafayette Rd. (603) 926-8718. 🆆 **hamptonchamber.com**

One of New Hampshire's oldest towns, Hampton is situated at the geographic center of the many state parks and public beaches that line Highway 1A, the coast road. Public recreation areas stretch from Seabrook Beach, a sandy shore dotted with dunes, to the rugged shoreline of **Odiorne Point State Park** in Rye to the north. The park has biking trails, tidal pools, and a boardwalk spanning a saltwater marsh. The park's Science Center also runs interpretive nature programs that are especially appealing to young visitors. Ten miles (6 km) to the south of the factory outlet shopping center in North Hampton, travelers will come upon the popular **Hampton Beach**. This miniature version of Atlantic City (without the gambling) comes complete with a venue that hosts big-name entertainers and

Exterior of the American Independence Museum in Exeter

an old-fashioned boardwalk lined with video arcades, ice-cream shops, and stalls selling T-shirts and tacky souvenirs. Open year-round, Hampton Beach is busiest during hot summer months, when vacationers come to enjoy the miles of clean, golden beaches, including a separate area designated for surfers. Swimmers and jet skiers test the waters, parasailors soar overhead, and deep-sea fishing and whale-watching charter boats are available from Hampton Harbor. Hampton Beach is not the place for people looking for quiet, but it is geared toward family fun, with game arcades, water slides, magic shows, and a series of free concerts and fireworks.

🌳 Odiorne Point State Park
Rte. 1A, Rye Beach. **Tel** (603) 436-7406. 🏛 Science Center: **Tel** (603) 436-8043. **Open** 10am–5pm daily (Nov–Mar: only Sat–Mon). **Closed** Jan 1, Thanksgiving, & Dec 25. 📷 ♿ Park: **Open** year-round: 8am–dusk. 📷

🏖 Hampton Beach
Tel (603) 926-8717. 🆆 **hamptonbeach.org**

Away from the casino and busy boardwalk, the blue skies and tranquil surf of Hampton Beach

❹ America's Stonehenge

Haverhill Rd., N. Salem. **Tel** (603) 893-8300. **Open** 9am–5pm daily. **Closed** Thanksgiving, Dec 25. 🅿️
Ⓦ stonehengeusa.com

Although not nearly as imposing as its British namesake, this is an intriguing place nonetheless. Believed to be one of the oldest man-made complexes this side of the Atlantic, the 1,306,800-sq-ft (121,400-sq-m) grounds of America's Stonehenge are scattered with standing stones, walls, and stone chambers. Archaeologists, historians, and astronomers have argued for decades about the origins of the site, with credit going to everyone from ancient Greeks to wayward aliens. Today one of the most popular theories has Native American tribes constructing this megalithic complex as a giant calendar to measure the movements of the sun and the moon. Excavations have turned up a wealth of ancient remains, including stone pottery, tools, and petroglyphs that purport to date from between 3,000 and 4,000 years ago. One of the more gruesome parts of the site is the 5-ton (4.5-tonne) so-called Sacrificial Table, carved with grooves that sensationalists say may have been troughs for collecting the blood of victims. Special events are held at the site during the spring and fall equinox and at the winter and summer solstice.

Mount Monadnock, popular with climbers and hikers

❺ Monadnock State Park

Off Rte. 124, W of Jaffrey. **Tel** (603) 532-8862. Campground reservations: (877) 647-2757. **Open** year-round. 🅿️ 🏕️
Ⓦ nhstateparks.org

Standing some 3,165 ft (965 m) high, Mount Monadnock has two claims to fame. It is said to be one of the world's most climbed mountains (it is not unusual to find several dozen hikers milling around its peak) and it has spawned a geological term. A "monadnock" is an isolated hill or mountain of resistant rock rising above a plain that has been created by glacial activity.

The mountain's popularity has a lot to do with its camp-grounds, scenic picnic areas, and numerous hiking trails. Within the 8-sq-mile (20-sq-km) park, there are 40 miles (64 km) of trails, many of which lead to the summit. The climb to the peak of the metamorphic schist pinnacle takes more than 3 hours, but on clear days intrepid hikers are rewarded with gorgeous views of all six New England states. Markers along the trails have been erected in memory of such men of letters as Ralph Waldo Emerson (1803–82) and Henry David Thoreau (1817–62), both of whom climbed to the peak. The visitor center gives an overview of the hiking trails and information about the local flora and fauna.

The campgrounds are open year-round and in the winter months the trails are popular with cross-country skiers.

❻ Rhododendron State Park

Off Rte. 119, W of Fitzwilliam. **Tel** (603) 532-8862. **Open** year-round: dawn–dusk daily. 🅿️ ♿ partial.

New England's largest grove of wild rhododendrons bursts into a celebration of pink and white in June through mid-July. The 4.2-sq-mile (10.9-sq-km) park has more than 696,950 sq ft (64,750 sq m) of giant rhododendron bushes. Walking through the rhododendrons, some of which grow to more than 20 ft (6 m) high, is a feast for the senses in summer, but there are floral highlights in other seasons as well. In the spring the woodland park is carpeted with trilliums. By May the apple trees are heavy with blossoms. During summer, visitors will find flowering mountain laurel and wildflowers such as jack-in-the-pulpit and delicate pink lady slippers. The park is equipped with picnic areas and hiking trails that offer spectacular views of Mount Monadnock and the surrounding peaks.

Ancient ruins of America's Stonehenge

❼ Keene

25,350. 58 miles (93 km) W of Manchester. 48 Central Sq. (603) 352-1303.

Keene is the largest town in southern New Hampshire's Monadnock region. The nation's first glass-blowing factory was founded in nearby Temple in 1780, and soon after Keene became one of the region's hotbeds of arts and crafts. By the 19th century the town was famous for the production of high-quality glass and pottery and for its thriving wool mill. The **Horatio Colony Museum** is the former home of a descendant of the mill-owning family. Its period furnishings give a good idea of upper-class life in the mid-19th century. Today the focus of Keene's thriving cultural life is Keene State College, located on what is reputed to be the widest Main Street in the world. The college has several theaters and art studios where events are staged throughout the year.

Horatio Colony Museum
199 Main St. **Tel** (603) 352-0460. **Open** May–mid-Oct: 11am–4pm Wed–Sun. obligatory.

Environs

Half a dozen covered bridges *(see p267)* lie within a 10-mile (16-km) radius of Keene, giving the region the nickname "Currier and Ives country." Road markers direct drivers to each span. These "kissing bridges," where young couples would steal secret embraces as they rode their buggy through them, have long been favorite subjects of photographers.

West Swanzey or Thompson Covered Bridge near Keene

❽ Manchester

105,250. 1 Airport Rd. 54 Hanover St. (603) 666-6600. (603) 622-7531.

In 1805 a modest mill was built on the east bank of the Merrimack River. Fueled by water power, the Amoskeag Mill continued to expand until by the beginning of the 20th century it claimed the title as the largest textile mill in the world. At its peak, the operation employed some 17,000 people and its complex of brick buildings stretched for more than 1 mile (1.5 km). Today the structures that once held workers and heavy machinery are used for restaurants, college classrooms, and even residential housing.

This former industrial center is now known for the **Currier Museum of Art**, New Hampshire's premier art museum. In order to display more of its impressive collection of fine and decorative arts, the museum has undergone an ambitious renovation program that added a massive 33,000 sq ft (3,050 sq m) of space. The entire second floor is dedicated to 18th- and 19th-century American artists, including the Impressionists and members of the Hudson River School. The museum's holdings of modern paintings and sculptures include works by Pablo Picasso (1881–1973) and Henri Matisse (1869–1954). A gallery features regional artists, while a café occupies the sky-lit Winter Garden.

The museum's largest piece is the nearby Zimmerman House, designed in 1950 by pioneering American architect Frank Lloyd Wright (1867–1959) as an exemplar of his Usonian homes. Shuttles take visitors from the museum to the house, and guided tours (by advance reservation April through December) of its interior highlight textiles and furniture designed by Wright.

Currier Museum of Art
150 Ash St. **Tel** (603) 669-6144. **Open** 11am–5pm Wed–Mon (from 10am Sat). Zimmerman House: **Open** Apr–Dec (call for tour hours). **currier.org**

The granite and marble façade of the State House, in Concord

❾ Concord

37,500. 25 miles (49 km) N of Manchester. 40 Commercial St. (603) 224-2508.

New Hampshire's capital is a quiet little town, but thanks to its prominent political position it has been associated with a number of important historical figures. Mary Baker Eddy

Concord Coaches

In 1827 Concord-based wheelwright Lewis Downing and coach builder J. Stephens Abbot built the first Concord Coach, designed to withstand the unforgiving trails of the undeveloped West. The 1-ton (1-tonne) stagecoaches were, in their own way, as revolutionary as the Internet is today, because they helped facilitate communications across the vast emerging hinterland. Wells Fargo, the famous transportation company, relied heavily on the coaches during the California Gold Rush (1848–55) to carry mail and passengers on parts of the route between New York City and San Francisco.

(1821–1910), founder of the Christian Science Church, spent much of her life here. The **Pierce Manse** was the one-time home of Franklin Pierce (1804–69), the 14th president of the US.

The 1819 **State House**, built from New Hampshire granite and Vermont marble, is one of the oldest in America. Inside the building are several hundred paintings of the state's better-known residents and political figures.

In its heyday, the Eagle Hotel on Main Street, which is now used as an office building, hosted the likes of presidents Andrew Jackson and Benjamin Harrison, as well as aviator Charles Lindbergh, and former First Lady Eleanor Roosevelt.

Concord schoolteacher Christa McAuliffe (1948–86) unfortunately gained her fame through tragedy. On January 28, 1986, McAuliffe boarded the *Challenger* space shuttle as the first civilian to be launched into space by NASA. Seventy-three seconds after the liftoff, with her husband and children watching from the ground, the shuttle

exploded into a fireball and crashed, killing McAuliffe and her six fellow astronauts.

McAuliffe's memory lives on at **The McAuliffe-Shepard Discovery Center**, which also honors New Hampshire native and astronaut Alan Shepard, who was the first American to be launched into space. The futuristic center is capped by a giant glass pyramid. In addition to exhibits and planetarium shows, visitors can see a scale model of a space shuttle and a replica of the Mercury-Redstone rocket from Shepard's flight on May 5, 1961.

🏠 Pierce Manse
14 Horseshoe Pond Lane. **Tel** (603) 225-4555. **Open** mid-Jun–early Sep: 11am–3pm Tue–Sat; early Sep–mid-Oct: noon–3pm Sat & Sun. 🛑 🔲 🔲

🏠 State House
107 N Main St. **Tel** (603) 271-2154. Visitor center: **Open** year-round: 8am–4pm Mon–Fri. 🛑 🔲

🏛 The McAuliffe-Shepard Discovery Center
2 Institute Dr. **Tel** (603) 271-7827. **Open** 10:30am–4pm Fri–Sun (late Jun–Aug: daily). Call for show times. 🛑 🛑 🔲 🔲 starhop.com

Sightseeing boat on Lake Sunapee

⑩ Lake Sunapee Region

ℹ 143 Main St., New London (603) 526-6575 or (877) 526-6575.

This scenic region, dominated by 2,743-ft- (835-m-) high Mount Sunapee and the 10-mile- (16-km-) long lake at its feet, is a major drawing card for outdoor enthusiasts, particularly boaters and skiers. Many locals have vacation and weekend homes here, and an increasing number of retirees are also moving to the region, attracted not only by the scenery but also by the activity-oriented lifestyle.

Lake Sunapee (its name is said to be derived from the Penacook Indian words for "wild goose water") has been attracting visitors for well over a century. In the mid-19th century, trains and steamships used to transport tourists to hotels that rimmed the lake. The steamships have long since gone, but vacationers can rent canoes, picnic on the beach, or take a narrated trip on a sightseeing boat. **Mount Sunapee State Park**'s namesake peak attracts hikers and climbers during the summer months and skiers during the winter. The Mount Sunapee resort in the park is the largest ski area between Boston and the White Mountains.

🎿 Mount Sunapee State Park
Rte. 103. **Tel** (603) 763-5561. **Open** Jun–Labor Day. 🛑 🛑 Mount Sunapee Resort: **Tel** (603) 763-4020.

⓫ Canterbury Shaker Village

Founded in 1792, this Shaker community remained active until the last sister died in 1992, making it one of the longest-lasting communities of the religious group in the US. Shakers also lived in nearby Enfield *(see p266)*. This museum presents the Shaker legacy of entrepreneurship, innovative design, and simple living through 25 restored original, and four reconstructed, Shaker buildings, plus 1 sq mile (2.8 sq km) of forests, fields, gardens, and trails. Guided tours and self-guided exhibits are available. Visitors have basement-to-attic access to the 1793 Dwelling House.

Canterbury Shaker Village
The village is dominated by the central Dwelling House *(below)*.

Shaker Brooms
The common flat broom was invented in 1798 by Shaker Brother Theodore Bates. Shakers believed that cleanliness mirrored spiritual purity.

★ Dining Room
This area once held as many as 60 Shakers per sitting.

KEY

① **The Chapel Wing** was added in 1837.

② **The distinctive belfry** contains a bell made by Revere and Sons.

③ **Dormer rooms** were used for summer sleeping.

Key

- Illustrated building
1. Trustees' Office
2. The Infirmary
3. Meeting House
4. Dwelling House
5. Sisters' Shop
6. Carriage House
7. Creamery
8. Carpenter Shop
9. Fire House/Power House
10. Laundry
11. Shaker Box Lunch and Farm Stand
12. School House
13. Syrup Shop
14. Shaker Table
15. Visitor Center

VISITORS' CHECKLIST

Practical Information
288 Shaker Rd., Canterbury.
Tel (603) 783-9511.
Open mid-May–Oct: 10am–5pm daily; Nov & Dec: some weekends.
🅿 🅲 🅳 🅴 🅵 **W** shakers.org

Popular Stop
Historic buildings, a restaurant, and a gift shop make Canterbury a favorite tourist destination.

★ Shaker Design
A display shows how a uniformity of design was maintained within and across all Shaker communities.

★ Hands to Work
Exhibits in the Dwelling House show the simple hand tools the Shakers used to produce their spare but elegant furniture.

⑫ New London

🏠 3,700. ✈ 28 miles (45 km) NW in
Lebanon. 🚌 ℹ Main St. (603) 526-
6575 or (877) 526-6575.
🌐 sunapeevacations.com

New London's perch atop a
crest gives it an enviable view of
the surrounding forests during
the fall foliage season. The
bucolic setting also serves as a
wonderful backdrop for the
town's rich collection of colonial
and early 19th-century
buildings. Of these, the
architectural centerpiece is
Colby-Sawyer College, an
undergraduate liberal arts
school founded in 1837. The
college organizes numerous
cultural programs, including
plays, lectures, films, concerts,
and art exhibitions. More
cultural fun can be had farther
down the street at the **New
London Barn Playhouse**.
Housed in a refurbished 1820s
barn, the theater stages popular
plays and musicals during the
summer months.

🏛 **Colby-Sawyer College**
Main St. **Tel** (603) 526-2010.
Open year-round: 9am–5pm Mon–
Fri. 🚻 ♿ 🅿 🌐 colby-sawyer.edu

🎭 **New London Barn Playhouse**
84 Main St. **Tel** (603) 526-4631 or (603)
526-6710. **Open** mid-Jun–Sep: call for
hours. 🅿 🌐 nlbarn.org

⑬ Enfield Shaker Museum

Rte. 4A, Enfield. **Tel** (603) 632-4346.
Open 10am–5pm Mon–Sat, noon–
5pm Sun (winter: closes 4pm). 🅿
♿ 🅿 🌐 shakermuseum.org

Facing religious persecution in
Britain in the mid-18th century,
several groups of Shakers, a sect
that broke away from the
Quakers, fled to North America
under the spiritual guidance of
Mother Ann Lee (1736–84). The
Shaker village at Enfield was
founded in 1793, one of 18 such
communities in the US.
    Between the founding of
Enfield and the 1920s, the
Shakers constructed more
than 200 buildings, of which
13 remain. And while they
farmed more than 4.6 sq miles

Colby-Sawyer College in New London

(12 sq km) of land, property was
under the ownership of the
community, not individuals.
Members were celibate and
they were strict pacifists,
devoting their "hands to work
and hearts to God." At one time
the Enfield Shakers numbered
over 300, but, as in similar
communities, their numbers
gradually dwindled. In 1923 the
last 10 members moved to the
Canterbury Shaker
Village *(see pp264–5)*
north of Concord. The
last Canterbury
Shaker died in 1992 at
the age of 96.
    The exhibits at the
museum illustrate how
the Shakers lived and
worked. Visitors will
come across fine
examples of Shaker
ingenuity, including
one of their many
inventions: sulfur
matches. The buildings are
filled with the simple but
practical wooden furniture for
which the Shakers, who were
consummate craftspeople,
were famous. The 160-year-old
Great Stone Dwelling, the

Saint-Gaudens'
angel

largest such structure ever
built by these industrious
people, is a model of
stately workmanship.

⑭ Saint-Gaudens National Historic Site

Rte. 12A N of Cornish-Windsor Bridge.
Tel (603) 675-2175. Buildings:
Open late May–Oct: 9am–4:30pm
daily. Grounds: **Open** year-round.
🅿 🎫 🅿 🌐 nps.gov/saga

This national historic site
celebrates the life of Augustus
Saint-Gaudens (1848–1907),
the preeminent US sculptor of
his time. When he began to
summer here in 1885, it marked
the beginning of the town's
evolution into an art colony.
Artists, writers, and musicians
alike were attracted to
the town by the talent
of Saint-Gaudens,
whose family had
emigrated to the US
from Ireland when
he was just a baby.
Something of a world
traveler, Saint-Gaudens
became an apprentice
cameo cutter in New
York and later studied
at the Ecole des
Beaux-Arts in Paris.
He also won several
commissions in Rome. By the
time that he returned to New
York, his reputation as a brilliant
sculptor had been well
established. His work, usually
of heroic subject matter, can
be found throughout the

Great Stone Dwelling in the Enfield Shaker Museum

country. New England is home to many Saint-Gaudens masterpieces, including Boston's Shaw Memorial (1897).

Eventually Saint-Gaudens grew tired of the big-city pace, buying an old tavern near the Connecticut River and turning it into a home and studio. Many of his greatest

Model for Boston's Shaw Memorial

works were created here, including the famous statue of Abraham Lincoln (1809–65) in Lincoln Park, Chicago. Today this historic 1805 structure is filled with the sculptor's furniture and samples of his small, detailed sketches for large bronzes. A number of his sculptures are scattered around the 0.2-sq-mile (0.6-sq-km) property, which is laid out with formal gardens and pleasing walking trails flanked by tall pines and hemlocks.

Environs

Just 2 miles (3 km) south of the Saint-Gaudens site, visitors will come upon the Cornish-Windsor Bridge. Spanning the Connecticut River between New Hampshire and Vermont, the structure is the longest covered bridge in New England at 460 ft (140 m). Three other covered bridges can be found in the vicinity of Cornish.

ⓐ Hanover

 9,200. ✈ 6 miles (10 km) SE in Lebanon. 🚌 *i* 216 Nugget Arcade Building (603) 643-3115.
w hanoverchamber.org

Hanover, with a traditional village green ringed by historic brick buildings, is the archetypal New England college town. Situated in the upper valley region of the Connecticut River, it is a pleasant stop for visitors following the Appalachian Trail, which goes right through the center of town. Hanover is the home of **Dartmouth College**,

the northernmost of the country's Ivy League schools. The college was originally known as Moor's Indian Charity School, and was founded in 1769 to educate and convert Abenaki Natives. Today some 4,500 students participate in programs that include one of the oldest medical schools in America, the Thayer School of Civil Engineering (1867), and the Amos Tuck School of Business Administration (1900). The school's famous graduates include statesman Daniel Webster (1782–1852) and former vice president Nelson Rockefeller (1908–79).

The college has a number of noteworthy sights. The **Baker-Berry Memorial Library** is decorated by a series of thought-provoking murals tracing the history of the Americas painted by Mexican artist José Clemente Orozco (1883–1949) in the early 1930s. The **Hood Museum of Art** has a diverse collection that includes Native American and African art, early American and European paintings, and works by such noted modern artists as Pablo Picasso (1881–1973).

🏛 **Dartmouth College**
Tel (603) 646-1110. 🗓 ♿

🏛 **Baker-Berry Memorial Library**
Dartmouth College. **Tel** (603) 646-2560. **Open** year-round: call for hours. ♿

🏛 **Hood Museum of Art**
Dartmouth College. **Tel** (603) 646-2808. **Open** year-round: 10am–5pm Tue & Thu–Sat, 10am–9pm Wed, noon–5pm Sun. 🗓 ♿ 🚻 📷
w hoodmuseum.dartmouth.edu

Gallery in Dartmouth's Hood Museum of Art in Hanover

Covered Bridges

American bridge builders began covering their wooden spans in the early 19th century to protect the truss work and planking from the harsh weather. Originally the bridges were built by locals, meaning that each one had design elements specific to its region. Covered bridges built in farming communities were wide enough and tall enough to accommodate a wagon loaded with hay. Bridges leading into town had the added luxury of pedestrian walkways. The bridges, though, were more than just river crossings. Fishermen cast their lines beneath the spans, children used them as platforms from which to dive into the water below, birds nested among the rafters, and social dances were sometimes held beneath their roofs.

One of New Hampshire's covered bridges outside Cornish

⑯ Tour of Lake Winnipesaukee

This stunning lake has a shoreline that meanders for 240 miles (386 km), making it the biggest stretch of waterfront in New Hampshire. Ringed by mountains, Winnipesaukee is scattered with 274 islands. Around its shores are sheltered bays and harbors, with half a dozen resort towns where visitors can enjoy activities ranging from canoeing to shopping for crafts and antiques.

Tips for Drivers

Tour length: 70 miles (113 km).
Starting point: Alton, at junction of Hwys 11 & 28.
Stopping-off points: Popular Weirs Beach eateries include Donna Jean's Diner and Patio Garden Restaurant. In Center Sandwich, Corner House Inn oozes historic Yankee style. Wolfeboro has many places to eat, including Wolfetrap Grill, Bailey's Bubble, and West Lake Asian Cuisine.

④ **Squam Lake**
This pristine body of water was where the movie *On Golden Pond* (1981) was filmed. The lake is ideal for boating and fishing.

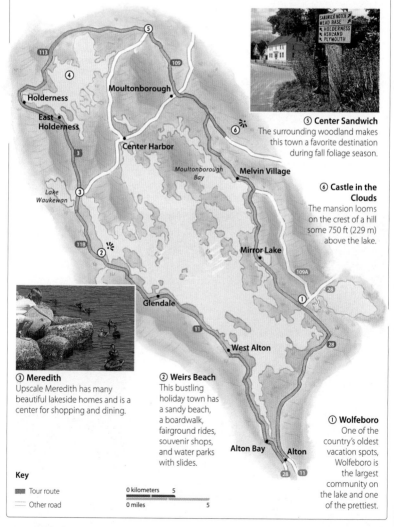

⑤ **Center Sandwich**
The surrounding woodland makes this town a favorite destination during fall foliage season.

⑥ **Castle in the Clouds**
The mansion looms on the crest of a hill some 750 ft (229 m) above the lake.

③ **Meredith**
Upscale Meredith has many beautiful lakeside homes and is a center for shopping and dining.

② **Weirs Beach**
This bustling holiday town has a sandy beach, a boardwalk, fairground rides, souvenir shops, and water parks with slides.

① **Wolfeboro**
One of the country's oldest vacation spots, Wolfeboro is the largest community on the lake and one of the prettiest.

Holderness
East Holderness
Moultonborough
Center Harbor
Lake Waukewan
Moultonborough Bay
Melvin Village
Mirror Lake
Glendale
West Alton
Alton Bay **Alton**

Key

▬▬ Tour route
═══ Other road

0 kilometers 5
0 miles 5

⑰ White Mountains/ White Mountain National Forest

ℹ️ Headquarters: 71 White Mountain Drive, Campton (603) 536-6100. ♿ 📷 🌐 **fs.fed.us/r9/ forests/white_mountain**
Camping: reservations: **Tel** (877) 444-6777. 🌐 **recreation.gov**

New Hampshire's heavily forested northland is an outdoor paradise, encompassing a national forest, several state parks, more than 1,200 miles (1,900 km) of hiking trails, several dozen lakes, ponds and rivers, and 23 campgrounds. The White Mountain National Forest, a small portion of which lies in neighboring Maine, sprawls over 1,203 sq miles (3,116 sq km).

The most beautiful wilderness area in the state, the National Forest is home to an abundance of wildlife, including a large population of moose. These giant members of the deer family are very shy, but they can be seen from the road at dawn or dusk, lumbering back and forth from their feeding grounds or standing in a swampy pond.

This region offers all manner of outdoor activities – from bird-watching and skiing to rock climbing and kayaking – but even less sporty travelers will revel in the spectacular scenery visible from their car. More than 20 summits soar to over 4,000 ft (1,200 m). Driving through the White Mountains,

Brightly colored engine of the Conway Scenic Railroad

Saco **RANGER STATION** WHITE MOUNTAIN *National* **Forest**
Ranger station marker

visitors encounter one scenic vista after another: valleys flanked by forests of pine, waterfalls tumbling over rocky outcrops, and trout rivers hissing alongside the meandering roads.

In 1998 a stretch of road, the 100-mile- (161-km-) long White Mountains Trail was designated as a National Scenic and Cultural Byway. The trail loops across the Mount Washington Valley, through Crawford Notch *(see p275)*, North Conway, and Franconia Notch *(see pp276–7)*.

Brilliant fall foliage colors, interspersed with evergreens, transform the rugged countryside into a living palette. The leaves of different trees manifest a rich variety of shades – flaming red maples, golden birch, and maroon northern red oaks. Driving during the fall can be a beautiful but slow-moving experience, since thousands of "leaf peepers" are on the roads.

Accommodations can also be difficult to find unless booked well in advance.

⑱ North Conway

🏔️ 2,500. ✈️ 70 miles (112 km) SE in Portland, ME. ℹ️ 2617 Main St (603) 356-3171 or (800) 367-3364.

The gateway to the sublime beauty of the White Mountains, North Conway is, surprisingly, also a bustling shopping center. This mountain village now has more than 200 factory outlets and specialty shops lining its Main Street. Prices are low in the first place, even for designer names such as Calvin Klein, Ralph Lauren, and Tommy Hilfiger, but, because there is no sales tax in New Hampshire, all purchases become even better bargains.

Locals are quick to point out that there are many other attractions in and around North Conway, including canoe trips on the Saco River and a ride into the mountains in an old-fashioned train aboard the **Conway Scenic Railroad**. At the **Story Land** theme park, children can ride on an antique German carousel, a pirate ship, or Cinderella's coach.

🚂 **Conway Scenic Railroad**
Rte. 16 in North Conway. **Tel** (603) 356-5251 or (800) 232-5251.
Open call for schedule. 🎟️ ♿ 🅿️
🌐 **conwayscenic.com**

🎠 **Story Land**
Rte. 16 in Glen. **Tel** (603) 383-4186.
Open Jul & Aug: 9am–6pm daily; late May–Jun & Labor Day–Columbus Day: 9:30am–5pm Sat–Sun. 🎟️ ♿

Cathedral Ledge, just outside North Conway

Red and white covered bridge leading into Jackson

⑲ Jackson

🏠 750. ✈ 77 miles (125 km) SE in Portland, ME. 𝑖 Rte. 16B (603) 383-9356 or (800) 866-3334.

This mountain village is tucked away on a back road off Route 16B, but drivers will not miss it, because the entrance is marked by its distinctive red and white covered bridge. The picturesque 200-year-old community is, along with the nearby villages of Intervale, Bartlett, and Glen, the main center for accommodation in the Mount Washington area.

Jackson was at one time a favorite getaway spot for big-city Easterners, but the hard times of the Great Depression of the 1930s saw the town slip into disrepair. Developers rediscovered this quiet corner of New Hampshire in the 1980s and began restoring several of the town's best hotels.

Jackson is a popular base camp for winter-sports enthusiasts because the region is blessed with more than 110 downhill ski runs and a network of more than 200 miles (320 km) of cross-country trails. The main ski centers are Black Mountain, the Wildcat Ski Area, and the Attitash Mountain Resort *(see p363)*. With 0.4 sq miles (1.1 sq km) of skiable terrain served by 12 lifts, Attitash is the state's biggest ski center.

Summer sports abound here as well. The region's numerous peaks and valleys make this prime hiking and mountain-biking country, and a restored 18-hole course gives golfers the chance to play a round against one of the most scenic backdrops in New England. After having worked up a sweat, bikers and hikers can cool off under the waterfalls of the Wildcat River in Jackson Village.

⑳ Pinkham Notch

𝑖 Rte. 16 N of North Conway (603) 466-2721. **Open** 6:30am–10pm daily.

Named after Joseph Pinkham, who according to local lore explored the area in 1790 with a sled drawn by pigs, this rocky ravine runs between Gorham and Jackson. The lofty Presidential Range girds the western flank of Pinkham Notch, while the 4,415-ft (1,346-m) Wildcat Mountain looms to the east.

Backcountry adventurers love this part of the state because of its great variety of activities. Skiing at the Wildcat Ski Area is among the best in the state, and its high elevation makes for a long season, running from November to April. In the summer, visitors can ride to the summit aboard the aerial gondola. Picnic areas at the top offer great views of Mount Washington and the Presidential Range.

Hiking trails lace Pinkham Notch, including a section of the fabled Appalachian Trail *(see pp26–7)*. These well-maintained paths range from less demanding nature walks suitable for whole families to lung-testing climbs best attacked by serious hikers. Along the way, visitors are led past some of the region's most captivating sights, including waterfalls, rivers, scenic overlooks, and pristine ponds tucked away in thick woodland.

Sublime beauty of the Presidential Range from Pinkham Notch

For hotels and restaurants in this region see pp317–18 and pp336–8

Striking exterior of the Mount Washington Hotel and Resort

Lucky travelers may spot raccoons, beaver, deer, and even the occasional moose.

㉑ Bretton Woods

🏔 550. ✈ 96 miles (155 km) SE in Portland, ME. ℹ (603) 745-8720 or (800) 346-3687.
🌐 visitwhitemountains.com

This tiny enclave situated on a glacial plain at the base of the Presidential Range has an unusual claim to fame: it hosted the United Nations Monetary and Financial Conference in 1944. The meetings established the International Monetary Fund and laid the groundwork for the World Bank, a response to the need for currency stability after the economic upheavals of World War II. The delegates also set the gold standard at $35 an ounce and chose the American dollar as the international standard for monetary exchange.

The setting for this vital meeting was the **Omni Mount Washington Hotel** *(see p317)*. It is easy to imagine the reaction of delegates when they first caught sight of this grand Spanish Renaissance-style hotel from a sweeping curve in the road. Opened in 1902, the hotel's sparkling white exterior and crimson roof stand out in stark contrast to Mount Washington, looming 6,288 ft (1,917 m) skyward behind the edifice. The hotel has entertained a host of distinguished guests, including British Prime Minister Sir Winston Churchill (1874–1965), inventor Thomas Edison (1847–1931), baseball star Babe Ruth (1895–1948), and three presidents.

Apart from its sublime setting, what makes the hotel so impressive is its sheer size. Designated a National Historic Landmark, the 200-room structure was built by 250 skilled craftsmen from Italy. Today the hotel is surrounded by more than 27 sq miles (70 sq km) of parkland, and its facilities include a 27-hole golf course laid out by the famous Scottish designer Donald Ross (1872–1948). Nearby Bretton Woods ski area *(see p363)* offers alpine skiing along with 62 miles (100 km) of cross-country trails.

Sir Winston Churchill, a Mount Washington visitor

🏨 Mount Washington Hotel and Resort

Rte. 302, Bretton Woods. **Tel** (603) 278-1000 or (800) 314-1752. ♿ 🏨
🌐 brettonwoods.com

Environs

The Mount Washington Valley, in which Bretton Woods is located, is dominated by the 6,288-ft (1,917-m) peak of Mount Washington, the highest in the northeastern United States. Other imposing peaks belonging to the Presidential Range – Adams, Jefferson, Madison, Monroe, and Eisenhower – surround Mount Washington, which has the dubious distinction of having the worst weather of any mountain in the world. Unpredictable snowstorms are not unusual, even during the summer months; the highest wind ever recorded on Earth was clocked here in April 1934: 230 mph (370 kph). During the last century, the mountain has claimed the lives of almost 100 people caught unaware by Mount Washington's temperamental climate. On clear days, however, when the mountain is in a good mood, nothing compares to the panoramic view from the top. Brave souls hike to the summit by one of the many trails, drive their own cars up the winding Mount Washington Auto Road, or puff their way slowly to the top in the deservedly famous **Mount Washington Cog Railroad**. Billed as "America's oldest tourist attraction," the railroad started operating in 1869.

The train, powered by steam locomotives, chugs its way up the cog track to the top of the mountain belching steam. The 3.5-mile (5.6-km) route to the top is one of the steepest tracks in the world, climbing at a heart-stopping 37 percent gradient at some points. At the top, passengers can visit the Sherman Adams Summit Building, with the Summit Museum, and Mount Washington Observatory, which records weather conditions and conducts research.

🏨 Mount Washington Cog Railroad

Off Rte. 302, Marshfield Base Station. **Tel** (603) 278-5404 or (800) 922-8825. **Open** Apr–Dec: call for hours and train schedule. 🚫 ♿ 🏨 ♿
🌐 thecog.com

Mount Washington Cog Railroad

A perfect spot on Chocorua Lake, with Mount Chocorua in the distance

㉒ Kancamagus Highway

Rte. 112 between Lincoln & Conway.
🛈 Saco District Ranger Station, 33 Kancamagus Hwy. (603) 447-5448.

Touted by many as the most scenic fall-foliage road in New England, this stretch of highway runs through the White Mountain National Forest (see p269) between Lincoln and Conway. The road covers about 34 miles (55 km) of Route 112 and offers exceptional vistas from the Pemi Overlook as it climbs 3,000 ft (914 m) through the

Sabbaday Falls, a highlight of the Kancamagus Highway

Kancamagus Pass. Descending into the Saco Valley, the well-traveled road joins up with the Swift River, following the aptly named waterway into Conway. The highway provides fishermen with easy access to the river, home to brook and rainbow trout.

Campgrounds and picnic areas along the entire length of highway give travelers ample opportunity to relax and eat lunch on the banks of cool mountain streams. Maintained by the US Forest Service, the campgrounds are equipped with toilets, and one has shower facilities; most are operated on a first-come, first-served basis. Well-marked trails also allow drivers to stretch their legs in the midst of some of the most beautiful scenery in the state. One of the most popular trails is the short loop that leads travelers to the oft-photographed Sabbaday Falls. Closer to Conway, road signs guide drivers to several scenic areas that afford views of cascades, rapids, and rivers.

The area is home to a wide variety of wildlife, including resident birds such as woodpeckers and chickadees, as well as migratory songbirds who breed here in the summer. Larger inhabitants include deer, moose, and the occasional black bear.

Clark's Trading Post in North Woodstock

㉓ Lincoln-Woodstock

🅰 1,300. ✈ 66 miles (106 km) SW in Lebanon. 🛈 Rte. 112 & Connector Rd., Lincoln (603) 745-6621 or (800) 227-4191. 🅆 lincolnwoodstock.com

Not including its convenient location near the White Mountains (see p269), the region's main attraction is **Clark's Trading Post**, a strange combination of circus acts, amusement park rides, and museums. Children especially love the trained bears and the over-the-top performers. A session at Clark's "blaster boat" marina, in which participants try to ram each other's boat, is where the younger set can blow off the steam that may have built up on a leaf-peeping drive.

Environs
Tiny Lincoln is located just 3 miles (5 km) northwest of North Woodstock. The town's location

◀ The expansive White Mountains

at the western end of the Kancamagus Highway and at the southern entrance to Franconia Notch State Park (see pp276–7) have turned it into a base camp for both backwoods adventurers and stick-to-the-road sightseers. Nearby **Loon Mountain** is one of the state's premier ski resorts. However, in the summer it offers a number of activities, from guided nature walks and tours of caves to horseback riding, mountain biking, and a gondola ride to the summit.

Clark's Trading Post
Rte. 3, Lincoln. **Tel** (603) 745-8913. **Open** late May–mid-Oct: call for hours & show times.

Loon Mountain
E of I-93, near Lincoln. **Tel** (603) 745-8111 or (800) 229-5666. **loonmtn.com**

Challenging climbing wall at Loon Mountain outside of Lincoln

The wilds of Crawford Notch State Park beyond Willey House

㉔ Crawford Notch State Park

Rte. 302 between Twin Mountains & Bartlett. (603) 374-2272 or (877) 647-2757. Camping: **Tel** (877) 647-2757 for reservations. **Open** mid-May–mid-Oct (campground until mid-Dec).

This narrow pass, which squeezes through the sheer rock walls of Webster and Willey mountains, gained notoriety in 1826. One night a severe rain sent tons of mud and stone careening into the valley below, heading straight for the home of innkeeper Samuel Willey and his family. Alerted by the sounds of the avalanche, the family fled outdoors, where all seven were killed beneath falling debris. Ironically the lethal avalanche bypassed the house, leaving it unscathed. Several writers, including New Englander Nathaniel Hawthorne (see p34), have immortalized the tragedy

in literature. The house still stands today and is now in service as a visitors center.

Once the notch was threatened by overlogging. However, the establishment of the state park in 1911 has ensured protection of this rugged wilderness. Today white-water boaters come here to test their mettle on the powerful Saco River, which carves its way through the valley. Fishermen ply the park's more tranquil ponds and streams in search of sport and a tasty dinner of trout or salmon.

People who prefer to keep their feet dry can still enjoy the water on a short hiking trail leading to the Arethusa Falls. Towering more than 200 ft (61 m) in the air, this magnificent cascade is New Hampshire's tallest waterfall. Elsewhere drivers will get wonderful views of the Silver Cascades and Flume Cascades waterfalls without leaving the comfort of their car.

Robert Frost and New Hampshire

The natural beauty of New Hampshire was an inspiration to one of America's best-loved poets: Robert Frost (1874–1963). Born in San Francisco, California, the four-time winner of the Pulitzer Prize moved to Massachusetts with his family when he was 11. After working as a teacher, a reporter, and a mill hand, Frost moved to England in 1912. Upon his return to the US in 1915, Frost settled in the Franconia Notch area (see pp276–7). The majestic setting inspired him to pen many of his greatest works, including his famous poem *Stopping by Woods on a Snowy Evening* (1923).

Robert Frost farm in Derry, New Hampshire

For hotels and restaurants in this region see pp317–18 and pp336–8

㉕ Franconia Notch State Park

This spectacular mountain pass carved between the Kinsman and Franconia ranges is graced with some of the state's most spectacular natural wonders. Foremost among them was the Old Man of the Mountain, a rocky outcropping on the side of a cliff that resembled a man's profile, until the nose and forehead came crashing down in 2003. Other attractions compensate for the loss including a boardwalk and stairways which lead visitors through the Flume Gorge, a narrow, granite chasm slashed in two by the Flume Brook, while an aerial tramway carries passengers to the summit of Cannon Mountain in eight minutes. Also within the park is Boise Rock, a picnic area by a mountain spring that offers views of the Cannon Cliffs and Echo Lake.

Glacial Boulder
This glacial boulder is one of the sights on the Flume Trail.

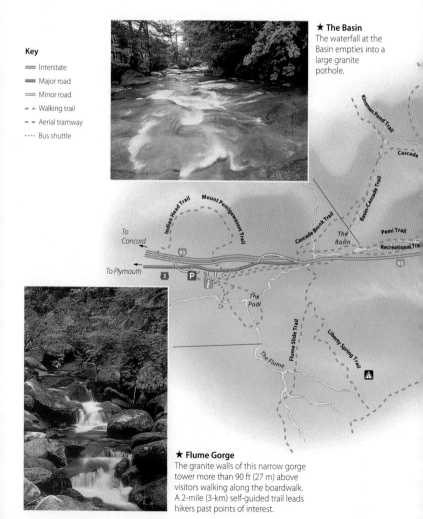

Key

- ▭▭▭ Interstate
- ▬▬▬ Major road
- ▭▭▭ Minor road
- – – Walking trail
- – – Aerial tramway
- ···· Bus shuttle

★ The Basin
The waterfall at the Basin empties into a large granite pothole.

Kinsman Pond Trail

Cascade

Basin-Cascade Trail

Indian Head Trail

Mount Pemigewasset Trail

Cascade Brook Trail

The Basin

Pemi Trail

Recreational Tra

To Concord

93

To Plymouth

3

P

i

The Pool

Flume Slide Trail

Liberty Spring Trail

The Flume

93

★ Flume Gorge
The granite walls of this narrow gorge tower more than 90 ft (27 m) above visitors walking along the boardwalk. A 2-mile (3-km) self-guided trail leads hikers past points of interest.

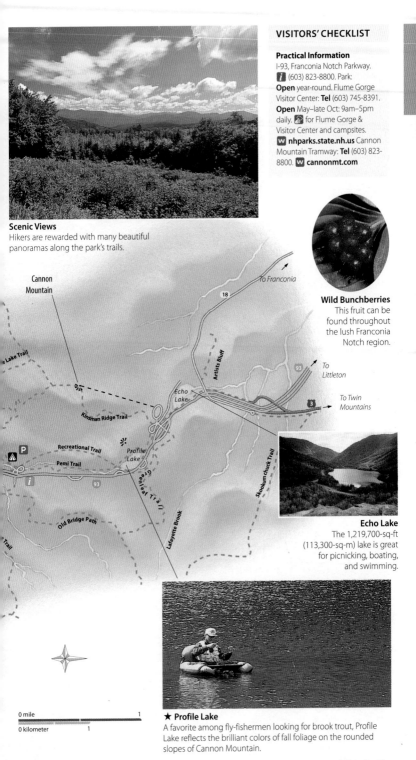

Scenic Views
Hikers are rewarded with many beautiful panoramas along the park's trails.

VISITORS' CHECKLIST

Practical Information
I-93, Franconia Notch Parkway.
i (603) 823-8800. Park:
Open year-round. Flume Gorge
Visitor Center: **Tel** (603) 745-8391.
Open May–late Oct: 9am–5pm
daily. ⚑ for Flume Gorge &
Visitor Center and campsites.
W nhparks.state.nh.us Cannon
Mountain Tramway: **Tel** (603) 823-
8800. **W** cannonmt.com

Wild Bunchberries
This fruit can be found throughout the lush Franconia Notch region.

Cannon Mountain

To Franconia

18

Artists Bluff

93

To Littleton

To Twin Mountains

Echo Lake

Lake Trail

Kinsman Ridge Trail

Recreational Trail

Pemi Trail

Profile Lake

Greenleaf Trail

Skookumchuck Trail

93

Old Bridge Path

Lafayette Brook

Echo Lake
The 1,219,700-sq-ft (113,300-sq-m) lake is great for picnicking, boating, and swimming.

0 mile   1
0 kilometer   1

★ Profile Lake
A favorite among fly-fishermen looking for brook trout, Profile Lake reflects the brilliant colors of fall foliage on the rounded slopes of Cannon Mountain.

For map symbols *see back flap*

Exploring Maine

Maine's most popular attractions are found dotted along its coast, beginning in the southeast with the beach playgrounds of Ogunquit *(see pp282–3)*, Old Orchard *(see p283)*, and the resort towns of the Kennebunks *(see p283)*. The scenery gets more dramatic as travelers move north through Boothbay Harbor *(see p289)*, Pemaquid Point *(see p289)*, and Muscongus Bay. The tiny villages are perfect starting points for sailing and kayaking excursions. Yachts and windjammers ply the waters of the Penobscot Bay region *(see pp290–91)*, while Acadia National Park *(see pp292–3)* stands as Maine's coastal jewel. Farther north, the rising sun first strikes the US at Cobscook Bay. World-class hiking, boating, and mountain-biking opportunities are found inland among the state's many mountains, lakes, and rivers.

Key

- ▬▬ Highway
- ▬▬ Major road
- ▭▭ Minor road
- ▬▬ Scenic route
- – – Track
- ▬▬ Main railway
- —— Minor railway
- ▬▬ International border
- ▬▬ State border
- △ Summit

Stone fortifications at Fort William Henry on Pemaquid Point

Getting Around

Interstate 95 is the only major artery in the state. As a result, the smaller scenic routes along the coastline are often congested with summer traffic. Many coastal towns can be reached from Boston by Greyhound bus line. Amtrak runs a service from Boston to Brunswick with stops en route. Maine State Ferry Service has numerous routes to and from various seashore destinations. Both Portland and Bangor have international airports. The scarcity of public roads in northern Maine means that occasionally logging roads are used, which are operated much like toll roads and are best tackled with four-wheel-drive vehicles.

For hotels and restaurants in this region see pp318–19 and pp338–9

Mount Katahdin, centerpiece of Baxter State Park

Sights at a Glance

Picturesque Stonington village on Deer Isle

For additional map symbols *see back flap*

❶ Kittery

🏠 9,500. ✈ 49 miles (78 km) NE in Portland. ℹ I-95 and US Rte. 1, (207) 439-1319. 🆆 mainetourism.com

The southern coast of Maine begins at the Piscataqua River and Kittery, a town with a split personality. Founded in 1647, Kittery boasts the oldest church in the state, the 1730 **First Congregational Church**. Many fine old mansions line the streets, including the John Bray House, one of the oldest dwellings in Maine. **Fort McClary**, now a state historic site, has fortifications dating to the early 1800s and a hexagonal blockhouse, and the **Kittery Historical and Naval Museum** is filled with ship models and exhibits explaining maritime history. Despite its wealth of historical attractions, Kittery is best known for a more contemporary lure – the more than 100 factory outlet stores promising bargains along Route 1, where shoppers can buy name brands at a discount.

🏛 First Congregational Church
23 Pepperrell Rd. **Tel** (207) 439-0650.
✝ 8am & 10am Sun.

🏰 Fort McClary State Historic Site
Rte. 103 E of Kittery. **Tel** (207) 384-5160. **Open** late May–Sep: 9am–dusk daily. 🅿

🏛 Kittery Historical and Naval Museum
Rogers Rd. **Tel** (207) 439-3080. **Open** Jun–mid-Oct: 10am–4pm Wed–Sun; call for winter hours. 🅿 ♿ partial.

Hexagonal Fort McClary blockhouse in Kittery

Environs
Four miles (6 km) from Kittery, visitors will come upon York Village. Settled in the 1630s, the village later grew into an important trading center, its wharves and warehouses filled with treasures from the lucrative West Indies trade. A collection of nine historic buildings maintained by the Old York Historical Society, **Old York** traces town history over three centuries. A repository for historical items, Old York has a superb collection of regional decorative arts housed in more than 30 period rooms and galleries. Tours begin at Jefferds' Tavern, a colonial hostelry, and include two historic homes, a 1745 one-room schoolhouse, and the John Hancock Warehouse, named after its owner, an original signatory of the Declaration of Independence. Down the street, the 1719 Old Gaol (jail) stands as one of the country's oldest public buildings. Dark, foreboding dungeons tell of harsh conditions

Lobster trap buoys

faced by the felons who served their sentences within the jail's 3-ft- (1-m-) thick walls.

🏛 Old York
Lindsay Rd. **Tel** (207) 363-1756. **Open** late May–mid-Oct: 10am–5pm Tue Sat, 1–5pm Sun. **Closed** early Sep–mid-Oct: Tue & Wed. 🅿 🗂 last tour at 4pm. 📷 📸 indoors. 🆆 oldyork.org

❷ Ogunquit

🏠 900. 🚌 36 miles (58 km) NE in Portland. ℹ 36 Main St. (207) 646-2939. 🆆 ogunquit.org

It is easy to see why the Abenaki Indians called this enclave Ogunquit, or "Beautiful Place by the Sea." Maine beaches do not come any better. From mid-May to Columbus Day, trolleys shuttle visitors to this powdery 3-mile (5-km) stretch of sand and dunes that curves around a backdrop of rugged cliffs. Atop the cliffs is the 1.25-mile (2-km) Marginal Way, a footpath that offers walkers dramatic vistas of the ocean. Perkins Cove, home of the only pedestrian drawbridge in the US, is a quaint jumble of fishermen's shacks now transformed into art galleries, shops, restaurants, and docks with fishing and cruise boats.

This picturesque outpost attracted an artist's colony as early as 1890, establishing it as a haven for the arts. The **Ogunquit Museum of American Art** was

Scenic ocean vista at Marginal Way in Ogunquit

For hotels and restaurants in this region see pp318–19 and pp338–9

built in 1952 by the eccentric but wealthy Henry Strater, who served as its director for more than 30 years. Constructed of wood and local stone, the museum has wide windows to allow views of the rocky cove and meadows. A 130,700-sq-ft (12,150-sq-m) sculpture garden and lawns also make the most of the breathtaking setting. The permanent collection includes art by many notable American painters.

🏛 **Ogunquit Museum of American Art**

543 Shore Rd. **Tel** (207) 646-4909. **Open** May–Oct: 10am–5pm daily. **Closed** Labor Day. 🅿
🌐 ogunquitmuseum.org

❸ The Kennebunks

🚗 30 miles (48 km) NE in Portland. ℹ 16 Water St., Kennebunk (207) 967-0857. 🌐 visitthekennebunks.com

First a thriving port and busy shipbuilding center, then a summer retreat for the wealthy, the Kennebunks are made up of two villages, Kennebunkport and Kennebunk.

The profusion of fine Federal and Greek Revival structures in Kennebunkport's historic village is evidence of the fortunes made in shipbuilding and trading from 1810 to the 1870s. With its 100-ft- (30-m-) tall white steeple and belfry, the 1824 South Congregational Church is a favorite subject for photographers. History of a different sort can be found at the **Seashore Trolley Museum**, where some 200 antique streetcars are housed, including one vehicle from New Orleans named Desire. Visitors can embark on a tour of the countryside aboard one of the restored trolleys.

The scenic drive along Route 9 offers views of surf along rocky Cape Arundel. At Cape Porpoise hungry travelers can sample lobster pulled fresh from the Atlantic. Kennebunk is

Maine's Lighthouses

For centuries mariners have been guided to safety by Maine's picturesque lighthouses. The coast is dotted with 63 such beacons, some accessible from the mainland and others perched on offshore islands. Portland Head Light was commissioned by the country's first president, George Washington (1732–99), and built in 1791, making it the oldest lighthouse in the state. It, like several other beacons, is open to the public and houses a small museum focusing on local marine and military history.

Nubble Lighthouse near Old York

famous for its beaches, most notably Kennebunk Beach, which is actually three connected strands. One of the town's most romantic historic homes is the 1826 Wedding Cake House. According to the local lore, George Bourne was unexpectedly called to sea before his marriage. Although a very hastily arranged wedding took place, there was no time to bake the traditional wedding cake. Instead, the shipbuilder vowed to his bride that upon his return he would remodel their home to look like a wedding cake. Today the Gothic spires, ornate latticework, and gingerbread trim offer proof that Bourne was a man of his word. Housed in four restored 19th-century buildings, **The Brick Store Museum** offers glimpses into the past with displays of decorative arts. It also offers architectural walking tours of the town's historic area (May–October).

Kennebunkport signpost

🏛 **Seashore Trolley Museum**
195 Log Cabin Rd., Kennebunkport. **Tel** (207) 967-2712. **Open** late May–mid-Oct: 10am–5pm daily; early May & late Oct: 10am–5pm Sat–Sun. 🅿
♿ 🌐 trolleymuseum.org

🏛 **The Brick Store Museum**
117 Main St., Kennebunk. **Tel** (207) 985-4802. **Open** year-round: 10am–4:30pm Tue–Fri, 10am–1pm Sat. **Closed** pub hols. 🅿
🌐 brickstoremuseum.org

❹ Old Orchard Beach

🏙 9,000. 🚗 13 miles (21 km) NE in Portland. 🚌 ℹ 11 First St. (207) 934-2500 or (800) 365-9386.

One of Maine's oldest seashore resorts, Old Orchard Beach's 7 miles (11 km) of sandy shoreline and low surf make it a favorite spot for swimming and boogie boarding. Kids love the pier, lined with shops and food stands, the games arcade, and the Palace Playland amusement park, which features a carousel, a Ferris wheel, a steel roller coaster, and other thrill rides.

Fresh lobster from the Cape Porpoise area in southern Maine

❺ Portland

Poet and Portland native Henry Wadsworth Longfellow (1807–82) described Maine's largest city as "the beautiful town that is seated by the sea." Longfellow was inspired by Portland's fortunate location on the crest of a peninsula with expansive views of Casco Bay and the Calendar Islands on three sides. Once a prosperous port and an early state capital, Portland has been devastated by no less than four major fires, resulting in a preponderance of sturdy stone Victorian buildings that line many of its streets today.

Exploring Portland
A thriving arts community and a downtown with interesting shopping and dining are all part of a stroll along Congress Street and through the restored Old Port Exchange area *(see pp286–7)*. The West End has fine homes and a splendid Western Promenade overlooking the water. The working waterfront and nearby beaches all add to the city's charm and atmosphere.

🏛 Neal Dow Memorial
714 Congress St. **Tel** (207) 773-7773. **Open** call for an appointment.
Neal Dow (1804–97), one of Portland's prominent citizens, built this Federal-style mansion in 1829. Twice serving as the city's mayor, Dow was an abolitionist and prohibitionist who also championed the causes of women's rights and prison reform. The Dow family's furnishings, paintings, china, and silver are displayed. The home is also the headquarters of The Maine Women's Christian Temperance Union.

🏛 Victoria Mansion
109 Danforth St. **Tel** (207) 772-4841. **Open** May–Oct: 10am–4pm Mon–Sat, 1–5pm Sun; late Nov & Dec: 11am–4:30pm daily. **Closed** Jan–Apr, Jul 4, Nov & Dec 25. 🚫 📷 every half-hour. 📷
This sumptuous brownstone villa was completed in 1860 to serve as the summer home of Ruggles hotelier Sylvester Morse (c.1816–93). The interior has striking decorative details, such as painted trompe l'oeil walls and ceilings, wood paneling, marble mantels, and a flying staircase.

🏛 Portland Museum of Art
7 Congress Sq. **Tel** (207) 775-6148. **Open** year-round: 10am–5pm Tue–Thu, Sat, Sun, 10am–9pm Fri; late May–mid-Oct: 10am–5pm Mon. 🚫 ♿ 🖥 portlandmuseum.org
Portland's fine art museum occupies three buildings in Federal, Beaux-Arts, and postmodern styles.

Distinctive building in Portland's downtown arts district

The museum has a rich collection of paintings and graphic art by Winslow Homer (1836–1910) and arranges seasonal tours to his studio on Prouts Neck. Other highlights include works by Andrew Wyeth (1917–2009), Fitz Henry Lane (1804–65), and Alex Katz (b.1927). Also on display are glass, ceramics, and furniture.

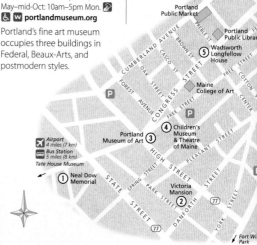

Victoria Mansion, with its lavishly decorated interior

Portland City Center
① Neal Dow Memorial
② Victoria Mansion
③ Portland Museum of Art
④ Children's Museum & Theatre of Maine
⑤ Wadsworth-Longfellow House

For hotels and restaurants in this region see pp318–19 and pp338–9

Coastal fishing on the outskirts of Portland

🏛 Children's Museum & Theatre of Maine

142 Free St. **Tel** (207) 828-1234. **Open**
year-round: 10am–5pm Tue–Sat,
noon–5pm Sun; May–Sep: 10am–5pm
Mon. **Closed** public hols. 🎫 🛗 📷

This historic brick building
houses three floors of interactive
exhibits, including a tidepool
touch tank, a replica space
shuttle, and a camera obscura.
Young actors occasionally
perform shows in
the Children's
Theatre.

🏛 Wadsworth-Longfellow House

489 Congress St. **Tel** (207) 879-0427.
Open May–Oct: 10am–4pm daily
(from noon Sun). 🎫 🛗 ♿ first
floor. 📷

Poet Henry Wadsworth
Longfellow grew up in this
1785 house, which contains
family mementos, portraits,
and furnishings.

🏛 Tate House Museum

1270 Westbrook St. **Tel** (207) 774-
6177. **Open** Jun–mid-Oct: 10am–
4pm Wed–Sat, 1–4pm Sun. **Closed**
Oct–May, Jul 4, & Labor Day. 🎫

In 1755 George Tate, an
agent of the British Royal
Navy, constructed an elegant
gambrel-roofed home
with rich wood paneling,
patterned floors, a
dogleg staircase, and
eight fireplaces. Now
a National Historic
Landmark, the house
has fine period furnishings.
Garden and architectural
tours can be arranged by
appointment.

🏛 Maine Narrow Gauge Railroad Co. & Museum

58 Fore St. **Tel** (207) 828-0814.
Open May–mid-Oct: 9:30am–4pm
Sat–Thu, noon–4pm Fri. ♿ Train ride:
Open running on the hour. 🎫

Scenic trips along a 3-mile
(5-km) stretch of the waterfront are the highlight of this
museum dedicated to the
railroad that served much
of Maine from the 1870s to
the 1940s. Exhibits include
vintage locomotives.

🏛 Portland Observatory

138 Congress St. **Tel** (207) 774-5561.
Open late May–mid-Oct: 10am–5pm
daily. **Closed** Jul 4. 🎫 🛗 ♿ 📷

Constructed in 1807, this
octagonal landmark is the last
surviving 19th-century signal
tower on the Atlantic. The
86-step climb to the upper deck
is worth the effort.

🏛 Museum at Portland Head Light at Fort Williams Park

1000 Shore Rd. **Tel** (207) 799-2661.
Open late May–Oct: 10am–4pm daily;
mid-Apr–May & Nov–mid-Dec:
10am–4pm Sat & Sun. 🎫 ♿

First illuminated in 1791 by
order of President George
Washington (1732–99), the
lighthouse has been the subject
of poetry, postage stamps, and
photographs. The keeper's
house is now a museum with
exhibits on the history of the
world's beacons. The large
surrounding park, just 4 miles
(6.5 km) from downtown, has
a beach and picnic areas.

Maine Narrow
Gauge Railroad Co.
& Museum

Convention, Visitors Bureau &
Information Center ℹ️

Maine
State Pier

United States
Customs House

Mariner's Church

Portland
Pier

0 meters 400
0 yards 400

Key

▫️ Street-by-Street map *see pp286–7*

Portland Observatory atop Munjoy Hill

Street-by-Street: Old Port

This once-decaying neighborhood near the harbor has been restored and is now the city's liveliest area, filled with shops, art galleries, restaurants, and bars. The Old Port's narrow streets are lined with classic examples of Victorian-era commercial architecture, including venerable structures that once served as warehouses and ships' chandleries. From the docks, ships take passengers out for deep-sea fishing excursions and harbor tours. Cruises include mail-boat rides and excursions to the Calendar Islands, where visitors can enjoy everything from cycling to sea kayaking.

Lively District
The Old Port has numerous pubs and outdoor terraces.

Centennial Block
has a façade made of Maine granite.

Charles Q. Clapp Block
This distinctive building was designed by self-taught architect Charles Quincy Clapp in 1866.

First National Bank is a typical example of Queen Anne commercial style. Its sandstone and brick exterior features a corner tower and tall chimneys.

Mary L. Deering Block, built for the prominent Deering family, is a mix of Italian and Colonial Revival styles.

Dolphins Statue
The statue is situated in the small cobblestone area in the middle of the Old Port district.

Seaman's Club
Built after the devastating fire of 1866, the building is known for its striking Gothic windows.

★ **United States Custom House**
Built following the Civil War (1861–5), this regal building contains gilded ceilings, marble staircases, and chandeliers.

Antique shops can be found throughout the Old Port district.

State of Maine Armory, now the Portland Regency Hotel, was designed to resemble a fortress and once was home to several units of the reserve militia known as the National Guard.

0 meters 50
0 yards 50

Key

— Suggested route

PEARL STREET

SILVER STREET

FORE STREET

COMMERCIAL STREET

★ **Mariner's Church**
Built in 1828, the building is an eclectic mix of Greek Revival and Federal styles, and is now used to house a variety of shops and businesses.

❻ Freeport

🏔 7,000. ✈ 17 miles (31 km) SW in Portland. ℹ 23 Depot St. (207) 865-1212. 🌐 **freeportusa.com**

Although Freeport dates back to 1789, shoppers would argue that it did not arrive on the scene until 1917, when the first L. L. Bean clothing store opened its doors. Today this retail giant is open 24 hours a day, 365 days a year, and, with more than 3.5 million customers annually, L. L. Bean is easily Maine's biggest man-made attraction. Since the 1980s, more than 150 other brand-name outlets have opened here.

Travelers who make it past the shops will discover a working harbor in South Freeport, where seal-watching tours and sailing cruises depart. The shoreline includes **Wolfe's Neck Woods State Park**, 0.4 sq miles (1 sq km) of tranquility wrapped along Casco Bay.

Freeport's most unusual sight is the **Desert of Maine**. Originally a late 1700s farm, the area was severely over-tilled and over-logged. The topsoil eventually disappeared altogether, giving way to glacial sand deposits and creating a 1,742,400-sq-ft (161,900-sq-m) desert of sand dunes. Visitors can walk the nature trails with a guide who narrates the history of the area, or ride on an open cart. The farm museum is housed in a 1783 barn.

L. L. Bean and Outlet Shopping

Leon Leonwood Bean (1872–1967) likely would be amazed if he could see the result of his dislike for cold, wet feet. The hunting shoe he developed in 1912 with leather uppers on rubber overshoe bottoms began a company that now claims more than a billion dollars in sales worldwide and carries anything needed for outdoor excursions. Bean's showroom has grown into a mammoth flagship store that includes a 785-sq-ft (73-sq-m-) pond stocked with trout.

Bust of L. L. Bean

🌳 **Wolfe's Neck Woods State Park**
Wolfe's Neck Rd. **Tel** (207) 865-4465.
Open 9am–dusk daily. 🚫 🅿 ♿

🏜 **Desert of Maine**
95 Desert Rd. **Tel** (207) 865-6962.
Open mid-May–mid-Oct: tours 9am–4:30pm daily. 🚫 ♿
🌐 **desertofmaine.com**

❼ Brunswick

🏔 21,000. ✈ 33 miles (53 km) SW in Portland. 🚌 ℹ 8 Venture Ave., Topsham (207) 725-8797.

Brunswick is best known as the home of Bowdoin College and as the land entry for the scenic panoramas of the town of Harpswell – a peninsula and three islands jutting out into Casco Bay.

Founded in 1794, the college claims a number of distinguished alumni, including explorers Robert Peary (1856–1920) and Donald MacMillan (1874–1970). The **Peary-MacMillan Arctic Museum** honors the two, who

Peary-MacMillan Arctic Museum on Bowdoin College campus

in 1909 became the first to reach the North Pole. Exhibits trace the history of polar exploration and display the journals of both men.

The **Pejepscot Historical Society** offers displays of Brunswick history in its three museums and offers tours of both Skolfield-Whittier House, a 17-room Italianate mansion built in 1858 by a shipyard

Seemingly endless acres of sand in Desert of Maine, Freeport

For hotels and restaurants in this region see pp318–19 and pp338–9

owner, and the Joshua L. Chamberlain House, a Civil War museum.

🏛 Peary-MacMillan Arctic Museum

Hubbard Hall, Bowdoin College. **Tel** (207) 725-3416. **Open** year-round: 10am–5pm Tue–Sat, 2–5pm Sun. **Closed** public hols. ♿

🏛 Pejepscot Historical Society

159 Park Row. **Tel** (207) 729-6606. **Open** Jun–Oct: call for opening hours and tour times. 🎫

Environs

Nine miles (14 km) east lies Bath, long a shipbuilding center. Its stately homes were built with the profits from this lucrative industry. In 1608 colonists constructed the *Virginia*, the first British boat produced in the New World. Since then, some 4,000 ships have been built here. The **Maine Maritime Museum** includes one of the country's few surviving wooden shipbuilding yards. The modern Maritime History Building annex is a repository of nautical models, paintings, and memorabilia.

Nautical art from the Maine Maritime Museum in Bath

🏛 Maine Maritime Museum

243 Washington St. **Tel** (207) 443-1316. **Open** 9:30am–5pm daily. **Closed** Jan 1, Thanksgiving, & Dec 25. 🎫 📷 call for times. ♿ partial. 📷

❽ Boothbay Harbor

🏘 2,500. ✈ 38 miles (61 km) N in Augusta. ℹ 192 Townsend Ave. (207) 633-2353 or (800) 266-8422. 🌐 boothbayharbor.com

The boating capital of the mid-coast, Boothbay Harbor bustles with the influx of summer tourists. Dozens of boating excursions cast off from the dock. Visitors might choose to take an hour's sail along the coast aboard a majestic windjammer, a 41-mile (66-km)

Boothbay Harbor's busy boardwalk area

cruise up the Kennebec River, or the popular trip to the artists' retreat on Monhegan Island *(see p291)*. Sightseers can participate in a wide range of activities, including puffin and whale-watching expeditions. The harbor is at its best in late June, when majestic tall ships parade in under full sail for the annual Windjammer Days festival.

Boothbay Harbor whale-watch sign

The town itself is chockablock with shops and galleries. **Maine State Aquarium**, a haven for parents of restless children on rainy days, is equipped with a large touch tank filled with sea creatures, which can be touched.

🐟 Maine State Aquarium

194 McKown Point Rd., West Boothbay Harbor. **Tel** (207) 633-9559. **Open** late May–Sep: 10am–5pm daily. **Closed** Sep: Mon & Tue. 🎫 📷 ♿

Environs

A scenic 30-mile (48-km) drive up the coast brings travelers to Pemaquid Point, complete with shelves of granite cliffs that jut from the sea. Rising dramatically above a bluff and offering panoramic views of the coast-line, the 1827 **Pemaquid Point Light** houses the Fisherman's Museum in the old lightkeeper's home. The Pemaquid Art Gallery is on the grounds and shows the work of local artists. There is a bonus for history buffs at the 348,500-sq-ft (32,350-sq-m) **Colonial Pemaquid State Historic Site**, which includes a 1695 graveyard and a replica of

Fort William Henry. English colonists fought French invaders at this spot in several forts that date from the early 17th century onward. A small museum contains a diorama of the original 1620s settlement and displays a collection of tools, pottery shards, and house-hold items that reflect the rustic lives of the early settlers.

🔆 Pemaquid Point Light

Rte. 130. **Tel** (207) 677-2492. **Open** mid-May–mid-Oct: 10:30am–5pm daily. 🎫 ♿ Fisherman's Museum: **Tel** (207) 677-2494. **Open** May–Oct: call for hours. ♿ Pemaquid Art Gallery: **Tel** (207) 677-2752. **Open** Jun–Oct: call for hours.

🔆 Colonial Pemaquid State Historic Site/Fort William Henry

Off Rte. 130. **Tel** (207) 677-2423. **Open** late May–early Sep: 9am–sunset. 🎫 📷

Pemaquid Point Light and the Fisherman's Museum

⑨ Penobscot Bay

Penobscot Bay is picture-book Maine, with high hills seemingly rolling straight into the ocean, wave- pounded cliffs, sheltered harbors bobbing with fishing boats, and lobster traps piled high on the docks. Windjammer sailboats, ferries, and numerous cruise ships carry passengers to offshore islands, setting sail from ports such as Rockland, Camden, and Lincolnville, popular stops on the bay's western shore. The former shipbuilding centers of Searsport and Bucksport lie beyond. The more remote eastern shore leads to serene, perfectly preserved villages such as Castine and Blue Hill.

Sailboats moored in the safe confines of Camden Harbor

Penobscot Bay

Exploring Penobscot Bay

To sail across Penobscot Bay covers a mere 35 miles (56 km) from its southernmost outpost of Port Clyde to its northern tip at Stonington. However, typical of Maine's ribboned coast, the same voyage takes almost 100 miles (160 km) by car. Either mode of transportation will offer stunning views of one of Maine's coastal highlights.

Rockland

🔢 1 Park Drive (207) 596-0376 or (800) 562-2529.

Long a fishing town and commercial center, Rockland is now evolving into a tourist destination. These days lobster boats share the harbors with excursion boats, state ferries, and the schooners of Maine's windjammer fleet. However, the Lobster Festival, on the first full weekend of August, remains the town's biggest event.

On land the Farnsworth Art Museum and Wyeth Center showcases artists inspired by the Maine landscape, including Rockwell Kent (1882–1971), Edward Hopper (1882–1967),

and N. C. (1882–1945), Andrew (1917–2009), and Jamie (b.1946) Wyeth. The Maine Lighthouse Museum has a superb collection of lenses and other artifacts, as well as a lighthouse-themed gift shop. Two miles (3.2 km) south of Rockland on Route 73, the Owls Head Transportation Museum houses aircraft, cars, bicycles, and carriages, and occasionally hosts air shows.

Camden

🔢 Commercial St., 2 Public Landing (207) 236-4404 or (800) 223-5459.
🌐 visitcamden.com

The compact village is ideal for exploring on foot. Shady streets are lined with elegant homes and spired churches, and a host of shops border the waterfront. Among the fine inns on High Street is the Whitehall, with a room dedicated to Pulitzer-Prize-winning poet Edna St. Vincent Millay (1892–1950), who went to school in Camden.

From mid-May to mid-October a short road at Camden Hills State Park on Route 1 is open to the top of 796-ft (242-m) Mount Battie. Standing on this point overlooking Penobscot

Bay, Millay was inspired to write her first volume of poetry.

Searsport

🔢 14 Main St., Belfast (207) 338-5900.

Searsport was once a major shipbuilding port. Now a handful of restored sea captains' homes on Church Street house the collection of the Penobscot Marine Museum (open late May to late October). An extensive collection of maritime art, ship models, navigational instruments and imported goods and displays of shipbuilding tools help tell the story of those glory days.

Considered to be the antiques capital of Maine, the town is chockablock with shops and has large flea markets on weekends in the summer.

Bucksport

🔢 52 Main St. (207) 469-6818. 🏨
Bucksport looks across the Penobscot River to the 0.2-sq-mile (0.5-sq-km) Fort Knox State Park that surrounds a pentagonal Civil War-era fortress. From May through

Vintage aircraft at Owls Head Transportation Museum

Searsport
Bucksport
15
166 199 • Blue Hill
Isleboro
Island • Castine
Dark
Harbor Deer
Lincolnville Isle
Sunshine
Camden North
Haven Stonington
Rockland Island
Vinalhaven
Island Isle au Haut
131

• Port Clyde
Matinicus
Matinicus
Island

Monhegan island

Penobscot Bay and its Islands

Penobscot Bay is famous for its islands. Although some are no more than a pile of bald granite boulders, others are lush paradises that cover thousands of acres and are prime territory for birders, hikers, and sea kayakers. While some of these retreats are inhabited, most are completely wild, home only to harbor seals and seabirds such as puffins and great cormorants.

Key
▬▬ Major road
▬▬ Minor road

0 kilometers 20
0 miles 10

October, visitors can explore barracks, storehouses, and underground passages. The park also features the Penobscot Narrows Bridge Observatory (open May to October), which provides 360-degree views from 420 ft (128 m) above the river.

Castine

ℹ️ Emerson Hall, Court St. (207) 326-4502.

Founded in the early 17th century and coveted for its strategic location overlooking the bay, Castine has flown the flags of France, Britain, the Netherlands, and the US.

Relics of Castine's turbulent past can still be seen at Fort George on Wadsworth Cove Road, the highest point in town. Fort George was built by the British in 1779 and witnessed the American Navy's worst defeat during the Revolutionary War, a battle in which more than 40 colonial ships were either captured or destroyed. The fort is always open. Across from Fort George on Battle Avenue is the Maine Maritime Academy.

On Perkins Street, the two-story Wilson Museum has a collection that includes everything from Balinese masks and pre-Inca pottery to minerals and farm tools. It is closed during the fall and winter months.

Blue Hill

ℹ️ 16B South St. (207) 374-3242.

Surrounded by fields of blueberries and with many of its white clapboard buildings listed on the National Historic Register, Blue Hill is a living postcard. Visitors will get a great view if they climb up Blue Hill Mountain.

Deer Isle

ℹ️ Rte. 15 at Eggemoggin Rd. (207) 348-6124.

Deer Isle, reached from the mainland via a graceful suspension bridge, is actually a series of small islands linked by causeways. Island highlights include the towns of Deer Isle and Stonington, and the famous Haystack Mountain School of Crafts.

Isle au Haut

ℹ️ Rte. 15 at Eggemoggin Rd., Deer Isle (207) 348-6124.

A mail boat from Stonington covers the 8 miles (13 km) to Isle au Haut. Almost half the island,

White-tailed deer, a common sight throughout the Penobscot Bay area

some 4 sq miles (11 sq km), belongs to Acadia National Park (see pp292–3) and offers 20 miles (32 km) of hiking.

Monhegan Island

ℹ️ (207) 596-0376 or (800) LOBCLAW.

This unspoiled enclave has no cars and no commotion. Only a half-mile (0.8 km) wide and 1.7 miles (2.7 km) long, this island is smaller than New York City's Central Park, and is a favored retreat for birders and hikers who enjoy rough trails along rocky cliffs and through deep forest. Painter Jamie Wyeth is one of the prominent current members of a summer artists' colony. Cruise companies operate round-trip excursions from Port Clyde, Boothbay Harbor, and New Harbor.

North Haven Island

ℹ️ (207) 867-4433.

Eight miles (13 km) long and 3 miles (5 km) wide, North Haven is a refined summer colony and home to 350 hardy year-round residents. Much of the island remains open fields and meadows filled with wildflowers.

Vinalhaven Island

ℹ️ (207) 863-4826.

Tiny Vinalhaven is a perfect place for a swim or a hike. Inland moors and green spaces are balanced by a granite shoreline and a harbor bustling with lobster boats.

⑩ Acadia National Park

Located primarily on Mount Desert Island, the 73-sq-mile (190-sq-km) Acadia National Park, a wild, unspoiled paradise, is heavily visited in summer. Wave-beaten shores and inland forests await travelers. The park's main attraction is the seasonal Loop Road, a 27-mile (43-km) drive that climbs and dips with the pink granite mountains of the east coast of the island before swinging inland past Jordan Pond, Bubble Pond, and Eagle Lake. Visitors who want a closer, more intimate look at the flora and fauna can do so on foot, bike, or horseback.

Vintage Carriage Roads
Forty-five miles (72 km) of old crushed-rock carriage roads can be used for hiking and cycling.

Acadia's Wildlife
The park is home to numerous animals including woodchucks, white-tailed deer, red foxes, and the occasional black bear.

★ **Bass Harbor Head**
Craggy Bass Harbor Head exemplifies Maine's rock-bound shoreline. The 1858 Bass Harbor Head lighthouse affords magnificent views of the ocean.

Thompson Island

Indian Point   Town Hill

Somesville

Round Pond

Pretty Marsh

Long Pond

Echo Lake

Echo Lake Beach

Seal Cove Pond

Seal Cove

Mount Desert Oceanarium

Seal Cove Road

Long Pond Road

Bass Harbor Marsh

Key

▬ Major road
▭ Minor road
▬ Scenic route
— Park boundary

0 kilometers   2
0 yards   2

Bass Harbor Head

★ Cadillac Mountain

The 1,527-ft- (465-m-) tall Cadillac Mountain is the highest point on the Atlantic Coast. Hiking trails and an auto road lead to spectacular panoramas at the summit.

Jordan Pond

Many visitors stop at beautiful Jordan Pond, where a restaurant serves lunch, tea, and dinner from late May to late October.

★ Sand Beach

Sand Beach is one of only two lifeguarded beaches in the park, but the ocean water, which rarely exceeds 55° F (15° C), discourages many swimmers.

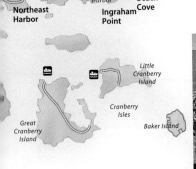

★ Thunder Hole

The ocean's relentless pounding on the island's cliffs has created the natural phenomenon known as the Thunder Hole. When the tide rises during heavy winds, air trapped in this crevice is compressed and expelled with a resounding boom.

For map symbols *see back flap*

Rolling hills near Eagle Lake on the outskirts of Bar Harbor

⓫ Bar Harbor

🏠 5,000. ✈ 11 miles (17 km) NW in Trenton. 🚌 Island Explorer (free). 🛈 1201 Bar Harbor Rd., Trenton, (800) 345-4617 or 93 Cottage St., Bar Harbor (mid-May–mid-Oct only). 🆆 **barharbormaine.com**

With a commanding location on Frenchman Bay, Bar Harbor is Mount Desert Island's lively tourist center. Artists Thomas Cole (1801–48) and Frederic Church (1862–1900) discovered the area's beauty in the 1840s and their brilliant work attracted the wealthy. In the 19th century, the town was a haven for the Astors and the Vanderbilts, among other rich American families.

Today Bar Harbor is a thriving waterside resort that attracts 5 million visitors a year. From here people can explore Acadia National Park *(see pp292–3)* or the mid-Maine coastline.

🏛 Bar Harbor Historical Society Museum

33 Ledgelawn Ave. **Tel** (207) 288-0000. **Open** mid-Jun–Oct: 1–4pm Mon–Fri.

In 1947 a fire destroyed 26.5 sq miles (69 sq km) of

wilderness and a third of Bar Harbor's lavish summer homes, all but ending the village's reign as a high-society enclave. A display of early photographs shows the grand old days and the devastating effects of the fire. Happily for visitors, several of the remaining summer showplaces have been turned into gracious inns.

🎭 Criterion Theater

35 Cottage St. **Tel** (207) 288-0829. 🎫 A perennial favorite, this is an Art Deco gem that is listed on the National Register of Historic Places. The theater offers films, live music, and theater performances.

🏛 Abbe Museum

26 Mount Desert St. **Tel** (207) 288-3519. **Open** late May–Nov: 10am–5pm daily; call for winter hours. **Closed** Jan. 🎫 ♿ 🎁

This museum celebrates Maine's Native American heritage with exhibits, hands-on programs and workshops taught by Native artists. There is a seasonal branch next to the Wild Gardens of Acadia, which has some 300 species of local plants.

ⓧ Mount Desert Oceanarium & Lobster Hatchery

Rte. 3. **Tel** (207) 288-5005. **Open** late May–Sep: 9am–5pm Mon–Sat. 🐾 🎁 ♿ 🎁

Mount Desert Oceanarium, 8.5 miles (14 km) northwest of town, is the place to learn about lobsters. The hatching and raising process is explained in the Lobster Hatchery, while a fishing program illustrates this Maine industry. Children enjoy the touch tank and a walk on a salt marsh.

ⓧ Kisma Preserve

Rte. 3 in Trenton. **Tel** (207) 667-3244. **Open** May–Oct: 10:30am–5pm daily. 🐾 ♿

This preserve is located in Trenton, across the bridge from Mount Desert Island. The pastures, streams, and woods are home to numerous species of animals, such as wolves, bears, lynx, and many birds, but it is difficult to predict which will be visible at any one time. All visits feature guided tours that provide background on the animals.

⓬ Northeast Harbor

✈ 12 miles (19 km) N in Trenton. 🛈 18 Harbor Dr. (207) 276-5040. 🆆 **mountdesertchamber.org**

Northeast Harbor is the center of Mount Desert Island's social scene. The village has a handful of upscale shops, a few dining places, many handsome but rambling summer mansions, and a scenic harbor where boats set sail for nearby Cranberry Islands.

Chartered cruise boat in Bar Harbor

🔵 Asticou Terrace and Thuya Lodge and Gardens

Rte. 3 S of Rte. 198 jct. **Tel** (207) 276-3727. **Open** May–Oct: call for hours. 🅿 for gardens **W** garden preserve.org

The Harbor can best be admired from the stunning Asticou Terraces. A granite path snakes along the hillside, yielding ever-wider vistas as it ascends, with benches and a gazebo placed at strategic viewpoints. At the top of the hill are Thuya Lodge, with collections of paintings and books, and Thuya Gardens, with flowerbeds and a reflecting pool that descends to the harbor's edge.

Environs

Somes Sound, a finger-shaped natural fjord that juts 5 miles (8 km) into Mount Desert Island, separates Northeast

Whimsical sculpture in Asticou Gardens

Harbor from quiet Southwest Harbor, famed for its yacht-builders Hinckley and Morris. The village is also home to the **Wendell Gilley Museum of Bird Carving**. The village artisan was a pioneer in the art of decorative bird carving, and the museum preserves about 100 of more than 10,000 birds he carved. It's a good introduction to local species. Museum workshops range from introductory classes to projects focused on specific birds. A drive or bike ride beyond Southwest Harbor leads to unspoiled villages, including Bass Harbor, where tourists are few and visitors can view the 1858 Bass Harbor Head Light.

🏛 Wendell Gilley Museum of Bird Carving

4 Herrick Rd. **Tel** (207) 244-7555. **Open** Jun–Oct: 10am–4pm Tue–Sat, noon–4pm Sun (to 5pm Jul & Aug); May, Nov & Dec: 10am–4pm Fri & Sat, noon–4pm Sun.

⓭ Machias

🏔 2,900. ✈ 91 miles (146 km) W in Bangor. ℹ 1 Main St. (207) 255-4402.

Situated at the mouth of the river of the same name, Machias retains many of the handsome homes that sprang up during its days as a prosperous 19th-century lumber center. The town's name comes from the Micmac Indians and means "bad little falls," a reference to the waterfall that cascades in the center of town. There is a good view of the falls from the footbridge in Bad Little Falls Park.

Machias proclaims itself as the wild blueberry capital of Maine. It also lays claim to the region's oldest building, the 1770 **Burnham Tavern**, now a museum with period furnishings, paintings, and historic photographs. It was here that plans were made for the first naval battle of the Revolutionary War in 1775 *(see pp47–9).* Following that meeting, local men sailed out into Machias Bay on the small sloop *Unity* and captured the British man-of-war HMS *Margaretta.* Models

Footbridge in Bad Little Falls Park in Machias

The Lobster Industry

Harbors filled with lobstering boats and piers piled high with traps are familiar sights in the state that is America's undisputed lobster capital. Maine harvests over 120 million lb (54 million kg) of this tasty crustacean each year. No visit is complete without a trip to a lobster pound, where patrons pick a live lobster from the tank, wait for it to be steamed, and savor the sweet meat at a picnic table overlooking the water.

Lobster fishermen

of the two ships can be seen at the **Gates House**, a restored 1807 Federal-style home in nearby Machiasport.

The town is set on the Machias River, a demanding canoeing route. **Roque Bluffs State Park** to the southwest of town offers swimming in a 2,613,600-sq-ft (242,800-sq-m) freshwater pond and a 1-mile-(1.6-km-) long sweep of beach. The park has a launching ramp for sea kayaks, which are popular in Machias Bay. Birders go to nearby Cutler for boat trips to Machias Seal Island, home to puffins, Arctic terns, and razorbill auks.

🏛 Burnham Tavern

Main St. **Tel** (207) 255-6930. **Open** mid-Jun–Oct: call for hours. 🅿 🚻

🏠 Gates House

344 Port Rd., Machiasport. **Tel** (207) 255-8461. **Open** Jul & Aug: 12:30–4:30pm Tue–Fri. 🅿

🔵 Roque Bluffs State Park

145 Shoppee Point Rd., Roque Bluffs. **Tel** (207) 255-3475. **Open** mid-May–Oct: 9am–dusk. 🅿 ♿

⑭ Campobello Island

In 1964 4.5 sq miles (11.5 sq km) of Campobello Island were designated as a memorial to President Franklin Delano Roosevelt (1882–1945). The main settlement of Welshpool was where the future president spent most of his summers, until 1921, when he contracted polio. Undaunted, Roosevelt went on to lead the US through the Great Depression and World War II. The highlight of the park – which actually lies in Canada – is Roosevelt Cottage, a 34-room summer home that displays Roosevelt's personal mementos. A passport is required for border crossing.

VISITORS' CHECKLIST

Practical Information
ℹ️ Rte. 774. **Tel** (506) 752-2922.
Cottage: **Open** late May–mid-
Oct: 9am–5pm daily. Grounds:
Open year-round. 🅿️ ♿
🅦 fdr.net

Key

▬▬ Major road
═══ Minor road
▭▭▭ Scenic route
—— Park boundary
= = = Walking trail

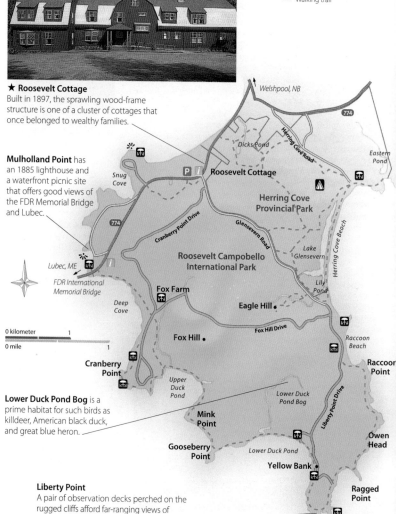

★ **Roosevelt Cottage**
Built in 1897, the sprawling wood-frame structure is one of a cluster of cottages that once belonged to wealthy families.

Mulholland Point has an 1885 lighthouse and a waterfront picnic site that offers good views of the FDR Memorial Bridge and Lubec.

Lower Duck Pond Bog is a prime habitat for such birds as killdeer, American black duck, and great blue heron.

Liberty Point
A pair of observation decks perched on the rugged cliffs afford far-ranging views of the coastline and the ocean.

Welshpool, NB

Dicks Pond

Eastern Pond

Roosevelt Cottage

Herring Cove Provincial Park

Snug Cove

Cranberry Point Drive

Glensevern Road

Lake Glensevern

Herring Cove Beach

Roosevelt Campobello International Park

Lily Pond

Lubec, ME

FDR International Memorial Bridge

Fox Farm

Deep Cove

Eagle Hill

Fox Hill Drive

Fox Hill

Raccoon Beach

Raccoon Point

0 kilometer   1
0 mile   1

Cranberry Point

Upper Duck Pond

Mink Point

Lower Duck Pond Bog

Liberty Point Drive

Owen Head

Gooseberry Point

Lower Duck Pond

Yellow Bank

Ragged Point

☀ **Liberty Point**

Privately owned Hamilton's Folly mansion in Calais

⓯ Calais

🏙 4,000. ✈ 229 miles (424 km) W in Bangor. ℹ 39 Union St. (207) 454-2211.

Perched on the west bank of the St. Croix River opposite St. Stephen, New Brunswick, Calais is Maine's busiest border crossing to Canada. The two countries share jurisdiction over nearby St. Croix Island, where in 1604 explorers Samuel de Champlain (1567–1635) and the Sieur de Monts (c.1560–1630) established the first white settlement in North America north of Florida. The island is accessible only by boat, a difficult trip due to strong currents and tides that can run as high as 28 ft (8.5 m).

Ripe blueberries in Calais

Calais was devastated by a gigantic fire in 1870. One of the few buildings that survived the conflagration is Hamilton's Folly mansion at No. 78 South Street. The Victorian house was so dubbed by locals because of its ostentatious design – a tribute to excess that bankrupted its owner.

Outdoor activities abound here. The St. Croix River is a challenging waterway for canoeists and a prime spot for salmon fishing. Three miles (5 km) southwest of Calais is the Baring Unit of the **Moosehorn National Wildlife Refuge**, 26.5 sq miles (69 sq km) of wilderness that beckons hikers, bird-watchers, and naturalists. Man-made eagle nesting platforms have been erected along Route 1 north

of town. Visitors should watch for the 400-sq-ft (120-sq-m) observation deck on this road for the best views. Also, there are a number of commercial farms that allow visitors to pick their own blueberries.

🦅 Moosehorn National Wildlife Refuge

103 Headquarters Rd., Baileyville. **Tel** (207) 454-7161. Park: **Open** year-round: sunrise–sunset daily. Office: **Open** year-round: 8am–4:30pm Mon–Fri. ♿

⓰ Bangor

🏙 32,700. ✈ 287 Godfrey Blvd. 🚌 ℹ 519 Main St. (207) 947-0307.

The world's leading lumber port in the 1850s, Bangor remains the commercial center of northern Maine. The town's Penobscot River harbor was once loaded with ships carrying pine logs from nearby sawmills. This past is saluted with a 31-ft (9.5-m), 3,200-lb (1,450-kg) statue of the mythical lumberjack Paul Bunyan on Main Street. Industrial might aside, Maine's second-largest city also draws visitors because of its ideal location as a base camp for treks to Acadia National Park (see pp292–3) and the forestlands that stretch to the north.

The city has a number of noteworthy residences from both the past and the present. The stately homes spared by a 1911 fire still line the West Market Square Historic District and the Broadway area. Maine-born horror author Stephen King lives in a mansion at No. 47 West Broadway, complete with a wrought-iron fence festooned with iron bats and cobwebs. The Greek Revival 1836 Thomas Hill House is headquarters for the **Bangor Historical Society** and offers historic walking tours.

One of Bangor's most pleasant green spaces is the **Mount Hope Cemetery**. Established in 1834, the cemetery is beautifully landscaped with ponds, bridges, and paved paths that attract strollers and inline skaters. This spirit of movement is also celebrated at the **Cole Land Transportation Museum**. The museum's collection contains more than 200 vehicles dating from the 19th century, ranging from fire engines and horse-drawn logging sleds to antique baby carriages.

🏛 Bangor Historical Society

159 Union St. **Tel** (207) 942-1900. **Open** Jun–Sep: 10am–4pm Tue, Thu & Sat. 🐾 📷 🌐 bangormuseum.org

⚰ Mount Hope Cemetery

State St. **Open** 7:30am–dusk Mon–Fri. 📷 ♿

🏛 Cole Land Transportation Museum

405 Perry Rd. **Tel** (207) 990-3600. **Open** May–early Nov: 9am–5pm daily. 🐾

Bangor's West Market Square Historic District

For hotels and restaurants in this region see pp318–19 and pp338–9

⑰ Augusta

🏛 19,000. ✈ 75 Airport Rd. 🚌
ℹ 21 University Dr. (207) 623-4559.

Maine's state capital is a relatively quiet city of 19,000. The 1832 **Maine State House**, the centerpiece of the government complex on the Kennebec River, was built of granite quarried from neighboring Hallowell. Major expansions have left only the center block from the original design by Boston architect Charles Bulfinch (1763–1844). Exhibits include political portraits and battle flags. Across the street, the **Blaine House** has been serving as the governor's mansion since 1919. The 28-room Colonial-style home was built in 1832 for a local sea captain.

The **Maine State Museum** has exhibits spanning "12,000 years of Maine history." One highlight is the "Made in Maine" exhibit, which re-creates a water-powered woodworking mill. The **Old Fort Western** is a restoration of one of New England's oldest surviving wooden forts, dating from 1754. The fort was built on the site where the Plymouth Pilgrims (see pp154–5) had established their trading post the previous century.

🏛 **Maine State House**
State & Capitol Sts. **Tel** (207) 287-1400.
Open year-round: 8am–5pm Mon–Fri.
🚗 ♿

Costumed interpreter at Old Fort Western in Augusta

Imposing façade of the Maine State House in Augusta

🏛 **Blaine House**
192 State St. **Tel** (207) 287-2031.
Open year-round: call for appt. 📞 call to arrange.

🏛 **Maine State Museum**
2301 State St. **Tel** (207) 287-2301.
Open year-round: 9am–5pm Mon–Fri, 10am–4pm Sat.
Closed public hols. 🚗 📷 ♿
🌐 mainestatemuseum.org

🏛 **Old Fort Western**
16 Cony St. **Tel** (207) 626-2385.
Open late May–mid-Oct: call for hours. 🚗 ♿
🌐 oldfortwestern.org

Lifeguard's chair on the shore of tranquil Sebago Lake

Environs

Heading southwest from Augusta, travelers will get a rare look at the last active Shaker community in the US. Established in the 18th century, the Sabbathday Lake Shaker Community is home to a handful of residents who still adhere to their traditional beliefs of simplicity, celibacy, and communal harmony. Tours of the 18-building village include a stop at the **Shaker Village Museum** to see the beautiful furniture and ingenious inventions that became Shaker trademarks.

Nestled at the feet of Maine's western mountain ranges, Poland Springs is famous for its water. Farther west is Sebago Lake, a favorite among fishermen for its landlocked salmon.

🏛 **Sabbathday Shaker Village Museum**
707 Shaker Rd., New Gloucester.
Tel (207) 926-4597. **Open** late May–mid-Oct: 10am–4:30pm Mon–Sat.
🚗 📷 ♿ 🌐 maineshakers.com

⑱ Bethel

🏛 2,500. ✈ 70 miles (113 km) S in Portland. ℹ 8 Station Place (207) 824-2282 or (800) 442-5826.
🌐 bethelmaine.com

A picturesque historic district, a major New England ski resort, and proximity to the White Mountains give Bethel year-round appeal. First settled in 1796, the town grew into a farming and lumbering center, and with the coming of the railroad in 1851 quickly became a popular resort. The lineup of classic clapboard mansions on the town green includes the Federal-style **Moses Mason House** (c.1813), which has period pieces and Rufus Porter murals on two floors.

Scenic drives are found in all directions, taking in tiny, unspoiled colonial hamlets such as Waterford to the south and beautiful mountain terrain to the north. **Sunday River Ski Resort** (see p362), 6 miles (10 km) north of town in Newry, has 8 mountains and more than 100 ski trails. Evans Notch, a natural pass through the White Mountain peaks, offers many memorable views, including the Roost, a suspension bridge high above the Wild River and a favorite with photographers. **Grafton Notch State Park** has even more spectacular scenery along its drives, hiking trails and picnic areas. The park's special spots include waterfalls bearing such fanciful names as Screw Auger and Mother Walker, and beautiful panoramic views from Table Rock and the top of Old Speck Mountain.

🏛 Moses Mason House
10–14 Broad St. **Tel** (207) 824-2908. **Open** Jul & Aug: 1–4pm Tue–Sat, or by appointment year-round. 🅿 🄲 ♿ 🆆 bethelhistorical.org

🎿 Sunday River Ski Resort
Off Rte. 2 in Newry. **Tel** (207) 824-3000 or (800) 543-2SKI. **Open** 9am–4pm Mon–Fri, 8am–4pm Sat & Sun. 🅿

🌲 Grafton Notch State Park
Rte. 26 NW of Newry. **Tel** (207) 824-2912. **Open** mid-May–mid-Oct. 🅿

⑲ Sugarloaf

ℹ (207) 237-2000 or (800) 843-5623.

Maine's highest ski mountain, Sugarloaf is the centerpiece of this touristic village packed with hotels, restaurants, and hundreds of condominiums. Downhill skiers have been flocking to the **Sugarloaf** ski center *(see p362)* for years, attracted by the more than 100 trails and a vertical drop of 2,800 ft (870 m). The center also offers cross-country skiing, snowshoeing, and ice skating.

In summer, the emphasis shifts to the resort's 18-hole golf course, boating on the lakes and rivers, and hiking in the surrounding Carrabassett Valley. The resort is also famous for a network of more than 50 miles (80 km) of mountain-biking trails through terrain ranging from flat trails to challenging circuits full of steep climbs and descents.

Screw Auger Falls in Grafton Notch State Park

🎿 Sugarloaf
Carrabassett Valley. **Tel** (207) 237-2000 or (800) 843-5623. **Open** 8:30am–3:50pm daily. 🅿 🄲 ♿ in lodge. 🍴 🆆 sugarloaf.com

⑳ Rangeley Lakes Region

ℹ 6 Park Rd. (207) 864-5571 or (800) 685-2537. 🆆 rangeleymaine.com

Set against a backdrop of mountains, this rustic area encompasses a series of pristine lakes that have long been a magnet for any kind of outdoor enthusiast. In summer fishermen ply the waterways for trout and salmon, while canoeists frequently spot a moose or two lumbering along the shoreline. The area is now

Moose crossing sign

popular with mountain bikers, but the beauty of the place has never been a secret. Hikers have been enjoying the vistas from the summit of **Bald Mountain** and tramping the section of the Appalachian Trail *(see pp26–7)* running along **Saddleback Mountain** for decades.

Elsewhere, the popular **Rangeley Lake State Park** provides vacationers with facilities for swimming, fishing, birding, boating, and camping, and 1.2 miles (2 km) of lakefront. Toward the southeast, **Mount Blue State Park** is home to Lake Webb, a favorite haunt of fishermen because of its plentiful population of black bass, trout, and salmon. The park is dominated by the towering 3,187-ft (971-m) Mount Blue.

🏔 Bald Mountain
Tel (207) 864-7311.

🏔 Saddleback Mountain
Tel (207) 864-5671. **Open** 9am–4pm Mon–Fri; daily during the ski season.

🌲 Rangeley Lake State Park
South Shore Dr., Rangeley. **Tel** (207) 864-3858. **Open** mid-May–Oct: 9am–dusk. 🅿

🌲 Mount Blue State Park
West Rd., Weld. **Tel** (207) 585-2347. **Open** daylight hours. Camping: **Tel** (207) 624-9950. 🅿 🄲 ♿

Snowboarding on Sugarloaf, Maine's second-highest mountain at 4,237 ft (1,290 m)

The dramatic 1,800-ft- (550-m-) high cliffs of Mount Kineo on Moosehead Lake

㉑ Moosehead Lake

🅘 Rte. 15, Greenville (207) 695-2702 or (888) 876-2778.
🆆 mooseheadlake.org

Forty miles (64 km) long and blessed with 320 miles (515 km) of mountain-rimmed shoreline, Moosehead Lake is one the largest bodies of fresh water within any state in the Northeast. A popular destination for hunters, fishermen, hikers, and canoeists since the 1880s, the region is attracting a whole new breed of outdoor enthusiasts: mountain bikers, skiers, and snowmobilers.

Greenville, the region's largest town, is the starting point for excursions into the deep boreal forests known as the Great North Woods, including seaplane services that fly visitors to remote fishing camps in the most extensive wilderness region of New England. Greenville is also the chief base for moose-watching expeditions, which can take the form of aerial reconnaissance, exploration of boggy sites via timber roads, or trips aboard canoes or inflatable boats to observe moose as they feed in shallow waters.

The **Moosehead Marine Museum** tells of the history of the steamboat in Greenville, beginning in 1836, when the town was a logging center. One of the museum's prized possessions is the *Katahdin*, a restored 1914 steamboat and the last of a fleet of 50 such boats that plied the lake during the peak lumbering years. The *Katahdin* offers lake cruises and

excursions to Mount Kineo, the sheer cliff face of which is the most prominent landmark on the lake. Local Native Americans considered the mountain sacred. The tiny settlement of Rockwood, the closest town to Mount Kineo, provides views of the mountain from rustic lakeside lodgings.

🏛 **Moosehead Marine Museum**

12 Lily Bay Rd., Greenville. **Tel** (207) 695-2716. Museum: **Open** late Jun–mid-Oct: 10am–4pm Mon–Sat. 🅿 Cruises: **Open** Tue–Sat: call for times. 🅰 🆆 katahdincruises.com

㉒ Baxter State Park

🅘 64 Balsam Dr, Millinocket (207) 723-9905. Office: **Open** 8am–4pm Mon–Fri; late May–mid-Oct: 8am–4pm daily. Park: **Open** mid-May–mid-Oct & Dec–Mar. 🅿 🆆 baxter stateparkauthority.com

This park was named for Governor Percival Proctor Baxter (1876–1969). Baxter was instrumental in the effort to preserve this magnificent land, purchasing more than 300 sq miles (800 sq km) and donating it to the state over 30-odd years with the stipulation that it was never to be developed. The park encompasses 46 mountain peaks, 18 of them over 3,000 ft (900 m), including Katahdin, Maine's tallest.

The park's 200 miles (320 km) of hiking trails

are unsurpassed, and range from demanding climbs to easy family walks. Henry David Thoreau *(see p34)* tried the trek in 1846, but never made it to the 5,267-ft (1,605-m) summit of Katahdin. However, hundreds of hikers are successful each year, and the trails can be crowded in summer and fall. Some hardy souls can be seen completing the last steps of the famous Appalachian Trail *(see pp26–7)*, which runs from Springer Mountain, Georgia, to its terminus atop Katahdin.

Deer, bear, raccoons, and other wildlife are abundant in this park, and ponds such as Grassy, Sandy Stream, and Russell are favorite watering spots for Maine's official state animal: the moose.

Majestic Mount Katahdin, a popular hiking destination

◀ Lake Millinocket in Baxter State Park, Maine

Autumn colors in Aroostook State Park

㉓ Aroostook County

ℹ 11 W. Presque Isle Rd., Caribou (888) 216-2463.
🅦 visitaroostook.com

Maine's largest and most northern county, Aroostook covers an area greater than the combined size of Connecticut and Rhode Island. The region is best known for agriculture, with some 1,550 sq miles (4,050 sq km) producing nearly 2 billion lb (907 million kg) of potatoes each year, plus lush crops of clover, oats, barley, and broccoli. In summer endless acres of potato fields are covered with blossoms, a vision in pink and white. Another 6,250 sq miles (16,200 sq km) of land is forested, mostly owned by paper companies that process the trees in 50 local pulp and paper mills.

Finely crafted tools of the trade for fly-fishermen

In summer, hikers trek the trails in **Aroostook State Park**, fly-fishermen plumb the streams for salmon and trout, and canoeists and kayakers paddle the Allagash River. When the heavy winter snows come, snowmobilers arrive in large numbers to explore the entire 3,500 miles (5,600 km) of the Interstate Trail System.

Aroostook County begins in the south in Houlton, a quiet town with a Market Square Historic District of 28 19th-century buildings. A French dialect can be heard in the northern St. John Valley, the legacy of Acadians who settled here in 1785. The **Acadian Village** consists of 16 original and reconstructed buildings from the early days. In New Sweden, a cluster of historic buildings, including a log house and a one-room school, recalls a Swedish colony that settled not far from Caribou in the late 19th century.

🏕 Aroostook State Park
87 State Park Rd., S of Presque Isle. **Tel** (207) 768-8341. **Open** year-round: for camping; mid-May–mid-Oct: daylight hours; accessible for cross-country skiing and snowmobiling in winter. 🚻 🅒 🅖

🏛 Acadian Village
Rte. 1, Van Buren. **Tel** (207) 868-5042. **Open** mid-Jun–mid-Sep: noon–5pm daily. 🚻

Environs
Starting at Lake Chamberlain and extending north for more than 90 miles (145 km), the **Allagash Wilderness Waterway** is one of New England's most stunning natural areas. The waterway and its many lakes and streams have been protected since 1966. The Allagash has also been

designated a National Wild and Scenic Rivers System.

The state owns the land flanking the waterway for 500 ft (150 m) on each side, assuring a protected habitat for dozens of animals and more than 120 bird species. Anglers will find numerous brook and lake trout, whitefish, and cusk.

A trek up or down the Allagash system is the ultimate canoe trip in the state, and one that generally takes between 5 and 10 days. Especially beautiful spots are Allagash Lake, a tranquil side trip where no motors are allowed, and Allagash Falls, a dramatic 40-ft (12-m) drop that necessitates carrying the canoe (called "portaging") for about a third of a mile (0.5 km). The canoeing season runs from late May to early October.

🏞 Allagash Wilderness Waterways
ℹ Maine Bureau of Parks and Lands. 106 Hogan Rd. Bangor (207) 941-4014 **Open** year-round 🚻

Frog in the protected habitat of the Allagash Wilderness Waterway

Maine's Great Rafting Rivers

Maine is famous for three whitewater rivers, the Kennebec, the Dead, and the west branch of the Penobscot. The first two rivers meet near the town called The Forks, southwest

Kennebec River rafters in the challenging whitewater

of Moosehead Lake, where more than a dozen rafting companies offer equipment and guided trips (see p357). The Millinocket area services paddlers bound for the Penobscot, famed among rafters for its challenging drop through a vertical walled canyon downriver from the Ripogenus Dam.

TRAVELERS'
NEEDS

WHERE TO STAY

The incredibly varied accommodations of the New England states are tailored to suit virtually all tastes and budgets. If you are looking to commune with nature and save a few dollars at the same time, you can take your pick of campsites *(see p356–7)* sprinkled liberally throughout the six states. Rustic country inns and bed and breakfasts (B&Bs) are plentiful, offering travelers quaint facilities and a more personal touch. Hotels and motels are also popular choices, conveniently located in or around busy tourist destinations and on major roads throughout the region. From the most posh hotel in Boston to a historic Vermont B&B or a rugged back-country camping experience in Maine, New England has suitable accommodations for everyone. During the summer vacation season, lodgings can sometimes be hard to come by, so it is always best to book in advance. This is also true during the busy fall-foliage season.

Foxwoods Resort Casino near Mystic, Connecticut *(see p315)*

Hotels

New England has no shortage of hotel chains. The majority of the large chains, such as Holiday Inn, Hilton, Hyatt, Marriott, and Holiday Inn, offer standard amenities that include such things as a bar, dining room, and exercise facilities. Although one hotel room is generally indistinguishable from the next, they are all impeccably clean and come equipped with a television, room service, and a private bathroom – comforts not always found in B&Bs. Luxury hotels, usually found in city centers, can be very lavish. Lush decor, fine dining, and valet services are the earmarks of such establishments. The area's large casinos and resorts are also known for their lavishness.

Most hotels will hold your reservation only until 6pm, especially during the tourist season. It is always best to notify the reservation clerk should you be arriving late.

Motels

If you are on a budget, motels offer you the best and most flexible value for your money. Often found on the outskirts of cities and towns, motels also dot the New England roads most frequented by travelers. While you will not find the same amenities as in the big hotels, motels will offer you convenience and comfort at significantly lower prices. A standard motel room is equipped with a private bathroom, color TV, and heat and air conditioning. The more modern places usually have two double or queen beds, making it easier to accommodate the whole family in a single room.

Bed and Breakfasts and Inns

American B&Bs can differ greatly from their European counterparts. Very often they are not the cozy one- or two-room guest lodgings located in the owner's personal residence like those you would come across in Europe. Increasingly, New England B&Bs are professionally operated businesses in which guests live in separate accommodations from the owner or caretaker. This style of B&B tends to be larger in size and have more rooms than its more traditional counterpart. The loss of intimacy usually comes with the added bonus of private bathrooms and added services. Of course, traditionalists can still find small, cozy B&Bs throughout New England. Regardless of size, all B&Bs offer distinctive lodgings and breakfast, which may vary in size and style from one establishment to another. Like B&Bs, inns come in all shapes and sizes, from the very rustic to the large resort-style lodging. Not only do inns serve breakfast and dinner, the larger ones can come with such "extras" as swimming pools, gardens, and taverns. Depending on their location, many are affiliated with local tennis or golf clubs.

Rose Farm Inn *(see p314)*, in a quiet country setting on Rhode Island's Block Island

◀ Interior of the dome of Quincy Market

Omni Mount Washington Hotel in Bretton Woods, New Hampshire *(see p317)*

Because some B&Bs and inns are historic homes appointed with beautiful antique furniture, they usually prohibit smoking and often do not allow children. The **New England Inns and Resorts Association**, or one of its state branches, is a good lodging resource.

Prices and Reservations

Rates and availability can fluctuate from season to season. Prices are generally highest during peak tourist periods (July–August and mid-September–late October) and in the cities, coastal areas, and other prime vacation destinations. The reverse is true with ski resorts, when winter months are the most expensive. Booking your accommodations well in advance is always the safest way to avoid complications. This is especially true if you are looking forward to staying at a B&B or inn in which rooms are limited.

Many hotels in urban areas such as Boston cater to business travelers and may offer reduced rates from Friday to Sunday. Conversely, many of the rural lodgings, popular with the weekend crowd, slash their prices substantially during the week.

Always inquire about package deals offered by motels and hotels. Discounted meals and free passes to local attractions are sometimes thrown in as added incentives for you to stay

Beautiful room at the Red Lion Inn in Stockbridge, Massachusetts *(see p314)*

with them. Some inns and B&Bs also work in conjunction with each other to promote inn-to-inn tours for cyclists and cross-country skiers, offering special rates for accommodations along the tour route. To avoid unpleasant surprises, it is always prudent to ask about any restrictions, including those on children, pets, and smoking.

How to Make Reservations

Most hotels have toll-free reservation numbers, and some offer discounts on Internet bookings. Room rates are usually quoted for two people sharing a room, including tax (and breakfast, if it is offered); all B&Bs, of course, provide a morning meal. For longer stays, it is customary to prepay one night in advance.

Sleek interiors at XV Beacon, Boston, Massachusetts *(see p313)*

Hidden Extras

You should be aware that the prices quoted for many accommodations do not include taxes, which can increase the bill significantly – even in the haven of New Hampshire, which has no sales tax, but does have lodging and restaurant taxes. Hotels in large urban areas often charge for their parking facilities, sometimes substantially. In Boston, for example, parking costs could amount to $35–$45 per day. Also be aware of added service fees which can sometimes be as high as 15 percent.

Business Travelers

As access to high-speed wireless Internet rapidly becomes a common amenity, even in modest motels and many B&Bs, the modern business traveler can stay connected to the office and the world at large. Internet access is often free at small properties but pricey at major chain hotels. Some modern urban hotels offer multi-line phones, in-room fax machines, and private voice mail.

Disabled Travelers

Although federal law requires that all businesses provide access and facilities for the disabled, the practical reality is that this is not always the case. The vast majority of large private and chain hotels are modern enough to be equipped with the necessary facilities, including visual notification of the fire alarm, incoming phone calls, and the doorbell. Many also have some suites designated specifically for the disabled. However, many of New England's older buildings and B&Bs have narrow hallways that can obstruct wheelchairs and have no ramps. As always, it is best to check in advance.

Where to Stay in Boston

The centrally located Back Bay has the greatest concentration

Bedroom at the Inn on Covered Bridge Green *(see p316)* in Arlington, Vermont

of hotels, convenient for tourists as well as for business travelers. In the gentrifying South End, an increasing number of restored Victorian town houses have been converted into B&Bs. Accommodations in the downtown Financial District near the waterfront cater to business people during the week, but often offer good value to vacationers on the weekends. Across the Charles River, Cambridge has a large number of hotels, particularly around Harvard Square and among the Kendall Square office towers. In more suburban Brookline along the Green Line Trolley routes west of the Back Bay, several guesthouses as well as more upscale B&Bs offer additional alternatives. One plus for travelers: Boston hotels now house many of the city's top restaurants, including Clio in the Eliot Hotel, and L'Espalier at the Mandarin Oriental.

Boston hotels are particularly busy in May and June for college graduations, July and August for summer vacations, and September and October for the fall-foliage season. Throughout the course of a year, many Boston hotels, including the hotels around the Boston Convention and Exhibition Center and in Cambridge's Kendall Square, cater to business travelers. This means that the rates are often lowest on weekends.

The city does have a good selection of smaller hotels and B&Bs, often offering more personal service and charm than the big convention hotels. If you are looking for a classic B&B – a room or two in the owner's home – you should contact one of the B&B booking agencies, such as the **Bed & Breakfast Agency of Boston**, or the **Bed and Breakfast Associates Bay Colony, Ltd**. A popular trend is the "boutique" hotel, a small, elegantly appointed accommodation with solicitous service. Be warned: these luxury boutiques are among the most expensive lodging options.

Hostels

Hostels have long been a way for people – especially students – to slash their traveling budget. However, unlike the more extensive European model, New England's hostel network

Boston's Seaport Hotel *(see p312)*, busy during the summer

is somewhat underdeveloped. The good news is that some of the region's prime locations (including Boston and Cape Cod) do have hostels. A list of member hostels and their locations is available from **Hostelling International – American Youth Hostels (HI/AYH)**. **HI/AYH Eastern New England Council** provides information on hostels in New Hampshire, Maine, and Massachusetts. Located in the heart of the Theater District, the modern HI-Boston Hostel offers a variety of rooms, including some very affordable six-bed dormitories and several private rooms with en-suite bathroom. Guests enjoy free Wi-Fi and daily continental breakfast.

The stylish Hotel Pemaquid *(see p319)* in New Harbor, Maine

Luxurious room at the Taj Boston Hotel, Massachusetts *(see p310)*

Recommended Hotels

The lodging options featured in this guide have been selected across a wide price range for their excellent facilities, good location, and value. From rustic, family-owned inns and relaxing beachfront resorts to stylishly modern boutique hotels, these hotels run the gamut across all price levels and environments. For the finest in service and amenities, consider a stay in one of New England's award-winning luxury hotels. For a more intimate experience, the region contains numerous acclaimed inns and B&Bs, and some of the nation's most historic lodging options. Key urban areas host plenty of full-service business hotels ideal for the working traveler, and those who don't mind sacrificing a bit of comfort and location can find wallet-friendly motels on the edge of town.

Hotels are listed by area, and within these areas by price. For the best of the best, look out for hotels featured as "DK Choice". These establishments have been highlighted in recognition of an exceptional feature – a stunning location, notable history, inviting atmosphere. The majority of these are exceptionally popular among local residents and visitors, so be sure to inquire regarding reservations or you may be left on the outside looking in.

DIRECTORY

Bed and Breakfast and Inn Agencies

Bed & Breakfast Agency of Boston
Tel (800) 248-9262 or (617) 720-3540; (0800) 895-128 from UK.
Ⓦ boston-bnb agency.com

Bed and Breakfast Associates Bay Colony, Ltd.
PO Box 57166, Babson Park Branch, Boston, MA 02457-0166.
Tel (888) 486-6018 or (617) 720-0522.
Ⓦ bnbboston.com

New England Inns and Resorts Association
PO Box 1089, North Hampton, NH 03862-1089.
Tel (603) 964-6689.
Ⓦ newenglandinnsand resorts.com

Hostels and Budget Accommodations

Best Western International
Tel (800) 528-1234.
Ⓦ bestwestern.com

Boston International Youth Hostel
12 Hemenway St., Boston, MA 02115.
Tel (617) 536-9455.
Ⓦ bostonhostel.org

Days Inn
Tel (800) 329-7466.
Ⓦ daysinn.com

Fairfield Inn
Tel (800) 228-2800.
Ⓦ marriott.com/ fairfield-inn/travel.mi

Hostelling International
8401 Colesville Rd., Suite 600, Silver Spring, MD, 20910.
Tel (301) 495-1240 (membership information).
Tel (800) 909-4776 (reservation service).
Ⓦ hiusa.org

Hostelling International Eastern New England Council
218 Holland St., Somerville, MA 02144.
Tel (617) 718-7990.
Ⓦ hinewengland.org

Cape Cod Chamber of Commerce
5 Patti Page Way, Centerville, MA 02632.
Tel (508) 362-3225.
Ⓦ capecodchamber.org

North of Boston Convention and Visitors Bureau
10 State St., Suite 309, Newburyport, MA 01950.
Tel (978) 225-1559.
Ⓦ northofboston.org

Where to Stay

Boston

Back Bay and South End

82 Chandler Bed & Breakfast **$$**
Inn/B&B   Map 4 D3
82 Chandler St., 02116
Tel *(617) 482-0408*
W 82chandler.com
These five Victorian-style rooms
with private baths and air
conditioning can be a good
deal, especially in the summer.

**Best Western
Roundhouse Suites** **$$**
Business
891 Massachusetts Ave.
Tel *(617) 989-1000*
W bestwestern.com
Limited public transportation is
the only drawback at this hotel
in a former railroad roundhouse.
Modern, spacious suites.

Chandler Inn **$$**
Boutique   Map 4 D3
26 Chandler St., 02116
Tel *(617) 482-3450*
W chandlerinn.com
This stylish 55-room hotel sits in
the South End, convenient to the
Theatre District and Back Bay.

Charlesmark **$$**
Boutique   Map 3 C2
655 Boylston St., 02116
Tel *(617) 247-1212*
W charlesmarkhotel.com
The small rooms here are very
chic, and the price is right for
Copley Square. Breakfast included.

Clarendon Square Inn **$$**
Inn/B&B   Map 3 C4
198 West Brookline St., 02118
Tel *(617) 536-2229*
W clarendonsquare.com
This South End brick town house
inn features large modern suites
with many amenities. Some have
marble fireplaces; one has a
private bamboo garden.

Eliot Hotel **$$**
Luxury   Map 3 A2
370 Commonwealth Ave., 02215
Tel *(617) 267-1607*
W eliothotel.com
Each suite at this boutique
hotel is an elegant apartment
created by a top Boston designer.
Conveniently located for
sightseeing and dining.

Gryphon House **$$**
Inn/B&B
9 Bay State Rd., 02215
Tel *(617) 375-9003*
W gryphonhouseboston.com

Eight huge, elegant rooms with
fireplaces in an 1895 brownstone
offer discreet luxury between
Back Bay and the Fenway.

Hotel 140 **$$**
Boutique   Map 3 C3
140 Clarendon St., 02116
Tel *(617) 585-5600*
W hotel140.com
A veritable bargain, this hotel sits
just outside Copley Square. The
room decor is very modern.

Lenox Hotel **$$**
Luxury   Map 3 B2
710 Boylston St., 02116
Tel *(617) 536-5300*
W lenoxhotel.com
A family-run Edwardian
landmark, the Lenox offers
intimate rooms and splendid
corner suites.

Midtown Hotel **$$**
Motel   Map 3 B4
220 Huntington Ave., 02115
Tel *(617) 262-1000*
W midtownhotel.com
Close to Symphony Hall, but
removed from the rest of Back
Bay, this nicely updated 1960s-
style motor inn with secure
parking and connecting rooms
is often the best deal in town.

Newbury Guest House **$$**
Inn/B&B   Map 3 B2
261 Newbury St., 02116
Tel *(617) 670-6000*
W newburyguesthouse.com
Spread across three town houses,
the 32 rooms here vary in size.
The Newbury is just a few blocks
from glam shopping.

Colonnade Hotel **$$$**
Luxury   Map 3 B3
120 Huntington Ave., 02116
Tel *(617) 424-7000*
W colonnadehotel.com
Large, comfortable rooms in
Back Bay are complemented
by the city's only outdoor
rooftop pool and a great bar.

Fairmont Copley Plaza **$$$**
Historic   Map 3 C2
138 St. James Ave., 02116
Tel *(617) 267-5300*
W fairmont.com
The New York Plaza's sister hotel
features opulent public areas and
a few exceptionally grand suites.

Hotel Commonwealth **$$$**
Luxury
500 Commonwealth Ave., 02215
Tel *(617) 933-5000*
W hotelcommonwealth.com
In the midst of Boston University,
near Fenway Park, this luxe hotel
is renowned for its great dining
and bar.

Mandarin Oriental **$$$**
Luxury   Map 3 B2
776 Boylston St., 02199
Tel *(617) 535-8888*
W mandarinoriental.com
Featuring all the bells and
whistles one would expect of
Mandarin hospitality, this hotel
is in the heart of Back Bay.

DK Choice

Taj Boston **$$$**
Luxury   Map 4 D2
15 Arlington St., 02116
Tel *(617) 536-5700*
W tajhotels.com/boston
First opened in 1927 as the
original Ritz-Carlton, this is
one of New England's most
inviting hotels. Most of the
city's major attractions are
within walking distance.
This *grande dame* epitomizes
opulence, decorum, and "old
Boston" style. The lobby bar
is legendary.

Elegant interiors at the Taj Boston hotel, Boston

Beacon Hill and the Theater District

Courtyard Boston Downtown Hotel $$
Historic   Map 3 E2
275 Tremont St., 02116
Tel *(617) 426-1400*
W marriott.com
This Theater District dowager hotel takes a star turn as a modernized spot with hints of earlier glamor.

John Jeffries House $$
Inn/B&B   Map 1 B3
14 David G. Mugar Way, 02114
Tel *(617) 367-1866*
W johnjeffrieshouse.com
Classy and historic, this Beacon Hill inn is perfect for downtown sightseeing. Many rooms have kitchenettes.

Beacon Hill Hotel $$$
Boutique   Map 1 B4
25 Charles St., 02114
Tel *(617) 723-7575*
W beaconhillhotel.com
Compact but chic rooms await at the base of Beacon Hill, in a convenient spot for sightseeing. Breakfast at the bistro is included.

Four Seasons $$$
Luxury   Map 4 E2
200 Boylston St., 02116
Tel *(617) 338-4400*
W fourseasons.com
Rock stars, royalty, and dignitaries choose this luxurious but low-key hotel for the combination of comfort, convenience, and discretion. Impeccable service.

Liberty Hotel $$$
Luxury   Map 1 B3
215 Charles St., 02114
Tel *(617) 224-4000*
W libertyhotel.com
Often booked by professional sports teams, this exciting hotel is a striking redesign of the iconic former Charles Street jail. Its bars are key spots to be seen.

Ritz-Carlton Boston Common $$$
Luxury   Map 1 C5
10 Avery St., 02111
Tel *(617) 574-7100*
W ritzcarlton.com
At the downtown edge of the Theater District, this elegant high-rise hotel has some rooms with views of Boston Common.

W Hotel $$$
Luxury   Map 1 B5
100 Stuart St., 02116
Tel *(617) 261-8700*
W starwoodhotels.com
This style-driven chain hotel is so chic it could make the cover

Entrance to Irving House B&B, Cambridge, Massachusetts

of *Vogue*. It also boasts a prime location in the Theater District.

Brighton

Days Hotel $
Budget
1234 Soldiers Field Rd., Brighton, 02135
Tel *(617) 254-1234*
W dayshotelboston.com
This five-story hotel on Charles River is a short ride from Harvard Square. Free parking offsets poor public transportation.

Brookline

Beech Tree Inn $$
Inn/B&B
83 Longwood Ave., Brookline, 02446
Tel *(617) 277-1620*
W thebeechtreeinn.com
This Victorian-style B&B features rooms with private baths and a common parlor. Close to eateries, but not too convenient for sights.

Bertram Inn $$
Inn/B&B
92 Sewall Ave., Brookline, 02446
Tel *(617) 566-2234*
W bertraminn.com
The early 20th-century home of a wealthy merchant is now an inn with spacious rooms, many with working fireplaces. Located about 20 minutes to downtown via streetcar.

Inn at Longwood Medical Center $$
Budget
342 Longwood Ave., Brookline, 02115
Tel *(617) 731-4700*
W innatlongwood.com
This low-key inn charges special rates for families of patients at Children's Hospital. There are some rooms with kitchenettes.

Cambridge

A Friendly Inn at Harvard $$
Inn/B&B
1673 Cambridge St., Cambridge, 02138
Tel *(617) 547-7851*
W afinow.com
Featuring 17 large rooms, this Queen Anne-style house is located a quick walk from Harvard Square. Guests, who are often affiliated with local colleges, tend to develop a strong sense of camaraderie in the public areas.

Harvard Square Hotel $$
Budget
110 Mt Auburn St., Cambridge, 02138
Tel *(617) 864-5200*
W harvardsquarehotel.com
In the heart of the city's cultural core, this former motor inn offers modern rooms and friendly service.

Holiday Inn Express $$
Budget
250 Monsignor O'Brien Hwy., Cambridge, 02141
Tel *(617) 577-7600*
W hiecambridge.com
Rooms at this Holiday Inn come with microwaves and fridges, as well as a hot breakfast and free parking. Lechmere MBTA stop is a 10-minute walk away.

Hyatt Regency Cambridge $$
Budget
575 Memorial Dr., Cambridge, 02139
Tel *(617) 492-1234*
W cambridge.hyatt.com
Popular with groups of academics, this riverfront hotel has stepped floors to maximize the river views. The limited access to public transit keeps the price down.

Irving House $$
Inn/B&B
24 Irving St., Cambridge, 02138
Tel *(617) 547-4600*
W irvinghouse.com
In a convenient location near Harvard Square, this old rooming house is a peaceful retreat. Rooms with shared bath are much cheaper.

Isaac Harding House $$
Inn/B&B
288 Harvard St., Cambridge, 02139
Tel *(617) 876-2888*
W harding-house.com
This 1860s Victorian home offers comfortable, spacious rooms – some with shared baths.

For more information on types of hotels *see p309*

Modern rooms at the Royal Sonesta, Cambridge, Massachusetts

The Kendall Hotel $$
Boutique
350 Main St., Cambridge, 02142
Tel *(617) 577-1300*
Ⓦ kendallhotel.com
A former historic firehouse
near MIT and the buzzing
Kendall dining scene is now
a hotel. Features include
spacious designer rooms
filled with quilts and antique-
style furnishings.

Le Meridien Cambridge $$
Boutique
20 Sidney St., Cambridge, 02139
Tel *(617) 577-0200*
Ⓦ lemeridiencambridge.com
Favored by MIT affiliates and
biotech and robotics executives,
this contemporary hotel is
situated close to the Central
Square dining scene.

Mary Prentiss Inn $$
Inn/B&B
6 Prentiss St., Cambridge, 02140
Tel *(617) 661-2929*
Ⓦ maryprentissinn.com
Some of the rooms at this
Greek Revival house sporting
traditional "historic B&B"-style
decor have fireplaces and
whirlpool tubs.

Royal Sonesta $$
Business
*5 Cambridge Pkwy., Cambridge,
02142*
Tel *(617) 806-4200*
Ⓦ sonesta.com
Filled with striking modern
art, this sleek riverfront hotel
boasts a number of top
restaurant and bars.

The Charles Hotel $$$
Luxury
1 Bennett St., Cambridge, 02138
Tel *(617) 864-1200*
Ⓦ charleshotel.com
A chic hotel with a personal
touch, The Charles also has
a jazz club, and a leading
Boston restaurant.

Hotel Marlowe $$$
Luxury
*25 Edwin H. Land Blvd.,
Cambridge, 02141*
Tel *(617) 868-8000*
Ⓦ hotelmarlowe.com
Located near the Museum of
Science and attached to a
shopping mall, this elegant hotel
hosts evening wine receptions
and loans bicycles and kayaks to
guests. It is noted for being
particularly pet-friendly.

Hotel Veritas $$$
Boutique
*1 Remington St., Cambridge,
02138*
Tel *(617) 520-5000*
Ⓦ thehotelveritas.com
This stylish establishment near
the Harvard campus provides
intimate but chic rooms, plus
a hip cocktail lounge.

Charlestown

Constitution Inn $$
Budget   Map 2 D1
*150 3rd Ave., Charlestown Navy Yard,
Charlestown, 02129*
Tel *(617) 241-8400*
Ⓦ constitutioninn.org
Built to give military families
modestly priced accommodations,
this hotel welcomes all. A pool,
sauna, and kitchenettes are
among the amenities.

North End and the
Waterfront

Harborside Inn $$
Boutique   Map 2 D3
185 State St., 02109
Tel *(888) 723-7565*
Ⓦ harborsideinnboston.com
Stylish, contemporary rooms
occupy a handsome spice
warehouse dating back to 1858.
There are windowless quarters
for light sleepers, plus free HBO
and a movie library. Prices swing
wildly based on demand.

Seaport Hotel $$
Business   Map 2 F5
1 Seaport Lane, 02210
Tel *(617) 385-4000*
Ⓦ seaportboston.com
Comfortable rooms offer large
workspaces and flatscreen TVs.
The hotel is adjacent to the
South Boston waterfront
dining and nightlife scene.

Boston Harbor Hotel $$$
Luxury   Map 2 E4
70 Rowes Wharf, 02110
Tel *(617) 439-7000*
Ⓦ bhh.com
Renowned for its winter wine
festival and summer entertainment series, this hotel also
has plush rooms, plus such
amenities as an on-site spa.

Old Boston and the
Financial District

Millennium Bostonian $$
Luxury   Map 2 D3
26 North St., 02109
Tel *(617) 523-3600*
Ⓦ millenniumhotels.com
Rooms in this elegant oasis, close
to Faneuil Hall Marketplace, run
the gamut from tiny to palatial.

Nine Zero $$
Boutique   Map 1 C4
90 Tremont St., 02108
Tel *(617) 772-5800*
Ⓦ ninezerohotel.com
This contemporary luxury hotel
offers in-room spa services and
a hosted evening wine hour.

Omni Parker House $$
Historic   Map 2 D4
60 School St., 02108
Tel *(617) 227-8600*
Ⓦ omniparkerhouse.com
America's oldest hotel still
in operation, this opulent
downtown landmark has
elegant rooms and suites.

The Langham Boston $$$
Luxury   Map 2 D4
250 Franklin St., 02110
Tel *(617) 451-1900*
Ⓦ langhamhotels.com
Classic British elegance and style
are the hallmarks of this luxurious
hotel in a landmark building
overlooking Post Office Square.

Ames Hotel $$$
Boutique   Map 2 D3
1 Court St., 02108
Tel *(617) 979-8100*
Ⓦ ameshotel.com
Housed in a historic downtown
skyscraper, the posh Ames Hotel
is located just steps from the core
of the Freedom Trail.

XV Beacon $$$
Luxury   Map 1 C4
15 Beacon St., 02108
Tel *(617) 670-1500*
w xvbeacon.com
This chic boutique hotel has design-conscious decor. All rooms feature high-tech extras.

Somerville

La Quinta Inn and Suites $$
Budget
23 Cummings St., Somerville, 02145
Tel *(617) 625-5300*
w lq.com
In addition to spacious rooms, this hotel has a complimentary shuttle service and breakfast.

Massachusetts

AMHERST: Allen House Inn $$
Inn/B&B
599 Main St., 01002
Tel *(413) 253-5000*
w allenhouse.com
This Victorian B&B celebrates the English and American Arts & Crafts movement.

CHARLEMONT: Warfield House Inn $$
Inn/B&B
200 Warfield Rd., 01339
Tel *(413) 339-6600*
w warfieldhouseinn.com
Each room at this mountaintop inn with sweeping views features a hot tub and a fireplace.

CHATHAM: Chatham Wayside Inn $$$
Historic
512 Main St., 02633
Tel *(508) 945-5550*
w waysideinn.com
A modern wing has been added to this original stagecoach inn. Some room offer whirlpool tubs and private patios.

Exterior of the XV Beacon, Boston, Massachusetts

DK Choice

CONCORD: Colonial Inn $$
Historic
48 Monument Sq., 01742
Tel *(978) 369-9200*
w concordscolonialinn.com
Located in the center of historic Concord, this inn has a section with 15 rooms dating from the 18th century. The rest of the lodgings are decorated in modern Colonial Revival style. Old North Bridge and other sites of the American Revolution are a short walk away.

CONCORD: North Bridge Inn $$
Historic
21 Monument St., 01742
Tel *(978) 371-0014*
w northbridgeinn.com
This renovated 1885 home has six suites, each named for a local 19th-century author.

EDGARTOWN: Winnetu Oceanside Resort $$$
Luxury
31 Dunes Rd., 02539
Tel *(508) 310-1733*
w winnetu.com
Bright rooms, suites, and cottages offer luxurious stays where few whims cannot be satisfied. There are also plenty of kid-friendly activities on offer.

FALMOUTH: Palmer House Inn $$
Inn/B&B
81 Palmer Ave., 02540
Tel *(508) 548-1230*
w palmerhouseinn.com
Antique furnishings, canopy beds, and lace provide pleasant historic touches at this Queen Anne-style inn and adjacent guesthouse.

GREAT BARRINGTON: Monument Mountain Motel $
Motel
247 Stockbridge Rd., 02130
Tel *(413) 528-3272*
w monumentmountainmotel.com
This updated vintage budget motel is located near a range of outdoor activities and events. Some rooms can connect, making them ideal for families, and there is an outdoor pool.

IPSWICH: Inn at Castle Hill $$
Inn/B&B
280 Argilla Rd., 01938
Tel *(978) 412-2555*
w theinnatcastlehill.com
Located within a preserve noted for its birdlife, this is a tranquil inn. A nearby beach features sand dunes and hiking trails.

NANTUCKET: Century House $$
Luxury
10 Cliff Rd., 02554
Tel *(508) 228-0530*
w centuryhouse.com
The island's oldest family-run inn is a short walk from the town center. Modern amenities complement a graceful 19th-century ambience.

NEW MARLBOROUGH: Old Inn on the Green $$
Historic
134 New Marlborough Branch Rd., 01230
Tel *(413) 229-7924*
w oldinn.com
Dating back to 1760, this historic inn is located on the village green. Spacious rooms feature antiques, quilts, and folk art.

NORTH ADAMS: Porches Inn $$
Inn/B&B
231 River St., 01247
Tel *(413) 664-0400*
w porches.com
Early 20th-century millworkers' buildings form this gracious inn near the Massachusetts Museum of Contemporary Art.

PLYMOUTH: John Carver Inn $$
Inn/B&B
25 Summer St., 02360
Tel *(508) 746-7100*
w ohncarverinn.com
This Colonial-Revival-style inn has a Pilgrim-themed indoor pool featuring an 80-ft (24-m) water slide.

PROVINCETOWN: Seaglass Inn & Spa $$
Luxury
105 Bradford St. Ext., 02657
Tel *(508) 487-1286*
w seaglassinnandspa.com
Notably family-friendly, this quiet, private accommodations has luxuriant gardens, a large heated pool, and several decks.

SALEM: Hawthorne Hotel $$
Inn/B&B
18 Washington Square West, 01970
Tel *(978) 744-4080*
w hawthornehotel.com
Book well in advance during fall foliage and Halloween: this Federal-style hotel is famous for its Halloween costume ball.

SANDWICH: Sandy Neck Motel $
Motel
669 Route 6A, 02537
Tel *(508) 362-3992*
w sandyneck.com
Near the dunes and marshes of Sandy Neck Beach, this motel on manicured grounds has some units with kitchenettes. All rooms share lawn BBQ stations.

For more information on types of hotels *see p309*

SOUTH WELLFLEET:
Wellfleet Motel & Lodge $$
Motel
170 Route 6, 02663
Tel *(508) 349-3535*
W wellfleetmotel.com
At the edge of the Cape Cod
Rail Trail and convenient for
reaching National Seashore,
this complex offers many
different room configurations.

SPRINGFIELD: La Quinta Inn
& Suites Springfield $
Budget
100 Congress St., 01104
Tel *(413) 781-0900*
W lq.com
A pocket-friendly option near
some major attractions, La
Quinta provides microwaves
and fridges in every room, plus
a continental breakfast.

DK Choice
STOCKBRIDGE:
Red Lion Inn $$$
Luxury
30 Main St., 01262
Tel *(413) 298-5545*
W redlioninn.com
This historic stagecoach inn
with an iconic rocker-filled
porch forms part of a complex
of town-center buildings. Some
rooms are on the small side,
but the suites are huge and
represent real country luxury.

STURBRIDGE: Comfort Inn $$
Budget
215 Charlton Rd., 01566
Tel *(508) 347-3306*
W sturbridgecomfortinn.com
Featuring both indoor and
outdoor pools, this modern
establishment also has well-
maintained grounds.

WEST DENNIS: GuestLodge $
Budget
221 Main St., 02670
Tel *(508) 394-8472*
W guestlodge.net
A two-story motor inn with
many room options and a nice
pool, the GuestLodge sits
between Hyannis and Chatham,
on Route 28.

WILLIAMSTOWN:
The Williams Inn $$
Inn/B&B
1090 Main St., 01267
Tel *(413) 458-9371*
W williamsinn.com
A genteel option for the
Williamstown Theatre Festival
and Clark Museum, this decorous
three-story inn is located on the
Williams College campus.

Rhode Island

BLOCK ISLAND: 1661 Inn
and Hotel Manisses $$
Inn/B&B
5 Spring St., 02807
Tel *(401) 466-2421*
W blockislandresorts.com
The 21-room inn is open year-
round, while the Victorian-style
hotel closes mid-Oct to Mar. Some
rooms lack TVs and share baths.

BLOCK ISLAND: Rose Farm Inn $$
Inn/B&B
1005 High St., 02807
Tel *(401) 466-2034*
W rosefarminn.com
This hotel is located in a romantic
setting with plenty of wildlife. No
air conditioning or TVs. Open
mid-Apr to mid-Oct.

BRISTOL: Bristol Harbor Inn $$
Inn/B&B
259 Thames St., 02809
Tel *(401) 254-1444*
W bristolharborinn.com
A former distillery and warehouse
in this cute East Bay village
has been turned into a well-
appointed boutique hotel.
Rooms are furnished in a style
that recalls the area's 19th-
century trading heyday.

CHARLESTOWN: General
Stanton Inn $
Historic
4115 Old Post Rd., 02813
Tel *(401) 364-8888*
W generalstantoninn.com
Parts of this historic inn with low
ceilings and open fireplaces date
from the early 18th century.
Guest rooms are more modern,
with air conditioning and TVs.

MIDDLETOWN: Newport Beach
Hotel and Suites $$
Luxury
1 Wave Ave., 02840
Tel *(401) 846-0310*
W newportbeachhoteland
suites.com

In an excellent location, this
hotel has well-appointed rooms
and great facilities.

NEWPORT: Castle Hill Inn
and Resort $$$
Luxury
590 Ocean Dr., 02840
Tel *(401) 849-3800*
W castlehillinn.com
Epitomizing the luxurious leisure
of America's yachting class, this
mansion on a headland has
rolling lawns, beachfront
cottages, and a great restaurant.

NEWPORT: The Chanler at
Cliff Walk $$$
Luxury
117 Memorial Blvd., 02840
Tel *(401) 847-1300*
W thechanler.com
A boutique hotel in a sprawling
mansion with an amazing porch,
The Chanler offers excellent
ocean views and individually
appointed rooms.

NEWPORT: Hyatt Regency
Newport $$$
Luxury
1 Goat Island, 02840
Tel *(401) 851-1234*
W newport.hyatt.com
Rooms here feature deluxe
amenities and water views.
Guests enjoy outdoor activities
on the broad lawns and gardens.

NEWPORT: Vanderbilt
Grace Hotel $$$
Luxury
41 Mary St., 02840
Tel *(401) 846-6200*
W vanderbiltgrace.com
Formerly the famous Vanderbilt
Hall mansion, this hotel features
indoor and outdoor pools and a
charming terrace garden.

NORTH KINGSTOWN:
Hamilton Village Inn $
Inn/B&B
642 Boston Neck Rd., 02852
Tel *(401) 295-0700*
W hamiltonvillageinn.com

Rich interiors at the Red Lion Inn, Stockbridge, Massachusetts

This year-round inn with simple rooms is good for exploring the Narragansett and Rhode Island's South County area. In summer, Newport is an hour away via two bridges.

DK Choice

PROVIDENCE: Hotel Providence $
Luxury
311 Westminster St., 02903
Tel *(401) 861-8000*
W hotelprovidence.com
This leading boutique hotel blends modern design with classic formality. Combining European flair and New England charm, it boasts a handy location in the heart of the city's thriving arts and theater district.

WESTERLY: Sand Dollar Inn $
Budget
171 Post Rd., 02891
Tel *(401) 322-2000*
W sandmotel.info
Situated 6 miles (10 km) from Watch Hill beach, this no-frills inn is the least expensive option in the area.

WOONSOCKET: Pillsbury House B&B $
Inn/B&B
341 Prospect St., 02895
Tel *(401) 766-7983*
W pillsburyhouse.com
This 1875 home full of Victorian style is an excellent base for exploring the Blackstone Valley.

Connecticut

BRIDGEPORT: Holiday Inn $
Business
1070 Main St., 06604
Tel *(203) 334-1234*
W holidayinn.com
Cheerful staff make this budget chain with a convenient location and inexpensive parking the best choice in Bridgeport.

COVENTRY: Daniel Rust House $$
Historic
2011 Main St., 06238
Tel *(860) 742-0032*
W thedanielrusthouse.com
An inn since 1800, this country hotel has four guest rooms. The atmospheric dining room and tavern have a cozy fireplace.

ESSEX: The Griswold Inn $
Historic
36 Main St., 06426
Tel *(860) 767-1776*
W griswoldinn.com

Antique furnishing and original Currier & Ives lithographs make this charming inn from 1776 feel historic but not stuffy.

GREENWICH: The Cos Cob Inn $$
Inn/B&B
50 River Rd., 06830
Tel *(203) 661-5845*
W coscobinn.com
This Federal-style inn is filled with reproductions of American Impressionist paintings.

GREENWICH: The Delamar $$$
Luxury
500 Steamboat Rd., 06830
Tel *(203) 661-9800*
W delamargreenwich.com
Old-world charm combines with bespoke services and modern technology at this elegant hotel.

GROTON: Best Western Olympic Inn $
Budget
360 Route 12, 06340
Tel *(860) 445-8000*
W bestwestern.com
Large, modern rooms and free parking facilities make this motel a good base for sightseeing in nearby Mystic or for visiting the Indian casinos.

KENT: Fife 'N Drum $$
Inn/B&B
53 North Main St., 06757
Tel *(860) 927-3509*
W fifendrum.com
A historic inn and adjacent house are just a short stroll from upscale boutiques and galleries.

LEDYARD: Stonecroft Country Inn $$
Inn/B&B
515 Pumpkin Hill Rd., 06339
Tel *(860) 572-0771*
W stonecroft.com
A former sea captain's home from 1807, this elegant country retreat sits between Foxwoods and Mystic Seaport. Many rooms have fireplaces. Full breakfast is included.

MADISON: Madison Beach Hotel $$$
Luxury
93 West Wharf Rd., 06443
Tel *(203) 245-1404*
W madisonbeachhotel.com
All rooms at this contemporary resort in a beachfront Victorian building have balconies and direct access to a sandy beach.

MASHANTUCKET: Foxwoods Resort Casino $$
Luxury
350 Trolley Line Blvd., 06338
Tel *(860) 312-3000*
W foxwoods.com

The atmospheric Daniel Rust House, Coventry, Connecticut

One of the world's largest casino resorts, Foxwoods offers six casinos, more than 25 restaurants, five hotels, and endless shopping opportunities.

MONTVILLE: Mohegan Sun $$
Luxury
1 Mohegan Sun Blvd., 06382
Tel *(888) 226-7711*
W mohegansun.com
This is an all-purpose entertainment destination with casinos, famous performers, gourmet dining, shopping, and many amenities. Every room in the 1,200-room hotel is at least 450 sq ft (42 sq m).

MYSTIC: Hyatt Place $$
Business
224 Greenmanville Ave., 06355
Tel *(860) 536-9997*
W mystic.place.hyatt.com
Close to Mystic Seaport, this Hyatt is aimed at vacationers rather than business execs. Big rooms have large TVs and Wi-Fi. Hot breakfast is included.

MYSTIC: Whaler's Inn $$
Inn/B&B
20 East Main St., 06355
Tel *(860) 536-1506*
W whalersinnmystic.com
Spread across five buildings, this friendly inn is close to the shops. It requires a minimum two-night stay on weekends and holidays, except in winter.

NEW HAVEN: Omni New Haven $$
Luxury
155 Temple St., 06510
Tel *(203) 772-6664*
W omnihotels.com
This large hotel near Yale University, museums, and other attractions has elegant interiors. It charges for Wi-Fi unless you belong to its loyalty program.

For more information on types of hotels *see p309*

DK Choice

NEW HAVEN: Study at Yale $$
Luxury
1157 Chapel St., 06511
Tel *(203) 503-3900*
W studyhotels.com
This sleek hotel across from Yale School of Art has rooms with large flatscreen TVs, leather reading chairs, seersucker robes, and iPod docking stations. A farm-to-table restaurant completes the picture.

NORWALK: EVEN Hotel $
Budget
426 Main Ave., 06851
Tel *(203) 849-9355*
W ihg.com
Close to the restaurants in South Norwalk, this hotel has lots of fitness options, hypoallergenic fabrics and healthy breakfasts.

OLD LYME: Bee & Thistle Inn $$
Inn/B&B
100 Lyme St., 06371
Tel *(860) 434-1667*
W beeandthistleinn.com
This charming inn features carved staircases, canopy and four-poster beds, and Oriental carpets.

OLD SAYBROOK: Saybrook Point Inn $$$
Luxury
2 Bridge St., 06475
Tel *(860) 395-2000*
W saybrook.com
This intimate spa hotel offers private balconies, whirlpool tubs, and working fireplaces.

SIMSBURY: Iron Horse Inn $
Budget
969 Hopmeadow St., 06070
Tel *(860) 658-2216*
W ironhorseinnofsimsbury.com
Simple, functional rooms have fridges and microwaves. There's no elevator, so the property is not suitable for wheelchair users.

SOUTHPORT: The Delamar $$
Boutique
275 Old Post Rd., 06890
Tel *(203) 259-2800*
W delamarsouthport.com
This upscale luxury hotel features custom furnishings, marble floors, and museum-quality art.

STONINGTON: The Inn at Stonington $$
Inn/B&B
60 Water St., 06378
Tel *(860) 535-2000*
W theinnatstonington.com
This clapboard-style inn overlooks Fisher Sound; most rooms have a fireplace and luxury bath.

WOODBURY: Curtis House Inn $
Historic
506 Main St., 06798
Tel *(203) 263-2101*
W curtishouseinn.com
Connecticut's oldest inn (1735) has an old-time, quirky style and very low prices. Breakfast included.

WOODSTOCK: Inn at Woodstock Hill $$
Inn/B&B
94 Plaine Hill Rd., 06281
Tel *(860) 928-0528*
W woodstockhill.com
In summer, this classic, rambling 19th-century country inn is often booked for weddings.

Vermont

ARLINGTON: Inn on Covered Bridge Green $$
Historic
3587 River Rd., 05250
Tel *(802) 375-9489*
W coveredbridgegreen.com
Fully equipped cottages and rooms are available at this 1792 farmhouse, the former home of illustrator Norman Rockwell.

BRATTLEBORO: Latchis Hotel $
Business
50 Main St., 05301
Tel *(802) 254-6300*
W latchis.com
This Art Deco hotel has a movie theater and modest rooms with refrigerators and coffee-makers.

BURLINGTON: Hotel Vermont $$
Boutique
41 Cherry St., 05401
Tel *(802) 651-0080*
W sheratonburlington.com
Stylish and contemporary, this hotel sits in downtown Burlington, a short stroll from both Church Street Marketplace and the Lake Champlain waterfront.

Exterior of the Bee & Thistle Inn, Old Lyme, Connecticut

BURLINGTON: Willard Street Inn $$
Inn/B&B
349 South Willard St., 05401
Tel *(800) 577-8712*
W willardstreetinn.com
This charming 19th-century mansion is filled with antiques and reproduction Victorian furniture.

CHITTENDEN: Mountain Top Inn $$
Inn/B&B
195 Mountain Top Rd., 05737
Tel *(802) 483-2311*
W mountaintopinn.com
Rates cover breakfast and many sporting activities at this inn with rooms, chalets, and pet-friendly cabins.

EAST MIDDLEBURY: Waybury Inn $$
Inn/B&B
457 East Main St., 05740
Tel *(802) 388-4015*
W wayburyinn.com
Updated rooms include private baths at this hotel, said to have been Robert Frost's favorite.

ESSEX: Essex Culinary Resort & Spa $$
Luxury
70 Essex Way, 05452
Tel *(802) 878-1100*
W vtculinaryresort.com
Some rooms have fireplaces at this resort focusing on cooking classes and gourmet getaways. They even make treats for pets.

GRAFTON: The Grafton Inn $$
Historic
92 Main St., 05146
Tel *(802) 843-2231*
W graftoninnvermont.com
The old-fashioned rooms above this historic tavern offer tranquil rest without TVs. Larger and more modern rooms are available in guesthouses around the village.

KILLINGTON: The Inn at Long Trail $
Inn/B&B
709 Route 4, 05751
Tel *(800) 325-2540*
W innatlongtrail.com
This rustic lodge is legendary among the hikers and skiers of the Appalachian and Long Trails.

KILLINGTON: Mountain Meadows Lodge $$
Inn/B&B
285 Thundering Brook Rd., 05751
Tel *(802) 775-1010*
W mountainmeadowslodge.com
On a glacial lake within the Appalachian Trail, this is the ideal base for outdoor enthusiasts.

Woodstocker Inn, Woodstock, Vermont

MANCHESTER: The Equinox Resort $$
Historic
3567 Main St., 05254
Tel *(802) 362-4700*
W equinoxresort.com
Stunning public spaces and large rooms at this 18th-century resort make all stays feel special. Activities range from fly-fishing to golf.

MIDDLEBURY: Swift House Inn $$
Inn/B&B
25 Stewart Lane, 05753
Tel *(802) 388-9925*
W swifthouseinn.com
Rooms at Swift House are spread among a Federal-era main inn, a modernized carriage house, and a gatehouse on a hill.

MONTPELIER: The Inn at Montpelier $$
Inn/B&B
147 Main St., 05602
Tel *(802) 223-2727*
W innatmontpelier.com
In two Federal-era homes, this stately inn has a large veranda and wood-burning fireplaces.

NORTH HERO: North Hero House Inn $$
Inn/B&B
3643 Route 2, 05474
Tel *(802) 372-4732*
W northherohouse.com
Rooms are spread over four historic buildings at this inn on a Lake Champlain island. Open May–Nov.

SHELBURNE: Inn at Shelburne Farms $$
Inn/B&B
1611 Harbor Rd., 05482
Tel *(802) 985-8498*
W shelburnefarms.org/staydine
Stay in a 19th-century mansion on a farm that features highly in the local food movement and makes its own acclaimed cheese.

STOWE: Alpenrose Motel $$
Inn/B&B
2619 Mountain Rd., 05672
Tel *(802) 253-7277*
W gostowe.com/saa/alpenrose
Modest rooms cater mainly to winter-sports enthusiasts. Some units are pet-friendly.

STOWE: Stowe Mountain Lodge $$$
Luxury
7412 Mountain Rd., 05672
Tel *(802) 253-3560*
W stowemountainlodge.com
An all-seasons resort, this is a good base for nature lovers. Custom-designed rooms feature warm tones and comfy furnishings.

DK Choice

STOWE: Trapp Family Lodge $$$
Inn/B&B
700 Trapp Hill Rd., 05672
Tel *(802) 253-8512*
W trappfamily.com
This is the world-famous resort of the family that inspired *The Sound of Music*. Set within massive grounds, the 96-room property features a large Austrian-style main lodge and 100 cozy guest chalets. Guests enjoy nightly live entertainment, a range of recreational activities (sleigh rides, cross-country skiing, maple sugaring), and exquisite cuisine that pairs nicely with beer from the on-site brewery.

WOODSTOCK: The Woodstocker Inn $$$
Inn/B&B
61 River St., 05091
Tel *(802) 457-3896*
W woodstockervt.com
The Woodstocker is a "green" B&B that prides itself on using organic and energy-efficient products.

New Hampshire

ALTON BAY: Bay Side Inn $$
Inn/B&B
86 Route 11D, 03810
Tel *(603) 875-5005*
W bayside-inn.com
This family-operated inn on Lake Winnipesaukee has a lakeside sundeck. Open May–Oct.

BETHLEHEM: Adair Country Inn $$$
Inn/B&B
80 Guider Lane, 03754
Tel *(603) 444-2600*
W adairinn.com
Built in 1927 as a private retreat, this genteel country hideaway features antique decor. Some rooms have fireplaces, too. Full hot breakfast is included.

DK Choice

BRETTON WOODS: Omni Mount Washington Hotel $$$
Luxury
310 Mt Washington Hotel Rd., 03585
Tel *(603) 278-1000*
W brettonwoods.com
Built in 1902 as one of the last White Mountains grand hotels, this resort offers high-quality service in a beautiful natural setting. The Neoclassical style fits its distinguished history: the international monetary system was created here in 1944. Besides many public areas and dining facilities, guests enjoy a signature spa, a thrilling year-round canopy tour, and a Donald Ross-designed golf course.

BRIDGEWATER: Inn on Newfound Lake $$
Inn/B&B
1030 Mayhew Turnpike, 03222
Tel *(603) 744-9111*
W newfoundlake.com
The welcoming restaurant and lively lounge at this classic country stagecoach inn dating from 1840 attract patrons from miles away.

CONCORD: The Centennial Inn $$
Inn/B&B
96 Pleasant St., 03301
Tel *(603) 227-9000*
W thecentennialhotel.com
Sleek, contemporary rooms can be found inside this 1892 Victorian mansion. The turret suites are much-sought-after hideaways.

For more information on types of hotels *see p309*

Old-fashioned decor at the Franconia Inn, New Hampshire

EXETER: The Exeter Inn $$
Inn/B&B
90 Front St., 03833
Tel *(603) 772-5901*
W theexeterinn.com
Built in 1932 on a prep school
campus, this Georgian-style inn
exudes old-school style.

FRANCONIA:
The Franconia Inn $
Inn/B&B
1172 Easton Rd., 03580
Tel *(603) 823-5542*
W franconiainn.com
A former farmhouse, the Franconia
is a good base for sports fanatics.
The country decor adds charm.

HAMPTON: Ashworth by
the Sea $$
Inn/B&B
295 Ocean Blvd., 03842
Tel *(800) 345-6762*
W ashworthhotel.com
This 1912 beachfront hotel has
been carefully modernized over
the years. Many rooms have
balconies and ocean views.

HANOVER: Hanover Inn $$$
Historic
2 East Wheelock St., 03755
Tel *(603) 643-4300*
W hanoverinn.com
Overlooking Dartmouth Green,
the Hanover Inn epitomizes
Colonial-style sophistication.

KEENE: Carriage Barn B&B $
Inn/B&B
358 Main St., 03431
Tel *(603) 357-3812*
W carriagebarn.com
The four rooms in this country
home near Keene State College
and downtown shopping area
are furnished with local antiques.

KEENE: Fairfield Inn & Suites
Keene Downtown $$
Historic
30 Main St., 03441
Tel *(603) 357-7070*
W thelaneinn.com
This handsome brick building
was a department store for a
century before becoming a hotel.

MANCHESTER: Econo Lodge $
Budget
75 W. Hancock St., 03102
Tel *(603) 624-0111*
W econolodge.com
Near the Merrimack River, this
pet-friendly redbrick hotel offers
basic, comfortable rooms.

MANCHESTER: Hilton Garden
Inn Manchester Downtown $$
Budget
101 S. Commercial St., 03101
Tel *(603) 669-2222*
W hilton.com
This modern hotel overlooks the
baseball stadium of Manchester's
minor league team.

NEW CASTLE: Wentworth by
the Sea $$$
Luxury
588 Wentworth Rd., 03854
Tel *(603) 422-7322*
W wentworth.com
Dating from 1874, this historic
waterfront hotel features a spa,
swimming pools, tennis courts,
restaurants, and beautiful gardens.

NORTH SUTTON: Follansbee
Inn $$
Inn/B&B
2 Keyser St., 03260
Tel *(603) 927-4221*
W follansbeeinn.com
On Kezar Lake, this historic inn
offers kayaks, canoes, bicycles,
and snowshoes. The Game Room
is a favorite winter hideaway.

WEIRS BEACH: Lake
Winnipesaukee Motel $
Motel
350 Endicott North, 02347
Tel *(603) 366-5502*
W lakewinnipesaukeemotel.com
This small motel has simple, well-
maintained rooms on a tree-lined
property with a swimming pool.
Open mid-May–mid-Oct.

WHITFIELD: Mountain View
Grand Resort & Spa $$
Historic
101 Mountain View Rd., 03598
Tel *(855) 837-2100*
W mountainviewgrand.com

With splendid mountain views
from the front porch, this is one of
the state's last few grand hotels.

WOLFEBORO: The
Wolfeboro Inn $$
Inn/B&B
90 North Main St., 03894
Tel *(603) 569-3016*
W wolfeboroinn.com
A historic lakeside inn with a
private beach, The Wolfeboro has
rooms with country-squire-style
decor and a popular tavern.

Maine

BANGOR: Fairfield Inn $$
Budget
300 Odlin Rd., 04401
Tel *(207) 990-0001*
W marriott.com
Contemporary rooms feature
bright color palettes and mini-
refrigerators. Close to the airport.

BAR HARBOR: Atlantic Eyrie
Lodge $$
Inn/B&B
6 Norman Rd., 04609
Tel *(207) 288-9786*
W atlanticeyrielodge.com
Simply furnished rooms have
ocean or mountain views, plus
cooking facilities. Open May–Oct.

BAR HARBOR: Mira Monte
Inn $$
Inn/B&B
69 Mount Desert St., 04609
Tel *(207) 288-4263*
W miramonte.com
Rooms at this family-owned
Victorian B&B are lavishly
decorated. Open May–Oct.

BELFAST: Colonial Gables
Oceanfront Village $
Inn/B&B
7 Eagle Ave., 04915
Tel *(207) 338-4000*
W colonialgables.com
Motel rooms and small cottages
(some with kitchenettes) occupy a
hillside sloping down to a beach.

BETHEL: Bethel Inn Resort $$
Luxury
21 Broad St., 04217
Tel *(207) 824-2175*
W bethelinn.com
This popular resort is renowned
for its golf course and its winter
network of Nordic ski trails.

CAMDEN: Camden Maine
Stay Inn $$
Historic
22 High St., 04843
Tel *(207) 236-9636*
W camdenmainestay.com

In an 1802 building, this hotel
has luxurious, traditional rooms
and a lovely garden.

CAPE ELIZABETH: Inn by the Sea $$$
Luxury
40 Bowery Beach Rd., 04107
Tel *(207) 799-3134*
W innbythesea.com
Accommodations range from
individual rooms to suites with
kitchens at this modern property.

CARIBOU: Caribou Inn and Convention Center $
Budget
19 Main St., 04736
Tel *(207) 498-3733*
W caribouinn.com
This pet-friendly inn is located on
Maine's snowmobile trail and is
especially popular during winter.

CARRABASSETT VALLEY: Sugarloaf Mountain Resort $$
Inn/B&B
5092 Sugarloaf Rd., 04947
Tel *(207) 237-2000*
W sugarloaf.com
This popular ski resort offers a
full-service hotel, a casual slope-
side inn, and condominium units.

FREEPORT: Harraseeket Inn $$
Inn/B&B
162 Main St., 04032
Tel *(207) 865-9377*
W harraseeketinn.com
A short walk from Freeport's
outlet shopping, this inn has two
restaurants and an indoor pool.

FRYEBURG: Oxford House Inn $$
Inn/B&B
548 Main St., 04037
Tel *(207) 935-3442*
W oxfordhouseinn.com
A 1913 Mission-style inn, Oxford
House has four elegant guest
rooms, a fine-dining restaurant,
and a more casual pub.

GREENVILLE: Kineo View Motor Lodge $
Motel
50 Overlook Dr., 04441
Tel *(207) 695-4470*
W kineoview.com
This modest lodge's rooms and
suites have water or mountain
views. Deluxe and corner rooms
have private balconies.

GREENVILLE: Greenville Inn $$
Inn/B&B
40 Norris St., 04441
Tel *(207) 695-2206/(888) 695-6000*
W greenvilleinn.com
A former Victorian lumber baron's
estate, this retreat offers a choice
of rooms, suites, and cottages.

KENNEBUNKPORT: Captain Jefferds Inn $$$
Historic
5 Pearl St., 04046
Tel *(800) 839-6844*
W captainjefferdsinn.com
Built in 1804, this sea captain's
mansion retains its antique
charm and has beautiful gardens.

KENNEBUNKPORT: The Colony Hotel $$$
Inn/B&B
140 Ocean Ave., 04046
Tel *(207) 967-3331*
W thecolonyhotel.com
Rooms in this 1914 oceanfront
resort are located in five separate
buildings and have ocean, river,
or garden views. Private beach.

DK Choice

KENNEBUNKPORT: The White Barn Grace $$$
Historic
37 Beach Ave., 04043
Tel *(207) 967-2321*
W gracehotels.com
The heart of this luxury complex
is a late 19th-century home with
well-appointed rooms. There are
also suites and garden rooms in
other buildings on the property.
A large pool and spa treatments
help to round out the
experience. The on-site
restaurant is renowned for
its local, seasonal cuisine.

MONHEGAN ISLAND: The Island Inn $$
Inn/B&B
Monhegan Harbor, 04852
Tel *(207) 596-0371*
W islandinnmonhegan.com
The bright rooms at this 1816 inn
have sweeping harbor views but
no TVs. Those with a shared bath
are the best bargains. Open late
May–early Oct.

NEW HARBOR: Hotel Pemaquid $
Historic
3098 Bristol Rd., 04554
Tel *(207) 677-2312*
W hotelpemaquid.com
Traditional rooms and suites are
spread across ten buildings at
this relaxed property, just steps
from Pemaquid Lighthouse.
Open late May–mid-Oct.

NEWCASTLE: Newcastle Inn $$
Inn/B&B
60 River Rd., 03907
Tel *(207) 563-5685*
W newcastleinn.com
Rooms and suites occupy the
main inn and a carriage house at
this elegant property, a great base
for exploring the mid-Maine coast.

OGUNQUIT: The Cliff House Resort & Spa $$
Historic
591 Shore Rd., 03907
Tel *(207) 361-1000*
W cliffhousemaine.com
All rooms at this 1872 oceanfront
resort have balconies with sea
views. Open Apr–mid-Dec.

PORTLAND: The Inn at St. John $$
Inn/B&B
939 Congress St., 04102
Tel *(800) 636-9127*
W innatstjohn.com
Built in 1897, this convenient inn
offers rooms decorated in either
Victorian or modern style.

PORTLAND: Portland Regency Hotel $$
Historic
20 Milk St., 04101
Tel *(207) 774-4200*
W theregency.com
Portland's 1895 Armory, in the
Old Port, is now a hotel with
elegant, traditional furnishings.

RANGELEY: Rangeley Inn $
Inn/B&B
2443 Main St., 04970
Tel *(207) 864-3341*
W therangeleyinn.com
This late 19th-century lakeside inn
has comfortable, simply furnished
rooms. Open Jun–Mar.

ROCKLAND: Limerock Inn $$
Inn/B&B
96 Limerock St., 04841
Tel *(207) 594-2257*
W limerockinn.com
Eight rooms occupy this Queen-
Anne-style mansion, which has a
big porch and lovely gardens.

TENANTS HARBOR: East Wind Inn $$
Inn/B&B
21 Mechanic St., 04860
Tel *(207) 372-6366*
W eastwindinn.com
This waterfront hotel gives a taste
of Maine's fishing and boating
way of life. Open mid-May–Oct.

The White Barn Grace, Kennebunkport, Maine

For more information on types of hotels *see p309*

WHERE TO EAT AND DRINK

To many outsiders, New England has long been synonymous with simple, hearty, somewhat boring fare. While it is true that a traditional meal of the past often consisted of cod or boiled beef and cabbage served with potatoes, the contemporary regional menu is substantially more varied and tempting. Local cheeses, fruits, and vegetables from rural areas complement the exquisite seafood, often caught fresh the same day, which is found up and down the coast. In addition, the New England dining experience includes a host of ethnic flavors,

thanks to a steady stream of immigrants into the large urban areas. Boston (Massachusetts), Portland (Maine), and Providence (Rhode Island) are the region's top dining destinations. Boston's restaurant scene is particularly vibrant. The city's top restaurants often serve farm-to-table menus with preparations liberally adapted from French, Italian, and Spanish kitchens. Asian influences are less common in Boston than in California, but immigrants have opened many ethnic restaurants representing Southeast Asia and Latin America.

Opening Hours

Most restaurants serve breakfast from 6am or 7am until 11am or noon. Some serve breakfast all day. The choice is varied, with some spots offering little more than a bagel and a coffee and others whipping up portions of eggs, bacon, and sausages hefty enough to keep you going almost all day. Lunch can run anytime from 11:30am until 2:30pm, and is equally varied. In downtown areas, businesspeople can be seen gulping down a sandwich at the counter of a local deli or sitting down to enjoy a sumptuous restaurant meal. In many places, the lunch menu is the same as it is for dinner, with smaller portions and significantly lower prices. Some restaurants close for a few hours between lunch and dinner, while smaller family run places may stay open throughout the afternoon, making them a good bet for eating at more unusual times.

Traditionally, New Englanders tend to serve up large dinners.

Radio Room at the Good News Café *(see p335)* in Woodbury, Connecticut

You can usually sit down between 5:30pm and 10:30pm. Some Boston restaurants, notably those in Chinatown and Kenmore Square, stay open late, supported mostly by the ravenous crowds heading home from the dance clubs and bars. As a general rule, urban areas will have a much higher percentage of dinner-only establishments, while finding a casual eating spot open after 3pm in the countryside can be challenging. State and local laws vary on the hours during which alcohol may be served, but in most parts of New England bars begin to close at midnight, with a few staying open until 1am or 2am in the urban areas. Food service, even at bars, usually finishes by 10pm or 11pm. On Sundays, alcohol sales are generally prohibited before noon, although some Boston establishments, notably in the South End, are allowed to serve cocktails with their amazing Sunday brunches. Hotels are also exempt from the alcohol prohibition and often

serve champagne cocktails with their Sunday brunches. It is not uncommon for restaurants to close on Mondays, as well as during quiet afternoon periods. As always, check in advance.

Reservations

Finer restaurants often require a reservation, though in most cases (especially weeknights) these can be made at short notice. In rural areas and small cities, reservations are only an issue during peak season – July and August on the coast and the Berkshires, September and October in the mountains, and December, January, and February in ski country.

Paying and Tipping

Waiters are generally paid fairly low wages and they earn the bulk of their income through tips. This means that all restaurants with table service expect some sort of gratuity at the end of the

Elegant dining room at Rialto, Cambridge, Massachusetts *(see p327)*

Casual outdoor seating at Local 188, Portland, Maine *(see p339)*

meal. Each state charges a different meal tax, but it is standard practice to leave 15–20 percent of the bill as the tip. If the service is particularly good or bad, adjust the tip accordingly.

Alcohol and Smoking

The legal drinking age is 21, so underage travelers should be aware that they will be denied access to most bars and will not be allowed to order wine with dinner in restaurants. Most places are strict about this and often require you to show photographic ID before you are served. Passports are generally the best form of identification, since many people are unfamiliar with driver's licenses from abroad. The legal age to purchase cigarettes is 18; identification may be required. Smoking is banned in almost all restaurants and bars throughout New England.

Dress Codes

New England is a relaxed place where people dress on the casual side when they are dining out. This is especially true along the coast, where the casual beach atmosphere carries over into restaurants. There, shorts and T-shirts are commonplace. However, some establishments do have strict dress codes. Formal evening wear is uncommon, but in some of the finest restaurants it will not appear out of place.

Children

Children are welcome in most mid-range restaurants, although restaurants in urban business

areas are often less accustomed to them. Avoid restaurants that feature a large bar and young crowds, as they are less likely to permit under-21s on the premises.

Entrance to L'Espalier in Boston, Massachusetts *(see p325)*

Disabilities

Federal and state legislation has made most restaurants in New England at least partially accessible by wheelchair and many more are accessible to people with other disabilities. Historic structures are sometimes exempted from the accessibility requirements. Entrances are generally ramped, doors may be

fitted with an automatic opener, and restrooms usually include the appropriate stalls and sinks.

Recommended Restaurants

The restaurants featured in this guide have been selected across a wide price range for their value, good food, atmosphere, and location. From authentic, no-frills seafood shacks to pricey temples of gastronomy, these restaurants run the gamut across all price levels and cuisine types. Bordering the chilly waters of the Atlantic Ocean, New England is renowned for its seafood offerings. Large cities such as Boston, Providence, and New Haven all have large Italian communities with a preponderance of acclaimed Italian and pizza eateries on offer. Many of the region's most acclaimed, restaurants serve French and New American fare. Ethnic restaurants also abound, serving tasty Chinese, Thai, and Indian fare to budget-minded diners.

Restaurants are listed by area, and within these areas by price. Since venues often host private events or close unexpectedly due to any number or issues, it's always wise to consult a restaurant's homepage or call before visiting. For the best of the best, look out for restaurants featuring the "DK Choice" symbol. These establishments have been highlighted in recognition of an exceptional feature – a celebrity chef, exquisite food, an inviting atmosphere. The majority of these are popular among local residents and visitors, so be sure to inquire regarding reservations or you may be facing a lengthy wait for a table.

New England's Maple Syrup

During the spring thaw in late March and early April, New England farmers hammer spigots into the trunks of their sugar maple trees in order to collect the trees' clear, slightly sweet sap in buckets. Traditionally sap is then poured into vats back at the "sugarhouse" and boiled for hours. When most of the excess water has been evaporated, an amber-colored syrup is left – a highly concentrated, thoroughly delicious product that is distinctly New England. The finest-quality syrup goes best on pancakes and waffles and over ice cream.

The Flavors of New England

The geography and history of New England have produced some fine and highly distinctive culinary traditions. The long coastline accounts for the region's abundance of superb seafood, while the ethnic make-up of the area has led to some gastronomic highlights. Native Americans enjoyed staples such as corn, maple syrup, and cranberries. Early settlers brought dishes from England and Ireland, including hearty stews (known as boiled dinners) and puddings that remain popular to this day. Thanks to several Italian communities, New England boasts some of the best and most authentic pizza in America, and recipes from Portuguese fishermen pepper many menus.

New England apples

Typical lobster dish served at a beachfront restaurant

Gifts from the Sea

Seafood is at the heart of New England cuisine. The cold waters along the coast yield a bounty of delicious fish such as scrod (young cod), haddock, and swordfish. Maine lobster is a coveted delicacy. Tanks of live lobsters are shipped to restaurants all around America, but nowhere are they as succulent and sweet as they are in their home state. Lobster is at its best when eaten at one of the informal outdoor lobster pounds that are found all along the shoreline. Here, diners can choose their own freshly caught specimen from a tank and then sit back and enjoy the view, while it is being steamed or boiled. Lobster is usually served with melted butter in which to dip the meat, and cups of clear steaming seafood broth.

The Mighty Clam

No food is more ubiquitous in the region than clams. They are served in so many different ways: steamed, stuffed, baked, minced in fish cakes, or in the famous New England clam chowder. Fried clams, a dish said to have been invented in Essex, Massachusetts, are found on almost every seafood menu. The large hard-shelled quahog clam – a delicacy from Rhode Island – is used to make stuffed

Corn on the cob   Baked potato   Steamed clams   Melted butter   Boiled lobster

A typical New England clambake dinner

Local Dishes and Specialties

Like most Americans, New Englanders tend to have a light lunch and their main meal in the evening. Some New England dining experiences are too good to miss. Breakfasts are hearty, perhaps because of the cold winters, and at least one should include wild blueberry pancakes or muffins, and another an omelette made with tangy Vermont cheddar. Other musts are a lunch of lobster roll (chunks of sweet lobster meat in a mayonnaise-based dressing, stuffed into a toasted bun), New England clam chowder, and one of the region's famous clambake dinners. A visit to Boston is hardly complete without sampling the superb local scrod and the rich classic cream pie, both found on menus all over the city along with Vermont's favorite ice cream, Ben & Jerry's.

Maple Syrup

Blueberry pancakes Wild blueberries are stirred into batter to make a stack of these thick pancakes.

Colorful display of pumpkins at a local farmers' market

clams known as "stuffies". There is also a distinctive Rhode Island-style chowder which is made with a clear broth, unlike the more usual chowder, which is enriched with either milk or cream.

Sweet Offerings

Sugar maples, which bring a dazzling display of color to the hillsides in fall, yield yet more riches in late winter, when the trees can be tapped and their sap boiled down to produce maple syrup. This is served on pancakes and made into sweets (candy) and sauces. New England also produces vast acres of wild blueberries, apples, and pumpkins that lend themselves to a variety of delectable desserts. Well into the 19th century, molasses from the Caribbean was used as a sweetener, and is still added to many traditional sweet dishes, such as Indian pudding, a delicious slow-baked confection of spiced cornmeal, molasses, eggs, and milk.

Freshly picked wild blueberries, from the bumper summer harvest

Dairy Delights

Vermont is home to over 1,500 dairy farms, where herds of well-fed cows produce the milk that goes into some of New England's famous dairy produce. This includes a selection of rich ice creams and the highly acclaimed Vermont cheddar cheese. Some of the best and most widely available cheeses are produced by the Cabot Creamery Cooperative, which is owned directly by a group of dairy farmers. The Vermont Cheese Council offers a map showing 39 dairies that make a variety of cheeses. Some welcome visitors.

WHAT TO DRINK

Poland Spring water This bottled water from Maine is the local favorite.

Frappé A New England-style milkshake made with ice cream and chocolate syrup.

Sakonnet Wines From Rhode Island, these are among the finest wines in the region.

Samuel Adams and Harpoon beers New England's best known brands are brewed in Boston.

Microbrewery beers Some of the best are made by Thomas Hooker in Hartford, Connecticut; Smuttynose in Portsmouth, New Hampshire; and Magic Hat in Burlington, Vermont.

Baked scrod Fillets of young cod (scrod) are rolled in breadcrumbs and baked, then served with tartare sauce.

New England clam chowder Fresh clams, either left whole or chopped, and chunks of potato fill this creamy soup.

Boston cream pie Layers of sponge cake, sandwiched with egg custard, are topped with chocolate icing.

Where to Eat and Drink

Boston

Back Bay and South End

B.Good $
American   Map 3 B2
272 Newbury St., 02116
Tel *(617) 236-0440*
Gourmet burgers, oven-finished fries, and salads make healthy fast-food meals. The leafy patio is a top choice for alfresco eats.

El Pelon Taquería $
Mexican
92 Peterborough St., 02215
Tel *(617) 262-9090*
This is a favorite grab-and-go spot for those heading to or from Fenway Park. Try the fish tacos and the *El Guapo* burrito.

Flour Bakery + Café $
American   Map 3 C5
1595 Washington St., 02118
Tel *(617) 267-4300*
Area residents and medical staff stop at this neighborhood spot for gourmet sandwiches, coffee, and freshly baked goods.

Mike's City Diner $
American   Map 3 C5
1714 Washington St., 02118
Tel *(617) 267-9393*
There's often a line outside for this breakfast- and lunch-only diner. Filling, greasy classics take up most of the menu.

Parish Café $
American   Map 3 B2
361 Boylston St., 02116
Tel *(617) 247-4777*
Creative sandwiches are designed by Boston's top chefs. In warm weather, the sidewalk patio offers terrific views of the street scene.

Trident Booksellers & Café $
American   Map 3 A3
338 Newbury St., 02115
Tel *(617) 267-8688*
The in-store café and bar serves light and casual meals ranging from breakfast eggs to lunch wraps, as well as dinner dishes such as lasagna.

Aquitaine $$
French   Map 4 D4
569 Tremont St., 02118
Tel *(617) 424-8577*
This Parisian-style bistro is popular for its snazzy wine bar and French cooking. Black truffle vinaigrette makes Aquitaine's steak-frites among Boston's best.

Audubon Circle Restaurant Bar $$
New American
838 Beacon St., 02215
Tel *(617) 421-1910*
Craft beers and imaginative New American fare make this lively bar, near both Fenway Park and Boston University, a firm favorite.

The Beehive $$
New American   Map 4 D4
551 Tremont St., 02116
Tel *(617) 423-0069*
Jazz rules at this hip restaurant/nightclub in the Boston Center for the Arts, where the cassoulet is as good as the craft cocktails.

Brasserie Jo $$
French   Map 3 B3
120 Huntington Ave., 02116
Tel *(617) 425-3240*
Hearty French classics such as steak *roquefort* and *coq au vin* pair nicely with the inviting wine list at this airy hotel-restaurant, which captures 1940s Paris.

Douzo $$
Japanese   Map 3 C3
131 Dartmouth St., 02116
Tel *(617) 859-8886*
One of the city's popular spots for sushi and intricate Japanese dishes, Douzo offers specialties such as Phoenix Rolls, Red Spider, and Spicy Tuna Crispy Rice.

Gaslight Brasserie $$
French   Map 4 E4
560 Harrison Ave., 02116
Tel *(617) 422-0224*
This stylish bistro specializes in the casual cuisine of the French provinces. Free parking is a rare added bonus.

The sophisticated and popular Clio, at the Eliot Hotel, Boston

Price Guide
Prices are based on a three-course meal per person, with a half-bottle of house wine, including tax and service.

$ under $35
$$ $35 to $60
$$$ over $60

Jae's Café $$
Asian   Map 3 B4
520 Columbus Ave., 02118
Tel *(617) 421-9405*
Light, fresh dishes drawn from Korea, Japan, China, and Southeast Asia, served in relaxed environs.

Joe's American Bar & Grill $$
American   Map 3 B2
181 Newbury St., 02116
Tel *(617) 536-4200*
Steak, pasta, burgers, and salads dominate this cheerful chain bar and grill. Kids are welcome too.

Masa $$
Southwestern   Map 4 D3
439 Tremont St., 02116
Tel *(617) 338-8884*
Masa's refined New American dishes with Southwestern accents are complemented by margaritas, colorful decor, and good wines.

Orinoco $$
Latin American   Map 3 C5
477 Shawmut Ave., 02118
Tel *(617) 369-7075*   **Closed** *Mon*
This cheerful dining room serves inviting, exotic Latin American and Venezuelan fare. The diverse cocktail list features something for every taste.

Tremont 647 $$
New American   Map 3 C4
647 Tremont St., 02118
Tel *(617) 266-4600*
The chef's barbecue has won national competitions. His menu is also filled with eclectic, New American eats. The sidewalk patio and "pajama brunch" are neighborhood favorites.

Bravo $$$
New American
465 Huntington Ave., 02116
Tel *(617) 369-3474*
The Museum of Fine Arts' dining destination focuses on light and healthy dishes like crisp salads and pastas tossed with vegetables.

Clio $$$
New American   Map 3 A2
370A Commonwealth Ave., 02215
Tel *(617) 536-7200*   **Closed** *Sun*
Local culinary titan Ken Oringer presides over the grand Eliot

Elegant interiors at the famed L'Espalier, Boston

Hotel's claim to fame. Luxurious entrées complement the richly appointed dining room.

Davio's $$$
Italian Map 4 D2
75 Arlington St., 02116
Tel *(617) 357-4810*
The menu at this Tuscan grill also features Northern Italian pastas, grilled vegetable dishes, and superb seafood.

Deuxave $$$
New American Map 3 A2
371 Commonwealth Ave., 02116
Tel *(617) 517-5915*
In chic surroundings, Deuxave serves highbrow cocktails and modern American fare made with local, seasonal ingredients.

Eastern Standard $$$
New American
468 Commonwealth Ave., 02215
Tel *(617) 375-0699*
The creative market-driven cooking here complements the extraordinary bar scene, which is acclaimed for its inventive cocktails and craft brews.

The Elephant Walk $$$
Asian-French
1415 Washington St., 02118
Tel *(617) 247-1500*
A vivid, sophisticated menu alternates between authentic Cambodian and French dishes. There is an extensive wine list.

Grill 23 & Bar $$$
Steakhouse Map 4 D2
161 Berkeley St., 02117
Tel *(617) 542-2255*
This big-ticket steakhouse harks back to the days of exclusive, Prohibition-era supper clubs. Prime-aged beef with an inventive spin is served in a sumptuously classic interior.

Island Creek Oyster Bar $$$
Seafood
500 Commonwealth Ave., 02215
Tel *(617) 532-5300*
Far more than the oyster bar it bills itself as, this large hotel-restaurant provides a plethora of creative, seasonal fare in casual surroundings.

DK Choice

L'Espalier $$$
French Map 3 B2
774 Boylston St., 02199
Tel *(617) 262-3023*
Staffed by impeccable waiters and brilliant cooks, this romantic destination restaurant serves some of New England's most acclaimed contemporary French cuisine. Chef-owner Frank McClelland's vegetarian entrées featuring produce from his own farm are every bit as sophisticated as those with meat. Inventive desserts, unrivaled cheese dishes, and a to-die-for wine list complete the gourmet scene.

SELECT Oyster Bar $$$
Seafood Map 3 B3
50 Gloucester St., 02116
Tel *(617) 239-8064*
Seafood dishes inspired by the cuisines of Greece, Portugal, Spain, and even Cuba make this elegant little spot near the Hynes Convention Center much more than a mere oyster bar. Russian caviar service is a plus.

Sonsie $$$
New American Map 3 A3
327 Newbury St., 02115
Tel *(617) 351-2500*
Local and sustainable meat and fish anchor a dynamic menu that is complemented by good wines at Sonsie.

Stephanie's on Newbury $$$
American Map 3 B2
190 Newbury St., 02116
Tel *(617) 236-0990*
This joint with a California-inspired menu is famed for lunch and dinner salads – and for having Back Bay's best sidewalk tables.

Summer Shack $$$
Seafood Map 3 A3
50 Dalton St., 02115
Tel *(617) 867-9955*
One of New England's legendary chefs delivers straightforward preparations of fresh seafood in casual, fun environs. The bar is a welcoming spot for solo diners.

Tapéo $$$
Spanish Map 3 B2
266 Newbury St., 02116
Tel *(617) 267-4799*
An authentic tapas bar, Tapéo bustles with the after-work crowd. The summer patio is filled with diners sharing sangría pitchers.

Toro $$$
Spanish Map 3 C5
1704 Washington St., 02118
Tel *(617) 536-4300*
It's a battle to secure a table at the city's most popular spot for upscale tapas and Latin fare. The menu is filled with trendy, imported items and hard-to-find-elsewhere dishes.

Beacon Hill and the Theater District

Anna's Taqueria $
Mexican Map 1 B3
242 Cambridge St., 02114
Tel *(617) 227-8822*
This cafeteria-style burrito chain is a dependable spot for no-frills Mexican bites. It is a favorite of neighborhood students and the medical community.

For more information on types of restaurants *see p321*

Fresh crabs on display at the New Jumbo Seafood Restaurant, Boston

King & I $
Thai   **Map** 1 B3
145 Charles St., 02114
Tel *(617) 227-3320*
Savory, well-priced Thai staples are served in a small, casual interior; the takeout is popular.

75 Chestnut $$
American   **Map** 1 B4
75 Chestnut St., 02108
Tel *(617) 227-2175*
A converted townhouse offers one of Beacon Hill's most welcoming dining experiences. The upscale bistro fare can be enjoyed while watching sports in the casual bar.

Figs $$
Italian   **Map** 1 B4
42 Charles St., 02114
Tel *(617) 742-3447*
Local celeb-chef Todd English delivers special thin-crust pizzas with gourmet toppings, hand-made pastas and home-made desserts at this popular spot.

Jacob Wirth $$
German-American   **Map** 1 B5
31 Stuart St., 02116
Tel *(617) 338-8586*
There is live piano music on Friday nights at this old-fashioned beer hall, which dates from 1868. A true Boston landmark.

Lala Rokh $$
Middle Eastern   **Map** 1 B4
97 Mount Vernon St., 02108
Tel *(617) 720-5511*
Authentic Persian cuisine is served in romantic surroundings. Citrus-based glazes and relishes give meats a lovely piquant flavor.

New Jumbo Seafood Restaurant $$
Chinese   **Map** 4 F3
5 Hudson St., 02111
Tel *(617) 542-2823*
A bustling Chinatown eatery that replicates the complex seafood

cuisine of China's Guandong province, New Jumbo features imported ingredients such as dried shrimp and jellyfish.

Panificio Bistro & Bakery $$
Italian   **Map** 1 B3
144 Charles St., 02114
Tel *(617) 227-4340*
This popular bakery specializes in rustic Italian breads, pastries, and well-made coffee drinks; it also serves light meals all day long in the homey dining room.

Penang $$
Asian   **Map** 1 C5
685 Washington St., 02111
Tel *(617) 451-6373*   **Closed** *Fri, Sat*
A largely Malaysian menu, Penang's fare ranges from inexpensive noodle staples and spicy curry dishes to more contemporary concoctions.

Shabu-Zen $$
Asian   **Map** 4 F2
16 Tyler St., 02111
Tel *(617) 292-8828*
One of Chinatown's busiest restaurants, Shabu-Zen is a

Entrance to the award-winning Beacon Hill Bistro, Boston

casual social joint for enjoying traditional hot-pot fare.

Artù $$$
Italian   **Map** 1 B2
89 Charles St., 02114
Tel *(617) 227-9023*   **Closed** *Mon, Wed*
Tuscan specialties including seasoned chicken and roasted vegetables are served straight from the exposed, sizzling grill directly to the table. Casual subterranean environs.

Beacon Hill Bistro $$$
French-American   **Map** 1 B4
25 Charles St., 02114
Tel *(617) 723-7575*
Enjoy a New American spin on simple French cuisine in this authentic bistro setting. The tiny bar is perfect for sampling from the well-chosen wine list.

Bristol Lounge $$$
New American   **Map** 4 D2
200 Boylston St., 02116
Tel *(617) 351-2037*
The Four Seasons' all-purpose restaurant is one of the city's best spots for afternoon tea, upscale dining with kids, or a romantic rendezvous.

No. 9 Park $$$
New American   **Map** 1 C4
9 Park St., 02108
Tel *(617) 742-9991*
Hobnob with the Beacon Hill high flyers in this bold bistro that overlooks Boston Common. Inventive gourmet fare pairs nicely with the imaginative wine list.

Scampo $$$
Italian   **Map** 1 B3
215 Charles St., 02114
Tel *(617) 536-2100*
Celebrity chef Lydia Shire wows customers with upscale Italian-accented fare in this restaurant in the trendy Liberty Hotel.

Teatro $$$
Italian   **Map** 4 E2
177 Tremont St., 02111
Tel *(617) 778-6841*   **Closed** *Mon*
A glamorous scene prevails at this flashy *trattoria*, serving Italian classics such as handmade pastas, grilled thin-crust pizzas, and fresh seafood.

Toscano Restaurant $$$
Italian   **Map** 1 B4
47 Charles St., 02114
Tel *(617) 723-4090*
Situated in the heart of scenic Charles Street, in relaxed environs, Toscano serves a straightforward menu of Italian favorites prepared with aplomb.

Key to Price Guide *see p324*

Troquet $$$
New American **Map** 1 B5
140 Boylston St., 02116
Tel *(617) 695-9463* **Closed** *Sun, Mon*
Wines get top billing at this
stylish restaurant, with suggested
plates of New American bistro
fare paired with the owner's
diverse wine selections.

Brookline

Zaftigs Delicatessen $$
American
335 Harvard St., Brookline, 02446
Tel *(617) 975-0075*
This great Jewish-style deli has a
ton of menu options, from filling
breakfast fare to towering
sandwiches and hearty soups.

Cambridge

Henrietta's Table $$
American
1 Bennett St., Cambridge, 02138
Tel *(617) 661-5005*
Serving generous portions of
classic American fare, the Charles
Hotel's inviting bistro amply
rewards hearty appetites. House-
infused liquors can be enjoyed
at the small, social bar area.

Viale $$
New American
*502 Massachusetts Ave., Cambridge,
02139*
Tel *(617) 576-1900*
Big flavors, fascinating wines
by the glass, and a casual if
boisterous atmosphere make
this Italian-influenced joint in
Central Square a delight with
foodies and barflies alike.

West Bridge $$
New American
1 Kendall Sq., Cambridge, 02141
Tel *(617) 945-0221*
This French-inspired bistro
serving New England fare is one
of Kendall Square's hot spots to
be seen. Despite a pricey menu,
service and ambience are casual.

Café ArtScience $$$
New American
650 Kendall St., Cambridge, 02142
Tel *(857) 999-2193* **Closed** *Sun*
Superb French and American
dishes, sometimes executed with
a grab bag of molecular-cuisine
tricks, deliver explosive flavors.

Catalyst $$$
New American
*300 Technology Sq., Cambridge,
02139*
Tel *(617) 576-3000*
This elegant room serves
innovative locavore dishes. Craft
beers draw the coders, while good

wines soothe the biotech execs.
The patio is a summertime plus.

Craigie on Main $$$
New American
853 Main St., 02138
Tel *(617) 497-5511* **Closed** *Mon*
French-inspired dishes are
prepared with local organic
ingredients. The menu changes
daily, based on the ingredients
available on the day. The bar-
area-only burger is legendary.

East Coast Grill $$$
American
1271 Cambridge St., Cambridge, 02139
Tel *(617) 491-6568*
This Pacific-Rim-influenced Inman
Square fish house also serves up
some of the area's best barbecue
fare. "Hell Nights" attract lovers of
exceptionally spicy fare.

EVOO $$$
New American
350 3rd St., Cambridge, 02142
Tel *(617) 661-3866*
The chef-owner packs deep
flavors into an inventive bistro
menu that changes constantly
to employ local food at its peak.
The lunch menu is a steal.

Oleana $$$
Mediterranean
*134 Hampshire St., Cambridge,
02139*
Tel *(617) 661-0505*
Award-winning chef Ana Sorton
favors Arabic-influenced corners
of the Mediterranean for her
spice-laden cuisine. Diners can
choose the casual but elegant
dining room or the serene patio.

Restaurant Dante $$$
Italian
*40 Edwin H Land Blvd., Cambridge,
02142*
Tel *(617) 497-4200*
The chef's Italian heritage shines
through in the appetizing family

Intimate seating at EVOO, Cambridge,
Massachusetts

recipes and home-made pastas
on the menu at this riverside
Cambridge hotel-restaurant. The
beautiful outdoor patio offers
scenic river views.

Rialto $$$
New American
1 Bennett St., Cambridge, 02138
Tel *(617) 661-5050*
One of New England's best-
known chefs, Jody Adams
takes a luscious approach
to Italian dining, with an
emphasis on fresh, local
ingredients. The comfortable
and soothing dining room is
ideal for special occasions.

Russell House Tavern $$$
New American
14 JFK St., Cambridge, 02138
Tel *(617) 500-3055*
Enjoy modern takes on American
classics and regional favorites at
Russell House Tavern. Diners
choose between the bustling bar
area, casual dining room, and
popular patio space.

The bar area at West Bridge in Cambridge, Massachusetts

For more information on types of restaurants *see p321*

The historic Warren Tavern, Charlestown, Massachusetts

Charlestown

Warren Tavern $
American
2 Pleasant St., Charlestown, 02129
Tel *(617) 241-8142*
This is one of the most historic pubs in America, dating back to 1780. Choose from a lenghty beer list and varied menu of familiar comfort fare.

North End and the Waterfront

James Hook & Co. $
Seafood **Map** 2 E5
15 Northern Ave., 02110
Tel *(617) 423-5501*
Enjoy the freshly cooked lobster, clams, crab, and fish to-go at this seafood market located right on Fort Point Channel.

Pizzeria Regina $
Italian **Map** 2 D2
11 1/2 Thatcher St., 02113
Tel *(617) 227-0765*
The city's best-known pizza spot hasn't changed much over the decades. Expect affordable wine and amazing brick-oven pies.

Barking Crab $$
Seafood **Map** 2 E5
88 Sleeper St., 02210
Tel *(617) 426-2722*
This colorful fish shack is most congenial in the summer, when diners can sit outdoors at picnic tables.

Daily Catch $$
Italian **Map** 2 D3
323 Hanover St., 02113
Tel *(617) 523-8567*
Many items are served in a sizzling pan at this closet-sized eatery catering to fans of classic Italian seafood dishes, heavy on the garlic.

No Name Restaurant $$
Seafood
15 Fish Pier St. W., 02210
Tel *(617) 423-2705*
Fish Pier's only restaurant serves fresh seafood, fried or broiled, in bare-bones environs. Popular with families and tour groups.

Bricco $$$
Italian **Map** 2 D3
241 Hanover St., 02113
Tel *(617) 248-6800*
Lively and stylish, Bricco is popular for socializing over Abruzzo-style pastas or rabbit casserole.

Legal Harborside $$$
Seafood
1 Seafood Way, 02210
Tel *(617) 530-9000*
Legal is legendary for impeccably fresh fish, an excellent raw bar, and its signature clam chowder. There are separate levels for bar, casual, and fine dining.

DK Choice

Maurizio's $$$
Italian **Map** 2 E2
364 Hanover St., 02113
Tel *(617) 367-1123*
Chef-owner Maurizio Loddo works his magic in a tiny open kitchen, using just-off-the-boat New England fish for bold cooking from his native Sardinia. Seating is on two levels, but the best tables are those where you can watch him prepare his signature fish, pasta, and lamb dishes. The carefully chosen wines, mostly from Sardinia and the rest of Italy, are good-value.

Meritage $$$
New American **Map** 2 E4
70 Rowes Wharf, 02110
Tel *(617) 439-3995* **Closed** *Sun, Mon*
Wine lovers truly appreciate this hotel-restaurant known for its varied menu. All items feature suggested wine pairings.

Prezza $$$
Italian **Map** 2 E2
24 Fleet St., 02113
Tel *(617) 227-1577*
One of the longest wine lists in town guarantees just the right glass to accompany hearty Tuscan fare and sinfully rich desserts.

Taranta $$$
Italian **Map** 2 D3
210 Hanover St., 02113
Tel *(617) 720-0052*
An artistic, eco-conscious blend of Southern Italian and Peruvian cuisine results in intricate recipes and intense flavors.

Trade $$$
New American **Map** 2 E5
540 Atlantic Ave., 02210
Tel *(617) 451-1234*
Downtown workers fill this airy, after-work hot spot for Mediterranean-inspired bites, craft beers, and designer cocktails.

Old Boston and the Financial District

Les Zygomates $$$
French **Map** 4 F2
129 South St., 02111
Tel *(617) 542-5108* **Closed** *Sun*
Dozens of wines by the glass complement the reasonably priced bistro fare. Live jazz most nights attracts young professionals.

Nebo $$$
Italian **Map** 2 E5
520 Atlantic Ave., 02210
Tel *(617) 723-6326* **Closed** *Sun*
Enjoy upscale pizzas and pastas in a clean, welcoming space. Notable for its gluten-free menu of traditional *trattoria* fare.

O Ya $$$
Japanese **Map** 2 D5
9 East St., 02111
Tel *(617) 654-9900* **Closed** *Sun, Mon*
One of the city's most acclaimed restaurants, O Ya serves modern

Diners at the popular fish shack – Barking Crab, Boston, Massachusetts

Bright decor at Redbones, Somerville, Massachusetts

Japanese fare. It's hard to find, tucked away near South Station.

Somerville

Dalí $$
Spanish
415 Washington St., Somerville, 02143
Tel *(617) 661-3254*
The area's most beloved spot for authentic tapas is hidden away on the Cambridge–Somerville border. A favorite with celebratory couples.

Diva $$
Indian
246 Elm St., Somerville, 02144
Tel *(617) 629-4963*
This sleekly appointed bistro, part of a local chain, serves carefully prepared classics and cocktails.

Redbones $$
Barbecue
55 Chester St., Somerville, 02144
Tel *(617) 628-2200*
A down-home kitchen slings some of the best Texas barbecue in the area. The young, upbeat crowd brings a raucous vibe. Free valet service for cyclists.

Wellesley

DK Choice

CK Shanghai $$
Chinese
15 Washington St., Wellesley, 02481
Tel *(781) 237-7500*
Chef C. K. Sau lured local foodies to Chinatown when he first came to Boston in 1993. Those in the know followed him to his new restaurant in the suburb of Wellesley to continue enjoying his creative versions of classic dishes from all over China. Dim sum brunch is served at weekends.

Blue Ginger $$$
Asian
583 Washington St., 02482
Tel *(781) 283-5790*
TV superchef Ming Tsai lures foodies to quiet Wellesley to sample his upscale Pan-Asian fare. An extensive wine list pairs nicely with the eclectic menu.

Massachusetts

AMHERST: Amherst Chinese Food $
Chinese
62 Main St., 01002
Tel *(413) 253-7835*
Spicy, flavorful Cantonese and Szechuan specialties (stir-fries, steamed dishes, vegetarian soups) are made using organic produce from a nearby farm.

AMHERST: Judie's $$
American
51 N. Pleasant St., 01002
Tel *(413) 253-3491*
American bistro fare in the evenings complements the daytime bakery/café menu, featuring burgers and popovers.

BREWSTER: Chillingsworth $$$
French
2449 Main St., 02631
Tel *(508) 896-3640*
Since 1976, this restaurant has been setting the fine-dining bar for Cape Cod with elegant French dishes and top-notch service. More casual fare is served in the bistro and bar areas.

DEERFIELD: Champney's $$$
American
81 Old Main St., 01342
Tel *(413) 774-5587*
The dining room of the historic Deerfield Inn features a field-to-table menu of classic American dishes and a bar where locals often gather.

DENNIS: Scargo Café $$
American
799 Main St., 02638
Tel *(508) 385-8200*
Scargo is located across the Cape Playhouse, and it is ideal for a pre-show bite. Diners enjoy creative, contemporary American fare and welcoming service.

ESSEX: Woodman's of Essex $$
Seafood
121 Main St., 01929
Tel *(978) 768-6057*
This is an old-time year-round favorite for world-famous fried clams, huge steamed lobsters, clam cakes, and other seafood treats. Casual, no-frills environment.

LENOX: Bistro Zinc $$$
French
56 Church St., 01240
Tel *(413) 637-8800*
The menu at this popular upscale bistro, with a long zinc bar and the atmosphere of a Provencal country *boîte*, is a mix of contemporary dishes and familiar French favorites.

MARTHA'S VINEYARD: Net Result $
Seafood
79 Beach Rd., Vineyard Haven, 02554
Tel *(508) 693-6071* **Closed** *Mon–Wed; Dec–May*
This fish market-cum-café churns out inexpensive fish dishes and sushi, as well as steamed lobster. It is operated by the island's largest seafood distributor.

MARTHA'S VINEYARD: Sweet Life Café $$$
New American
63 Circuit Ave., Oak Bluffs, 02557
Tel *(508) 696-0200* **Closed** *Fall/Winter*
Sweet Life is located in a Victorian house with three dining rooms and a garden terrace. On the menu is upscale New American cooking.

NANTUCKET: Brant Point Grill $$$
American
50 Easton St., 02554
Tel *(508) 325-1320* **Closed** *Oct–May*
Situated on the harbor, Brant Point Grill is an island favorite for its high-end wine list, fresh seafood, and artfully prepared dishes.

NANTUCKET: Ventuno $$$
Italian
21 Federal St., 02554
Tel *(508) 228-4242* **Closed** *Nov–May*
Northern Italian fare is presented with panache and often features the daily seafood catch, as well as vegetables farmed on the island and the Cape.

For more information on types of restaurants see p321

Romantic ambience at Old Inn on the Green, New Marlborough, Massachusetts

DK Choice

NEW MARLBOROUGH: Old Inn on the Green $$$
American
134 Hartsville New Marlborough Rd., 02130
Tel *(413) 229-7924* **Closed** *Mon & Tue*
The four dining rooms of this 18th-century inn all have fireplaces, but they've never had electricity, so all dining is by candlelight. Chef-owner Peter Platt creates new menus nightly based on what local farms are harvesting. The contemporary American bistro fare is fresh and innovative, designed to maximize flavors in beautiful presentations. *Prix-fixe* menus include a bargain Welcome Menu early in the week, while the weekend menu tends to be more extensive.

NORTH ADAMS: Gramercy Bistro $$$
New American
87 Marshall St., 01247
Tel *(413) 663-5300* **Closed** *Tue*
Conveniently located across the street from the Massachusetts Museum of Contemporary Art, the Gramercy offers contemporary cuisine with French and Italian touches.

NORTHAMPTON: Northampton Brewery $
American
11 Brewster Ct., 01060
Tel *(413) 584-9903*
One of New England's oldest brewpubs, this place serves up beer-friendly appetizers and dishes. Plenty of TVs for watching sports with rowdy local fans.

NORTHAMPTON: Eastside Grill $$
American
19 Strong Ave., 01060
Tel *(413) 586-3347*
An American grill menu with a New Orleans accent translates into great steaks, spicy gumbo, and killer jambalaya. Craft cocktails rule the bar.

PLYMOUTH: East Bay Grille $$
American
173 Water St., 02360
Tel *(508) 746-9751*
Steak tips, baked scrod, and seafood casseroles provide traditional fine dining in a relaxed dining room, with excellent water views from the patio.

PLYMOUTH: Lobster Hut $$
Seafood
25 Town Wharf, 02360
Tel *(508) 746-2270*
A local institution on the waterfront, just steps from the *Mayflower II*, Lobster Hut serves a classic fish-shack menu to a steady stream of hungry tourists and locals. Self-service.

ROCKPORT: Lobster Pool $$
Seafood
329 Granite St., 01966
Tel *(978) 546-7808* **Closed** *Oct–Apr*
This typical fish shack is renowned for fair prices and spectacular sunset views. Lobster is served in various forms, plus there is fresh local seafood and home-made pie.

SALEM: Finz Seafood & Grill $$$
Seafood
76 Wharf St., 01970
Tel *(978) 744-8485*
This cheerful waterfront restaurant serves fresh seafood

and New American fare. A lively bar scene picks up when musical performances are hosted in the lounge.

SANDWICH: Marshland Restaurant $
American
109 Route 6A, 02537
Tel *(508) 888-9824*
Classic Yankee cooking is executed with special care. Locals covet the recipe for stuffed *quahogs* (hard-shelled clams). Attached takeout bakery.

SANDWICH: Belfry Inne & Bistro $$$
Eclectic
8 Jarves St., 02563
Tel *(508) 888-8550* **Closed** *Jan*
A menu of "world's greatest hits" is served in an atmospheric, de-sanctified church. Impeccably executed dishes run the gamut from Thai noodles to lobster truffle risotto.

SAUGUS: Kowloon Restaurant $$
Chinese
948 Broadway, 01906
Tel *(781) 233-0077*
Old-time Chinese-American favorites such as sizzling *pupu* platters and sweet-and-sour-chicken feature at this giant eatery perched majestically atop a hill.

SPRINGFIELD: Student Prince $$
German
8 Fort St., 01103
Tel *(413) 734-7475*
A local institution, the Student Prince is one of the region's few German eateries. Home-made sausages and a beer stein collection complete the authentic experience.

STURBRIDGE:
Publick House $$$
American
277 Main St., 01566
Tel (508) 347-3313
This welcoming roadside inn has been feeding weary travelers since 1771 and to this day continues to serve old-school, warming, filling fare. Fittingly close to Old Sturbridge Village.

SUDBURY: Longfellow's
Wayside Inn $$
American
72 Wayside Inn Rd., 01776
Tel (978) 443-1776
A Colonial-era stagecoach inn, Longfellow's offers a number of seating options – from a Tap Room to the famous Old Bar Room – in which to enjoy retro-minded fare (lobster pie, prime rib, baked scrod).

DK Choice

WALTHAM: Il Capriccio $$$
Italian
888 Main St., 02453
Tel (781) 894-2234
One of the pioneering Northern Italian restaurants in eastern Massachusetts, Il Capriccio remains a flag-bearer for the clean fish and vegetable dishes of the Veneto and Liguria regions, while bringing a touch of wood smoke to Tuscan grill dishes. Like the food, the wine list ranges from the full-flavor whites of Friuli and Alto Adige to bold Barolos and Barbarescos and supple Chiantis and Brunellos.

WELLFLEET: Catch of the Day
Seafood Grill $$
Seafood
975 Route 6, 02667
Tel (508) 349-9090 **Closed** mid-Oct–late May
The town's famous oysters are on offer at this casual seafood eatery and market. Simply select your fish from the market and specify how you'd like it prepared, or enjoy a hearty fisherman's stew.

WILLIAMSTOWN: Gala
Steakhouse and Bistro $$$
New American
222 Adams Rd., 01267
Tel (413) 458-9590
One of the most romantic dining spots in western Massachusetts, this upscale dining room in the Orchards Hotel serves fine steaks and modern bistro fare.

The Tap Room at Longfellow's Wayside Inn, Sudbury, Massachusetts

Rhode Island

BLOCK ISLAND: Eli's $$
Italian
456 Chapel St., 02807
Tel (401) 466-5230 **Closed** Winter
This friendly eatery serves up imaginative pastas with flair. With only 50 seats, the casual dining room can get packed; arrive early or be prepared to wait.

BLOCK ISLAND: Atlantic Inn $$$
American
359 High St., 02807
Tel (401) 466-5883
Urbane locals favor this formal spot for its spectacular ocean views and sophisticated modern fare. The veranda tables are especially popular at sunset.

BLOCK ISLAND: Manisses
Dining Room $$$
American
5 Spring St., 02807
Tel (401) 466-2836 **Closed** Nov–Apr
The classy Hotel Manisses' formal boîte is an attractive place in which to sample freshly caught local seafood, home-made pastas, and elaborate desserts.

BRISTOL: Lobster Pot $$
Seafood
199 Hope St., 02809
Tel (401) 253-9100
Extremely fresh basic as well as sophisticated preparations are served across three dining rooms and a patio with harbor views.

CHARLESTOWN:
Nordic Lodge $$$
American
178 East Pasquisett Trail, 02813
Tel (401) 783-4515 **Closed** Mon–Thu; Jan–Apr
The all-you-can-eat buffet at this woodsy summer lodge includes unlimited lobster, oysters, prime rib, Alaskan crab and other pricey fare. Reservations not accepted.

GALILEE: George's of Galilee $$
Seafood
250 Sand Hill Cove Rd., 02882
Tel (401) 783-2306
Diners come to this bustling waterfront landmark in one of the region's leading fishing ports for the seafood platters, clam cakes, and chowders.

HARRISVILLE: Wright's
Farm Restaurant $
American
84 Inman Rd., 02830
Tel (401) 769-2856
All-you-can-eat chicken dinners are the drawing card at this legendary restaurant, hosting more than 1,000 diners weekly.

MIDDLETOWN: Atlantic
Beach Club $$$
American
55 Purgatory Rd., 02842
Tel (401) 847-2750
Choose between casual daytime patio dining and a more formal dining room. Local seafood is prepared in any number of ways, and the varied menu has something for everyone.

Veranda tables at the Atlantic Inn, Rhode Island

For more information on types of restaurants see p321

NARRAGANSETT: Coast Guard House $$$
American
40 Ocean Rd., 02882
Tel *(401) 789-0700*
In a renovated coastguard station, this place provides views of the beach, plus straightforward seafood offerings and large portions of familiar American fare. Popular Sunday brunch service.

NEWPORT: Crazy Dough's Pizza $
Italian
446 Thames St., 02840
Tel *(401) 619-3343* **Closed** *Mon*
Enjoy pocket-friendly eats in a sea of pricey tourist haunts. Award-winning pizzas and *calzoni* are made using fresh ingredients.

NEWPORT: Salvation Café $
Eclectic
140 Broadway, 02840
Tel *(401) 847-2620*
The laid-back staff mirrors the colorful atmosphere featuring vivid local art. The diverse menu incorporates everything from Thai fare to roasted local seafood.

NEWPORT: Brick Alley Pub $$
American
140 Thames St., 02840
Tel *(401) 849-6334*
One of Newport's most popular restaurants, this is always packed with families enjoying selections from a far-ranging casual menu. Many menu items come with an unlimited soup and salad buffet.

NEWPORT: Scales & Shells $$
Seafood
527 Thames St., 02840
Tel *(401) 846-3474*
This welcoming eatery sports a raw bar to go with its lengthy menu of seafood and pasta dishes. Many patrons stick to cold beer in these casual environs.

NEWPORT: The Black Pearl $$$
New American
Bannister's Wharf, 02840
Tel *(401) 846-5264* **Closed** *Jan & Feb*
A former run-down sail loft is now one of the city's most charming dining spots. Diners enjoy a varied menu featuring local seafood.

NEWPORT: The Mooring $$$
American
Sayers Wharf, 02840
Tel *(401) 846-2260*
Located on the historic Downtown Waterfront, The Mooring offers views of Narragansett Bay. Varied menu contains numerous seafood and steak offerings. Lively bar area.

NEWPORT: Restaurant Bouchard $$$
French
505 Thames St., 02840
Tel *(401) 846-0123* **Closed** *Tue*
French-trained chef Albert Bouchard wows the fussiest of gourmands with his elegant interpretations of French classics. Attentive service and classy environs make it a top choice for special occasions.

NEWPORT: White Horse Tavern $$$
American
26 Marlborough St., 02840
Tel *(401) 849-3600*
One of the oldest taverns in America, the White Horse serves upscale American fare in candlelit environs. Low-beamed ceilings, hearth fires, and colonial bric-a-brac complete the picture.

PROVIDENCE: Caserta Pizzeria $
Pizza
121 Spruce St., 02903
Tel *(401) 621-3618*
This old-time pizzeria churns out inexpensive pies in spartan environs. Families pop in for a quick pie or for takeout.

PROVIDENCE: East Side Pockets $
Middle Eastern
278 Thayer St., 02906
Tel *(401) 453-1100*
A favorite of bargain-seekers and vegetarians, this family-owned eatery serves inexpensive wraps and platters.

PROVIDENCE: Olneyville NY System Restaurant $
American
20 Plainfield St., 02903
Tel *(401) 621-9500*
This nondescript eatery has won national attention for its old-style hot dogs, a true state delicacy. Try the coffee-flavored milk.

PROVIDENCE: Rick's Roadhouse $
Barbecue
370 Richmond St., 02903
Tel *(401) 272-7675*
A wide selection of beers, bourbons, and whiskies pair well with smoky barbecue fare. The wood-fired grill provides an inviting aroma to the casual environs.

DK Choice

PROVIDENCE: Venda Ravioli $
Italian
265 Atwells Ave., 02903
Tel *(401) 421-9105*
This Italian gourmet shop features a huge selection of cheeses, cold cuts, prepared dishes, and pickled items, including a vast selection of olives. Although it is part of the same operation as a nearby restaurant, Venda Ravioli also has some tables ringing the central deli cases, where it serves bountiful and delicious Italian meals – from late breakfast through early supper.

Entrance to the Brick Alley Pub, Newport, Rhode Island

Bar area at Al Forno, Providence, Rhode Island

DK Choice

PROVIDENCE: Al Forno $$$
Italian
577 S. Main St., 02903
Tel *(401) 273-9760* **Closed** *Sun,
Mon*
Diners come from far and
wide to sample nationally
renowned, upscale Italian
fare. Wood-fire grilled meats,
thin-crust pizzas, and bubbling
baked pasta dishes all jockey
for attention. An extensive
wine list features something
for everyone. Seasonal, local
ingredients are dotted through-
out the menu. The kitchen's
talents have spawned
numerous cookbooks.

**PROVIDENCE:
Capital Grille** $$$
Steakhouse
1 Union Station, 02903
Tel *(401) 521-5600*
Pricey cuts of premium-aged
beef and big-ticket classics are
served with panache at this
top Providence steakhouse.

**PROVIDENCE:
Capriccio** $$$
Italian
2 Pine St., 02903
Tel *(401) 421-1320*
Grand style Continental cuisine
continues to hold forth in a
grotto-like, candlelit dining
room. Modern Northern Italian
dishes pair nicely with the
well-chosen wine list.

PROVIDENCE: Gracie's $$$
New American
194 Washington St., 02903
Tel *(401) 272-7811* **Closed** *Sun*
Possibly the city's most popular
restaurant, Gracie's serves
inspired farm-to-table meals in
prix-fixe or tasting menus, with or
without specific wine pairings.

**PROVIDENCE:
New Rivers** $$$
New American
7 Steeple St., 02903
Tel *(401) 751-0350* **Closed** *Sun*
A pair of 1870s storefronts
on College Hill, housing a
40-seat dining room and an
intimate bar, offer a bistro
menu packed with plenty
of culinary surprises.

**PROVIDENCE:
Siena** $$$
Italian
238 Atwells Ave., 02903
Tel *(401) 521-3311*
Siena serves Northern Italian fare
in the heart of Federal Hill. The
wood-grilled pizzas and roasted
meats are particularly popular.

Connecticut

DARIEN: Coromandel $$
Indian
25 Old Kings Hwy., 06820
Tel *(203) 662-1213*
One of the state's most lauded
Indian restaurants, Coromandel
serves South Indian specialties, but
also Goan and northern dishes.

FARMINGTON: Apricots $$$
New American
1593 Farmington Ave., 06032
Tel *(860) 673-5405*
This airy, two-story barn
overlooking a scenic river has a
wine list that matches the creative
cuisine. The pub downstairs is a
popular after-work haunt.

**GREENWICH: Burgers, Shakes
& Fries** $
American
302 Delavan Ave., 06830
Tel *(203) 531-7433* **Closed** *Sun*
Gourmet burgers, fresh side
orders, and creamy milkshakes
are served in a casual joint.

GREENWICH: Penang Grill $$
Asian
55 Lewis St., 06830
Tel *(203) 861-1988* **Closed** *Sun*
This stylish yet casual eatery
churns out Chinese-Malaysian
fare. Certain dishes are
exceptionally fiery; spice levels
can be adjusted on request.

**GUILFORD: Whitfield's on
Guilford Green** $$
American
25 Whitfield St., 06437
Tel *(203) 458-1300*
The varied menu at this
contemporary café in a late 18th-
century home filled with bright
artwork includes hearty steaks
and home-made pasta dishes, as
well as smaller plates for sharing.

**HARTFORD: City Steam
Brewery Café** $
Italian
942 Main St., 06103
Tel *(860) 525-1600* **Closed** *Sun*
A voluminous brewpub, City
Steam serves contemporary
pub fare and excellent beers
in a downtown 1887 steam
plant building.

HARTFORD: Black-Eyed Sally's $$
Barbecue
350 Asylum St., 06103
Tel *(860) 278-7427* **Closed** *Sun*
This downtown eatery churns out
Southern-style barbecue and
Cajun fare, with live music on the
side. Expect a crowd when there's
an event at the nearby arena.

HARTFORD: Max Downtown $$$
New American
185 Asylum St., 06103
Tel *(860) 522-2530*
Contemporary fare is served
in stylish environs at this flagship
of a local chain with locations in
the city and suburbs. A favorite
of the after-work crowd.

KENT: Fife 'n Drum $$
Eclectic
53 N. Main St., 06757
Tel *(860) 927-3509* **Closed** *Tue*
Live piano music often
accompanies the fine French,
Italian, and American meals here.
A lengthy wine list complements
the cuisine.

LEDYARD: Paragon $$$
New American
*Grant Pequot Tower, Foxwoods,
Route 2, 06339*
Tel *(860) 312-5130* **Closed** *Mon–Wed*
Elegant cuisine comes with views
of the countryside. Seasonal
menus spotlight gourmet ingre-
dients such as fresh oysters, Maine
lobsters, and dry-aged steaks.

For more information on types of restaurants *see p321*

Outdoor tables at Abbott's Lobster in the Rough, Noank, Connecticut

LITCHFIELD: West Street Grill $$$
New American
43 West St., 06759
Tel *(860) 567-3885*
Enjoy New American fare in a comfortably casual setting. Inexpensive, straightforward lunch offerings stand in contrast to the pricier, more creative dinner menu.

MANCHESTER: Cavey's $$$
French-Italian
45 E. Center St., 06040
Tel *(860) 643-2751*
Two rooms in this restaurant serve two cuisines: Northern Italian in the casual upstairs; gourmet modern French in the formal downstairs, where jackets are suggested for men.

MONTVILLE: Bobby Flay's Bar Americain $$$
New American
1 Mohegan Sun Blvd., 06382
Tel *(860) 862-8000*
The popular TV chef here treats diners to his interpretations of classic French bistro fare and top-notch seafood.

MYSTIC: Mystic Pizza $
Pizza
56 W. Main St., 06355
Tel *(860) 536-3700*
Famous from its role in the Julia Roberts movie of the same name, this no-frills institution remains popular for its tasty pies. Lots of TVs and a well-stocked bar.

MYSTIC: Oyster Club $$
American
13 Water St., 06355
Tel *(860) 415-9266* **Closed** *Tue*
Bistro-style seafood, including butter-poached hot lobster roll, is served in a rustic setting with an outdoor deck.

NEW BRITAIN: Staropolska $
Polish
252 Broad St., 06051
Tel *(860) 612-1711*
The home-style Polish cooking in this friendly space is popular with locals, who make up the state's largest Polish expat community.

NEW HAVEN: Frank Pepe's Pizzeria $
Pizza
157 Wooster St., 06511
Tel *(203) 865-5762*
Opened in 1925, this no-frills spot for thin-crust pizza attracts foodies from all over for what some consider to be the world's best white clam pizza.

DK Choice

NEW HAVEN: Louis' Lunch $
American
263 Crown St., 06511
Tel *(203) 562-5507* **Closed** *Sun, Mon*
While some may question it, most people agree that the humble hamburger can trace its origins back to this famed lunch counter, which first served a ground beef patty on a bun back when it opened in 1895. Today, it remains mostly unchanged, with an old-time environment that matches its small menu and low prices. Grilled in vintage vertical broilers, each burger provides a true taste of history.

NEW HAVEN: Bentara $$
Malaysian
76 Orange St., 06510
Tel *(203) 562-2511*
Authentic dishes are served in high-ceilinged dining rooms decorated with Asian artifacts. Most dishes blend sweet, pungent, spicy, and salty notes.

**NEW HAVEN:
Union League Café** $$$
French
1032 Chapel St., 06510
Tel *(203) 562-4299* **Closed** *Sun*
This acclaimed restaurant, in a historic setting, serves traditional French food with a contemporary twist, using local and organic produce and artisanal cheeses.

NEW HAVEN: Zinc $$$
New American
964 Chapel St., 06510
Tel *(203) 624-0507* **Closed** *Sun*
The stunning minimalist decor suits the vibrant, Asian-tinged modern cuisine made with local, organic ingredients. Situated directly on New Haven Green.

NOANK: Abbott's Lobster in the Rough $
Seafood
117 Pearl St., 06340
Tel *(860) 536-7719* **Closed** *Nov–May*
Fresh local seafood is served at plain picnic-style tables facing the harbor on Mystic River. Patrons are allowed to bring their own beer and wine.

OLD SAYBROOK: Fresh Salt $$$
New American
Saybrook Point Inn, 2 Bridge St., 06475
Tel *(860) 388-1111*
This upscale eatery puts a European spin on local produce and fresh seafood. The stellar raw bar is a prime spot for enjoying oysters on the half shell.

PLAINVILLE: Confetti $
Italian
393 Farmington Ave., 06062
Tel *(860) 793-8809*
Confetti is an oasis of hearty Italian fare in an inviting setting. The kitchen focuses on seafood, with ingredients like calamari offered in multiple preparations.

PLAINVILLE: The Cottage $$
American
427 Farmington Ave., 06062
Tel *(860) 793-8888* **Closed** *Sun, Mon*
Chef Patty Queen constantly invents new comfort food with the changing local harvest. Oyster dishes are especially good, and wine is a bargain.

SOUTH NORWALK: SoNo Seaport Seafood $$
Seafood
100 Water St., 06854
Tel *(203) 854-9483*
This casual dining spot serves fresh seafood, fried or grilled, with a view of working fishermen right outside. Takeout is available at the adjacent market.

STONINGTON: Noah's $$
Seafood
113 Water St., 06378
Tel *(860) 535-3925* **Closed** *Mon*
Noah's has been serving local seafood, Mediterranean dishes, and home-made desserts since 1979. The casual environs include one of the area's liveliest bars.

VERNON: Rein's Deli $
American
435 Hartford Tnpk., 06066
Tel *(860) 875-1344*
A popular, affordable stop along the NYC–Boston corridor, this NYC-style, family-owned deli has been satisfying motorists' sandwich cravings for decades.

WEST HARTFORD: Plan B Burger Bar $
American
138 Park Rd., 06119
Tel *(860) 231-1199*
This small gourmet burger chain is beloved for its huge menu. Some other food offerings are available, plus craft beers help draw the crowds.

WOODBURY: Good News Café $$$
American
694 Main St. S., 06798
Tel *(203) 266-4663* **Closed** *Tue*
Fresh organic ingredients from local farmers are the focus of this award-winning restaurant's menu.

Vermont

BURLINGTON: American Flatbread Burlington Hearth $
Pizza
115 St. Paul St., 05401
Tel *(802) 861-2999*
Gourmet wood-fired pizzas made with local, organic ingredients keep the crowds coming at this eco-friendly eatery. Craft beers and organic salads are also served.

BURLINGTON: India House Restaurant $
Indian
207 Colchester Ave., 05401
Tel *(802) 862-7800*
This casual spot specializes in traditional North Indian food and is one of the city's best options for vegetarians.

BURLINGTON: Penny Cluse Café $
American
169 Cherry St., 05401
Tel *(802) 651-8834*
Penny Cluse Café is a friendly spot that serves breakfast and lunch daily. The varied menu

runs from gingerbread pancakes to fish tacos. Especially popular for weekend brunch.

BURLINGTON: The Vermont Pub & Brewery $
American
44 College St., 05401
Tel *(802) 865-0500*
Vermont's oldest craft brewery serves hearty American fare alongside freshly brewed beers. The lengthy menu features lots of fun plates perfect for sharing.

BURLINGTON: Leunig's Bistro $$$
Eclectic
115 Church St., 05401
Tel *(802) 863-3759*
Located in a 1920s building, this award-winning grill and bistro serves a varied menu of French classics and Mediterranean-tinged American dishes.

BURLINGTON: Trattoria Delia $$$
Italian
152 St. Paul St., 05401
Tel *(802) 864-5253*
This family-run restaurant offers an old-world ambience and regional specialties. Stone walls, exposed beams, and a fireplace add to the atmosphere.

GRAFTON: Grafton Inn $$$
American
92 Main St., 05146
Tel *(800) 843-1801*
The menu at this restaurant, in an 1801 inn, incorporates modern global touches. Ingredients include

herbs from the inn's garden, and local meat and dairy products.

KILLINGTON: The Foundry at Summit Pond $$
American
Summit Pond & Killington Rd., 05751
Tel *(802) 422-5335*
Bistro-style fare is served in an atmospheric building that was designed to look like an old mill. It often features live entertainment.

LOWER WATERFORD: The Rabbit Hill Inn $$$
New American
48 Lower Waterford Rd., 05848
Tel *(802) 748-5168* **Closed** *Wed (except during peak foliage season)*
This tranquil 1795 country inn is the stage for one of the state's most acclaimed restaurants. New American fare is served à la carte or via a seasonal tasting menu.

MANCHESTER CENTER: Little Rooster Café $
American
Rte. 7A and Hillvale Dr., 05255
Tel *(802) 362-3496*
This is a popular stop for filling breakfasts and lunches. Belgian waffles and over-stuffed sandwiches are crowd favorites.

MIDDLEBURY: American Flatbread $
Pizza
137 Maple St., 05753
Tel *(802) 388-3300* **Closed** *Sun, Mon*
This popular pizzeria utilizes local, organic produce, and it is a great spot for sampling award-winning, local craft beers.

Exterior of the Grafton Inn, Vermont

For more information on types of restaurants *see p321*

MONTPELIER: La Brioche $
American
89 Main St., 05602
Tel *(802) 229-0443*   **Closed** *Sun*
The pastry chefs of tomorrow
train at this bakery-café operated
by the New England Culinary
Institute. The menu includes
soups, salads, and sandwiches.

MONTPELIER: NECI on Main $$
New American
118 Main St., 05602
Tel *(802) 223-3188*   **Closed** *Mon*
Students of the New England
Culinary Institute staff this spot,
located just down the street from
the school. The French-influenced
menu emphasizes the use of
fresh, local ingredients.

DK Choice

**QUECHEE: Simon Pearce
Restaurant** $$$
New American
1760 Quechee Main St., 05059
Tel *(802) 295-1470*
Located in a restored mill
overlooking the Ottauquechee
River, Simon Pearce enjoys a
scenic location. After checking
out the namesake glass-
blowing studio, where the
glassware and pottery used by
the restaurant are produced,
guests fill the romantic dining
room to enjoy fresh, modern
American cuisine and an award-
winning wine list.

**SHELBURNE: Restaurant at
the Inn at Shelburne Farms** $$$
New American
1611 Harbor Rd., 05482
Tel *(802) 985-8498*
The estate's gardens provide
many of the ingredients for
the true farm-to-table cuisine
served in the dining room of
this historic mansion, on a bluff
overlooking Lake Champlain.

Simple, classy interiors of NECI on
Main, Montpelier, Vermont

**STOWE: Depot Street
Malt Shop** $
American
57 Depot St., 05672
Tel *(802) 253-4369*
This casual spot with a 1950s-
style soda fountain and a big
menu for children is known for
its burgers, grilled sandwiches,
and fries. Ice cream is served
all year.

STRATTON: Verde $$$
New American
19 Village Lodge Rd., 05360
Tel *(802) 297-9200*
The contemporary, upscale
bistro fare featuring local
ingredients is the culinary star
of this mountain resort. Look
out for the grass-fed Vermont
beef on the menu.

**WATERBURY: Hen of
the Wood** $$$
New American
92 Stowe St., 05676
Tel *(802) 244-7300*   **Closed** *Sun,
Mon*
This restaurant's straightforward
preparations showcase the
wealth of premium ingredients

found nearby, in the lush Green
Mountains and Champlain Valley.

WESTON: Inn at Weston $$$
New American
630 Main St., 05161
Tel *(802) 824-6789*
The ever-changing menu of
the Inn at Weston is always
interesting. Members of the
Vermont Fresh network supply
top-notch, seasonal meat and
dairy produce.

**WOODSTOCK: Bentley's
Restaurant** $
American
3 Elm St., 05091
Tel *(802) 457-3232*
Bentley's is a friendly hangout
hosting trivia contests and
live music to go along with
its varied menu of hearty
American fare. Deep,
comfortable couches add to
the warm atmosphere.

**WOODSTOCK: Osteria
Pane e Salute** $$$
Italian
61 Central St., 05091
Tel *(802) 457-4882*   **Closed** *Mon–
Wed, Nov, Apr*
Spectacular Italian farmhouse
cooking and good wines make
Osteria Pane e Salute the most
sophisticated dining and
drinking spot in town.

New Hampshire

**BEDFORD: Bedford
Village Inn** $$$
New American
2 Olde Bedford Way, 03110
Tel *(603) 472-2001*
This luxury inn's restaurant
serves upscale regional cuisine
in eight unique dining rooms.
Oenophiles will delight in the
lengthy wine list.

**CENTER SANDWICH:
Corner House Inn** $$
American
22 Main St., 03227
Tel *(603) 284-6219*   **Closed** *Tue*
Comfort food gets a modern
twist at this venerable inn and
tavern, where vegetarian fare
gets equal billing with meat.

CONCORD: The Common Man $$
American
25 Water St., 03301
Tel *(603) 228-3463*
American comfort food is served
in relaxed environs. Choose
between the spacious downstairs
dining room or the inviting
upstairs pub.

Scenic location of the Simon Pearce Restaurant, Quechee, Vermont

DURHAM: Three Chimneys Inn $$
American
17 Newmarket Rd., 03824
Tel *(603) 868-7800*
Enjoy fine American cuisine in a beautiful 1649 mansion. A full menu is served in the elegant dining room, as well as the historic pub on the lower level.

EXETER: Epoch Restaurant and Bar $$
New American
2 Pine St., 03833
Tel *(603) 778-3762*
In addition to a strong menu of small plates, bar bites, sandwiches, and salads, Epoch also offers some pastas and roasted meat dishes in a casually elegant setting.

HANOVER: Lou's $
American
30 S. Main St., 03755
Tel *(603) 643-3321*
This is a go-to spot for hearty comfort fare. Over four generations of Dartmouth College students have filled their bellies with traditional breakfast and lunches.

HANOVER: Market Table $$
New American
44 S. Main St., 03755
Tel *(603) 676-7796*
Bold flavors and eco-conscious eating converge in this café, where seasonal farm-to-table fare is served all day. Prepared meals are also for sale.

HANOVER: Pine $$$
New American
2 S. Main St., 03755
Tel *(603) 643-4300*
Gourmet breakfast, lunch, and dinner options are available in a boutique hotel. Stunning views of the Dartmouth College campus, especially from the alfresco terrace.

KEENE: Elm City Brewing Company $
American
22 West St., 03431
Tel *(603) 355-3335*
Elm City serves handcrafted draft beers and hearty pub fare in a renovated 19th-century woolen mill. It's a college town hangout, so expect a boisterous atmosphere.

KEENE: Luca's Mediterranean Café $$
International
10 Central Sq., 03431
Tel *(603) 358-3335*
Luca's offers Mediterranean-inspired dishes served in casual environs. The menu showcases French, Italian, and Spanish classics, with occasional forays into North African, Greek, and Turkish fare.

Red Arrow Diner, Manchester, New Hampshire

LITTLETON: Miller's Café & Bakery $
American
16 Mill St., 03561
Tel *(603) 444-2146*   **Closed** *Mon*
This lunch-only café is housed in a former mill building with great views. The friendly staff mirrors the congenial surroundings.

MANCHESTER: Café Momo $
Nepali
1065 Hanover St., 03104
Tel *(603) 623-3733*   **Closed** *Mon*
Enjoy authentic Nepali cuisine in a colorful environment. The momos (traditional dumplings) and spicy curries prove popular.

MANCHESTER: Red Arrow Diner $
American
61 Lowell St., 03101
Tel *(603) 626-1118*
Dating back to 1922, this historic diner serves classic American fare 24 hours a day. Friendly service.

DK Choice

MEREDITH: Hart's Turkey Farm Restaurant $$
American
233 Daniel Webster Hwy., 03253
Tel *(603) 279-6212*
The country-style turkey dinner is a staple of New England dining. This restaurant specializes in serving up Thanksgiving on a plate every day, and also offers turkey pot pie, turkey livers, and even turkey tempura. A huge selection of non-turkey dishes is also available, such as prime rib and a full line of seafood.

NASHUA: MT's Local Kitchen & Wine Bar $$
New American
212 Main St., 03060
Tel *(603) 595-9334*
This eatery delivers fanciful modern bistro fare in style.

Exposed brick walls, white linen tablecloths, and a chic jazz bar all lend to the sophisticated vibe.

NEW CASTLE: Latitudes at Wentworth $$$
New American
588 Wentworth Rd., 03854
Tel *(603) 422-7322*
Scenic harbor views and a fireplace contribute to the romantic atmosphere at this restaurant. On the menu is upscale regional cuisine, with an emphasis on using fresh local ingredients.

NEW LONDON: The Coach House $$$
New American
353 Main St., 03257
Tel *(603) 526-2791*   **Closed** *Sun, Mon*
Tourists and locals alike enjoy the casual elegance and fine local fare served in a charming New England atmosphere at The Coach House. The wine list is impressive.

NEWMARKET: Rocky's Famous Burgers $
American
171 Main St., 03257
Tel *(603) 292-3393*
Rocky's is a popular eatery that serves a variety of half-pound burgers (beef, bison, chicken, and veggie) with a whimsical sense of humor; the fries are free if you can pin a photo of your pet dog on the wall.

NORTH CONWAY: Moat Mountain Smoke House and Brewing Co. $
Barbecue
3378 White Mtn. Hwy., 03860
Tel *(603) 356-6381*
Friendly and casual, this brewpub pairs its popular handcrafted ales with a variety of slow-cooked barbecued meats (pulled pork, ribs, and brisket).

For more information on types of restaurants *see p321*

Portsmouth Gas Light Co., New Hampshire

PORTSMOUTH: Portsmouth Gas Light Co. $$
American
64 Market St., 03801
Tel *(603) 430-8582*
Here you'll find American and Italian fare in the dining room, casual pizza downstairs, and a bar-nightclub on the third floor.

PORTSMOUTH: The Oar House $$$
New American
55 Ceres St., 03801
Tel *(603) 436-4025*
Upscale fare is served in a restored 1803 warehouse. The decor reflects the city's maritime heritage.

WALPOLE: L.A. Burdick Restaurant $
New American
47 Main St., 03608
Tel *(800) 229-2419* **Closed** *Sun*
Part of an ever-growing chocolate empire, this restaurant serves a bistro menu only in the afternoon, leading up to world-class desserts.

WEST LEBANON: Three Tomatoes Trattoria $$
Italian
1 Court St., 03766
Tel *(603) 448-1711*
Across from the Lebanon Green, this spot's thin-crust pizzas – made in a wood-fire oven – make it popular with college students.

Maine

BANGOR: Thistles Restaurant $$$
Mediterranean
175 Exchange St., 04401
Tel *(207) 945-5480* **Closed** *Sun, Mon*
This is the place for local seafood with a Spanish accent. Live music

makes it one of the most avant-garde spots in town.

BAR HARBOR: Lompoc Café and Brewpub $$
American
36 Rodick St., 04609
Tel *(207) 288-9392* **Closed** *Sun*
Enjoy house-made microbrews along with an interesting varied menu at this intimate café and bar, with a heated outdoor dining room and a *bocce* garden.

BAR HARBOR: West Street Café $$$
Seafood
76 West St., 04609
Tel *(207) 288-5242* **Closed** *Dec–May*
A welcoming eatery near the downtown waterfront, popular for its array of fresh seafood, steak, pasta dishes, and home-made pies.

BATH: Mae's Café & Bakery $
American
160 Centre St., 04530
Tel *(207) 442-8577*
This top-notch bakery-café serves dependable breakfast, brunch, and lunch in an old house.

BELFAST: Chase's Daily $$
Vegetarian
96 Main St., 04915
Tel *(207) 338-0555* **Closed** *Mon*
A bakery/restaurant/market, Chase's serves up creative vegetarian and vegan fare featuring organic veggies. Small but well-chosen wine and beer selection.

BETHEL: Millbrook Tavern & Grille $$
New American
21 Broad St., 04217
Tel *(207) 824-2175*
Located in the historic Bethel Inn, this tavern offers a mix of

seafood, steaks, and pizzas in a relaxed atmosphere, with outdoor seating in the summer.

BOOTHBAY HARBOR: Brown's Wharf Restaurant $$
Seafood
121 Atlantic Ave., 04538
Tel *(207) 633-5440* **Closed** *Sun, Mon; Oct–May*
A casual spot in the middle of the harbor, Brown's serves fresh seafood to a friendly mix of locals and tourists.

GREENVILLE: The Greenville Inn $$$
New American
40 Norris St., 04441
Tel *(207) 695-2206*
The Greenville Inn is a gourmet restaurant housed in an 1895 mansion in remote northern Maine. A round dining room and a smaller Victorian room have sweeping views.

KENNEBUNKPORT: The Clam Shack $
Seafood
2 Western St., 04046
Tel *(207) 967-2560* **Closed** *Oct–Apr*
Serving Maine's best lobster roll, the Clam Shack is a tiny takeout stand that is celebrated as a coastal legend. The menu's freshly cut onion rings are also popular standouts.

KENNEBUNKPORT: Stripers at Breakwater Inn & Spa $$$
New American
127 Ocean Ave., 04046
Tel *(207) 967-5333* **Closed** *Sep–Apr*
For local flavor, stick to the shellfish and multiple versions of lobster at this relaxed upscale spot, with breezy lawn seating for pre-dinner drinks.

KITTERY: Warren's Lobster House $$
Seafood
11 Water St., 03904
Tel *(207) 439-1630*
This vintage 350-seat seafood house is perched above the old Route 1 bridge. The house specialty is twin steamed lobsters.

LINCOLNVILLE BEACH: Lobster Pound $
Seafood
2521 Lincolnville Hwy., 04849
Tel *(207) 789-5550*
This restaurant serves classic seafood dishes such as stews, chowders, and boiled lobsters, plus steaks and burgers.

OGUNQUIT: Barnacle Billy's $
Seafood
70 Perkins Cove Rd., 03907
Tel *(207) 646-5575* **Closed** *Nov–Mar*
Offering bare-bones clam-shack fare at the harbor, Billy's is a real bargain – unless you order lobster.

PORTLAND: Duckfat $
New American
43 Middle St., 04101
Tel *(207) 774-8080*
This cozy eatery attracts crowds thanks to its signature namesake treat: duck-fat fried potatoes. Salads, sandwiches, and craft beers are also on offer.

PORTLAND: El Rayo Taqueria $
Mexican
101 York St., 04101
Tel *(207) 780-8226*
This converted gas station houses a popular spot for fresh, fiery Mexican fare.

PORTLAND: Local 188 $$
New American
685 Congress St., 04102
Tel *(207) 761-7909*
Blending a menu of Spanish-style tapas with a handful of

Diners at the bustling Local 188 in Portland's Arts District, Maine

rice and fish dishes, this colorful café with an open kitchen draws both foodies and singles looking for a lively scene.

PORTLAND: Fore Street $$$
New American
288 Fore St., 04101
Tel *(207) 775-2717*
The upscale American fare at Fore Street features fresh ingredients from Maine's community of farmers, fishermen, and cheesemakers. High-vaulted ceilings and a brick hearth add to the warm environs.

PORTLAND: Hugo's $$$
New American
88 Middle St., 04101
Tel *(207) 774-8538* **Closed** *Sun, Mon*
Hugo's is a nationally renowned restaurant that specializes in inventive modern fare, served in *prix-fixe* and tasting menus. The bar offers a less expensive, à la carte menu.

DK Choice

ROCKLAND: Primo Restaurant $$$
New American
2 S. Main St., 04841
Tel *(207) 596-0770* **Closed** *Mon–Wed, Nov–Apr*
This acclaimed restaurant, known for its innovative market cuisine, provides a complete farm-to-table experience. Dishes are prepared with locally sourced seafood and fresh vegetables. Choose between formal dining areas or a more casual bar area in which a less expensive menu is offered.

SOUTH FREEPORT: Harraseeket Lunch & Lobster $
Seafood
36 Main St., 04078
Tel *(207) 865-3535* **Closed** *Oct–Apr*
Head to the back counter for steamed lobsters to go at this time-honored lobster pound, serving up fried and steamed seafood right on the water's edge.

SOUTH THOMASTON: Waterman's Beach Lobster $
Seafood
343 Waterman Beach Rd., 04858
Tel *(207) 594-7518* **Closed** *early Sep–mid-Jun*
This iconic family-run shack sells lobster caught by the family themselves. It also serves a delicious blueberry pie.

WALDOBORO: Moody's Diner $
American
1885 Atlantic Hwy., 04572
Tel *(207) 832-7785*
Locals, vacationing families, and long-haul truck drivers all mix at this Maine institution. The old-school diner menu includes comfort fare such as blueberry pancakes and chicken pot pie.

WALDOBORO: Morse's Sauerkraut & European Deli $
German
3856 Washington Rd., 04572
Tel *(207) 832-5569* **Closed** *Wed*
An authentic German café and market, Morse's sells hard-to-find, imported specialties and award-winning, home-made sauerkraut and pickles.

WELLS: Billy's Chowderhouse $
Seafood
216 Mile Rd., 04090
Tel *(207) 646-7558* **Closed** *Jan*
Located behind the Wells barrier beach, this casual spot is ideal for whiling away an afternoon drinking beer and snacking on wine-steamed mussels.

Elegant interiors at the nationally acclaimed Primo, Rockland, Maine

For more information on types of restaurants *see p321*

SHOPPING IN NEW ENGLAND

New England offers a wide and ever-growing variety of high-quality stores and merchandise. For gifts with regional flavor, maple syrup and maple sugar candy, especially plentiful in the northern states of Vermont, New Hampshire, and Maine, fit the bill. Many coastal souvenir shops carry beautiful replicas of whalebone scrimshaw carvings. Regional arts and crafts can be found everywhere. Some of

New England's best-known shopping is in factory outlet stores in Freeport and Kittery, Maine, and North Conway, New Hampshire, where brand-name goods are sold at a discount. The region's best and most varied shopping is found in Boston. Long known as an excellent center for antiques, books, and quality clothing, the shopping options have evolved to become vibrant and eclectic.

Large glass atrium of the busy Shops at Prudential Center in Boston

store, the Eataly Italian gourmet complex, and many specialty stores. The city's most upscale shopping destination, **Heritage on the Garden** looks out over Boston's Public Garden, and features the boutiques of top European designers, fine jewelers, and stores selling other luxury goods.

Outside the center of town, across the Charles River, **Cambridgeside Galleria** has over 120 stores and a pond-side food court. For last-minute purchases, **Boston America!** at Logan Airport Terminal B has Boston-themed gifts and souvenirs.

Sales

There are two major sale seasons in New England. In July, summer clothes go on sale to make room for fall fashions, and in January, winter clothing and merchandise is cleared after the holidays. Most stores also have a sale section or clearance rack throughout the year.

Payment and Taxes

Major credit cards and traveler's checks with identification are accepted at most stores. Sales tax in the New England states ranges from 5.5 to 7 percent. In some states, clothing items may be exempt. New Hampshire is unique in that it has no sales tax.

Opening Hours

Most stores open at 10am and close at 6pm from Monday to Saturday, and from noon to 5pm or 6pm on Sunday. Many stores

stay open later on Thursday nights, and major department stores often stay open until 9pm during the week. Weekday mornings are the best times to shop. Saturdays, lunch hours and evenings can be very busy.

Shopping Malls in Boston

Shopping malls – clusters of stores, restaurants, and food courts all within one complex – have become top destinations for shopping, offering variety, dining, and entertainment. With long winters and a fair share of bad weather, New Englanders flock to malls to shop, eat, and, in the case of teenagers, simply hang out.

Copley Place, with its elegant restaurants and more than 75 stores over two levels, is based around a dazzling 60-ft (18-m) atrium and waterfall. Across a pedestrian overpass, **Shops at Prudential Center** encompasses Saks Fifth Avenue department

Department Stores in Boston

Boston's major department stores offer a large and varied selection of clothing, accessories, cosmetics, housewares, and gifts. Some also have restaurants and beauty salons, and provide a variety of personal services. **Macy's**, a branch of the legendary New

An elegant display of contemporary fashion at Barneys New York

York emporium, anchors Downtown Crossing *(see p74)*, a bustling shopping district between Boston Common and the Financial District. It offers fashions, cosmetics, housewares, and furnishings. Also in the area is a branch of **H&M**, the Swedish chain that offers the latest styles at bargain prices, and a number of smaller stores, including many that sell jewelry.

Heading uptown, through Boston Common and Public Garden to Boylston Street, you can spot the Prudential Tower, centerpiece of a once nondescript but fully revitalized complex of stores, offices, and restaurants. It includes the venerable **Saks Fifth Avenue**, which caters to its upscale clientele with renowned service, a luxurious ambience, and strikingly stylish displays. For the ultimate high-fashion, high-profile shopping experience, stop by **Neiman Marcus (NM)** in Copley Place, which specializes in haute couture, precious jewelry, furs, and gifts. The store is known for its Christmas catalog, with gift suggestions that have included authentic Egyptian mummies, vintage airplanes, a pair of $2-million diamonds, and robots to help out around the house.

Sign for Brattle Book Shop

Contrasting Manhattan chic against NM's Texas cheekiness, is **Barneys New York**, a large-scale outlet of the premier New York retail trendsetter. Not only can shoppers sample exotic perfumes inside "smelling columns," they can rely on the in-store concierge to book their theater tickets and make dinner reservations. Next door is **Lord & Taylor**, well-known for its classic American designer labels, junior and children's departments, and menswear. The store also carries a range of crystal, china, and gifts. Shoppers looking for bargains in the Back Bay should try **Marshalls**, which carries clothing for men, women, and children.

Near Fenway Park, the Target corporation opened its first **CityTarget** store on the East Coast in 2015 to cater to urbanites who are looking for fashionable clothing and small goods at reasonable prices.

Specialty Districts in Boston

From the fashionable boutiques to the many stores selling cosmopolitan home furnishings or ethnic treasures, to the varied

Boutiques of trendy Newbury Street

art and crafts galleries, Boston has evolved to cater to every shopping need. Charles Street has been one of the nation's leading centers of fine antiques for generations, while Newbury Street is known for couture and art galleries. A younger and more trendy gallery scene has emerged in the SoWa (south of Washington Street) section of the South End.

Home decor stores also tend to cluster in the South End, especially along the 1300 block of Washington Street. Shoppers seeking contemporary designer furniture find a treasure trove on the 1000 block of Massachusetts Avenue in Cambridge. Despite the inroads made by online book dealers, Harvard Square retains one of the greatest concentrations of bookstores in the United States *(See Specialty Dealers pp342–3).*

DIRECTORY

Shopping Malls

Boston America!
Terminal B Logan
International Airport,
East Boston.
w massport.com

Cambridgeside Galleria
100 Cambridgeside Pl.,
Cambridge.
Tel (617) 621-8666.

Copley Place
100 Huntington Ave.
Map 3 C3.
Tel (617) 262-2600.
w simon.com

Heritage on the Garden
300 Boylston St. **Map** 4
D2. **Tel** (617) 426-9500.

Shops at Prudential Center
800 Boylston St.
Map 3 B3. **Tel** (800) 746-7778.
w prudentialcenter.com

Department Stores

Barneys New York
5 Copley Place, 100
Huntington Ave. **Map** 3
C3. **Tel** (617) 385-3300.

CityTarget
1341 Boylston St.
Map 3 A3.
Tel (857) 317-5220.

H&M
350 Washington St.
Map 4 F1.
Tel (855) 466-7467.

Lord & Taylor
760 Boylston St.
Map 3 B3.
Tel (617) 262-6000.

Macy's
450 Washington St.
Map 4 F1.
Tel (617) 357-3000.

Marshalls
500 Boylston St.
Map 3 B3.
Tel (617) 262-6066.

Neiman Marcus
5 Copley Place,
100 Huntington Ave.
Map 3 C3.
Tel (617) 536-3660.

Saks Fifth Avenue
Prudential Tower
and Shopping Center.
Map 3 B3.
Tel (617) 262-8500.

Boston Fashion and Antiques

Bostonians have always preferred their traditions reinvigorated with an edge, making both clothing and decorative arts distinct from other parts of the country. While the top national names in apparel are well represented, so are virtual unknowns with fresh ideas. The city is also a major international center for fine arts in craft media as well as home to the region's top purveyors of antiques – some of which were made right here in Boston.

Men's Fashion

Gentlemen seeking the quintessential New England look should head to **Brooks Brothers** on Newbury Street, longtime purveyors of traditional, high-quality menswear. America's foremost fashion house, **Polo/Ralph Lauren** offers top-quality and high-priced sporting and formal attire, while **Jos. A. Bank Clothiers** sells private label merchandise as well as major brands at discounted prices. Professors and students alike patronize the venerable **Andover Shop** and **J. Press** in Cambridge for top-quality Ivy League essentials.

Women's Fashion

No woman need leave Boston empty-handed, whether her taste is for the haute couture of **Chanel** or the earthy ethnic clothing at **Nomad**. Newbury Street's high-fashion boutiques include **Kate Spade, Betsy Jenney**, and **Max Mara**. A branch of British retailer **Barbour** offers clothing for city and country wear. On Boylston Street, **Ann Taylor** is the first choice for modern career clothes, while **Talbots**, a Boston institution, features enduring classics.

Other Cambridge shops include **Tess & Carlos**, known for its pricey designer clothing; **Settebello**, with its elegant European apparel and accessories; and **Clothware**, which emphasizes natural fiber clothing by local designers.

Discount and Vintage Clothes

First among discount chains is **Marshall's**, promising "brand names for less" and offering bargains on clothing, shoes, and

accessories. Trendsetters head to **H&M**, the popular Swedish retailer, for the latest fashions for adults and kids.

Vintage aficionados love the vast collections at **Bobby from Boston**, a longtime costume source for Hollywood and top fashion designers. **Keezer's** has provided generations of Harvard students with used tuxedos and tweed sports jackets. **Second Time Around**, with locations in both Boston and Cambridge, offers a select array of top-quality, gently worn contemporary women's clothing.

Shoes and Accessories

Many Boston stores specialize in accessories. **Helen's Leather** is known for jackets, briefcases, purses, and shoes, as well as Western boots. At Downtown Crossing, **Foot Paths** carries a range of casual shoes from major manufacturers. Stylish Spanish shoes and bags are the specialty at **Stuart Weitzman** at Copley Place, while the adventurous will find more unusual shoes at **Berk's** and **The Tannery** in Cambridge.

For sports gear, **Niketown** shows video reruns of sports events while shoppers peruse the latest designs in clothing and footwear. Visitors don't mind going out of the way for huge discounts on athletic and street shoes and apparel at the **New Balance Factory Outlet** store.

Antiques

There are several multi-dealer antiques emporiums in town. **The Boston Antique Company** searches local estates for tableware, art, jewelry, and vintage corkscrews. In Cambridge, **Cambridge**

Antique Market encompasses more than 150 dealers, offering antiques, collectibles, furniture, jewelry and more.

Charles Street, Boston's antiques mecca, also features specialty shops for those with specific tastes. Collectors of fine Asian antiques should not miss **Alberts-Langdon, Inc.** and **Judith Dowling Asian Art**, for everything from screens and scrolls to lacquerware, ceramics, and paintings.

Antique jewelry is a specialty at **Marika's Antiques Shop**, along with paintings, porcelain, glass, and silver. **Twentieth Century Ltd.** excels in glittery costume jewelry from top designers.

Danish Country carries Scandinavian furniture, while **JMW Gallery**, near South Station, specializes in 19th- and early 20th-century American objects associated with the Arts and Crafts movement. Call ahead for an appointment.

Fine Crafts

Collectors with a more contemporary bent will find several distinguished galleries with a wide variety of American crafts. **Mobilia** in Cambridge has a national reputation for its jewelry, ceramics, and other objects. The **Society of Arts and Crafts**, established in 1897, has a shop and gallery, with exhibits from the 350 artists it represents. The **Cambridge Artists' Cooperative**, owned and run by over 200 artists, offers an eclectic collection ranging from hand-painted silk jackets to ornaments and jewelry. **Mudflat Gallery** is a showcase for the work of almost 50 ceramic artists.

Specialty Dealers

There are shops specializing in everything from posters to rare books, early maps to tribal rugs. Top-brand and vintage watches are a specialty at **European Watch Co.**, while the **Bromfield Pen Shop** has been the purveyor of new, antique, and limited edition pens since 1948. For vintage posters from the 19th and 20th centuries, try **International Poster Gallery** on Newbury Street. **Brattle Book Shop** has a huge selection of used, out-of-print and rare books, magazines, and vintage photographs. **Eugene Galleries** features antiquarian maps, prints, and etchings, as well as a comprehensive selection of books. Harvard Square is one of the best places in the United States for bookstores. Specialists abound, including the legendary **Grolier Poetry Book Shop**, and the comic book and graphic novel specialist **Million Year Picnic**. The **Harvard Coop Bookstore** has a nearly encyclopedic selection of new books, while **Harvard Bookstore** offers used and remaindered books in addition to a wide range of carefully chosen new titles.

DIRECTORY

Men's Fashion

Andover Shop
22 Holyoke St.,
Cambridge.
Tel (617) 876-4900.

Brooks Brothers
46 Newbury St.
Map 4 D2.
Tel (617) 267-2600.

J. Press
82 Mount Auburn St.,
Cambridge.
Tel (617) 547-9886.

Jos. A. Bank Clothiers
399 Boylston St.
Map 4 D2.
Tel (617) 536-5050.

Polo/Ralph Lauren
93/95 Newbury St. **Map** 3
C2. **Tel** (617) 424-1124.

Women's Fashion

Ann Taylor
800 Boylston St. **Map** 3
B3. **Tel** (617) 421-9097.

Barbour
79 Newbury St. **Map** 4
D2. **Tel** (617) 375-7829.

Betsy Jenney
114 Newbury St. **Map** 3
C2. **Tel** (617) 536-2610.

Chanel
6 Newbury St. **Map** 4 D2.
Tel (617) 859-0055.

Clothware
1773 Massachusetts
Ave., Cambridge.
Tel (617) 661-6441.

Kate Spade
117 Newbury St. **Map** 3
C2. **Tel** (617) 262-2632.

Max Mara
69 Newbury St. **Map** 3 C2.
Tel (617) 267-9775.

Nomad
1741 Massachusetts Ave.,
Cambridge.
Tel (617) 497-6677.

Settebello
52 Brattle St., Cambridge.
Tel (617) 864-2440.

Talbots
500 Boylston St. **Map** 3 C2.
Tel (617) 262-2981.

Tess & Carlos
20 Brattle St., Cambridge.
Tel (617) 864-8377.

Discount and Vintage Clothes

Bobby from Boston
19 Thayer St. **Map** 4 E4.
Tel (617) 423-9299.

H&M
350 Washington St. **Map**
4 F1. **Tel** (617) 482-7001.
100 Newbury St. **Map** 3
C2. **Tel** (855) 466-7467.

Keezer's
140 River St., Cambridge.
Tel (617) 547-2455.

Marshall's
500 Boylston St. **Map** 3
C2. **Tel** (617) 262-6066.

Second Time Around
176 Newbury St. **Map** 3
B2. **Tel** (617) 247-3504. 8
Eliot St., Cambridge.
Tel (617) 491-7185.

Shoes and Accessories

Berk's
50 John F. Kennedy St.,
Cambridge.
Tel (617) 492-9511.

Foot Paths
415 Washington St. **Map**
4 F1. **Tel** (617) 338-6008.

Helen's Leather
110 Charles St. **Map** 1 B3.
Tel (617) 742-2077.

New Balance Factory Outlet
173 Market St., Brighton.
Tel (617) 779-7429.

Niketown
200 Newbury St. **Map** 3
B2. **Tel** (617) 267-3400.

Stuart Weitzman
Copley Place. **Map** 3 C3.
Tel (617) 266-8699.

The Tannery
39 Brattle St., Cambridge.
Tel (617) 491-1811.

Antiques

Alberts-Langdon, Inc.
135 Charles St. **Map** 1 B3.
Tel (617) 523-5954.

The Boston Antique Company
119 Charles St. **Map** 1 B3.
Tel (617) 227-9810.

Cambridge Antique Market
201 Msgr. O'Brien Hwy,
Cambridge.
Tel (617) 868-9655.

Danish Country
138 Charles St. **Map** 1 B3.
Tel (617) 227-1804.

JMW Gallery
144 Lincoln St. **Map** 4 F2.
Tel (617) 338-9097.

Judith Dowling Asian Art
133 Charles St. **Map** 1 B3.
Tel (617) 523-5211.

Marika's Antiques Shop
130 Charles St. **Map** 1 B3.
Tel (617) 523-4520.

Twentieth Century Ltd.
73 Charles St. **Map** 1 B4.
Tel (617) 742-1031.

Fine Crafts

Cambridge Artists' Cooperative
59A Church St.,
Cambridge.
Tel (617) 868-4434.

Mobilia
358 Huron Ave.,
Cambridge.
Tel (617) 876-2109.

Mudflat Gallery
36 White St., Cambridge.
Tel (617) 491-7976.

Society of Arts and Crafts
175 Newbury St.
Map 3 B2.
Tel (617) 266-1810.

Specialty Dealers

Brattle Book Shop
9 West St. **Map** 1 C4.
Tel (617) 542-0210.

Bromfield Pen Shop
5 Bromfield St. **Map** 1 C4.
Tel (617) 482-9053.

Eugene Galleries
76 Charles St. **Map** 1 B4.
Tel (617) 227-3062.

European Watch Co.
232 Newbury St.
Map 3 B2.
Tel (617) 262-9798.

Grolier Poetry Book Shop
6 Plympton St.,
Cambridge.
Tel (617) 547-4648.

Harvard Bookstore
1256 Massachusetts Ave.,
Cambridge.
Tel (617) 661-1515.

Harvard Coop Bookstore
1400 Massachusetts Ave.,
Cambridge.
Tel (617) 499-2000.

International Poster Gallery
205 Newbury St.
Map 3 B2.
Tel (617) 375-0076.

Million Year Picnic
99 Mt. Auburn St.,
Cambridge.
Tel (617) 492-6763.

Shopping in New England

Although New England does not immediately conjure up images of unrestrained shopping, in reality there are bargains to be had on a huge variety of consumer goods as well as regional specialties. With a few notable exceptions including Boston (see pp310–4), the greatest concentration of stores generally occurs outside the downtown area, usually along the highways at the outskirts of town. Some of New England's best-known shopping experiences occur at the factory outlet stores in Freeport and Kittery in Maine, and North Conway in New Hampshire, where brand-name clothing and other goods are offered at discount prices.

Shopping Malls

With free parking and a wide range of stores gathered under one roof, malls are popular throughout the region. Here you can find fashions for the whole family, home furnishings, electronic goods, books, toys, music, beauty products, jewelry, sporting goods, food courts, and virtually anything else you could need.

Large department stores are increasingly serving as anchor stores to mall complexes. These "magnet" stores include upscale retailers such as Seattle-based Nordstrom, Lord & Taylor, and branches of Manhattan retail giant Macy's. For widest appeal, these pricey emporiums often share mall space with popular discount chains such as J. C. Penney, Kohl's, big-box electronics retailer Best Buy, and Sears.

The **Natick Mall**, New England's largest shopping complex, is located 15 miles (24 km) from Boston. In addition to 250 stores, the sprawling complex includes condominiums, multiple dining options, and plenty of parking space. **The Arcade** in Providence, Rhode Island, is considered the first indoor marketplace in America. **Providence Place**, a 566,300-sq-ft (52,600-sq-m) shopping complex in the heart of the city, has over 170 stores. Highlights include one of New England's few Nordstrom department stores, an IMAX theater and Dave & Buster's, a combination restaurant and amusement arcade.

Downtown Hartford, Connecticut, has been overshadowed by nearby malls. Only 7 miles (11.2 km) southwest,

Westfarms Mall boasts 160 shops, including the first Nordstrom in New England as well as Lord & Taylor for those with deep pockets. Twelve miles (19 km) east of Hartford, **The Shoppes at Buckland Hills**, one of the state's biggest and most successful malls, caters to families by offering a play area for children and a carousel in the large food court. The success of the mall has attracted many other retailers to the surrounding area. In an ironic nod to the past, **Evergreen Walk** is a recreation of a typical main street, lined with housewares shops such as Pottery Barn and Williams Sonoma; fashion retailers such as The Gap, J. Jill, and Talbots; and restaurants and ice-cream shops. For a different kind of experience, **Olde Mistick Village** in Mystic, Connecticut is designed to resemble a colonial village, with more than 40 shops and restaurants set among duck ponds and gardens. Along with clothing and household items, merchandise ranges from scrimshaw carvings to Christmas ornaments, from Irish imports to folk art.

In New Hampshire, options include the **Mall of New Hampshire** in Manchester with about 125 specialty stores as well as J. C. Penney, Sears, and Macy's anchor shops and the somewhat smaller **Steeplegate Mall** in Concord with about 75 shops. New Hampshire is the only state in New England that does not have a sales tax, making savings on shopping purchases even greater. The **Maine Mall**, only 6 miles (10 km) south of Portland, has not

reduced the lively boutique shopping scene at the Old Port. Nonetheless, it attracts a large crowd to its 140 stores, anchored by Macy's, Best Buy, and The Sports Authority, the country's largest full-line sporting goods dealer. The mall also boasts about 20 eateries.

In bucolic Vermont, the largest mall is **University Mall** in South Burlington, with about 70 shops, including toy and clothing stores for children, anchor stores Sears and J. C. Penney, and a food court.

Travelers looking for a unique shopping environment should visit **Thornes Marketplace** in Northampton, Massachusetts. A Victorian-era department store building was converted into a five-story mall with retailers offering something for everyone: upscale home accessories and clothing, trendy merchandise for college students, ethnic imports, crafts items, and organic foods.

Discount and Outlet Shopping

Dedicated bargain hunters will want to pay a visit to some of New England's famed outlet centers, where many top designers and major brand manufacturers offer late-season and over-stocked clothing and goods at big discounts. Generally sold at 20 to 30 percent less than retail prices, some items can be found reduced by as much as 75 percent. In addition to clothing, outlets are good places to find bargains on kitchen goods, linens, china, glassware, leather goods, luggage and sporting goods.

In Wrentham, Massachusetts, 33 miles (53 km) southwest of Boston, are the **Wrentham Village Premium Outlets**. The stores here sell designer clothing, housewares, and accessories from many leading manufacturers. Serving the upscale Long Island Sound community, the **Tanger Factory Outlet Center** in Westbrook, Connecticut, emphasizes fashion and style in its mix of about 65 shops. **Kittery** (see p282), Maine, is an even larger outlet destination, with about 120 shops lining a 1-mile (1.6-km) stretch of busy Route 1. Merchants offer everything from footwear and designer clothes to sports equipment, perfume, books, china, glass, and gifts. There are also numerous restaurants. Many shoppers prefer **Freeport**, farther up the coast, about a 20-minute drive north of Portland. Outlets, individual shops, and eateries mingle along the streets of the historic village, making it easy to park the car and stroll from Jones New York to J. Crew or to check out leather goods and luggage at Dooney & Bourke or Sea Bags.

The **Manchester Designer Outlets** in Manchester, Vermont, focus on some of the top names in the fashion world, such as Michael Kors, Escada, Giorgio Armani, and BCBG Max Azria, in addition to Jones New York, Polo/Ralph Lauren and Tse for

soft, luxurious cashmere. Other designers to look out for include Kenneth Cole and Kate Spade New York.

Settlers' Green Outlets in North Conway, New Hampshire, was one of the first major outlet centers in the region. The 3-mile (5-km) stretch along Route 16 is lined with factory outlets selling fashion, furniture, and outdoor gear.

Outdoor Outfitters

With mountains to climb, streams to fish, woods to hike, and lakes and oceans to paddle, New England has an abundance of outdoors outfitters who offer everything from custom flyrods to specialized rock-climbing gear. They also sell "outdoors chic" casual clothing for those more interested in looking the part than breaking a sweat. The regional leader in outdoor

sporting equipment (especially hunting and fishing gear) is **L. L. Bean**, which has its flagship store in Freeport, Maine. The hunting and fishing section is open daily around the clock. The 23,000-sq-ft (2150-sq-m) flagship store of **Orvis** in Manchester, Vermont (see p245), sits on the company's extensive campus, where visitors can tour the adjacent signature flyrod factory or practice flycasting in company trout ponds. **REI Boston** has outdoor gear for all seasons, including equipment for rent, and it operates outdoor classes for all levels. **Eastern Mountain Sports** focuses on climbing, trekking, mountain biking, and kayaking. Its flagship store is located in Peterborough, New Hampshire. Outdoor stores at the North Conway Factory Outlets include Eddie Bauer, Norm Thompson, and Chuck Roast who sell warm and durable winter outerwear.

Antiques, Crafts, Books, and Country Stores in New England

While the highway-side shopping centers are the focus of mercantile New England, the goods closely associated with the region are more likely to be found in shops along the byways or in the villages. Visitors looking for gifts with a regional flavor might consider maple syrup, found widely in Vermont and New Hampshire. Coastal shops often have excellent reproductions of scrimshaw whalebone carvings. The nostalgia-oriented country stores often sell the most typical goods of the region, from freshly ground cornmeal to carved wooden toys.

Antiques and Flea Markets

Perhaps the region's most famous antiquing event is the thrice-yearly Brimfield Antique Show (see p165) in Brimfield, Massachusetts. On Cape Cod, scenic Route 6 is peppered with antique shops, especially the charming towns of Dennis and Brewster. Up to 200 dealers fill the parking lot of the **Wellfleet Drive-In Theater** for the flea market on weekends from May through mid-October. The towns of the southern Berkshires are also known for antiquing. **Great Barrington Antiques Center** and the **Emporium Antique Center** cover a broad range of Americana. In Sheffield, **Painted Porch Country Antiques** displays rustic antiques from France, England, and Canada in decorator settings.

Shops continue as Route 7 crosses the border to Vermont. This state's largest antiques emporia is **Vermont Antique Mall** at Quechee Gorge Village, with more than 450 booths.

Connecticut's Litchfield Hills is another antiques hotbed. The town of Woodbury has dozens of high-quality shops, including **Country Loft Antiques**, which sells many wine implements. The **New Woodbury Antiques and Flea Market** operates on Saturdays all year, selling a wide range of new and collectible merchandise. The former mill town of Putnam has reinvented itself as an antiques center. Chief among the shops is **Antiques Marketplace**.

In Rhode Island, go to Spring Street and lower Thames Street in Newport for a variety of shops with select, upmarket merchandise. One of the state's largest flea markets is held on weekends from April through October at Charlestown's **General Stanton Inn**. Up to 200 dealers offer a wide range of antiques and collectibles.

In Maine, Route 1 between Kittery and Scarborough is lined with antiques shops and one of the largest is **Arundel Antiques** with more than 200 dealers. The seafaring town of Searsport has a mix of multi-dealer shops and weekend flea markets. In season, **Hobby Horse Flea Market** features indoor and outdoor stalls. For nautical antiques, quilts, and old tools, visit **Pumpkin Patch Antiques Center**.

New Hampshire's antiquing areas include Route 4 between Concord and Durham, Route 101A in Milford, and Route 119 in Fitzwilliam. The highly regarded **Northeast Auctions** conducts five major auctions a year in Manchester and Portsmouth, as well as smaller estate sales. The **Londonderry Flea Market** operates on weekends from mid-April through October.

Crafts Galleries

New Hampshire has the region's best-established program to support local craftspeople. The **League of New Hampshire Craftsmen** was founded in 1932 and its annual fair in early August is one of the most important in the region. The League also operates seven crafts galleries throughout the state.

The **Frog Hollow Vermont State Craft Center** began modestly in 1971 by offering pottery classes for children. Now it offers a wide array of programs and operates a gallery that displays traditional and contemporary work by about 250 Vermont artisans.

In Connecticut, the **Brookfield Craft Center** was founded in 1954. It offers classes, and showcases the work of American craftspeople through its exhibitions and gallery.

Fifteen Maine potters have formed a collective to market their work through the **Maine Potters Market** in Portland. The functional and decorative pieces represent a wide range of styles and colors. Nearby **Abacus American Craft Gallery** displays the work of American artists, including many from New England.

The Berkshire Hills of Massachusetts are home to many crafts artists, including ceramist Thomas Hoadley. His work and that of other local and national artists is displayed in the **Hoadley Gallery**.

Book Dealers

Specialists in antiquarian and used books abound in New England, but few stores have the variety of out-of-print volumes – especially of cookbooks and culinary titles – as **New England Mobile Book Fair**. For sheer volume of used books, check out **Old Number Six Book Depot** in Henniker, New Hampshire, or **Big Chicken Barn Books** in Ellsworth, Maine. Illustrated books and Vermontiana are specialties of **Monroe Street Books** in Middlebury, Vermont, while **Harbor Books** in Old Saybrook, Connecticut, has a broad range of new and used nautical books. **Tyson's Old & Rare Books** in Swansea, Massachusetts, specializes in American history, nautical themes, and Native American literature.

Country Stores

New England's country stores offer an old-fashioned atmosphere and specialize in local foods: honey, maple syrup, cheese, mustards, and jams. At **Brown & Hopkins Country Store** in Chepachet, Rhode Island, well-worn pine planks line the floors and a glass case of penny candy sits by the door. The **Williamsburg General Store** in Williamsburg, Massachusetts, is located in an 1870 building and offers delicious baked goods as well as kitchen tools, herbs, spices, mustards, jellies, and syrups. In Vermont, the **Weston Village Store** has a pressed tin ceiling and scuffed wooden floors. Sturdy pottery, weathervanes, and wooden bowls supplement the wide selection of cheese and fudge. The **Vermont Country Store** sells outdoor clothing, quirky but useful gadgets, and local foodstuffs. In Sugar Hill, New Hampshire, **Harman's Cheese & Country Store** is known for its aged white cheddar. **The Old Country Store and Museum** in Moultonborough also offers cheddar cheese, along with cast-iron cookware.

DIRECTORY

Antiques and Flea Markets

Antiques Marketplace
109 Main St., Putnam, CT.
Tel (860) 928-0442.
W putnamantiques.com

Arundel Antiques
Route 1, Arundel, ME.
Tel (207) 985-7965.

Country Loft Antiques
557 Main St. S., Woodbury, CT. **Tel** (203) 266-4500.
W countryloftantiques. com

Emporium Antique Center
319 Main St., Great Barrington, MA. **Tel** (413) 528-1660. W emporium antiquecenter.com

General Stanton Inn Flea Market
4115 Old Post Rd., Charlestown, RI. **Tel** (401) 364-1818. W general stantoninn.com

Great Barrington Antiques Center
964 S. Main St., Great Barrington, MA. **Tel** (413) 644-8848. W great barringtonantiques center.com

Hobby Horse Flea Market
383 Main St., Searsport, ME. **Tel** (207) 548-2981.
W hobbyhorseflea market.com

Londonderry Flea Market
RR 102 Londonderry, NH.
Tel (603) 883-4196.
W londonderryflea market.com

New Woodbury Antiques and Flea Market
44 Sherman Hill Rd., Woodbury, CT.
Tel (203) 263-6217.
W thenewwoodbury fleamarket.com

Northeast Auctions
W northeastauctions. com

Painted Porch Country Antiques
102 S. Main St., Sheffield, MA. **Tel** (413) 229-2700.
W paintedporch.com

Pumpkin Patch Antiques Center
15 W. Main St., Searsport, ME. **Tel** (207) 548-6047.

Vermont Antique Mall
Route 4, Quechee, VT.
Tel (802) 281-4147.
W vermontantique mall.com

Wellfleet Drive-In Theater Flea Market
Route 6, Wellfleet, MA.
Tel (508) 349-0541.
W wellfleetcinemas.com

Crafts Galleries

Abacus American Craft Gallery
44 Exchange St., Portland, ME.
Tel (207) 772-4880.
W abacusgallery.com

Brookfield Craft Center
286 Whisconier Rd., Brookfield, CT.
Tel (203) 775-4526.
W brookfield craft.org

Frog Hollow Vermont State Craft Center
85 Church St., Burlington, VT. **Tel** (802) 863-6458.
W froghollow.org

Hoadley Gallery
21 Church St., Lenox, MA.
Tel (413) 637-2814.
W hoadleygallery.com

League of New Hampshire Craftsmen
32 Main St., Center Sandwich, NH. **Tel** (603) 284-6831 (May–Oct only).
W nhcrafts.org
36 N. Main St., Concord, NH. **Tel** (603) 228-8171.
13 Lebanon St., Hanover, NH. **Tel** (603) 643-5050.
81 Main St., Littleton, NH.
Tel (603) 444-1099.
279 Daniel Webster Hwy., Meredith, NH. **Tel** (603) 279-7920.
98 Main St., Nashua, NH.
Tel (603) 595-8233. (May–Oct only.)
2526 White Mountains Hwy./Route 16. North Conway, NH. **Tel** (603) 356-2441.

Maine Potters Market
376 Fore St., Portland, ME.
Tel (207) 774-1633.
W mainepotters market.com

Book Dealers

Big Chicken Barn Books
1768 Bucksport Rd., Ellsworth, ME.
Tel (207) 667-7308.

Harbor Books
146 Main St., Old Saybrook, CT.
Tel (860) 388-6850.

Monroe Street Books
70 Monroe St. (Route 7 N.), Middlebury, VT.
Tel (802) 398-2200.

New England Mobile Book Fair
82–84 Needham St., Newton Highlands, MA.
Tel (617) 527-5817.

Old Number Six Book Depot
166 Depot Hill Rd., Henniker, NH.
Tel (603) 428-3334.

Tyson's Old & Rare Books
301 Seaview Ave., Swansea, MA.
Tel (508) 567-5795.

Country Stores

Brown & Hopkins Country Store
1179 Putnam Pike, Chepachet, RI.
Tel (401) 568-4830.

Harman's Cheese & Country Store
1400 Route 117, Sugar Hill, NH.
Tel (603) 823-8000.

The Old Country Store and Museum
1011 Whittier Hwy., Moultonborough, NH.
Tel (603) 476-5750.

Vermont Country Store
Route 100, Weston, VT.
Tel (802) 824-3184.

Weston Village Store
Route 100, Weston, VT.
Tel (802) 824-5477.

Williamsburg General Store
12 Main St., Williamsburg, MA. **Tel** (413) 268-3036.

ENTERTAINMENT IN BOSTON

From avant-garde performance art to serious drama, and from popular dance music to live classical performances, Boston offers an outstanding array of entertainment options, with something to appeal to every taste: the Theater District offers many excellent plays and musicals; the Wang Theatre hosts many touring productions; and Symphony Hall is home of the renowned Boston Symphony Orchestra. Boston is also well acquainted with jazz, folk, and blues, as well as being a center for more contemporary music, played in big city nightclubs. In summer, entertainment often heads outdoors, with many open-air plays and concerts, such as the famous Boston Pops at the Hatch Shell.

Practical Information

The best sources for information on current films, concerts, theater, dance, and exhibitions include the arts and entertainment sections of the *Boston Globe*, *Boston Herald*, and *Improper Bostonian*. Even more up-to-date listings can be found on the Internet at the following sites: www.bostonmagazine.com; www.boston.com; and www.bostonusa.com.

Boston. For advance tickets these are **Ticketmaster** and **Live Nation**. Tickets can be purchased from both of these agencies over the telephone, in person, or online.

Half-price tickets to the majority of non-commercial arts events as well as to some commercial productions are available from 10am on the day of the performance or 11am on Sundays at **BosTix** booths. Purchases must be made in person. BosTix also sells discount tickets in advance. Special Boston entertainment discount vouchers, available from hotel lobbies and tourist offices, may also offer savings on some shows.

Boston entertainment listings magazines

Booking Tickets

Tickets to popular musicals, theatrical productions, and touring shows often sell out far in advance, although theaters sometimes have a few returns or restricted-view tickets available. You can either get tickets in person at theater box offices, or use one of the ticket agencies in

Districts and Venues

Musicals, plays, comedies, and dance are generally performed at venues in the Theater District,

Tchaikovsky's *Nutcracker*, danced by the Boston Ballet *(see pp350–51)*

although larger noncommercial theater companies are distributed throughout the region, many being associated with colleges and universities.

The area around the intersection of Massachusetts and Huntington Avenues hosts a concentration of outstanding concert venues, including Symphony Hall, Berklee Performance Center at Berklee College of Music, and Jordan Hall at the New England Conservatory of Music.

Many nightclub and dance venues are on Lansdowne and nearby streets by Fenway Park and around Boylston Place in the Theater District. The busiest areas for bars and small clubs offering live jazz and rock music are Central and Harvard Squares in Cambridge, Davis Square in Somerville, and Allston. The principal gay scene in Boston is found in the South End, with many of the older bars and clubs in neighboring Bay Village.

Boston's Symphony Orchestra performing at Symphony Hall *(see pp350–51)*

Open-Air and Free Entertainment

The best free outdoor summer entertainment in Boston is found at the **Hatch Shell** *(see p100)*. The Boston Pops *(see p350)* performs here frequently during the week around July 4, and all through July and August jazz, pop, rock, and classical music is played. On Friday evenings from late June to the week before Labor Day, the Hatch Shell also shows free big-screen family films.

City Hall Plaza and Copley Plaza have free concerts at lunchtimes and in the evenings. Other free open-air entertainment includes productions of Shakespeare on the Boston Common in July and August, sponsored by **Commonwealth Shakespeare**, and concerts by artists from the Berklee College of Music at the **Institute of Contemporary Art** *(see p90)*.

Free open-air music concert outside Boston City Hall *(see p84)*

Entrance to the Shubert Theatre *(see p75)*

Most of the annual concerts and recitals of the **New England Conservatory of Music** *(see pp350–51)* are free, although some require advance booking.

Faneuil Hall Marketplace has a regular schedule of street performers, but Harvard Square is even better known for its nightly and weekend scene of musicians and other performers. Many recording artists paid their dues here, and hopefuls still flock to the square in hope of being discovered – or at least of earning the cost of dinner.

In the summer months, the **Blue Hills Bank Pavilion**, on the waterfront, hosts jazz, pop, and country music concerts. The **Museum of Fine Arts** *(see pp110–13)* hosts summer concerts in its courtyard. The **Isabella Stewart Gardner Museum** *(see p109)* presents classical, new music, and jazz performances from fall through spring.

Disabled Access

Many entertainment venues in Boston are wheelchair-accessible. **Very Special Arts Massachusetts** offers a full Boston arts access guide. Some places, such as **Jordan Hall**, the **Emerson Cutler Majestic Theatre**, and the **Wheelock Family Theatre**, have listening aids for the hearing impaired, while the latter also has signed and described performances.

DIRECTORY

Booking Tickets

BosTix
Faneuil Hall Marketplace.
Map 2 D3. Copley Sq.
Map 3 C2.
Tel (617) 262-8632.
W bostix.org

Live Nation
1 Hamilton Pl.
Map 1 C4. Various outlets.
Tel (800) 745-3000.
W livenation.com

Ticketmaster
Various outlets.
Tel (866) 448-7849.
W ticketmaster.com

Open-Air/Free Entertainment

Blue Hills Bank Pavilion
290 Northern Ave., South Boston. **Map** 2 F5.
Tel (617) 728-1600.
W bluehillsbank pavilion.net

Commonwealth Shakespeare
Parkman Bandstand, Boston Common. **Map** 1 C4. **Tel** (617) 426-0863.
W commshakes.org

Hatch Shell
Charles River Esplanade.
Map 3 C1.
W hatchshell.com

Institute of Contemporary Art
100 Northern Ave.
Map 2 E5.
Tel (617) 478-3100.
W icaboston.org

Isabella Stewart Gardner Museum
25 Evans Way.
Tel (617) 278-5156.
W isgm.org

Museum of Fine Arts
465 Huntington Ave.
Tel (617) 267-9300.
W mfa.org

New England Conservatory of Music
290 Huntington Ave.
Tel (617) 585-1260.
W necmusic.edu

Disabled Access

Emerson Cutler Majestic Theatre
219 Tremont St. **Map** 4 E2.
Tel (617) 824-8000.
W cutlermajestic.org

Jordan Hall
30 Gainsborough St.
Tel (617) 585-1260.
W necmusic.edu

Very Special Arts Massachusetts
89 South St. **Map** 4 F2.
Tel (617) 350-7713/6535 (TTY). W vsamass.org

Wheelock Family Theatre
200 Riverway, Brookline.
Tel (617) 879-2300/2150 (TTY). W wheelock familytheatre.org

The Arts in Boston

Although some theaters are closed on Mondays, there is rarely a night in Boston without performing arts. For classical music lovers, the season revolves around the Boston Symphony Orchestra, with many Brahmins (see p67) occupying their grandparents' seats at Symphony Hall. Bostonians are also avid theatergoers, opting for touring musical productions in historic theaters as well as ambitious contemporary drama at repertory theaters. (Occasionally shows preview in Boston before debuting on Broadway.) The prestigious Boston Ballet performs at the Opera House and other smaller venues. With huge student and expat populations, the city also enjoys a healthy cinema scene, with annual film festivals and a number of art-house theaters.

Classical Music and Opera

Two cherished Boston institutions, the **Boston Symphony Orchestra** and its popular-music equivalent, the Boston Pops, have a long history of being led by some of America's finest conductors. The BSO performs a full schedule of concerts at Symphony Hall from October through April. The Boston Pops takes over for May and June, performing at the Charles River Esplanade (see p100) for Fourth of July festivities that are the highlight of the summer season.

The students and faculty of the **New England Conservatory of Music** present more than 450 free classical and jazz performances each year, many in Jordan Hall (see p349). **Boston Lyric Opera** has assumed the task of reestablishing opera in Boston, through small-cast and light opera at venues around the city.

Boston's oldest musical organization is the **Handel & Haydn Society** (H&H), founded in 1815. As the first American producer of such landmark works as Handel's *Messiah* (performed annually since 1818), Bach's *B-Minor Mass* and *St. Matthew Passion*, and Verdi's *Requiem*, H&H is one of the country's musical treasures. Since 1986, the society has focused on performing and recording Baroque and Classical works using the period instruments for which the composers wrote. H&H gives regular performances in Boston at Symphony Hall, Jordan Hall, and other venues.

Classical music is ubiquitous in Boston. **Emmanuel Music**, for example, performs the entire Bach cantata cycle at regular services at Emmanuel Church on Newbury Street. The Isabella Stewart Gardner Museum (see p109) hosts a series of chamber music concerts, continuing a 19th-century tradition of professional "music room" chamber concerts in the homes of the social elite.

The **Celebrity Series of Boston** brings world-famous orchestras, soloists, and dance companies to Boston, often to perform at Jordan Hall and Symphony Hall.

Theater

Though much diminished from its heyday in the 1920s, when more than 40 theaters were in operation throughout Boston, today the city's Theater District (see pp62–75) still contains a collection of some of the most architecturally eminent, and commercially productive, early theaters in the United States. Furthermore, during the 1990s, many of the theaters that are currently in use underwent major programs of restoration to bring them back to their original grandeur, and visitors today are bound to be impressed as they catch a glimpse of these theaters' past glory.

The main, commercially run theaters of Boston – the **Emerson Colonial** and Shubert (see p75) theaters, and the **Opera House** and the Wang Theatre (see p75) – often present Broadway productions that have already premiered in New York and are touring the country. They also present Broadway "tryouts" and local productions.

In stark contrast to some of the mainstream shows on offer in Boston, the most avant-garde contemporary theater in the city is performed at the **American Repertory Theater** (ART), an independent, non-commercial company associated with Harvard University (see pp116–19). ART often premieres new plays, particularly on its second stage, but is best known for its often radical interpretations of traditional and modern classics. By further contrast, the **Huntington Theatre**, allied with Boston University, is widely praised for its traditional direction and interpretation. For example, the Huntington was the co-developer of Pulitzer Prize-winning plays detailing 20th-century African American life, by the late August Wilson, an important chronicler of American race relations.

Several smaller companies, including **Lyric Stage**, devote their energies to showcasing local actors and directors and often premiere the work of Boston-area playwrights. Many of the most adventurous companies perform on one of the four stages at the **Boston Center for the Arts**.

Dance

The city's largest and most popular resident dance company, the **Boston Ballet** performs an ambitious season of classics and new choreography between October and May at the opulent Opera House and other venues. The annual performances of the *Nutcracker* during the Christmas season are a Boston tradition.

The somewhat more modest **José Mateo Ballet Theatre** has developed a strong and impressive body of repertory choreography. The company performs in the neo-Gothic Old Cambridge Baptist Church, which is situated near Harvard Square. Modern dance in Boston is represented by many small companies, collectives, and independent choreographers, who often perform in the **Dance Complex** and **Green Street Studios** in Cambridge. Boston also hosts many other visiting dance companies, who often put on performances at the **Emerson Cutler Majestic Theatre**.

Cinema

Situated in Harvard Square (see p114) close to Harvard Yard, the **Brattle Theater**, one of the very last repertory movie houses in the Greater Boston area, primarily shows classic films on a big screen. For example, the Brattle was instrumental in reviving moviegoers' interest in the Humphrey Bogart, black-and-white classic *Casablanca*. Something of a Harvard institution, the Brattle has long served as a popular "first date" destination.

Serious students of classic and international cinema patronize the screening programs of the **Harvard Film Archive**, for its range of foreign, art, and historical films. The **Kendall Square Cinema** multiplex is the city's chief venue for non-English language films, art films, and documentaries. Multiplex theaters showing mainstream, first-run Hollywood movies are found throughout the Boston area. Some of the most popular are **AMC Loews Boston Common 19**, located at Boston Common, and the **Regal Fenway 13** in the suburb of Brookline.

Tickets for every kind of movie in Boston are often discounted for first shows of the day.

DIRECTORY

Classical Music and Opera

Boston Lyric Opera
Various venues.
Tel (617) 542-6772.
ⓦ blo.org

Boston Symphony Orchestra
Symphony Hall, 301 Massachusetts Ave.
Map 3 A4.
Tel (617) 266-1200, (617) 266-1492.
ⓦ bso.org

Celebrity Series of Boston
Various venues.
Tel (617) 482-6661.
ⓦ celebrityseries.org

Emmanuel Music
Emmanuel Church, 15 Newbury St.
Map 4 D2.
Tel (617) 536-3356.
ⓦ emmanuelmusic.org

Handel & Haydn Society
Various venues.
Tel (617) 266-3605.
ⓦ handelandhaydn.org

New England Conservatory of Music
Jordan Hall, 30 Gainsborough St.
Map 3 A4.
Tel (617) 585-1260.
ⓦ necmusic.edu

Theater

American Repertory Theater
Loeb Drama Center, 64 Brattle St., Cambridge.
Tel (617) 547-8300.
ⓦ amrep.org

Boston Center for the Arts
539 Tremont St.
Map 4 D3.
Tel (617) 933-8600.
ⓦ bcaonline.org

Emerson Colonial Theatre
106 Boylston St.
Map 4 E2.
Tel (617) 482-9393.
ⓦ citicenter.org

Huntington Theatre
264 Huntington Ave.
Map 3 B4.
Tel (617) 266-0800.
ⓦ huntingtontheatre.org

Lyric Stage
140 Clarendon St.
Map 3 C3.
Tel (617) 585-5678.
ⓦ lyricstage.com

Opera House
539 Washington St.
Map 4 E1.
Tel (617) 259-3400.
ⓦ bostonoperahouse.com

Dance

Boston Ballet
Various venues.
Tel (617) 695-6955.
ⓦ bostonballet.org

Emerson Cutler Majestic Theatre
219 Tremont St.
Map 4 E2.
Tel (617) 824-8000.
ⓦ cutlermajestic.org

Dance Complex
536 Massachusetts Ave., Cambridge.
Tel (617) 547-9363.
ⓦ dancecomplex.org

Green Street Studios
185 Green St., Cambridge.
Tel (617) 864-3191.
ⓦ greenstreet studios.org

José Mateo Ballet Theatre
400 Harvard St., Cambridge.
Tel (617) 354-7467.
ⓦ ballettheatre.org

Cinema

AMC Loews Boston Common 19
Boston Common.
Map 4 E2.
Tel (617) 423-5801.
ⓦ amctheatres.com

Brattle Theater
40 Brattle St., Cambridge.
Tel (617) 876-6837.
ⓦ brattlefilm.org

Harvard Film Archive
24 Quincy St., Cambridge.
Tel (617) 495-4700.
ⓦ hcl.harvard.edu/hfa

Kendall Square Cinema
1 Kendall Square, Cambridge.
Tel (617) 621-1202.
ⓦ landmarktheatres.com

Regal Fenway 13
201 Brookline Ave.
Tel (617) 424-6266.

Music Venues in Boston

Boston's mix of young professionals and tens of thousands of college students produces a lively nightlife scene, focused on live music, clubs, and bars. Since the 1920s, Boston has been especially hospitable to jazz, and it still has an interesting jazz scene, with the world-renowned Berklee College of Music playing an important part. Cambridge is an epicenter of folk and acoustic music revivals and alt-rock, while Lansdowne Street (behind Fenway Park) is the main district for rock clubs. Virtually every neighborhood has a selection of friendly bars, many with live music. The city's audiences, considered to be among the country's most eager and receptive, make Boston a must-stop destination for national touring acts.

Rock Music

The **House of Blues** chain of clubs specializing in indoor rock and blues concerts began in Harvard Square in 1992. In 2009, a giant House of Blues opened in the Fenway district. Heavily booked throughout the year with both established and up-and-coming rock and pop acts – many from New England – the venue occasionally offers a popular Sunday brunch that features Southern-style food accompanied by live gospel music. In keeping with this theme, a box of mud from the Mississippi Delta is buried beneath the main stage.

Royale, one of Boston's most popular clubs, offers the occasional big-time concert with international performers including Robyn and Ziggy Marley, but it makes its name by hosting some of the city's most raucous club nights, with world-famous DJs and hordes of scantily clad clubbers.

Located on the edge of Boston University's campus, the **Paradise Rock Club** has long been a local institution (the likes of U2, Coldplay, and the Police have all graced the stage). The front lounge offers a relaxed spot for an inexpensive pre-show meal and sometimes hosts smaller acts.

In a city that's chock full of historical sites, the **Orpheum Theatre** stands out as the oldest concert venue. The original home of the New England Conservatory of Music (see pp350–51) dates back to 1852

and serves as Boston's premier venue for acts that are too big for the clubs but can't quite fill an arena. While the sightlines are above average, the venue loses major points for having a no food or beverage policy in the stands (concertgoers are forced to enjoy their overpriced beers in the stuffy lobby).

Arena-level acts head to the 18,000-seat **TD Garden**, home of the Boston Bruins (NHL) and Celtics (NBA), or Boston University's **Agganis Arena**, which is roughly half the size of the Garden. Come summertime, those same acts head outdoors to play the massive **Xfinity Center** – located 30 miles (48 km) southwest of Boston – and smaller **Blue Hills Bank Pavilion** (see p349), which enjoys scenic skyline views from its South Boston waterfront home.

At the other end of the size spectrum are places like the **Green Dragon Tavern** near Quincy Market, known for its Irish and cover bands; **Midway Café**, in Jamaica Plain, for live local blues and rock; and the **Brighton Music Hall**, a diminutive venue that hosts an assortment of local and national acts.

The Middle East, Cambridge's premier all-purpose club, offers three distinct stages in which to enjoy everything from local folk collectives and belly dancing to national rock acts. The eponymous restaurant provides a relaxed spot for a pre- or post-show drink or snack.

Some Cambridge stalwarts of the alt-rock circuit closed in 2015, but other venues more than compensate. The bare-bones **Lilypad** mixes up punk, jazz, classical, and rock, while **Sinclair** showcases world music, singer-songwriter acts, and small rock bands.

Also located in Cambridge are the **Lizard Lounge** and **Atwood's Tavern**, tiny clubs that host wildly eclectic schedules, and **Plough & Stars** and **Toad**, both of which are popular with local singer-songwriters.

Away from the city center, up-and-coming Somerville is home to **P. A.'s Lounge** and **Sally O'Brien's**, a pair of dive bars that are good for cheap drinks and local rock acts.

Jazz and Blues

As one would expect from one of the nation's most respected music schools, **Berklee Performance Center** houses the best acoustics and sight-lines in Boston. The auditorium hosts everything from jazz legends and big-band revues to contemporary acts. The only drawback is that no food or drink is allowed in the seats.

On a nondescript stretch of Massachusetts Avenue resides **Wally's Cafe**, one of the city's hidden gems. This atmospheric jazz club hosts live music 365 days a year, with bebop, swing, and Afro-Cuban Latin jazz. Now and then professionals pop up, but most lineups comprise students and amateurs. On weekends, there's usually a line.

The majority of national jazz touring acts stick to one of three clubs: **Regattabar** (in Harvard Square's swish Charles Hotel), **Ryles Jazz Club** (in Cambridge's Inman Square), and **Scullers Jazz Club** (in the Doubletree Hotel, on the Brighton-Cambridge border).

Those looking to avoid paying steep cover charges stick to lower-key spots like Central Square's **Cantab Lounge**, Allston's **Wonder Bar**, and **Les Zygomates**, a stylish French bistro in Boston's gentrifying Leather District that hosts free live jazz most nights.

Folk and World Music

Since 1958, Harvard Square has been home to **Club Passim**, one of the country's seminal folk clubs. The small venue held the Northeast's first hootenanny, and has seen everyone from Bob Dylan to Joan Baez play here. **Loretta's Last Call**, near Fenway Park, is Boston's country and cowboy haven, with live bands on weekends, and line dancing, country karaoke, and singer-songwriter nights during the week. There's a live jazz brunch and blues jam on Sunday's. The **Somerville Theatre** is popular with world music acts, while just down the street is **The Burren**, an Irish pub run by musicians that hosts lively sessions. The Museum of Fine Arts' **Remis Auditorium** has wonderful acoustics for world music gigs. International acts ranging from Afro-pop to ska play at large venues across Boston in a concert series presented by promoters **World Music**.

DIRECTORY

Rock Music

Agganis Arena
925 Commonwealth Ave., Boston.
Tel (617) 358-7000.
w bu.edu/agganis

Atwood's Tavern
877 Cambridge St., Cambridge.
Tel (617) 864-2792.
w atwoodstavern.com

Blue Hills Bank Pavilion
290 Northern Ave.
Tel (617) 728-1600.
w bluehillsbank pavilion.net

Brighton Music Hall
158 Brighton Ave., Allston, MA.
Tel (617) 779-0140.
w crossroadspresents. com/brighton-music-hall

Green Dragon Tavern
11 Marshall St.
Tel (617) 367-0055.
w somerspubs.com

House of Blues
13–15 Lansdowne St.
Tel (888) 693-2583.
w houseofblues.com

Lilypad
1353 Cambridge St., Cambridge, MA.
Tel (617) 055-7729.
w lilypadinman.com

Lizard Lounge
1667 Massachusetts Ave., Cambridge, MA.
Tel (617) 547-0759.
w lizard loungeclub. com

The Middle East
472/480 Massachusetts Ave., Cambridge.
Tel (617) 864-3278.
w mideastclub.com

Midway Café
3496 Washington St., Jamaica Plain.
Tel (617) 524-9038.
w midwaycafe.com

Orpheum Theatre
1 Hamilton Place. **Map** 1C4. **Tel** (617) 482-0106.
w crossroadspresents. com/orpheum-theatre

P. A.'s Lounge
345 Somerville Ave., Somerville.
Tel (617) 776-1557.
w paslounge.com

Paradise Rock Club
967 Commonwealth Ave.
Tel (617) 562-8800.
w crossroadspresents. com/paradise-rock-club

Plough & Stars
912 Massachusetts Ave., Cambridge.
Tel (617) 576-0032.
w ploughandstars.com

Royale
279 Tremont St.
Tel (617) 338-7699.
w royaleboston.com

Sally O'Brien's
335 Somerville Ave., Somerville, MA.
Tel (617) 666-3589.
w sallyobriensbar.com

Sinclair
52 Church St., Cambridge, MA **Tel** (617) 547-5200.
w sinclaircambridge. com

TD Garden
1 Causeway St. **Map** 1C2.
Tel (617) 624-1000.
w tdgarden.com

Toad
1912 Massachusetts Ave., Cambridge.
Tel (617) 497-4950.
w toadcambridge.com

Xfinity Center
885 S Main St., Mansfield, MA. **Tel** (508) 339-2331.
w thexfinitycenter.com

Jazz and Blues

Berklee Performance Center
Berklee College of Music, 136 Massachusetts Ave.
Map 3 A3.
Tel (617) 266-7455.
w berkleebpc.com

Cantab Lounge
738 Massachusetts Ave., Cambridge.
Tel (617) 354-2685.
w cantab-lounge.com

Les Zygomates
129 South St.
Tel (617) 542-5108.
w winebar129.com

Regattabar
Charles Hotel, 1 Bennett St., Cambridge.
Tel (617) 395-7757.
w regattabarjazz.com

Ryles Jazz Club
212 Hampshire St., Cambridge.
Tel (617) 876-9330.
w rylesjazz.com

Scullers Jazz Club
Doubletree Guest Suites, 400 Soldiers Field Rd., Brighton.
Tel (617) 562-4111.
w scullersjazz.com

Wally's Cafe
427 Massachusetts Ave.
Tel (617) 424-1408.
w wallyscafe.com

Wonder Bar
186 Harvard Ave., Allston, MA.
Tel (617) 351-2665.
w wonderbarboston. com

Folk and World Music

The Burren
247 Elm St., Somerville, MA.
Tel (617) 776-6896.
w burren.com

Club Passim
47 Palmer St., Cambridge.
Tel (617) 492-7679.
w clubpassim.com

Loretta's Last Call
1 Lansdowne St.
Tel (617) 421-9595.
w lorettaslastcall.com

Remis Auditorium, Museum of Fine Arts
465 Huntington Ave.
Tel (617) 267-9300.
w mfa.org

Somerville Theatre
55 Davis Square, Somerville, MA.
Tel (617) 625-5700.
w somervilletheatre online.com

World Music
Various venues.
Tel (617) 876-4275.
w worldmusic.org

Pubs, Clubs, and Sports Bars

While large-scale events and concerts abound, the regular nightlife of Boston revolves primarily around drinking establishments. The legal drinking age here is 21, and you may be asked to show proof of identification *(see p367)* if you appear to be under 35. Not all bars and clubs are clearly marked, but they can usually be identified by their address and the cluster of smokers puffing away near the entrance in all weather. (Smoking is not permitted in clubs and bars in New England.) Ironically, the window for nightlife is short, as most venues don't liven up until 10pm, and Boston's drinking laws shut off alcohol service at 1am or 2am, depending on the neighborhood.

Sports Bars

Bostonians love sports, and while most bars have at least one game on the television over the bar, hard-core fans want more, and the city's dozens of sports bars oblige with multiple channel offerings. The **Cask 'N' Flagon**, adjacent to Fenway Park (to the west of Back Bay), is perfect for celebrating victory or softening the pain of defeat, while **Jillian's Boston** is just up the street, drawing a mixed-gender crowd for billiards and sports-watching. At **Kings**, big-screen sports televisions vie with bowling lanes, while **Jerry Remy's Sports Bar** has giant, wall-to-wall televisions. The area near North Station is filled with bars catering to Boston Celtics and Boston Bruins fans. One of the most notable is **The Fours**, where the sandwiches are named for sports legends and the memorabilia extends beyond basketball and hockey to boxing and baseball. One of the friendliest neighborhood sports bars of South Boston is the **Boston Beer Garden**, where locals refer to the city's hockey team as the "Broonz."

Pubs and Brewpubs

With the largest per capita population of Irish descendants in the US, it's not surprising that Boston has many Irish pubs, which offer a convivial setting for good hearty food, pints of Guinness and live music. Among these are **Kinsale**, near Government Center, where the entire bar was transported brick by brick from Ireland; the **Phoenix Landing Bar and Restaurant**, a mock Irish pub in Cambridge's Central Square lined with mahogany and screening local and international sports; **The Burren**, which has some of the finest musicians in the city; and the smaller **Druid**, where, as the evening wears on, crowds of young professionals give way to recent Irish immigrants. **The Independent** in Somerville's Union Square is a good place to catch Irish bands, as well as unplugged rock. Darts and stout are the main draws at **The Field**, which is reputed to serve more Guinness on draft than any other bar in the US. The **Plough and Stars** ranks as one of the city's most seriously literary bars. It also features English League football on weekends.

Boston was in the forefront of the national brewpub craze in the 1980s, but of that first wave of artisanal brewers, only **John Harvard's Brew House** in Harvard Square and **Cambridge Brewing Company** in Kendall Square continue to flourish. Successful newcomer **Boston Beer Works** has a built-in clientele by virtue of its location next to Fenway Park and Boston University. No serious drinker or student of Boston history should miss **Doyle's Café**, famous for its continuing role in Boston political campaigns and a flagship bar for nearby Boston Beer Co., which debuts its seasonal Sam Adams brews here.

Gay Clubs and Bars

Boston's gay scene comes into sharpest focus in the South End and Bay Village, but bars and clubs are found throughout the city that hold gay nights. These events are often a staple of otherwise straight nightclubs. **Club Café Bar & Lounge** runs separate front and back dance rooms with different themes every night. Wednesday is Karaoke Kween night, Saturday gets sweaty with a video dance party, and Sunday features an old-fashioned tea dance. A suave cabaret scene can be found in the venue's **Napoleon Room**. Boston's longest-running gay club, **Jacques**, features raucous drag shows and cabarets, as well as occasional karaoke sessions that lure wild crowds. The leather and denim set are drawn to the sociable, mellow Ladder District bar, **The Alley**, and to Boston's largest gay cruise bar, **Machine** in the Fenway. The weekly *Bay Windows* newspaper provides more information, as do other listings.

Nightclubs

Boston has a club for almost every type of dance music. Little happens until at least 11pm. The **Emerald Lounge**, is a swanky hotel venue that attracts crowds with its trendy environs and lively DJ nights. The **Grand Canal** near North Station spins techno and house music for a youthful clientele and has live bands on some weekends. Located in the rear of a stylish downtown restaurant, **Whisky Saigon** draws an upscale crowd with its DJ nights and craft cocktails. More middle-of-the-road is the **Royale** in the Theater District, with classy touches like doormen instead of bouncers, marble walls, and a vast dance floor. On the other side of the river, in Cambridge's Central Square, **Phoenix Landing** features electronica and a frenetic dance floor, while **Middlesex** has a hip (sometimes hip-hop) dance scene.

Comedy Clubs

Many clubs and bars program occasional evenings of stand-up comedy, and several specialize in it. **Nick's Comedy Stop**, on the other hand, tends to focus on homegrown talent, grooming performers who often go on to the "big time." Located in Cambridge's nightlife-busy Central Square, **Improv Boston** mixes audience-participation cabaret, skit comedy, revues, the occasional hootenanny, and even serious theater. The very name of **Improv Asylum** explains it all: lunatic comedy based on audience suggestions. Local comedian Dick Doherty hosts the shenanigans (including open mic nights) at **Dick's Beantown Comedy Vault**. Somewhat edgier laughs from newcomers and television comedy writers can be had at **The Comedy Studio**. National comedy acts and stand-up performances by TV stars are held at the **Wilbur Theatre**.

DIRECTORY

Sports Bars

Boston Beer Garden
732 East Broadway, South Boston.
Tel (617) 269-0990.
W bostonbeergarden.com

Cask 'N' Flagon
62 Brookline Ave.
Tel (617) 536-4840.
W casknflagon.com

The Fours
166 Canal St.
Map 1 C2.
Tel (617) 720-4455.
W thefours.com

Jerry Remy's Sports Bar
1265 Boylston St.
Tel (617) 236-7369.
W jerryremys.com

Jillian's Boston
145 Ipswich St.
Tel (617) 437-0300.
W jilliansboston.com

Kings
50 Dalton St. Map 3 A3.
Tel (617) 266-2695.
W kingsbowlamerica.com

Pubs and Brewpubs

Boston Beer Works
61 Brookline Ave.
Tel (617) 536-2337.
W beerworks.net

The Burren
247 Elm St., Somerville.
Tel (617) 776-6896.
W burren.com

Cambridge Brewing Company
1 Kendall Sq., Building 100.
Tel (617) 494-1994.
W cambrew.com

Doyle's Café
3484 Washington St., Jamaica Plain.
Tel (617) 524-2345.
W doylescafeboston.com

Druid
1357 Cambridge St., Cambridge.
Tel (617) 497-0965.
W druidpub.com

The Field
20 Prospect St. (Central Sq.), Cambridge.
Tel (617) 354-7345.
W thefieldpub.com

The Independent
75 Union Sq., Somerville.
Tel (617) 440-6022.
W theindo.com

John Harvard's Brew House
33 Dunster St., Cambridge.
Tel (617) 868-3585.
W johnharvards.com

Kinsale Irish Pub & Restaurant
2 Center Plaza.
Map 1 C3.
Tel (617) 742-5577.
W classicirish.com

Phoenix Landing Bar and Restaurant
512 Massachusetts Ave., Cambridge.
Tel (617) 576-6260.
W phoenixlandingbar.com

Plough and Stars
912 Massachusetts Ave., Cambridge.
Tel (617) 576-0032.
W ploughandstars.com

Gay Clubs and Bars

The Alley
14 Pi Alley. Map 2 D4.
Tel (617) 263-1449.

Club Café Bar & Lounge
209 Columbus Ave.
Map 4 D3.
Tel (617) 536-0966.

Jacques
79 Broadway.
Map 4 F4.
Tel (617) 426-8902.

Machine
1254 Boylston St.
Tel (617) 536-7950.

Napoleon Room
209 Columbus Ave.
Map 4 D3.
Tel (617) 536-0966.

Nightclubs

Emerald Lounge
200 Stuart St.
Map 2 B5.
Tel (617) 457-2626.
W emeraldnightlife.com

Grand Canal
57 Canal St.
Map 2 D2.
Tel (617) 523-1112.

Middlesex
315 Massachusetts Ave., Cambridge.
Tel (617) 868-6739.
W middlesexlounge.us

Royale
279 Tremont St.
Map 4 E2.
Tel (617) 338-7699.

Whisky Saigon
116 Boylston St.
Tel (617) 482-7799.

Comedy Clubs

The Comedy Studio
Hong Kong Restaurant, 3rd Floor, 1238 Massachusetts Ave., Cambridge.
Tel (617) 661-6507.
W thecomedystudio.com

Dick's Beantown Comedy Vault
184 High St.
Map 2 E4.
Tel (800) 401-2221.
W dickdoherty.com

Improv Asylum
216 Hanover St.
Map 2 D3.
Tel (617) 263-6887.
W improvasylum.com

Improv Boston
40 Prospect St., Cambridge.
Tel (617) 576-1253.

Nick's Comedy Stop
100 Warrenton St.
Tel (617) 963-6261.
W nickscomedystop.com

Wilbur Theatre
246 Tremont St.
Map 4 E2.
Tel (617) 248-9700.
W thewilbur.com

OUTDOOR ACTIVITIES

Squeezed within New England's relatively compact borders there is a wealth of outdoor activities. Mountain ranges, forests, rivers, and miles of coastline have been preserved as natural playgrounds for outdoor enthusiasts ranging from people just looking for a quiet afternoon in the sun to serious backcountry trekkers. While the majority of unspoiled, rugged wilderness is found in the northern states of New Hampshire, Vermont, and Maine, there are still plenty of outdoor adventures to be had in the much more densely populated south. Visitors will find plenty to do on sea and land throughout Massachusetts, Rhode Island, and Connecticut.

Visitors camping on the coast of Maine

Camping

Always a popular activity in New England, camping can also save you money on accommodations – depending on how much you are willing to rough it. While there are designated primitive camping areas in the backcountry of selected national forests, the more established campgrounds make up the majority of sites. Standard campgrounds, usually found in state and national forests, are equipped with facilities such as toilets, garbage disposal, and often facilities for hot showers. The tent sites at such places are usually spaced well apart and cost between $12 and $35 a night. For the hard-core camper, primitive campgrounds found in national forests offer only the bare minimum: rudimentary cooking areas, pit toilets, and cold running water. These sites are perfect for the frugal outdoor enthusiast, usually costing around $10 a night.

On the opposite end of the spectrum, private campgrounds are models of luxury. Most cater to large recreational vehicles (RVs) and motor homes, with running water and electrical hookups. Hot showers and sewage hookups are often provided as well. Many upscale campgrounds have a host of recreational facilities that range from swimming to miniature golf courses. These sites are somewhat more expensive, costing $20 to $40 or more a night.

Government-run campgrounds usually follow the summer season from the end of May through to early October. For the most part, private campgrounds have a much longer season, with some staying open year-round. Regardless of the type of camping that will be done, it is always a good idea to reserve a campground early, especially during the busy summer months. Contact the **National Park Service** or the **National Recreation Reservation Service** for campground information and reservations. As a safety measure, always remember to notify someone of your itinerary and your approximate time of arrival at your destination, should you decide to camp or hike by yourself.

Hiking

Hiking trails crisscross almost all of New England, with the two most popular being the New England section of the **Appalachian Trail** *(see pp26–7)* and Vermont's 265-mile (426-km) Long Trail. Both trails can be quite challenging in spots, with extremely steep mountain climbs to stunning vistas. Maine's Baxter State Park *(see p302)* and New Hampshire's White Mountain National Forest *(see p269)* are both well-known for their extensive networks of demanding trails.

Not all nature walks need be difficult, however. Acadia National Park *(see pp292–3)* in Maine has an excellent system of easier hiking trails that lead past some of the most breathtaking coastal scenery. The **Rails-to-Trails Conservancy**

Boston's Swan Boats offering gentle cruises *(see pp68–9)*

provides information and maps on 1,359 trails along abandoned railroad tracks that have been converted into convenient and accessible paths for cyclists and pedestrians alike. These paths stretch across a vast portion of New England.

In Vermont, **Inn to Inn** provides guides for day hikes or custom multi-day itineraries for groups of four people or more. Trips can be geared to your fitness and experience level.

Easy biking amid New England wildflowers

Hiking at Center Sandwich, New Hampshire

Biking

In addition to the more formal bike paths, the region possesses hundreds of miles of quiet back roads that are a cyclist's paradise. The pastoral scenery is beautiful, but the distances between towns are rarely so great that you will feel isolated. Cape Cod *(see pp158–63)* is famous for its wonderful bike paths, as is Nantucket *(see p157)*, with its network of easy trails leading to pristine beaches. Many people believe that the best way to see Martha's Vineyard *(see pp156–7)*, Block Island *(see pp196–7)*, and the Litchfield Hills *(see pp212–13)* is by bike. Various outfitters such as **VBT** offer organized bike tours for some of New England's most scenic regions, supplying everything from bicycles and protective gear to maps and accommodations.

Mountain bikers also have plenty to choose from. Some ski areas let bikers use their lifts and slopes in the summer, and many of the region's forests are open to biking. Acadia National Park, Mount Desert Island *(see pp292–3)*, and the White *(see p269)* and Green *(see p248)* Mountains all have excellent facilities. To avoid damaging the surrounding environment, mountain bikers should stick to the marked trails. Cyclists should wear helmets and other protective gear.

DIRECTORY

Canoeing and Rafting

Maine Island Trail Association
58 Fore St., Portland, ME 04101. **Tel** (207) 761-8225.
Ⓦ mita.org

Raft Maine
PO Box 78, West Farms, ME 04985.
Tel (800) 723-8633.
Ⓦ raftmaine.com

Hiking and Biking

Appalachian Trail Conservancy
799 Washington St., PO Box 807, Harpers Ferry, WV 25425-0807.
Tel (304) 535-6331.
Ⓦ appalachiantrail.org

Green Mountain Club
4711 Waterbury-Stowe Rd., Waterbury Center, VT 05677.
Tel (802) 244-7037.
Ⓦ greenmountainclub. org

Inn to Inn
52 Park St., Brandon, VT, 05733.
Tel (802) 247-3300 or (800) 838-3301.
Ⓦ inntoinn.com

Rails-to-Trails Conservancy
2121 Ward Ct NW, Washington, DC 20037.
Tel (202) 331-9696.
Ⓦ railstotrails.org

VBT
614 Monkton Rd., Bristol, VT 05443.
Tel (800) 245-3868.
Ⓦ vbt.com

Technical or Rock Climbing

Acadia Mountain Guides Climbing School
92 Main St., Orono, ME 04473 or 228 Main St., Bar Harbor, ME 04609 (summer only).
Tel (888) 232-9559 or (207) 288-8186.
Ⓦ acadiamountain guides.com

New England Climbing
Ⓦ neclimbs.com

Rhinoceros Mountain Guides
55 Mountain View Rd., Campton, NH 03223.
Tel (603) 520-5696.
Ⓦ rhinoguides.com

Fishing

If you like to fish, you will love New England. Deep-sea fishing is best at Point Judith in Rhode Island, where you can rent boats through the **Rhode Island Party and Charterboat Association**. Farther up the coast at Cape Cod, surfcasters test the waters for striped bass and bluefish, which are most plentiful between July and October. Brook trout, walleye, and bass are plentiful in the inland streams and lakes, especially in Maine. Contact the **Maine Sporting Camp Association** for information regarding the state's top fishing camps and lodges. Fly-fishermen seeking to hone their skills can do so in one of the highly regarded programs run by **Orvis** in Manchester, Vermont. Fresh-water fishing licenses are mandatory throughout New England and can be obtained at fishing supply stores.

Turbulent rapids in one of New England's mountain rivers

Canoeing, Kayaking, and White-Water Rafting

Maine is the premier destination for paddlers, beginning with sea kayakers who flock here each summer to ply the waters along the 3,500-mile (5,630-km) coast. One of the state's most popular excursions is the 375-mile (605-km) Maine Island Trail, which goes from Kittery to Canada.

Maine's latticework of rivers is ideal for canoeing, with its most famous trek being down the challenging Allagash Wilderness Waterway *(see p303)*. New Hampshire's Androscoggin River is another demanding waterway best tested by experienced paddlers. Canoeists

Whale-watching on a regional cruise ship

looking for a more leisurely ride can skim across the calm waters of northern New England's lakes and ponds.

White-water rafting is the paddler's roller-coaster ride and, once again, Maine is the region's best theme park. The state's three major rivers, the Penobscot, Kennebec, and Dead, offer gut-wrenching tests of rafters' skills. **Raft Maine** will put you in touch with the proper outfitter. New Hampshire's Saco River is another favorite among the white-water set.

Boating

New England's reputation as one of the world's great cruising areas is well deserved. The thousands of miles of shoreline are dotted with hundreds of anchorages. Penobscot Bay, Maine, and Newport, Rhode Island, are both considered sailing meccas. For those who want something a little calmer than the Atlantic Ocean, New England has countless lakes, large and small, including popular cruising destinations such as Sebago Lake, Lake Champlain, and Lake Winnipesaukee.

Boat rentals are available at many seaside and lakeside resorts in New England. A few outlets will rent a large sailboat for a day or night. These so-called "bareboat charters" are only for experienced sailors, particularly in Maine, where water and weather conditions can be treacherous. **Hinckley Yacht Charters** in Southwest Harbor, Maine, is one of the area's larger companies, with 25 sail and power crafts available. This company will also provide fully crewed yacht charters. Top-notch windsurfing sites and windsurfing equipment rentals are also available at many locations up and down the New England coast.

Cruises

Whale-watching cruises have become one of the region's most popular activities, with more and more coastal towns trying to cash in. Not quite an exact science, a successful whale-watching trip relies both on the experience of the ship's captain and on the guidance offered by high-tech sounding gear to find these majestic mammals. Many companies will offer a rain check if no whales are sighted.

Plan whale-watching trips carefully. Choose a calm day. Choppy water causes most people to become seasick. If you fear you will get sick, buy some ginger capsules at a health food store and take the recommended dose just before boarding.

Sightseeing and nature cruises are also available throughout New England. For a different view of the city, **Boston Harbor Cruises** offers sunset tours throughout the summer. River cruises are available on several New England waterways, including both the Charles and the

Group rafting run on the Cold River at Charlemont, Massachusetts

Boats at pier in Edgartown Harbor, Martha's Vineyard

Connecticut rivers in Massachusetts and Connecticut's Mystic River.

Maine has prime waters for multi-day windjammer trips. Day sails dominate elsewhere.

Bird-Watching

With its diverse habitats, ranging from mountains to coastal marshes and sand flats to conifer and mixed hardwood forests, New England offers some of the most interesting birding in the U.S.

Massachusetts, home to the first Audubon Society in America, is famous for several areas, most notably the northeast coast at Newburyport, Cape Cod, and around the Berkshires. At Machias Seal Island, Maine, birders have a good opportunity to sight nesting colonies of Atlantic puffins. Special boat excursions to the island are offered by local charters.

National parks along with national wildlife refuges and protection areas are often the best places to bird, since they are protected and unspoiled. **The US Fish and Wildlife Service** can provide information on the location of refuges and the birding opportunities at each. Every state's **Audubon**

Society will provide information on birding in the state as well as on Audubon field trips to various hotspots.

Golf

New England has more than its share of outstanding golf courses – in all price ranges and at all levels of difficulty. Dedicated golf vacationers have a choice between some stunning coastal and mountain resorts. Of the former, Samoset Resort, located in Rockport, Maine, stands out above all the rest.

With ocean views on 14 holes, Samoset has been called the most visually appealing course in New England. Two other terrific coastal links, the Seaside course at New Seabury and the Ocean Edge Resort and Golf Club, are located on Cape Cod.

For a full-fledged mountain golf holiday, consider the Equinox resort in Manchester, Vermont. It features a championship 1927 Walter J. Travis design surrounded by the Green Mountains. Some famous ski

destinations offer great golf, as well. In western Maine, Sugarloaf Golf Club presents a memorable Robert Trent Jones, Jr. layout that *Golf Digest* has ranked among the top ten for both memorability and aesthetics. Mount Snow is ranked as one of Vermont's top five courses. Both courses also offer summer golf schools, as does Quechee in Vermont. Other worthwhile mountain courses include The Balsams in northeastern New Hampshire and Cranwell Resort and Golf Club in the Berkshires.

The signature of New England: a beautiful, well-kept golf course

Technical or Rock Climbing

With New England's Green Mountains and White Mountains, it's little surprise that this part of the country offers some great climbing.

In Maine the vast majority of cliff climbing falls along its rugged south coast, with high-quality routes in a setting that is truly stunning. **Acadia National Park** is the most popular destination. Alpine climbers will also find a worthy test in Maine. Mount Katahdin, the state's highest peak, has some of the longest routes in New England.

New England's best climbing, however, is found in New Hampshire, where Cannon Cliff, Cathedral Ledge, and Whitehorse Ledge make up a triumvirate of diverse, challenging peaks. New Hampshire also offers bouldering and sport climbing at several sites, the best of which is Rumney in the center part of the state.

Connecticut and Rhode Island are not especially famed for their climbing, but both offer several quite good bouldering sites, most notably at Lincoln Woods, Rhode Island.

Climbing in Massachusetts is varied, with the central area of the state offering longer scenic routes and Boston providing some of the country's best urban cragging.

Vermont has few developed sites, though the treacherous sport of ice climbing is practiced at Smuggler's Notch and Lake Willoughby.

Hunting

With its wide range of game spread across its diverse woodlands, New England offers something for every hunter. Among the big game are white tail deer, bear, and moose, while small game includes rabbit, hare, and squirrel. For those interested in bird-hunting,

Climber in bold ascent of New Hampshire's White Mountains

turkey, duck, goose, pheasant, quail, and grouse can be found. The hunting seasons are concentrated in the late summer and fall, with limited exceptions. Hunters in all six states require licenses. In most cases, the fees are significantly higher for out-of-state hunters. Guns must be kept unloaded during transport in all states, and in some of them, a secure transport case is mandatory. There are also regulations that govern transport of game out-of-state. For specific information on regulations in each state, contact the government

Ruffed grouse

department responsible for wildlife management in that state.

Hang Gliding and Paragliding

Good hang-gliding and paragliding sites abound in New England. That's no surprise, considering the large number of accessible places throughout the Green Mountains and the White Mountains. The best place to start is **Morningside Flight Park** in Charlestown, New Hampshire. It is the only full-time flight school and flying center in New England, and it has a 450-ft (137-m) summit launch site on the premises. Not far away in Vermont, Mount Ascutney is known as the premier cross-country hang gliding site in New England, with flights having reached the Atlantic coast.

Southern New England is not without its advantages, however. Two of the best sand cliff launches are located in Cape Cod, Massachusetts, and Block Island, Rhode Island. Training is essential before attempting these sports. It is important to check local regulations before making any flight. You will find that many sites require memberships or have strict guidelines about landing areas. At state sites in Vermont, gliders must sign a waiver before making any flight. Contact the state association or a local club before making any jump.

Daring way to view the Berkshires at North Adams, Massachusetts

DIRECTORY

Bird-Watching

Audubon Society of New Hampshire
84 Silk Farm Rd., Concord, NH 03301.
Tel (603) 224-9909.
w nhaudubon.org

Audubon Society of Rhode Island
12 Sanderson Rd., Smithfield, RI 02917-2600.
Tel (401) 949-5454.
w asri.org

Audubon Vermont
255 Sherman Hollow Rd., Huntington, VT 05462.
Tel (802) 434-3068.
w vtaudubon.org

Connecticut Audubon Society
2325 Burr St., Fairfield, CT 06430.
Tel (203) 259-6305 or (800) 996-8747.
w ctaudubon.org

Maine Audubon Society
20 Gilsland Farm Rd., Falmouth, ME 04105.
Tel (207) 781-2330.
w maineaudubon.org

Massachusetts Audubon Society
208 S Great Rd., Lincoln, MA 01773.
Tel (781) 259-9500 or (800) 283-8266.
w massaudubon.org

United States Fish and Wildlife Service
Regional Office, 300 Westgate Center Dr., Hadley, MA 01035-9589.
Tel (413) 253-8200.
w fws.gov/northeast

Boating

Hinckley Yacht Charters
Great Harbor Marina, PO Box 950, Southwest Harbor, ME 04679.
Tel (207) 244-5531.
w hinckleycharters.com

Camping

Connecticut Campground Owners Association
1728 Route 198, Woodstock, CT 06281.
Tel (860) 521-4704.
w campconn.com

Department of Environmental Protection
79 Elm St., Hartford, CT 06106.
Tel (860) 424-3000.
w ct.gov/deep

Maine Campground Owners Association
10 Falcon Rd., Suite 1, Lewiston, ME 04240.
Tel (207) 782-5874.
w campmaine.com

Maine Department of Conservation
18 Elkins Lane, Augusta, ME 04333.
Tel (207) 287-3821.
w maine.gov/dacf/parks

Massachusetts Department of Conservation and Recreation
251 Causeway St., Suite 600, Boston, MA 02114.
Tel (617) 626-1250.
w mass.gov/dcr

National Park Service Northeast Region
Custom House, 200 Chestnut St., Philadelphia, PA 19106.
Tel (800) 365-2267 or (215) 597-7013.
w nps.gov/nero

National Recreation Reservation Service
Tel (518) 885-3639 or (877) 444-6777.
w recreation.gov

New Hampshire Campground Owners Association
PO Box 1074, Epsom, NH 03234.
Tel (800) 822-6764.
w ucampnh.com

New Hampshire Division of Parks and Recreation
PO Box 1856, Concord, NH 03302.
Tel (603) 271-3556.
w nhparks.state.nh.us

Rhode Island State Parks
1100 Tower Hill Rd., North Kingstown, RI 02852. **Tel** (401) 667-6200.
w riparks.com

Vermont State Parks
1 Nation Life Drive, Montpelier, VT 05620.
Tel (888) 409-7579.
w vtstateparks.com

Cruises

Bar Harbor Whale Watch Company
1 West St., Bar Harbor, ME 04609.
Tel (207) 288-2386 or (800) WHALES-4.
w whalesrus.com

Boston Harbor Cruises
One Long Wharf, Boston, MA 02110.
Tel (617) 227-4320 or (877) 733-9425.
w bostonharborcruises.com

Fishing and Hunting

Maine Sporting Camp Association
HC 76, Box 620, Greenville, ME 04441.
w mainesportingcamps.com

Maine Windjammer Association
Tel (800) 807-9463.
w sailmainecoast.com

Orvis
Rte. 7A, Manchester, VT 05254.
Tel (802) 362-3750 or (888) 235-9763.
w orvis.com

Rhode Island Party and Charterboat Association
PO Box 171, Wakefield, RI 02880.
w rifishing.com

Hang Gliding and Paragliding

Morningside Flight Park
357 Morningside Lane, Charlestown, NH 03603.
Tel (603) 542-4416.
w flymorningside.kittyhawk.com

Vermont Hang Gliding Association
w vhga.aero

Winter Activities

Far from lamenting the end of the stunning fall-foliage season, New Englanders instead begin readying themselves for winter activities. Skis and snowboards are pulled out and dusted off, snowmobiles are tuned up, and skates are sharpened in anticipation of cold weather and the slate of outdoor fun it brings. In New England top-notch ski hills and cross-country ski and snowmobiling trails are never far away. This is especially true in the region's northernmost reaches, where the annual blanket of snow is thickest and, for outdoor enthusiasts, most inviting.

Sleigh ride through Hancock Shaker Village in Pittsfield, Massachusetts

Skiing

People have been downhill skiing on New England's rounded peaks for more than a century. While the region does not have the elevation of the Rockies, it does offer many large hills, some with a vertical rise of more than 2,000 ft (610 m). The best skiing and snowboarding is concentrated in the three northern states. Vermont has the most high-quality peaks, with **Killington** offering the most trails at 212. But it is **Stowe** that can claim the title of New England's ski capital. A world-famous resort set in the quaint village of the same name, Stowe has the state's highest peak and offers excellent trails for skiers of all levels. For the experienced skier, **Mad River Glen** near Waitsfield provides a stern test in one of the most pristine settings in the world. It also forbids snowboarding.

The White Mountains in New Hampshire have a plethora of good ski hills; downhill, alpine, and cross-country trails are arguably the best in the Northeast. In Maine, **Sugarloaf** and **Sunday River** are considered to be the best hills in the state.

Downhill ski trails in New England are accurately rated following a standard code: Easier = green circle; More Difficult = blue square; Most Difficult = black diamond; and Expert = double diamond. Rental equipment is available at all resorts, as are skiing and snowboarding lessons for all levels. Where price is concerned, in general, the larger, more famous resorts charge more for lift tickets. If you have time, look for off-site sellers. They typically offer reduced prices. Also ask about package deals and senior or child discounts.

Cross-country ski trails are also plentiful in New England. Towns such as Craftsbury Common, Vermont, and **Jackson**, New Hampshire have miles of groomed trails. State parks also often provide good trails. These are good areas for other winter activities such as sliding and snowshoeing. **Catamount Trail**, set aside for skiers and snowshoers, runs 300 miles (482 km) down the length of Vermont. Many renowned downhill resorts also offer cross-country trails. The trails at the **Trapp Family Lodge Ski Center** in Stowe are considered among the best in New England.

Low in the turn at Vermont's majestic Stowe resort

Snowmobiling

Snowmobiling is extremely popular all across New England, but Maine is truly the mecca for this activity. The state is interconnected by 12,500 miles (20,000 km) of trails and has more than 85,000 registered snowmobiles using them. Resorts such as **Northern Outdoors** in The Forks and the **New England Outdoor Center** in Millinocket will rent snowmobiles and accommodations, and supply guides for excursions. Most agencies require that renters have a valid driver's license.

Skating

In winter, New England has plenty of frozen lakes and rivers for skating. Always check with local authorities to be sure the ice is safe.

Winter also brings droves of bundled-up skaters to the Boston Common Frog Pond in Boston. Rentals are available in the warm-up shed or at the **Beacon Hill Skate Shop**. In Providence, Rhode Island, the rink at the **Alex & Ani City Center** sits in the shadow of the city's tallest building. Rentals are available.

Freestyle skiing, common at New England ski resorts

DIRECTORY

Skiing

Attitash Mountain Resort
PO Box 508, Rte. 302, Bartlett, NH 03812.
Tel (800) 223-7669 or (603) 374-2368.
ⓦ attitash.com

Bretton Woods Mount Washington Resort
Rte. 302, Bretton Woods, NH 03575.
Tel (800) 314-1752 or (603) 278-1000.
ⓦ brettonwoods.com

Catamount Trail Association
1 Main St., Suite 350, Burlington, VT 05401.
Tel 802-864-5794.
ⓦ catamounttrail.org

Jackson Ski Touring Foundation
PO Box 216, 153 Main St., Jackson, NH 03846.
Tel (800) 927-6697 or (603) 383-9355.
ⓦ jacksonsc.org

Killington
4763 Killington Rd., Killington, VT 05751.
Tel (800) 621-MTNS or (802) 422-6200.
ⓦ killington.com

Mad River Glen
Rte. 17, Fayston, VT 05673.
Tel (802) 496-3551.
ⓦ madriverglen.com

Ski Maine Association
Box 7566, Portland, ME 04112.
Tel (207) 773-7669.
ⓦ skimaine.com

Ski New Hampshire
PO Box 528, North Woodstock, NH 03262.
Tel (603) 745-9396 or (800) 887-5464.
ⓦ skinh.com

Ski Vermont
26 State St., PO Box 368, Montpelier, VT 05601.
Tel (802) 223-2439.
ⓦ skivermont.com

Stowe Mountain Resort
5781 Mountain Rd., Stowe, VT 05672.
Tel (800) 253-4754 or (802) 253-3000.
ⓦ stowe.com

Sugarloaf
5092 Access Rd., Carrabassett Valley, ME 04947.
Tel (800) THE-LOAF or (207) 237-2000.
ⓦ sugarloaf.com

Sunday River Ski Resort
Sunday River access road, Newry, ME 04261.
Tel (800) 543-2SKI or (207) 824-3000.
ⓦ sundayriver.com

Trapp Family Lodge Ski Center
700 Trapp Hill Rd., Stowe, VT 05672.
Tel (800) 826-7000 or (802) 253-8511.
ⓦ trappfamily.com

Snowmobiling

Maine Snowmobile Association
PO Box 80, Augusta, ME 04332.
Tel (207) 622-6983.
ⓦ mesnow.com

New England Outdoor Center
PO Box 669, Millinocket, ME 04462.
Tel (800) 634-7238.
ⓦ neoc.com

New Hampshire Snowmobile Association
614 Laconia Rd., Tilton, NH 03276.
Tel (603) 273-0220.
ⓦ nhsa.com

Northern Outdoors
PO Box 100, 1771 Route 201, The Forks, ME 04985.
Tel (800) 765-7238.
ⓦ northernoutdoors.com

Snowmobile Association of Massachusetts
PO Box 386, Conway, MA 01341.
Tel (413) 369-8092.
ⓦ sledmass.com

Skating

Alex & Ani City Center
2 Kennedy Plaza, Providence, RI 02903.
Tel (401) 331-5544.
ⓦ alexandanicitycenter.com

Beacon Hill Skate Shop
135 South Charles St., Boston, MA 02116.
Tel (617) 482-7400.

SURVIVAL
GUIDE

PRACTICAL INFORMATION

New England offers a wide variety of recreational activities within a relatively small area. Vacationers can hike the White Mountains of New Hampshire in the morning, swim at Maine's Ogunquit Beach in the afternoon, and take in the Boston Symphony Orchestra at night. Tourism is a major part of the local economy, with numerous agencies and facilities geared toward ensuring that visitors have an enjoyable stay. Accommodations and restaurants (see pp306–39) come in all price ranges, allowing you to sleep and eat in comfort even on a limited budget. For people without cars, transportation is readily available in Boston and throughout the six states (see pp376–9). The following pages offer some practical advice for people traveling around New England, from general guidelines on personal security and health (see pp370–71) to some basic financial and media information (see pp372–3).

When to Go

New England is a four-season vacation destination, but it is particularly popular in the summer and fall. Generally speaking, the peak tourist period is from mid-June, when schools let out, through October. During this time, accommodations and restaurant reservations can be hard to come by, especially in the busy resort towns along the coast.

Fall-foliage season (see pp24–5) means heavily trafficked roads from mid-September to late October. During this month-long stretch, the hotels and B&Bs farther inland near the woods are booked solid.

The length of the ski season depends entirely on the weather. It is not unheard of for New England winters to run from late November right through March, during which time New Hampshire and Vermont, which possess the bulk of New England's

Enough signs to keep visitors busy in Center Sandwich, New Hampshire

ski centers (see pp362–3), are busiest.

If you are planning a backwoods vacation, it is prudent to avoid wooded areas in April and May, when the ground can be extremely muddy and swarms of hungry black flies fill the air. Don't be fooled by their small size; they have a nasty bite.

Visas and Passports

All travelers to New England and the US, including Canadians, should have a machine-readable biometric passport that is valid for six months longer than their intended period of stay. Holders of a valid EU, Australian, or New Zealand passport in possession of a return ticket do not need visas if staying 90 days or less in the US. However, visitors must apply for entry in advance via the Electronic System for Travel

Authorization, or ESTA (https://esta.cbp.dhs.gov). Applications must be made at least 72 hours before travel. Sometimes foreign visitors must prove they carry sufficient funds. Ask your travel agent, check with the US Department of State (travel. state.gov), or contact the US embassy in your home country for current requirements.

Customs Information

Visitors over the age of 21 are allowed to enter the US with two pints (1 liter) of alcohol; 200 cigarettes, 50 cigars, or 4 lb (2 kg) of smoking tobacco; and gifts worth up to $100. Prohibited items include meat products, dairy products aged less than 90 days, and all fresh fruit. Travelers entering the country with more than $10,000 in cash or traveler's checks must declare the money to customs officials upon entry.

Snowboarding, popular with the young, daring, and fit

◀ Clay cliffs lining Lucy Vincent Beach on Martha's Vineyard, Massachusetts

Acadia National Park Visitor Center, Maine

Tourist Information

The state tourism offices are great sources of information, and they can provide road maps, brochures, and listings of accommodations, events, and attractions free of charge. Some offices also hand out discount vouchers for lodgings and restaurants. Many towns have a visitors' bureau that dispenses local information. State Welcome Centers found along motorways also provide information for tourists.

Admission Prices

While some of New England's attractions are free to visit, many have an admission charge. Check in advance for admission information, and ask about special discounts for groups, children, and seniors. Some museums offer an evening slot when admission is free or by voluntary donation.

Opening Hours

Most stores open from 9am or 10am to 6pm Monday to Saturday, although they often stay open until 9pm or 10pm on Thursday and Friday. Many stores are open on Sunday too.

Most New England banks are open from 9am to 4pm or 5pm Monday to Friday. Many banks are also open on Saturday mornings from 9am to noon or 1pm.

The larger museums are usually open from 10am–5pm Tuesday to Sunday, but always check in advance. Smaller museums may have seasonal hours and even be closed during the winter.

Many gas stations and convenience stores stay open 24 hours a day. Offices are generally open from 9am to 5pm Monday to Friday and do not close for lunch.

Etiquette and Smoking

The legal drinking age throughout New England is 21. Most young people will be asked to produce a photo ID as proof of age in order to buy alcohol or enter a bar; your passport is usually your best bet. Drinking in public spaces is against the law, and the penalties for driving under the influence of alcohol are severe, including the loss of your driver's license.

Cigarettes can be sold only to people aged 18 or over. It is against the law to smoke in public buildings, such as hospitals, and on public conveyances, including subways and buses. A few restaurants permit smoking in designated outdoor sections, though most are completely smoke-free.

Accessibility to Public Conveniences

Tourist information booths and welcome centers are equipped with toilets, and rest areas are usually found upon entering states on major highways.

There are several automatic coin-operated toilets around Boston. Public libraries and government buildings also provide a handy stop for those in need of a restroom during business hours, and most coffee shops and bars require only a small purchase in order to use their facilities.

Taxes and Tipping

Listed prices rarely include applicable taxes or expected gratuities. All New England states, with the exception of New Hampshire, levy their own sales tax. All states charge taxes on hotel rooms and restaurant meals, and some cities have extra taxes, too. Many accommodations tack on additional surcharges to bills, such as housekeeping and parking fees; these can increase the total by up to 15 percent. To avoid unpleasant surprises at the end of a stay, inquire about any extra charges before checking in.

A gratuity is given for most services. Travelers should give waiters 15–20 percent of the bill, bartenders $1–$2 per drink, barbers 10–15 percent of the bill, and taxi drivers between 10 and 20 percent of the fare. Porters usually get $1 per piece of luggage, and hotel maids at least $1 per night.

A tip of 15–20 percent of the bill is expected by waiters

Taxes in New England

State	Lodging	Meal	Sales
Connecticut	12%	6.35%	6.35%
Maine	7%	7%	5.5%
Massachusetts	12.5–15%	6.25–7%	6.25%
New Hampshire	9%	9%	–
Rhode Island	13%	8%	7%
Vermont	9%	9%	6%

Youngsters enjoying water-based activities at a lakeside wharf

Travelers with Special Needs

While US federal law requires that businesses are accessible to the disabled, some historic buildings may have limited facilities for wheelchair users. Most hotels and restaurants are equipped for people with special needs, and an increasing number of small inns are refitting their rooms. Many outdoor recreation areas, including all national parks, also provide restrooms and facilities for the disabled, including tour buses and wheelchair-friendly trails.

Disabled travelers visiting New England are advised to call venues in advance or to contact organizations such as the **Society for Accessible Travel and Hospitality** or **Mobility International** for help. Both groups provide information and comprehensive guides on disabled access throughout the region.

Traveling with Children

New England is a fairly child-friendly place. Many museums, zoos, and aquariums offer hands-on and interactive exhibits that encourage younger participants. The multitude of state parks, forests, and public beaches give children lots of space to burn excess energy.

Many establishments and services cater to families by having children's menus and reduced admission rates. Most hotels and motels make cots or roll-away beds available (sometimes for a nominal fee) so that children can stay in the same room as their parents. The same is generally not true for inns and bed and breakfasts (B&Bs), some of which will not take children under a certain age.

Senior Travelers

Senior travelers are eligible for myriad discounts, ranging from car rentals and lodgings to entry to museums and national parks. Depending on the place, the minimum qualifying age for seniors can be as low as 50. A valid form of ID is required. For more information, visitors to New England should contact

Senior travelers getting around in Lenox, Massachusetts

the **American Association of Retired Persons (AARP)** or **Elderhostel**, also known as Road Scholar. This Boston-based international senior-travel organization offers educational tours in New England and throughout the US, for those over 50.

Gay and Lesbian Travelers

New England has a number of vibrant gay communities, including Provincetown (see pp160–61), on the far end of Cape Cod; Ogunquit (see pp282–3), Maine; Northampton (see p167), Massachusetts; and Boston's South End (see pp97–105). New England was historically one of the leading regions of the US in banning discrimination based on sexual orientation. As of 2015, gay marriage is legal throughout the US.

Bay Windows, New England's largest gay and lesbian newspaper, includes arts and cultural listings for all six states.

International Student Identity Card (ISIC)

Traveling on a Budget

Students from abroad should buy an **International Student Identity Card (ISIC)** from the ISIC website before traveling to New England. Numerous discounts are available to cardholders at such places as hostels, museums, and theaters. This is especially true in Boston. The **Student Advantage Card** offers a similar deal, but this is available only to American university students.

Budget-minded travelers should look out for lunch menus, which are commonly less expensive at restaurants than dinner menus. Some establishments also offer unlimited lunch buffets. To save money on accommodations, check out www.airbnb.com for casual rooms in private homes, or a hotel consolidator like www.hotwire.com.

What to Take

Given the region's notoriously inconsistent weather – "if you don't care for the weather, wait a few minutes and it's likely to change" is a common adage – it's wise to pack for an array of conditions. Layers are recommended, as is rain gear.

All of New England's main cities are easily manageable on foot, so comfortable footwear is a must. Foreign travelers visiting remote parts of the region may have a difficult time finding electrical converters to purchase, so they should therefore come prepared.

Electricity

Electricity flows at the standard US 110–120 volts AC (alternating current). Foreign-made electrical appliances may require a US-style plug adapter and a voltage converter.

Responsible Tourism

Long considered one of America's most environmentally conscious regions, New England continues to gain national acclaim for its forward-thinking initiatives and policies. Examples include state zoning laws requiring LEED (Leadership in Energy and Environmental Design) certification for certain developments and a requirement that all Boston taxicabs go hybrid by 2015. Organizations like **Boston Green Tourism** help guide out-of-towners toward the area's numerous eco-certified hotels. The "green movement" has spread throughout New England's economic landscape. Visitors find it easier and easier to be environmentally aware while touring the area, as recycling bins are quite common and community farmers' markets selling local produce and artisan foodstuffs can be found in every corner of every state.

DIRECTORY

Tourist Information

Connecticut Office of Tourism
One Constitution Plaza, Hartford, CT 06103.
Tel (888) 288-4748.
🅦 ctvisit.com

Greater Boston Convention and Visitors Bureau
2 Copley Place, Suite 105, Boston, MA 02116. **Map** 3 C3. **Tel** (888) 733-2678 or (617) 536-4100.
🅦 bostonusa.com

Maine Office of Tourism
59 State House Station, Augusta, ME 04333-0059.
Tel (207) 287-5711 or (888) 624-6345.
🅦 visitmaine.com

Massachusetts Office of Travel & Tourism
10 Park Plaza, Suite 4510, Boston, MA 02116. **Map** 1 B5. **Tel** (617) 973-8500 or (800) 227-6277.
🅦 massvacation.com

New Hampshire Division of Travel & Tourism Development
172 Pembroke Rd., PO Box 1856, Concord, NH 03302.
Tel (603) 271-2665 or (800) 386-4664.
🅦 visitnh.gov

Rhode Island Tourism Division
315 Iron Horse Way, Suite 101, Providence, RI 02908.
Tel (800) 556-2484.
🅦 visitrhodeisland.com

Vermont Department of Tourism and Marketing
National Life Drive, 6th Floor, Montpelier, VT 05260.
Tel (800) VERMONT.
🅦 vermontvacation.com

Travelers with Special Needs

Mobility International
🅦 miusa.org

Society for Accessible Travel and Hospitality
2175 Hudson St., Fort Lee, NJ 07024.
Tel (212) 447-7284.
🅦 sath.org

Senior Travelers

American Association of Retired Persons (AARP)
601 E. St. NW, Washington, DC 20049.
Tel (888) 687-2277.
🅦 aarp.org

Elderhostel (Road Scholar)
11 Ave. de Lafayette, Boston, MA 02111. **Map** 4 F2. **Tel** (800) 454-5768.
🅦 roadscholar.org

Gay and Lesbian Travelers

Bay Windows
Tel (617) 464-7280.
🅦 baywindows.com

Traveling on a Budget

International Student Identity Card (ISIC)
🅦 isic.org

Student Advantage Card
61 Brown Rd., Ithaca, NY 14850.
Tel (800) 333-2920.
🅦 studentadvantage.com

Responsible Tourism

Boston Green Tourism
🅦 bostongreentourism.org

Useful Websites

City of Boston
🅦 cityofboston.gov

Boston Globe Online
🅦 boston.com

Visit New England
🅦 visitnewengland.com

Yankee Magazine
🅦 yankeemagazine.com

Personal Security and Health

New England's comparatively low crime rate makes it a safe vacation destination. Even the region's largest metropolitan area, Boston, is considered quite safe. Nonetheless, it is a good idea for travelers to exercise a few simple precautions to ensure that they remain out of harm's way. This same rule of thumb applies to the wilderness areas. Despite being almost free of crime, these areas possess a number of natural hazards that can be minimized with a little effort.

Motorized police patrol on Surfside Beach, Nantucket, Massachusetts

Police

Three agencies share law enforcement duties: city police, sheriffs (who patrol county areas), and the state Highway Patrol, which deals with traffic accidents and offenses outside city boundaries. Law enforcement officials are friendly and often helpful when not otherwise engaged in official duties. Their uniforms are dark blue or khaki.

What to be Aware of

As with all large urban centers, New England's major cities – Boston, Burlington, Worcester, Springfield, New Haven, Hartford, Providence, and Portland – have pockets of crime. Generally speaking, the main tourist areas are safe, as most of the problems occur in neighborhoods not usually frequented by visitors. It is best to avoid wandering into areas that are off the beaten track. The number of street people, or panhandlers, in cities is on the rise, but these people are almost always harmless.

Pickpockets are sometimes at work in the busy centers and will target anyone who looks like a tourist. Your best defense is common sense. Avoid wearing expensive jewelry and carry cameras and camcorders securely. Carry only small amounts of cash, and opt instead for credit cards and traveler's checks. Money belts or pouches worn under your clothing provide maximum security against pickpockets, especially in crowded areas such as buses and malls. While theft in hotels is not common, it is prudent to store valuables in the safe when you are out.

Always lock your car when leaving it unoccupied. Valuables left in the open in unattended cars are easy targets for smash-and-grab thieves, so store them in the trunk. In major urban areas, avoid walking through parks and strange neighborhoods at night. Always use automatic teller machines (ATMs) on busy, well-lit streets.

Before you leave home, make a photocopy of all important documents, such as your passport and visa or ESTA application number, and take it with you, keeping it separate from the originals. Also make a note of the numbers of your traveler's checks and credit cards, in case they are stolen.

In an Emergency

For emergency medical, fire, or police services, call 911. The call is free from public phones. Emergency phone boxes are located along major highways and connect instantly to the emergency services. The **Travelers' Aid Society** may provide assistance or referrals to stranded travelers.

Lost and Stolen Property

Although the chances of retrieving lost or stolen property are very slim, you should report all missing items to the police and get a copy of the police report for your insurance claim. A stolen passport should be reported to your embassy or consulate. Most credit card companies have toll-free numbers to report a lost or stolen card, as do **American Express** and **Thomas Cook** for lost traveler's checks, which can often be replaced within a few hours. In the event of loss or theft, it is useful to have a record of your valuables' serial numbers and receipts as proof of possession. If you have lost something, try retracing your steps and think of the taxi companies and bus or train routes you were using when the item went missing. Most taxi and transport companies run a Lost and Found service, which can be reached via their general access phone numbers (see p377).

A crowded Boston street, where pickpockets can operate

Fire engine

Ambulance

Police car

Hospitals and Pharmacies

New England has a number of acclaimed hospitals and research facilities, such as **Massachusetts General Hospital**, should you need medical treatment. If you need a prescription dispensed, there are pharmacies (drugstores) in every city in the region, some staying open 24 hours, such as **CVS Pharmacy**. Ask your hotel for the nearest one. Those with known medical issues visiting small towns and remote areas should take precautions and locate the nearest medical facility in advance. If you need to see a dentist, some clinics offer emergency care, including **Tufts Emergency Dental Clinic**.

Outdoor Safety

A wide variety of outdoor recreational activities are on offer in New England, some of which entail certain risks. Helmets and other protective items are essential, and often mandatory, for such activities as white-water rafting and mountain biking, as are life jackets for all types of boating. Hikers should always stay on marked trails; those who are

hiking or camping alone should notify someone of their destination and estimated time of arrival. Campers should never feed animals and are advised to suspend food from a tree branch to avoid visits from bears. If you see a bear, don't look it in the eyes. Back away slowly and do not run. Extinguish campfires carefully using water. Mountain hikers and rock climbers should always be prepared for sudden changes in the weather, while ocean swimmers are advised to use beaches with lifeguards and ask about undertows.

Wear a hat and apply sunblock in the summer. Hikers should wear bright-colored clothes and avoid forests and fields during hunting season (May and the fall). To avoid any risk of catching Lyme disease from ticks, cover up well when walking through woods and fields.

Travel and Health Insurance

As the US does not have a government health program, emergency medical and dental care, though excellent, can be very expensive. Medical travel insurance is highly recommended in order to defer some of the costs of an unscheduled stop in a US hospital. Even with medical coverage, you may have to pay for services when you receive them, then claim reimbursement from your insurance company later. Ensure the policy you choose covers trip cancellation, baggage, document loss, emergency medical care, and accidental death. You may need extra cover for certain activities.

Hiking trail marker

Banks and Local Currency

Outside of Boston, not many banks exchange foreign currency, so visitors from abroad should use credit or automatic teller machine (cash machine) cards. Never carry all your money and credit cards with you at the same time, and keep in mind that most banks and foreign currency exchanges are closed on Sundays.

Banks and Foreign Exchange Bureaus

Most New England banks are open 9am–5pm Monday to Friday. Many are also open 9am–noon or 1pm on Saturdays. Most banks are closed on Sundays, and all are closed on public holidays. Foreign exchange bureaus tend to be open 9am–5pm weekdays.

Traveler's checks can usually be cashed at banks with a recognized photo ID, such as a passport. The main branches of national banks in large urban areas will exchange foreign currency for a small fee, but outside the major cities not many facilities offer this service. Among the best-known agencies for changing currency are American Express Travel Agency and Travelex Currency Services.

Always ask about hidden charges or commissions before making a transaction. For the best rates, avoid exchanging your money at airports or train and bus stations. In general, you will get the best rates at big city banks or private exchange bureaus in larger centers.

ATMs

Automatic teller machines (ATMs) are available throughout New England, even in tiny villages. Look for them in foyers or by the entrances of banks. ATMs are also found in airports, train stations, shopping malls, supermarkets, large gas stations, and along the streets of major cities. Widely found bank-card networks include Cirrus, Plus, NYCE, and Interlink. The machines will also dispense money to credit cards such as VISA and MasterCard.

Before leaving home, ask your bank if your card can be used in the US.

Credit Cards

The most commonly accepted credit cards in New England are MasterCard, VISA, and American Express, with Diners Club and the Discover Card sometimes accepted as well. Credit and debit cards can be used at most restaurants, retail stores, hotels, and gas stations, as well as to reserve tickets over the phone and to book a rental car. The biggest benefit of credit cards is that they offer you much more security than carrying around large sums of cash, and they can be very useful to have in emergency situations (see p371).

Bills and Coins

The US currency is the dollar. There are 100 cents to a dollar. Bills come in denominations of $1, $5, $10, $20, $50, and $100, while coins come in 1-, 5-, 10-, 25-, and 50-cent pieces. Gold-tone $1 coins are also in circulation, though not very popular; you will receive them mainly as change from vending machines. Each coin has a popular name: 25-cent pieces are called quarters; 10-cent pieces, dimes; 5-cent pieces, nickels; and 1-cent pieces, pennies.

1-dollar bill ($1)

5-dollar bill ($5)

10-dollar bill ($10)

20-dollar bill ($20)

50-dollar bill ($50)

100-dollar bill ($100)

25-cent coin (a quarter)

10-cent coin (a dime)

5-cent coin (a nickel)

1-cent coin (a penny)

Communications and Media

Many cities and towns in New England offer free wireless Internet access in public places, and a copy of a daily local newspaper (some of which are free) is never far away. For updates on the news, traffic, and weather, consult the numerous specialized websites that residents count on in their day-to-day lives.

International and Local Telephone Calls

Local phone calls are fairly inexpensive, but long-distance calls incur additional charges. Check rates by dialing 0 and asking the operator, but do not get the operator to put the call through, since this costs extra. The cheapest way to make long-distance calls is with a disposable calling card. These can be purchased for as little as $5 at convenience stores and train station kiosks.

Cell Phones

If you wish to bring your own cell phone, ask your provider if they offer an international plan that covers the US. However, it may be easier and cheaper to buy a disposable phone in the US. Pre-paid cell phones can be bought from around $25 throughout New England. Replacement chargers and adapters can be found in any electronics store.

Public Telephones

Public phones may be found in train stations and shopping centers. All pay phones accept coins, and many also take phone and credit cards. Local calls cost 50¢–$1 for three minutes; long-distance rates vary and include both a fixed call charge and a per-minute charge. All numbers with an 800, 866, 877, or 888 prefix are free of charge, as are calls from a pay phone to directory assistance (411 for local, 00 for international) and the emergency services (911). Operator assistance (0 for local, 01 for international) has a charge. Making a call from a hotel room can carry a hefty surcharge, and it is usually cheaper to use the pay phone in the lobby.

Internet and Email

Internet-enabled cell phones have led to the decline of the cybercafé, though **FedEx**, of which there are numerous locations throughout New England, have computers with Internet access available for rental. Terminals with online access can also be found in the **Boston Public Library** and in many hotels, though you may have to pay. Some colleges and universities allow visitors to use their Internet terminals for free. From coffee shops to public parks, wireless Internet hot spots dot the region.

Postal Services

Post offices are open 9am–5pm weekdays, with some branches offering a Saturday service. All are closed on Sundays and federal holidays. Letters and small parcels (less than 13 oz (370 g)) with the correct postage can be placed in any blue mailbox. Domestic mail takes one to five days for delivery; faster if you use Priority Mail or Express Mail's next-day delivery. Use airmail when sending mail overseas. Couriers like **FedEx**, **UPS**, and **DHL** provide a faster service but also cost more.

Boston post office, Charles Street

DIRECTORY

Internet and Email

Boston Public Library
700 Boylston St., Boston, MA 02116. **Map** 3 C2.
Tel (617) 536-5400.
Ⓦ bpl.org

FedEx
187 Dartmouth St., Boston, MA 02116. **Map** 3 C2. **Tel** (617) 262-6188. Ⓦ local.fedex.com

Postal Services

Boston Main Post Office (extended hours)
25 Dorchester Ave., Boston, MA 02210.
Tel (617) 654-5302.

Cambridge Main Post Office (extended hours)
770 Massachusetts Ave., Cambridge, MA 02139. **Map** 3 C5.
Tel (617) 575-8700.

DHL
420 E St., Boston, MA 02127.
Tel (800) 225 5345.

FedEx Office Print & Ship Center
125 Tremont St., Boston, MA 02116. **Map** 4 E1.
Tel (617) 423-0234.

UPS Customer Center
647 Summer St., Boston, MA 02127. **Tel** (800) 742-5877.

Newspapers and Magazines

The *Boston Globe* is the most widely read newspaper in New England. The *Boston Herald* is a popular tabloid-style daily. National publications like the *New York Times*, *Wall Street Journal*, and *USA Today* are also easily available.

Television and Radio

Hotels usually have access to the main networks (CBS, NBC, Fox, ABC), as well as some cable channels such as ESPN (for sports) and CNN (news). Public station PBS has classic films and documentaries.

Radio stations on FM frequencies tend to stick to a particular type of music (rock, jazz, Top 40, and so on). AM stations are usually geared toward talk-radio shows.

TRAVEL INFORMATION

The most common ways to get to New England are by plane or by car. However, trains and buses also provide decent access to many areas, particularly the southern states in the region. Boston's Logan International Airport handles international and domestic flights, and some of the longest journeys within the region can be accomplished by

a quick flight on a regional carrier. Boston is also the hub for rail and bus services coming in from all over the US and parts of Canada. Amtrak is the only rail option, but the presence of several bus carriers competing with one another has led to greatly reduced fares, with direct Boston to New York services at very low prices.

The international check-in area at Boston Logan International Airport

Arriving by Air

Boston's **Logan International Airport** (BOS) is the region's busiest, although some domestic and international carriers use **Manchester Boston Regional Airport** (MHT), in New Hampshire, which serves Vermont and Maine; **T. F. Green Airport** (PVD) in Warwick, Rhode Island, which serves Providence; and **Bradley International Airport** (BDL) in Windsor Locks, Connecticut, which serves Hartford. A few major commercial airlines also fly into Bangor (BGR) and Portland (PWM), Maine; and Burlington (BTV), Vermont. Other gateways to New England include Montreal, Quebec, and, of course, New York City's three major airports.

Tickets and Fares

Planning your vacation early will allow you to shop around for the best fares. Even with the small fees they may charge, travel agents are often your best bet in your search for savings. Alternatively, **Expedia** is a good online source of inexpensive tickets, while **Kayak** gives you instant access to the best published prices on the web. Flights are busiest between

June and October, as well as around the major holidays (Easter, Labor Day, Thanksgiving, Christmas). Book well in advance if you wish to fly during these times. In general, you will get the lowest fares if you travel at non-peak times – prices usually drop substantially after Columbus Day, for instance.

Internal Flights

Small domestic airlines cover specific geographical regions, and also offer a few national flights. With fewer flights than the major carriers, they often have much lower fares. Some regional commuter airlines shuttle passengers around with small, single-prop planes flying to various destinations including islands off the coast. **Cape Air** flies smaller routes throughout New England and is especially useful for those

Passenger jet in flight

Airport	Information	Distance from City
Logan International Airport (Boston, MA)	(800) 235-6426	3 miles (4.8 km) from Downtown Boston ⓦ massport.com/logan
Manchester Boston Regional Airport (Manchester, NH)	(603) 624-6556	6 miles (9.5 km) from Downtown Manchester ⓦ flymanchester.com
T. F. Green Airport (Warwick, RI)	(401) 737-8222	10 miles (16 km) from Downtown Providence ⓦ pvdairport.com
Bradley International Airport (Windsor Locks, CT)	(860) 292-2000	12 miles (19 km) from Downtown Hartford ⓦ bradleyairport.com

visiting Cape Cod. **Nantucket Airlines** fly between Hyannis (Cape Cod) and Nantucket.

On Arrival

International travelers will be given a customs and immigration form to complete during their flight and to hand in to customs officials at the airport. At the immigration area there are two lines – one for US citizens and another for non-US citizens. If you are entering the country via New York's busy JFK, be warned that the immigration lines there are often long and the process can be time-consuming.

Arriving by Train

Amtrak is the major railroad in the US. One of its busiest routes serves southern and central New England up to Boston. Amtrak's high-speed Acela regional train links New York to Boston, cutting about 45 minutes off the regional service's regular travel time of four hours. While Acela is available at a premium price, it is still cheaper than most airfares and has the added benefit of taking you from downtown to downtown without the added expense of taxis or shuttle buses.

A rail service also runs between Boston and Portland, Maine; in the summer, there is a stop at Maine's popular Old Orchard Beach.

Arriving by Car

Beginning in Florida, I-95 (known as Route 128 in the Boston area) is one of the most popular drives for travelers from the South. This major highway sticks close to the

A modern Greyhound bus

coast as it passes through Connecticut and Providence, Rhode Island, en route to the outskirts of Boston. Circumventing the city, the highway continues up through New Hampshire and Maine before crossing the border into Canada. Truck traffic on I-95 can be heavy, especially when the route approaches Boston.

From the north, the two major gateways into New England are I-89 and I-91. The latter crosses from Canada into Vermont at Derby Line, then follows a relatively straight line south along the Vermont/New Hampshire border, through Massachusetts and Connecticut all the way down to New Haven. I-89 starts in Vermont's northwesternmost corner, then cuts diagonally from Burlington to Concord, New Hampshire, where it links up with I-93 into Boston.

The major western points of entry into New England are I-84 and I-90 (toll road) from New York state.

Arriving by Bus

You can get just about anywhere in New England by bus, so long as you are not in a hurry. Many of the bus companies serve particular sections of the region. **Concord Coach Lines** has routes in Maine

and New Hampshire, while **Peter Pan** has stops in Connecticut, Rhode Island, New Hampshire, and western Massachusetts. Other parts of Massachusetts, such as Cape Cod and the South Shore, are served by **Plymouth & Brockton**. **Greyhound Lines** is a nationwide carrier with stops throughout New England. Greyhound works in conjunction with Peter Pan lines.

Most major bus lines offer discounted rates for students and seniors (with proper ID).

DIRECTORY

Tickets and Fares

Expedia
Ⓦ expedia.com
Kayak
Ⓦ kayak.com

Internal Flights

Cape Air
Tel 800-227-3247.
Ⓦ flycapeair.com

Nantucket Airlines
Tel 800-635-8787.
Ⓦ nantucketairlines.com

Arriving by Train

Amtrak
Tel (800) 872-7245.
Ⓦ amtrak.com

Arriving by Bus

Concord Coach Lines
Tel (617) 426-8080.
Ⓦ concordcoachlines.com

Greyhound Lines
Tel (617) 526-1800.
Ⓦ greyhound.com

Peter Pan
Tel (800) 343-9999.
Ⓦ peterpanbus.com

Plymouth & Brockton
Tel (508) 746-0378.
Ⓦ p-b.com

Train station in North Conway, New Hampshire

Getting Around Boston

The public transportation network in Boston and Cambridge is very good. In fact, it is considerably easier to get around by public transit than by driving, with the added benefit of not having to find a parking space. All the major attractions in the city are easily accessible by subway, bus, or taxi. The central sections of the city are also extremely easy to navigate on foot.

One of Boston's MBTA buses

Green Travel

Most places in the Boston area can be easily reached by public transit. The city's public transportation network, the MBTA (Massachusetts Bay Transportation Authority), is committed to providing alternatives to the car and works with the Environmental Protection Agency on projects such as locomotive-engine pollution control devices. The MBTA is also replacing its diesel-powered buses with natural gas-powered vehicles.

Boston's tourism moniker of "America's Walking City" hints at how easy it is to see the city on foot. Most attractions require nothing more than sensible shoes, while the Esplanade Trail along the Charles River and the Minuteman Bikeway offer ample opportunities for bikers, joggers, and walkers.

Websites such as https:// boston.hopstop.com offer public transport and walking directions to almost anywhere.

Finding Your Way in Boston

Much of Boston is laid out organically, rather than in the sort of strict grid found in most American cities. When trying to orient yourself, it helps if you think of Boston as enclaves, or neighborhoods around a few central squares. In general, uphill from Boston Common is Beacon Hill, downhill is Downtown, while Back Bay begins west of Arlington Street. The North End sticks out from the north side of Boston, while the Waterfront is literally that – where Boston meets the sea.

MBTA Subway and Trolley Buses

Run by the **MBTA**, Boston's combined subway and trolley network is known as the "T". The T operates 5am–12:45am daily (from 6am on Sundays). Weekday service is every 3–15 minutes; less frequent at weekends. There are five lines: Red, from south of the city to Cambridge; Green, from the Museum of Science westward into the suburbs; Blue, from near the Government Center to Logan Airport and on to Revere; Orange, linking the northern suburbs to southwest Boston; and Silver, a surface bus that runs from Roxbury to Logan Airport via South Station. Maps of the system are available at Downtown Crossing MBTA station.

Admission to subway stations is via turnstiles into which you insert a paper "Charlie" ticket ($2.65) or plastic "Charlie" card ($2.10). These can be bought from MBTA vending machines. Day or week Link passes for unlimited travel can be purchased at Downtown Crossing, South Station, Back Bay, Government Center, and North Station subway stops

MBTA Buses

The MBTA bus system expands the transit network to cover more than 1,000 miles (1,600 km). Buses are often crowded, though, and schedules can be hard to get. Two useful sightseeing routes are Haymarket–Charlestown (from near Quincy Market to Bunker Hill) and Harvard–Dudley (from Harvard Square via Massachusetts Avenue through Back Bay and South End to Dudley Square in Roxbury). Cash, a paper "Charlie" ticket ($2.10), or a plastic "Charlie" card ($1.60) is required for the fare.

Taxis

Finding a taxi in Boston and Cambridge is easy, except when it rains. Taxis can be found at stands in tourist areas or hailed on the street. Taxis may pick up fares only in the city for which they are licensed – Boston taxis only in Boston, Cambridge taxis only in Cambridge. If you need to be somewhere on time, it is wise to call a taxi company and arrange a pickup time and place in advance.

Rates are calculated by both mileage and time of day, beginning with a $2.60 pickup fee when the meter starts running. Taxis in Boston and Cambridge tend to be more expensive than in other US cities.

Boston taxis waiting for fares at one of the city's many taxi stands

Taxis to and from Logan Airport are required to charge an airport fee ($2.75); taxis coming into the city from the airport also charge for the harbor tunnel toll ($5.25). Other surcharges may apply late at night. A full schedule of fares should be posted inside the cab.

Visitors with a valid **Uber** account on their smart phones may find the alternative ride-hailing service less costly than a taxi.

Walking in Boston

Boston is a great walking city: it is compact, and virtually all streets are flanked by sidewalks. It is nonetheless essential to wear comfortable walking shoes with adequate cushioning and good support. Boston is mainly a city of neighborhoods, so it is usually best to use public transportation to reach a particular area, and then walk around to soak up the

atmosphere. Walking also allows you to see parts of the city that are impractical to explore by car because the streets are too narrow – for example, Beacon Hill, parts of the North End, and Harvard Square.

Traveling by Boat

With more than 6,000 miles (9,656 km) of coastline, New England offers numerous public boats and ferries for both leisure and transport purposes. Some attractions, like the Boston Harbor Islands, are reachable only by boat, with ferries by **Boston Harbor Cruises** departing from Long Wharf. Ships also make longer journeys to Salem or Provincetown on Cape Cod. **Baystate Cruise Company** also offers ferries to Cape Cod. From there, ferries make the trip to Nantucket and Martha's Vineyard.

DIRECTORY

Subway, Trolley Buses, and Buses

MBTA
Tel (617) 222-3200. **w** mbta.com

Taxis

Boston Cab Dispatch, Inc
Tel (617) 262-2227 (Boston).

Boston Town Taxi
Tel (617) 536-5000 (Boston).

Cambridge Taxi
Tel (617) 649-7000 (Cambridge).

Checker Cab of Cambridge
Tel (617) 497-9000 (Cambridge).

Uber
w uber.com

Traveling by boat

Baystate Cruise Company
Tel 877-783-3779.

Boston Harbor Cruises
Tel (617) 227-4321.

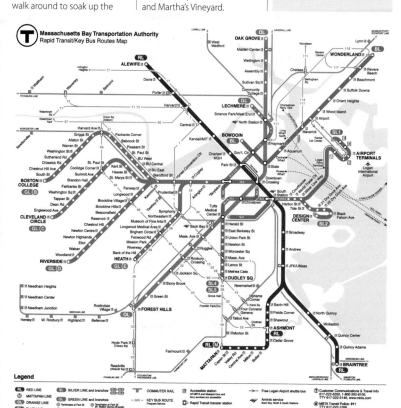

Massachusetts Bay Transportation Authority
Rapid Transit/Key Bus Routes Map

Driving in New England

While flying is the fastest and most efficient way to get to New England, driving is by far the best way to explore the region. In fact, much of this area's charm is found along scenic jaunts down the coast and driving tours during fall-foliage season. It is important to remember that large parts of the region are essentially wild, so you should always be prepared for any eventuality, such as a breakdown. This is doubly true in the winter, when sudden blizzards and whiteouts caused by blowing snow can leave motorists stranded. Boston's public transit system makes it easy to be without a car *(see pp376–7)*, but once outside the city you will need a vehicle to do your best exploring.

Country roads beckoning drivers to leave the crowds behind

A rented convertible, perfect for exploring in good weather

Car Rental

The major car rental chains have outlets in most of New England's largest cities and airports. These national chains include **Avis**, **Budget**, **Enterprise**, **Hertz**, **National**, **Rent-A-Wreck**, and **Thrifty**. While their rates are somewhat higher than those offered by smaller local companies, they usually provide an extremely efficient service.

In order to rent a car, you must be 21 and possess a valid driver's license. People under the age of 25 will usually have to pay an additional fee. A major credit card is normally required as well, unless you are prepared to put down a hefty cash deposit. Credit cards sometimes provide coverage against damage or theft of the vehicle, but it is wise to check what the terms are with your credit card company prior to traveling. Make sure that your car rental agreement includes Collision

Damage Waiver (CDW) – also known as Loss Damage Waiver (LDW) – or else you will be liable for any damage to the car, even if it was not your fault. This supplemental insurance can cost between $10 and $20 extra a day.

Sightseeing by car, stopping where and when you want

Speed Limits

It is important to pay attention to road signs, since speed limits can vary from one place to the next depending on your proximity to a town or city. In general, the maximum speed on an interstate highway ranges from 55 to 65 mph (88–105 km/h). On smaller highways, it can range between 30 and 55 mph (50–88 km/h). Cities and towns set their speed limits between 20 and 35 mph (32–56 km/h), and drastically lower around hospitals and schools.

Police pick strategic points along highways – often right after a sign requesting drivers to lower their speed – to set up their radar equipment in order to catch those who are going too fast. Do not try to pay tickets or fines directly to the police officer who pulled you over; this can be interpreted as attempted bribery and can land you deeper in hot water.

Driving Tours

There are a number of books on the market listing the best driving tours of the region. Some magazines, such as **Yankee**, which can be purchased at most newsstands, might include a complete itinerary of recommended routes, historic stops, and the best places to eat and stay. Tours vary from a single day to an entire week and take in everything from dramatic coastal scenery and tiny fishing villages to mountainous terrain and country towns. Of course, the favorite season for drivers is the fall, when the rural roads are flanked by the brilliant colors of leaves (see pp24–5).

State tourism offices (see p369) can give you the contact details of organizations that arrange foliage tours. Each state also has a **Foliage Hotline** number that gives frequently updated foliage reports. Remember, though, that traffic on New England's roads peaks during the fall.

Parking

New England is one of the most densely populated regions in America, and space is at a premium. As a result parking spaces can be hard to find in some destinations. Larger cities tend to provide a variety of parking options, from cheaper municipal lots and highly contested metered spaces to pricier private lots and valet services. First-time visitors to the region's cities should allow extra time when driving to more popular destinations. Also be aware of marked towing zones.

Gasoline

Except when driving through remote areas, motorists will rarely have trouble locating a gas station. However, many locations close at night, with 24-hour stations hard to come by, even in the larger cities. Prices fluctuate wildly; in general, gas stations in smaller, remote towns charge more than those in more densely populated areas. Without fail, motorists can save money by pumping their own gas rather than opting for full service.

Safety Tips

The steps listed below will help to ensure a safe road trip. The National Highway Traffic Safety Administration website (www.nhtsa.gov) has more information on road safety.

- Passengers should wear their seat belts at all times. Infants and young children should be secured in a car seat in the back seat. Follow child-seat instruction manuals precisely. A rear-facing child seat should NEVER be placed in the front seat of a vehicle equipped with an air bag.

- Check your oil, radiator reservoir, brake fluids, and your fan belt before setting off on a long drive. Also check your tires for tread wear and the correct air pressure, and see that your spare tire is roadworthy.

- In winter, be sure you have extra gloves, boots, and warm clothes. If you get stuck in an out-of-the-way place, stay in your car. Keep the motor running for warmth, but open your window slightly to guard against carbon monoxide buildup. Make sure your exhaust pipe is clear of snow.

- Check road conditions on the radio, especially in winter. Heavy snowfalls can leave many areas impassable. Individual state transportation departments often have hotlines dispensing up-to-date information.

- Be wary of large animals on the road. Hitting a moose poses more of a threat to you than it does to the animal.

Sign on a Vermont highway warning drivers to watch for moose

General Index